Related Books of Interest

DB2 Developer's Guide

By Craig Mullins
ISBN: 0-13-283642-4

The field's #1 go-to source for on-the-job information on programming and administering DB2 on IBM z/OS mainframes.

Now, three-time IBM Information Champion Craig S. Mullins has thoroughly updated this classic for the newest versions of DB2 for z/OS: DB2 V9 andV10.

This Sixth Edition builds on the unique approach that has made previous editions so valuable. It brings together condensed, easy-to-read coverage of all essential topics: information otherwise scattered through dozens of IBM and third-party documents. Throughout, Mullins offers focused drill-down on the key details DB2 developers need to succeed, with expert, field-tested implementation advice and realistic examples.

DB2 SQL Tuning Tips for z/OS Developers

By Tony Andrews
ISBN: 0-13-303846-7

The Definitive Solutions-Oriented Guide to IBM® DB2® for z/OS®: Now Fully Updated for Both v9 and v10!

DB2 tuning expert Tony Andrews ("Tony the Tuner") draws on more than 20 years of DB2-related experience, empowering you to take performance into your own hands, whether you're writing new software or tuning existing systems. Tony shows you exactly how to clear bottlenecks, resolve problems, and improve both speed and reliability.

This book fully reflects the latest SQL programming best practices for DB2 V9 and DB2 V10 on z/OS: techniques that are taught in no other book and are rarely covered in general DB2 SQL courses.

Related Books of Interest

DB2 9 for Linux, UNIX, and Windows
DBA Guide, Reference, and Exam Prep, Sixth Edition

By George Baklarz and Paul C. Zikopoulos
ISBN: 0-13-185514-X

The sixth edition of this classic offers complete, start-to-finish coverage of DB2® 9 administration and development for Linux®, UNIX®, and Windows® platforms, as well as authoritative preparation for the latest IBM® DB2 certification exam. Written for both DBAs and developers, this definitive reference and self-study guide covers all aspects of deploying and managing DB2 9, including DB2 database design and development; day-to-day administration and backup; deployment of networked, Internet-centered, and SOA-based applications; migration; and much more.

You'll also find an unparalleled collection of expert tips for optimizing performance, availability, and value. Download Complete DB2 V9 Trial Version. Visit ibm.com/db2/9/ download.html to download a complete trial version of DB2, which enables you to try out dozens of the most powerful features of DB2 for yourself—everything from pureXML™ support to automated administration and optimization.

DB2 pureXML Cookbook
Master the Power of the IBM Hybrid Data Server

By Matthias Nicola and Pav Kumar-Chatterjee
ISBN: 0-13-815047-8

DB2® pureXML® Cookbook provides hands-on solutions and best practices for developing and managing XML database applications with DB2.

More and more database developers and DBAs are being asked to develop applications and manage databases that involve XML data. Many are utilizing the highly praised DB2 pureXML technology from IBM®. In *DB2 pureXML Cookbook*, two leading experts from IBM offer the practical solutions and proven code samples that database professionals need to build better XML solutions faster. Organized by task, this book is packed with more than 700 easy-to-adapt "recipe-style" examples covering the entire application lifecycle—from planning and design through coding, optimization, and troubleshooting.

 Listen to the author's podcast at:
ibmpressbooks.com/podcasts

Related Books of Interest

Enterprise Master Data Management
An SOA Approach to Managing Core Information

By Allen Dreibelbis, Eberhard Hechler,
Ivan Milman, Martin Oberhofer, Paul van
Run, and Dan Wolfson
ISBN: 0-13-236625-8

Enterprise Master Data Management provides an authoritative, vendor-independent
MDM technical reference for practitioners:
architects, technical analysts, consultants,
solution designers, and senior IT decision
makers. Written by the IBM® data management innovators who are pioneering
MDM, this book systematically introduces
MDM's key concepts and technical themes,
explains its business case, and illuminates
how it interrelates with and enables SOA.

Drawing on their experience with cutting-
edge projects, the authors introduce MDM
patterns, blueprints, solutions, and best
practices published nowhere else—everything you need to establish a consistent,
manageable set of master data, and use it
for competitive advantage.

An Introduction to IMS
Klein, Long, Blackman, Goff,
Nathan, Lanyi, Wilson,
Butterweck, Sherrill
ISBN: 0-13-288687-1

IBM Cognos 10 Report Studio: Practical Examples
Draskovic, Johnson
ISBN: 0-13-265675-2

Patterns of Information Management
Chessell, Smith
ISBN: 0-13-315550-1

IBM Cognos Business Intelligence v10
Gautam
ISBN: 0-13-272472-3

Decision Management Systems
Taylor
ISBN: 0-13-288438-0

Data Integration Blueprint and Modeling
Giordano
ISBN: 0-13-708493-5

DB2®
Essentials

DB2®
Essentials

Understanding DB2 in a
Big Data World

Raul F. Chong

Clara Liu

IBM Press
Pearson plc
Upper Saddle River, NJ • Boston • Indianapolis • San Francisco
New York • Toronto • Montreal • London • Munich • Paris •
Madrid • Cape Town • Sydney • Tokyo • Singapore • Mexico City

ibmpressbooks.com

The authors and publisher have taken care in the preparation of this book, but make no expressed or implied warranty of any kind and assume no responsibility for errors or omissions. No liability is assumed for incidental or consequential damages in connection with or arising out of the use of the information or programs contained herein.

IBM Press Program Managers: Steven M. Stansel, Ellice Uffer
Cover design: IBM Corporation
Associate Publisher: Dave Dusthimer
Marketing Manager: Stephane Nakib
Executive Editor: Mary Beth Ray
Publicist: Heather Fox
Editorial Assistant: Vanessa Evans
Development Editor: Jeff Riley
Managing Editor: Kristy Hart
Cover Designer: Alan Clements
Senior Project Editor: Lori Lyons
Copy Editor: Apostrophe Editing Services
Indexer: Heather McNeill
Senior Compositor: Gloria Schurick
Proofreader: Sherri Cain
Manufacturing Buyer: Dan Uhrig

Published by Pearson plc
Publishing as IBM Press

IBM Press offers excellent discounts on this book when ordered in quantity for bulk purchases or special sales, which may include electronic versions and/or custom covers and content particular to your business, training goals, marketing focus, and branding interests. For more information, please contact

U. S. Corporate and Government Sales
1-800-382-3419
corpsales@pearsontechgroup.com.

For sales outside the United States, please contact

International Sales
international@pearsoned.com.

Library of Congress Control Number: 2013946725

ISBN-13: 978-0-13-346190-9
ISBN-10: 0-13-346190-4

Text printed in the United States on recycled paper at Courier in Westford, Massachusetts.
First printing: October 2013

I would like to thank my wife Jin, and my two daughters Meylin and Isabelle,
for their understanding, patience, support, and love.
The many weekends and nights spent writing this book meant many sacrifices,
and quality family time lost.
But you all kept me going to complete this book!
I would also like to thank my parents, in-laws,
and siblings for their constant support and love.

Raul F. Chong

I didn't think I would write another book after completing
my fourth one a couple years ago.
I would like to sincerely thank Raul for his encouragement (and convincing)
to become THE co-author of this book.
It is indeed a proud achievement to find five books (so far)
listed when my name is "googled."
I want to dedicate this book to my lovely family: Heison, Kristen, Ansel,
my parents, and my in-laws.
I thank you for your support on giving me private time to work on the chapters
over weekends and late nights.
We missed our annual Ride for Heart event this year, didn't we?
Finally, congratulations to the entire DB2 for LUW team. We did it again!

Clara Liu

Contents at a Glance

Contents

Chapter 3   Installing DB2   89

Foreword

To meet the rapidly growing demand for information, IT infrastructures must not only work faster to provide analytics, they must also work smarter with new database technology created for the era of Big Data. DB2® 10.5 with BLU Acceleration offers businesses a faster, easier and significantly more affordable approach to analytics.

This book describes the increasing interest and demand for Big Data, and introduces big data technologies such as IBM® InfoSphere® Streams, IBM InfoSphere BigInsights™, and IBM InfoSphere Data Explorer. The authors highlight the value of DB2 for data warehouse simplification.

In the last two editions, the authors received great feedback about the visual illustrations throughout the book. With this third edition of the Understanding DB2 series, this book continues to keep the visual learning style with clear explanations for every chapter. Each chapter introduces a topic with a "big picture". Figures are used extensively and explained thoroughly. The "big pictures" are excellent for beginners to understand the concept and see how each component complements and interacts with others. They are also excellent references for database professionals at intermediate levels.

After "visually" learning the concepts in the chapters, the full case studies that follow will illustrate how to put theory into practice in real life scenarios. There are concept review questions to help you prepare for your DB2 certification exams. This provides a complete introduction as well as practical guide with study material.

This book has been fully updated with DB2 10.1 and 10.5 functions and features. New topics include introducing BLU Acceleration, Adaptive Compression, multi-temperature data management, the newly simplified DB2 portfolio, the complementary tool - IBM Data Studio, and many other new capabilities.

The authors have effectively compiled valuable information into this book that has been collected through their experience of working in the DB2 development lab as well as from working with many DB2 customers and partners globally. As with the previous editions, it will continue to earn a place on the must-read list for every DB2 professional. Enjoy the book!

Judy Huber
Vice President, Distributed Data Servers and Data Warehousing
Director, IBM Canada Laboratory

Preface

We are living in exciting times where data is being heralded as the new gold. The confluence of Big Data Technologies and Cloud Computing is enabling us to analyze vast amounts of data in ways never done before, and allowing the discovery of new information that is impacting everyone's lives. But for those in the Information Technology (IT) field, keeping up with the skills to be successful on the job is becoming more and more challenging. Understanding new algorithms, new programming paradigms, and new technologies in general require significant time commitment. Although you cannot avoid the time investment needed on your own education, choosing books written in a clear, concise, and visual manner can help you get the most of your investment. This book was designed with this in mind, to minimize the time, money, and effort required to learn DB2 for Linux®, UNIX®, and Windows®. The book visually introduces and discusses the latest version of DB2, DB2 10.5. This version introduces and important feature, BLU acceleration technology, which is particularly important in the big data world.

Who Should Read This Book?

This book is intended for anyone who works with data, and specifically databases, such as database administrators (DBAs), application developers, system administrators, and consultants. This book is a great introduction to DB2, whether you have used it before or you are a beginner. It is also a good study guide for anyone preparing for the IBM DB2 10 Certification exams 610 (DB2 10.1 Fundamentals), or 611 (DB2 10.1 Database Administrator for Linux, UNIX and Windows).

This book will save you time and effort because the topics are presented in a clear and concise manner, and we use figures, examples, case studies, and review questions to reinforce the material as it is presented. The book is different from many others on the subject because of the following.

- Visual learning. The book relies on visual learning as its base. Each chapter starts with a "big picture" to introduce the topics to be discussed in that chapter. Numerous graphics are used throughout the chapters to explain concepts in detail. We feel that figures allow for fast, easy learning and longer retention of the material. If you forget some of the concepts discussed in the book or just need a quick refresher, you will not need to read the entire chapter again. You can simply look at the figures quickly to refresh your memory. For your convenience, some of the most important figures are provided in color on the book's Web site (www.ibmpressbooks.com/title/9780133461909). These figures in color can further improve your learning experience.

- Clear explanations. We have encountered many situations when reading other books where paragraphs need to be read two, three, or even more times to grasp what they are describing. In this book we have made every effort possible to provide clear explanations so that you can understand the information quickly and easily.

- Examples, examples, examples. The book provides many examples and case studies that reinforce the topics discussed in each chapter. Some of the examples have been taken from real life experiences that the authors have had while working with DB2 customers.

- Sample exam questions. All chapters end with review questions that are similar to the questions on the DB2 Certification exams. These questions are intended to ensure that you understand the concepts discussed in each chapter before proceeding, and as a study guide for the IBM Certification exams. Appendix A contains the answers with explanations.

Getting Started

If you are new to DB2 and would like to get the most out of this book, we suggest you start reading from the beginning and continuing with the chapters in order. If you are new to DB2 but are in a hurry to get a quick understanding of the product, you can jump to Chapter 2, "DB2 at a Glance: The Big Picture." Reading this chapter will introduce you to the main concepts of DB2. You can then go to other chapters to read for further details. If you are new to DB2 but have knowledge of Oracle database products, you can review first Appendix C, "A Comparison of DB2 and Oracle Terminology."

If you would like to follow the examples provided with the book, you need to install DB2. Chapter 3, "Installing DB2," gives you the details to handle this task.

A Word of Advice

In this book we use figures extensively to introduce and examine DB2 concepts. Although some of the figures may look complex, don't be overwhelmed by first impressions! The text that accompanies them explains the concepts in detail. If you look back at the figure after reading the description, you will be surprised by how much clearer it is.

This book only discusses DB2 for Linux, UNIX, and Windows, so when we use the term DB2, we are referring to DB2 on those platforms. DB2 for i®, DB2 for z/OS®, and DB2 for VSE and VM are mentioned only when presenting methods that you can use to access these databases from an application written on Linux, UNIX, or Windows. When DB2 for i®, DB2 for z/OS®, and DB2 for VSE and VM are discussed, we refer to them explicitly.

This book was written prior to the official release of DB2 10.5. The authors used a beta copy of the product to obtain screen shots, and perform their tests. It is possible that by the time this book is published, and the product is officially released, some features and screenshots may have changed slightly.

Conventions

Many examples of SQL statements, XPath/XQuery statements, DB2 commands, and operating system commands are included throughout the book. SQL statement keywords are written in uppercase. For example: Use the SELECT statement to retrieve data from a DB2 database.

XPath and XQuery statements are case sensitive—for example: /employee/DEPT/Id

DB2 commands are shown in lowercase mono—for example: The list applications command lists the applications connected to your databases.

You can issue many DB2 commands from the Command Line Processor (CLP) utility, which accepts the commands in both uppercase and lowercase. In UNIX operating systems, program names are case-sensitive, so be careful to enter the program name using the proper case. For instance, on UNIX, db2 must be entered in lowercase. (See Chapter 2, "DB2 at a Glance: The Big Picture," for a detailed discussion of this.)

Keywords are written in uppercase, unless the keyword is part of a command statement or syntax, or the particular program language uses lowercase.

Database object names used in our examples are shown in italic. For example: The *COUNTRY* table has a *City* column.

Italic is also used for variable names in the syntax of a command or statement. If the variable name has more than one word, it is joined with an underscore. For example: CREATE SEQUENCE *sequence_name*.

In code listings, some code lines are too long to fit the width of the page. When a code line wraps to another line, you will see a code continuation character (➡) at the beginning of the runover line:

```
Number of pooled fenced processes          (FENCED_POOL) =
➡AUTOMATIC(MAX_COORDAGENTS)
```

Where a concept of a function is new in DB2 10.1 or DB2 10.5, we signify this with an icon as follows:

V10

Note that the DB2 certification exams only include material of DB2 version 10.1, not version 10.5

Contacting the Authors

We are interested in any feedback that you have about this book. Please contact us with your opinions and inquiries at udb2book@ca.ibm.com.

Depending on the volume of inquiries, we may be unable to respond to every technical question but we'll do our best. The DB2 forum at https://www.ibm.com/developerworks/community/forums/html/forum?id=11111111-0000-0000-0000-000000000842 is another great way to get assistance from IBM employees and the DB2 user community.

What's New

This book, though with a different title, is an update of the book *Understanding DB2 – Learning Visually with Examples* (2nd Edition), which received great reviews. Though our intention was to keep the same title and same depth in each topic, the size of the book became an issue. As more features are added into the DB2 product, more pages are required to describe them. Rather than reduce the depth of each topic, we decided to split the book. *DB2 Essentials* covers the core topics every DB2 professional should know at the beginner-to-intermediate level. More advanced concepts have been left for another book, which at the time of this writing is in the planning stage.

Since the time the second edition of *Understanding DB2: Learning Visually with Examples* was published, there have been four releases or versions of DB2 for Linux, UNIX, and Windows in that time: DB2 9.7, DB2 9.8, DB2 10.1, and now DB2 10.5; this section highlights what's new with each of them.

The core of DB2 and its functionality remains mostly the same as in previous versions; therefore, some chapters required minimal updates. On the other hand, some other chapters such as Chapter 4, "Using Database Tools and Utilities," required substantial changes since most DB2 GUI Tools were deprecated with DB2 9.7, and then discontinued with DB2 10.1 and replaced by IBM Data Studio.

To indicate where something has changed from the previous version of the book, or was added in DB2 10.1 or DB2 10.5, we have used the icon shown below. This is particularly useful for those who have bought the second edition of the *Understanding DB2* book and quickly want to identify what's new.

V10

As you will see next, there is only one main feature introduced in DB2 10.5 (BLU acceleration technology) that we discuss in this book; therefore we did not use different icons to distinguish changes or additions between version 10 and version 10.5.

The following sections will briefly introduce the changes or additions in each of these new versions of DB2.

DB2 9.7

DB2 9.7 introduced many features to help administrators and developers of other relational database products migrate their databases and applications to DB2. For example, with DB2 9.7 a migration from an Oracle database to DB2 that would take months in the past, could now be performed in a few hours or days. This was possible because DB2 9.7 introduced several data types, and support for non-standard SQL statements used in Oracle. In addition, the CLPPlus tool was introduced which has a very similar interface and behavior to Oracle's SQL*Plus. Moreover, Oracle's PL/SQL language often used in stored procedures could be easily understood in DB2; therefore Oracle's stored procedures could run with minimal or no modification in DB2. Appendix C, "A Comparison of DB2 and Oracle Terminology," has a section with more information about this. Other improvements in this release included compression, pureXML®, and security enhancements.

DB2 9.8

DB2 9.8 introduced pureScale® technology, a solution architected based on DB2 on the mainframe data-sharing technology. With pureScale, different DB2 servers share the same data in a cluster environment. DB2 servers can be added to the cluster as the data grows, allowing for scalability, but also, extreme availability. In this book we discuss the basic concepts of pureScale.

DB2 10.1

DB2 10.1 introduced many features and enhancements in different areas. Most of these enhancements are discussed in detail in the book:

- Adaptive compression, for deep compression using dictionaries at the page and table levels.
- Time Travel Query, which allows users to query data in the past, the present or the future.
- Multi-temperature data management, ideal for data warehousing environments where data is classified based on how often it is accessed; thus, assigning the most frequently used data (hot data) to faster devices, and the least frequently used data (cold data) to slower devices.
- Row and Column Access Control (RCAC), which provides security granularity at both, row and column levels.

DB2 10.5

DB2 10.5 introduces new packaging of the product to fit different needs at different price points. One single image is created for most editions, as opposed to one different image per edition. This means that to upgrade from one edition to the other, you don't need to uninstall the previous edition of DB2, simply apply the license of the new edition, and any feature specific to the new edition would be unlocked. This is particularly helpful in environments where the company's IT policy required safety procedures in place for new installations of a product. With this approach, there is no new installation required.

Probably the key feature of DB2 10.5 is BLU Acceleration technology, a revolutionary approach of storing data rows in columnar fashion. This is ideal for data warehousing environments, and allows for performance improvements in order of magnitude for analytic workloads. BLU Acceleration is a technology that enables users to work with big data as it dramatically helps with performance. It is also remarkable the ease in which this technology can be implemented by users. All complexities are hidden from regular users who don't even need to create indexes.

One common denominator in all the new features and changes made to DB2 in these four new versions or releases is that many of the new features and functions were developed to make your life easier!

Acknowledgments

Raul and Clara would like to thank Cristian Molaro and Kshitij Kohli for their extensive technical review of the book. Their suggestions and corrections were invaluable.

Steven Stansel, Susan Visser, and Mary Beth Ray provided guidance and invaluable help throughout the whole process of planning, writing, and publishing the book. Without their help, this book would never have been completed as smoothly as it has been.

About the Authors

Raul F. Chong is a Senior DB2, Big Data and Cloud Program Manager and Technical Evangelist based at the IBM Canada Laboratory. He leads the development and design of several offerings for the Information Management (IM) brand of IBM, with the goal of increasing awareness and growing communities around IBM IM products, such as IBM InfoSphere® BigInsights™, IBM InfoSphere Streams, DB2 database software, IBM Data Studio, InfoSphere Data Architect, and pureQuery® technology. As part of the IM Cloud Computing Center of Competence at the Toronto Lab, Raul leads the development and deployment of projects by the community using DB2 on the Cloud, such as bigdatauniversity.com, and db2oncampus.org. As a technical evangelist, Raul travels worldwide delivering presentations and workshops targeting customers, IBM business partners and the Academia. Raul develops and leads the development of collateral material such as articles, books, videos, courses, and DVDs that help educate users in IBM IM products. He has also participated actively in the development of training material and offerings of IBM IM Certification programs. Raul joined IBM in 1997 and has worked as a DB2 consultant, DB2 technical support specialist, and DB2 Information Developer. Raul has summarized many of his DB2 experiences through the years in the first and second editions of the book Understanding DB2—Learning Visually with Examples for which he is the lead author. He has also co-authored the book DB2 SQL PL Essential Guide for DB2 UDB on Linux, UNIX, Windows, i5/OS, and z/OS (ISBN 0131477005), and other books that are part of the DB2 on Campus book series. In his spare time, Raul enjoys playing with his two little daughters. Raul is fluent in Spanish as he was born and raised in Peru, but he keeps some of the Chinese traditions from his grandparents. He also enjoys reading history and archeology books.

Clara Liu was recently appointed to be the Program Manager of IBM Cross Brand Technical Initiatives. She manages leading edge strategic projects across IBM brands. Her prior management role was with the DB2 Planning team. Her previous consulting experience gave her an insight and solid understanding of customers' needs. Based on market demand, competition pressure, and objectives of maximizing return of investment, she drives software enhancements into the product with the right balance between leading edge technology and business needs. In many DB2, Warehouse, PureData™ Systems versions and releases, Clara held key responsibilities such as planning product enhancements, managing product offer portfolio and license entitlement, making software available on fulfillment systems for customers, and planning for smooth migration paths for customers when products reach end of life. Over the years, she delivered many product hands-on and video demonstrations with her team. Those are great assets for the IBM Sales and Marketing team and customers who want to 'see' and 'play' with the technologies. Due to the board involvement in numerous phases of the database product life cycle, Clara has established great networking within the development organization as well as across the business teams. As a mother of two, Clara had coauthored five books (including this one), all focusing in her technical expertise, DB2 for Linux, UNIX and Windows.

## CHAPTER 1

Introduction to DB2

DATABASE 2 (DB2) for Linux, UNIX, and Windows is a relational data server developed by IBM. Version 10.5, available since June 2013 is the most current version of the product and the one on which we focus in this book.

In this chapter, you learn about

- The history of DB2
- DB2 in the big data world
- DB2 for Linux, UNIX, and Windows product portfolio
- Syntax diagram conventions

A Brief History of DB2: From Past to Present

Since the 1970s, when IBM Research invented the Relational Model and the Structured Query Language (SQL), IBM has developed a complete family of data servers. Development started on mainframe platforms such as Virtual Machine (VM), Virtual Storage Extended (VSE), and Multiple Virtual Storage (MVS™). In 1983, DB2 for MVS Version 1 was born. "DB2" was used to indicate a shift from hierarchical databases—such as the Information Management System (IMS™) popular at the time—to the new relational databases. DB2 development continued on mainframe platforms as well as on distributed platforms.[1] Figure 1.1 shows some of the highlights of DB2 history with different names and versions of the product up until the most current one, DB2 10.5.

---

1. Distributed platforms, also referred to as *open system platforms*, include all platforms other than mainframe or midrange operating systems. Some examples are Linux, UNIX, and Windows.

In 1996, IBM announced the release of DB2 Universal Database™ (UDB) Version 5 for distributed platforms. With this version, DB2 was able to store all kinds of electronic data, including traditional relational data, as well as audio, video, and text documents. It was the first version optimized for the web, and it supported a range of distributed platforms. This universal database was able to run on a variety of hardware, from uniprocessor systems and symmetric multiprocessor (SMP) systems to massively parallel processing (MPP) systems and clusters of SMP systems.

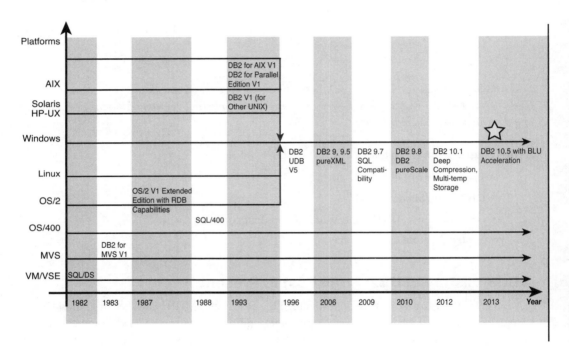

Figure 1.1   DB2 timeline

Since DB2 UDB was introduced, IBM delivered numerous releases of DB2 over the years. In every release, cutting-edge technologies were brought to the industry. For example, in 2006 DB2 9 introduced pureXML, a technology that provides better support to store XML documents. This feature made DB2 a hybrid or multi-structured data server because relational data and hierarchical data (XML) could be natively stored and because SQL with XQuery could be combined in a single query. DB2 9.5 further enhanced the pureXML capabilities by bringing improvements in installation, manageability, scalability and performance, workload management, and application development support for business partners. In 2009, DB2 9.7 introduced the DB2 SQL compatibility feature. With this feature, an entire new library was developed in DB2 from scratch to support nonstandard SQL syntax used by other database vendors. The main objective of this feature was to make it easier for users of those products to migrate to DB2. When working in

DB2, they could take advantage of other DB2 features such as data compression to further lower their ongoing database ownership costs.

IBM's innovations did not slow down with DB2 9.7; six months after its release, DB2 pureScale was added to the DB2 offering. DB2 pureScale is a shared-disk clustering technology on distributed platforms. With this technology you can add more DB2 servers to the cluster as your data grows. This allows you to maintain your query response time because you are adding more resources to handle more data. When you add servers to the cluster, the databases can remain online. Therefore pureScale delivers transparent application scalability and extreme availability.

In 2012, IBM released DB2 10.1 with several features to reduce operational costs. For example, with multi-temperature storage, you can classify your data in storage classes: "Hot" data (data that is accessed often) resides in the fastest and typically more expensive devices, and "cold" data (data that is rarely used) resides in slower, cheaper devices. Distributing your data in this matter helps reduce overall administration and storage costs. Other key functionalities delivered with DB2 10 include support for new "no SQL" applications with the addition of user-defined functions that could access a Hadoop cluster; adaptive data compression, which ensures high compression ratios over time; and advanced and flexible data access control with Row and Column Access Control.

In 2013, IBM released its latest DB2 version, DB2 10.5. With this version, IBM introduces **BLU Acceleration**, a memory-based column store that leverages parallel vector processing power, dynamic memory capabilities, and advanced storage disk technology. BLU Acceleration eliminates the need for indexes, aggregates, or time-consuming database tuning to achieve top performance and storage efficiency, and it is ideal to handle analytic workloads in a data warehouse environment. DB2 BLU Acceleration is discussed in more detail in Chapter 7, section "Column-Organized Tables (a.k.a. DB2 BLU Acceleration)."

NOTE

The term "Universal Database" or "UDB" was dropped from the name for simplicity starting from DB2 version 9.

Note that new release numbers are not necessarily consecutive within a version. For example, DB2 version 10 release 1 (DB2 10.1) was released in 2012, and DB2 10.5 was released in 2013. There were no DB2 10.2, DB2 10.3 or DB2 10.4 in between. Going from DB2 10.1 to DB2 10.5 directly signifies major changes or new features added in the product.

The Role of DB2 in the Big Data World

Big data is one of the hottest areas in the Information Technology (IT) field these days. There is no formal definition of big data, but many people use this term to describe large collections of data that can be structured or unstructured and grow so large and quickly that it is difficult to manage with regular database or statistics tools.

If we talk about having 1 gigabyte of data, are we talking about big data? How about 1 terabyte or 1 petabyte? Big data is a generic term, and there is no set number to indicate that anything equal or above to that number should be called big data and anything below it should not. However, one thing that is almost certain about big data is that it requires a cluster of computers to process it to obtain the desired information in reasonable time.

Big data has probably existed for a long time, but the term and hype started when the Apache Hadoop technology started to gain momentum in 2010. This technology relies on commodity hardware (typically inexpensive) to scale its computing power, a distributed file system with a built-in replication algorithm for handling failures (expected in commodity hardware) and a new programming paradigm called MapReduce that allows code to be sent and run at the nodes or servers where the data to be processed resides as opposed to bringing the data to be processed to the servers were the code resides.

When big data was starting to gain popularity, it was fortunate that the cloud computing model was also gaining momentum. Cloud computing facilitates big data because it provides the commodity hardware Hadoop clusters need, and it provisions these resources on demand and at low cost. Its utility-like billing model is a winner with companies and governments and makes it ideal for test and development environments. As these two technologies continue to grow and become more robust, it is likely Cloud computing environments will run most production workloads as well.

The description of big data in this section might seem to imply that relational databases such as DB2 might no longer be needed; however, this is not true. Relational databases and big data technologies complement each other, and can be integrated as you see in the next sections.

Characteristics of Big Data

Four key characteristics of big data include

- **Volume:** The volume of data is growing and coming from multiple sources: Sensors, RFID devices, social networks, and so on. Experts predict that the volume of data in the world will grow to 25 zettabytes in 2020. (A zettabyte is one billion terabytes.) This also applies to every business—their data is growing at an exponential rate.

- **Variety:** The type of data being generated is not necessarily structured data that can be easily stored and analyzed in relational databases. Most of the data out there is unstructured in nature—audio, video, the contents of an email, insurance claim forms, and so on. In fact, studies suggest that 80% of the world's data is unstructured. If we apply this same number to companies, we can say that 80% of a company's data is unstructured and likely discarded, or archived and not analyzed. This means that CEOs of companies are making mission-critical decisions only with 20% of the data they have.

- **Velocity:** Data is being generated at increasingly high speeds, and this is continuing to accelerate. Consider Twitter generates 400 million tweets per day today. By the time you read this book, it might have doubled. Data is coming at us at record speeds, and to make the most of it, it needs to be processed quickly, maybe even in real time.

- **Veracity:** Is the data that is being collected trustworthy? How can you act on information if you don't trust it? Establishing trust in big data presents a huge challenge as the sources and the variety grows. Some social media accounts are not credible and should be flagged as such so that anything that comes from those accounts is filtered out.

These characteristics correlate to the three "I"s in IBM's Smarter Planet® message:

"The world is becoming more and more Instrumented, Interconnected, and Intelligent."

With a world that is Instrumented and interconnected, we are collecting huge amounts of data at great speeds. We've also gotten more data about things: You can put 32 and 64 -bit microprocessor technology into lots of things and capture more information about physical infrastructures (with sensors), business processes, human interactions, and so on. You can do things today that just were not possible a decade ago. The interconnect infrastructure that supports us all is extraordinary in the level of bandwidth that's available.

With this vast amount of data we are collecting, the world is getting more "intelligent" by analyzing this data using technologies like Apache Hadoop.

Types of Big Data

There are three types of big data:

- **Big Data in motion:** This type of big data is constantly flowing; it is a stream of information that never ends. Most solutions in this space analyze the data as it is flowing; in other words, they perform real-time analytics. Take a stream or a river as an analogy. Imagine standing on a bridge and looking down to see the stream pass by. As it is flowing, you can see small fish passing by, a branch of a tree, and so on. So you analyze the stream "on the go." Likewise, if we now think of this stream as a stream of data, with software like IBM InfoSphere Streams, you can analyze it as it flows. You don't need to wait for the data to be filtered and collected in tables to later create your data warehouse and then start examining the data. With streams analytics, you get *real-time* processing of the information. Potentially, you can also reduce storage costs given that the desired analytics have already been obtained and all that needs to be stored are the results.

  For example, in a project involving a hospital, a university, and IBM, vital signs of premature babies were collected and analyzed in real time. The objective was to detect life-threatening conditions of the babies as they happened. Prior to this solution, nurses had to monitor babies manually and record the vital signs on a computer. After 24 hours, they would run queries in the computer to analyze the data collected. With the new solution doctors are able to act on the problem right away.

  Other examples of big data in motion are Twitter feeds, Facebook comments, stock market data, sensors to predict the weather, and so on.

- **Big Data at rest:** This type of big data has been archived during the years and that keeps growing as more data is archived. Take an ocean as an analogy; it is huge and not really flowing. Imagine being in the middle of the Atlantic Ocean and having to analyze all the different type of fish and other specimens. Just like streams normally end up in the ocean, data in motion that has streamed will normally end up as big data at rest. Most solutions in this space analyze this data for exploration and discovery purposes or to tackle data that had never been examined before. Typically, most of the data collected is unstructured.

  For example, in a project involving an energy and services company, petabytes of information where collected from sensors to determine the best location to install wind turbines. Using IBM InfoSphere BigInsights, a software that uses Apache Hadoop technology, this analysis was performed in substantially shorter time than with previous solutions.

  Other examples of big data at rest are emails, insurance claim forms, web logs, machine data collected over time, and so on.

- **Big Data in place:** This type of data refers to existing data a company has in many different repositories. Think of lakes as the analogy for these repositories. You don't want to get all water of all the lakes together before you analyze all of it. In the same way, when we talk about data in different repositories, you don't want to merge all of these data into one repository to perform analytics. Instead, you can leave all of the data where it is, in place, and build an external index that can access the data in all the repositories. With the index built, you can present all the data in a dashboard and run federated queries behind the scenes. Depending on which user is accessing the dashboard, he can see data from all repositories (respecting, of course, his security clearance). Moreover, you can bring external sources to this dashboard, which can help him correlate internal information with external data. IBM InfoSphere Data Explorer can be used to manage big data in place.

The IBM Big Data Platform

IBM's definition of big data and big data technologies is not confined to Hadoop-related data or Hadoop-related workloads; it is more than that. As we saw in the earlier section, in IBM we talk about different types of big data. In this section, we discuss the platform that can handle each type of big data.

Figure 1.2 illustrates the IBM Big Data Platform. The outer circle describes common customers' pain points or needs. The middle circle shows the different products of the platform that can provide solutions to those problems.

IBM Big Data Platform

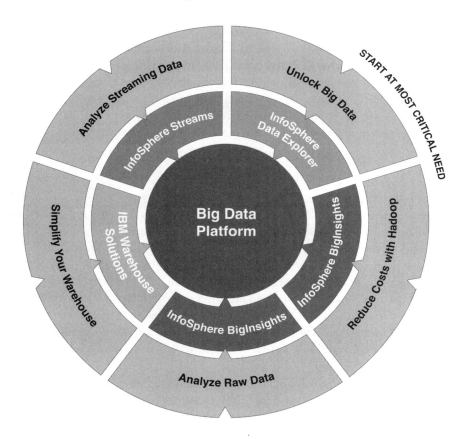

Figure 1.2   The IBM Big Data Platform—solving customers' needs

The fact that IBM has a platform for big data does not mean customers need to purchase all the products in a platform. They can simply choose the products that can help them with their immediate needs; however, as their needs grow, having a product that is part of a platform can help reuse any prior work performed because the products in the platform are integrated. For example, text analytics annotators are programs that can be used to extract specific words or phrases you choose. You can write a text analytics annotator to work with IBM InfoSphere BigInsights, but that same annotator can be used to work with IBM InfoSphere Streams.

Following is further explanation detailing each customer's needs from Figure 1.2 and how the IBM Big Data Platform helps.

Unlock Big Data

This is the situation where a company has many repositories of data but is unable to understand it because it is isolated and assigned to independent silos. Attempts to expose the data might require copying it to a central location accessible by the company's content management system. This can be costly and time-consuming. One way to get up and running quickly and discover and retrieve relevant big data is to use IBM InfoSphere Data Explorer (Data Explorer). With this software, the company can search and navigate big data in place from federated sources.

Analyze Raw Data

As discussed earlier, many companies have been either discarding or archiving raw data. This is the data they cannot process or analyze, such as unstructured data. Imagine a software company collecting thousands of emails sent to its support team. The problems reported in those emails might have been addressed one at a time and then archived. From a management point of view, it would be more beneficial for the company to analyze the contents of *all* of those emails to determine the top ten most common issues reported and make changes to its software appropriately.

With Hadoop technology, a company can now ingest the raw data as-is and derive insight from it. There is no need to convert unstructured data to a structured format. Hadoop enables companies to process large volumes of diverse data relatively fast. They can also combine insights with their existing data warehouses. If a company wanted to test a new hypothesis where they would modify the analytic models in the data warehouse, they can validate it by running a low cost ad-hoc analysis with Hadoop.

The IBM product applicable to this customer need is IBM InfoSphere BigInsights (BigInsights). This software is based on Apache Hadoop. IBM has not forked the Apache Hadoop project, but it uses it as its core. Whenever a new version of Hadoop is released, typically the next release of BigInsights will use it. On top of Hadoop, new added-value features have been built such as

- An integrated installer where all open source components that have been tested together are installed at once, rather than having to download and install each component separately
- A web console for Hadoop cluster administration and application development
- A spreadsheet-like tool called BigSheets to enable business users to work with big data right away
- A text analytics processing engine and library of annotators that enable developers to query and identify items of interest in documents and messages

- An application ecosystem for developers with a BigInsights Eclipse Tools plug-in
- Built-in accelerators, which are templates that can speed up application development
- Enterprise software integration with DB2 and related products
- Additional security and performance features
- ...and many more

Reduce Costs with Hadoop

Many customers would like to reduce the overall cost to maintain data in the warehouse. DB2 has a feature called multi-temperature data management, discussed in Chapter 7, "Working with Database Objects," that can help reduce storage costs. If the amount of data in the warehouse that is seldom used and kept "just in case" is very large, and if the company has already invested in a Hadoop cluster, an alternative to the multi-temperature data management feature is to offload the seldom used data to the Hadoop cluster. This lowers costs because this data is moved to commodity hardware but is still available for querying; the data in the Hadoop system is automatically replicated at the software layer, providing for fault tolerance. For this customer need, BigInsights is the product that can be used (see Figure 1.3).

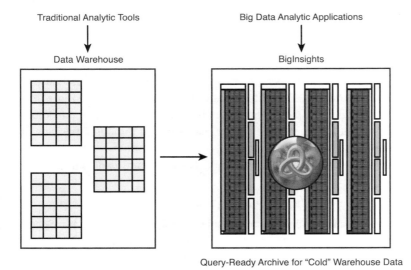

Query-Ready Archive for "Cold" Warehouse Data

Figure 1.3   Reducing costs with Hadoop by moving cold warehouse data to BigInsights

Analyze Streaming Data

In situations where customers need to analyze streaming data in real time—for example, when monitoring networks for possible intrusion to the company's systems or when monitoring emails text to ensure no confidential information is being sent outbound—software like IBM InfoSphere Streams can be used. This type of software can also be used for competitive advantage by analyzing a stream of data coming from social networks. The analysis can be used to determine the customer sentiment on a product or service, so respondents can react quickly based on these findings. It is often used in Telco companies that need to analyze Call Detail Records (CDRs) for customer churn prevention.

Analyzing streaming data can also provide storage savings; there is no need to store the data in the flow because it has already been analyzed.

Simplify Your Warehouse

An enterprise data warehouse can be encumbered by too much data for too many purposes. Administrators have to devote numerous hours trying to improve general-purpose data warehouse performance and optimize queries that take hours to run. They need to have the ability to ingest huge volumes of structured data and run multiple concurrent, deep analytic queries.

IBM has several solutions that can simplify customers' warehouses. Its offerings can provide simplicity to administer and tune the warehouse and at the same time, deliver 10 to 100 times faster performance. This can be achieved using technology such as DB2 BLU Acceleration. With this technology, you don't need to create indexes, and the data is automatically compressed. Internally, the data is organized by columns in data pages (rather than by rows); this new way of organization is particularly advantageous for analytical workloads of a data warehouse.

In addition to DB2 BLU technology, IBM offers PureData systems, which are more than appliances—they are expert systems. This means that not only is hardware, software, and configuration built into the system, but also the expertise IBM has acquired through thousands of different customer engagements.

The IBM PureData System comes in a number of models with more to come in the near future:

- **IBM PureData System for Transactions** is an expert integrated system tuned specifically for the demands of transactional data processing. Its core infrastructure is a tightly integrated environment that combines computing resources, memory, storage layer, channels to the storage layer, and high-speed interconnectivity. The complete infrastructure optimizes for ideal transaction system characteristics, such as high availability, high-level throughput, extreme scalability, and fast response time. DB2 pureScale technology is at the heart of the PureData System for Transactions.

- **IBM PureData System for Operational Analytics** is an optimized data warehouse system for high performance operational analytics of both historical and operational data. It is designed to run both analytics and operational queries. This PureData System uses the DB2 warehouse and data partitioning capability.

- **IBM PureData System for Analytics** is a highly optimized system for customer analytic environment. Customers can load petabytes of information and write complex queries and reports with minimal administration. This system is powered by the Netezza® technology. The built-in expertise helps drive up to 100 times performance improvement compared to traditional customized systems.

- **IBM PureData System for Hadoop** integrates IBM InfoSphere BigInsights Hadoop-based software, server, and storage into a single, easy-to-manage system. The built-in expertise accelerates big data time to value, simplifies big data adoption and consumption, and implements enterprise-class big data.

Different workloads require systems to be optimized differently, which is why there are different models to handle and manage data.

By now, it should be clear what the role of DB2 is in the big data world, but let's summarize it:

DB2 is at the core of technologies and offerings like BLU acceleration and PureData systems used in data warehouse solutions. Data warehouses are part of big data. Though big data's hype started with Apache Hadoop, this does not mean that only Hadoop-related data is big data. As some experts say, big data is all data!

Integration of DB2 with BigInsights (Hadoop)

Earlier, in the section "Reduce Costs with Hadoop," you saw how a data warehouse (which could be based on DB2) and a Hadoop cluster (which could be using BigInsights) can work together. This section describes two other cases of integration between a relational database (mainly DB2) and BigInsights.

Obtaining Data from DB2 by a BigInsights Client and Vice Versa

Figure 1.4 shows a BigInsights cluster on the left and several traditional relational databases on the right.

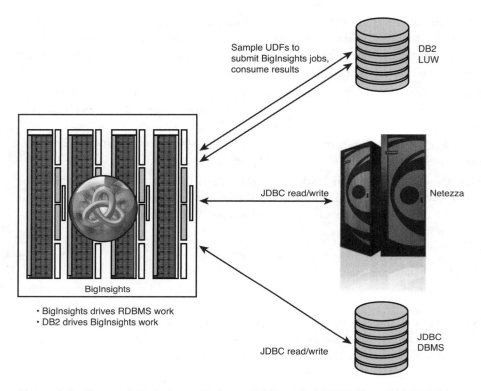

Figure 1.4   Connectivity between Netezza, DB2 or other RDBMS, and BigInsights

As you can see from the figure, BigInsights can drive Relational Database Management System (RDBMS) work by behaving as a database client and retrieving information from an RDBMS. This is mainly performed using JDBC and an open source language called Jaql (http://www-01.ibm.com/software/data/infosphere/hadoop/jaql/). In addition, the BigInsights web console also includes a database import/export application. The primary objective of this support is to provide dynamic transfers of data between BigInsights and the target DBMS.

In addition, you can have DB2 LUW initiate a Jaql job on BigInsights (DB2 as a client to BigInsights). DB2 includes sample user-defined functions (UDFs) to support this.

With either approach, users can write queries and applications that integrate data managed by BigInsights and an RDBMS or warehouse.

BigInsights Filtering, Aggregating, and Transforming Data for the Data Warehouse

After storing raw data in BigInsights, firms can manipulate, analyze, and summarize the data to gain new insights as well as feed downstream systems. In this manner, both the original (raw) data and modified forms are accessible for further processing.

One potential deployment approach involves using BigInsights as a source for a data warehouse. BigInsights can sift through large volumes of unstructured or semi-structured data, capturing relevant information that can augment existing corporate data in a warehouse. Figure 1.5 illustrates such a scenario, which offers firms the ability to broaden their analytic coverage without creating an undue burden for their existing systems. When in the warehouse, traditional business intelligence and query/report writing tools can work with the extracted, aggregated, and transformed portions of raw data stored in BigInsights.

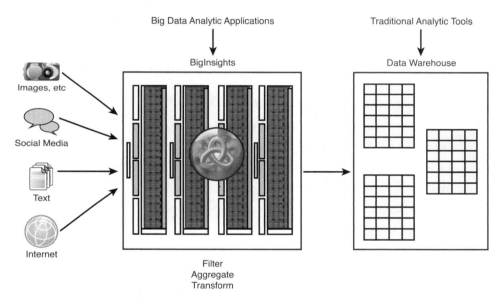

Figure 1.5   BigInsights filtering, aggregating, and transforming data for the data warehouse

DB2 Editions

DB2 for Linux, UNIX, and Windows (sometimes referred to as **LUW**) is developed using the C/C++ language. More than 90 percent of the code is common among these platforms. The remaining code is unique to take full advantage of the underlying platform architecture; however, the database functionality on all of these platforms is the same.

DB2 for z/OS, DB2 for VM/VSE, and DB2 for i use a different code base than that used by DB2 LUW. Note, however, that the Linux operating system extends across all of IBM's servers: System x®, System p®, and System z®. DB2 for Linux on all of these server platforms is the same. Thus, DB2 for Linux on System z uses the same code base and is licensed in the same way as DB2 for Linux on a System x (Intel®) platform.

Prior to DB2 10.5, each edition was built on top of the other by linking modules or object files that contained additional functionality. The core of the DB2 code was common across all editions. In this model each DB2 Edition had its own separate install image; if you wanted to upgrade from one DB2 Edition to a higher-end one to gain extra functionality, you had to install a separate image. Considering that some enterprises have IT policies where any new software installation requires full application testing and certification, this would incur a lot of unnecessary delays.

In DB2 10.5, selected editions share a common install image. There is no need to install new DB2 code if you want to upgrade an existing installation to a higher-end edition. A simple license certificate (also known as license key) update unlocks new capabilities in your existing DB2 installation. This makes it easy to deploy and start taking advantage of the more advanced DB2 editions in your enterprise. Chapter 3, "Installing DB2," provides more details about installing licenses.

There are seven editions and one feature offering in DB2 10.5:

- DB2 Advanced Enterprise Server Edition (AESE)
- DB2 Advanced Workgroup Server Edition (AWSE)
- DB2 Enterprise Server Edition (ESE)
- DB2 Workgroup Server Edition (WSE)
- DB2 Express Server Edition
- DB2 Express-C
- DB2 Developer Edition
- DB2 Advanced Recovery Feature

The DB2 10.5 offering portfolio gives you options to deploy DB2 in a single-server or multi-server clustered environment. The underlying technology in the portfolio can handle transactional processing, analytical processing, and mixed transactional and warehouse workloads. DB2 10.5 gives you incredible deployment flexibility without having to compromise on functionality or performance.

NOTE

All functionality and tools offered in prior versions of DB2 for Linux, UNIX, and Windows and InfoSphere Warehouse editions and features are consolidated and available in the DB2 10.5 offerings.

Four DB2 editions, namely AESE, AWSE, ESE, WSE, share a common install image. Applying the corresponding license certificate unlocks new capabilities or disable capabilities in your existing DB2 installation.

Figure 1.6 gives you an overview of all seven DB2 editions. Let's discuss each of these editions starting with DB2 Express-C, the entry-level offering at the bottom of the diagram.

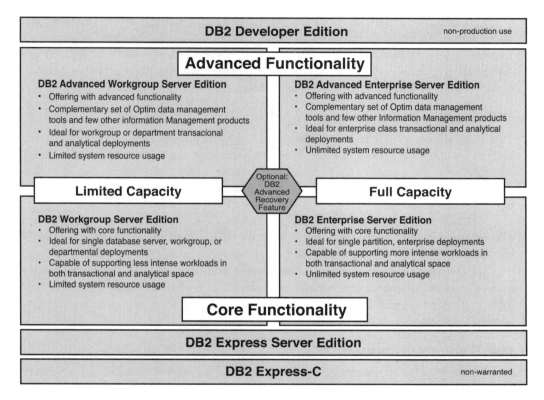

Figure 1.6   DB2 10.5 Editions

DB2 Express-C

DB2 Express-C is a DB2 data server available for download and deployment at no charge. The C stands for Community; this means it is an edition for the community of database enthusiasts. It is an ideal data server for small businesses and developers who develop database applications for their clients. The core code of DB2 Express-C is the same as the other DB2 editions. DB2 Express-C can be used in production or in a commercial setting. In addition, businesses can embed and distribute DB2 Express-C as part of their application also for free. DB2 Express-C does not impose limits on the number of instances per server or the number of users. However, it does have some system resource usage limitations. DB2 Express-C is available on Windows and Linux (on x86, x86–64, and Power), and Solaris on x86–64 systems. At the time of writing, it is also available on the Mac for DB2 10.1. It can utilize at most 16GB of memory and 2 processor cores. The memory resource limit is significantly lifted compared to previous versions of DB2 Express-C.

You can obtain DB2 Express-C technical assistance through a free community-based online forum. An optional renewable 12-month subscription license can be purchased for DB2 Express-C to obtain IBM DB2 Technical support (24/7) and also support for the SQL replication and the High Availability and Disaster Recovery (HADR) functionality. For further details, refer to the DB2 Express website: www.ibm.com/software/data/db2/express-c/.

DB2 Express Server Edition

DB2 Express Server Edition (DB2 Express) is ideal for businesses that require a data server but have minimal in-house database skills. This edition provides the same support as the other DB2 editions, but it also features simple installation, enhanced self-management, and other ease-of-use features. Businesses developing applications that require a database can embed DB2 Express as part of their solutions.

DB2 Express is available on Windows and Linux (on x86–64 and Power) and Solaris on x86–64 systems. DB2 Express can utilize at most 64GB of memory and 8 processor cores. The system resource limit is doubled compared to previous versions of DB2 Express.

DB2 Express includes complementary support entitlement of IBM Data Studio and a suite of database features such as time travel query, pureXML storage, text search, PL/SQL compatibility, advanced security management, and high availability capability including High Availability Disaster Recovery (HADR).

DB2 Workgroup Server Edition

DB2 Workgroup Server Edition (DB2 WSE) is a data server with functionalities suitable for single database server, workgroup, or medium-sized business environments. In addition to functions that come with DB2 Express, DB2 WSE enables table partitioning, and platform support is extended to also include AIX®, Solaris on SPARC, and HP-UX.

System resource usage allowed in a DB2 WSE deployment is doubled the amount of DB2 Express. DB2 WSE can use at most 128GB of memory and 16 processor cores. The resource limits of DB2 WSE is also lifted in DB2 10.5.

DB2 Enterprise Server Edition

DB2 Enterprise Server Edition (DB2 ESE) is a DB2 offering targeted for mid to large enterprises. It provides high performance, scalability, accessibility, and extensibility functionalities that make it one of the most popular choices for many enterprises.

DB2 ESE includes all the capabilities in DB2 WSE and additional functionalities to support more intense workloads in single database server environments for both transactional and analytical processing. DB2 ESE deployments also enjoy query parallelism capability, multi-temperature storage, warehouse cubing services, and few other warehouse tools.

DB2 ESE can run on Linux, UNIX, and Windows servers, and it has no limit in the amount of system resources it can use.

DB2 Advanced Workgroup Server Edition

DB2 Advanced Workgroup Server Edition (DB2 AWSE) is a new offering added to the DB2 family. DB2 AWSE is a fully functional offering that includes BLU Acceleration, DB2 pureScale, database partitioning, deep data compression, workload management, comprehensive warehouse capabilities, and various advanced replication technologies.

With three highly valuable deployment models, DB2 AWSE gives you the choice of the following options:

- Use BLU Acceleration to handle terabytes of data for speed of thought analytics and reporting.
- Use DB2 pureScale to handle millions of daily transactions requiring a mix of data reads and writes.
- Use database partitioning to run complex analytics while handling operational reads and writes for real-time decision making.

A suite of complementary Optim™ tools to manage database performance, deployment, administration, monitoring, and availability is included in DB2 AWSE. Database tools are discussed in more detail in Chapter 4, "Using Database Tools and Utilities."

Like DB2 WSE, DB2 AWSE can utilize at most 128GB of memory and 16 processor cores. This offering is ideal for mid-size to large-size businesses that need optimal and high performance of the three deployment models just discussed.

DB2 Advanced Enterprise Server Edition

DB2 Advanced Enterprise Server Edition (DB2 AESE) is the most complete data server offering, ideal for enterprise class transaction and analytical environments.

DB2 AESE is a fully functional edition that includes the three highly valuable deployment models described earlier for DB2 AWSE, adaptive data compression, workload management, full warehouse management capabilities, a complementary suite of Optim tools, and advanced replication and database federation support required for today's complex data environment.

In addition to the database support provided by the core DB2 server, both DB2 advanced editions bundle a few other IBM Information Management products, such as

- **IBM Cognos® Business Intelligence Reporting:** This tool provides a comprehensive set of reporting capabilities and collaborative reporting features. It helps you to make smarter business decisions.
- **IBM Mobile Database solution:** Delivers mobile capabilities that expand and modernize the infrastructure for DB2 to work seamlessly in the mobility space.

This edition imposes no system resource restrictions.

DB2 Developer Edition

DB2 Developer Edition (DB2 Developer) was previously known as the IBM Database Enterprise Developer Edition (DEDE). DB2 Developer is a product bundle that contains all the DB2 editions (except Express-C) just described. It comes with overriding license terms that provide a DB2 Developer customer entitlement to use all the underlying products and DB2 functionalities for *non-production use*. You can use the data servers under the DB2 Developer terms in development and test environments for non-production activities. Non-production activities include but are not limited to testing, performance tuning, fault diagnosis, internal benchmarking, staging, and quality assurance activities.

 NOTE

All DB2 editions are only available in 64-bit with the exception of DB2 Express-C and the DB2 Developer Edition, which also come in 32-bit for either Windows or Linux platforms.

DB2 Advanced Recovery Feature

DB2 Advanced Recovery Feature is an add-on offering that includes three products:

- DB2 Recovery Expert
- DB2 Merge Backup
- Optim High Performance Unload

These tools help you with database backup and recovery tasks, improve data availability, and mitigate risk in case of database failure.

The Advanced Recovery Feature is the only separately priced feature available in DB2 10.5. It can be purchased with any DB2 editions except DB2 Express-C.

NOTE

To find out more about what each DB2 edition offers, please refer to the DB2 Information Center at http://pic.dhe.ibm.com/infocenter/db2luw/v10r5/topic/com.ibm.db2.luw.licensing.doc/doc/r0053238.html.

IBM Data Server Clients and Driver Packages

To enable client applications to access one or more remote DB2 data servers, you can use the IBM data server clients and driver packages. The **IBM data server clients** are also known as the **common clients** because they support a number of IBM data servers, namely DB2 for LUW, DB2 for z/OS, DB2 for i, and Informix® data servers.

The data server clients are available in different packages to provide different types of support. There are five types of IBM data server clients and drivers:

- **IBM Data Server Driver Package:** Has everything you need to run applications using ODBC, CLI, .NET, OLE DB, PHP, Ruby, JDBC and SQLJ. This driver package is an ideal solution for application distribution in a mass deployment scenario. In Windows, this driver is available as an installable image (known as the merge modules) so that you can embed the driver in a Windows-based installation.

- **IBM Data Server Driver for JDBC and SQLJ:** Provides support for JDBC and SQLJ applications, Java™ stored procedures, and user-defined functions. JDBC 3.0 is supported by drivers db2jcc.jar and sqlj.zip. JDBC 4.0 is supported by drivers db2jcc4.jar and sqlj4.zip.

- **IBM Data Server Driver for ODBC and CLI:** Also known as the "CLI" driver, this type provides runtime support for ODBC and CLI applications.

- **IBM Data Server Runtime Client:** Has all the functionality from IBM Data Server Driver Package. In addition, it provides the interface to process commands for remote server administration.

- **IBM Data Server Client:** Provides runtime support of the programming languages just mentioned. It also comes with First Steps documentation, replication tools, samples, and tutorials.

You can download the data server clients and driver packages at no charge from the IBM web page at http://www.ibm.com/support/docview.wss?uid=swg21385217. Every DB2 server edition also comes with the clients and drivers. With an active DB2 server support and subscription, you also receive support for the client and driver packages.

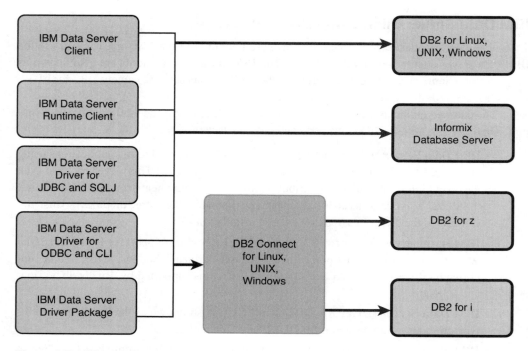

Figure 1.7   IBM data server client and driver packages

Mainframe Host Connectivity

DB2 Connect™ is a software product containing the license files required to communicate from a DB2 distributed client (also known as the **DRDA Application Requester**) to a host DB2 server (a **DRDA Application Server**). DRDA—Distributed Relational Database Architecture—is the standard that defines formats and protocols for providing transparent access to remote data. Host DB2 servers include DB2 for z/OS, DB2 for VM/VSE, and DB2 for i.

> **NOTE**
>
> DB2 Connect license entitlement is only required when connecting from DB2 LUW to a host DB2 server, such as DB2 for z/OS; it is *not* required in the other direction, for example, when DB2 for z/OS behaves as the client, and DB2 LUW is the server. DB2 Connect license entitlement can be obtained from the DB2 Connect software or apply the DB2 Connect license certificate to a Data Server Client installation.

Database Federation Support

Database Federation allows you to query and manipulate data stored on other servers. Target data source can be a relational database, a flat file, or a spreadsheet. When you issue an SQL statement in a federated environment, you might actually be accessing information from multiple databases and potentially multiple data servers, as illustrated in Figure 1.8.

Database federation support, accessing another DB2 for LUW and Informix databases, is included in all DB2 editions (including DB2 Express-C). To federate with DB2 for z/OS or DB2 for i databases, you need to acquire the DB2 Connect product or the IBM InfoSphere Federation Server.

IBM InfoSphere Federation Server provides federated support by making remote data sources from IBM or different vendors appear as if they were part of the same database. The federation server uses wrappers to communicate with and retrieve data from those other data sources; it encapsulates any conversions required from the source database and presents them to the target database as tables.

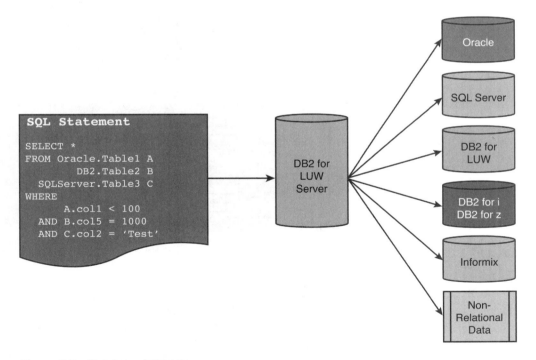

Figure 1.8 Database federation

Database Replication Support

Database Replication enables you propagate data to different servers to keep multiple databases synchronized. This can be useful in situations where a single server is used for day-to-day transaction operations and where issuing reporting queries at the same time would be costly for performance. By replicating the data to another server, the secondary server could be used for reporting without disturbing the primary server. There are a few replication technologies DB2 servers support. Figure 1.9 illustrates an overview of the SQL replication implementation, which is the most mature replication technology.

In the figure, you can see that the data changes captured at one server are later applied to another (target) server. The box on the far left box shows the source server, and the box on the far right shows the target server. The second and third boxes contain the "capture" and "apply" components, respectively.

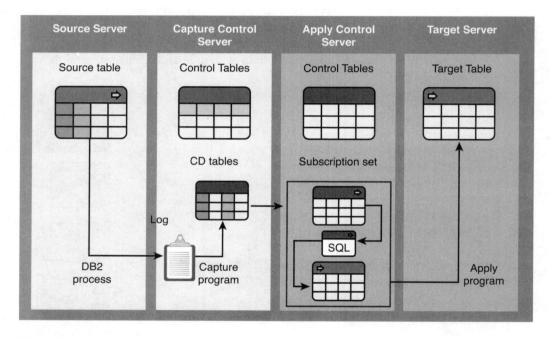

Figure 1.9   DB2 replication environment

All DB2 editions (except DB2 Express-C) have built-in support for SQL replication when both source and target databases are DB2 for LUW or Informix databases. For databases from Oracle or SQL Server, DB2 for z/OS, or DB2 for i, the IBM InfoSphere Data Replication software is required.

IBM InfoSphere Data Replication supports three replication technologies:

• SQL replication

• Q replication

• Change data capture (CDC) replication

As previously mentioned, SQL replication is included in most DB2 LUW editions. Q replication and CDC replication are more advanced replication technologies included only in the DB2 AWSE and AESE offerings.

> **NOTE**
>
> IBM InfoSphere Federation Server and IBM InfoSphere Data Replication were formerly known as WebSphere Information Integrator.

DB2 Syntax Diagram Conventions

DB2 supports a comprehensive set of statements for data access and manipulation. These statements are documented online in the DB2 Information Center, which gives you access to all information about DB2 as well as major DB2 features and components. It can be conveniently accessed by using a browser, as shown in Figure 1.10. The DB2 Information Center is available at http://pic.dhe.ibm.com/infocenter/db2luw/v10r5/index.jsp.

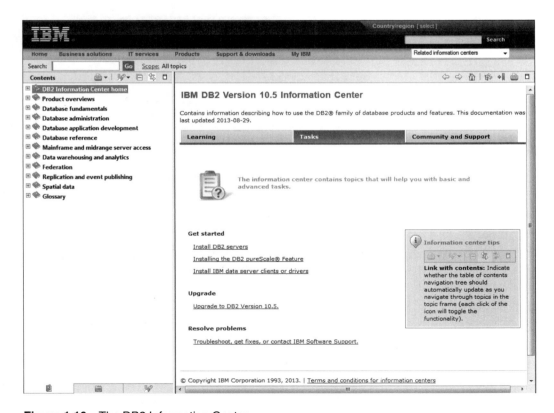

Figure 1.10   The DB2 Information Center

   You can find the syntax of any commands or statements we introduce in this book in the DB2 Information Center. Understanding how to read the syntax diagrams helps you use the numerous options available with many of the statements.

   Syntax diagrams are all read from left to right and top to bottom, following the path of each line. Table 1.1 summarizes a few of the most commonly used symbols in a syntax diagram.

Table 1.1   Summary of Some Symbols Used in Syntax Diagrams

Symbol	Description
>>---	Indicates the beginning of a syntax diagram
--->	Indicates that the syntax is continued on the next line
>---	Indicates that the syntax is continued from the previous line
---><	Indicates the end of a syntax diagram

   When a mandatory field is required, it appears on the horizontal line (the main path) like this.

```
>>-mandatory_field------------------------------------><
```

   Optional fields appear below the main path.

```
>>-mandatory_field--+---------------+------------------><
                    '-optional_field-'
```

   If an optional field appears above the main path, it means that it is the default option.

```
                    .-default_field-.
>>-mandatory_field--+---------------+------------------><
                    '-optional_field-'
```

   If two or more mandatory choices are available, one of the mandatory choices appears in the main path, and the rest appear in a stack. You must choose one of these options.

```
>>-mandatory_field--+-mandatory_choice1-+--------------><
                    '-mandatory_choice2-'
```

   An arrow returning to the left, above the main line, indicates an option can be repeated. In this example, repeated options are separated by one or more blanks.

```
                     .----------------.
                     V                |
>>-mandatory_field----repeatable_field-+---------------><
```

   If the repeat arrow contains a comma, you must separate repeated items with a comma.

```
                     .-,--------------.
                     V                |
>>-mandatory_field----repeatable_field-+---------------><
```

Example 1:

```
>>---- Word1---- Word2 --------------------------------<>>
>>--------- Word3---- Word4 ---------------------------<><
```

Output: Word1 Word2 Word3 Word4

All tokens that are in sequence must be included in the order in which they are listed.

Example 2:

```
>>----Word1----+---------------+-----------------------<><
               '-optionalWord---'
```

Output 1: Word1

Output 2: Word1 optionalWord

The optionalWord token is optional and does not have to be included in the statement.

Example 3:

```
              .-,-----------.      .----Word2----.
              V             |      V             |
>>----Word1-------Variable--+-----------------------------<><
```

Output 1: Word1

Output 2: Word1 Variable1, Variable 2, Variable 3

Output 3: Word1 Word2

Output 4: Word1 Variable 1 Word2

You should now feel comfortable reading syntax diagrams in the DB2 documentation. Browse through the DB2 online documentation and review some examples there.

```
>>-+-STOP--+-DATABASE MANAGER-+-+-----------------------------">
   |       +-DB MANAGER-------+ |
   |       '-DBM-------------' |
   '-db2stop------------------'

>--+-----------------------------+-------------------------">
   '-+---------------+--identifier-'
     +-DBPARTITIONNUM-+
     +-MEMBER---------+
     '-CF------------'

>--+---------------------------------+--+-----------------+---">
   '-INSTANCE ON--hostname--+-------+-'  '-PROFILE--profile-'
                            '-FORCE-'

>--+---------------------------------+-------------------------">
   '-DROP DBPARTITIONNUM--identifier-'

>--+----------------------------------------------+------------">
   '-FORCE--+----------------------------------+-'
            '-+---------------+----identifier---'
              +-DBPARTITIONNUM-+
```

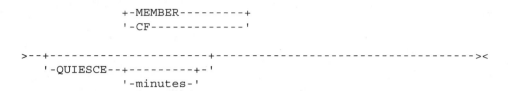

```
                    +-MEMBER---------+
                    '-CF------------'

>--+---------------------+------------------------------------>< 
   '-QUIESCE--+---------+-' 
              '-minutes-'
```

Case Study

John recently graduated from Pennsylvania State University, where he learned DB2 as part of the IBM Academic Initiative program (http://www-03.ibm.com/ibm/university/academic/pub/page/academic_initiative), a program that provides DB2 and other IBM software for free to teach database skills.

While at school, he worked with a DB2 Enterprise Server Edition installed on a System p machine at the university computer lab. He was given SYSADM authority and was able to see connections from many different clients to all created databases using the list applications command. John wanted to develop a Java application using the JDBC Type 4 driver, so he downloaded and installed on his laptop the 90-Day Try-and-Buy version of DB2 Express Server Edition. With this edition, he was able to build, test, and run his application and connect to the database created on his laptop. Because the client and data server were both on his laptop, he was dealing with a local client connection.

John wanted to test whether his application would work as a remote client, so he used the client software that comes with DB2 Express to test his application against the database he had created earlier on the university's System p machine. This also worked, and John was feeling like a DB2 guru.

Eager to show his program to his colleagues, he emailed the executable to his friend Peter, who had just bought a new laptop with Microsoft® Windows installed. Peter detached the file and tried to run the application against John's database on the University's pSeries server. After spending a few hours trying to figure out why he couldn't, he dropped by John's place. John realized that Peter had to download and install either an IBM Data Server Runtime Client, an IBM Data Server Client, or just the IBM Data Server JDBC and SQLJ driver, as he needed the JDBC Type 4 driver on his laptop. Given that Peter was not going to develop a new program nor administer a database, John asked Peter to download just the IBM Data Server JDBC and SQLJ driver from the IBM website—and after installation, voila! the program ran successfully.

After John's graduation, he applied for a position at a medium-sized company in his hometown. To prepare for his interview, John again tested the program he had written against his laptop database, but the Try-and-Buy evaluation period had expired. John figured that he would always need DB2 on his laptop, so he decided to buy the permanent license. When John received the license file after the purchase, he installed it on his laptop with the command db2licm -a filename. With this problem resolved, John demonstrated his program during the job interview and was immediately hired.

The company John worked for was using DB2 Workgroup, His manager wanted to expand and modify the application running on DB2 LUW to also connect to a DB2 for z/OS host data server. In general, applications built for DB2 LUW work fine with DB2 for z/OS. However there are some commands and SQL that might not be compatible. John used "SQL Reference for Cross-Platform Development" (http://www.ibm.com/developerworks/data/library/techarti cle/0206sqlref/0206sqlref.html) to help identify and handle the incompatibilities. John led the project and demonstrated that no changes were needed for the application; it simply needed to also connect to the database on DB2 for z/OS. However DB2 Workgroup does not come with the DB2 Connect software component, so the company would need to purchase this software or get the DB2 Developer Edition, as it would be cheaper and have most of the software for all DB2 editions. DB2 Developer is licensed per developer. This company did not have that many developers, so this option satisfied their needs. If the company decided to use DB2 in a production environment, they would have to buy the appropriate edition and license.

Given that the company was expanding, the marketing and sales team in his company needed to make real-time decisions to be responsive and competitive. John performed a study to collect requirements from these teams and realized that structured and unstructured data would be growing exponentially in the near term and that this would impact performance. Moreover, new queries with analytic workloads would cripple the existing system if left untouched. After his thorough study, he recommended the IBM PureData System family to the Chief Technology Officer (CTO). They reviewed the features and benefits of each PureData System model and felt that the IBM PureData System for Operational Analytics fit their needs perfectly.

John contacted IBM and participated in the PureExperience™ program. His technical team and IBM performed a proof of concept with the company's applications and the PureData System. The optimized data warehouse system satisfied what John and his company were looking for

- Leveraged the PureData System built-in expertise and received high performance analysis of both historical and operational data
- Deployed the PureData System in hours and provided insights into new areas of the business immediately
- Simplified and reduced IT life cycle and costs significantly

After a successful implementation of the IBM PureData system in his company, John was happy with the results. However, he knows that to keep competitive, his company needs to be ahead of the curve. John stays on top of new offerings added to the IBM PureData family and monitors IBM marketing programs to utilize the investment already made and the skill set his team already has.

Summary

This chapter gave you a brief history of DB2, from the past to the present. Each DB2 release has brought breakthrough technologies and new value propositions to customers. DB2 10.5 is not an exception. With its BLU Acceleration capability, it provides significant response time improvements in reporting and analytics workloads and significant storage space savings.

The chapter also discussed the concepts of big data, cloud computing, and smarter planet, and explained where DB2 fit in the IBM Big Data platform. In this platform, we also talked about the IBM PureData System for Transactions and IBM PureData System for Operational Analytics, both of which use DB2 as their core. IBM PureData Systems offer built-in expertise, integration by design, and a simplified experience throughout the life cycle.

You have also seen the new DB2 10.5 product offering portfolio. You can choose to start with DB2 editions with core functionality and limited system resource capacity. As your business needs grow, you can easily update to a more advanced edition with a seamless upgrade path that might require a simple license key update to your existing installation. This would unlock other functionalities in the product.

DB2 is a client-server data management product. This chapter also discussed the types of clients available with DB2. You can use the traditional full Data Server Client or the individual lightweight Data Server drivers. Different drivers are available to provide different types of application interface support, such as JDBC, SQLJ, ODBC, CLI, .NET, OLE DB, PHP, and Ruby On Rails.

Review Questions

1.   Why is DB2 called "DATABASE 2?"

2.   What DB2 for LUW technology is used in the IBM PureData System for Transaction?

3.   Can an application developed for DB2 Express Server Edition work with DB2 Enterprise Server Edition?

4.   Is DB2 Connect required to connect from a DB2 for z/OS client to a DB2 for Linux, UNIX, and Windows server?

5.   What is the name of the technology in DB2 for LUW that provides memory-based column store?

6.   With any edition of DB2 for LUW installed, is IBM InfoSphere Federation Server entitlement needed to set up a federation environment between a DB2 LUWserver and an Informix server?

7.   Why are there different models of PureData System?

8.   Does DB2 for Linux, UNIX, and Windows have one single file that is used for installation in any of these platforms?

9.   What does the DB2 database partitioning enable you to do?

10. What should you do when your Try-and-Buy license period expires and you would like to buy a permanent license?

11. Which of the following products is the minimum required on the Windows client to *run* a DB2 application accessing a DB2 database on UNIX?

    A. DB2 Enterprise

    B. DB2 Express-C

    C. DB2 Connect

    D. IBM Data Server Runtime Client

12. Which of the following products is the minimum required to *run* a DB2 application using JDBC Type 4?

    A. IBM Data Server Client

    B. IBM Data Server Runtime Client

    C. Data Server Driver for JDBC and SQLJ

    D. Data Server Client

13. Which of the following DB2 editions can I choose from if I need warehouse and data partition functionality?

    A. DB2 Workgroup

    B. DB2 Express

    C. DB2 Enterprise

    D. DB2 Advanced Workgroup

14. Which of the following DB2 Edition does *not* include SQL replication technology?

    A. DB2 Workgroup

    B. DB2 Express-C

    C. DB2 Express

    D. DB2 Enterprise

15. Which of the following DB2 edition does *not* have system resource usage limitation?

    A. DB2 Workgroup

    B. DB2 Advanced Workgroup

    C. DB2 Express

    D. DB2 Enterprise

16. In a small start-up software development company, there are three developers developing and testing their existing Oracle application to also support DB2 for LUW. Due to the tight software release cycle, they need to install DB2 on multiple servers to leverage their testing system in parallel. Which of the following products fits their need the most?

    A. DB2 Enterprise

    B. DB2 Advanced Enterprise

    C. DB2 Developer

    D. DB2 Advanced Workgroup

17. A software development company would like to test an application that connects to both DB2 for LUW as well as DB2 for z/OS. Which of the following would suit its needs the best?

    A. DB2 Enterprise Server Edition

    B. DB2 Workgroup Server Edition

    C. DB2 Connect Enterprise Edition

    D. DB2 Developer Edition

18. Which of the following software can run on a System z server?

    A. DB2 for Linux, UNIX, and Windows

    B. DB2 for iSeries

    C. DB2 Connect

    D. Data Server Runtime Client

19. Which of the following is the most suitable client for application distribution in a mass deployment scenario?

    A. IBM Data Server Driver Package

    B. IBM Data Server Driver for ODBC and CLI

    C. IBM Data Server Runtime Client

    D. IBM Data Server Client

20. Which IBM data server client provides support for JDBC and SQLJ applications? (Choose all that apply.)

    A. IBM Data Server Driver Package

    B. IBM Data Server Driver for JDBC and SQLJ

    C. IBM Data Server Runtime Client

    D. IBM Data Server Client

## CHAPTER 2

DB2 at a Glance:
The Big Picture

This chapter is like a book within a book: It covers a vast range of topics that provide you with not only a good introduction to DB2 core concepts and components, but also an understanding of how these components work together and where they fit in the DB2 scheme of things. After reading this chapter you should have a general knowledge of the DB2 architecture that will help you better understand the topics discussed in the rest of the book. Subsequent chapters revisit and expand what has been discussed here.

In this chapter, you learn about

- SQL statements, XQuery statements, and DB2 commands
- Database tools and utilities
- The DB2 environment
- The DB2 database partitioned environment
- DB2 pureScale
- Database federation
- Use of uppercase versus lowercase in DB2

A DB2 environment is made up of many components. You interact with DB2 by issuing SQL statements, XQuery statements, and DB2 commands. You can issue these statements and commands from an application, or you can use graphical interface tools. Statements and commands arrive at the DB2 server for processing. This is shown in Figure 2.1.

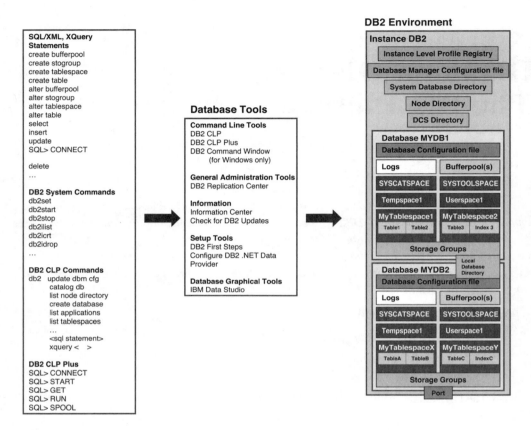

Figure 2.1   DB2 at a glance

SQL Statements, XQuery Statements, and DB2 Commands

SQL is the standard language used for retrieving and modifying data in a relational database. An SQL council formed by several leading companies in the industry determines the standard for these SQL statements, and the different relational database management systems (RDBMSs) follow these standards to make it easier for customers to use their databases. Recent additions to the standard include XML extension functions. These are also referred to as SQL/XML extension functions. This section introduces the different categories of SQL statements and presents some examples.

The XML Query Language (XQuery) specification is a language used for querying XML documents. XQuery includes the XML Path Language (XPath), which is also used to query XML documents. The XQuery specification is managed by W3C, a consortium formed by several industry leaders and academia. In this section, we provide a few simple XQuery and XPath examples.

DB2 commands are directives specific to DB2 that allow you to perform tasks against a DB2 server. There are four types of DB2 commands:

- DB2 System commands
- Command Line Processor (CLP) commands
- Command Line Processor Plus (CLPPlus) commands
- DB2 Text Search commands

> **NOTE**
>
> SQL statements and DB2 commands can be specified in uppercase or lowercase. However, in Linux or UNIX some of the commands are case-sensitive; see section "Use of Uppercase Versus Lowercase in DB2" for an explanation of the use of uppercase versus lowercase in DB2.

SQL Statements

SQL statements allow you to work with the relational and XML data stored in your database. The statements are applied against the database you are connected to, not against the entire DB2 environment. There are three different classes of SQL statements: Data Definition Language (DDL), Data Manipulation Language (DML), and Data Control Language (DCL).

DDL statements create, modify, or drop database objects. For example

```
CREATE INDEX ix1 ON t1 (salary);
ALTER TABLE t1 ADD COLUMN hiredate DATE;
DROP VIEW view1;
```

DML statements insert, update, delete, or retrieve data from the database objects. For example

```
INSERT INTO t1 VALUES (10,'Johnson','Peter');
UPDATE t1 SET lastname = 'Smith' WHERE firstname = 'Peter';
DELETE FROM t1;
SELECT * FROM t1 WHERE salary > 45000;
SELECT lastname
  FROM patients
 WHERE xmlexists ($p/address[zipcode='12345'] passing
                  PATIENTS.INFO as p)
   AND salary > 45000;
```

DCL statements grant or revoke privileges or authorities to perform database operations on the objects in your database. For example

```
GRANT  select ON employee TO peter;
REVOKE update ON employee FROM paul;
```

> **NOTE**
>
> SQL statements are commonly referred to simply as "statements" in most relational data-base management systems (RDBMS) books. For an introduction to SQL, refer to *Appendix B*. For detailed syntax of SQL statements, see the *DB2 Information Center, under Data-base fundamentals > SQL*.

XQuery Statements

XQuery statements enable you to work with relational and XML data. The statements are applied against the database you are connected to, not against the entire DB2 environment. There are two main ways to work with XML documents in DB2:

- **Xpath:** XPath is part of XQuery. Working with XPath is like working with the Change Directory (cd) command in Linux or Windows. Using the cd operating system com-mand, one can go from one subdirectory to another subdirectory in the directory tree. Similarly, by using the slash (/) in XPath, you can navigate a tree, which represents the XML document. For example, Figure 2.2 shows an XML document in both serialized format and parsed hierarchical format.

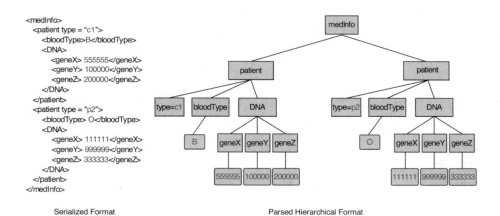

Serialized Format   Parsed Hierarchical Format

Figure 2.2   An XML document in serialized and parsed hierarchical format

Table 2.1 shows some XPath expressions and the corresponding values obtained using the XML document in Figure 2.2 as input.

Table 2.1   Sample XPath Expressions

XPath Expression	Value to Be Returned
/medInfo/patient/@type	c1 p2
/medInfo/patient/bloodType	\<bloodType>B\</bloodType> \<bloodType>O\</bloodType>
/medInfo/patient/DNA/geneX	\<geneX>555555\</geneX> \<geneX>111111\</geneX>

- **XQuery FLWOR expression:** FLWOR stands for

  - **FOR:** Iterates through an XML sequence, binds variables to items.
  - **LET:** Assigns an XML sequence to a variable.
  - **WHERE:** Eliminates items of the iteration; use for filtering.
  - **ORDER:** Reorders items of the iteration.
  - **RETURN:** Constructs query results; can return another XML document or even HTML.

  For example, using the XML document as shown in Figure 2.2, an XQuery expression could be

```
    for $g in db2-fn:xmlcolumn('GENOME.INFO')/medInfo
    let $h := $g//DNA/geneX/text()
  where $g/patient/@type = "c1"
return <geneXList>
          {$h}
       </geneXList>
```

which would return:

```
       <geneXList>
           555555
       </geneXList>
```

DB2 System Commands

You use DB2 system commands for many purposes, including starting services or processes, invoking utilities, and configuring parameters. Most DB2 system commands do not require the instance—the DB2 server engine process—to be started (instances are discussed later in this chapter). DB2 system command names are prefixed with db2. For example:

```
db2start
db2set
db2icrt
```

> **NOTE**
>
> Many DB2 system commands provide a quick way to obtain syntax and help information about the command by using the -h option. For example, typing db2set -h displays the syntax of the db2set command, with an explanation of its optional parameters.

DB2 Command Line Processor (CLP) Commands

DB2 Command Line Processor (CLP) commands are processed by the CLP utility (introduced in the next section). These commands typically require the instance to be started, and they can be used for database and instance monitoring and for parameter configuration. For example

```
list applications
create database
catalog tcpip node
```

You invoke the Command Line Processor by entering db2 at an operating system prompt. If you enter db2 and press the Enter key, you are then working with the CLP in interactive mode, and you can enter the CLP commands as just shown. On the other hand, if you don't want to work with the CLP in interactive mode, precede each CLP command with db2. For example

```
db2 list applications
db2 create database
db2 catalog tcpip node
```

Many books, including this one, display CLP commands as db2 CLP_command for this reason. Chapter 4, "Using Database Tools and Utilities," explains the CLP in greater detail.

> **NOTE**
>
> On the Windows platform, `db2` must be entered in a DB2 Command Window, not at the operating system prompt.

> **NOTE**
>
> A quick way to obtain syntax and help information about a CLP command is to use the question mark (?) character followed by the command. For example
>
> `db2 ? catalog tcpip node`
> or just
>
> `db2 ? catalog`
> For detailed syntax of a command, refer to the DB2 Information Center.

DB2 Command Line Processor Plus (CLPPlus) Commands

DB2 Command Line Processor Plus (CLPPlus) is a command-line interface introduced in DB2 9.7. Like the CLP, CLPPlus enables you to develop, edit, and execute SQL statements and compile and run SQL stored procedures and functions. CLPPlus provides a quick and easy way for database administrators (DBAs) and application developers familiar with Oracle's SQLPlus to work with scripts and run command-line reports.

CLPPlus must be started before any CLPPlus commands can be run. You get an `SQL>` prompt when CLPPlus is started. Chapter 4 explains CLPPlus in greater detail.

Following are some example CLPPlus commands:

```
SQL> CONNECT db2inst1@localhost:50000/sample
SQL> START resourceReport.sql
SQL> GET resourceReport.sql
SQL> RUN
```

DB2 Text Search Commands

DB2 Text Search commands, as the name implies, are used to administer and manage your DB2 Text Search environment. DB2 Text Search is powered by the IBM Enterprise Content Management (ECM) Text Search server. It enables you to issue SQL, SQL/XML, and XQuery statements to perform text search queries on data stored in a DB2 database. After DB2 Text Search server is successfully installed, you need to start the text search instance service with this command:

```
db2ts "START FOR TEXT"
```

Then enable the database for text search with the command

```
db2ts "ENABLE DATABASE FOR TEXT"
```

You can use the SQL and XML built-in search functions enable you to perform matches with search patterns. The three built-in search functions are

- **CONTAINS:** Returns a NULL or an INTEGER value of 0 or 1 depending on whether the input text document matches the text search condition.

- **xmlcolumn-contains:** Returns a NULL or an INTEGER value 1 or 0 depending on whether the input text document of XML data type matches the text search condition.

- **SCORE:** Returns a NULL or DOUBLE value between 0 and 1, indicating the extent to which the text document meets the search criteria.

To improve performance of your text search queries, you can create text search indexes and populate the indexes with data. After you enable a database for DB2 Text Search, you can create text search indexes on columns that contain the text that you want to search. DB2 Text Search commands must begin with `db2ts`. For example

- `db2ts CREATE INDEX mytitleidx FOR TEXT ON books(title) LANGUAGE AUTO` command creates a text search index for the text column. The column data can then be searched using the text search functions.

- `db2ts DROP INDEX mytitleidx` drops the text search index associated with a text column.

- `db2ts UPDATE INDEX mytitleidx` populates the text search index based on the current contents of a text column.

Database Tools and Utilities

DB2 comes with a comprehensive set of tools and utilities to help you manage your data and applications. The tools and utilities are mainly categorized into command-line tools and graphical tools. Chapter 4 covers these tools in more detail. For now, let's get familiarized with them.

Command-Line Tools

Command-line tools, as the name implies, enable you to issue DB2 CLP commands, DB2 CLP-Plus commands, DB2 Text Search commands, SQL statements, and XQuery statements from a command-line interface. The three text-based interfaces are the Command Window, Command Line Processor, and the Command Line Processor Plus. The Command Window is available only on Windows, but the CLP and CLPPlus are available on all other platforms.

On Windows, you can launch the command-line tools from the Windows menu, as shown in Figure 2.3.

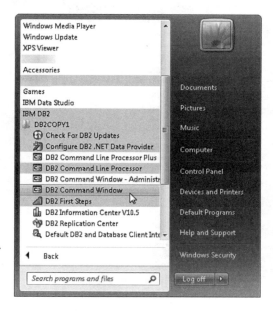

Figure 2.3 DB2 menu on Windows

IBM Data Studio

IBM Data Studio is an Eclipse-based integrated development environment (IDE). The software is available for download and use at no charge and with no time restrictions. It can be downloaded from the IBM website. Support entitlement of the IBM Data Studio is included in every DB2 edition. IBM Data Studio provides a single environment for database administration and application development. You can perform tasks that are related to database modeling and design, develop database applications, administer and manage databases, tune SQL performance, and monitor databases all in one single tool. This is an ideal tool that fosters teamwork with team members having different roles and responsibilities.

Figure 2.4 illustrates the IBM Data Studio Task Launcher, which provides you with a quick way to get started based on specific tasks.

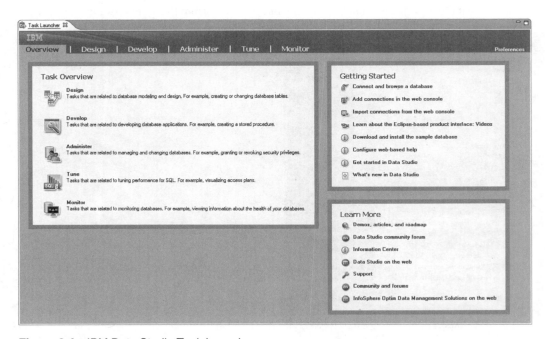

Figure 2.4   IBM Data Studio Task Launcher

In each tab in Data Studio, key and primary tasks are listed in the box on the left, as shown in Figure 2.5, and are described in more detail next. To learn more about the tasks and be able to perform more advanced functionality, advanced tools available in the InfoSphere Optim portfolio are listed in the *Learn More* box.

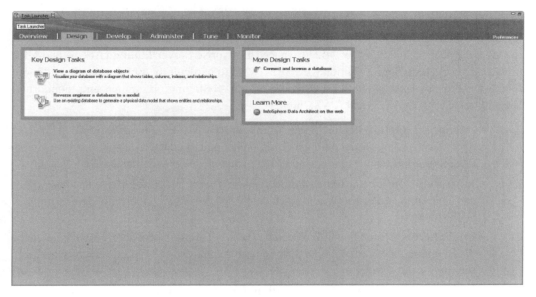

Figure 2.5 IBM Data Studio Task Launcher—Design tab

- **Design tab:** Provides a diagram of database objects and enables you to reverse-engineer a database to a model. If you need a more advanced tool to design a database, InfoSphere Data Architect is recommended.

- **Develop tab:** Provides you guidance on development tasks such as creating and running SQL statements, stored procedures, coding Java SQL applications using pureQuery syntax, and managing database routines deployment.

- **Administer tab:** Brings you a guided assist feature to administer and manage the database, database objects, SQL scripts, database jobs, and security privileges.

- **Tune tab:** Provides wizards to tune SQL queries, query workloads, and compare data access plan.

- **Monitor tab:** Helps you to monitor the health of the database, provides a summary of health alerts and indicators across your database. You can also view currently connected applications of the database, read-write statistics of the applications, and the table space usage summary.

Chapter 4 provides more details to get you started with IBM Data Studio and IBM Data Studio Web Console.

Design, Configuration, Tuning, and Monitoring Tools

In addition to IBM Data Studio, a comprehensive set of advanced tools in the InfoSphere Optim portfolio are also included in the DB2 Advanced Enterprise Server Edition (AESE) and DB2 Advanced Workgroup Server Edition (AWSE). They are particularly useful in larger and more complex enterprise environments for database design, configuration, tuning, and monitoring. The additional tools in AESE and AWSE are

- **InfoSphere Optim Performance Manager (OPM) Extended Edition:** This is a performance analysis and tuning tool for managing DB2 databases by using a web interface. It offers extended monitoring of DB2 databases as well as database applications.
- **InfoSphere Optim Configuration Manager:** This is a tool to manage database client configurations, track configuration changes, and record and analyze activities in your DB2 systems.
- **InfoSphere Optim Query Workload Tuner:** This is a tool that provides advance query tuning capabilities. It can also be used to analyze and monitor query workloads running on the data servers.
- **InfoSphere Optim pureQuery Runtime for LUW:** This tool is used to deploy pure-Query applications. pureQuery runs on top of Java DataBase Connectivity (JDBC). It is a simple, straightforward programming model for data access and simplifies database application development.
- **InfoSphere Data Architect (IDA):** This tool provides a comprehensive development environment for data modeling, detecting and mapping related data structures, and developing database applications.

Setup Tools

The following tools help you set up your system, provide tutorials, and install add-ins for development:

- **First Steps** is a good starting point for new DB2 users who wish to become familiar with the product. This tool enables you to create a sample database and provides tutorials that help you familiarize yourself with DB2.
- **Configure DB2 .NET Data Provider** enables you to easily configure this provider for .NET applications.
- **Default DB2 and Database Client Interface Selection Wizard** (Windows only) enables you to choose the DB2 installation copy to use as the default. Multiple DB2 installations are possible on the same machine, but one of them should be chosen as the default copy. This tool also helps you choose the default IBM database client interface (ODBC/CLI driver and .NET provider) copy.

   • **Replication Center** helps you set up and manage your replication environment. Use
   DB2 replication when you want to propagate data from one location to another.

Information Tools

The **DB2 Information Center** contains topics for you to learn about the product and help you
with basic and advanced tasks. You can install the Information Center locally on your computer
or intranet server or access it via the Internet.

   The **Check for DB2 Updates** menu option is used to obtain the most up-to-date information about the DB2 product.

The DB2 Environment

Several items control the behavior of your database system. We first describe the DB2 environment in a single-partition database. In sections "Data Partitioning" and "DB2 pureScale,"
we expand the material to include concepts relevant to multi-partition database systems and
DB2 pureScale, respectively (we don't want to overload you with information at this stage in the
chapter).

   Figure 2.6 provides an overview of the DB2 environment. Consider the following when
you review this figure:

   • The figure might look complex, but don't be overwhelmed by first impressions! Each
     item in the figure is discussed in detail in the following sections.

   • Because we reference Figure 2.6 throughout this chapter, *we strongly recommend that
     you bookmark page 44*. This figure is available for free in color as a GIF file on the
     book's website (www.ibmpressbooks.com/title/0131580183). Consider printing it.

   • The commands shown in the figure can be issued from the Command Window on Win-
     dows or the operating system prompt on Linux and UNIX. Chapter 4 describes equiva-
     lent methods to perform these commands using the database graphical tools.

   • Each arrow points to a set of three commands. The first command in each set (in blue if
     you printed the figure using a color printer) inquires about the contents of a configura-
     tion file; the second command (in black) indicates the syntax to modify these contents;
     and the third command (in purple) illustrates how to use the command.

   • The numbers in parentheses in Figure 2.6 match the superscripts in the headings in the
     following subsections.

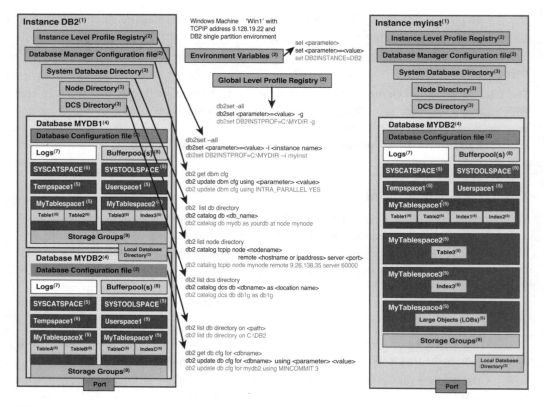

Figure 2.6   The DB2 environment

An Instance[1]

In DB2, an instance provides an independent environment where databases can be created for applications to access. Because the environments are independent, databases in separate instances can have the same name. For example, in Figure 2.11 the database called *MYDB1* is associated to instance *DB2*, and another database called *MYDB2* is associated with instance *myinst*. Instances enable users to have separate, independent environments for different purposes such as for development, testing, and production use.

When DB2 is installed on the Windows platform, an instance named *DB2* is created by default. In Linux and UNIX environments, if you choose to create the default instance, it is called *db2inst1*.

To create an instance explicitly, use

```
db2icrt <instance_name>
```

To drop an instance, use

```
db2idrop <instance_name>
```

To start the current instance, use

```
db2start
```

To stop the current instance, use

```
db2stop
```

When an instance is created on Linux and UNIX, logical links to the DB2 executable code are generated. For example, if the server in Figure 2.6 was a Linux or UNIX server and the instances *DB2* and *myinst* were created, both of them could be linked to the same DB2 libraries and binaries. A logical link works as an alias or pointer to another program. For non-root Linux and UNIX installations as we see in Chapter 3, each instance has its own local copy of the DB2 code under the sqllib directory. On Windows, you can also have multiple DB2 installations (same or different levels) installed on the server. *DB2* instances can be created running on any one of the DB2 installations.

The Database Administration Server

The Database Administration Server (DAS) is a daemon or process running on the database server that allows for remote graphical administration from remote clients such as IBM Data Studio. If you don't need to administer your DB2 server from a remote client, you don't need to start the DAS. Note that the DAS needs to be running at the data server you are planning to administer remotely, not at the DB2 client. There can only be one DAS per server regardless of the number of instances or DB2 install copies on the server.

To start the DAS, use the following command:

```
db2admin start
```

To stop the DAS, use this command:

```
db2admin stop
```

DB2 Profile Registries[2] and DB2 Configuration Files[2]

Like many other RDBMSs, DB2 uses different mechanisms to influence the behavior of the database management system. These include

- Environment variables
- DB2 profile registry variables
- DB2 configuration parameters

Environment Variables

Environment variables are defined at the operating system level. On Windows, you can create a new entry for a variable or edit the value of an existing one by choosing **Control Panel > System > Advanced system settings > Advanced tab > Environment Variables**. On Linux and UNIX, you can normally add a line to execute the script db2profile (Bourne or Korn shell) or db2cshrc (C shell) (provided after DB2 installation) to the instance owner's *.login* or *.profile* initialization files.

The DB2INSTANCE environment variable enables you to specify the instance to which all commands apply by default. If DB2INSTANCE is set to *myinst*, then issuing the command CRE-ATE DATABASE mydb creates a database associated to instance *myinst*. If you wanted to create this database in instance *DB2*, you would first change the value of the DB2INSTANCE variable to DB2. Using the Control Panel (Windows) or the user profile (Linux or UNIX) to set the value of an environment variable guarantees that value is used the next time you open a window or session. If you only want to change this value temporarily while in a given window or session, you can use the operating system set command on Windows or export on Linux or UNIX. The following command sets the value of the DB2INSTANCE environment variable to DB2.

```
set DB2INSTANCE=DB2 (on Windows)
```

or

```
export DB2INSTANCE=DB2 (on Linux and UNIX)
```

A common mistake when using the command is to leave spaces before and/or after the equal sign (=); no spaces should be entered. To check the current setting of this variable, you can use any of these three commands:

```
echo %DB2INSTANCE%   (Windows only)
set DB2INSTANCE
db2 get instance
```

For a list of all available instances in your system, issue the following command:

```
db2ilist
```

The DB2 Profile Registry

The word *registry* always causes confusion when working with DB2 on Windows. The DB2 profile registry variables, or simply the DB2 registry variables, have no relation whatsoever with the Windows Registry variables. The DB2 registry variables provide a centralized location where some key variables influencing DB2's behavior reside.

> **NOTE**
>
> Some of the DB2 registry variables are platform-specific.

The DB2 Profile Registry is divided into four categories:

- The DB2 global-level profile registry
- The DB2 instance-level profile registry
- The DB2 instance node-level profile registry
- The DB2 user-level profile registry

The first two are the most common ones. The main difference between the global-level and the instance-level profile registries, as you can tell from their names, is the scope to which the variables apply. Global-level profile registry variables apply to all instances on the server. In Figure 2.6, this registry has been drawn outside of the two instance boxes. Instance-level profile registry variables apply to a specific instance. You can see separate instance-level profile registry boxes inside each of the two instances in the figure.

To view the current DB2 registry variables, issue the following command:

```
db2set -all
```

You might get output like this:

```
[i] DB2INSTPROF=C:\PROGRAM FILES\IBM\SQLLIB
[g] DB2SYSTEM=PRODSYS
```

As you might have already guessed, `[i]` indicates the variable has been defined at the instance level, and `[g]` indicates that it has been defined at the global level.

The following are a few other commands related to the DB2 registry variables. To view all the registry variables that can be defined in DB2, use this command:

```
db2set -lr
```

To set the value of a specific variable (in this example, DB2INSTPROF) at the global level, use

```
db2set DB2INSTPROF="C:\PROGRAM FILES\IBM\SQLLIB" -g
```

To set a variable at the instance level for instance *myinst*, use

```
db2set DB2INSTPROF="C:\MY FILES\SQLLIB" -i myinst
```

Note that for these commands, the same variable has been set at both levels: the global level and the instance level. When a registry variable is defined at different levels, DB2 always chooses the value at the lowest level, in this case the instance level.

For the `db2set` command, like the `set` command discussed earlier, there are no spaces before or after the equal sign.

By default, changes to many registry variables take effect immediately. In some other cases, you must explicitly include the IMMEDIATE keyword in the `db2set` command. Some other registry variables require an instance stop and start (`db2stop`/`db2start`) for the change to take effect. Other registry variables do not have this requirement. Refer to the DB2 Information Center for a list of variables that have this requirement.

Configuration Parameters

Configuration parameters are defined at two different levels: the instance level and the database level. The variables at each level are different (not like DB2 registry variables, where the same variables can be defined at different levels).

At the instance level, variables are stored in the database manager configuration file (*dbm cfg*). Changes to these variables affect all databases associated to that instance, which is why Figure 2.6 shows a database manager configuration file box defined per instance and outside the databases.

To view the contents of the database manager configuration file, issue the command

```
db2 get dbm cfg
```

To update the value of a specific parameter, use

```
db2 update dbm cfg using <parameter> <value>
```

For example

```
db2 update dbm cfg using INTRA_PARALLEL YES
```

Many of the database manager configuration parameters are **online configurable**, meaning changes to their values are dynamic—you don't need to stop and start the instance for the new values to take effect. You can use this command:

```
db2 get dbm cfg show detail
```

If you prefer graphical tools, from IBM Data Studio right-click the desired instance and choose **Configure** to view and update the database manager configuration parameters. In the Configure Parameters Editor, the *Immediate* column indicates whether the parameter is online configurable or not. In addition, many of these parameters are also noted as "Automatic," meaning that DB2 automatically calculates the best value depending on your system setup or utilization at that time.

At the database level, parameter values are stored in the database configuration file (*db cfg*). Changes to these parameters only affect the specific database the configuration file applies to. In Figure 2.6, you can see that the database configuration file box resides inside each of the databases.

To view the contents of the database configuration file, issue the command

```
db2 get db cfg for <dbname>
```

For example

```
db2 get db cfg for mydb2
```

To update the value of a specific variable, use

```
db2 update db cfg for <dbname> using <parameter> <value>
```

For example

```
db2 update db cfg for mydb2 using MINCOMMIT 3
```

If you are connected to the database, you can omit the `for <dbname>` clause in these commands.

Many database configuration parameters are also online configurable. Changes to the online configurable parameters are dynamic. You do not need to disconnect all connections to the database for the change to take effect. You can use this command:

```
db2 get db cfg for <dbname> show detail
```

If you prefer graphical tools, from IBM Data Studio you can use the same Configure Parameters Editor described earlier to view and update database configuration parameters of the database you have selected. Similarly, the Immediate column indicates whether the parameter is online configurable or not. The Automatic column indicates if the parameter can be adjusted by DB2 automatically.

Connectivity and DB2 Directories[3]

In DB2, directories are used to store connectivity information about databases and the servers on which they reside. There are four main directories, which are described in the following sub-sections. The corresponding commands to set up the database and server connectivity are also included.

Chapter 6, "Configuring Client and Server Connectivity," discusses all the commands and concepts described in this section in detail.

System Database Directory

The system database directory (or system db directory) is like the main "table of contents" that contains information about all the databases to which you can connect from your DB2 server. As you can see from Figure 2.6, the system db directory is stored at the instance level.

To list the contents of the system db directory, use the command

```
db2 list db directory
```

Any entry from the output of this command containing the word *Indirect* indicates that the entry is for a local database; that is, a database that resides on the data server on which you are working. The entry also points to the local database directory indicated by the *Database drive* item (Windows) or *Local database directory* (Linux or UNIX).

Any entry containing the word *Remote* indicates that the entry is for a remote database—a database residing on a server other than the one on which you are currently working. The entry also points to the node directory entry indicated by the *Node name* item.

To enter information into the system database directory, use the `catalog` command:

```
db2 catalog db <dbname> as <alias> at node <nodename>
```

For example

```
db2 catalog db mydb as yourdb at node mynode
```

The `catalog` commands are normally used only when adding information for remote databases. For local databases, a catalog entry is automatically created after creating the database with the `CREATE DATABASE` command.

Local Database Directory

The local database directory contains information about databases residing on the server where you are currently working. Figure 2.6 shows the local database directory overlapping the database box. This means that there will be one local database directory associated to all of the databases residing in the same location (the drive on Windows or the path on Linux or UNIX). The local database directory does not reside inside the database itself, but it does not reside at the instance level either; it is in a layer between these two. (After you read the "Directory Structure of Your DB2 Environment" section in this chapter, it will be easier to understand this concept.)

Note also from Figure 2.6 that there is no specific command used to enter information into this directory, only to retrieve it. When you create a database with the CREATE DATABASE command, an entry is added to this directory under the covers.

To list the contents of the local database directory, issue the command

```
db2 list db directory on drive / path
```

where drive can be obtained from the item *Database drive* (Windows) or path from the item *Local database directory* (Linux or UNIX) in the corresponding entry of the system db directory.

Node Directory

The node directory stores all connectivity information for remote database servers. For example, if you use the TCP/IP protocol, this directory shows entries such as the host name or IP address of the server where the database to which you want to connect resides and the port number of the associated *DB2* instance.

To list the contents of the node directory, issue the command:

```
db2 list node directory
```

To enter information into the node directory, use

```
db2 catalog tcpip node <node_name>
    remote <hostname or IP_address>
    server <tcpip_service_name or port_number>
```

For example:

```
db2 catalog tcpip node mynode
    remote 192.168.1.100
    server 60000
```

You can obtain the port number of the remote instance to which you want to connect by looking at the SVCENAME parameter in the database manager configuration file of that instance. If this parameter contains a string value rather than the port number, you need to look for the corresponding entry that maps this string to the port number in the TCP/IP services file. Check with your system administrator for the location based on the operating system you are using.

Database Connection Services Directory

The Database Connection Services (DCS) directory contains connectivity information for host databases residing on System z or System i server. You need to have the DB2 Connect license certificate installed.

To list the contents of the DCS directory, issue the following command:

```
db2 list dcs directory
```

To enter information into the DCS directory, use

```
db2 catalog dcs db <dbname> as <location_name>
```

For example

```
db2 catalog dcs db mydb as db1g
```

Databases[4]

A database is a collection of information organized into interrelated objects like table spaces, tables, and indexes. Databases are closed and independent units associated to an instance. Because of this independence, objects with the same name can be defined in two or more databases. For example, Figure 2.6 shows a table space called *MyTablespace1* inside the database *MYDB1* associated to instance *DB2*. Another table space with the name *MyTablespace1* is also used inside the database *MYDB2*, which is also associated to instance *DB2*.

Because databases are closed units, you cannot perform queries involving tables of two different databases in a direct way. For example, a query involving *Table1* in database *MYDB1* and *TableZ* in database *MYDB2* is not readily allowed. For an SQL statement to work against tables of different databases, you need to use *database federation* (see the section, "Database Federation," later in the chapter).

You create a database with the command CREATE DATABASE. This command automatically creates three table spaces, a buffer pool, and several configuration files, which is why this command can take a few seconds to complete.

> **NOTE**
>
> Although CREATE DATABASE looks like an SQL statement, it is considered a DB2 command.

Table Spaces[5]

Table spaces are logical objects used as a layer between logical tables and physical containers. **Containers** are where the data is physically stored in files, directories, or raw devices. When you create a table space, you can associate it to a specific buffer pool (database cache) and to specific containers.

The three table spaces automatically created are

- *SYSCATSPACE* (holding the DB2 catalog tables)
- *TEMPSPACE1* (system temporary space)
- *USERSPACE1* (the default user table space)

> **NOTE**
>
> Two other system table spaces, *SYSTOOLSPACE* and *SYSTOOLTMPSPACE* are also created—not when a database is created, but when any tools or SQL administrative routines are used for the first time. They are used in support of these tools and administrative routines.

SYSCATSPACE and *TEMPSPACE1* can be considered system structures, as they are needed for the normal operation of your database. *SYSCATSPACE* contains the catalog tables containing **metadata** (data about your database objects) and must exist at all times. Some other RDBMSs call this structure a **data dictionary**.

> **NOTE**
>
> Do not confuse the term "catalog" in this section with the `catalog` command mentioned earlier; they are used in different context.

A system temporary table space is the work area for the database manager to perform operations, such as joins and overflowed sorts. There must be at least one system temporary table space in each database.

The *USERSPACE1* table space is created by default. You can choose to drop this table space and create another table space with customized settings. To create a table in a given table space, use the `CREATE  TABLE` statement with the `IN table_space_name` clause. If a table space is not specified in this statement, the table is created in the first user-created table space.

Figure 2.6 shows other table spaces that were explicitly created with the CREATE TABLESPACE statement (in brown in the figure if you printed the softcopy version). Chapter 7, "Working with Database Objects," discusses table spaces in more detail.

Tables, Indexes, and Large Objects[6]

A table is an unordered set of data records consisting of columns and rows. An index is an ordered set of pointers associated with a table, and is used for performance purposes and to ensure uniqueness. Nontraditional relational data, such as video, audio, and scanned documents, are stored in tables as large objects (LOBs). Tables and indexes reside in table spaces. Chapter 7 describes these in more detail.

Database Transaction Logs[7]

Database transaction logs are used by DB2 to record every operation against a database. In case of a failure, logs are crucial to recover the database to a consistent point.

Buffer Pools[8]

A buffer pool is an area in memory where all index and data pages other than LOBs are processed. DB2 retrieves LOBs directly from disk. Buffer pools are one of the most important objects to tune for database performance. Chapter 7 discusses buffer pools in more detail.

Storage Groups[9]

A storage group is a collection of storage paths that have similar characteristics, and a storage path is just a piece of storage, such as a drive, a path, or filesystem. Rather than assigning containers with explicit definitions to table spaces, you can now assign them storage groups.

Directory Structure of your DB2 Environment

We have already discussed DB2 registry variables, configuration files, and instances. In this section we illustrate how some of these concepts physically map to directories and files in the Windows environment. The structure is a bit different in Linux and UNIX environments, but the main ideas are the same. Figures 2.7, 2.8, and 2.9 illustrate the DB2 environment internal implementation that corresponds to Figure 2.6.

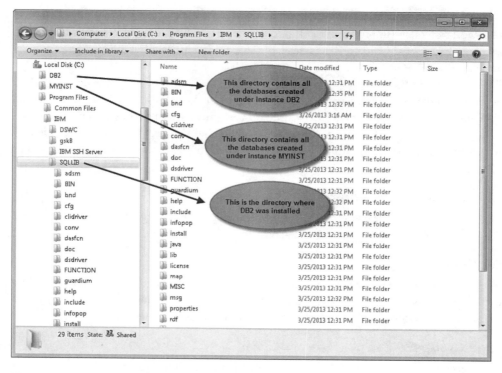

Figure 2.7   Directory structure of a DB2 environment on Windows

Figure 2.7 shows the directory where DB2 was installed: C:\Program Files\IBM\SQLLIB. The SQLLIB directory contains several subdirectories and files that belong to DB2, including the binary code that makes DB2 work.

At the top of the figure, there is a directory C:\DB2. This directory contains all the databases created under the C: drive for instance *DB2*. Similarly, the C:\MYINST directory contains all the databases created under the C: drive for instance *myinst*.

Figure 2.8 shows an expanded view of the C:\ProgramData\IBM\DB2\DB2COPY1\DB2 directory. This directory contains information about the instance DB2. The db2systm binary file contains the database manager configuration (*dbm cfg*). The other file (*db2nodes.cfg*) highlighted in the figure is discussed later in this book. The figure also points out the directories where the system database, node, and DCS directories reside. Note that the node and DCS directories don't exist if they don't have any entries.

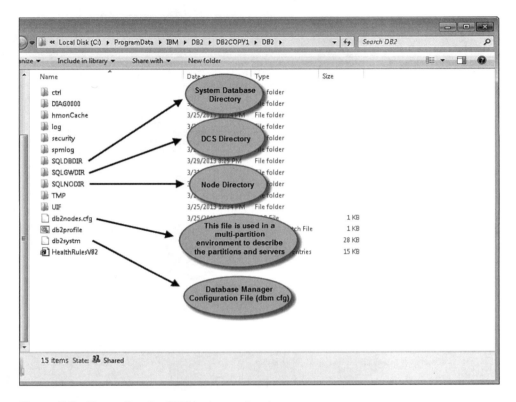

Figure 2.8   Expanding the DB2 instance directory

In Figure 2.9, the C:\DB2 and C:\MYINST directories have been expanded. The subdirectories SQL00001 and SQL00002 under C:\DB2\NODE0000 correspond to the two databases created under instance DB2. To map these directory names to the actual database names, you can review the contents of the local database directory with this command:

```
list db directory on c:
```

Chapter 6 shows sample output of this command. Note that the local database directory is stored in the subdirectory SQLDBDIR. This subdirectory is at the same level as each of the database subdirectories; therefore, when a database is dropped, this subdirectory is not dropped. Figure 2.8 shows two SQLDBDIR subdirectories, one under C:\DB2\NODE0000 and another one under C:\MYINST\NODE0000.

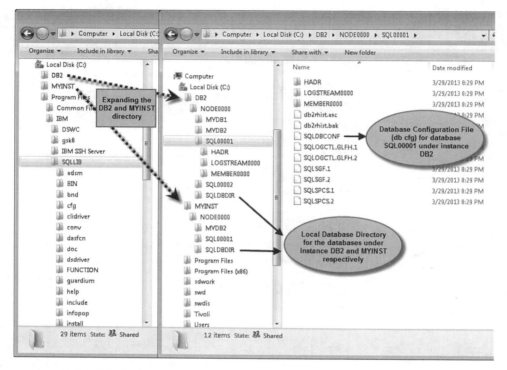

Figure 2.9   Expanding the directories containing the database data

Knowing how the DB2 environment is physically mapped out can help you understand the DB2 concepts better. For example, looking back at Figure 2.6 (the one you should have printed!), what would happen if you dropped the instance *DB2*? Would this mean that databases *MYDB1* and *MYDB2* are also dropped? The answer is no. Figure 2.8 clearly shows that the directory where the instance information resides (C:\ProgramData\IBM\DB2\DB2COPY1\DB2) and the directory where the data resides (C:\DB2) are totally different. When an instance is dropped, only the subdirectory created for that instance is dropped.

Similarly, let's say you uninstall DB2 at a given time, and later you reinstall it on the same drive. After reinstallation, can you access the "old" databases created before you uninstalled DB2 the first time? The answer is yes. When you uninstalled DB2, you removed the SQLLIB directory; therefore, the DB2 binary code, as well as the instance subdirectories, were removed, but the databases were left untouched. When you reinstall DB2, a new SQLLIB directory is created with a new default *DB2* instance; no other instance is created. The new *DB2* instance will have a new empty system database directory (db2systm). So even though the directories containing the database data were left intact, you need to explicitly put the information in the DB2 system database directory for DB2 to recognize the existence of these databases. For example, if you would like to access the *MYDB1* database of the *DB2* instance, you need to issue this command to add an entry to the system database directory:

```
catalog db mydb1 on c:
```

If the database you want to access is *MYDB2*, which was in the *myinst* instance, you would first need to create this instance, switch to it, and then issue the catalog command, as shown next.

```
db2icrt myinst
set DB2INSTANCE=myinst
catalog db mydb2 on c:
```

It is a good practice to regularly back up the contents of all your configuration files as shown here:

```
db2 get dbm cfg > dbmcfg.bk
db2 get db cfg for database_name > dbcfg.bk
db2set -all > db2set.bk
db2 list db directory > systemdbdir.bk
db2 list node directory > nodedir.bk
db2 list dcs directory > dcsdir.bk
```

Notice that all of these commands redirect the output to a text file with a .bk extension.

CAUTION

The purpose of this section is to help you understand the DB2 environment by describing its physical implementation. We strongly suggest that you *do not tamper with the files and directories discussed in this section*. You should only modify the files using the commands described in earlier sections.

Database Partitioning

In this section, we introduce you to the DB2 database partitioning capability. DB2 database partitioning lets you partition your database across multiple servers or within a large symmetric multiprocessor (SMP) server. Each server contains a collection of system resources including processes, memory, disk storage, and communications. The multiple database partitions are working in parallel in a **shared-nothing environment**. This environment allows for scalability because you can add new servers and spread your database across them. That means more CPUs, more memory, and more disks from each of the additional servers for your database.

DB2 database partitioning is ideal to manage large databases, whether you are doing data warehousing, data mining, online analytical processing (OLAP), also known as Decision Support Systems (DSS), or working with online transaction processing (OLTP) workloads. Users connect to the database and issue queries as usual without the need to know that the database is spread among several partitions.

Up to this point, we have been discussing a single partition environment and its concepts, all of which apply to a multi-partition environment as well. We now point out some implementation differences and introduce a few new concepts, including database partitions, partition groups, and the coordinator partition, that are relevant only to a multi-partition environment.

 NOTE

In DB2 10.5, the database partition capability is included in the DB2 Advanced Enterprise Server Edition, the DB2 Advanced Workgroup Server Edition, and the DB2 Developer Edition.

Database Partitions

A database partition is an independent part of a partitioned database with its own data, configuration files, indexes, and transaction logs. You can assign multiple partitions across several physical servers or to a single physical server. In the latter case, the partitions are called logical partitions, and they can share the server's resources.

A single-partition database is a database with only one partition. We described the DB2 environment for this type of database in the section, "DB2 Environment." A multi-partition database (also referred to as a partitioned database) is a database with two or more database partitions. Depending on your hardware environment, there are several topologies for database partitioning. Figure 2.10 shows single partition and multi-partition configurations with one partition per server. The illustration at the top of the figure shows an SMP server with one partition (single-partition environment). This means the entire database resides on this one server.

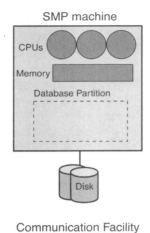

Single Partition Configurations

I) Single-partition on a
   Symmetric Multiprocessor (SMP)
   machine

**Multi-Partition Configurations
(one partition per machine)**

II) Multiple partitions on a cluster of SMP
    machines (also known as a
    Massively Parallel Processing (MPP)
    environment)

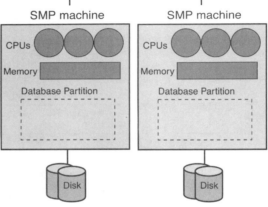

Figure 2.10   Database partition configurations with one partition per server

The illustration at the bottom of the figure shows two SMP servers, one partition per server
(multi-partition environment). This means the database is split between the two partitions.

NOTE

In Figure 2.10, the SMP systems could be replaced by uniprocessor systems.

Figure 2.11 shows multi-partition configurations with multiple partitions per server. Unlike Figure 2.10 where there was only one partition per server, this figure illustrates two (or more) partitions per server.

Multi-Partition Configurations Partitions (several partitions per machine)

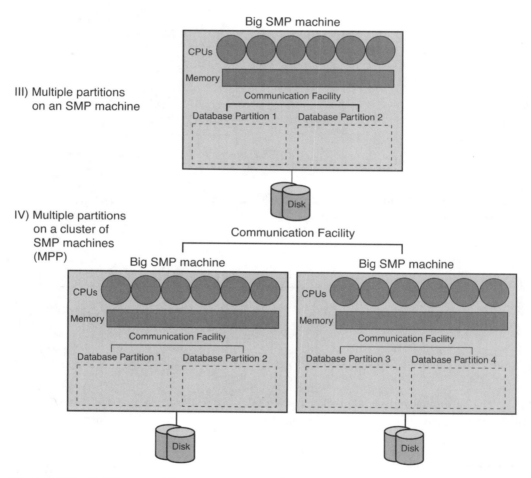

Figure 2.11   Database partition configurations with multiple partitions per server

To visualize how a DB2 environment is split into multiple database partitions, Figure 2.12 illustrates a partial reproduction of Figure 2.6 and shows it split into three physical partitions, one partition per server. (We changed the server in the original Figure 2.6 to use the Linux operating system instead of the Windows operating system.)

NOTE

Because we reference Figure 2.12 throughout this section, *bookmark page 60*. Alternatively, since this figure is available in color on the book's website, www.ibmpressbooks.com/title/9780133461909, consider printing it.

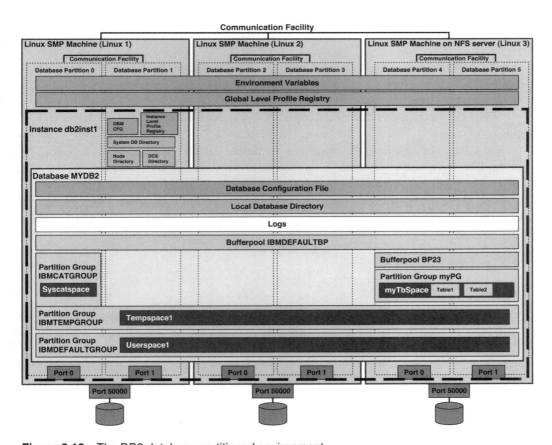

Figure 2.12   The DB2 database partitioned environment

In Figure 2.12, the DB2 environment is "split" so that it now resides on three servers running the same operating system (Linux, in this example). The partitions are also running the same DB2 version, but it is important to note that different Fix Pack levels are allowed. This figure shows where files and objects would be located on a new installation of a multi-partition system.

It is also important to note that all of the servers participating in a database partitioning environment have to be interconnected by a high-speed communication facility that supports

the TCP/IP protocol. TCP/IP ports are reserved on each server for this "interpartition" communication. For example, by default after installation, the services file on Linux (/etc/services) is
updated as follows (assuming you chose to create the *db2inst1* instance):

```
DB2_db2inst1          60000/tcp
DB2_db2inst1_1        60001/tcp
DB2_db2inst1_2        60002/tcp
DB2_db2inst1_END      60003/tcp
db2c_db2inst1         50000/tcp
```

This will vary depending on the number of partitions on the server. By default, ports 60000
through 60003 are reserved for interpartition communication. You can update the services file
with the correct number of entries to support the number of partitions you are configuring.

When the partitions reside on the same server, communication between the partitions still
requires this setup.

For a Data Server client to connect to a partitioned database system, you issue `catalog`
commands at the client to populate the system and node directories. In the example, the port
number to use in these commands is 50000 to connect to the *db2inst1* instance, and the host name
can be any of the servers participating in the DB2 database partitioning environment. The server
used in the `catalog` command becomes the coordinator unless the DBPARTITIONNUM option
of the `connect` statement is used. The concept of coordinator is described later in this section.
Chapter 6 discusses the `catalog` command in detail.

> **NOTE**
>
> Each of the servers participating in the DB2 database partitioning environment have their
> own separate services file, but the entries in those files that are applicable to DB2 interparti-
> tion communication must be the same.

The Node Configuration File

The node configuration file (*db2nodes.cfg*) contains information about the database partitions
and the servers on which they reside that belong to an instance. Figure 2.13 shows an example of
the *db2nodes.cfg* file for a cluster of four UNIX servers with two partitions on each server.

In Figure 2.13, the partition number, the first column in the *db2nodes.cfg* file, indicates
the number that identifies the database partition within DB2. You can see that there are eight
partitions in total. The numbering of the partitions must be in ascending order, can start from any
number, and gaps between the numbers are allowed. The numbering used is important, because it
is taken into consideration in commands or SQL statements.

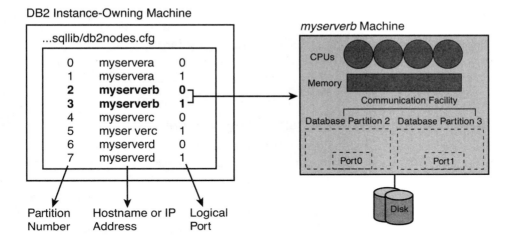

Figure 2.13   An example of the db2nodes.cfg file

The second column is the *hostname* or TCP/IP address of the server where the partition is created.

The third column, the *logical port*, is required when you create more than one partition on the same server. This column specifies the logical port for the partition within the server and must be unique within a server. In Figure 2.13, you can see the mapping between the *db2nodes.cfg* entries for partitions 2 and 3 for server *myserverb* and the physical server implementation. The logical ports must also be in the same order as in the db2nodes.cfg file.

The fourth column (not shown in diagram) in the *db2nodes.cfg* file, the *netname*, is required if you are using a high-speed interconnect for interpartition communication or if the *resourceset-name* column is used.

The fifth column (not shown in diagram) in the *db2nodes.cfg* file, the *resourcesetname*, is optional. It specifies the operating system resource that the partition should be started in.

In Windows, the *db2nodes.cfg* file uses the *computer name* column instead of the *resource-setname* column. The *computer name* column stores the computer name for the server on which a partition resides. Also the order of the columns is slightly different: *partition number*, *hostname*, *computer name*, *logical port*, *netname*, and *resourcesetname*.

The *db2nodes.cfg* file must be located

- Under the SQLLIB directory for the instance owner on Linux and UNIX
- Under the SQLLIB*instance_name* directory on Windows

In Figure 2.12, this file would be on the Linux3 server, as this server is the Network File System (NFS) source server for which the server whole disk(s) can be shared.

On Linux and UNIX, you can edit the *db2nodes.cfg* file with any ASCII editor or use DB2 commands to update the file. In Windows, you can only use the `db2ncrt` and `db2ndrop` commands to create and drop database partitions; the *db2nodes.cfg* file should not be edited directly.

On any platform, you can also use the `db2start` command to add and/or remove a database partition from the *DB2* instance and update the *db2nodes.cfg* file using the `add dbpartitionnum` and the `drop dbpartitionnum` clauses, respectively.

An Instance in the DB2 Database Partitioning Environment

Partitioning is a concept that applies to the database, not the instance; you partition a database, not an instance. In a DB2 database partitioning environment an instance is created once on an NFS source server. The instance owner's home directory is then exported to all servers where DB2 is to be run. Each partition in the database has the same characteristics: the same instance owner, password, and shared instance home directory.

On Linux and UNIX, an instance maps to an operating system user; therefore, when an instance is created, it has its own home directory. In most installations, /home/*user_name* is the home directory. All instances created on each of the participating servers in a DB2 database partitioning environment must use the same name and password. In addition, you must specify the home directory of the corresponding operating system user to be the same directory for all instances, which must be created on a shared file system. Figure 2.14 illustrates an example of this.

In Figure 2.14, the instance *myinst* has been created on the shared file system, and *myinst* maps to an operating system user of the same name, which in the figure has a home directory of /home/myinst. This user must be created separately in each of the participating servers, but they must share the instance home directory. In some cases, the same user on each server must have the same uid (OS user ID) and gid (OS group ID) to avoid file access issues. As shown in Figure 2.14, all three Linux servers share directory /home/myinst, which resides on a shared file system local to Linux3. Because the instance owner directory is locally stored on the Linux3 server, this server is considered to be the DB2 instance-owning server.

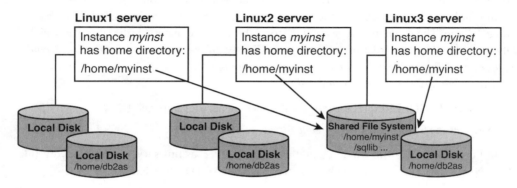

Figure 2.14   An instance in a partitioned environment

Figure 2.14 also shows that the Database Administration Server user db2as is created locally on each participating server in a partitioned database environment. There can only be one DAS per physical server regardless of the number of partitions that server contains. The DAS user's home directory cannot be mounted on a shared file system. Alternatively, different user IDs and passwords can be used to create the DAS on different servers.

> **NOTE**
>
> Make sure the passwords for the instances are the same on each of the participating servers in a partitioned database environment; otherwise, the partitioned system will look like it is hanging because the partitions are not able to communicate.

Partitioning a Database

When you want to partition a database in a DB2 database partitioning environment, simply issue the CREATE DATABASE command as usual. For example, if the instance owner home directory is /home/myinst, when you execute this command

```
CREATE DATABASE mydb2
```

the structure created for a partitioned database in a single file system is as shown here:

```
/home
    /myinst
        /NODE0000
            /SQL00001
        /NODE0001
            /SQL00001
        /NODE0002
            /SQL00001
```

If you don't specify a path in your CREATE DATABASE command, by default the database is created in the directory specified by the database manager configuration parameter DFTDB-PATH, which defaults to the instance owner's home directory. This partitioning is not optimal because all of the database data would reside in one file system that is shared by the other servers across a network.

We recommend that you create a directory with the same name, locally in each of the participating servers. For the environment in Figure 2.14, let's assume the directory /data has been created locally on each server. When you execute the command

```
CREATE DATABASE mydb2 on /data
```

the following directory structure is automatically built for you:

```
/data/instance_name/NODExxxx/SQLyyyyy
```

The /data directory is specified in the CREATE DATABASE command, but the directory must exist *before* executing the command. *instance_name* is the name of the instance; for example, *myinst*. NODE*xxxx* distinguishes which partition you are working with, where *xxxx* represents the number of the partition specified in the db2nodes.cfg file. SQL*yyyyy* identifies the database, where *yyyyy* represents a number. If you have only one database on your system, then *yyyyy* is equal to 00001; if you have three databases on your system, you have different directories as follows: SQL00001, SQL00002, SQL00003. To map the database names to these directories, you can review the local database directory using the following command:

```
list db directory on /data
```

Figure 2.15 illustrates a partitioned database created in the /data directory.

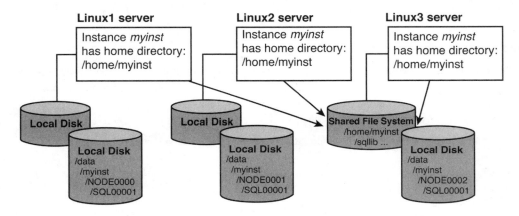

Figure 2.15   A partitioned database across several file systems

NOTE

Before creating a database, be sure to change the value of the dbm cfg parameter, DFTDB-PATH, to an existing path created locally with the same name on each of the participating servers of your partitioned database environment. Alternatively, make sure to include this path in your CREATE DATABASE command. The path would become part of the default storage group. The CREATE DATABASE command is described in more detail in Chapter 7.

The Catalog Partition

As stated previously, when you create a database, several table spaces are created by default. One of them, the catalog table space *SYSCATSPACE*, contains the DB2 system catalogs. In a partitioned environment, *SYSCATSPACE* is not partitioned but resides on a partition known as the catalog partition. The partition from which the CREATE DATABASE command is issued becomes the catalog partition for the new database. All access to system tables must go through this catalog partition. Figure 2.12 shows *SYSCATSPACE* residing on server Linux1, so the CREATE DATABASE command was issued from this server.

For an existing database, you can determine which partition is the catalog partition by issuing the command list db directory. The output of this command has the field *Catalog database partition number* for each of the entries, which indicates the catalog partition number for that database.

Partition Groups

A partition group is a logical layer that provides for the grouping of one or more database partitions. A database partition can belong to more than one partition group. When a database is created, DB2 creates three default partition groups, and these partition groups cannot be dropped. Refer to Figure 2.12 to see how partition groups relate to other components visually.

- **IBMDEFAULTGROUP:** This is the default partition group for any table you create. It contains all database partitions defined in the *db2nodes.cfg* file. This partition group cannot be modified. Table space *USERSPACE1* is created in this partition group.

- **IBMTEMPGROUP:** This partition group is used by all system temporary tables. It contains all database partitions defined in the *db2nodes.cfg* file. Table space *TEMPSPACE1* is created in this partition group.

- **IBMCATGROUP:** This partition group contains the catalog tables (table space *SYSCATSPACE*). It only includes the database's catalog partition. This partition group cannot be modified.

To create new database partition groups, use the CREATE DATABASE PARTITION GROUP statement. This statement creates the database partition group within the database, assigns database partitions that you specified to the partition group, and records the partition group definition in the database system catalog tables.

The following statement creates partition group *pgrpall* on all partitions specified in the *db2nodes.cfg* file:

```
CREATE DATABASE PARTITION GROUP pgrpall ON ALL DBPARTITIONNUMS
```

To create a database partition group *pg23* consisting of partitions 2 and 3, issue this command:

```
CREATE DATABASE PARTITION GROUP pg23 ON DBPARTITIONNUMS (2,3)
```

Other relevant partition group statements/commands are

- `ALTER DATABASE PARTITION GROUP` (statement to add or drop a partition in the group)
- `DROP DATABASE PARTITION GROUP` (statement to drop a partition group)
- `LIST DATABASE PARTITION GROUPS` (command to list all your partition groups; note that *IBMTEMPGROUP* is never listed)

Buffer Pools in a DB2 Database Partitioning Environment

Refer to Figure 2.12—it shows buffer pools defined across all of the database partitions.

Interpreting this figure for buffer pools is different than for the other objects because the data cached in the buffer pools is not partitioned as the figure implies. Each buffer pool in a DB2 database partitioning environment holds data only from the database partition where the buffer pool is located.

You can create a buffer pool in a partition group using the `CREATE BUFFERPOOL` statement with the `DATABASE PARTITION GROUP` clause. This means that you have the flexibility to define the buffer pool on the specific partitions defined in the partition group. In addition, the size of the buffer pool on each partition in the partition group can be different. The following statement creates buffer pool *bpool_1* in partition group *pg234*, which consists of partitions 2, 3, and 4:

```
CREATE BUFFERPOOL bpool_1 DATABASE PARTITION GROUP pg234
      SIZE 10000
      EXCEPT ON DBPARTITIONNUM (3 TO 4) SIZE 5000
```

Partition 2 in partition group *pg234* has a buffer pool *bpool_1* defined with a size of 10,000 pages, and Partitions 3 and 4 have a buffer pool of size 5,000 pages.

As an analogy, think of it as if you were issuing the `CREATE BUFFERPOOL` statement on each partition separately, with the same buffer pool name for each partition but with different sizes. That is

- On partition 2: `CREATE BUFFERPOOL bpool_1 SIZE 10000`
- On partition 3: `CREATE BUFFERPOOL bpool_1 SIZE 5000`
- On partition 4: `CREATE BUFFERPOOL bpool_1 SIZE 5000`

Note that we use these statements only to clarify the analogy; they do not work as written. In executing each of these commands as shown you attempt to create the same buffer pool on all partitions. It is not equivalent to using the `DATABASE PARTITION GROUP` clause of the `CREATE BUFFERPOOL` statement.

Buffer pools can also be associated with several partition groups. This means that the buffer pool definition is applied to the partitions in those partition groups.

Table Spaces in a Partitioned Database Environment

You can create a table space in specific partitions, associating it to a partition group by using the CREATE TABLESPACE statement with the IN DATABASE PARTITION GROUP clause. This allows users to have flexibility as to which partitions actually store their tables. In a partitioned database environment with three servers, one partition per server, the following statement creates the table space *mytbls*, which spans partitions 2, 3, and 4 (assuming *pg234* is a partition group consisting of these partitions):

```
CREATE TABLESPACE mytbls IN DATABASE PARTITION GROUP pg234
      MANAGED BY SYSTEM USING ('/data')
      BUFFERPOOL bpool_1
```

In addition, the table space is associated with buffer pool *bpool_1* defined earlier. Note that creating a table space would fail if you provide conflicting partition information between the table space and the associated buffer pool. For example, if *bpool_1* was created for partitions 5 and 6, and table space *mytbls* was created for partitions 2, 3, and 4, you would get an error message when trying to create this table space.

The Coordinator Partition

In simple terms, the coordinator partition is the partition where the application connects to.

In general, each database connection has a corresponding DB2 agent handling the application connection. An *agent* can be thought of as a thread for all platforms that performs DB2 work on behalf of the application. There are different types of agents. One of them, the coordinator agent, communicates with the application, receiving requests and sending replies. It can either satisfy the request itself or delegate the work to multiple subagents to work on the request.

The coordinator partition of a given application is the partition where the coordinator agent exists. You use the SET CLIENT CONNECT_NODE command to set the partition that is to be the coordinator partition. Any partition can potentially be a coordinator, so in Figure 2.12 we do not label any particular partition as the coordinator node.

Issuing Commands and SQL Statements in a Database Partitioned Environment

Imagine you have 20 physical servers, with two database partitions on each. Issuing individual commands to each physical server or partition would be quite a task. Fortunately, DB2 provides a command that executes on all database partitions.

Use the db2_all command when you want to execute a command or SQL statement against all database partitions. For example, to change the db cfg parameter LOGFILSIZ for the database *sample* in all partitions, you would use

```
db2_all ";db2 UPDATE DB CFG FOR sample USING LOGFILSIZ 500"
```

When the semicolon (;) character is placed before the command or statement, the request runs in parallel on all partitions.

NOTE

In partitioned environments, the operating system command `rah` performs commands on all servers simultaneously. The `rah` command works per server, while the `db2_all` command works per database partition. The `rah` and `db2_all` commands use the same characters. For more information about the `rah` command, refer to your operating system manuals.

The DB2NODE Environment Variable

In the section, "The DB2 Environment," we talked about the DB2INSTANCE environment variable used to switch between instances in your database system. The DB2NODE environment variable is used in a similar way, but to switch between partitions on your partitioned database environment. By default, the current partition is the one defined with the logical port number of zero (0) in the *db2nodes.cfg* file for a server. To switch the current partition, change the value of the DB2NODE variable using the SET command on Windows and the `export` command on Linux or UNIX. Be sure to issue a `terminate` command for all connections from any partition to your database after changing this variable, or the change will not take effect.

Using the settings for the *db2nodes.cfg* file shown in Table 2.3, you have four servers, each with two logical partitions. If you log on to server *myserverb*, any commands you execute affect partition 2, which is the one with logical port zero on that server and the default coordinator partition for that server.

Table 2.3   Sample Partition Information

Partition	Server Name	Logical Port
0	Myservera	0
1	Myservera	1
2	Myserverb	0
3	Myserverb	1
4	Myserverc	0
5	Myserverc	1
6	Myserverd	0
7	Myserverd	1

If you want to make partition 0 the current partition, make this change on a Linux or UNIX system:

```
DB2NODE=0
export DB2NODE
db2 terminate
```

Note that partition 0 is on server *myservera*. Even if you are connected to *myserverb*, you can make a partition on *myservera* the current one. To determine which is your current partition, you can issue this statement after connecting to a database:

```
db2 "values (current dbpartitionnum)"
```

Distribution Maps and Distribution Keys

By now, you should have a good grasp of how to set up a partitioned database environment. It is now time to understand how DB2 distributes data across the partitions. Figure 2.16 shows an example of this distribution.

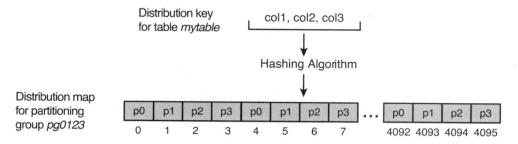

Figure 2.16   Distributing data rows in a partitioned database environment

A distribution map is an internally generated array containing 4,096 entries for multi-partition database partition groups or a single entry for single-partition database partition groups. The partition numbers of the database partition group are specified in a round-robin fashion in the array.

A distribution key is a column (or group of columns) that determines the partition on which a particular row of data is physically stored. You define a distribution key explicitly using the CREATE TABLE statement with the DISTRIBUTE BY clause.

When you create or modify a database partition group, a distribution map is associated with it. A distribution map in conjunction with a distribution key and a hashing algorithm determine which database partition will store a given row of data.

For the example in Figure 2.16, let's assume partition group *pg0123* has been defined on partitions 0, 1, 2, and 3. An associated distribution map is automatically created. This map is an array with 4,096 entries containing the values 0, 1, 2, 3, 0, 1, 2, 3. . . . (note that this is shown in Figure 2.21 as p0, p1, p2, p3, p0, p1, p2, p3 . . . to distinguish them from the array entry numbers). Let's also assume table *mytable* has been created with a distribution key consisting of columns *col1*, *col2*, and *col3*. For each row, the distribution key column values are passed to the hashing algorithm, which returns an output number from 0 to 4,095. This number corresponds to one of the entries in the array that contains the value of the partition number where the row is to be stored. In Figure 2.16, if the hashing algorithm had returned an output value of 7, the row would have been stored in partition *p3*.

NOTE

The terms DISTRIBUTION MAP and DISTRIBUTION KEY terms are sometimes known as PARTITIONING MAP and PARTITIONING KEY, respectively.

DB2 pureScale

In the previous section, you learned about DB2 database partitioning, a technology that works on a clustered environment using a share-nothing architecture. This architecture is ideal for scalability and mainly appropriate for analytics or reporting workloads of a data warehouse. Because the database is partitioned across different severs, a failure in one of those servers could render the database inaccessible. However, DB2 has different mechanisms to prevent this from happening. Refer to the DB2 Information Center for details.

This section introduces you to DB2 pureScale, a technology that works on a clustered environment and uses a data-sharing architecture. This architecture is ideal for scalability and mainly appropriate for transaction processing. In this environment, the data being accessed is shared by all servers in the cluster. If there is a failure in one of the servers, or if it needs to be brought down for maintenance purposes, the rest of the members that continue to be online in the cluster take over the work, thus providing transparent availability to the data at all times.

DB2 pureScale is based on robust technology that has been running on mainframe production systems for more than a decade. Like with DB2 database partitioning, with DB2 pureScale there is no need for application developers to write their code in any special way.

DB2 pureScale Architecture Overview

A DB2 pureScale environment is made up of members running DB2 with pureScale technology. Each member cooperates with one another to provide coherent access to the same shared copy of the database. The database is stored on a shared disk accessible by all members. Figure 2.17 illustrates a pureScale cluster with four members each running a copy of DB2. All members are sharing the data of a single-partitioned database. Each member maintains its own set of transaction log files on the shared disk, each set in a separate log path. The top of the figure shows clients executing queries to access the database; these queries are automatically rerouted to the members of the cluster so there is workload balancing; this ensures no single member is overloaded with work.

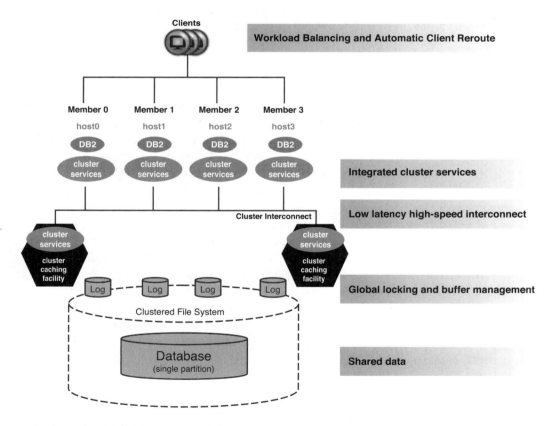

Figure 2.17   DB2 pureScale members operating in a data-sharing architecture

The figure also shows cluster services in each member and a cluster interconnect (low latency high-speed interconnect) to two cluster caching facilities, in addition to other concepts and components such as the clustered file system, global locking and buffer management, and so on. All of these technologies and components, which are described in more detail in the next section, help pureScale achieve transparent scalability and high availability. For a thorough discussion of the technology, refer to the DB2 Information Center.

> **NOTE**
>
> DB2 pureScale can also be deployed on a virtualized environment. For example, a physical server running two virtual machines can have DB2 pureScale installed on both. In a production environment, it is recommended to have each member on its own single physical host computer to provide optimal high availability and scalability.

Cluster Interconnect

DB2 pureScale members and other components of the technology shared data and other information between themselves. A high-speed, low-latency interconnect is needed for extremely fast communication. The remote direct memory access (RDMA) technology plays a key role to achieve this goal.

RDMA is a feature of the network interface card that allows one host to access memory of another host directly. It bypasses the operating systems, avoids data traversing from application memory to kernel memory, requires no IP socket calls, no context switching, and no interrupts. Hence it is also referred as interrupt-free RDMA.

DB2 pureScale is designed and optimized to work with the interconnect fabric of Infiniband and RDMA over Converged Ethernet (RoCE). Infiniband is an industry standard for interconnect architecture for server and storage connectivity. This technology is very mature as it was established in 1999. On the other hand, the RoCE specification was released around 2010. It is a light-weight RDMA transport over Ethernet. RoCE provides support of 10 Gigabit Ethernet (10GE), 40GE networks. DB2 pureScale demands a high speed communication network that uses an InfiniBand network or a 10GE network. A mixture of these two networks in the pureScale cluster is not supported.

 > **NOTE**
>
> DB2 pureScale only supports AIX and Linux on System x. pureScale supports Infiniband and RoCE networks. RoCE support for pureScale on AIX was added in DB2 10.1.

Cluster Caching Facility (CF)

The cluster caching facility (CF) is specialized software that provides global locking management, group buffer pool service, and a few other services.

When a member requires a row or table lock to process a transaction, the member's local lock manager communicates to the CF's global lock manager using RDMA. Dedicated threads on the CF server then immediately processes the request.

Similarly, when a member tries to access a data page, its local buffer pool requests the latest copy of the page from the CF using RDMA. The CF's group buffer pool service manages a global cache for frequently accessed pages (also referred as hot pages) in the cluster. If the requested page is in the group buffer pool, the page is transferred to the member's local buffer pool. The group buffer pool also maintains a page registry, which records which pages are buffered in each member. If a page is updated, the group buffer pool informs all the members that the page is no longer valid based on the page registry.

It is strongly recommended to use two CFs to provide redundancy and to eliminate a single point of failure within the cluster.

DB2 Cluster Services (CS)

DB2 pureScale comes with an integrated component called DB2 Cluster Services (CS). CS runs on every member and CFs in the pureScale cluster. It is used to detect member failure, drive automated recovery of the member, and manage access to the shared data for the member. These services are provided by three different IBM software products that are tightly integrated inside the DB2 engine:

- **IBM Reliable Services Clustering Technology (RSCT):** Enables the ability to detect member failure.
- **Tivoli Systems Automation for Multi Platforms (TSAMP):** Allows for automatic recovery.
- **IBM General Parallel File System (GPFS):** Provides the clustered shared file system.

Although these are three separate IBM products, they are seamlessly integrated in DB2 pureScale. For example, CS interfaces with RSCT and GPFS when there is a member failure. Before the recovered member regains access to the GPFS file system, RSCT must first recognize and allow the member back into the cluster.

Cluster File System

GPFS is the cluster file system used with DB2 pureScale. It provides concurrent access from all pureScale members to the pureScale instance files and the database files, such as table space containers and logs.

GPFS has its own management tool; however to provide seamless experience for DB2 database administrators, they can use the `db2cluster -cfs` command to create, mount, and configure the file systems. There is a list of options made available to the `db2cluster` command. Different options require different DB2 authorization levels, such as SYSADM, SYSCTL, or SYSMAINT.

DB2 pureScale Instance

In a pureScale cluster, you can define one pureScale instance. Within the instance, multiple active databases are supported. Like in the database partitioned environment, DB2 pureScale also uses the node configuration file (*db2nodes.cfg*) to maintain information about the hosts of the cluster. Specifically, it stores information about each pureScale member and CF, the hostname, and the network interface name. Here is a sample *db2nodes.cfg* file with four member hosts and two CFs.

```
0       host0       0       host0-ib0       MEMBER
1       host1       0       host1-ib0       MEMBER
2       host2       0       host2-ib0       MEMBER
3       host3       0       host3-ib0       MEMBER
4       host4       0       host4-ib0         CF
5       host5       0       host5-ib0         CF
```

During installation and configuration of DB2 pureScale, the DB2 Setup Wizard updates the node configuration file based on the cluster interconnect network names you specify.

To get an overview of the health of the pureScale cluster, you can use the `db2instance -list` command. For example, you would receive a listing similar to the following:

```
ID    TYPE     STATE    HOME_HOST    CURRENT_HOST    STATE     INSTANCE_STOPPED    ALERT

0     MEMBER   STARTED    host0          host0      ACTIVE                  NO        NO

0     MEMBER   STARTED    host1          host1      ACTIVE                  NO        NO

0     MEMBER   STARTED    host2          host2      ACTIVE                  NO        NO

0     MEMBER   STARTED    host3          host3      ACTIVE                  NO        NO

0        CF    PRIMARY    host4          host4      ACTIVE                  NO        NO

0        CF    CATCHUP    host5          host5      ACTIVE                  NO        NO
```

A DB2 administrative view, `DB2_GET_CLUSTER_HOST_STATE`, provides similar information. For example, you can use the following SQL statement to query the cluster status.

```
SELECT varchar(HOSTNAME,10) AS HOST,
       varchar(STATE,8) AS STATE,
       varchar(INSTANCE_STOPPED,7) AS STOPPED,
       ALERT
FROM SYSIBMADM.DB2_GET_CLUSTER_HOST_STATE
HOST         STATE    STOPPED ALERT
----------   -------- ------- --------
HOST4        ACTIVE   NO      NO
HOST2        ACTIVE   NO      NO
HOST0        ACTIVE   NO      NO
HOST1        ACTIVE   NO      NO
HOST5        ACTIVE   NO      NO
HOST3        ACTIVE   NO      NO
  6 record(s) selected.
```

In a clustered environment like pureScale, you might wonder where the pureScale related
files are stored. Recall that DB2 is installed on each member as shown in Figure 2.17. Therefore
each host has a local sqllib directory just like the DB2 non-pureScale environment. Under the
sqllib directory, there is a combination of directories and files local to the member, as well as files
that point to the installation directory.

DB2 node configuration file *db2nodes.cfg*, database manager configuration file db2systm,
log files—these files are common to members belonging to the pureScale instance. They are
located in the `sqllib_shared` directory on the clustered shared file system.

See Figure 2.18 to get an idea of how the files are mapped to the `sqllib_shared`
directory.

NOTE

Members of a DB2 pureScale cluster can also be configured to be at different sites, which
minimizes risk of total outage in case the entire data center is disabled due to fire or power
failure. This configuration is known as the geographically dispersed DB2 pureScale cluster
(GDPC).

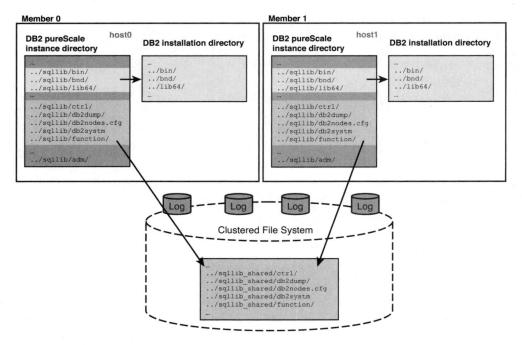

Figure 2.18   DB2 pureScale instance directory

As you can see, DB2 pureScale has specific system hardware and software dependencies, which require additional configuration steps. Details can be found in the DB2 Information Center, where dedicated topics on pureScale are available.

Database Federation

Database federated support in DB2 allows tables from multiple databases to be presented as local tables to a DB2 server. The databases may be local or remote; they can also belong to different relational or nonrelational databases. Chapter 1, "Introduction to DB2," briefly introduced federated support, but this section provides an overview of how federation is implemented.

First of all, make sure that your server allows federated support: The database manager parameter `federated` must be set to `yes`. Default setting is `no`. You would need to update the parameter and restart the instance for this change to take in effect.

DB2 uses NICKNAME, SERVER, WRAPPER, and USER MAPPING objects to implement federation. Let's consider the example illustrated in Figure 2.19.

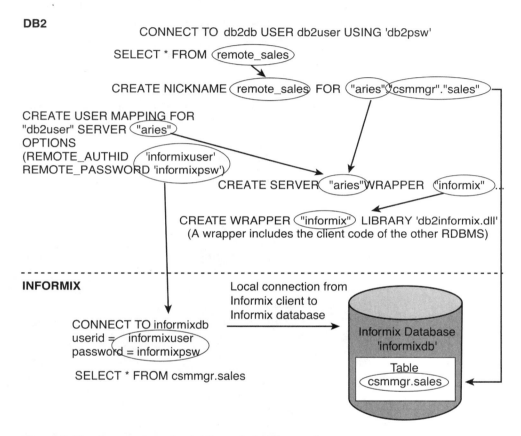

Figure 2.19 An overview of a database federation environment

The DB2 user *db2user* connects to the database *db2db*. He then issues the following statement:

```
SELECT * FROM remote_sales
```

The table remote_sales, however, is not a local table but a *nickname*, which is a pointer to a table in another database, possibly in another server and from a different RDBMS. A nickname is created with the CREATE NICKNAME statement and requires a SERVER object (*aries* in the example) and the schema and table name to be accessed at this server (*csmmgr.sales*).

A SERVER object is associated to a WRAPPER. A wrapper is associated to a library that contains all the code required to connect to a given RDBMS. For IBM databases like Informix, these wrappers or libraries are provided with DB2. For other RDBMSs, you need to obtain the IBM InfoSphere Federation Server software. In Figure 2.19, the wrapper called *informix* was created, and it is associated to the library *db2informix.dll*.

To access the Informix table *csmmgr.sales*, however, you cannot use the DB2 user ID and password directly. You need to establish a mapping between the DB2 user ID and an Informix user ID that has the authority to access the desired table. This is achieved with the CREATE USER MAPPING statement. Figure 2.19 shows how the DB2 user *db2user* and the Informix user *informixuser* are associated with this statement.

Use of Uppercase Versus Lowercase in DB2

Table 2.4 identifies which kinds of statements, commands, parameters, objects, and data are case-sensitive in DB2 and gives examples.

Table 2.4   Case-Sensitivity Requirements in DB2

Category	Description	Examples
DB2 system commands (including the *db2* executable)	You can treat DB2 system commands like any other program or application launched from the operating system.	These work in Linux, UNIX, and Windows: db2 db2start db2ilist
	In Windows, the case does *not* matter.	These only work in Windows: dB2 db2STARt DB2ILIST
	In Linux and UNIX, the case *does* matter, and because all DB2 system commands are named in lowercase, you need to issue the commands in lowercase.	
CLP commands	You can invoke CLP commands from the DB2 Command Line Processor or the DB2 Command Window (Windows only). These tools do *not* care about the case of the command.	These work in Linux, UNIX, and Windows: list applications LIST apPLicatIONs Or if working with the CLP in non-interactive mode: db2 list applications db2 LIST apPLicatIONs

Category	Description	Examples
SQL statements	You can invoke SQL statements within an application or tool like the CLP. DB2 tools do *not* care about the case of the SQL statement.	These work in Linux, UNIX, and Windows: select * from employee SELECT * frOM emPLOYee
	When you create database objects, you can specify the object name in any case. However, DB2 usually stores names in the DB2 catalog in uppercase unless you use double quotes enclosing the object name when you create the object.[1]	These work in Linux, UNIX, and Windows: create table Tab1 ... create table taB1 ... (*TAB1* is stored in the DB2 catalog tables.) create table "taB1" (*taB1* is stored in the DB2 catalog tables.)
XQuery statements	All XQuery statements start with the keyword `xquery` which can be written in any case.	These work in Linux, UNIX, and Windows: `XqueRy db2-fn:xmlcolumn('CUSTOMER.INFO')`
	Column and table names inside the XQuery statement must be in uppercase.	These work in Linux, UNIX, and Windows: `xquery db2-fn:xmlcolumn('CUSTOMER.INFO')` This returns an error saying the table cannot be found: `xquery db2-fn:xmlcolumn('CustOMER.InfO')`

1. Using the CLP in Windows to create an object in mixed case by using double quotes will not work. Use the IBM Data Studio instead.

Category	Description	Examples

	Any other XQuery expression or XPath expression is case-sensitive.	This returns an error because the clauses in the FLWOR expression must be lowercase, and in this example, fOr uses mixed case.
		
		`xqueryfOr $i in ...`
		
		The following does not return an error, but an incorrect output if the actual XPath is `/customerinfo/phone`:
		
		`SELECT XMLQUERY (`
		`  $d/CustomerInfo/Phone'`
		`passing INFO as "d" ) FROM`
		`CUSTOMER`
		
		This returns the correct output. Note that the SQL part of the statement is not case-sensitive, but the XPath part of the statement is
		
		`SelEcT XMLQUERY (`
		`  $d/customerinfo/phone'`
		`passing INFO as "d" ) FROM`
		`cuSToMer`

DB2 registry variables	Case-insensitive on all platforms.	These work in Linux, UNIX, and Windows: db2options DB2optIOns
DB2 configuration parameters	Case-insensitive on all platforms.	These work in Linux, UNIX, and Windows: INTRA_PARALLEL intra_PARAllel

User data stored in the database	DB2 stores the data in your database exactly the way you inserted it.	In Linux, UNIX, and Windows, if you issue the following:
		`insert into mytable (col2)`
		`values ('RAul')`
		
		Then column *col2* in table *mytable* has the value *RAul*, just as it was inserted.

Category	Description	Examples
Database object names or any system data already stored in DB2 catalog tables	Typically any database object names or system-related data stored implicitly by DB2 itself is in uppercase. However, the object name can be in mixed case if it was created using double quotes. Keep this in mind when you refer to these objects in a query.	In Linux, UNIX, and Windows if you issue this: `create table t1 (col2 integer)` *t1* is stored as *T1*, and *col2* is stored as *COL2* in DB2 catalog tables. If double quotes enclose the object `create table "t1" (col2 integer)` *t1* is stored as *t1* and *col2* is stored as *COL2* in DB2 catalog table.

Case Study

> **NOTE**
>
> Several assumptions have been made in this case study and the rest of the case studies in this book, so if you try to follow them, some steps may not work for you. If you do follow some or all of the steps in the case studies, we recommend you use a test computer system.

You recently attended a DB2 training class and would like to try things out on your own laptop at the office. Your laptop is running Windows 2008 R2, and DB2 Enterprise Server Edition has been installed. You open the Command Window and take the following steps:

1. First, you want to know how many instances you have in your computer, so you enter
   `db2ilist`

2. Next, to find out which of these instances is the current one, you enter
   `db2 get instance`
   With the `db2ilist` command, you find out there are two instances defined on this computer, *DB2* and *myinst*. With the `db2 get instance` command, you learn that the *DB2* instance is the current instance.

3. You now need to list the databases in the *myinst* instance. Because this one is not the current instance, you first switch to this instance temporarily in the current Command Window:
   `set DB2INSTANCE=myinst`

4. You again issue `db2 get instance` to check that *myinst* is now the current instance, and you start it using the `db2start` command.

5. To list the databases defined on this instance, you issue

   ```
   db2 list db directory
   ```

   This command shows that you only have one database (*MYDB2*) in this instance.

6. You want to try creating a new database called *TEMPORAL*, so you execute

   ```
   db2 create database temporal
   ```

   The creation of the database takes some time because several objects are created by default inside the database. Issuing another `list  db  directory` command now shows two databases: *MYDB2* and *TEMPORAL*.

7. You connect to the *MYDB2* database (`db2 connect to mydb2`) and check which tables you have in this database (`db2 list tables for all`). You also check how many table spaces are defined (`db2 list tablespaces`).

8. Next, you want to review the contents of the database configuration file (db cfg) for the *MYDB2* database:

   ```
   db2 get db cfg for mydb2
   ```

9. To review the contents of the Database Manager Configuration file (dbm cfg), you issue

   ```
   db2 get dbm cfg
   ```

10. At this point, you want to practice changing the value of a dbm cfg parameter, so you pick the INTRA_PARALLEL parameter, which has a value set to NO. You change its value to YES as follows:

    ```
    db2 update dbm cfg using INTRA_PARALLEL YES
    ```

11. You learned at the class that this parameter is not configurable online, so you know you have to stop and start the instance. Because there is a connection to a database in the current instance (remember you connected to the *MYDB2* database earlier from your current Command Window), DB2 does not allow you to stop the instance. Enter the following sequence of commands:

    ```
    db2 terminate (terminates the connection)
    db2stop
    db2start
    ```

And that's it! In this case study, you reviewed some basic instance commands like `db2ilist` and `get  instance`. You have also reviewed how to accomplish the following:

- Switch to another instance
- Create and connect to a database
- List the databases in the instance
- Review the contents of the database configuration file and the database manager configuration file
- Update a database manager configuration file parameter
- Stop and start an instance

Summary

This chapter provided an overview of the DB2 core concepts using a "big picture" approach. It introduced SQL statements and their classification as Data Definition Language (DDL), Data Manipulation Language (DML), and Data Control Language (DCL) statements. You have seen some examples of XQuery with XPath and the FLWOR expression.

DB2 commands were classified into four groups—system commands, CLP commands, CLPPlus commands, and DB2 text search commands. DB2 commands are directives specific to DB2 that enable you to perform tasks against a DB2 server.

An interface is needed to issue SQL statements, XQuery statements, and commands to the DB2 engine. Three text-based interfaces were mentioned—the Command Line Processor (CLP), the Command Line Processor Plus (CLPPlus), and the Command Window.

Every DB2 edition is packaged with a separate graphical tool called IBM Data Studio. This is an Eclipse-based tool that provides a single integrated environment for database administration and application development. In addition, a suite of InfoSphere Optim tools is included in the DB2 Advanced Enterprise Server Edition and DB2 Advanced Workgroup Server Edition for larger and complex enterprise environments.

The concepts of instances, databases, table spaces, storage groups, buffer pools, logs, tables, indexes, and other database objects were discussed. The chapter also described the different levels of configuration for the DB2 environment, including environment variables, DB2 registry variables, and configuration parameters at the instance (dbm cfg) and database (db cfg) levels.

DB2 can be configured in a multi-partitioned database environment. The partitions work in parallel using a shared-nothing architecture. Data is spread across all the nodes made available to DB2. DB2 database partitioning is ideal for data mining and OLAP type of workloads.

You were also introduced to DB2 pureScale data-sharing technology. Since DB2 10.1, DB2 pureScale is available in the same codebase and installation image as rest of the DB2 offerings. DB2 pureScale provides extreme availability, scalability, and application transparency and is optimized for transactional processing. Cluster network interconnect, cluster services, cluster caching facility, clustered file systems are all superb technologies used in the DB2 pureScale environment.

In the rest of the book, most of these topics are discussed in more detail.

Review Questions

1. How are DB2 commands classified?

2. What are the different classes of SQL statements?

3. What are the key differences between the DB2 partitioned database environment and DB2 pureScale?

4. What command is used to create a DB2 instance?

5. What are the key benefits of CLPPlus?

6. What command can be used to get a list of all instances on your server?

7. What is the default instance that is created on Windows?

8. What is the technology DB2 pureScale used to achieve interrupt-free communication between members?

9. How can the DB2 environment be configured?

10. Which DB2 editions include a suite of InfoSphere Optim graphical tool products?

11. Which of the following commands start your DB2 instance?
    A. `startdb`
    B. `db2 start`
    C. `db2start`
    D. `start db2`

12. Which of the following commands list all of the registry variables that are set on your server?
    A. `db2set -a`
    B. `db2set -all`
    C. `db2set -lr`
    D. `db2set -ltr`

13. Say you are running DB2 on a Windows server with only one hard drive (C:). If the DB2 instance is dropped using the `db2idrop` command, after recreating the DB2 instance, which of the following commands lists the databases you had prior to dropping the instance?
    A. `list databases`
    B. `list db directory`
    C. `list db directory all`
    D. `list db directory on C:`

14. If the `list db directory on C:` command returns the following,

```
Database alias                          = SAMPLE
Database name                           = SAMPLE
Database directory                      = SQL00001
Database release level                  = a.00
Comment                                 =
Directory entry type                    = Home
Catalog database partition number       = 0
Database partition number               = 0
```

which of the following commands must be run before you can access tables in the database?

    A. `catalog db sample`

    B. `catalog db sample on local`

    C. `catalog db sample on SQL00001`

    D. `catalog db sample on C:`

15. If there are two DB2 instances on your Linux server, *inst1* and *inst2*, and if your default DB2 instance is *inst1*, which of the following commands needs to be run first from your Linux shell for you to connect to databases in the *inst2* instance from the same Linux shell?

    A. `export inst2`

    B. `export instance=inst2`

    C. `export db2instance=inst2`

    D. `connect to inst2`

16. Which of the following runs on every member and cluster caching facility in a pureScale cluster?

    A. Workload balancing

    B. Cluster services

    C. Cluster file system

    D. Automatic client reroute

17. Which of the following tools is used to run commands on all partitions in a multi-partition DB2 database?

    A. `db2_part`

    B. `db2_all`

    C. `db2_allpart`

    D. `db2`

18. Which of the following allows federated support in your server?

    A. `db2 update db cfg for federation using FEDERATED ON`

    B. `db2 update dbm cfg using FEDERATED YES`

    C. `db2 update dbm cfg using NICKNAME YES`

    D. `db2 update dbm cfg using NICKNAME, WRAPPER, SERVER, USER MAPPING YES`

19. Which environment variable needs to be updated to change the current logical database partition?

    A. DB2INSTANCE
    B. DB2PARTITION
    C. DB2NODE
    D. DB2PARTITIONNUMBER

20. Which of the following statements can be used to determine the value of the current database partition?

    A. values (current dbpartitionnum)
    B. values (current db2node)
    C. values (current db2partition)
    D. values (current partitionnum)

## CHAPTER 3

Installing DB2

Now that you have seen the big picture of DB2, the next step is to install the software and start using it. DB2 offers several installation methods to suit your needs.

In this chapter, you learn about

- The DB2 installation methods
- Checking the installation requirements for DB2 servers
- Root and non-root installation on Linux and UNIX
- The user IDs and groups required to install DB2
- Installing DB2 using the DB2 Setup Wizard
- Installing DB2 using the silent install method
- Installing DB2 licenses
- Reducing DB2 product installation image size
- Installing multiple DB2 copies on the same server
- Installing DB2 fix packs
- Upgrading to DB2 10 from previous DB2 versions

DB2 Installation: The Big Picture

Figures 3.1, 3.2, and 3.3 give you an overview of all the pieces needed for a complete DB2 installation on the Windows, Linux, and UNIX platforms, respectively. On Linux and UNIX platforms, installation can be performed by root users and non-root users. There are few capability and directory structure differences between the two as shown in Figures 3.2 and 3.3. More information about non-root installation is discussed in section "Root and Non-Root Installation on Linux and UNIX."

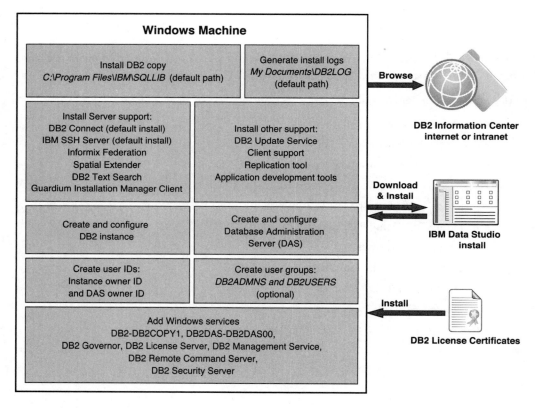

Figure 3.1   The big picture: DB2 installation on Windows

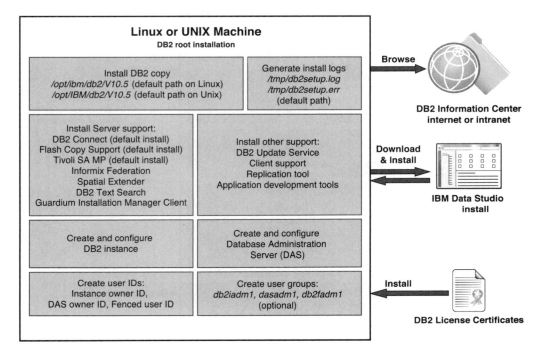

Figure 3.2 The big picture: DB2 root installation on Linux and UNIX

There are two methods for installing DB2 on Windows and four methods for installing DB2 on Linux and UNIX. Table 3.1 summarizes these installation methods.

Table 3.1 Installation Methods by Operating System

Installation Method	Windows	Linux and UNIX
Graphical base install—DB2 Setup Wizard (recommended)	Yes	Yes
Silent install—DB2 Response File installation (recommended for embedded install and mass install deployment)	Yes	Yes
Text base install—`db2_install` script	No	Yes
Advanced install and manual configuration—DB2 payload files	No	Yes

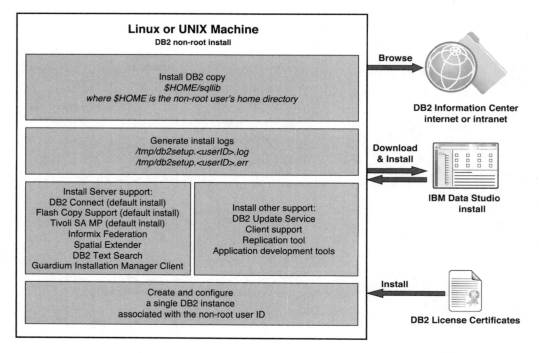

Figure 3.3   The big picture: DB2 non-root installation on Linux and UNIX

The **DB2 Setup Wizard** provides an easy to use graphical interface for installing DB2. In addition to creating a DB2 instance and any required user IDs, it also sets up some initial configuration parameters. It guides you through the installation tasks listed in Figures 3.1, 3.2, and 3.3. After the installation is complete, DB2 is ready for use. We recommend using the DB2 Setup Wizard for all platforms wherever possible and focus on this tool in this chapter.

NOTE

The DB2 Setup Wizard is a graphical installer. You must have X Window software capable of rendering a graphical user interface for the DB2 Setup Wizard to run on your machine. Ensure that the X Window server is running.

The DB2 silent install is a method that allows you to install DB2 without requiring user interaction. The key to this installation method is the response file, a text file that contains setup and configuration values. You pass this file as input to the DB2 setup program (`setup.exe` on Windows and `db2setup` on Linux and UNIX), and the setup program installs DB2 according to the values specified in the response file. Silent install is appropriate in situations where you have to install DB2 on hundreds or thousands of machines. Rather than manually answering the prompts of an interactive installation tool like the DB2 Setup Wizard, you can have DB2 automatically get the responses to these questions from the response file. Silent install is also appropriate when you are developing an application that embeds the DB2 software. As part of your application installation, you can invoke the DB2 setup program so it transparently installs DB2 while it installs your application. Silent install is discussed in detail in section "Silent Install Using a Response File."

The `db2_install` script installation method is only available on Linux and UNIX platforms. This install method prompts you for a DB2 product keyword and then installs all components for the DB2 product you specify. You cannot select or deselect components or specify the language to be used. This method does not perform user and group creation, instance creation, or configuration; it simply installs the DB2 components onto your system. You might prefer this method of installation if you want to customize the instances and their configurations yourself.

V10 **NOTE**

The `db2_install` script is deprecated in DB2 10. Deprecation means that the script may no longer be available in the next DB2 release. Start using the `db2setup` command instead.

The last installation method to install DB2 on Linux and UNIX platforms requires the user to manually install the DB2 payload files. A payload file is a compressed tarball file that contains all installation files and metadata required for an installable component. This requires advanced knowledge of both DB2 and your operating environment. You must manually perform user and group creation, instance creation, and configuration. This method is not recommended for most users. Instructions on how to install payload files can be found in section "Manually Installing the DB2 Payload Files."

V10 **NOTE**

You can now install DB2 pureScale with the DB2 SERVER image. DB2 pureScale has specific system and hardware requirements. For example, you can install DB2 pureScale on AIX and Linux x86-64 servers only. Your system must also meet some network, hardware, firmware, and storage requirements.

If you have purchased DB2, you can obtain the DB2 installation images by downloading them from IBM Passport Advantage® (http://www.ibm.com/software/howtobuy/passportadvantage/) or by ordering the DB2 product media. Refer to http://www.ibm.com/software/rational/howtobuy/index.html for more information. IBM Passport Advantage offers customers a secure web experience, enabling them to manage their IBM software quotes, offerings, purchases, and proof of entitlements.

If you want to try out DB2, trial copies of the DB2 editions are available at http://www.ibm.com/software/data/db2/linux-unix-windows/download.html. As described in Chapter 1, "Introduction to DB2," you might also find the no-charge DB2 Express-C at http://www-01.ibm.com/software/data/db2/express-c/download.html.

NOTE

Starting in DB2 V10.5, the DB2 SERVER image is all you need to install any DB2 server edition (except DB2 Express-C). After launching the DB2 SERVER installation image, you have the option to start installation of a particular DB2 Server Edition.

DB2 Installation System Requirements

When planning for a DB2 installation, the system requirement summary list (http://www.ibm.com/software/data/db2/linux-unix-windows/sysreqs.html) and http://pic.dhe.ibm.com/infocenter/db2luw/v10r5/topic/com.ibm.db2.luw.qb.server.doc/doc/r0025127.html are handy references. It provides you with the latest DB2 installation requirements for each DB2 release.

NOTE

References of the Windows file location made in this book are based on a Window 7 system.

Before you start the DB2 installation process, you can also use the db2prereqcheck command to check if your system meets the system requirements for a specific DB2 version and fix pack.

The db2prereqcheck command uses an XML file called DB2prereqs.xml. It contains system requirements for the DB2 version specified in the DB2Level XML tag. For example, <DB2Level value="10.5.0.0"> indicates prerequisites for DB2 10.5. Do not modify the contents of the XML file.

In Figure 3.4, the db2prereqcheck command confirms that the system requirements are met for DB2 V10.5.0.0, V10.1.0.2. However, this system does not meet the requirement for DB2 version 9.8.0.x, which is the DB2 pureScale feature.

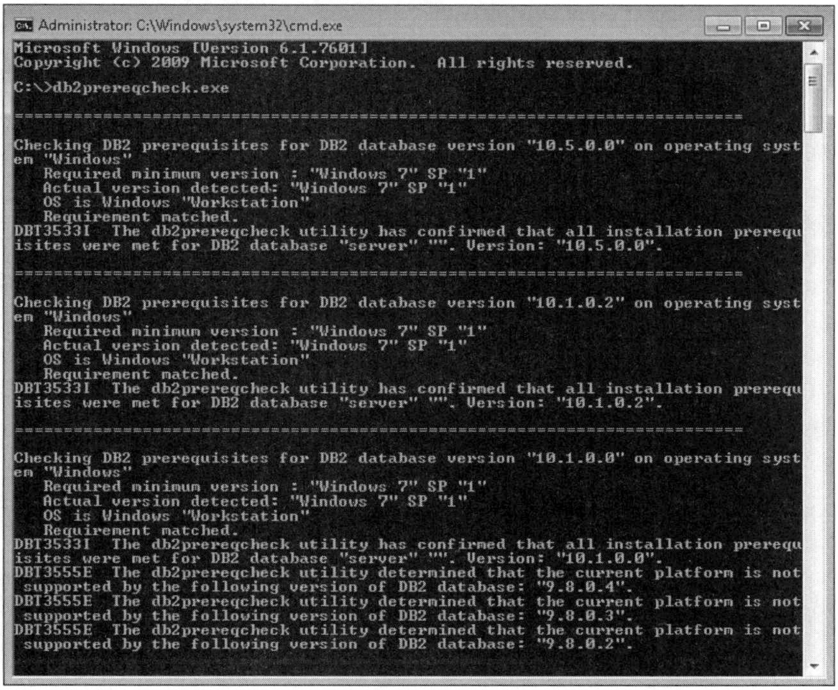

Figure 3.4   Output of the `db2prereqcheck` command

Installing DB2 Using the DB2 Setup Wizard

The DB2 Setup Wizard uses a step-by-step method to guide you through the installation process, perform the tasks listed in Figure 3.1, and keep an installation log. This section highlights the key installation steps and tips for using the DB2 Setup Wizard. Note that there are different first steps for Windows, Linux, and UNIX, but the procedure is mostly the same. Moreover, when handling tasks such as user and instance creation and configuration, the DB2 Setup Wizard goes through different steps in non-root installations versus those in root installations on Linux and UNIX.

> **NOTE**
>
> For simplicity, this section provides screen shots of an installation of the DB2 server image on Windows. Refer to the DB2 Information Center (http://pic.dhe.ibm.com/infocenter/db2luw/v10r5/topic/com.ibm.db2.luw.qb.server.doc/doc/c0024080.html) for complete installation instructions for other platforms.

Launch the DB2 Setup Wizard on Windows

To start the installation of DB2 on Windows, you must log on to the system with a user ID that belongs to the local Administrators group. Alternatively, the user ID must belong to the Windows elevated privilege setting that is properly configured to allow a non-Administrator user to perform an installation.

If you have the DB2 product DVD, insert it into the drive. The auto-run feature automatically starts the DB2 Setup Launchpad. If you downloaded the DB2 product image from Passport Advantage, run the executable file to extract the installation files. Double-click the **setup** icon to start the DB2 Setup Launchpad.

The launchpad determines your system's language and launches the setup program in that language. If you want to run the setup program in a different language, or if the setup program fails to start automatically, you can start the launchpad manually and use the /i option to specify a language. Click **Start > Run**. In the Open field, enter the following command:

```
DB2-install-image\setup /i language
```

where `DB2-install-image` represents the root directory of the installation image, and `language` is the territory identifier for your language (for example, `EN` for English). Other language identifiers can be found in the DB2 Information Center (http://pic.dhe.ibm.com/infocenter/db2luw/v10r5/topic/com.ibm.db2.luw.qb.server.doc/doc/r0007940.html).

If the /i flag is not specified, the installation program runs in the default language of the operating system.

From the launchpad, you have the option to view the installation prerequisites, release notes, migration information, or select **Install a Product** to proceed directly to the installation. You have the choice to install

- DB2 Workgroup, Enterprise, Advanced Workgroup, and Advanced Enterprise Edition
- DB2 Express Edition
- IBM Data Server Client
- IBM Database Add-Ins for Visual Studio
- DB2 Connect Server

To install DB2, select **Install New** under DB2 Enterprise Server Edition to launch the DB2 Setup Wizard. Refer to the section "DB2 Editions" in this chapter for descriptions of the DB2 products.

 NOTE

Starting in DB2 V10.5, DB2 Workgroup, Enterprise, Advanced Workgroup, and Advanced Enterprise Server Edition share the same install installer. You can choose to move from one edition to another by simply installing the associated license certificate. No additional DB2 installation is required. Refer to the "Installing a DB2 License" section to apply the appropriate license certificates as the post installation step.

Next, you are presented with the DB2 product license agreement. Make sure you take the time to read and understand the software license agreement. You can also print out the terms from this panel for easier reading.

Before we continue with the rest of the install steps, the next section shows you how to launch the DB2 Setup Wizard on Linux and UNIX.

Launch the DB2 Setup Wizard on Linux and UNIX

The DB2 Setup Launchpad and Wizard are also available on Linux and UNIX platforms. You must have X Window software capable of rendering a graphical user interface (GUI) for the DB2 Setup Launchpad and Wizard to run on your machine.

If you have the DB2 product DVD, change to the directory where the DVD is mounted. If you downloaded the DB2 product image from Passport Advantage, extract and untar the product file.

Extract the product file:

```
gzip -d product.tar.gz
```

In Linux, untar the product file:

```
tar -xvf product.tar
```

In UNIX, untar the product file:

```
gnutar -xvf product.tar
```

Start the DB2 Setup Launchpad with the command

```
./db2setup
```

Just like the DB2 Setup Launchpad on Windows, you have the option to view the installation prerequisites, release notes, or migration information or select **Install a Product** to proceed directly to the installation. You have the choice to install

- DB2 Workgroup, Enterprise, Advanced Workgroup, and Advanced Enterprise Edition
- DB2 Express Edition
- IBM Data Server Client
- DB2 Connect Server

Select **Install New** under DB2 Workgroup, Enterprise, Advanced Workgroup, and Advanced Enterprise Edition to launch the DB2 Setup Wizard.

Next, you are presented with the DB2 product license agreement. Make sure you take the time to read and understand this agreement. Refer to the section "Installing a DB2 License" to find out how to apply the appropriate license certificates as the post-installation step.

Generate a Response File

A response file captures installation choices and configuration data. It allows you to perform DB2 installation on other computers in an unattended mode. Refer to the "Silent Install Using a Response File" section for information on how to do this).

You can chose to either install DB2 Enterprise Server Edition on this computer, save the settings to a response file only, or both. If you need to install DB2 with the same configuration on other computers, it is a good idea to create a response file and install the DB2 code. The default path of the response file on Windows 7 is C:\Users\username\Documents\PROD_SERVER.rsp and /root/db2server.rsp for non-root installation on Linux.

Select Features to Be Installed

If you selected the Custom installation method, you have the opportunity to pick and choose the feature support and tools to install. Figure 3.5 shows that under the "Server support" category, DB2 Connect Support, IBM Secure Shell (SSH) Server for Windows, and Guardium Installation Management Client are selected by default.

Note that you need a separate DB2 Connect entitlement to use the Connect functionality. Refer to Chapter 1 to learn more about the DB2 Connect offerings.

The IBM SSH Server installation is only available on the Windows platform. Linux and UNIX typically already come with some SSH support.

If you already have some other SSH support installed and configured on the Windows machine, you can choose not to install this component. You are also given the option to auto or manual start the IBM SSH Server at system startup time.

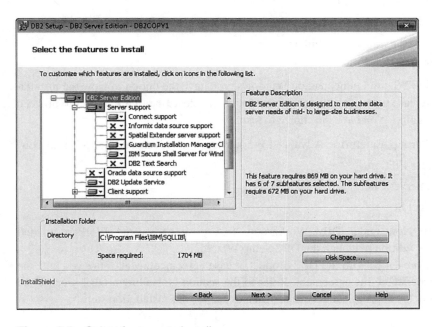

Figure 3.5   Select features to install

Specify a Unique DB2 Copy Name

You can install DB2 several times on the same computer. Each installation is called a DB2 copy, and these copies can be at the same or different code levels. Each DB2 copy is known by its copy name, which must be unique. The DB2 copy name is used to uniquely identify the installation path.

When you install a second or subsequent DB2 copy, the *Set this as the default DB2 copy on this computer* option identifies the copy you are installing as the default copy on the machine.

Set User Information for the DB2 Administration Server

The DAS is a special service needed to support the IBM Data Studio and Replication Tool and assist with administrative tasks on local and remote DB2 servers. Each server can have only one DAS. During installation the DAS is configured to start when the operating system is started.

You can specify either a local user or a domain user. If specifying a domain user, click the **domain** drop-down list and choose the domain. Otherwise, leave it as *None – use local user account*. If the user does not already exist, it is created and granted the appropriate rights. If the user already exists, DB2 grants it the appropriate rights.

If you are creating a domain user, the user ID you are using for this installation must belong to the administrator group of the domain.

Create and Configure the DB2 Instance

By default, a DB2 instance named DB2 is created on Windows. Subsequent copies of DB2 installed on the server would be by default named DB2COPY1, DB2COPY2, and so on.

On Linux and UNIX, the default instance created is called *db2inst1*. The DB2 Setup Wizard automatically detects the communication protocols configured on the server and generates communication parameter values for the instance to use for each detected protocol. The supported communication protocols are TCP/IP (for Windows, Linux, and UNIX) and Named Pipes (for Windows only).

Click the **Configure** button to display the settings for instance configuration. Figure 3.6 shows a list of the supported protocols on Windows: TCP/IP and Named Pipes. If a protocol is installed and configured correctly, the *Configure* option is selected. Otherwise, the *Do not configure at this time* option is selected. You can use the default values or enter different values.

In Figure 3.6, the TCPIP tab is selected; therefore the *service name* and the *port number* fields are displayed. The port number specifies the port where the instance will be listening for TCPIP requests by local applications that use TCP/IP and by remote DB2 clients. The service name is a string you can use as an alias for the port. If the service name is provided, an entry in the *services* file is created that matches the port number. For example, an entry similar to this is added:

```
db2c_DB2      50000/tcp
```

On Windows, the *services* file is typically located under *x*:\Windows\System32\drivers\ etc\services, where *x* represents the install drive. On Linux and UNIX, the file is located in /etc/ services.

If you want to specify a different port number, make sure that this number does not already exist in the *services* file because you cannot use the same port for two different applications.

More information about connectivity configuration can be found in Chapter 6, "Configuring Client and Server Connectivity."

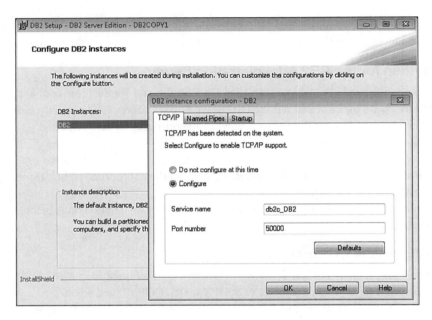

Figure 3.6   Configuring the DB2 instance and its communication protocols

Enable Operating System Security for DB2 Objects (Windows Only)

Extended security is a feature that allows for protection of DB2 objects at the operating system level. This means that only specific users can have access to files used by DB2, for example. If this feature is enabled, DB2 creates two user groups in the operating system. Their default names are DB2ADMNS and DB2USERS. You can specify different group names to adhere to your enterprise security policy.

After successfully completing a DB2 installation, you can add users to the DB2ADMNS or the DB2USERS groups to give them access to DB2. Users in the DB2ADMNS groups have complete control over all DB2 objects in the instance; users in the DB2USERS group have read and execute privileges only.

If you choose not to enable the extended Windows security feature now, you can still do so after the installation completes by running the command db2extsec.exe, which can typically be found in db2-installation-folder\BIN.

When you enable this security feature using the db2extsec.exe command, you have two options for backing out. If you made *any* changes after running the db2extsec.exe command to the system, you *must* use the second option.

- **Option 1:** Run the db2extsec.exe -r command again immediately *without* making any additional changes to the system.
- **Option 2:** Uninstall DB2, delete all the relevant DB2 directories (including the database directories), and then reinstall the DB2 database system without extended security enabled. This is the safest method.

Option 2 can be quite tedious, so make plans to decide if it will benefit your environment before enabling extended security. Additional information about this topic can be found in Chapter 8, "Implementing Security."

Review Installation Settings and Start the Installation

Just before starting the installation, the DB2 Setup Wizard displays a window summarizing the components that are going to be installed.

If you specified in the previous step to save your setting in a response file, the file information is displayed at the end of the summary. Review this window carefully. Click **Back** to make any changes; click **Finish** to start the installation.

After a successful DB2 installation, the DB2 First Steps tool is automatically launched. From this tool, you have the option to check for DB2 product updates, browse the DB2 Information Center (online manuals), create a sample database, or download IBM Data Studio.

Root and Non-Root Installation on Linux and UNIX

DB2 installation on Linux and UNIX allows both root and non-root users to install DB2. In many customer environments with strict enterprise security policies, root installation might not be practical. A non-root installation, as its name implies, is an installation of DB2 where a user other than root can install the product. This is useful in many scenarios. For example, application developers typically do not have root authority but need to install and use DB2 products to develop applications. Another example is for applications that embed DB2; the application installation would not need mandatory root authority.

Although non-root installation of DB2 products results in a fully functioning DB2 instance, there are differences and limitations between the two.

Table 3.2 summarizes the differences between root and non-root installations.

Table 3.2   Differences Between Root and Non-Root Installations

Criteria	Root Installations	Non-Root Installations
User can select installation directory	Yes	No. DB2 image is always placed in the $HOME/sqllib directory, where $HOME represents the non-root user's home directory.
Number of DB2 instances allowed	Multiple	One DB2 installer automatically creates and configures a single non-root instance during the installation.
Files deployed during installation	DB2 image files only. Instances are created after installation.	DB2 image files and instance files. An instance is automatically created and configured during installation.
Upgrade version and instance	No	No need to uninstall the old version before installing the new version. Install new version and upgrade the instance together.

Limitations of Non-Root Installations

There are several limitations for non-root installations, as listed in Table 3.3. Understanding the limitations can help you decide when to use a non-root installation.

Table 3.3   Limitations of Non-Root Installations

Limitations	Description
Product	Some DB2 products are not supported in non-root installations: • DB2 Net Search Extender • Locally installed DB2 Information Center
Database Partitioning Feature (DPF)	Partitioned databases are not supported in non-root installations.
DB2 Copies	Each non-root user can have only one copy of a DB2 product installed.
Features and Tools	The following features and tools are not supported in non-root installations: • DB2 Administration Server (DAS) • The ability for db2governor to increase priority • The agent priority set in the DB2 Work Load Manager is ignored even though the operation is allowed.

Limitations	Description
DB2 Instance Operations	The following DB2 instance operations are not supported in non-root installations:
	• Automatic start of DB2 instances at system reboot
	• User instance commands: `db2icrt`, `db2iupdt`, `db2idrop`, `db2imigr`
	• DAS instance commands: `dascrt`, `dasdrop`, `daslist`, `dasmigr`, and `dasupdt`
	The output produced by the `db2ls` command, when running as a non-root user, is different than the output produced when running as a root user.
Migration	Root instances cannot be migrated to a non-root instance.
Health Monitor	The following health monitor features are not supported in non-root installations
	• Running script or task actions on alert occurrences
	• Sending alert notifications

Installing DB2 with a Non-Root User

Most DB2 products can be installed with a non-root user. There isn't anything special required for a non-root user to install a DB2 product, other than being logged in as a non-root user.

To perform a non-root installation:

- Log in as a non-root user.
- Install the DB2 product using one of the methods listed in Table 3.1, such as the DB2 Setup Wizard.
- After the installation, you need to log in as the same user via a new login session to use the non-root DB2 instance. Alternatively, you can use the same login session if you source the DB2 instance profile (for example, $HOME/sqllib/db2profile) in the session. An example to source a file is `source filename` or `. filename`

When installing a DB2 product as a non-root user, a single instance is automatically created and configured. If the non-root user instance needs to be manually configured or updated afterward, you can use the `db2nrcfg` configuration tool or the `db2nrupdt` update command, respectively. In addition, the only way to drop a non-root user instance is to uninstall the product.

Enabling Some Root-Based Features in Non-Root Installations

Some root-based features and abilities are initially unavailable in non-root installations but can be enabled by running the `db2rfe` command with the root authority.

The following features and abilities can be enabled with the db2rfe command:

- Operating system-based authentication
- High Availability (HA) feature
- The ability to reserve service names in the /etc/services file
- The ability to increase user data limits (ulimits) on AIX

To enable those features and abilities in non-root installations:

1. Locate the *db2rfe.cfg* configuration file of the db2rfe tool under the $HOME/sqllib/ instance directory, where $HOME is the non-root user's home directory.

2. Make a copy of the configuration file for the recovery purpose.

3. Update the original configuration file accordingly.

   The example that follows shows an updated configuration file that enables the following features and abilities:

   - (HA) High Availability
   - Operating system-based authentication
   - Reserve DB2 Text search with a service name of db2j_db2inst1 and a port value of 55000

   ```
   INSTANCENAME=db2inst1
   SET_ULIMIT=NO
   ENABLE_HA=YES
   RESERVE_REMOTE_CONNECTION=NO
           **SVCENAME=db2c_db2inst1
           **SVCEPORT=50000
   RESERVE_TEXT_SEARCH_CONNECTION=YES
               SVCENAME_TEXT_SEARCH=db2j_db2inst1
               SVCEPORT_TEXT_SEARCH=55000
   ```

4. Log in as a user with root authority.

5. Run the db2rfe command located under the $HOME/sqllib/instance directory, using the following syntax:

   ```
   db2rfe -f config_file
   ```

   where config_file is the configuration file edited in Step 3.

Required User IDs and Groups

As shown in the big picture of DB2 installation (Figures 3.1 and 3.2), several user IDs and user groups are created during the DB2 on Windows install or the root installation on Linux and UNIX. For companies that have strict security policies, the user IDs and user groups can be precreated by the system administrator prior to the DB2 installation. This section discusses the basic requirements of those user IDs and groups, which are different for Windows than for Linux or UNIX.

User IDs and Groups Required for Windows

In addition to requiring an installation user ID to install the DB2 product on Windows, to operate DB2 you need two other user IDs:

- The **Instance owner** owns and controls the DB2 instance.
- The **DB2 Administration Server** (DAS) **user** runs the DB2 administration server service on your system. The DB2 GUI tools also use this ID to perform administration tasks against the local server database instances and databases.

Table 3.4 describes these user IDs in more detail.

Table 3.4   User IDs and Groups for DB2 on Windows

	Installation User ID	Instance Owner User ID	DAS User ID
Authority of the User ID	A local or domain user account that is part of the administrator group on the server where you are installing DB2 or a non-administrative ID with elevated rights to installation. The user right "Access this computer from the network" is required. You can also use the built- in Local System account to run the installation for all products except DB2 Enterprise Edition. If you want to have the DB2 Setup Wizard create a domain user account for the Instance owner or the DAS user, the installation ID must have authority to create domain user accounts.	A local or domain user account that belongs to the administrator group on the server.	A local or domain user account that belongs to the administrator group on the machine. The built-in Local System account can also be used.

	Installation User ID	Instance Owner User ID	DAS User ID
When to Create It	Before installation.	Before installation or during installation by the DB2 Setup Wizard. Either way, the necessary rights are granted during the installation process.	Same as Instance Owner User ID.
Rights Granted During Installation	Act as part of the operating system. • Create a token object. • Lock pages in memory. • Increase quotas. • Replace a process-level token.	Act as part of the operating system. • Debug programs. • Create a token object. • Increase quotas. • Lock pages in memory. • Log on as a service. • Replace a process-level token.	Same as Instance Owner User ID.

NOTE

The user installing DB2 on Windows does not need to be part of the Administrators group. You can install DB2 using a non-administrative ID. Just make sure that a Windows Administrator configures the elevated privileges feature in Windows before installing DB2.

User IDs and Groups Required for Linux and UNIX

For root installations on Linux and UNIX, you need to sign in as a root user to perform the DB2 installation. In addition, you need three users and three groups to operate DB2:

- The DB2 **Instance owner** controls all DB2 processes and owns all file systems and devices used by the databases contained within the instance.
- The **Fenced user** runs fenced user-defined functions (UDFs) and stored procedures. Fenced UDFs and stored procedures execute outside of the address space used by the DB2 instance and therefore cannot interfere with the execution of the instance. If you do not need this level of security, you can use the instance owner as your fenced user.
- The same as on Windows, the **DAS user** runs the DB2 Administration Server process on your system. This user ID is also used by the DB2 GUI tools to perform administration tasks against the local server database instances and databases.
- Three separate user groups must also be created for the Instance Owner, the Fenced User, and the DAS user.

Table 3.5 describes these user IDs and groups in more detail.

Table 3.5 User IDs and Groups Required for Installing DB2 on Linux and UNIX Platforms

	Instance Owner User ID	Fenced User ID	DAS User ID
When to Create It	During installation when using the DB2 Setup Wizard or Silent install. After installation when using the db2_install script or native OS install tool.	Same as Instance Owner User ID.	Same as Instance Owner User ID.
Default User ID Created by DB2 Installer	db2inst1 If db2inst1 already exists, the DB2 installer then searches for the user db2inst2. If that user doesn't exist, it creates that user. If that user does exist, the DB2 installer continues its search (db2inst3, db2inst4, and so on) until it finds an available user.	db2fenc1 Uses the same algorithm as Instance Owner User ID.	db2as (AIX only) dasusr1 (all other Linux and UNIX platforms). Uses the same algorithm as Instance Owner User ID.
Example Primary Group Name	db2iadm1	db2fadm1	dasadm1
Example Secondary Group Name	dasadm1	Not applicable	db2iadm1

Silent Install Using a Response File

When you need to install DB2 on a number of computers, you might want to install it using a response file to reduce the amount of work involved. With a response file, you can install DB2 unattended. This installation method is available on all DB2-supported platforms.

A response file is a text file with the extension *.rsp*. It specifies configuration and setup parameters such as the destination directory (Windows only) and the products and components to install. It can also be used to

- Create instances
- Set up global DB2 registry variables
- Set up the database manager configuration

Listing 3.1 shows the response file, *PROD_SERVER.rsp*, which can be used to perform one of the DB2 Server Edition installations on Windows.

Listing 3.1   A Response File Excerpt (Created by the DB2 Setup Wizard)

```
PROD=DB2_SERVER_EDITION
LIC_AGREEMENT=ACCEPT
FILE=C:\Program Files\IBM\SQLLIB\
INSTALL_TYPE=CUSTOM
COMP=APPLICATION_DEVELOPMENT_TOOLS
COMP=BASE_CLIENT
COMP=CONNECT_SUPPORT
COMP=DEBUGGING_SYMBOLS
COMP=DOTNET_DATA_PROVIDER
COMP=FIRST_STEPS
COMP=SPATIAL_EXTENDER_CLIENT_SUPPORT
COMP=DB2_UPDATE_SERVICE
COMP=JAVA_RUNTIME_SUPPORT
COMP=JDBC_SUPPORT
COMP=JDK
COMP=LDAP_EXPLOITATION
COMP=ODBC_SUPPORT
COMP=OLE_DB_SUPPORT
COMP=REPL_CLIENT
COMP=DB2_SAMPLE_DATABASE
COMP=SQLJ_SUPPORT
COMP=SSH_SERVER
COMP=WMI_PROVIDER
LANG=EN
DAS_CONTACT_LIST=LOCAL
INSTANCE=DB2
DB2.NAME=DB2
DEFAULT_INSTANCE=DB2
DB2.SVCENAME=db2c_DB2
DB2.DB2COMM=TCPIP
DB2_OLEDB_GUID={7D9B266E-8077-4216-95E6-13486623BB92}
DB2_OLEDB_ADVANCED_PAGE_GUID={9CC2778B-D353-42D6-BEEA-0ED7934E1260}
DB2_OLEDB_CONNECTION_PAGE_GUID={D24F08DF-E426-4739-83A8-5FFCE313887C}
DB2_OLEDB_ENUMERATOR_GUID={316BB619-C414-43D0-948C-53E7C7DC6E2A}
```

```
DB2_OLEDB_ERROR_LOOKUP_GUID={C764A109-BF76-44E0-BC93-9C141A6EC315}
DB2.PORT_NUMBER=50000
SSH_SERVER_INSTALL_DIR=C:\Program Files\IBM\IBM SSH Server\
AUTOSTART_SSH_SERVER=YES
DB2.AUTOSTART=YES
DB2.USERNAME=db2admin
DB2.PASSWORD=
ENCRYPTED=DB2.PASSWORD
DAS_USERNAME=db2admin
DAS_PASSWORD=
ENCRYPTED=DAS_PASSWORD
DAS_SMTP_SERVER=mailhub01
CREATE_DAS=YES
DB2_EXTSECURITY=YES
DB2_USERSGROUP_NAME=DB2USERS
DB2_ADMINGROUP_NAME=DB2ADMNS
DB2_COMMON_APP_DATA_TOP_PATH=C:\ProgramData
RSP_FILE_NAME=C:\Users\<username>\Documents\PROD_SERVER.rsp
DB2_COPY_NAME=DB2COPY1
DEFAULT_COPY=YES
DEFAULT_CLIENT_INTERFACE_COPY=YES
```

As shown in Listing 3.1, a response file consists of keywords and their values. For example, the PROD keyword specifies the DB2 product you are installing. The FILE keyword specifies the install location, and the INSTALL_TYPE keyword specifies whether to perform a TYPICAL install, a COMPACT install, or a CUSTOM install. These are the values you would have to enter interactively if you were installing DB2 using the DB2 Setup Wizard.

Creating a Response File Using the DB2 Setup Wizard

There are three ways to create a response file for your installation and not have to actually install the product:

- Using the DB2 Setup Wizard to save the setup and configuration data.
- Modifying a sample response file to create a custom response file.
- Using the response file generator (Windows only).

If you use the DB2 Setup Wizard to install DB2, you have the option to create a response file. This response file records all the parameters you input to the DB2 Setup Wizard, and you can use this file to perform installations on other computers. The DB2 Setup Wizard created the response file excerpt shown in Listing 3.2.

Creating a Custom Response File Using a Sample Response File

You can manually edit the response file created by the DB2 Setup Wizard or the sample response files provided on the DB2 installation image. Each DB2 product has sample response files. They are located at the *db2-install-image/*db2/*platform/*samples directory (where *platform* refers to the appropriate hardware platform). Listing 3.2 shows a sample Windows response file.

Listing 3.2   A Sample Windows Response File

```
** General Options
** ---------------


** Only one product can be specified for the following PROD keyword. Specifying
** multiple products in an installation is not supported.
PROD                   = DB2_SERVER_EDITION


** The FILE keyword determines the base installation path. If you specify a
** path that does not yet have any DB2 product installed, this will install a
** new copy.  Otherwise, this will install the product to the same copy. This
** is an optional keyword.
*FILE                  = C:\Program Files\IBM\SQLLIB
INSTALL_OPTION         = SINGLE_PARTITION


** Modify the value of the following LIC_AGREEMENT keyword to indicate that you
** have read and agreed to the license agreement file in the db2/license
** directory on the CD.
LIC_AGREEMENT          = DECLINE      ** ACCEPT or DECLINE


** INSTALL_TYPE keyword is used to select the installation type. If you specify
** a TYPICAL or a COMPACT install type, no COMP keywords are required. In this
** case the installer will select the appropriate components for you.  All COMP
** keywords are ignored by the installer unless the INSTALL_TYPE is set  to
** CUSTOM. If you select the CUSTOM install type, then ensure that you enable
** all of the COMP keywords that are required for your database environment.
**
** Note: The install type is not related to the language selection.
** ------------------------------------------------------------------------
INSTALL_TYPE           = TYPICAL      ** TYPICAL, COMPACT, CUSTOM


** The following components are part of all TYPICAL installations. If you
** perform a typical installation, all of these components will be installed on
** your computer.
** ------------------------------------------------------------------------
```

```
** Connect Support provides the ability to connect to host, AS/400, and iSeries
** systems.
*COMP                   = CONNECT_SUPPORT                  ** Connect Support

** This component contains source code to create DB2 sample databases.
*COMP                   = DB2_SAMPLE_DATABASE              ** Sample Database

** DB2 Update Service is a Web tool that lists the available DB2 product
** updates, and provides details about product updates. The DB2 Update Service
** requires an Internet connection.
*COMP                   = DB2_UPDATE_SERVICE               ** DB2 Update Service

** First Steps is a graphical tool that will help familiarize you with DB2
** features and functions.
*COMP                   = FIRST_STEPS                      ** First Steps

** Guardium Installation Manager Client component will place the Guardium
** Installation Manager(GIM) Client under DB2 Install Path.
*COMP                   = GUARDIUM_INST_MNGR_CLIENT        ** Guardium
                         .                                    Installation Manager
                                                              Client

.

.
```

All the entries in the sample response files are commented out with asterisks (*). You need to remove the asterisks to activate the corresponding entries. The possible values are listed to the right of the equal sign.

Creating a Response File Using the Response File Generator (Windows Only)

The response file generator utility, db2rspgn, creates a response file from an existing installed and configured DB2 product.

The syntax for db2rspgn is

```
db2rspgn -d path [-i instance] [-noctlsrv]
```

where

- -d specifies the target directory for the response file and any instance files. This parameter is required.
- -i (optional) specifies a list of instances for which you want to create a profile. The default is to generate an instance profile file for all instances.
- -noctlsrv (optional) indicates that an instance profile file will not be generated for the Replication Control Server instance.

For example

```
db2rspgn d:\temp
```

generates two files in the *d:\temp* directory. One is the response file, *PROD_SERVER.rsp*
(assuming DB2 Server Edition is the product installed), and the other file is *DB2.INS*, which contains information such as the registry variables and database manager configurations.

Installing DB2 Using a Response File on Windows

To perform a DB2 installation using a response file, use the `setup` command:

```
db2-install-image/setup [-i language] [-l log_file]
[-t trace_file] [-p install_directory] -u response_file
```

where

`db2-install-image` represents the location of the DB2 installable image.

* `-i` (optional) specifies the two-letter language code of the language in which to perform
  the installation.
* `-l` (optional) specifies the fully qualified log file name, where setup information and
  any errors occurring during setup are logged. If you do not specify the log file's name,
  DB2 names it *db2.log* and puts it in the My Documents/db2log folder.
* `-p` (optional) changes the installation path of the product. Specifying this option overrides the installation path that is specified in the response file.
* `-t` (optional) specifies the full path name of a file to trace install information.
* `-u` specifies the full path name of the response file.

For example

```
setup -u d:\temp\PROD_SERVER.rsp
```

Installing DB2 Using a Response File on Linux and UNIX

To perform a DB2 installation using a response on Linux and UNIX, use the `db2setup` command (ensure that you log on with the proper user ID based on the root or non-root installation
type):

```
db2-install-image/db2setup [-i language] [-l log_file] [-t
trace_file] -r response_file
```

where

`db2-install-image` represents the location of the DB2 install image.

`response_file` represents the full path name of the response file.

* `-i` (optional) specifies the two-letter language code of the language in which to perform
  the installation.

- `-l` (optional) specifies the fully qualified log file name, where setup information and any errors occurring during setup are logged. If you do not specify the log file's name, DB2 names it *db2.log* and puts it in the /tmp directory.
- `-t` (optional) specifies the full path name of a file to trace install information.
- `-r` specifies the full path name of the response file.

For example

```
db2setup -r /usr/tmp/PROD_SERVER.rsp
```

> **NOTE**
>
> DB2 response files are version-sensitive. That means response files created in DB2 V9 cannot be used to install a DB2 V10 product and vice versa. This is primarily because of mandatory keywords that are new in DB2 V10.

Advanced DB2 Installation Methods (Linux and UNIX Only)

DB2 supports two additional methods for installing DB2 on Linux and UNIX:

- Using the `db2_install` script
- Manual installation

These two methods require a certain level of operating system knowledge. Tasks such as user and instance creation and configuration that would be performed for you by the DB2 Setup Wizard or during a response file installation must be performed after the product is installed. We do not recommend using either of these methods if you are new to DB2 on Linux or UNIX.

Installing DB2 Using the db2_install Script

The `db2_install` script is located in the root directory on your DB2 product install media. To perform a DB2 installation using the `db2_install` script, follow these steps:

1. Log in with a proper user ID based on the root or non-root installation type.

2. Insert and mount the appropriate product DVD or access the file system where the installation image is stored.

3. If you downloaded the DB2 product, decompress and untar the product file.

4. Change the directory to the product directory.

5. Run the `db2_install` command:

   ```
   db2_install [-b install_path] [-p product_ID] [-c image_
   location] [-n] [-L language] [-l log_file] [-t trace_file]
   ```

where

- -b (optional) specifies the path where the DB2 product is to be installed in root installations. This parameter is mandatory if the -n parameter is selected. The default installation path is
  - for AIX, HP-UX, or Solaris /opt/IBM/db2/V10.5
  - for Linux, /opt/ibm/db2/V10.5
- -p (optional) specifies the DB2 product to be installed. Enter the keyword for the product you want to install. If you specify more than one product keyword, separate the key words with spaces in quotation marks. A list of DB2 product keywords is shown in Table 3.6, or it can be found in the file *ComponentList.htm* located in the /db2/*platform* directory on the install media (where *platform* is the platform on which you are installing).
- -c (optional) specifies the product image location.
- -n (optional) specifies noninteractive mode. If selected, you must also specify the -b install_path parameter.
- -L (optional) specifies national language support. By default, English is always installed.
- -l (optional) specifies the log file. The default log file is /tmp/db2_install.log$$, where $$ is the process ID.
- -t (optional) turns on the debug mode.

For example

```
./db2_install
```

or

```
./db2_install -p ese -b /db2/newlevel -n
```

Table 3.6   Keywords Used by the `db2_install` Script

DB2 Product	Keyword
Data Server Client	CLIENT
Data Server Runtime Client	RTCL
DB2 Connect Servers	CONSV
DB2 Express	EXP
DB2 Workgroup, Enterprise, Advanced Workgroup, Advanced Enterprise	ESE

Manually Installing the DB2 Payload Files

A payload file is a compressed tarball that contains all of the files and metadata for an installable component. This method is an advanced installation method that is not recommended for most users. It requires the user to physically install payload files.

To manually install payload files,

1. Log in with a proper user ID based on the root or non-root installation type.

2. Insert and mount the appropriate media or access the file system where the installation image is stored.

3. Locate the DB2 component you want to install. Refer to the component list in Listing 3.1, or it can be found in the file *ComponentList.htm* located in the /db2/*<platform>* directory on the media (where *platform* is the platform on which you are installing).

4. The DB2 payload file is compressed and uses the same format for all supported operating systems. You can uncompress the payload file with the following commands:

   • For AIX, HP-UX, or Solaris:

   ```
   cd DB2DIR
   gunzip -c /cd/db2/platform/FILES/filename.tar.gz |
   tar -xf -
   ```

   • For Linux:

   ```
   cd DB2DIR
   tar xzf /cd/db2/platform/FILES/filename.tar.gz
   ```

   where

   DB2DIR is the full path name where you are installing.

   • For root installations, the default path for AIX, HP-UX, or Solaris is /opt/IBM/db2/V10.5.

   • For Linux, the default path is /opt/ibm/db2/V10.5.

   • For non-root installations, DB2DIR must be $HOME/sqllib. This directory must be empty.

   cd represents the mount point of the DB2 media.

   filename is the name of the DB2 component you are installing.

5. To ensure the embedded library search path on each DB2 executable and library file uses the installation path, enter

   ```
   DB2DIR/install/db2chgpath
   ```

6. For non-root installations, run $HOME/sqllib/db2nrcfg to configure the non-root instance.

7. For non-root installations, after the DB2 product is installed, open a new login session to use the non-root DB2 instance. Alternatively, you can use the same login session if you source the DB2 instance profile (that is, $HOME/sqllib/db2profile) in the session.

After the product is installed, tasks such as user and instance creation and configuration will have to be performed for root installations. This method is not recommended. Instead, install DB2 products, components, and features using the DB2 Setup Wizard or by using a response file.

> **NOTE**
>
> You *cannot* manually install a DB2 product, component, or feature using an operating system's native installation utility such as rpm, SMIT, swinstall, or pkgadd.

Installing a DB2 License

After a successful DB2 installation, you must install the license certificate(s) that comes with your DB2 purchase. This ensures the functionality is properly enabled on your installed image, ensures you can generate a proper license compliance report for software inventory and audit purposes, and ensures you can receive proper service support entitlement.

License certificates (also known as license keys) are located in the associated DB2 product Quick Start and Activation media. License certificates are DB2 edition-specific, DB2 version and release-specific, charge metric option-specific, but platform *nonspecific*. For example, say you purchased the DB2 Advanced Enterprise Server Edition (AESE) 10.5 with Processor Value Unit (PVU) charge metric option. The license certificate you receive can only be installed on a DB2 Server Edition 10.5 installation. This means you cannot install the certificate on a DB2 Express Edition and/or DB2 AESE 9.7 installation. However, you can choose to install the license certificate on any supported operating system where DB2 Server Edition 10.5 is installed.

You can use the db2licm command to list, add, remove, and modify DB2 licenses registered on the local system.

You can either log in as a root user or an instance owner to install a license. In non-root installations, the only option is to install a license as the instance owner.

On Linux and UNIX, as an instance owner, use

DB2PATH/adm/db2licm -a *filename*.lic

On Linux and UNIX, as a root user for root installations, use

/opt/ibm/db2/V10.5/adm/db2licm -a *filename* (on Linux)

or /opt/IBM/db2/V10.5/adm/db2licm -a *filename* (on all UNIX platforms)

filename is the full pathname and filename for the license file that corresponds to the product you purchased.

On Windows, use `DB2PATH\bin\db2licm -a filename.lic` where `DB2PATH` is where the DB2 instance was created and `filename` is the full pathname and filename for the license file that corresponds to the product you purchased.

The license file is located in the /db2/license directory at the root directory of the DB2 Quick Start and Activation electronic image or media. Here is a sample output of the command after the license file *db2aese_c.lic* is added to the DB2 installation.

```
C:\>db2licm -a db2aese_c.lic
LIC1402I License added successfully.
LIC1426I This product is now licensed for use as outlined in your
License Agreement. USE OF THE PRODUCT CONSTITUTES ACCEPTANCE OF THE
TERMS OF THE IBM LICENSE AGREEMENT, LOCATED IN THE FOLLOWING DIRECTORY:
"C:\PROGRA~1\IBM\SQLLIB\license\en"
```

After the DB2 product license key is installed, use the `db2licm` command and the `-l` option to list the registered license.

Listing 3.3 is a sample output of the `db2licm -l` command. It shows that the DB2 installation is permanently licensed for the DB2 Advanced Enterprise Server Edition (AESE) 10.5 CPU option (also known as the PVU option).

Listing 3.3 Sample Output of the `db2licm -l` Command

```
C:\>db2licm -l
Product name:                 "DB2 Advanced Enterprise Server Edition"
License type:                 "CPU Option"
Expiry date:                  "Permanent"
Product identifier:           "db2aese"
Version information:          "10.5"
Enforcement policy:           "Soft Stop"
```

All DB2 editions (except DB2 Express-C) offer the Try and Buy program. You can download trial copies of the DB2 editions at http://www.ibm.com/software/data/db2/linux-unix-windows/download.html. You have a 90-day trial period from the moment the software is installed. After the trial period, you can purchase the software and install the license certificate as just described. This essentially turns a DB2 trial installation to a fully licensed DB2 installation without any additional software installation required (if you choose to keep the existing feature options). Note that all the DB2 instances and databases you created during the trial period are all maintained.

Reducing DB2 Product Installation Image Size

When you install DB2, you can choose the components to install with the DB2 installation image. In many cases, your application might *not* need everything shipped in the image. For example, you might not need the Spatial Extender and the Federated support, and you might only need the English language support. The components you don't need can increase the DB2 installation program footprint unnecessarily.

Using the db2iprune utility, you can customize and prune the install image to meet your own needs. The DB2 product installation image size is reduced. The new, customized, and smaller DB2 installation image can still be installed using the regular DB2 installation methods discussed earlier in this chapter. This can be helpful when you want to embed DB2 as part of your application or to provide a better user experience and ease of deployment.

Customizing DB2 Installation Images

The db2iprune utility is available to automate the process of pruning the install image. For example on Windows, the utility removes the Windows cabinet (.cab) files associated with those features as well as any languages that are marked for pruning based on the pruning input file. A sample input file (.prn file) is available on the installation media.

On Windows, the sample *db2iprune* input file is located at

`<DB2 installation image>\db2\Windows\utilities\db2iprune.`

On Linux and UNIX, the sample *db2iprune* input file is located at

`< DB2 installation image>/db2/platform/utilities/db2iprune.`

The input file, which resembles a response file, lists the features and languages you can prune from the installation image. Using the sample input file, simply remove the asterisk (*) to uncomment the product, component, or language you want to prune. Listing 3.4 shows part of the sample input file.

Listing 3.4   Sample Input File Used with the db2iprune Utility

```
** The following products are available to prune. At least one must not be
** pruned.
** ----------------------------------------------------------------------
PRUNE_PROD = CLIENT
*PRUNE_PROD = DB2_SERVER_EDITION


** The following components are available to prune. See the COMP descriptions
** below for more information about these options.
** ----------------------------------------------------------------------


** The Base Application Development Tools component contains tools and files
** (including header files, libraries, and a precompiler) that are needed for
** developing applications that work with DB2.
```

```
PRUNE_COMP   = APPLICATION_DEVELOPMENT_TOOLS      ** Base Application
                                                    Development Tools
```

```
** Connect Support provides the ability to connect to host, AS/400, and iSeries
** systems.
PRUNE_COMP   = CONNECT_SUPPORT                      ** Connect Support
```

```
** This component contains source code to create DB2 sample databases.
PRUNE_COMP   = DB2_SAMPLE_DATABASE                  ** Sample Database
. . .
** Enables users and applications to submit distributed requests for data
** managed by Informix systems.
PRUNE_COMP   = INFORMIX_DATA_SOURCE_SUPPORT         ** Informix data source
                                                      support
```

```
** JDBC Support allows Java samples, not containing embedded SQL (SQLJ), to be
** built and run using the JDBC driver.
*PRUNE_COMP  = JDBC_SUPPORT                         ** JDBC Support
```

```
** LDAP Exploitation allows DB2 to use an LDAP directory to store database
** directory and configuration information.
*PRUNE_COMP  = LDAP_EXPLOITATION                    ** LDAP Exploitation
```

```
** ODBC Support provides support for applications that use Open Database
** Connectivity (ODBC) to access data.
*PRUNE_COMP  = ODBC_SUPPORT                         ** ODBC Support
```

```
** OLE DB Support provides a set of interfaces that allow applications to
** uniformly access data stored in different data sources.
*PRUNE_COMP  = OLE_DB_SUPPORT                       ** OLE DB Support
```

```
** The Replication Tools help you administer, operate, and monitor SQL and Q
** replication.
PRUNE_COMP   = REPL_CLIENT                          ** Replication Tools
```

```
** Spatial Extender Client provides the support required for communicating with
** a Spatial Extender Server.
PRUNE_COMP   = SPATIAL_EXTENDER_CLIENT_SUPPORT      ** Spatial Extender Client
```

```
** Provides Spatial Extender support for the DB2 server, providing the storing
** and query of geographical information in DB2 tables.
```

```
PRUNE_COMP   = SPATIAL_EXTENDER_SERVER_SUPPORT      ** Spatial Extender Server
                                                       Support


** The following languages are available to prune.  You cannot prune English.
** ------------------------------------------------------------------------
PRUNE_LANG   = ALL               ** Remove all except English
 . . .
```

The lines in bold in Listing 3.4 are the components to be pruned. For example, the Data Server Client, DB2 Connect support, Sample database, Informix Federation support, Replication tools, Spatial Extender, and all non-English languages will not be included in the newly customized installation image.

When you have a customized input file ready, run the db2iprune command as follows:

```
db2iprune -r input_file_path -p root_directory_path
-o destination_directory_path -l log_file
```

> **NOTE**
>
> The db2iprune utility is not supported for a DB2 pureScale installation.

> **NOTE**
>
> The db2iprune utility can be used with DB2 fix pack images given that fix packs are full installation images.

Installing DB2 Using a Pruned Installation Image

You can use any of the regular DB2 installation methods to install a pruned DB2 installation image.

If you choose to use the DB2 Setup Wizard to install the pruned image, a typical installation would install all the regular typical components without the components removed by the db2iprune utility. A compact installation would install all the regular compact components without the components removed by the db2iprune utility. A custom installation would only have a list of the remaining components displayed in the feature selection panel.

If you choose to use silent install with a response file, make sure you specify only the components and languages available in the pruned installation image. If you select a component that has been removed, an error will be encountered during the silent install.

Installing Multiple DB2 Versions and Fix Packs on the Same Server

Imagine you are working on a high-risk project that requires a particular DB2 version and fix pack. The new server you ordered will not arrive for another week, and your manager is breathing down your neck asking for status updates. There is an active development server that has the minimum resources you need to run your tests, but the server is already running DB2 at a lower version and fix pack. Can you use the active development server to run a different version of DB2 and fix pack? Can you install different versions of DB2 on the same Windows machine at the same time? Can you test a particular version of DB2 on the same server as your production and then simply migrate it after the tests are successful? The answer to all of these questions is yes!

You can install and run multiple DB2 copies on the same computer. A **DB2 Copy** refers to one or more installations of DB2 database products in a particular location on the same computer. Each DB2 copy can be at the same or different code levels. This is done by installing multiple DB2 product codes in different paths on the same machine. Other benefits of this feature include

- **Install anywhere:** You can install DB2 using any valid path you choose.
- **Install any number of times:** You can install two or more copies of the same DB2 code on one machine. The code levels can be the same or different.
- **Maintain each copy independently:** You can update one copy without affecting any of the other copies.

Coexistence of Multiple DB2 Versions and Fix Packs (Windows)

You have the ability to install multiple DB2 server and client copies on the same machine. DB2 installs each DB2 copy into different installation paths and uses separate registry keys. Each DB2 installation copy can either be at the same DB2 level or at a different level. During installation, a unique DB2 copy name is generated, which you can later change.

When there is only one installation of DB2, that DB2 copy automatically becomes the default DB2 copy. The default DB2 copy is required for your applications to access DB2 databases through the default or native interface. In other words, any applications that have not been coded to target a specific DB2 copy will access the databases within the default DB2 copy. When you install subsequent versions of DB2, you can choose to work with an existing copy or install a new one. Working with an existing copy enables you to update the functionality of your current DB2 copy, whereas installing a new copy creates a new unique DB2 copy on the machine. If previous DB2 versions exist on the server, you have the option to *Install New* or *Migrate* the DB2 copy.

After you have installed multiple copies of DB2 on your machine, you might need to change which copy is your default DB2 copy. You can to do this, for example, in situations where you are promoting a test environment into production. For your current applications to connect successfully to the new production DB2 copy, you need to set the new production DB2 copy as the default. If you want to access a nondefault copy of DB2 (for testing purposes for example), you can use the following two methods:

- Using the DB2 command window from the Start > Programs > IBM DB2 > <*DB2 Copy Name*> > Command Line Tools > DB2 Command Window (see Figure 3.7).
- Using db2envar.bat from a command window:

Open a command window.

Run the db2envar.bat file using the fully qualified path for the DB2 copy you want the application to use, such as X:\DB2_01\bin\db2envar.bat.

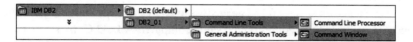

Figure 3.7   Selecting the DB2 copy instance to use

You can change which copy of DB2 becomes the default DB2 copy by using the Global Switcher, db2swtch.exe command. You can either launch this as a graphical interface or run it as a command. To launch the Default DB2 Selection wizard, type db2swtch.exe without any arguments at the command window. Note that local Administrator authority is needed. Figure 3.8 shows you the Welcome panel that greets you. Click **Next**.

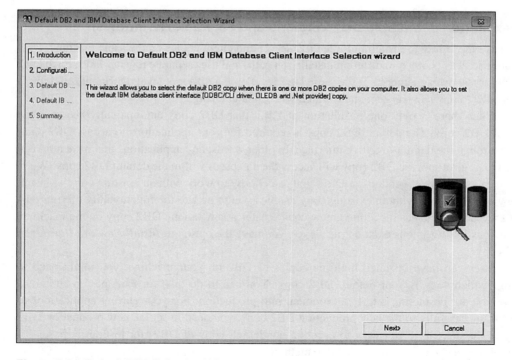

Figure 3.8   Default DB2 Selection Wizard

In Figure 3.9, you can see your current default DB2 copy and all other installation copies available on your system. For this exercise, we selected the DB2COPY2 DB2 copy and made that our default DB2 copy. Highlight **DB2COPY2** and click **Next**.

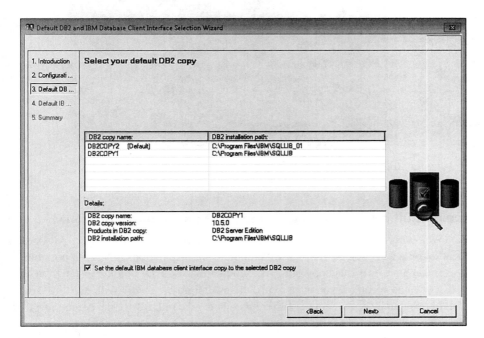

Figure 3.9   Select your default DB2 copy

You now see that the switch of your new default DB2 copy is successful. Your new default DB2 copy is now DB2COPY2. Click **Finish** to complete the process.

You can also switch the default DB2 copy by running the db2swtch.exe command with special arguments, such as

```
db2swtch.exe -l -d <installation name>
```

where

- -l displays a list of DB2 database product installations on the system
- -d <installation name> sets the default DB2 copy

Figure 3.10 provides an example of how to do this from the command line.

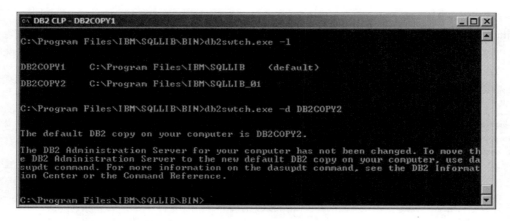

Figure 3.10   Using the db2swtch.exe command

Coexistence of Multiple DB2 Versions and Fix Packs (Linux and UNIX)

Similar to Windows, with root installations you can install multiple versions and fix packs of DB2 to any location on a Linux or UNIX server. With non-root installations this is not possible; each non-root user can have only one copy of a DB2 product installed. During the installation or migration process, you can specify if you want to install new, migrate, or work with existing DB2 copies. Each DB2 copy can be at the same or different code levels. In DB2 10, the default installation path for root installations is as follows:

- /opt/IBM/db2/V10.5 for AIX, HP-UX, or Solaris
- /opt/ibm/db2/V10.5 for Linux

You can specify your desired installation path or let DB2 specify it for you. If the default path is already used (by another DB2 copy), DB2 uses the following naming convention:

- /opt/IBM/db2/V10.5_## for AIX, HP-UX, or Solaris
- /opt/ibm/db2/V10.5_## for Linux

where ## is a sequential number ranging from 01 to 99. For example, if you decide to install two copies of DB2 on your Linux machine, then by default, DB2 installs the first in /opt/ibm/db2/V10.5 and the second in /opt/ibm/db2/V10.5_01.

The db2ls Command (Linux and UNIX)

The command db2ls is used to provide information about DB2 database systems and features installed on your Linux and UNIX systems. You can use the db2ls command to list where DB2 products are installed on your system and list the DB2 product level for each DB2 copy. You can also list all or specific DB2 products and features in a particular installation path. The db2ls command is available in the /usr/local/bin directory. db2ls can be used without any parameters.

To find information about a specific installation path or feature, here are few parameters you can use:

```
db2ls -q -f feature_id -a -p -b base-install-path -l logfile
```

where

- `-q` queries the list of installed DB2 products and features. By default, only the visible components or features are displayed unless the `-a` parameter is also specified.
- `-f feature_id` (optional) queries if the specified feature is installed on the system.
- `-a` (optional) lists all hidden components as well as visible features.
- `-p` (optional) lists products installed on the system only.
- `-b base-install-path` specifies which installation directory you are querying.
- `-l logfile` (optional) produces a trace file for debugging purposes in the path in which you ran the `db2ls` command.

Different feature listings are obtained depending on the root versus non-root type of DB2 installation and the user running the command. For example, to query if all DB2 database features are installed to a particular path, issue

```
db2ls -q -a -b /opt/ibm/db2/V10.5
```

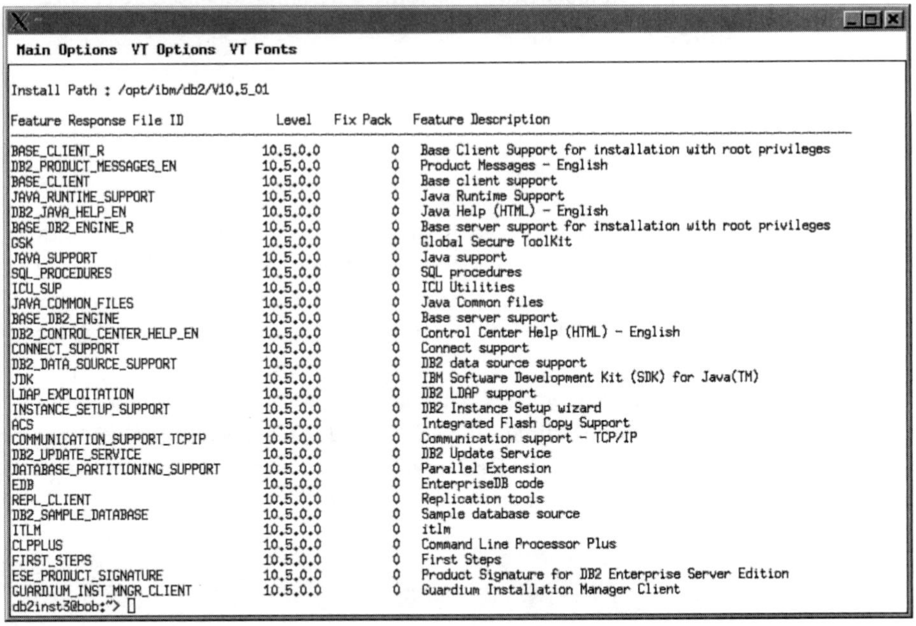

```
Main Options  VT Options  VT Fonts

Install Path : /opt/ibm/db2/V10.5_01

Feature Response File ID          Level     Fix Pack  Feature Description
---------------------------------------------------------------------------------------------
BASE_CLIENT_R                     10.5.0.0  0  Base Client Support for installation with root privileges
DB2_PRODUCT_MESSAGES_EN           10.5.0.0  0  Product Messages - English
BASE_CLIENT                       10.5.0.0  0  Base client support
JAVA_RUNTIME_SUPPORT              10.5.0.0  0  Java Runtime Support
DB2_JAVA_HELP_EN                  10.5.0.0  0  Java Help (HTML) - English
BASE_DB2_ENGINE_R                 10.5.0.0  0  Base server support for installation with root privileges
GSK                               10.5.0.0  0  Global Secure ToolKit
JAVA_SUPPORT                      10.5.0.0  0  Java support
SQL_PROCEDURES                    10.5.0.0  0  SQL procedures
ICU_SUP                           10.5.0.0  0  ICU Utilities
JAVA_COMMON_FILES                 10.5.0.0  0  Java Common files
BASE_DB2_ENGINE                   10.5.0.0  0  Base server support
DB2_CONTROL_CENTER_HELP_EN        10.5.0.0  0  Control Center Help (HTML) - English
CONNECT_SUPPORT                   10.5.0.0  0  Connect support
DB2_DATA_SOURCE_SUPPORT           10.5.0.0  0  DB2 data source support
JDK                               10.5.0.0  0  IBM Software Development Kit (SDK) for Java(TM)
LDAP_EXPLOITATION                 10.5.0.0  0  DB2 LDAP support
INSTANCE_SETUP_SUPPORT            10.5.0.0  0  DB2 Instance Setup wizard
ACS                               10.5.0.0  0  Integrated Flash Copy Support
COMMUNICATION_SUPPORT_TCPIP       10.5.0.0  0  Communication support - TCP/IP
DB2_UPDATE_SERVICE                10.5.0.0  0  DB2 Update Service
DATABASE_PARTITIONING_SUPPORT     10.5.0.0  0  Parallel Extension
EDB                               10.5.0.0  0  EnterpriseDB code
REPL_CLIENT                       10.5.0.0  0  Replication tools
DB2_SAMPLE_DATABASE               10.5.0.0  0  Sample database source
ITLM                              10.5.0.0  0  itlm
CLPPLUS                           10.5.0.0  0  Command Line Processor Plus
FIRST_STEPS                       10.5.0.0  0  First Steps
ESE_PRODUCT_SIGNATURE             10.5.0.0  0  Product Signature for DB2 Enterprise Server Edition
GUARDIUM_INST_MNGR_CLIENT         10.5.0.0  0  Guardium Installation Manager Client
db2inst3@bob:~>
```

Figure 3.11 Example of `db2ls` output

> **NOTE**
>
> The db2ls command is the only method to query a DB2 product. You cannot query DB2 products using the native Linux and UNIX utilities such pkgadd, rpm, SMIT, or swinstall.

DB2 Administrative Server (DAS) and Multiple DB2 Copies

You can only operate one active DAS on any given system at any given time, regardless of the number of DB2 installation copies that are installed on the machine. This is unchanged from previous versions. The DAS can be from any version of DB2 that is currently installed on the machine. If the DAS is created on DB2 10, then it can administer both DB2 9 and DB2 10 instances. If the DAS is created on DB2 9, then it can only administer DB2 9 instances. You can choose to either drop the DB2 9 DAS, migrate the DB2 9 DAS to DB2 10, or create a new DB2 10 DAS to administer both version instances. You will need to run the dasimgr command to switch the DAS when you switch the default DB2 copy.

> **NOTE**
>
> DAS is deprecated since DB2 9.7. DAS is required when remote administration task is performed. Start using Secure Shell protocol (SSH) for remote administration. For example, you can configure IBM Data Studio to run SQL statements on remote servers using the SSH protocol.

Installing DB2 Fix Packs

A DB2 fix pack provides fixes to program defects. A fix to a program defect is also known as an Authorized Program Analysis Report (APAR). APARs can be discovered during IBM testing or reported by customers in test or production environments. Every fix pack is accompanied by a document known as the APAR List (APARLIST.TXT), which describes the fixes that particular fix pack contains.

All fix packs are full DB2 installation images. They accumulate all updates of the previous fix packs on the same DB2 version. For example, fix pack 3 (FP3) includes all the fixes present in FP1 and FP2. It is recommended to keep your DB2 environment running at the latest fix pack level to ensure you receive the latest software updates.

> **NOTE**
>
> DB2 fix packs are full DB2 installation images. If a permanent DB2 license is not installed, the fix pack install acts like a trial install. It will be usable for 90 days and then will expire.

You can download the latest DB2 fix pack from the IBM DB2 and DB2 Connect Online Support website at http://www.ibm.com/support/entry/portal/Overview/Software/Information_ Management/DB2_for_Linux_UNIX_and_Windows. Each fix pack also contains a set of Release Notes and a Readme file. The Readme file provides instructions for installing the fix pack for each operating system.

When you apply a DB2 regular fix pack, you are in fact refreshing the DB2 code by overwriting some or all of the DB2 binaries. You then need to re-establish the links to an existing instance using the `db2iupdt` program on Linux and UNIX (this step is not required on Windows). Applying a fix pack does not affect the data in the databases. Figure 3.12 shows an example of what happens after applying fix pack 1 to DB2 10.5.

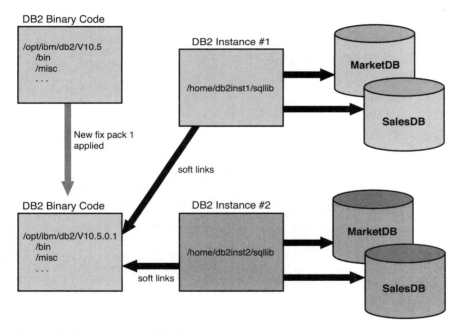

Figure 3.12 Applying a DB2 fix pack

If you have multiple DB2 copies on your system, each copy is treated as a separate entity. Applying a fix pack on one copy does not affect any other copies. You can choose to apply a new fix pack at a certain level to one DB2 copy and apply another fix pack of a different level to another DB2 copy on the same system.

> **NOTE**
>
> If you want to upgrade a DB2 instance to a DB2 copy of a different release, you use the `db2iupgrade` command.

Applying Fix Packs to a Non-Root Installation

The task of applying fix packs to a non-root installation on Linux and UNIX platforms is essentially the same as applying fix packs to a root installation with a few exceptions.

Before applying fix packs to a non-root installation, you must log on with the same user ID that was used to install the non-root installation. In addition, if you had root-based features enabled in your non-root installation, you should run the db2rfe command again as a post-fix pack operation to update and re-enable those root-based features.

Upgrading to the Latest DB2 Version

Upgrading DB2 servers involves upgrading your existing instances and databases so that they can run properly in the latest DB2 version. The upgrade paths from previous DB2 versions to DB2 10 are

- DB2 9.5 -> DB2 9.7 or DB2 10.1 -> DB2 10.5
- DB2 9.7 -> DB2 10.5
- DB2 10.1 -> DB2 10.5

> **NOTE**
>
> The term *migrate* is commonly used to indicate an upgrade from one version of DB2 to another. This is a bit confusing because the same term often refers to the process of making an application that works with other database software able to work with DB2. We use the term *upgrade* instead to refer to a DB2 version upgrade.

Case Study 1

Your company has chosen DB2 10.1 Enterprise Server Edition (ESE) on a Windows machine as your data server. Currently you have DB2 10.1 Express Edition (Express) installed on that machine because you were learning DB2 on your own time. To install DB2 ESE, you do not need to uninstall DB2 Express; you can either install a new copy or move your existing DB2 10.5 Express to DB2 ESE. You decide to install a new copy because you want to try out some advanced functionality offered in the DB2 ESE.

After the DB2 ESE installation completes successfully, you issue the command db2licm -l to confirm you installed the correct product and to review the license status. Figure 3.13 shows the output of the command.

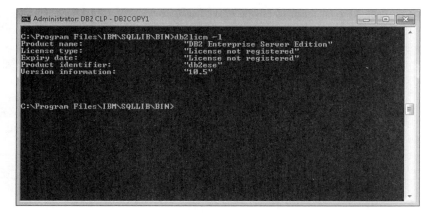

Figure 3.13   Output from the `db2licm` command

The output of the command confirms that you have DB2 Enterprise Server Edition installed, but now you realize it is not yet *registered*; that is, a license has not been applied. You inform your manager about this. The manager calls the 1-800-IBM-SERV number to purchase a permanent license.

Next, you issue the `db2level` command to ensure you are at the latest fix pack level. Figure 3.14 shows the command's output.

Figure 3.14   Output from the `db2level` command

You notice that the installation is at Fix Pack 0, also known as base level or General Availability (GA) level. Know that Fix Pack 1 has just been released, you go to the IBM Support website (http://www-01.ibm.com/support/docview.wss?uid=swg27007053) and download Fix Pack 1.

After applying Fix Pack 1, you again issue the db2level command to confirm it now shows the correct Fix Pack level.

Now your company is ready to start working with DB2!

Case Study 2

You've been asked to install DB2 Enterprise Server Edition (ESE) from scratch on a different machine and to record all responses in a response file so that it can be used for other installations. You decide to use the DB2 Setup Wizard, which is the recommend DB2 installation method. These are the steps you follow:

1. Download the DB2 10.5 Server trial image from the download site (http://www.ibm. com/software/data/db2/linux-unix-windows/download.html).

2. Select the DB2 Data Server Trial link.

3. Sign up and get an IBM ID.

4. Select your preferred operating system.

5. After the DB2 trial installation image is downloaded, run the db2prereqcheck command to determine if the system satisfies the DB2 installation prerequisites.

   On Linux and UNIX:
   ```
   ./db2prereqcheck -v 10.5.0.0 -o syscheck.rpt
   ```

   On Windows:
   ```
   db2prereqcheck -v 10.5.0.0 -o syscheck.rpt
   ```

6. Confirm that your system meets the software requirements. Run the setup program to launch the DB2 Setup Launchpad.

7. Select **Install New** under DB2 Server Edition to launch the DB2 Setup Wizard.

8. Read the Software License Agreement; if you accept, click **Next**.

9. Select **Custom** installation type. Click **Next**.

10. Select **Install DB2 Server Edition on this computer and save my settings in a response file**. Click **Next**.

11. Under Server Support, select only the **Connect support, IBM Secure Shell Server for Windows**, and **DB2 Text Search**. Click **Next**.

12. Select **English**. Click **Next**.

13. On the IBM SSH Server Startup Option page, select **Do not autostart the IBM SSH server**. Click **Next**.

14. On the DB2 copy name page and the location of the DB2 Information Center page, use the default options. Click **Next**.

15. On the user information for DB2 Administrator Server page, enter the user name and password that runs DAS. Select the **Use the same account for the remaining DB2 services** option. Click **Next**.

16. On the instance configuration page, configure the TCPIP support. Enter Service name **db2service_myinst**, port number **70000**. Click **Next**.

17. Keep the default settings for the rest of the pages. Review the options you have selected in the Summary page. Click **Finish** to start the installation process.

18. After the installation is completed, review the install logs.
    - On Windows 7, the logs are in My Documents\DB2LOG
    - On Linux and UNIX, the logs are in /tmp/db2setup.log and /temp/db2setup.err

19. If you have purchased DB2 ESE, download the license certificate (.lic file) from IBM Passport Advantage. The license certificate is stored in the DB2 Enterprise Server Edition Quick Start and Activation CD.

20. Install the DB2 product license certificate (for example, `db2ese_u.lic`) with the command
    ```
    db2licm -a db2ese_u.lic
    ```

21. Verify the installation. Start the database manager by entering the `db2start` command on a Command Window or at the Linux/UNIX shell.

22. Create the SAMPLE database with the command `db2sampl`.

You have successfully installed DB2 ESE on your system! If you did not install a permanent license to this installation in step 20, it will be a trial installation for 90 days. After 90 days, you will not be able to start up the instance unless a DB2 ESE 10 license certificate is applied to the installation.

It is recommended that you keep your DB2 installation up to date by downloading and installing DB2 fix packs from the IBM Support Portal (http://www.ibm.com/support/entry/portal/Overview/Software/Information_Management/DB2_for_Linux,_UNIX_and_Windows).

You should also sign up and subscribe to DB2 product support notifications.

Summary

In this chapter, we discussed four DB2 installation methods:

- Using the DB2 Setup Wizard
- Using a response file
- Using the `db2_install` script
- Using manual installation of DB2 payload files

The first two methods are available on all supported platforms; the last two are only available on Linux and UNIX platforms. The recommended method to install DB2 is by using the DB2 Setup Wizard. The silent install using the DB2 response file is also useful for applications that embed DB2 and/or mass deployment of DB2 installation.

On Linux and UNIX platforms, you can perform a root or non-root installation option.

Even as a non-root user, you can install products, apply and roll back fix packs, configure instances, add features, or uninstall products. If you use the DB2 Setup Wizard or the response file methods, you have the choice to create a DB2 instance and the DAS except during the non-root installation on Linux and UNIX. The instance owner user ID and the DAS user ID are also created. If you use the other two methods in root installations, you must manually create the user IDs and the instance after the installation is complete. If you use the manual install method, you must also install the DB2 license manually.

A DB2 copy is a separate installation copy of the DB2 code. Each DB2 copy can be at the same or different code levels. The benefits of DB2 copies include

- The ability to run applications that require different DB2 versions on the same machine at the same time.
- The ability to run independent copies of DB2 products for different functions.
- The ability to test on the same computer before moving the production database to the latter version of the DB2 product.

A DB2 copy can contain one or more different DB2 products. This refers to the group of DB2 products that are installed at the same location. On Linux and UNIX, non-root installations allow only one DB2 copy for each valid non-root user.

A DB2 fix pack contains updates and fixes for problems or defects found during IBM testing, and customer reports. These fixes are also known as Authorized Program Analysis Reports (APARs). Fix packs are cumulative, and it is recommended that you keep your DB2 environment running at the latest fix pack level to ensure a low-incident operation.

Review Questions

1. What DB2 installation methods are available on Windows?

2. With a non-root installation, can the user select an installation directory?

3. What is the name of the default instance created by the DB2 Setup Wizard during installation on Linux and UNIX?

4. What command can you run before performing a DB2 installation to ensure system requirements are met?

5. On Linux and UNIX, where are installation logs generated by default? Can you redirect them to a different location?

6. On Windows, where are installation logs generated by default? Can you redirect them to a different location?

7. Two user groups are optionally created on Windows during a DB2 install. What are they?

8. What command needs to be run after you install a DB2 fix pack in a root installation on Linux or UNIX?

9. What user rights are granted to an instance owner during installation on Windows?

10. What authority must a user have to install DB2 on Windows?

11. Which of the following is a valid method for installing DB2 on Windows?

    A. The `db2_install` script

    B. The DB2 Setup Wizard

    C. The `db2setup.exe` program

    D. Using the operating system's Add or Remove program utility under the Control Panel

12. Which of the following allows you to install DB2 unattended?

    A. The `db2_install` script

    B. The DB2 Setup Wizard

    C. A response file

    D. Smitty on AIX

13. Which of the following is the TCP/IP port the DB2 Setup Wizard uses to configure the very first default DB2 instance during installation (assuming TCP/IP is enabled on the system)?

    A. 6000

    B. 20000

    C. 50000

    D. 5000

14. What authority is required for a user to run the db2rfe command in a non-root installation on Linux and UNIX?

    A. Instance owner authority

    B. DAS user authority

    C. Local Administrator authority

    D. Root authority

15. Which of the following user IDs is used by the Replication Tool to perform administration tasks against the local server database instances and databases?

    A. The DAS user ID

    B. The instance owner user ID

    C. The fenced user ID

    D. The DB2 user ID

16. Which of the following is *not* a valid method of creating a response file on Windows?

    A. Using the DB2 Setup Wizard to save the setup and configuration data

    B. Using the `db2_install` script to save the setup and configuration data

    C. Using the response file generator

    D. Modifying one of the sample response files that are provided

17. During installation, which of the following methods prompts you to enter the product keyword (e.g., DB2.ESE, DB2.EXP) for the product you want to install?

    A. The DB2 Setup Wizard

    B. A response file install

    C. The `db2_install` script

    D. Smitty on AIX

18. Which of the following commands should be used to install DB2 on Linux and UNIX using a response file?

    A. `db2setup -r response_file`

    B. `setup /U response_file`

    C. `install -r response_file`

    D. `response_install /U response_file`

19. Which of the following is used to install a DB2 license?

    A. The `db2licm -a` command

    B. The `db2licm -r` command

    C. The DB2 Setup Wizard

    D. The `db2_install` script

20. Which command is used to provide information about DB2 database systems and features installed on your Linux and UNIX systems?

    A. The `db2licm` command

    B. The `db2cc` command

    C. The `db2ls` command

    D. The `db2level` command

## CHAPTER 4

Using Database Tools and Utilities

How do you work with DB2? How do you issue SQL and/or XQuery statements and enter DB2 commands? Are there graphical tools that can make your administration tasks easier? This chapter provides the answers to all of these questions. DB2 provides a wide range of tools, both graphical and command-driven, to help you work with DB2.

In this chapter, you learn about

- DB2 command line tools
- IBM Data Studio
- IBM Data Studio Web Console
- Set up tools
- DB2 information tools
- DB2 problem determination tools

Database Tools: The Big Picture

DB2 comes with a comprehensive and complimentary set of tools for you to perform basic database administration and development tasks. Figure 4.1 shows a high level overview of tools available with DB2. They are categorized into command line tools, graphical tools, and other tools to assist you with setup. In most cases you can perform the same DB2 commands, SQL statements, and XQuery statements using the command line and graphical tools.

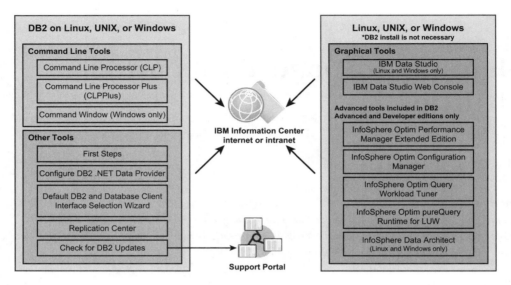

Figure 4.1   Database tools the big picture

 NOTE

The Control Center tools and all related components such as wizards and advisors were discontinued in DB2 10. IBM Data Studio can be used to manage DB2 environment and DB2 data-centric applications. IBM Data Studio comes with every DB2 edition.

The Command-Line Tools

All DB2 operations are invoked by DB2 commands, SQL statements, or XQuery statements. For example, to back up a database, you use the BACKUP DATABASE command. To create a table, you use the CREATE TABLE SQL statement. To parse an XML document you use the FLWOR expression. All of these commands, SQL statements, and XQuery statements can be entered using the command-line tools.

The command-line tools consist of the Command Line Processor (CLP), the Command Line Processor Plus (CLP Plus), and the Command Window (Windows platform only). Because they are command-driven, you must have some knowledge of DB2 commands and SQL statements to use them. Figure 4.2 demonstrates the relationship between them. Compare each line in the Windows machine versus the Linux/UNIX machine. The equivalent line in each machine has been aligned in the figure.

> **NOTE**
>
> In this chapter, we use the generic term **DB2 commands** to refer to DB2 system commands, DB2 CLP, and DB2 CLP Plus commands. When a section is only applicable to a given type of command, it is indicated. Refer to section "SQL Statements, XQuery Statements, and DB2 Commands," for an explanation about the differences between these commands.

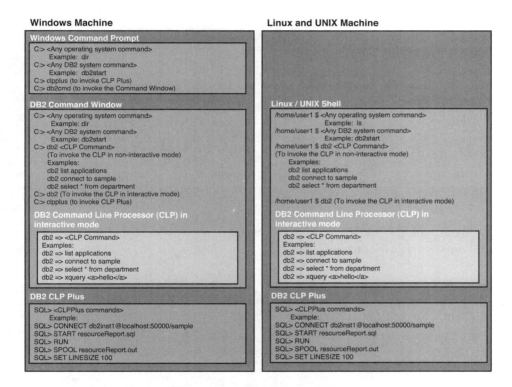

Figure 4.2   The CLP, CLP Plus, and the DB2 Command Window

The DB2 Command Window

The DB2 Command Window is only available on Windows; this is due to some architecture differences in Windows versus Linux and UNIX. If you are familiar with the Linux and UNIX platforms, you can think of the Command Window on Windows as the Linux/UNIX shell. Figure 4.2 illustrates this: The commands and statements inside the DB2 Command Window box to the left of the figure are equivalent to the ones inside the Linux/UNIX shell box on the right.

To start the Command Window, click **Start > Programs > IBM DB2 > DB2COPY1 (Default) > Command Window**. Alternatively, to invoke the Command Window from a

Windows command prompt, issue the command db2cmd. This command spawns another window that displays DB2 CLP in the title bar. Note that the Command Window looks like any Windows command prompt except for this title bar.

From the Windows command prompt, you can perform operating system commands and DB2 system commands but not DB2 CLP commands, DB2 CLPPlus commands, SQL statements, or XQuery statements. However, you can perform all of these from a DB2 Command Window.

Refer to the DB2 Information Center, under Database administration > Interfaces > Commands, for a complete list of different types of commands. Figure 4.2 shows a few examples. From the Windows command prompt you can execute the following:

Operating system commands:	dir
DB2 system commands:	db2start

In the DB2 Command Window, you can perform these commands as well as DB2 CLP commands and SQL statements:

DB2 CLP commands:	db2 list applications
SQL statements:	db2 SELECT * FROM department
XQuery statements:	db2 "xquery <a>hello</a>"

If you try to execute a CLP command, SQL statement, or XQuery statement from a Windows command prompt, you receive the following error as illustrated in Figure 4.3.

```
DB21061E Command line environment not initialized
```

In the figure, you also see how the same statement works from the DB2 Command Window after it is invoked with the db2cmd command.

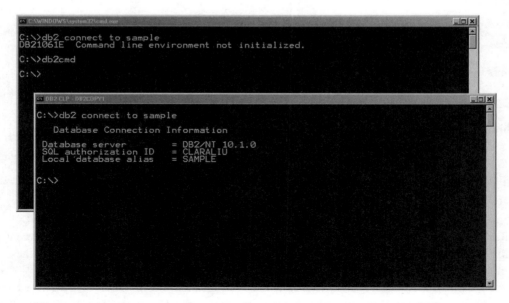

Figure 4.3   Invoking the DB2 Command Window from a Windows command prompt

The DB2 Command Line Processor

The DB2 Command Line Processor (CLP) is an application written in the C language that contains embedded SQL. It provides you with a text-based interface to the DB2 engine that lets you issue CLP commands, SQL statements, and XQuery statements. The CLP executable is called db2, and it is stored under the DB2_install_directory/sqllib/bin directory.

> **NOTE**
>
> We recommend you learn how to use the Command Line Processor, as it is the common tool available with all DB2 versions and clients.

Methods to Work with the CLP

There are three ways to issue a DB2 command or SQL statement with the CLP: interactive mode, noninteractive mode, and noninteractive mode using a file as input. These methods are discussed in the following sections.

Method 1: Interactive Mode

You start the CLP in interactive mode by clicking **Start > Programs > IBM DB2 > DB2COPY1 (Default) > Command Line Processor**. Alternatively, from the Command Window or Linux/UNIX shell, you start the CLP in interactive mode by entering db2 and pressing **Enter**, as shown in Figure 4.4.

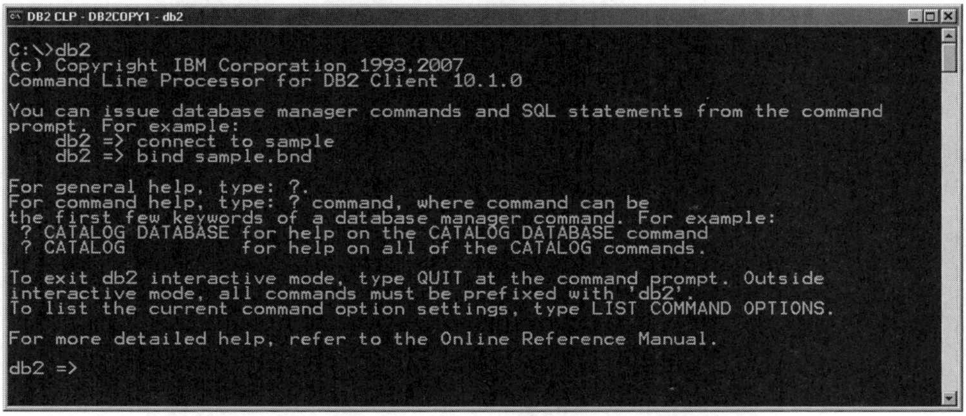

```
DB2 CLP - DB2COPY1 - db2
C:\>db2
(c) Copyright IBM Corporation 1993,2007
Command Line Processor for DB2 Client 10.1.0

You can issue database manager commands and SQL statements from the command
prompt. For example:
    db2 => connect to sample
    db2 => bind sample.bnd

For general help, type: ?.
For command help, type: ? command, where command can be
the first few keywords of a database manager command. For example:
 ? CATALOG DATABASE for help on the CATALOG DATABASE command
 ? CATALOG          for help on all of the CATALOG commands.

To exit db2 interactive mode, type QUIT at the command prompt. Outside
interactive mode, all commands must be prefixed with 'db2'.
To list the current command option settings, type LIST COMMAND OPTIONS.

For more detailed help, refer to the Online Reference Manual.

db2 =>
```

Figure 4.4   The Command Line Processor in interactive mode

After you invoke the CLP in interactive mode, a few messages appear on the screen, and then your command prompt changes to db2 =>. This prompt indicates that you are in interactive mode and you can type any DB2 CLP command, SQL statement, or XQuery statement.

Table 4.1 lists some common CLP interactive mode commands. The underlined letter in the command shows the shortcut that you can use to invoke the command. Figure 4.5 shows a few examples of the commands in Table 4.1 in action.

Table 4.1   Useful CLP Commands for Working with the CLP in Interactive Mode

Command	Explanation	Example
history	Lists the last 20 commands entered and prefixes each with a number. The maximum number of commands kept in memory can be customized with the DB2 registry variable DB2_CLP_HISTSIZE (see Chapter 5 for information about DB2 registry variables).	History
runcmd <n>	Re-executes command number *n* from the list given by the history command. If *n* is not specified (or *n* = -1), the previous command is invoked.	To re-execute the third command in the history list: r 3
edit <n>	Edits the command number *n* using an editor defined by the DB2 registry variable DB2_CLP_EDITOR. If not set, this uses the vi editor on Linux/UNIX and Notepad on Windows.	To edit the fifth command in the history list: e 5
Exclamation mark (!)	This is the escape character that enables you to issue operating system commands from within the CLP interactive mode.	!dir

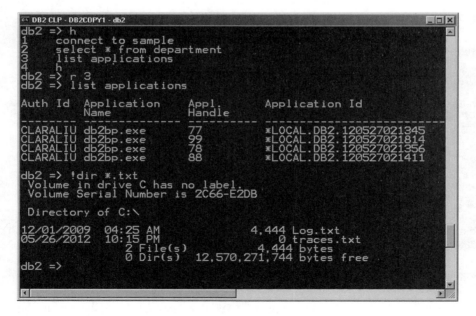

Figure 4.5   Examples of CLP commands in interactive mode

Method 2: Noninteractive Mode

Working with the CLP in noninteractive mode is equivalent to working with the DB2 Command Window (on Windows) or the Linux/UNIX shell. If you start the CLP in interactive mode, entering the `quit` command takes you to the CLP in noninteractive mode. In this mode you need to prefix the CLP command or SQL statement with db2, which calls the db2 executable. Otherwise, you receive an error. For example

```
db2 connect to sample
db2 list applications all
db2 select * from employee
db2 "xquery <name>Raul</name>"
```

Using this method you can execute operating system commands in addition to DB2 commands, SQL statements, and XQuery statements from the same window or session.

In practice, many DB2 users prefer to work in the CLP noninteractive mode environment because they can use some shortcut key strokes, such as pressing the up arrow key to repeat the last commands on Windows or taking advantage of operating system mechanisms like piping the output of the CLP to the `more` command on Linux and UNIX to display the output in portions.

Every time you issue the db2 executable, a "CLP session" is created where a front-end process is invoked. This takes the rest of the statement as input and then closes the process. For example, you issue the following command:

```
db2 list db directory
```

db2 invokes a CLP front-end process that takes `list db directory` as input. After the CLP digests this command, it implicitly issues the `quit` command to end the CLP front-end process. The front-end and back-end processes are discussed in more detail later in this chapter. Figure 4.6 shows the CLP in noninteractive mode.

When invoking the CLP in noninteractive mode, enclosing the CLP command, SQL statement, or XQuery statement double quotes (") might be required if these contain special characters that the operating system interprets as wildcard characters. This is especially important on Linux and UNIX platforms. If double quotes are not used, the error message that DB2 reports vary depending on where the wildcard character is used in the statement. For example, you issue this statement:

```
db2 select * from employee
```

You *might* receive the following error message because the asterisk (*) is a wildcard character:

```
SQL0104N An unexpected token "*" was found following "select "
```

To avoid parsing errors, use double quotes as shown here:

```
db2 "select * from employee"
```

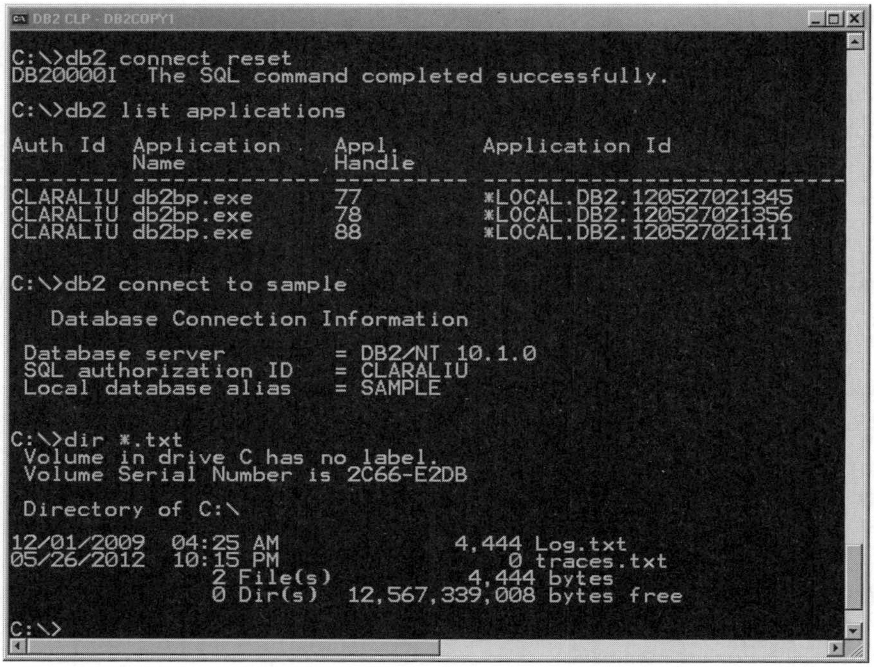

```
C:\>db2 connect reset
DB20000I  The SQL command completed successfully.

C:\>db2 list applications

Auth Id  Application .  Appl.      Application Id
         Name           Handle
-------- -------------- ---------- ------------------------------
CLARALIU db2bp.exe      77         *LOCAL.DB2.120527021345
CLARALIU db2bp.exe      78         *LOCAL.DB2.120527021356
CLARALIU db2bp.exe      88         *LOCAL.DB2.120527021411

C:\>db2 connect to sample

   Database Connection Information

 Database server        = DB2/NT 10.1.0
 SQL authorization ID   = CLARALIU
 Local database alias   = SAMPLE

C:\>dir *.txt
 Volume in drive C has no label.
 Volume Serial Number is 2C66-E2DB

 Directory of C:\

12/01/2009  04:25 AM              4,444 Log.txt
05/26/2012  10:15 PM                  0 traces.txt
               2 File(s)          4,444 bytes
               0 Dir(s)  12,567,339,008 bytes free

C:\>
```

Figure 4.6   The Command Line Processor in noninteractive mode

A more deceiving example occurs when you use the greater than (>) character. Here is an example:

```
db2 select lastname from employee where salary > 10000
```

The command is first parsed by the operating system, which interprets `>` `10000` as the redirection of the output to the file *10000*. After executing the statement just given, your current directory has a new file with the name *10000* containing a DB2 syntax error message because only `select lastname from employee where salary` was passed to DB2. Again, to resolve this problem, make sure to enclose the statement in double quotes.

```
db2 "select lastname from employee where salary > 10000"
```

This is particularly important as well when working with XQuery because XML documents use tags enclosed in angle brackets (< and >), which the operating system interprets completely differently.

Method 3: Noninteractive Mode Using a File as Input

The CLP can use a file containing one or more CLP commands or SQL statements and process them one after the other. This is ideal to develop DB2 database scripts. For example, Figure 4.7 shows the contents of the file *myInput.txt*, which we use as input to the CLP.

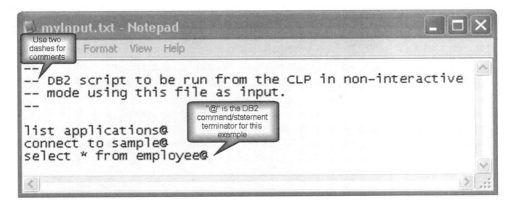

Figure 4.7   Input file to be used by the CLP

To execute this DB2 script file, the -f command option (for *file*) followed by the file name is required to indicate to the CLP that this file contains the input. (CLP command options are described in detail in the next section.) If the input file contains a statement terminator character, the -t command option (for *terminator*) is required to indicate a terminator character is present. By default, the statement terminator is a semicolon (;). If you want to use a different terminator, the –dcharacter option (for *delimiter*) indicates which delimiter character is being used as the terminator. Use the -v option (for *verbose*) to echo the command you are executing. Figure 4.8 provides an example of invoking the CLP using these command options.

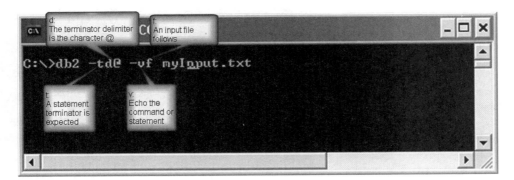

Figure 4.8   Invoking the CLP in noninteractive mode using a file as input

> **NOTE**
>
> The input file must be a text file. Be aware that invisible characters can cause DB2 CLP fail to process the file. If using the Notepad application on Windows, for example, saving the text file with Unicode encoding rather than ANSI encoding causes the following error:
>
> DB21007E End of file reached while reading the command.

If you prefix each of the CLP commands with `db2` (the CLP executable) in a file and remove the terminator characters, you are effectively converting this file into an operating system script rather than a DB2 script. Depending on the operating system, you might have to make additional modifications. For example, on Windows, you need to use `rem` for comments. You might also need to change the file name so that the *.bat* extension is used. Figure 4.9 shows this for the file *myOS_Input.bat*.

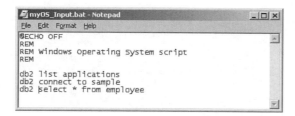

Figure 4.9   Invoking DB2 CLP commands and SQL statements in a Windows script file

On Linux and UNIX platforms, use the pound sign (#) for comments. You might also need to change the permissions of the file so that it is executable. Typically you can use this command to change the file permissions:

```
chmod +x myOS_Input.txt
```

Figure 4.10 shows the same script for a Linux or UNIX platform.

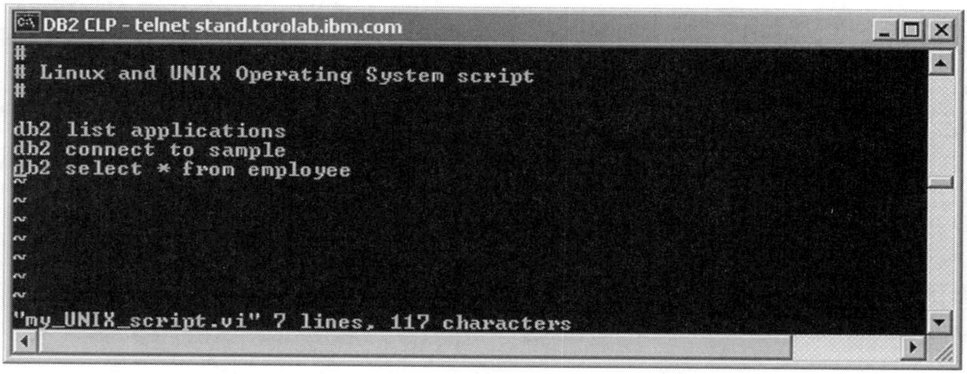

Figure 4.10   Invoking DB2 CLP commands and SQL statements in a Linux/UNIX script file

NOTE

DB2 scripts do not accept parameters, but operating system scripts do. In other words, if you need to invoke your scripts with parameters, you need to use operating system scripts.

CLP Command Options

The CLP is just another program designed to interact with DB2. Like many other programs, the CLP has been designed to accept several parameter options. The CLP command `list command options` displays the available CLP command option parameters (see Figure 4.11).

```
DB2 CLP - DB2COPY1

C:\>db2 list command options
        Command Line Processor Option Settings

Backend process wait time (seconds)      (DB2BQTIME) = 1
No. of retries to connect to backend     (DB2BQTRY) = 60
Request queue wait time (seconds)        (DB2RQTIME) = 5
Input queue wait time (seconds)          (DB2IQTIME) = 5
Command options                          (DB2OPTIONS) =

Option   Description                             Current Setting
------   -----------                             ---------------
  -a     Display SQLCA                               OFF
  -c     Auto-Commit                                 ON
  -d     Retrieve and display XML declarations       OFF
  -e     Display SQLCODE/SQLSTATE                     OFF
  -f     Read from input file                        OFF
  -i     Display XML data with indentation           OFF
  -l     Log commands in history file                OFF
  -m     Display the number of rows affected         OFF
  -n     Remove new line character                   OFF
  -o     Display output                              ON
  -p     Display interactive input prompt            ON
  -q     Preserve whitespaces & linefeeds            OFF
  -r     Save output to report file                  OFF
  -s     Stop execution on command error             OFF
  -t     Set statement termination character         OFF
  -v     Echo current command                        OFF
  -w     Display FETCH/SELECT warning messages       ON
  -x     Suppress printing of column headings        OFF
  -z     Save all output to output file              OFF

C:\>
```

Figure 4.11   CLP command options

To turn on an option, use a dash (-) in the command line. To turn off an option, use a plus symbol (+). Some options are on (or off) by default. For example, to enable auto-commit, invoke the CLP as follows.

```
db2 -c insert into employee (firstnme) values ('Raul')
```

After you execute this command, a COMMIT statement is automatically issued because auto-commit is enabled. (As you can see in Figure 4.11, the Auto-Commit option was already on by default, so including -c in this example is not necessary.)

To disable auto-commit, invoke the CLP as follows.

```
db2 +c insert into employee (firstnme) values ('Raul')
```

Note that specifying a command option in the db2 command applies only to that session of the CLP. Issuing the db2 command without an option uses the default command option values, or the ones contained in the DB2OPTIONS registry variable, which we discuss later in this section.

You can also change a command option when working with the CLP in interactive mode using the following command:

```
update command options using option1 value1 option2 value2 ...
```

Figure 4.12 shows an example where the v option (verbose) is used. This option causes the command or statement to be repeated or echoed when executed as discussed earlier. In Figure 4.12, note that the SELECT * FROM department statement is echoed.

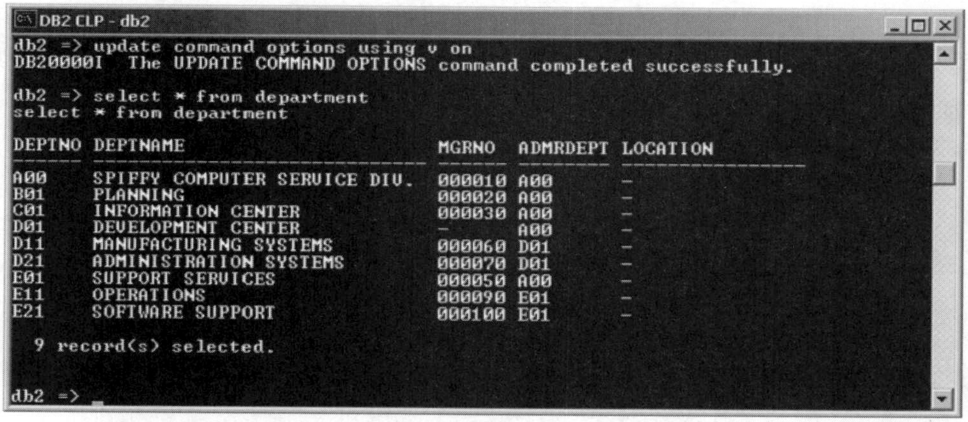

Figure 4.12   The CLP in interactive mode

If you would like the changes to your CLP options to be effective across all your CLP sessions, you can set the DB2OPTIONS registry variable with the desired options. In the command shown next, the DB2OPTIONS registry variable is set so that any command executed is echoed (-v option), and the output is spooled in the file *myfile.log* (-z myfile.log option). The changes take effect immediately for the current session and for any other new CLP sessions you start.

```
db2set db2options="-v -z myfile.log"
```

To reset the values to the default, issue this command:

```
db2set db2options=
```

To displays all defined values for the current instance:

```
db2set -all
```

DB2 registry variables are explained in detail in Chapter 5, "Understanding the DB2 Environment, DB2 Instances, and Databases."

Obtaining Help Information from the CLP

One of the most useful CLP commands is the help command represented by a question mark (?). This command provides help on SQL error codes (SQLCODE), DB2 messages, and CLP command syntax. For example

```
db2 ? SQL0104N
db2 ? DB21004E
db2 ? list applications
```

In addition, using the help command by itself displays the entire list of CLP commands, as shown in Figure 4.13.

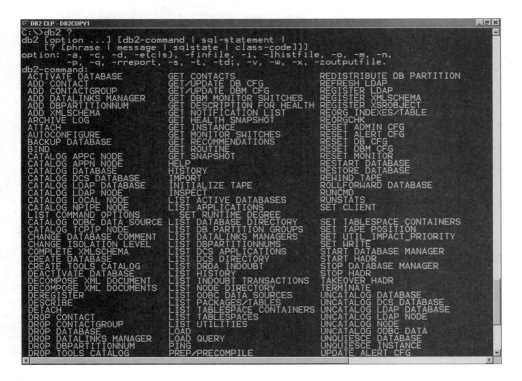

Figure 4.13 Output of the command db2 ?

NOTE

The help (?) command can display CLP command syntax, but not SQL statement syntax.
Refer to the *DB2 Information Center* for SQL statement syntax.

Figure 4.14 shows more examples of the help (?) command.

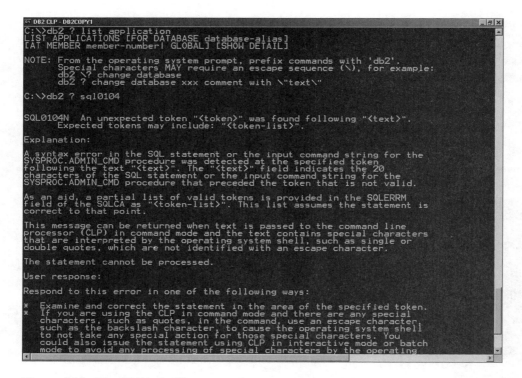

Figure 4.14   The CLP help (?) command

Using Line Continuation

There are two ways to use line continuation from the CLP: with the backslash character and with
the delimiter terminator character.

Method 1: Using the Backslash (\) Character

You can use the backslash (\) character in either interactive or noninteractive mode. Figure 4.15 first shows an example of using the interactive mode, followed by an example of using noninteractive.

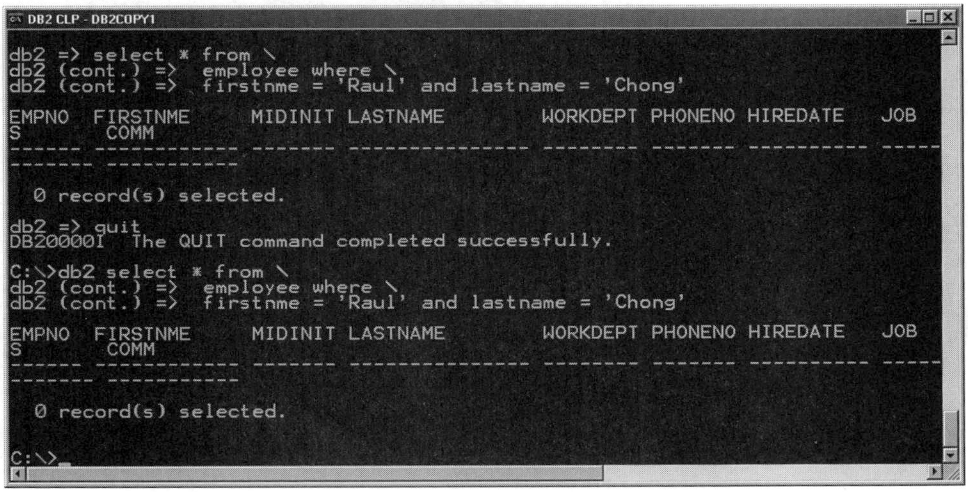

```
DB2 CLP - DB2COPY1                                                    _□×

db2 => select * from \
db2 (cont.) =>  employee where \
db2 (cont.) =>  firstnme = 'Raul' and lastname = 'Chong'

EMPNO  FIRSTNME     MIDINIT LASTNAME          WORKDEPT PHONENO HIREDATE   JOB
S      COMM
------ ----------- ------- ---------------- -------- ------- ---------- -----
------ -----------

  0 record(s) selected.

db2 => quit
DB200001  The QUIT command completed successfully.

C:\>db2 select * from \
db2 (cont.) =>  employee where \
db2 (cont.) =>  firstnme = 'Raul' and lastname = 'Chong'

EMPNO  FIRSTNME     MIDINIT LASTNAME          WORKDEPT PHONENO HIREDATE   JOB
S      COMM
------ ----------- ------- ---------------- -------- ------- ---------- -----
------ -----------

  0 record(s) selected.

C:\>
```

Figure 4.15   Line continuation in the CLP using the backslash continuation character

Notice that after entering \ and pressing Enter, the prompt changes to

```
db2 (cont.) =>
```

Method 2: Using a Delimiter Terminator Character with the CLP in Interactive Mode

Using this method, the CLP is invoked in interactive mode using the terminator delimiter option. For example

```
db2 -td!
```

After entering this command and pressing Enter, the CLP is invoked in interactive mode. You can wrap commands onto multiple lines until you type the terminator character, which is the exclamation mark (!) in the example shown in Figure 4.16.

```
DB2 CLP - DB2COPY1 - db2 -td!                                              _ □ ×
C:\>db2 -td!
(c) Copyright IBM Corporation 1993,2007
Command Line Processor for DB2 Client 10.1.0

You can issue database manager commands and SQL statements from the command
prompt. For example:
    db2 => connect to sample
    db2 => bind sample.bnd

For general help, type: ?.
For command help, type: ? command, where command can be
the first few keywords of a database manager command. For example:
  ? CATALOG DATABASE for help on the CATALOG DATABASE command
  ? CATALOG           for help on all of the CATALOG commands.

To exit db2 interactive mode, type QUIT at the command prompt. Outside
interactive mode, all commands must be prefixed with 'db2'.
To list the current command option settings, type LIST COMMAND OPTIONS.

For more detailed help, refer to the Online Reference Manual.

db2 => select * from
db2 (cont.) => employee where
db2 (cont.) => firstnme = 'Raul' and lastname = 'Chong'
db2 (cont.) => !

EMPNO   FIRSTNME     MIDINIT LASTNAME          WORKDEPT PHONENO HIREDATE    JOB
S       COMM
------- ------------ ------- ----------------- -------- ------- ---------- -----
------- -----------

   0 record(s) selected.

db2 =>
```

Figure 4.16   Line continuation in the CLP using a delimiter termination character in interactive mode

Use this method when you have statements that include carriage returns. If you copy and paste one of these statements into the CLP, the carriage returns cause the statement to continue in another line, which is acceptable because the CLP processes the command after the terminator character is entered.

The following statement has one carriage return character after `staff` and one after `Edwards`; therefore, use a delimiter termination character described in method 2 to start the DB2 CLP in interactive mode:

```
select * from staff
where name = 'Edwards'
and job = 'Sales'
```

After you copy and paste the statement into the CLP, enter the terminator character and press Enter to execute it. Remember that the termination character is an exclamation mark (!) in this example.

The CLP Front-End and Back-End Processes

The CLP has both front-end and a back-end processes. The front-end allows you to perform actions without connecting to a database. For example, issuing the command `db2 list db directory` does not require a connection to a database.

The back-end process is needed when you perform actions against a database. It is created when you connect to the database in a CLP session and can be identified by the application name db2bp. Figure 4.17 shows the output of the `list applications` command, which shows this thread, indicating a connection to the *SAMPLE* database.

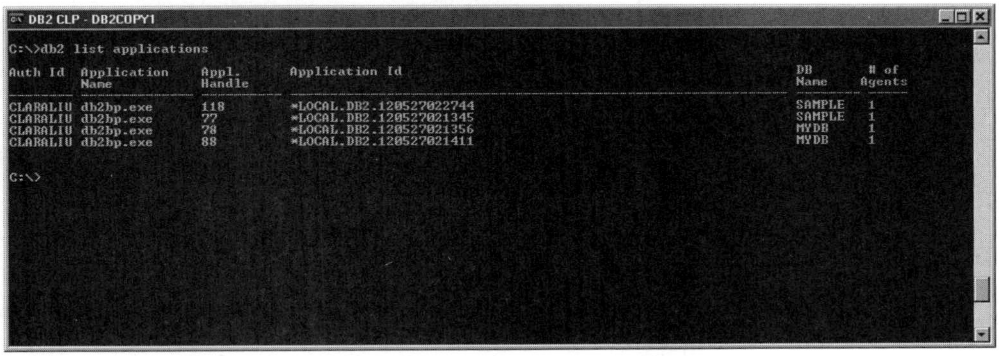

Figure 4.17   The CLP back-end process

To remove the connection to a database, issue the `connect reset` statement, the `terminate` command, or the `disconnect` statement. `Connect reset` and `terminate` work even if the process is in the middle of a unit of work. `Disconnect` only works when there is no active unit of work. Closing a window or session without previously issuing a `terminate` command closes the CLP application and front-end process and removes the connection to the database, but it does not guarantee that the back-end process will be terminated.

> **NOTE**
>
> The `terminate` command is the only one that guarantees the back-end process is indeed terminated. Even if the `list applications` command does not display the *db2bp* back-end process running, use the `terminate` command to be certain.

It is important to make sure that the back-end process is terminated because in some circumstances, a change to a parameter, environment variable, or DB2 registry variable does not take effect until this is performed.

> **NOTE**
>
> We recommend issuing a terminate command before a db2stop command. This prevents the back-end process from maintaining an attachment to an instance that is no longer active.

The DB2 Command Line Processor Plus

The DB2 Command Line Processor Plus (CLPPlus) is command-line user interface that enables you to

- Execute Operating system commands
- Execute DB2 system commands
- Develop, edit, and execute SQL statements and XQuery statements
- Compile and run DB2 stored procedures and functions
- Work with scripts and run command-line reports
- Support SQL*Plus scripts that many DBAs and application developers are familiar with

To start the CLPPlus, on Windows 7, click **Start > Programs > IBM DB2 DB2COPY1 (Default) > Command Line Processor Plus**. Alternatively, issue the command `clpplus` on the Windows command prompt or the Linux and UNIX shell. You get the `SQL>` prompt as shown in Figure 4.18.

Take a look at the program icon on the top left corner of the CLPPlus window. The icon is a Java application icon. That's right. CLPPlus is a Java application. CLPPlus requires Java 1.5 or later to execute. In DB2 10, Java 1.7 is installed and its path is set up with DB2 installation. If you encounter CLPPlus start-up issue, ensure Java is in your `PATH`.

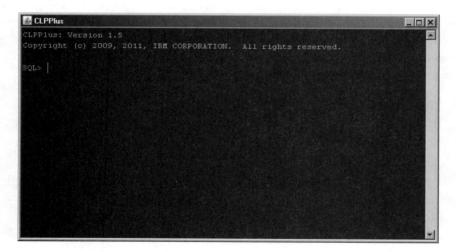

Figure 4.18   The CLPPlus Window

CLPPlus can run both OS and DB2 commands. To run OS commands, simply use the
! (exclamation mark) operator. Figure 4.19 illustrates how to use the `ls` and `grep` commands in
CLPPlus.

Figure 4.19 Use of the ! operator in CLPPlus

To work with the DB2 database from the CLPPlus, you need to first connect to the database. In Figure 4.20, it shows you two methods to connect to the database in CLPPlus. The first example is simply to enter the CONNECT command. CLPPLUS prompts you for the database name, hostname, port number, user ID, and password. You may also enter all these information in the CONNECT command as follows.

```
CONNECT demoadm@bob:50001/sample
```

To disconnect from the database, enter DISCONNECT.

NOTE

CLPPlus supports many commands. Refer to the DB2 Information Center for the list of commands and usage example.

Figure 4.20   Using the `CONNECT` command in CLPPlus

Working with the SQL Buffer

The **SQL buffer** is an in-memory working area where CLPPlus keeps copies of the most recently entered SQL statements or SQL Procedural Language (SQL PL) block. CLPPlus provides many commands to help manage the SQL buffer.

Let's use an example to demonstrate how to work with the SQL buffer. In Listing 4.1, you can see that a compound statement is used. A **compound statement** is bound by the keywords BEGIN and END that contain multiple statements. In this example, it uses the DECLARE variable statement that is part of SQL PL, a SET statement to assign a value to the variable, and an INSERT statement. If you are following the example on your system, you need to first create the CUSTOMER_STATISTICS table as shown in Listing 4.2.

Listing 4.1   Example of a Compound Statement Stored in File sqlpl.txt

```
BEGIN ATOMIC
  DECLARE v_custCount INTEGER;
  -- find out customer count and store value in variable v_custCount
  SET v_custCount = (SELECT COUNT(*) FROM customer);
```

```
-- insert the answer back in the table
INSERT into customer_statistics
VALUES (CURRENT DATE, v_custCount);
END
```

Listing 4.2 Sample Table Used in the Compound Statement Example

```
CREATE TABLE CUSTOMER_STATISTICS
    ( RECORD_DATE      DATE
    , CUSTOMER_COUNT INTEGER)
```

The compound statement is stored in the *sqlpl.txt* file. First, load the file into the SQL buffer with the GET command. Then RUN the script (see Figure 4.21).

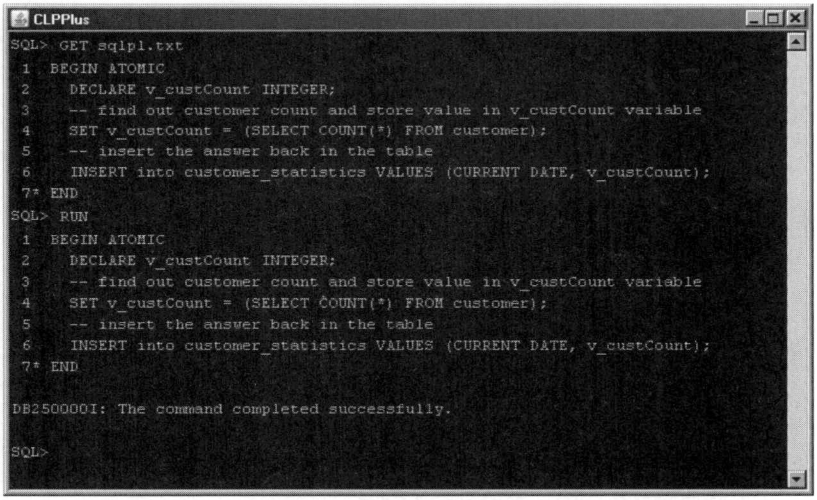

Figure 4.21 GET and RUN scripts in CLPPlus

After reviewing the output here, you decided to print the customer count returned from the compound statement. You can update the script from the CLPPlus using the EDIT command. The default editor is used. In this example, Notepad is used.

The line CALL DBMS_OUTPUT.PUT_LINE (highlighted in Figure 4.22) is added to print an output comment on the screen after the INSERT statement is executed successfully.

```
afiedt.buf - Notepad                                             _□×
File  Edit  Format  View  Help
BEGIN ATOMIC                                                      ▲
    DECLARE v_custCount INTEGER;
    -- find out customer count and store value in v_custCount variable
    SET v_custCount = (SELECT COUNT(*) FROM customer);
    -- insert the answer back in the table
    INSERT into customer_statistics VALUES (CURRENT DATE, v_custCount);

    CALL DBMS_OUTPUT.PUT_LINE('SUCCESS: Customer Count for ' || CURRENT DATE ||
                              ' is ' || VARCHAR(v_custCount));
END
/
                                                                  ▼
```

Figure 4.22   `EDIT` script in CLPPlus

After you save the file and exit the editor, the SQL buffer is updated with the new version
of the script.

To display the output comment you just added to the standard output (that is the screen),
you need to `SET SERVEROUTPUT ON`. The output from the `DBMS_OUTPUT` message buffer is
redirected to the standard output. Then run the script again with the `RUN` command. You now get
the customized output as shown in Figure 4.23.

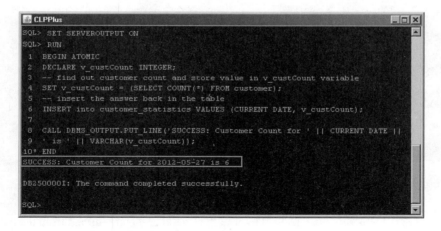

Figure 4.23   Output after script is updated

Formatting CLPPlus output

CLPPlus has a lot of options for working with reports. Here is a simple query to display the employee information. As you can see in Figure 4.24, the output is wrapped, and it is hard to read. You can improve the appearance of the report by using some CLPPlus options to format and customize the output of the query.

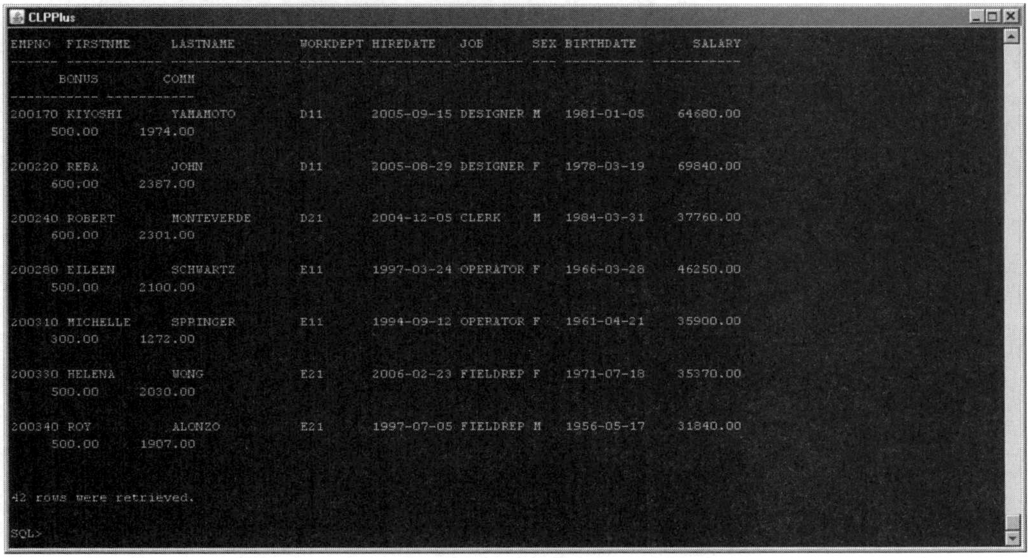

```
CLPPlus
EMPNO  FIRSTNME     LASTNAME        WORKDEPT HIREDATE   JOB      SEX BIRTHDATE       SALARY
------ ------------ --------------- -------- ---------- -------- --- ---------- -----------
      BONUS        COMM
----------- -----------
200170 KIYOSHI      YAMAMOTO        D11      2005-09-15 DESIGNER M   1981-01-05    64680.00
     500.00     1974.00

200220 REBA         JOHN            D11      2005-08-29 DESIGNER F   1978-03-19    69840.00
     600.00     2387.00

200240 ROBERT       MONTEVERDE      D21      2004-12-05 CLERK    M   1984-03-31    37760.00
     600.00     2301.00

200280 EILEEN       SCHWARTZ        E11      1997-03-24 OPERATOR F   1966-03-28    46250.00
     500.00     2100.00

200310 MICHELLE     SPRINGER        E11      1994-09-12 OPERATOR F   1961-04-21    35900.00
     300.00     1272.00

200330 HELENA       WONG            E21      2006-02-23 FIELDREP F   1971-07-18    35370.00
     500.00     2030.00

200340 ROY          ALONZO          E21      1997-07-05 FIELDREP M   1956-05-17    31840.00
     500.00     1907.00

42 rows were retrieved.

SQL>
```

Figure 4.24 Output of query of all employees

A few formatting options are used as described here. See Figure 4.25 for the customized output.

Set the line size to 120 characters for the output the better fit the screen.

```
SET LINESIZE 120
```

Apply formatting rules to the *salary*, *comm*, and *bonus* columns. Add dollar signs in front of the values and add a comma at the unit of thousand:

```
COLUMN salary FORMAT $999,999.99
COLUMN comm   FORMAT $99,999.99
COLUMN bonus  FORMAT $99,999.99
```

Do not print the column *firstnnme*:

```
COLUMN firstnme NOPRINT
COLUMN midinit  NOPRINT
```

Display the values of the *lastname* column right-justified:

```
COLUMN lastname JUSTIFY RIGHT
```

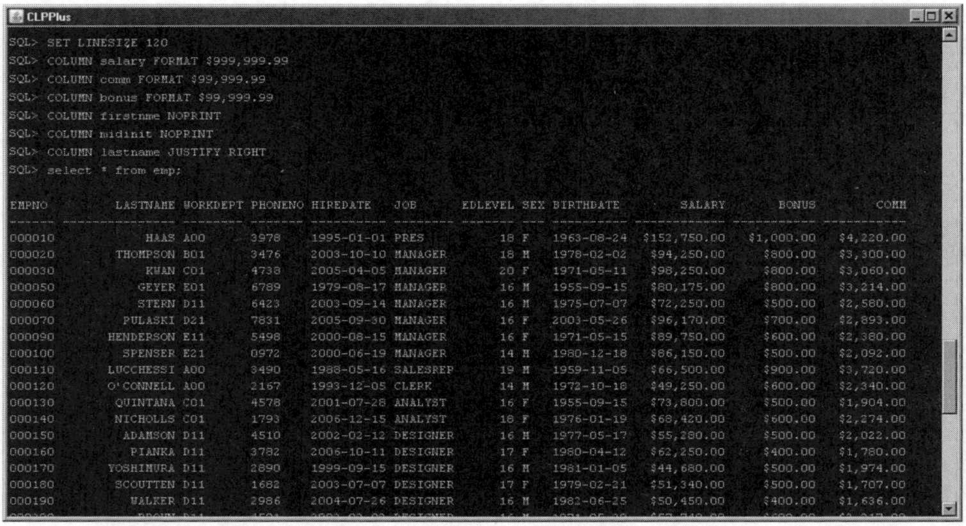

Figure 4.25   Formatted output of the query

IBM Data Studio

IBM Data Studio is included in every DB2 edition. IBM Data Studio provides a single integrated environment for database administration and application development. You can perform tasks that are related to database modeling and design, developing database applications, administering and managing databases, tuning SQL performance, and monitoring databases all in one single tool. It is an ideal tool that can greatly benefit a team environment with different roles and responsibilities.

IBM Data Studio comes in three favors: full client, administration client, and web console.

The full client includes both the database administrative and the application development capabilities. The development environment is Eclipse-based. This offers a collaborative development environment by integrating with other advanced Eclipse-based tools such as InfoSphere Data Architect and InfoSphere Optim pureQuery Runtime. Note that some of the advanced InfoSphere tools are only included in the DB2 Advanced editions and the DB2 Developer Edition. You can also separately purchase the advanced tools.

The administration client is a subset of the full client. It still provides a wide range of database administrative functionality such as DB2 instance management, object management, data management, and query tuning. Basic application development tasks such as SQL Builder, query formatting, visual explain, debugging, editing, and running DB2 routines are supported. Use the full client for advanced application development features.

The web console, as the name implies, it is a web-based browser interface that provides health monitoring, job management, and connection management.

> **NOTE**
>
> IBM Data Studio also provides collaborative database development tools for DB2 for z/OS, DB2 for i, Informix, and other non-IBM databases. To see a list of IBM Data Studio features by data server, refer to the documentation at http://www.ibm.com/support/docview. wss?uid=swg27022148.

IBM Data Studio Workspace and the Task Launcher

When you have successfully installed the IBM Data Studio, you are asked to provide a workspace name. A **workspace** is a folder that saves your work and projects. It refers to the desktop development environment, which is an Eclipse-based concept.

Task Launcher is displayed, which highlights the following category of tasks:

- Design
- Develop
- Administer
- Tune
- Monitor

Each category is described in more detail in its own tab. Click any tab, and you see the key and primary tasks listed in the box on the left. See Figure 4.26 to get an idea on how to navigate the Task Launcher.

As an example, the figure shows you the Develop tasks. You can find the key development tasks on the left. On the top right, it lists more tasks related to development. On the bottom right, IBM Data Studio provides a few documentation links where you can learn more about development. Where appropriate, it also suggests the advanced tools available in the InfoSphere Optim portfolio that apply to the task you have selected.

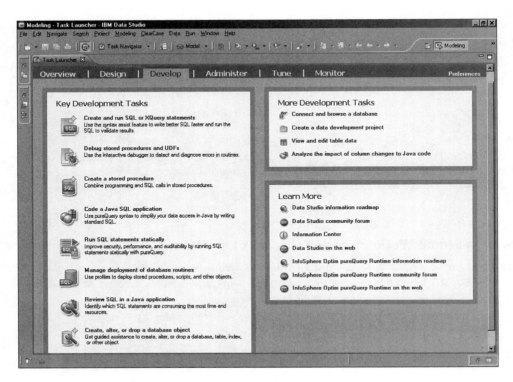

Figure 4.26   The IBM Data Studio Task Launcher

Connection Profiles

Every task you were to perform against a database requires to first establish a database connection. To connect to a database from IBM Data Studio, open the **Database Administration**
perspective. On the top right corner, click the **Open Perspective** icon and select **Database
Administration**.

On the **Administration Explorer**, right-click the white space or under the **New** menu,
select **New Connection** to a database. From the *New Connection* window, you see that you can
use the IBM Data Studio to connect to different IBM data sources, as well as non-IBM data
sources. Select the database manager and enter the necessary connection parameters. Figure 4.28
shows an example.

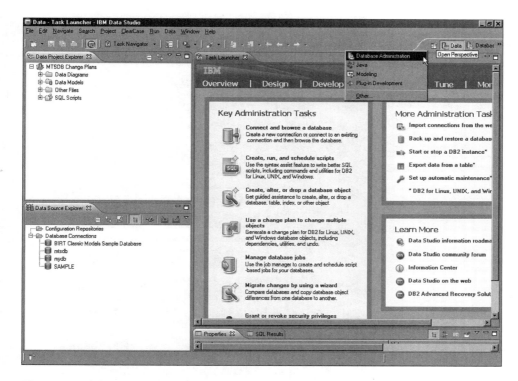

Figure 4.27 Open the Database Administration perspective

Pull down the JDBC driver drop-down menu, and you can select the type of JDBC driver to use. JDBC type 4 driver is used by default.

Use the **Test Connection** button to ensure the connection information you enter is valid. Click **Finish**.

At this point, you have created a connection profile. Connection profiles contain information about how to connect to a database such as indicating the type of authentication to be used when connecting the database, specifying default schema, and configuring tracing options. Other team members can import the connection profiles to their own IBM Data Studio and be able to deploy a set of consistent connection settings.

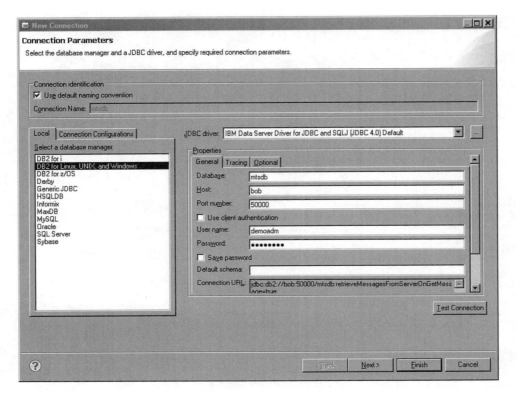

Figure 4.28   Creating a new database connection

To update the connection profile, right-click the database and select **Properties**. Properties for the database are displayed as shown in Figure 4.29.

General Database Administration Tools

There are few other useful administration tasks available in the menu illustrated in Figure 4.29.

The *Manage Connection* function enables you to rename the connection profile, delete the connection profile, change the user ID and password, and duplicate the profile. The *Back Up and Restore* function enables you to setup a database or table space backups. In the appropriate editor, you can specify the type of backup, location of the backup images, and performance options for the backup. Database backup and recovery is discussed in Chapter 10, "Maintaining, Backing Up, and Recovering Data."

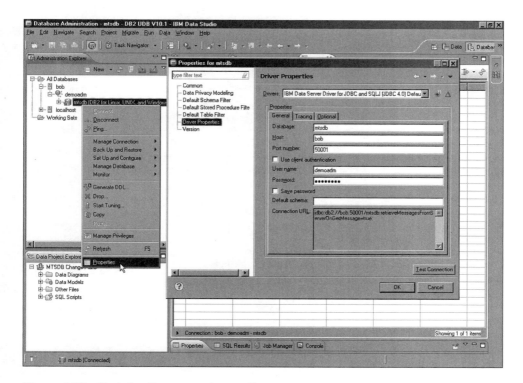

Figure 4.29   Updating the connection profile

The *Set Up and Configure* function enables you to configure the database. Database configuration and this IBM Data Studio function are covered in detail in Chapter 5. Notice from the menu, you can launch the Configure Automatic Maintenance editor. DB2 provides automatic maintenance capabilities for performing database backups, reorganizing tables and indexes, and updating the database statistics as necessary. The editor enables you customize the automatic maintenance policy (see Figure 4.30).

The *Manage Database* function enables you to start and stop the database. In DB2, that means activating and deactivating the database. Activating a database allocates all the necessary database memory and services or processes required. Deactivating a database releases the memory and stops DB2 services and processes.

The *Monitor* function launches the IBM Data Studio Web Console. Refer to the section, "IBM Data Studio Web Console," for introduction of the tool.

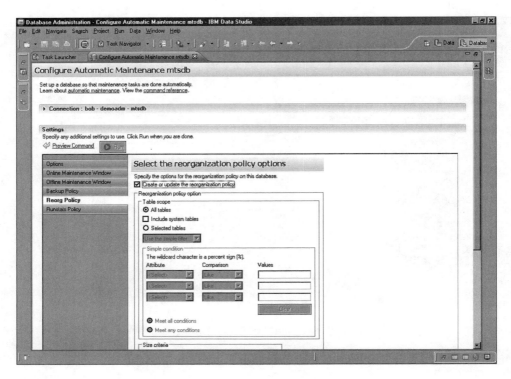

Figure 4.30   Select the Automatic Maintenance policy options

The *Generate DDL* function uses the DB2 command-based tool db2look to extract the Data Definition Language (DDL) statements for the identified database objects or the entire database. This function and tool come handy when you want to mimic a database, a set of database objects, or the database statistics to another database. As a result of the Generate DDL function in IBM Data Studio or the DB2 command db2look, you receive a DDL script. The script contains statements to re-create the database objects you have selected. See Figure 4.31 for a reference of the types of statements you can generate using the IBM Data Studio.

For complete options for the DB2 command db2look, refer to the DB2 Information Center.

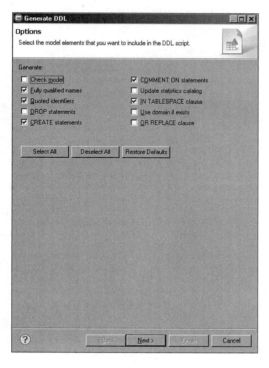

Figure 4.31 Generate DDL function in the IBM Data Studio

The *Start Tuning* function configures the database to enable query tuning. You might receive a warning indicating that you need to activate the InfoSphere Optim Query Workload Tuner (OQWT) license for advanced tuning capability. Note that IBM DB2 Advanced Enterprise Server Edition comes with OQWT. Follow the instructions to apply the product license or click **Yes** to configure the database server for tuning with the features complementary in the IBM Data Studio.

When the database is configured to use the tuning advisors and tools, you are presented with the Query Tuner Workflow Assistant, as shown in Figure 4.32.

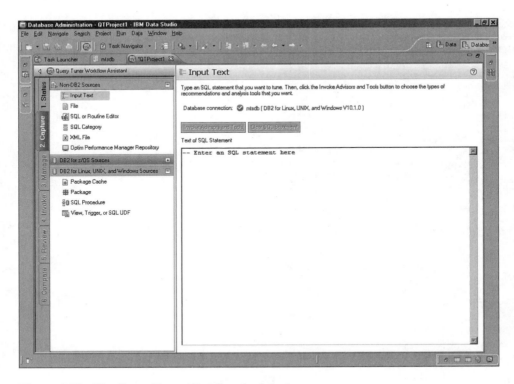

Figure 4.32   The Query Tuner Workflow Assistant

From the *Query Tuner Workflow Assistant*, you can obtain a statement from various sources and tune the statement. In the Capture view, it gives you a list of sources where you can capture the statements. Figure 4.33 shows an example on capturing the SQL statements from the Package Cache. This example captures over 100 statements. Right-click the statement in which you are interested and select **Show SQL statement** or **Run Single-Query Advisors and Tools on the Selected Statement**.

Run the query advisors and tools on the selected statement. You can now enter the Invoke view. The tool collects information and statistics and generates a data access plan (see Figure 4.34).

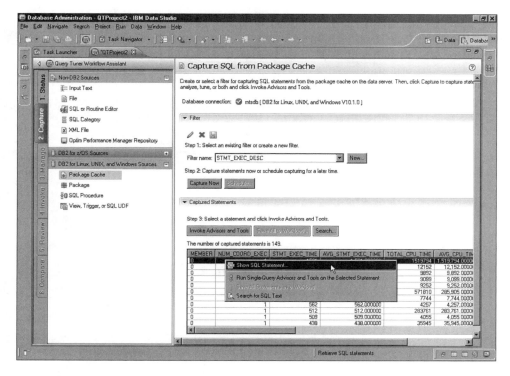

Figure 4.33 Capturing SQL statements for tuning

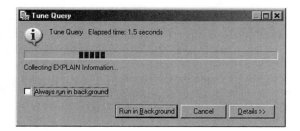

Figure 4.34 Tune query in progress

When the query tuning activities are complete, you are brought to the Review view. It presents you the analysis results and an advisor recommendation, such as the one shown in Figure 4.35. The tool documentation recommends gathering and re-collecting all of relevant statistics of the query.

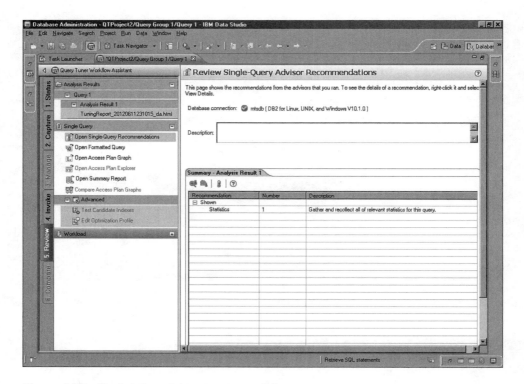

Figure 4.35   Review the advisor recommendation

You can also review the access plan graph generated by the DB2 explain function (see Figure 4.36 for an example). Remember to save the analysis for future references and compare them if needed.

The *Manage Privileges* function allows you to grant database privileges to the users. Refer to Chapter 8, "Implementing Security," for details about privileges and database access controls.

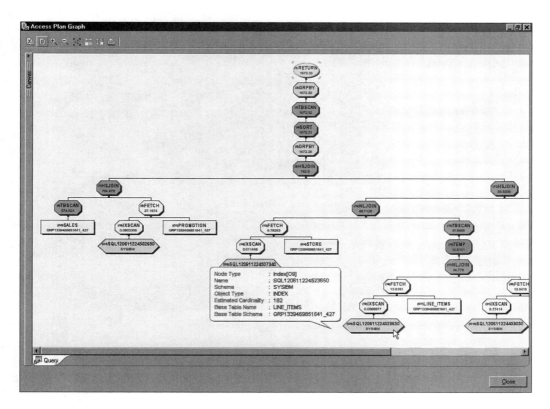

Figure 4.36 Sample access plan graph

General Database Development Tools

IBM Data Studio consolidates the database administration and database development capabilities. From the *Task Launcher – Develop*, you find a list of key development tasks such as creating and running SQL statements, debugging stored procedures, and user-defined functions (UDFs). Each task brings you to a tool that helps you accomplish it.

SQL and XQuery Editor

The SQL and XQuery editor helps you create and run SQL scripts that contain more than one SQL and XQuery statements. To launch the editor, open the **Data Project Explorer**; under SQL Scripts select **New > SQL or XQuery Script**. As shown in Figure 4.37, a sample SQL script is entered. You can configure the run options for the script.

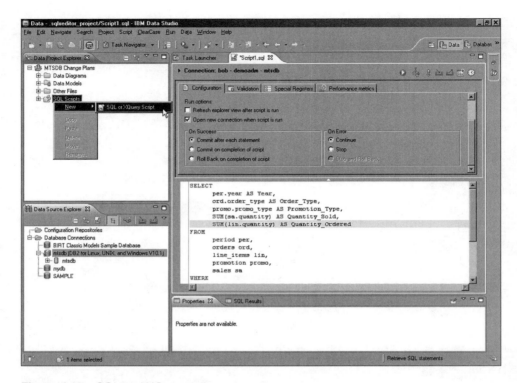

Figure 4.37   SQL and XQuery editor

The editor formats the SQL statements nicely and provides syntax highlights for easier reading as you enter the SQL statements. The functionality content assist is also very useful. It lists all the existing schemas in the database so that you can just select one from the drop-down menu. The editor also parses the statement and validates the statement syntax. You can validate the syntax in scripts with multiple database parsers and run scripts against multiple database connections.

SQL Query Builder

The SQL Query Builder enables you to create a single SQL statement, but it does not support XQuery. As the name implies, the tool helps you build an SQL statement. It helps you look at the underlying database schema or build an expression, as shown in Figure 4.38.

> **NOTE**
>
> To get to the SQL Query Builder, click the Data perspective button available at the top right of the window. In the Data Project Explorer view, expand the data profile, right-click the **SQL Scripts** folder, and then click **New** > **SQL or XQuery Script**. This launches the SQL Query Builder.

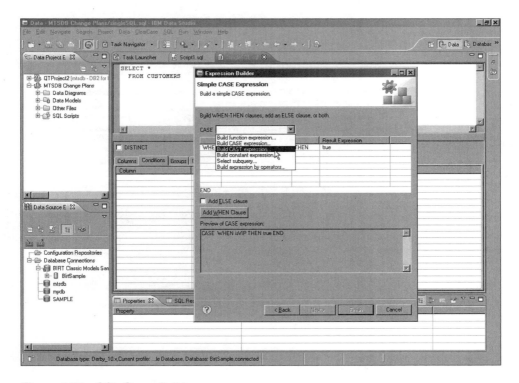

Figure 4.38   SQL Query Builder

Database Routines Editor and Debugger

Stored procedures and user-defined functions (UDFs) are database application objects that encapsulate application logic at the database server rather than in application-level code. Use of application objects help reduce overhead of SQL statements and the results that are passed through the network. Stored procedures and UDFs are also called routines. IBM Data Studio supports routines development and debugging.

From the Data Project Explorer, create a new Data Development Project. In the project, you can create various types of database application objects such as stored procedures and UDFs (see Figure 4.39). To debug a routine, right-click the routine and select **Debug**.

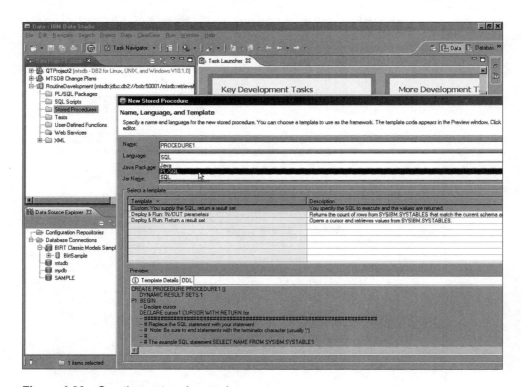

Figure 4.39   Creating a stored procedure

IBM Data Studio Web Console

As a database administrator, it is important to have a good understanding of your database environment. Some of the things you need to know are the kinds of activities that are happening on the system, the data server status, and the database connection status. The IBM Data Studio Web Console provides health monitoring, job management, and connection management for DB2 databases. It can be used in a single-user environment or a multiuser environment to share monitored features and analysis across database servers.

The web console is comprised of a server component and a client component. The server component must be running to monitor database health, issue alerts, and manage scheduled database maintenance jobs. The client component is a web interface used to create and manage jobs and view and analyze alerts.

Shown in Figure 4.40 are the key web console tasks:

- View health summary
- View alerts
- View application connections
- Manage database jobs

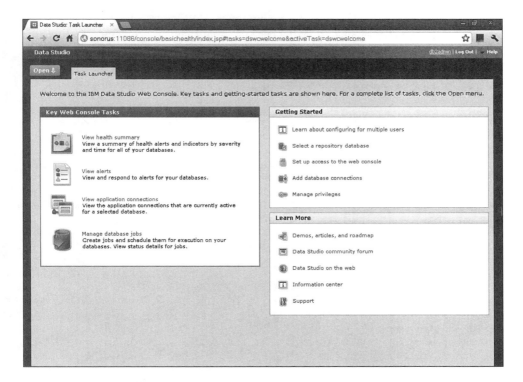

Figure 4.40 IBM Data Studio Web Console Task Launcher

Set-Up Tools

DB2 comes with a number of tools to help you setup the environment. Using these tools, you can create the *SAMPLE* database, which can be used to explore DB2 features. Other tools are Configure DB2 .NET Data Provider, First Steps, Default DB2 and Database Client Interface Selection Wizard, and the Replication Center.

Configure DB2 .NET Data Provider

As its name implies, the Configure DB2 .NET Data Provider tool helps you configure the DB2 .NET Data provider, also known as the IBM Data Server Provider for .NET. There are 32-bit and 64-bit versions of the IBM Data Server Provider for .NET, each supporting the 32-bit and 64-bit versions of the .NET Framework version 2.0, 3.0, 3.5, and 4.0 CLR, respectively.

First Steps

The IBM DB2 First Steps tool is a good starting point for new DB2 users who want to get familiar with the product. It can be launched from the DB2 program menu on Windows or execute the db2fs command. Figure 4.41 shows the operations you can perform using this tool.

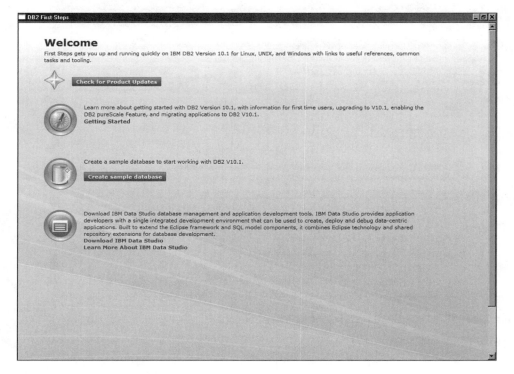

Figure 4.41   The DB2 First Steps

The Create Sample Database button enables you to create a database called *SAMPLE* on your local system. This database is provided with the DB2 product for testing and learning purposes. It comes with a set of predefined tables. You can work with this database just like any other. The equivalent DB2 command to create the *SAMPLE* database is db2sampl.

After the database is created, you can create tables using the IBM Data Studio or SQL statements. The SQL statements to create database objects are described in Chapter 7, "Working with Database Objects."

Default DB2 and Database Client Interface Selection Wizard

This tool only applies to Windows platforms. The Default DB2 and Database Client Interface Selection Wizard (available from the DB2 Programs menu) enables you to select or change the default DB2 install copy on your computer when there is one or more DB2 copies on it. Applications use this DB2 install copy by default. This tool can also be used to set the default IBM database client interface (ODBC/CLI driver and .NET provider) copy. You can also launch this wizard by running the db2swtch.exe command located in the sqllib\bin directory of your DB2 install copy. Figure 4.42 shows the Default DB2 and Database Client Interface Selection Wizard.

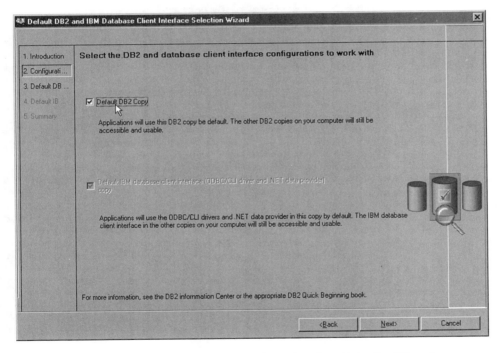

Figure 4.42 The Default DB2 and Database Client Interface Selection Wizard

The Replication Center

The Replication Center enables you set up and manage your replication environment. You can easily follow the required steps by using the Replication Center Launchpad. Use DB2 replication when you want to propagate data from one location to another. For example, let's say your users perform transactional queries to your database throughout the day. At the same time, another group of users performs reporting queries to the same database several times a day. When both types of queries are executed at the same time, the performance of your database degrades because the type of workload is different, causing a lot of contention. To solve this problem, you can replicate the database so that one database is used for transactional queries through the day, and the other database, the replicated one, is used for reporting queries. Figure 4.43 shows the Replication Center.

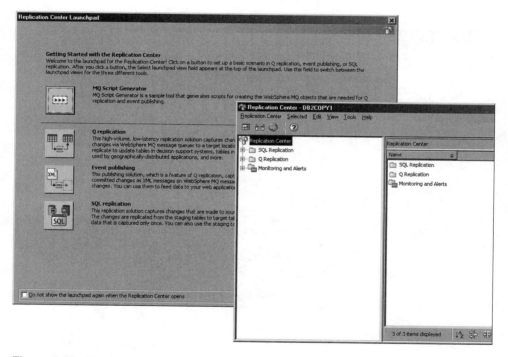

Figure 4.43   The Replication Center

Information Tools

To keep DB2 users informed on current and new product information, IBM offers valuable information via different channels such as webcasts, best practice documentations, and product videos. Additionally, every DB2 edition ships two information tools, namely the DB2 Information Center and the Check for DB2 Update tool.

DB2 Information Center

The DB2 Information Center gives you access to all DB2 documentation. It comes with a fast search engine, enabling you to search on any given topic. The DB2 Information Center can be accessed in three different ways:

- Dynamically through the Internet at http://pic.dhe.ibm.com/infocenter/db2luw/v10r5/ index.jsp.
- Locally on the database server after installing the DB2 Information Center from a separate media DVD.
- Through a designated server on your company's intranet. The DB2 Information Center must be installed on that server.

Figure 4.44 shows the Information Center accessed through the Internet. On the left panel there is a list of topics from which you can choose. Each of these topics can be drilled down to subtopics, and selecting a specific subtopic makes the contents panel on the right side display more information. At the top left corner of the Information Center, you find the Search field. Use this field to input any topic or keyword you want to search in the DB2 manuals. Then click the **GO** button.

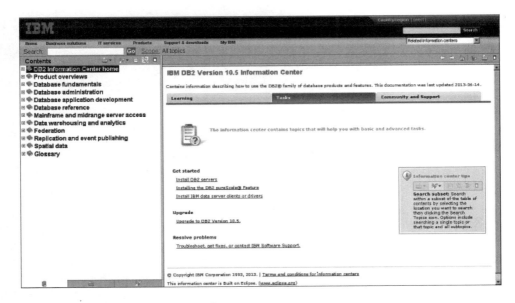

Figure 4.44   The DB2 Information Center

Checking for DB2 Updates

The Information Center website is periodically updated with new documentation; however, if you have installed the Information Center locally, make sure to check for updates regularly. Use the Check For DB2 Updates option in the DB2 menu to launch the InstallShield Update Service, which is shown in Figure 4.45.

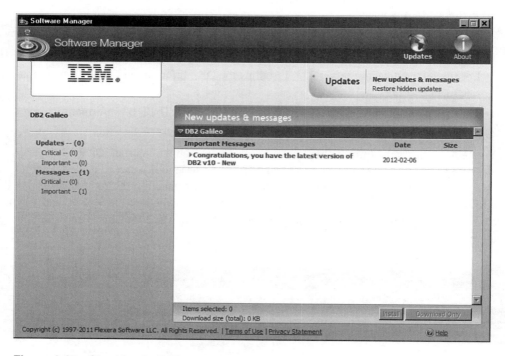

Figure 4.45   Checking for DB2 updates

From this site, you can download the refreshed DB2 Information Center image and install it on your server. You can also obtain information about updates to the DB2 code and news about DB2 in general.

Problem Determination Tools

Although people never want to encounter problems in their database systems, it happens, so it is important to be able to perform a logical and systematic diagnosis of a database system to identify source of problems. One of the best ways to collect diagnostic data in DB2 data is by using the db2pd tool.

The db2pd Tool

The db2pd tool is a command-line monitoring and troubleshooting tool that collects immediate statistics for DB2 instances and databases. This tool does not degrade the DB2 engine performance because it acquires the information directly from memory, rather than gathering data on the fly. Use this tool for troubleshooting, problem determination, database monitoring, performance tuning, and as an aid in application development design.

The db2pd tool provides many options to display information about database transactions, table spaces, table statistics, dynamic SQL, database configurations, and many other database details; for example

- To display the operating system information, issue

  db2pd -osinfo
- To display all instance-related information, issue

  db2pd -inst
- To display all database-related information to the *sample* database, issue

  db2pd -db sample
- Use the db2pd -help command to display all the available options. This tool is not available through the graphical interface.

Case Study 1

You recently installed DB2 Express-C on your Windows laptop. During the installation, the *DB2* instance was created. Now you want to start using DB2 by creating a database. Because you are new to DB2, you decide to use the DB2 First Steps tool (refer to Figure 4.41).

You click the **Create Sample Database** button from the First Steps. Next you choose the option **XML and SQL objects and data**, which creates a Unicode database, and click **OK**. Wait for a few minutes for the *sample* database to be created. Alternatively, you can create the *sample* database from a Windows command prompt or a Linux/UNIX shell using this command:

    db2sampl -sql -xml

After the database is created, you launch the DB2 Command Line Processor by choosing **Start > Programs > IBM DB2 > DB2COPY1 > Command Line Processor**. You should see a prompt like this: db2 =>, which is the DB2 CLP prompt. From the prompt, connect to the *sample* database.

    connect to sample

You want to examine the table spaces created by the tool; issue the following command:

    list tablespaces

Five table spaces are created by default. You wonder what sample user tables were created. The following command lists all tables defined under the schema of the user ID currently connected to the database.

```
list tables
```

To list tables of a specific schema (xyz, for example), use this command:

```
list tables for schema xyz
```

Issue `quit` to exit the CLP interactive mode. Sample codes and scripts are installed with the installation that works with the *SAMPLE* database. Run the file *tbread.db2* that contains SQL statements to query the sample tables. Issue the following in the CLP.

```
db2 -tvf ..\samples\clp\tbread.db2
```

You now want to get familiar with the CLPPlus. Issue the command `clpplus` to start the command line interface. But first, connect to the *SAMPLE* database.

```
CONNECT userid@localhost:50001/sample
```

Load a sample file into the SQL buffer with the `GET` command.

```
GET ..\samples\sqlpl\rsultset.db2
```

Run the script with the RUN command. You get an error complaining about the end label "@". Use the `EDIT` command to remove the @ sign at the end of the file. Save and close the editor.

Run the script again. This time it should work, and a stored procedure is successfully created. Call the stored procedure with the following command:

```
CALL median_result_set(?)
```

Congratulations! You have successfully created a Unicode database, queried few tables, and executed SQL scripts using the command-line tools CLP and CLPlus.

Case Study 2

Using the *SAMPLE* database you created in the First Steps, you now explore the IBM Data Studio graphical interface. Launch the IBM Data Studio full client. Open the Database Administration Explorer and create a database connection to the *SAMPLE* database. After a database connection is established, navigate to the *SAMPLE* database folder.

The *SAMPLE* database already has a set of tables defined in it. However, you decide to create a table of your own. To do so, you right-click the **Tables** folder and choose **Create Table**. You are presented with the following selections:

- Identify the schema for the new table. Select the user ID you logged in with. We discuss the significance of schemas in Chapter 7; for now it is sufficient to enter your user ID.

- The Properties pane is opened. Enter the name of the table you want to create, for example, **Table1**.

- Go to the Columns tab, click the **Add** icon. Enter the name of the first column for **Table1**, for example, **Col1**. Choose the data type from the pull-down menu, for example, **INTEGER**. You could create more columns by repeating this step, but one column is sufficient for now.

There are other tabs in which you can define the properties for the new table. However, completing these two windows is enough to create the table. Click the **Review and deploy changes** icon to generate the CREATE TABLE statement. Click the **Advanced Options** button to customize the deployment such as generating REORG and RUNSTATS commands. Click **Run** to run the statements now. Note that you can also schedule to deploy these changes some other time, such as the next maintenance window.

Table1 is displayed under the Tables view. To display the contents of the table, right-click on the table name and choose **Browse data**. Since nothing has been inserted into Table1, no contents are displayed. To insert a row into the table, right-click the table name, and click **Edit Data**. Enter a value under Col1. Click the **Play** button to commit the changes.

Your colleague, who is a DB2 expert, drops by your office and offers his help for any problems you may have. You tell him you would like to get familiar with how to tune SQL statements. He asks you to right-click on the database name, and select **Start Tuning.**

In the **Capture** tab, you enter the SQL statement you want to tune and get advise on. Click the **Invoke Advisors and Tools** button to run the explain command against the statement.

You are now in the **Review** tab where you are presented with recommendations based on the query, the current database statistics, and existing indexes defined in the database. You also check out the Access Plan Graph to understand how the query result is obtained. Lastly, you review the summary report and save the report for future reference.

Though you have not finished exploring all the functionality in IBM Data Studio, this exercise has made you realize how easy to use and powerful it is!

Summary

This chapter introduced most of the tools that are available in DB2. They come in two categories: the command-driven and the graphical user interface (GUI) tools. To use the command-line tools you need to have some knowledge of DB2 commands and SQL statements. If you aren't familiar with these, the GUI tools come in handy.

The command-line tools include the Command Line Processor (CLP), the CLP Plus, the Command Window (only on the Windows platform), and the Command Editor. The IBM Data Studio is a GUI that comes with every DB2 edition. From the IBM Data Studio, you can launch different perspectives to manage and administer your instances and databases. The SQL and XQuery editor helps you create and run SQL scripts. If you want to leverage the power of routines such as stored procedures, user-defined functions, and triggers, the database routines editor and debugger is what you need. It helps you with many tasks from developing and testing the routines to deploying and debugging the routines.

The IBM Data Studio Web Console provides health monitoring, job management, and connection management for DB2 databases. It can be used in a single-user environment or a multiuser environment to share monitored features and analysis across database servers.

The web console generates reports and keep track of your databases according to criteria you provide. These reports are handy for investigating performance problems and setting benchmarks for your database.

Review Questions

1. Which IBM tool can be used to schedule SQL scripts in DB2?

2. The DB2 Command Window is only available on Windows. What is the equivalent tool on the Linux/UNIX platforms?

3. Which registry variable needs to be changed to set `autocommit` to *off* permanently for the CLP?

4. When is it handy to start the CLP in interactive mode with a different terminator character as in `db2 -td!`?

5. Which command is necessary to guarantee the CLP back-end process is terminated?

6. When would you choose to use CLPPlus over CLP?

7. Which tool can be used to develop SQL user-defined functions?

8. Can the IBM Data Studio be used to perform database development for DB2 for i databases?

9. It's 9:00 a.m., and you would like to investigate a problem that happened at 3:00 a.m. Where do you look for more information?

10. How can you obtain the most current information about a given DB2 topic?

11. Which of the following tools can be used to execute SQL statements against a DB2 database?

    A.   Command Window

    B.   Command Editor

    C.   Command Line Processor

    D.   Command Line Processor Plus

12. Which of the following is the default termination character for files processed by the DB2 CLP?

    A.   :

    B.   ;

    C. |

    D. $

13. If you have the following CLP input file named *samp.sql*, how many commits will occur during the processing of the db2 -tvf samp.sql command?

```
connect to sample;

select * from org;

select * from dept;

connect reset;
```

    A.   0

    B.   1

    C.   2

    D.   3

    E.   4

14. In which function of the IBM Data Studio would you be able to view a data access explain plan visually?

    A.   Configure Automatic Maintenance editor

    B.   IBM Data Studio Web Console

    C.   SQL and XQuery Editor

    D.   Query Tuner Workflow Assistant

15. Which of the followings are tasks of the IBM Data Studio Web Console?

    A.   View alerts

    B.   Manage database jobs

    C.   View data access plan graphs

    D.   Deploy and debug stored procedures

    E.   Manage data connection profiles

16. If you have the following CLP input file named *samp.sql*, how many commits will occur during the processing of the db2 +c -tvf samp.sql command?

```
connect to sample;
select * from org;
select * from dept;
```

    A.   0

    B.   1

    C.   2

    D.   3

    E.   4

17. If you have the following CLP input file named *samp.sql*, which of the following commands will run this file successfully?

    connect to sample@
    ```
    select * from org@
    select * from dept@
    connect reset@
    ```

    A.   db2 –t@f samp.sql

    B.   db2 -td@ -f samp.sql

    C.   db2 -t@ -f samp.sql

    D.   db2 -td@f samp.sql

18. If your application receives the SQL code -911, which of the following commands can be used to get its description?

    A.   db2 ? -911

    B.   db2 ? 911N

    C.   db2 ? SQL-911

    D.   db2 ? SQL911N

19. Which of the following commands cannot be run from the CLP in interactive mode?

    A.   History

    B.   Edit

    C.   Runcmd

    D.   Repeat

20. Which two of the following can be performed from the CLP in interactive mode?

    A.   db2 ? SQL911N

    B.   db2stop

    C.   list applications

    D.   select * from staff

## CHAPTER 5

Understanding the DB2 Environment, DB2 Instances, and Databases

You need to understand the DB2 environment and the concepts of DB2 instances and databases to work effectively with DB2. DB2 instances and the DB2 environment control many factors that influence DB2's behavior by using configurable parameters at different levels and locations.

In this chapter, you learn about

- The big picture of the DB2 Environment, DB2 instances, and databases
- The environment variables
- The DB2 profile registries (also known as DB2 registry variables)
- How to manage and configure DB2 instances
- How to manage and configure the Database Administration Server (DAS)
- How to manage and configure databases
- The Configuration Advisor
- What to consider when designing instances and databases

The DB2 Environment, DB2 Instances, and Databases: The Big Picture

Figure 5.1 illustrates the different levels in which you can configure your DB2 environment.

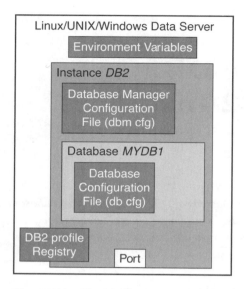

Figure 5.1   The big picture of the DB2 environment, instances, databases, and the various configuration levels

You can use

- Environment variables at the operating system level
- The DB2 profile registry variables at the operating system and instance levels
- The Database Manager (DBM) Configuration file at the instance level
- The Database (DB) Configuration file at the database level

In the following sections, you learn in detail each configuration level and how to work with all of these variables.

NOTE

DB2 provides several levels of configuration that allow users to control the DB2 environment with more flexibility. If you are not an experienced DB2 user, the *Configuration Advisor* tool can set parameter values based on information you provide about your system. Refer to the section "The Configuration Advisor" for more detail.

The DB2 Environment

The DB2 environment consists of environment variables and DB2 profile registry variables. These manage, monitor, and control the behavior of a DB2 system.

Environment Variables

You set environment variables at the operating system level. Most environment variables applicable to DB2 are set automatically during the DB2 installation. For example, the PATH environment variable is updated to point to the DB2 executable code directory.

The most important environment variable applicable to DB2 is DB2INSTANCE. This variable determines the current instance to which commands and configuration changes would apply.

To review the contents of an environment variable like DB2INSTANCE, you can do the following:

- On Windows

```
echo %DB2INSTANCE%
```

  or

```
set DB2INSTANCE
```

- On Linux and UNIX

```
export | grep DB2INSTANCE
```

  or

```
set | grep DB2INSTANCE
```

To change the value of an environment variable *temporarily* for the current session, use the `set` operating system command on Windows or `export` on Linux and UNIX as shown in the following examples.

- On Windows

```
set DB2INSTANCE=myinst
```

- On Linux and UNIX, it would depend on the shell that is used.

  - For the Korn shell

```
DB2INSTANCE=myinst
export DB2INSTANCE
```

  - For the Bourne shell

```
export DB2INSTANCE=myinst
```

  - For the C shell

```
setenv DB2INSTANCE myinst
```

This setting is lost after you close the window or end the session. Setting the environment variable temporarily can be useful to test certain behavior before making it permanent.

> **NOTE**
>
> A common mistake when using the `set` (Windows) or `export` (Linux and UNIX) commands is to leave spaces before and/or after the equal sign (`=`). No spaces must be used!

To create a new or modify an existing environment variable *permanently*, you can do the following:

- On Windows platforms, use the Control Panel. Figure 5.2 shows an example of using the Control Panel under Windows and viewing the environment variable DB2INSTANCE. In the figure, **System** was selected followed by the **Advanced** tab, and then the **Environment Variables** button.

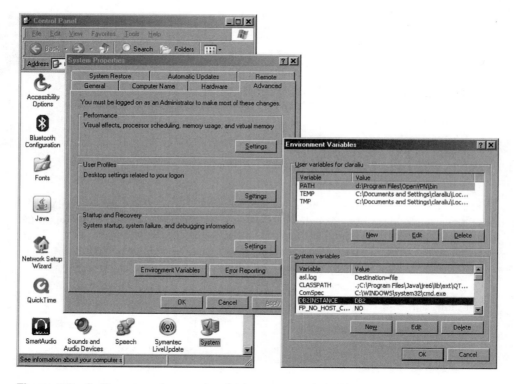

Figure 5.2   Setting an environment variable permanently in Windows

- On Linux and UNIX platforms, you can permanently change an environment variable by adding the `export` command in the `.login` or `.profile` startup scripts. However, rather than making this change directly, you can edit the script that comes with DB2 to set up the default DB2 environment. Then invoke this script from `.login` or `.profile`. DB2 provides the `db2profile` (for the Bourne and Korn shells) script and `db2cshrc` (for the C shell) script, which contain all the required commands to set up this default DB2 environment. These script files are located under the *INSTHOME*/sqllib directory, where *INSTHOME* represents the instance owner's home directory.

Listing 5.1 shows the `db2profile` script. Note that the DB2INSTANCE environment variable is set in the script file.

Listing 5.1 The `db2profile` Script File for a Linux and UNIX Machine

```
###############################################################
#
# Licensed Materials - Property of IBM
#
# "Restricted Materials of IBM"
#
# (C) COPYRIGHT IBM Corp. 1993, 2012 All Rights Reserved.
#
# US Government Users Restricted Rights - Use, duplication or
# disclosure restricted by GSA ADP Schedule Contract with IBM Corp.
#
###############################################################
#
# NAME:      db2profile
#
# FUNCTION: This script sets up a default database environment for
#           Bourne shell or Korn shell users.
#
# USAGE:     . db2profile
#           This script can either be invoked directly as above or
#           it can be added to the user's .profile file so that the
#           database environment is established during login.
#
#           #### DO NOT EDIT THIS FILE ####
#
###############################################################
DB2DIR=/opt/ibm/db2/V10.5
# Remember the current DB2INSTANCE environment variable
CUR_INSTNAME=${DB2INSTANCE:=""}
#--------------------------------------------------------------
# DB2INSTANCE [Default null, values: Any valid instance name]
# Specifies the instance that is active by default.
#--------------------------------------------------------------
DB2INSTANCE=demoadm
export DB2INSTANCE
INSTHOME=/home/demoadm
```

```
# Function to add or remove certain path to or from the specified
# environment variable.
. . . <content trimmed for better readability>
#---------------------------------------------------------------
# If DB2 instance environment is being switched from one instances to
another,
# the entries for old DB2 instance in the original instance environment
# are cleaned up.
#---------------------------------------------------------------
if [ -n "${CUR_INSTNAME?}" ]; then
    CUR_INSTHOME=`${INSTHOME?}/sqllib/bin/db2usrinf -d ${CUR_
➥INSTNAME?}`
    path_list="bin adm misc db2tss/bin"
    class_list="java/db2java.zip java/db2jcc.jar java/sqlj.zip
➥function \
       java/db2jcc_license_cisuz.jar java/db2jcc_license_cu.jar \
             java/runtime.zip"
    for tmp_entry in ${path_list?}; do
       AddRemoveString PATH ${CUR_INSTHOME?}/sqllib/${tmp_entry?} r
    done
    for tmp_entry in ${class_list?}; do
       AddRemoveString CLASSPATH ${CUR_INSTHOME?}/sqllib/${tmp_entry?} r
    done
    for path_name in LD_LIBRARY_PATH LIBPATH SHLIB_PATH LD_LIBRARY_
➥PATH_32 \
       LD_LIBRARY_PATH_64; do
       for tmp_path in lib lib32 lib64; do
          AddRemoveString ${path_name?} ${CUR_INSTHOME?}/sqllib/${tmp_
➥path?} r
       done
    done
    for path_name in PATH CLASSPATH LD_LIBRARY_PATH LIBPATH SHLIB_PATH
\
       LD_LIBRARY_PATH_32 LD_LIBRARY_PATH_64; do
       eval path_value=\$$path_name
       if [ "X${path_value}" = "X" ]; then
          unset ${path_name?}
       else
          export ${path_name?}
       fi
```

```
      done
      unset CUR_INSTNAME path_list class_list tmp_entry path_name path_
➡value
fi
. . . <content trimmed for better readability>
  for path_name in PATH LIBPATH SHLIB_PATH LD_LIBRARY_PATH; do
        if [ "X${path_name}" = "X" ]; then
            unset ${path_name?}
        else
            export ${path_name?}
        fi
  done
fi
. . . <content trimmed for better readability>
#---------------------------------------------------------------
# The following variables are used for JDBC support
#---------------------------------------------------------------
CLASSPATH=${CLASSPATH:-""}
if [ -f ${INSTHOME?}/sqllib/java/db2java.zip ]; then
    AddRemoveString CLASSPATH ${INSTHOME?}/sqllib/java/db2java.zip a
fi
if [ -f ${INSTHOME?}/sqllib/java/db2jcc.jar ]; then
    AddRemoveString CLASSPATH ${INSTHOME?}/sqllib/java/db2jcc.jar a
fi
if [ -f ${INSTHOME?}/sqllib/java/sqlj.zip ]; then
    AddRemoveString CLASSPATH ${INSTHOME?}/sqllib/java/sqlj.zip a
fi
if [ -d ${INSTHOME?}/sqllib/function ]; then
    AddRemoveString CLASSPATH ${INSTHOME?}/sqllib/function a
fi
if [ -f ${INSTHOME?}/sqllib/java/db2jcc_license_cisuz.jar ]; then
    AddRemoveString CLASSPATH ${INSTHOME?}/sqllib/java/db2jcc_license_
cisuz.jar a
fi
if [ -f ${INSTHOME?}/sqllib/java/db2jcc_license_cu.jar ]; then
    AddRemoveString CLASSPATH ${INSTHOME?}/sqllib/java/db2jcc_license_
cu.jar a
fi
AddRemoveString CLASSPATH . a
export CLASSPATH
```

```
LD_LIBRARY_PATH=${LD_LIBRARY_PATH:-""}
AddRemoveString LD_LIBRARY_PATH ${INSTHOME?}/sqllib/lib64 a
AddRemoveString LD_LIBRARY_PATH ${INSTHOME?}/sqllib/lib32 a
export LD_LIBRARY_PATH
#----------------------------------------------------------------
# Any user changes to the environment goes into userprofile.
Modifications
# to db2profile may be overwritten in fixpaks.
#----------------------------------------------------------------
if [ -f ${INSTHOME?}/sqllib/userprofile ]; then
    . ${INSTHOME?}/sqllib/userprofile
fi
```

For the *DB2* instance owner, a line to invoke the db2profile/db2cshrc script file is automatically added to the .login or .profile file during the instance creation. If you are a DB2 user who is not the instance owner, add the following line to your .login or .profile startup scripts:

. INSTHOME/sqllib/db2profile (for Bourne and Korn shells; the dot at the beginning of the line is required)

or

source INSTHOME/sqllib/db2cshrc (for C shell)

Executing the preceding commands guarantees your database environment is configured to use DB2.

DB2 Profile Registries

Most DB2-related information is stored in a centralized repository called the DB2 profile registry. Depending on the operating system platform where DB2 is installed, variables stored in the DB2 profile registries may be different. The DB2 profile registry variables are commonly referred to as **DB2 registry variables**.

> **NOTE**
>
> The word "registry" always causes confusion when working with DB2 on the Windows platform. The DB2 profile registry variables have no relationship to the Windows registry variables.

The DB2 profile registry consists of the following registries:

- **The DB2 Instance-Level Profile Registry:** Variables set at this level apply only to a specific instance.

- **The DB2 Global-Level Profile Registry:** Variables set at this level apply globally to all instances.

- **The DB2 Instance Node-Level Profile Registry:** Variables at this level apply to a specific partition in a multi-partitioned DB2 environment.

- **The DB2 Instance Profile Registry:** This contains a list of all instances in the system. The command `db2ilist`, which lists all instances in a system, uses this registry as input.

> **NOTE**
>
> All variables in the DB2 registries *except* those in the DB2 Instance Profile Registry are the same. The difference is the level at which you set the variable. For example, you can set the DB2COMM registry variable at the instance-level, global-level, or node-level profile registries.
>
> The list of DB2 registries and their usage can be found in the DB2 Information Center.

The DB2 registries are stored as binary or text files in different locations depending on the operating system. To modify these registries, do not edit these files directly; instead, use the `db2set` command. Figure 5.3 shows the `db2set` command with the `-all` option, which lists all of the currently set DB2 profile registry variables.

Figure 5.3   The `db2set` -all command

Notice that each registry variable is preceded with a letter in square brackets. This indicates in which level the variable is set.

- **[i]** indicates the variable has been set at the DB2 Instance-Level Profile Registry using the -i option (which is the default). For example, in Figure 5.3 *[i] DB2COMM=SSL* was set using the following command in instance *myinst*:

```
db2set DB2COMM=SSL -i myinst
```

- **[g]** indicates the variable has been set at the DB2 Global-Level Profile Registry using the -g option. This setting applies to all instances defined on the DB2 server. For example, in Figure 5.3, *[g] DB2COMM=SSL* was set using this command:

```
db2set DB2COMM=SSL -g
```

- **[e]** indicates a DB2 registry variable has been set as an environment variable using the set command (Windows) or export command (Linux and UNIX). For example, in Figure 5.3 *[e] DB2COMM=TCPIP* was set using this command:

```
set DB2COMM=tcpip
```

Although most DB2 registry variables can be set as environment variables, we recommend setting them as DB2 registry variables using the db2set command. Changes to DB2 registry variables might require DB2 instance stop and start and do not require a server reboot, but changes to environment variables could require a reboot.

To set a registry variable at the DB2 Instance Node-Level Profile Registry level, use a command with this syntax:

```
db2set registry_variable=value -i instance_name partition_number
```

> **NOTE**
> Similar to the set operating system command, do not leave spaces before and/or after the equal sign (=) when using the db2set command.

> **NOTE**
> The db2set command validates the values assigned to the DB2 registry variables. For example in Figure 5.3, if you set DB2COMM to the value of netbios, a value that is no longer supported, you will receive an error DB11301E Invalid value.

In Figure 5.3, the DB2COMM registry variable was set three times with different values each at the [e], [i], and [g] levels. When a registry variable is defined at different levels, DB2 chooses the value using the following search order:

1. Environment variable set using the `set/export` operating system commands.

2. DB2 Instance Node-Level Profile Registry

3. DB2 Instance-Level Profile Registry

4. DB2 Global-Level Profile Registry

Based on this search order, for the example in Figure 5.3, the value *tcpip* for the DB2COMM registry variable is the one that takes precedence as it has been set temporarily at the environment level.

Some registry variables require that you stop and start the instance (`db2stop/db2start`) for the change to take effect. Refer to the DB2 Information Center for such list of registry variables.

V10 With DB2 10, you can now use the `-info` option to show you whether this is the case for the variable. For example, to find out if DB2 registry variable DB2COMM requires a `db2stop/db2start` for a new value to take effect, issue

```
db2set -info DB2COMM
```

and you get:

```
Immediate change supported : NO
Immediate by default :      NO
```

This means an immediate value change is not supported for DB2COMM, therefore a `db2stop/db2start` is needed.

If the variable supports immediate change and immediate is not the default for the variable, you can specify the `-immediate` option in the `db2set` command:

```
db2set DB2_registry_variable -immediate
```

Table 5.1 summarizes other options commonly used with the `db2set` command.

Table 5.1   Common `db2set` Command Options

Command	Explanation
`db2set -all`	Lists all the currently set DB2 registry variables.
`db2set -lr`	Lists all the DB2 registry variables that can be set.
`db2set -h`	Displays help information about the `db2set` command.
`db2set DB2_registry_variable=`	Deletes a variable from the DB2 registry. Note that a blank space follows the equal sign (=).
`db2set -info DB2_registry_variable`	Displays if the DB2 registry variable requires `db2stop/db2restart` for the new value to take effect

The DB2 Instance

From a user's perspective, a *DB2* instance provides an independent environment where database objects can be created and applications can run. Several instances can be created on one server, and each instance can have a multiple number of databases, as illustrated in Figure 5.4.

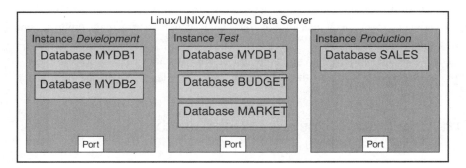

Figure 5.4   A DB2 instance from a user's perspective

Because of these independent environments, one instance cannot "see" the contents of another instance even they are defined on the same server. Therefore objects of the same name can exist in two or more instances. Each instance can be running with different levels of DB2 as well. In Figure 5.4, the database called MYDB1 is associated with instance *Development*, and another database also called MYDB1 is associated with instance *Test*. Instances allow users to have different environments for production, test, and developmental purposes. In addition, independent environments let you perform instance and database operations without affecting other instances. For example, if you stop and start the instance *Test*, the other two instances are not affected.

From an architectural perspective, an instance serves as a layer between the DB2 binary code and the user database objects. It is important to understand that this is just an association of the DB2 code to the database objects. There is a common misconception among new DB2 users that dropping an instance also drops the databases associated with that instance; this is not necessarily true. When an instance is dropped, the association to the user databases is broken, but it can later be re-established, as discussed in Chapter 2, "DB2 at a Glance: The Big Picture."

Figure 5.5 shows examples of two instances in a Linux and UNIX environment. Databases MarketDB and SalesDB are associated with instance *#1*. Databases TestDB and ProdDB are associated with instance *#2*. Each instance has its own configuration files. In this example, both instances are pointing to the same DB2 binary code for DB2 10.5 using *soft links*. On Linux and UNIX, a soft link behaves like an alias to another file. Soft links are also referred to as *symbolic links* or *logical links*.

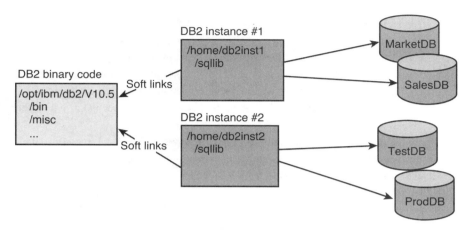

Figure 5.5   The DB2 instance in Linux and UNIX from an architectural perspective

NOTE

On Linux and UNIX, there are two types of installations, namely root installation and non-root installation. Instance creation and administration, in some cases, are different between the two installation types. In this chapter we focus on root installations, however we point out the difference for non-root installations when appropriate. Root and non-root installations were discussed in detail in Chapter 3, "Installing DB2."

NOTE

On Linux and UNIX, soft links are used as pointers from the instance *sqllib* directory to the DB2 binary code. However, in non-root installations, the *sqllib* directory contains all of the DB2 product files and instance files with no soft links. On Windows, there is a shared install path, and all instances access the same libraries and executables.

NOTE

In Figure 5.5, the path /opt/IBM/db2/V10.5 is applicable to UNIX only. For Linux, the path is /opt/ibm/db2/V10.5. We use the Linux path in most examples in this book.

Creating DB2 Instances

When you install DB2 on the Windows platform, an instance called *DB2* is created by default. On Linux and UNIX you can choose to create the default instance during the installation, change the instance owner's name, or not create an instance so that you can create one later. If you choose to create the default instance on these platforms, this instance is called *db2inst1*. DB2 creates an operating system user with the same name as the instance. This user is known as the *instance owner*.

You can also create new, additional instances on your server using the db2icrt command. Figure 5.6 summarizes the db2icrt command and provides examples.

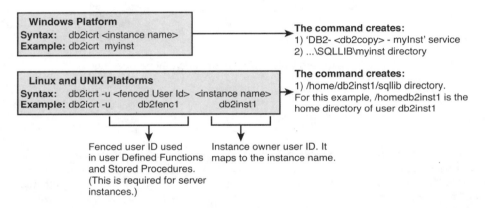

Figure 5.6   The db2icrt command

> **NOTE**
>
> In non-root installations on Linux and UNIX, the db2icrt command is not supported, as you cannot create other instances. You can only work with the instance created at installation time.

On Windows, the db2icrt command can be run by a user with Local Administrator authority. The command creates a subdirectory under the sqllib directory with the name of the instance just created. In addition, a Windows service *DB2 – db2copy_name – instance_name* is created. The first qualifier in DB2-related Windows services is always *DB2*.

> **NOTE**
>
> Several independent copies of DB2 can be installed at different release and Fix Pack levels. On Windows, to differentiate the Windows services created for each copy, the DB2 copy name—an arbitrary name given to a particular copy of the DB2 code—is incorporated in the service name as show here:
>
> ```
> DB2 - db2copy_name - instance_ name.
> ```
>
> This was described in Chapter 3.

On Linux and UNIX, you must have root authority or else you need to have the system administrator run the db2icrt command for you. You can either use the fully qualified path name to the program or change into the directory to run this command as shown here:

- Run the command **/opt/ibm/db2/V10.5/instance/db2icrt**

    or

- Change into the directory **/opt/ibm/db2/V10.5/instance** and then invoke the db2icrt command.

In addition, on Linux and UNIX, the instance name must match an existing operating system user ID, which becomes the instance owner. This operating system user must exist prior to executing the db2icrt command. The db2icrt command creates the subdirectory sqllib under the home directory of this user.

DB2 on Linux and UNIX also requires a fenced user to run stored procedures and user-defined functions (UDFs) as fenced resources—that is, in a separate address space other than the one used by the DB2 engine. This ensures that problems with these objects do not affect your database or instance. If you have thoroughly tested your stored procedures and UDFs and are confident they will run with no problems, you can use the same ID for the fenced user and the instance owner.

> **NOTE**
>
> The terms *instance* and a *DB2 instance* are used interchangeably. On Windows, the default name of the DB2 instance is *DB2*. This sometimes confuses new DB2 users.

Creating Client Instances

In general, when we talk about instances in this book we are referring to server instances: fully functional instances created at the DB2 server where your database resides. There are other types of instances that can be created. One of them, the **client instance**, is used for cataloging nodes and databases to which you want to connect using this machine. A client instance cannot be started or stopped, and databases cannot be created on this type of instance. Database connectivity and different types of clients are discussed in Chapter 6, "Configuring Client and Server Connectivity."

You create a DB2 client instance using the -s option. For example

```
db2icrt -s CLIENT myclinst
```

creates the client instance *myclinst*. On Linux and UNIX, the operating system user *myclinst* must exist before executing this command. On Windows, an instance does not map to a user ID, so this would not be a requirement.

On a Windows client, the entire machine is considered the DB2 client regardless of the user. On a Linux and UNIX machine the DB2 client is associated with an operating system user.

You need to have a client instance if you have two physically separate Linux and UNIX machines, one containing the DB2 client code (assume it is an application server machine) and the other one containing the DB2 server code (the DB2 server machine). On the client machine a client instance must be created that associates it to a given operating system user. Logging on as this user enables you to perform the commands required to set up connectivity to the DB2 server machine.

If the client and server reside on the same machine containing the DB2 server code, there would be no need to create a client instance because the operating system user used as the client can "source" the instance owner profile in sqllib/db2profile as described in the section, "Environment Variables."

Creating DB2 Instances in a pureScale Environment

If you installed DB2 pureScale Feature, a DB2 pureScale instance is created by default. If you chose not to create the instance during installation, you can create the DB2 pureScale instance with the db2icrt command or the db2isetup command, which launches the DB2 Instance Setup wizard. Note that DB2 pureScale was introduced in Chapter 2, section "DB2 pureScale"

Using the DB2 Instance Setup Wizard is the recommended method because it enables you to create multiple hosts—members and a cluster caching facility (CF) for the cluster. With the db2icrt command, on the other hand, you can only create two hosts—one CF and one member.

Dropping an Instance

You can drop an instance if you no longer need it. Before you drop one, though, make sure that it is stopped. Additionally, on Linux and UNIX ensure that all memory and inter-process communications (IPCs) owned by the instance have been released; this can be done by issuing the ipclean command as the instance owner. You can then run the db2idrop command to drop the *DB2* instance. For example, to drop the instance *myinst*, use the command

```
/opt/ibm/db2/V10.5/instance/db2idrop myinst
```

> **NOTE**
>
> Always use the `db2idrop` command to drop the instance. Unless instructed by DB2 Support, do not remove the instance manually. Improper manual instance removal can leave the instance registration behind that the DB2 copy would still recognize.

Listing the Instances in Your System

You can list all instances on your server using the `db2ilist` command. On Windows you can run this command from any Command Window. On Linux and UNIX you might need to change the directory to the path where this command resides, which is under the directory where DB2 was installed (/opt/ibm/db2/V10.5) before running this command.

IBM Data Studio is a "database-centric" tool rather than an "instance-centric" tool. You cannot list instances on your system from IBM Data Studio, but you can create a database connection. When a database connection is completed, the instance where the database is defined is listed on IBM Data Studio, as shown in Figure 5.7.

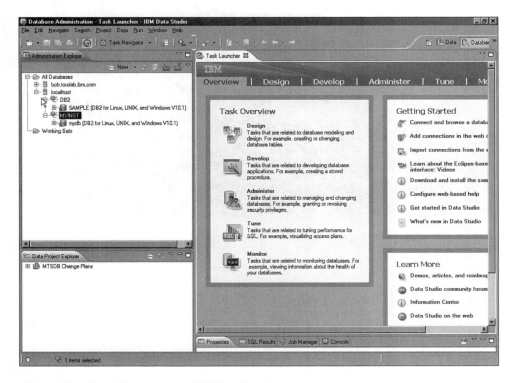

Figure 5.7   List of instances in IBM Data Studio

Using the DB2INSTANCE Environment Variable

Use the DB2INSTANCE environment variable to indicate which instance will be affected by your commands, that is, which instance is the active one for your commands. It is particularly important to have this variable set correctly when you have multiple instances in the same DB2 server. For example, if you have two instances, *myinst1* and *myinst2*, and DB2INSTANCE is set to *myinst2*, any command you execute is directed to the *myinst2* instance. On Linux and UNIX you can switch to another instance by logging on or switching to the corresponding instance owner user ID.

Because DB2INSTANCE is an operating system environment variable, you set this value like any other environment variable for your operating system, as discussed in section "Environment Variables." Figure 5.8 illustrates setting the DB2INSTANCE environment variable temporarily in the Windows platform using the `set` operating system command. It also illustrates the methods used to determine its current value such as using the command `get instance` (which works on any platform), using the `echo` operating system command, or the `set` operating system command.

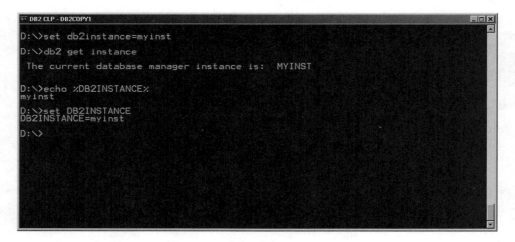

Figure 5.8   Working with the DB2INSTANCE variable

Starting a DB2 Instance

An instance must be started before you can work with it. You can choose to start the instance manually or automatically every time you reboot your machine. To start an instance manually, use the `db2start` command. On Windows, because *DB2* instances are created as services, you can also start an instance manually using the NET START command. To start an instance automatically on Windows, look for the service corresponding to the *DB2* instance by opening the Control Panel, choosing the *Administrative Tools* folder, and then double-clicking *Services*. A Services window similar to the one displayed in Figure 5.9 appears.

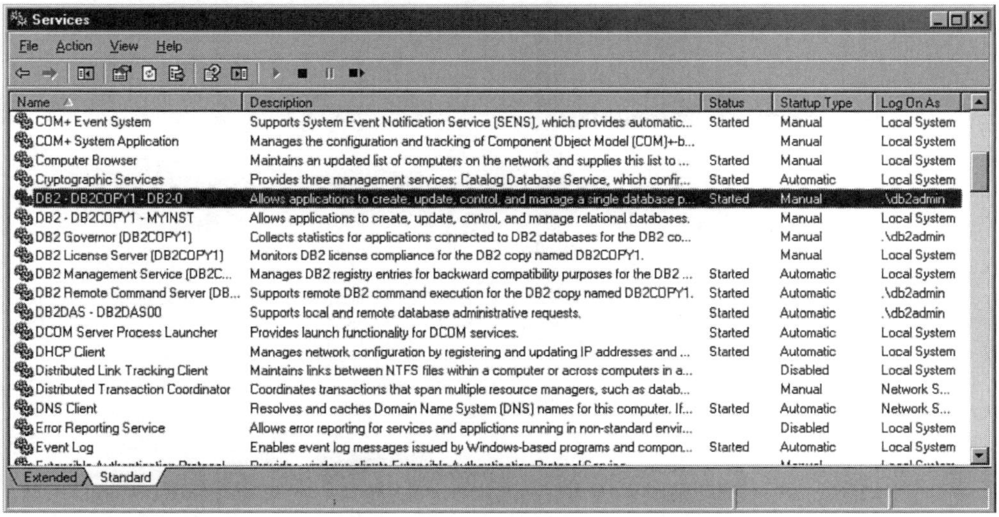

Figure 5.9 Windows services for DB2

Several DB2 services are listed in Figure 5.10. All of the DB2 services can be easily identified as they are prefixed with *DB2* and include the DB2 installation copy name. For example, the service *DB2 – DB2COPY1 – MYINST* represents the instance *MYINST* using the DB2 installation copy *DB2COPY1*. The service *DB2 – DB2COPY1 – DB2* highlighted in the figure represents the instance named *DB2* using installation copy *DB2COPY1*. As you can see from the figure, this service is set up to be manually started, so you would need to execute a db2start command every time the system is restarted for the *DB2* instance to be able to work with your databases.

You can set up the instance to be automatically started by right-clicking the *DB2 – DB2COPY1 – DB2-0* service and choosing **Properties** from the drop-down menu. When the Properties panel appears, you can change the **Startup type** from **Manual** to **Automatic** (see Figure 5.10).

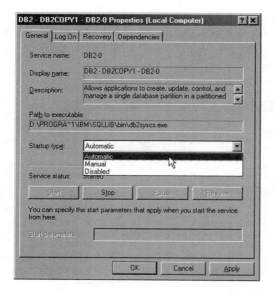

Figure 5.10   Service properties for the instance *DB2*

You can also start a *DB2* instance using the green database icon on the Windows taskbar as shown in Figure 5.11.

Figure 5.11   Windows task icon of DB2

On Linux and UNIX, to automatically start the *DB2* instance every time the server is started, use the `db2iauto` command. To set up the *db2inst1* instance to be started automatically, run the command

```
db2iauto -on db2inst1
```

NOTE

On Linux, UNIX, and Windows operating systems, an instance created by using `db2icrt` is set as a manual start.

> **NOTE**
>
> The DB2INSTANCE variable indicates which instance is your current instance, that is, the one to which your commands would apply. This is different from instances that are *started*. Many instances can be started at the same time, but only one is your current instance.

> **NOTE**
>
> On Linux and UNIX, the automatic starting of non-root DB2 instances at system reboot is not supported.

Stopping a DB2 Instance

You can use the `db2stop` command to stop a *DB2* instance that is currently running. On Windows, verify that the DB2INSTANCE environment variable is correctly set before issuing this command, as discussed in the "Environment Variables" section. On Linux and UNIX ensure you are logged on as the instance owner of the instance you wish to stop.

On Windows because the *DB2* instances are created as services, you can also stop the instances using the NET STOP command or stop the service from the Control Panel. To stop an instance from the Control Panel on Windows, right-click the service and select **Stop** from the drop-down menu. When the service is stopped the *Status* column will be blank.

You cannot stop the instance if there is a database that is active in the instance or if there are databases with one or more connections. You must first deactivate the database and/or reset the connections. In many cases you have a large number of DB2 client machines running applications that connect to the database server, and you cannot go to each machine to close the application to terminate the connection. In this case you can use the `force` option with the `db2stop` command to force off all active connections and/or activations to stop the instance:

```
db2stop force
```

> **NOTE**
>
> A `db2stop force` command has the same effect as issuing the `force applications all` command followed by the `db2stop` command. However, `db2stop force` prevents new connections from happening while the instance is being stopped. The `force applications` command is discussed in detail in Chapter 9, "Understanding Concurrency and Locking."

> **NOTE**
>
> In many DB2 customer environments, the process of issuing a `db2stop` followed by a `db2start` command is called one or more of the following:
>
> - Recycling the instance
> - Bringing the instance down and up
> - Bouncing the instance
> - Stopping and (re)starting the instance
> - Issuing a DB2 stop and start

Attaching to an Instance

To perform instance-level maintenance tasks, you first need to attach to the instance with the `attach` command. Some instance-level operations are

- Listing applications connected to your databases
- Forcing off applications
- Monitoring a database
- Updating the Database Manager Configuration parameters

Users often confuse attaching to an instance and connecting to a database. When in doubt as to which one to use, determine whether the operation is to affect the instance or a particular database. For example, the `list applications` command lists all the applications connected to all the databases in your active instance. This is not an operation you would perform at the database level because you want to list all connections to all databases, so an attachment is what is required in this case.

> **NOTE**
>
> Chapter 6 discusses setting up database connections in detail. In it, we describe the node directory, which is used to encapsulate connectivity information, such as the hostname of a remote DB2 database server and the port number of the instance.

> **NOTE**
>
> Attachments are only applicable at the instance level; connections are only applicable at the database level.

When you attach to an instance, it can be a local instance or a remote instance. Each instance has a corresponding entry in the node directory. A local instance resides on the same machine where you issue the `attach` command, while a remote instance resides on some other machine. Other than the current instance specified in the DB2INSTANCE variable, DB2 looks for connectivity information in the node directory for any other instance.

The syntax to attach to the current instance is

```
attach to instance_name_as_indicated_in_DB2INSTANCE
```

for example

```
attach to DB2
```

To attach to a local or remote instance that is not your current instance, use

```
attach to node_name [user userId] [using password]
```

for example

```
attach to mynode user peter using myudbpsw
```

where `mynode` is an entry in the node directory.

Attaching to the current instance (as specified in DB2INSTANCE) is normally done implicitly. However, there are special occasions where you do need to explicitly attach to the current instance, as you see in following sections.

To detach from the current attached instance, issue the `detach` command:

```
attach to mynode
detach
```

Configuring an Instance

You can set DB2 configuration parameters at the instance level (also known as the database manager level) and at the database level. At the instance level, variables are stored in the Database Manager (DBM) Configuration file. Changes to these variables affect *all* databases associated with this instance. At the database level, variables are stored in the Database Configuration file. Changes to these variables only affect that specific database. In this section, we discuss the DBM Configuration file in detail.

When you install DB2 and create an instance, the instance is assigned a default DBM configuration. You can view this configuration by running the `get dbm cfg` command. Listing 5.2 shows the output of this command on a Windows machine.

Listing 5.2 Contents of the DBM Configuration File

```
C:\Program Files\IBM\SQLLIB\BIN>db2 get dbm cfg
          Database Manager Configuration

      Node type = Enterprise Server Edition with local and remote
clients

  Database manager configuration release level          = 0x0f00

  CPU speed (millisec/instruction)               (CPUSPEED) = 1.023413e-006
```

```
Communications bandwidth (MB/sec)        (COMM_BANDWIDTH) =
1.000000e+002
Max number of concurrently active databases    (NUMDB) = 32
Federated Database System Support        (FEDERATED) = NO
Transaction processor monitor name      (TP_MON_NAME) =
Default charge-back account          (DFT_ACCOUNT_STR) =
Java Development Kit installation path      (JDK_PATH) = D:\PROGRA~1\
IBM\SQLLIB~1\java\jdk
Diagnostic error capture level            (DIAGLEVEL) = 3
Notify Level                            (NOTIFYLEVEL) = 3
Diagnostic data directory path             (DIAGPATH) = C:\DOCUME~1\
ALLUSE~1\APPLIC~1\IBM\DB2\DB2COPY2\DB2_01\
Current member resolved DIAGPATH                      = C:\DOCUME~1\
ALLUSE~1\APPLIC~1\IBM\DB2\DB2COPY2\DB2_01\DIAG0000\
Alternate diagnostic data directory path (ALT_DIAGPATH) =
Current member resolved ALT_DIAGPATH                  =
Size of rotating db2diag & notify logs (MB)  (DIAGSIZE) = 0
Default database monitor switches
  Buffer pool                        (DFT_MON_BUFPOOL) = OFF
  Lock                                  (DFT_MON_LOCK) = OFF
  Sort                                  (DFT_MON_SORT) = OFF
  Statement                             (DFT_MON_STMT) = OFF
  Table                                (DFT_MON_TABLE) = OFF
  Timestamp                        (DFT_MON_TIMESTAMP) = ON
  Unit of work                          (DFT_MON_UOW) = OFF
Monitor health of instance and databases   (HEALTH_MON) = OFF
SYSADM group name                        (SYSADM_GROUP) =
SYSCTRL group name                      (SYSCTRL_GROUP) =
SYSMAINT group name                    (SYSMAINT_GROUP) =
SYSMON group name                        (SYSMON_GROUP) =
Client Userid-Password Plugin          (CLNT_PW_PLUGIN) =
Client Kerberos Plugin                (CLNT_KRB_PLUGIN) = IBMkrb5
Group Plugin                             (GROUP_PLUGIN) =
GSS Plugin for Local Authorization    (LOCAL_GSSPLUGIN) =
Server Plugin Mode                      (SRV_PLUGIN_MODE) = UNFENCED
Server List of GSS Plugins       (SRVCON_GSSPLUGIN_LIST) =
Server Userid-Password Plugin         (SRVCON_PW_PLUGIN) =
Server Connection Authentication         (SRVCON_AUTH) = NOT_
➥SPECIFIED
Cluster manager                                      =
```

```
Database manager authentication          (AUTHENTICATION) = SERVER
Alternate authentication          (ALTERNATE_AUTH_ENC) = NOT_
➥SPECIFIED
Cataloging allowed without authority     (CATALOG_NOAUTH) = NO
Trust all clients                        (TRUST_ALLCLNTS) = YES
Trusted client authentication            (TRUST_CLNTAUTH) = CLIENT
Bypass federated authentication             (FED_NOAUTH) = NO
Default database path                        (DFTDBPATH) = D:
Database monitor heap size (4KB)           (MON_HEAP_SZ) =
➥AUTOMATIC(66)
Java Virtual Machine heap size (4KB)      (JAVA_HEAP_SZ) = 2048
Audit buffer size (4KB)                   (AUDIT_BUF_SZ) = 0
Size of instance shared memory (4KB)  (INSTANCE_MEMORY) =
➥AUTOMATIC(602394)
Instance memory for restart light (%) (RSTRT_LIGHT_MEM) =
➥AUTOMATIC(10)
Agent stack size                        (AGENT_STACK_SZ) = 16
Sort heap threshold (4KB)                   (SHEAPTHRES) = 0
Directory cache support                      (DIR_CACHE) = YES
Application support layer heap size (4KB)    (ASLHEAPSZ) = 15
Max requester I/O block size (bytes)          (RQRIOBLK) = 32767
Workload impact by throttled utilities(UTIL_IMPACT_LIM) = 10
Priority of agents                            (AGENTPRI) = SYSTEM
Agent pool size                         (NUM_POOLAGENTS) =
➥AUTOMATIC(100)
Initial number of agents in pool        (NUM_INITAGENTS) = 0
Max number of coordinating agents      (MAX_COORDAGENTS) =
➥AUTOMATIC(200)
Max number of client connections        (MAX_CONNECTIONS) =
➥AUTOMATIC(MAX_COORDAGENTS)
Keep fenced process                         (KEEPFENCED) = YES
Number of pooled fenced processes          (FENCED_POOL) =
➥AUTOMATIC(MAX_COORDAGENTS)
Initial number of fenced processes       (NUM_INITFENCED) = 0
Index re-creation time and redo index build   (INDEXREC) = RESTART
Transaction manager database name           (TM_DATABASE) = 1ST_CONN
Transaction resync interval (sec)       (RESYNC_INTERVAL) = 180
SPM name                                      (SPM_NAME) = CLARALIU
SPM log size                           (SPM_LOG_FILE_SZ) = 256
SPM resync agent limit                   (SPM_MAX_RESYNC) = 20
```

```
SPM log path                            (SPM_LOG_PATH) =
TCP/IP Service name                        (SVCENAME) = 60000
Discovery mode                             (DISCOVER) = SEARCH
Discover server instance              (DISCOVER_INST) = ENABLE
SSL server keydb file                  (SSL_SVR_KEYDB) =
SSL server stash file                  (SSL_SVR_STASH) =
SSL server certificate label           (SSL_SVR_LABEL) =
SSL service name                        (SSL_SVCENAME) =
SSL cipher specs                     (SSL_CIPHERSPECS) =
SSL versions                            (SSL_VERSIONS) =
SSL client keydb file                 (SSL_CLNT_KEYDB) =
SSL client stash file                 (SSL_CLNT_STASH) =
Maximum query degree of parallelism   (MAX_QUERYDEGREE) = ANY
Enable intra-partition parallelism     (INTRA_PARALLEL) = NO
Maximum Asynchronous TQs per query    (FEDERATED_ASYNC) = 0
No. of int. communication buffers(4KB)(FCM_NUM_BUFFERS) =
➥AUTOMATIC(4096)
No. of int. communication channels    (FCM_NUM_CHANNELS) =
➥AUTOMATIC(2048)
Node connection elapse time (sec)         (CONN_ELAPSE) = 10
Max number of node connection retries (MAX_CONNRETRIES) = 5
Max time difference between nodes (min) (MAX_TIME_DIFF) = 60
db2start/db2stop timeout (min)        (START_STOP_TIME) = 10
WLM dispatcher enabled                 (WLM_DISPATCHER) = NO
WLM dispatcher concurrency            (WLM_DISP_CONCUR) = COMPUTED
WLM dispatcher CPU shares enabled (WLM_DISP_CPU_SHARES) = NO
WLM dispatcher min. utilization (%) (WLM_DISP_MIN_UTIL) = 5
Communication buffer exit library list (COMM_EXIT_LIST) =
```

Note that the *Node type* entry field at the top of the output identifies the type of instance. For example, in Listing 5.2 this field has the value *Enterprise Server Edition with local and remote clients*. This means it is a server instance. For a client instance the value of this field would be *Client*.

In this book you learn some of the more important parameters for the DBM Configuration file. For a full treatment of all DBM Configuration parameters, refer to the **DB2 Information Center > Database fundamentals > Configuring > Database configuration parameters**.

To update one or more parameters in the DBM Configuration file, issue the command

```
update dbm cfg
     using parameter_name value parameter_name value ...
```

For example, to update the `INTRA_PARALLEL` DBM Configuration parameter, issue the following command:

```
update dbm cfg using INTRA_PARALLEL YES
```

Issuing the `get dbm cfg` command after the `update dbm cfg` command shows the newly updated values. However, this does not mean that the change will take effect right away. Several parameters in the DBM Configuration file require a `db2stop` followed by a `db2start` for the new values to be used. For other parameters, the update is dynamic, so a `db2stop/db2start` is not required as the new value takes effect immediately. These parameters are called **configurable online parameters**. If you are updating a configuration parameter of a DB2 client instance, the new value takes effect the next time you restart the client application or if the client application is the CLP after you issue the `terminate` command.

> **NOTE**
>
> Configurable online parameters of the DBM Configuration file can be updated dynamically only if you first explicitly attach to the instance. This also applies to local instances. If you have not performed an instance attachment, the parameter is not changed until you perform a db2stop/db2start.

In addition to the command `db2set -info` to find out if a parameter is configurable online, IBM Data Studio can also be used to provide the list of DBM Configuration parameters and indicates which ones are configurable online. Refer to the section, "Working with an Instance from IBM Data Studio," for details.

To get the current, effective setting for each configuration parameter and the value of the parameter the next time the instance is stopped and restarted, use the `show detail` option of the `get dbm cfg` command. This option requires an instance attachment:

```
db2 attach to <instance name>
```

If you run this command after changing the `INTRA_PARALLEL` configuration parameter as just shown, you see that the current value is NO, but the next effective or delayed value is YES. The related output from the `get dbm cfg show detail` command would look like the following:

```
C:\Program Files\SQLLIB\BIN>db2 get dbm cfg show detail
Description                          Parameter       Current Value   Delayed Value
-----------------------------------------------------------------------------

...

Enable intra-partition parallelism   (INTRA_PARALLEL) = NO           YES
```

Note that the `get dbm cfg` command also lists the actual value of parameters listed as AUTOMATIC. For example, when you issue the `get dbm cfg` command while attached to an instance, you might see output as follows for the INSTANCE_MEMORY parameter:

```
C:\Program Files\SQLLIB\BIN>db2 get dbm cfg
...
Size of instance shared memory (4KB)  (INSTANCE_MEMORY) = AUTOMATIC(602394)
```

To reset all the DBM Configuration parameters to their default value, use `reset dbm cfg`.

Working with an Instance from IBM Data Studio

Many of the instance configuration operations described in the previous sections can also be performed in IBM Data Studio. Figure 5.12 shows IBM Data Studio in the Database Administration view with the instance *MYINST* selected.

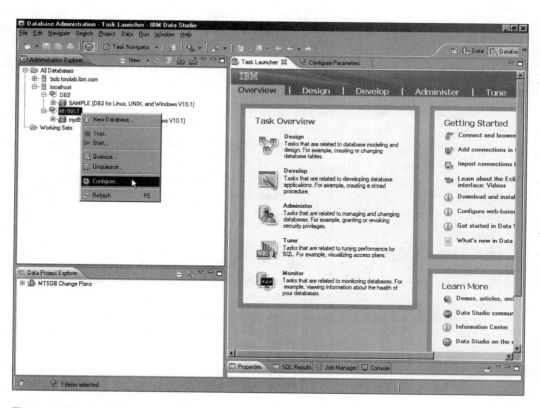

Figure 5.12 Available instance operations in Data Studio

When you right-click the instance, a menu with several options is displayed. To stop and instance, click **Stop**. To start an instance, click **Start**.

To configure the instance, select the **Configure** option. The **Configure Parameters** tab appears as shown in Figure 5.13. The column *Value* indicates the current value of the parameter, and the *Pending Value* indicates the new value of the parameter. *Automatic* and *Immediate* columns indicate whether the change will take effect automatically and/or immediately.

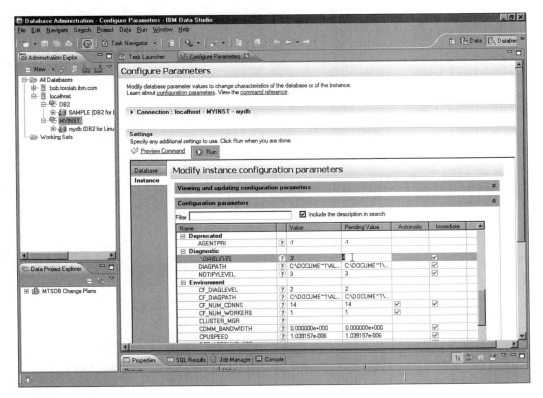

Figure 5.13   Configuring an instance from IBM Data Studio

To change values for the parameters, click the **Pending Value** cell and enter the new value. Notice also that the parameter is marked with an asterisk (*), indicating that there is a change but the change is not saved yet.

When you are ready, you can review the command generated by IBM Data Studio with the **Preview Command** link. From there, you can choose to edit, run, and save the command.

> **NOTE**
>
> IBM InfoSphere Configuration Manager, a separate offering, can provide further support to manage configurations of your instances. For example, this tool can provide information of historic configuration changes.

Using the DB2 Commands at the Instance Level

Table 5.2 summarizes the most common DB2 commands used at the instance level.

Table 5.2   DB2 Instance-Level Commands

Command	Explanation
db2start	Starts an instance.
db2stop	Stops an instance.
db2icrt	Creates a new instance.
db2idrop	Drops an instance.
db2ilist	Lists all available instances in your system.
get dbm cfg	Displays the Database Manager Configuration file.
update dbm cfg	Updates the Database Manager Configuration file.
reset dbm cfg	Resets the Database Manager Configuration file to its default values.

The Database Administration Server (DAS)

The Database Administration Server (DAS) is a background process that allows for remote graphical administration of your databases. If you use graphical administration tools such as the IBM Data Studio and the Replication Center graphical tools, you must have the DAS process up and running. There can only be one DAS per machine, even if there are several DB2 installation copies. Note that a DB2 10.x DAS can administer DB2 9.x instances, and a DB2 Version 9 DAS can only administer DB2 Version 9.x instances; therefore, if you have both DB2 10.x and DB2 9.x on a data server, the recommendation is to use the DAS of the latest Version 10.x.

On Linux and UNIX, a DAS user needs to be created. The DB2 profile registry variable DB2ADMINSERVER contains the value of the DAS user. Normally, it is set to *DB2DAS00* on Windows and *dasusr1* on Linux and UNIX.

> **NOTE**
>
> DB2 Administration Server and Database Administration Server are used interchangeably to refer to the DAS process.

> **NOTE**
>
> IBM Data Studio Web Console, a graphical tool that can do most of your administrative operations does not need a DAS. Learn more about this tool in Chapter 4, "Using Database Tools and Utilities."

Using the DAS Commands

Table 5.3 summarizes the most common commands for the DAS.

Table 5.3 DAS Commands

Command	Explanation
db2admin start	Starts the DAS.
db2admin stop	Stops the DAS.
dascrt	Creates the DAS in Linux and UNIX.
dasdrop	Drops the DAS in Linux and UNIX.
db2admin create	Creates the DAS in Windows.
db2admin drop	Drops the DAS in Windows.
get admin cfg	Displays the DAS admin configuration file.
update admin cfg	Updates the DAS admin configuration file.
reset admin cfg	Resets the DAS admin configuration file to its default values.

Configuring a Database

Database configuration and instance configuration are fairly similar. We use the same format to describe database configuration as we used to discuss instance configuration earlier in this chapter. Database concepts are discussed in more detail in Chapter 7, "Working with Database Objects."

A database is set up with a default configuration when you create it. You can view this configuration by running the get db cfg for *database_name* command. Listing 5.3 shows the output of this command on a Windows machine.

Listing 5.3 The Contents of the Database Configuration File

```
C:\Program Files\IBM\SQLLIB\BIN>db2 get db cfg for sample
        Database Configuration for Database sample
Database configuration release level                = 0x0f00
Database release level                              = 0x0f00
Database territory                                  = US
Database code page                                  = 1208
Database code set                                   = UTF-8
Database country/region code                        = 1
Database collating sequence                         = IDENTITY
Alternate collating sequence        (ALT_COLLATE) =
Number compatibility                                = OFF
```

```
Varchar2 compatibility                                             = OFF
Date compatibility                                                 = OFF
Database page size                                                 = 8192
Statement concentrator                          (STMT_CONC)        = OFF
Discovery support for this database             (DISCOVER_DB)      = ENABLE
Restrict access                                                    = NO
Default query optimization class                (DFT_QUERYOPT)     = 5
Degree of parallelism                           (DFT_DEGREE)       = 1
Continue upon arithmetic exceptions     (DFT_SQLMATHWARN)          = NO
Default refresh age                     (DFT_REFRESH_AGE)          = 0
Default maintained table types for opt  (DFT_MTTB_TYPES)           = SYSTEM
Number of frequent values retained      (NUM_FREQVALUES)           = 10
Number of quantiles retained             (NUM_QUANTILES)           = 20
Decimal floating point rounding mode    (DECFLT_ROUNDING)          = ROUND_HALF_
➥EVEN
Backup pending                                                     = NO
All committed transactions have been written to disk              = NO
Rollforward pending                                                = NO
Restore pending                                                    = NO
Multi-page file allocation enabled                                 = YES
Log retain for recovery status                                     = NO
User exit for logging status                                       = NO
Self tuning memory                      (SELF_TUNING_MEM)          = OFF
Size of database shared memory (4KB)    (DATABASE_MEMORY)          =
➥AUTOMATIC(37536)
Database memory threshold                       (DB_MEM_THRESH)    = 10
Max storage for lock list (4KB)                 (LOCKLIST)         = 4096
Percent. of lock lists per application          (MAXLOCKS)         = 22
Package cache size (4KB)                         (PCKCACHESZ)       = (MAXAPPLS*8)
Sort heap thres for shared sorts (4KB)  (SHEAPTHRES_SHR)           = 5000
Sort list heap (4KB)                            (SORTHEAP)         = 256
Database heap (4KB)                              (DBHEAP)          =
➥AUTOMATIC(600)
Catalog cache size (4KB)                (CATALOGCACHE_SZ)          = (MAXAPPLS*5)
Log buffer size (4KB)                           (LOGBUFSZ)         = 256
Utilities heap size (4KB)                (UTIL_HEAP_SZ)            = 5000
Buffer pool size (pages)                        (BUFFPAGE)         = 250
SQL statement heap (4KB)                        (STMTHEAP)         =
➥AUTOMATIC(2048)
Default application heap (4KB)                   (APPLHEAPSZ)       =
➥AUTOMATIC(256)
```

```
Application Memory Size (4KB)              (APPL_MEMORY) =
➡AUTOMATIC(10000)
Statistics heap size (4KB)               (STAT_HEAP_SZ) =
➡AUTOMATIC(4384)
Interval for checking deadlock (ms)         (DLCHKTIME) = 10000
Lock timeout (sec)                         (LOCKTIMEOUT) = -1
Changed pages threshold                 (CHNGPGS_THRESH) = 60
Number of asynchronous page cleaners    (NUM_IOCLEANERS) = AUTOMATIC(2)
Number of I/O servers                   (NUM_IOSERVERS) = AUTOMATIC(3)
Index sort flag                             (INDEXSORT) = YES
Sequential detect flag                      (SEQDETECT) = YES
Default prefetch size (pages)          (DFT_PREFETCH_SZ) = AUTOMATIC
Track modified pages                        (TRACKMOD) = NO
Default number of containers                           = 1
Default tablespace extentsize (pages)     (DFT_EXTENT_SZ) = 32
Max number of active applications            (MAXAPPLS) =
➡AUTOMATIC(40)
Average number of active applications       (AVG_APPLS) = AUTOMATIC(1)
Max DB files open per application            (MAXFILOP) = 32768
Log file size (4KB)                          (LOGFILSIZ) = 1000
Number of primary log files                 (LOGPRIMARY) = 3
Number of secondary log files               (LOGSECOND) = 10
Changed path to log files                   (NEWLOGPATH) =
Path to log files                                      = D:\DB2_01\
➡NODE0000\SQL00002\LOGSTREAM0000\
Overflow log path                      (OVERFLOWLOGPATH) =
Mirror log path                         (MIRRORLOGPATH) =
First active log file                                  =
Block log on disk full                 (BLK_LOG_DSK_FUL) = NO
Block non logged operations             (BLOCKNONLOGGED) = NO
Percent max primary log space by transaction  (MAX_LOG) = 0
Num. of active log files for 1 active UOW(NUM_LOG_SPAN) = 0
Percent log file reclaimed before soft chckpt (SOFTMAX) = 100
HADR database role                                     = STANDARD
HADR local host name                    (HADR_LOCAL_HOST) =
HADR local service name                  (HADR_LOCAL_SVC) =
HADR remote host name                   (HADR_REMOTE_HOST) =
HADR remote service name                 (HADR_REMOTE_SVC) =
HADR instance name of remote server    (HADR_REMOTE_INST) =
HADR timeout value                          (HADR_TIMEOUT) = 120
HADR target list                        (HADR_TARGET_LIST) =
```

```
HADR log write synchronization mode     (HADR_SYNCMODE) = NEARSYNC
HADR spool log data limit (4KB)      (HADR_SPOOL_LIMIT) = 0
HADR log replay delay (seconds)     (HADR_REPLAY_DELAY) = 0
HADR peer window duration (seconds)   (HADR_PEER_WINDOW) = 0
First log archive method                  (LOGARCHMETH1) = OFF
Archive compression for logarchmeth1     (LOGARCHCOMPR1) = OFF
Options for logarchmeth1                    (LOGARCHOPT1) =
Second log archive method                 (LOGARCHMETH2) = OFF
Archive compression for logarchmeth2     (LOGARCHCOMPR2) = OFF
Options for logarchmeth2                    (LOGARCHOPT2) =
Failover log archive path                   (FAILARCHPATH) =
Number of log archive retries on error    (NUMARCHRETRY) = 5
Log archive retry Delay (secs)          (ARCHRETRYDELAY) = 20
Vendor options                                (VENDOROPT) =
Auto restart enabled                        (AUTORESTART) = ON
Index re-creation time and redo index build  (INDEXREC) = SYSTEM
➥(RESTART)
Log pages during index build             (LOGINDEXBUILD) = OFF
Default number of loadrec sessions      (DFT_LOADREC_SES) = 1
Number of database backups to retain    (NUM_DB_BACKUPS) = 12
Recovery history retention (days)       (REC_HIS_RETENTN) = 366
Auto deletion of recovery objects      (AUTO_DEL_REC_OBJ) = OFF
TSM management class                        (TSM_MGMTCLASS) =
TSM node name                                (TSM_NODENAME) =
TSM owner                                       (TSM_OWNER) =
TSM password                                 (TSM_PASSWORD) =
Automatic maintenance                         (AUTO_MAINT) = ON
  Automatic database backup               (AUTO_DB_BACKUP) = OFF
  Automatic table maintenance             (AUTO_TBL_MAINT) = ON
    Automatic runstats                     (AUTO_RUNSTATS) = ON
      Real-time statistics               (AUTO_STMT_STATS) = ON
      Statistical views               (AUTO_STATS_VIEWS) = OFF
      Automatic sampling                  (AUTO_SAMPLING) = OFF
    Automatic statistics profiling      (AUTO_STATS_PROF) = OFF
      Statistics profile updates          (AUTO_PROF_UPD) = OFF
    Automatic reorganization                 (AUTO_REORG) = OFF
Auto-Revalidation                             (AUTO_REVAL) = DEFERRED
Currently Committed                           (CUR_COMMIT) = ON
CHAR output with DECIMAL input           (DEC_TO_CHAR_FMT) = NEW
Enable XML Character operations           (ENABLE_XMLCHAR) = YES
```

```
WLM Collection Interval (minutes)        (WLM_COLLECT_INT) = 0
Monitor Collect Settings
Request metrics                          (MON_REQ_METRICS) = BASE
Activity metrics                         (MON_ACT_METRICS) = BASE
Object metrics                           (MON_OBJ_METRICS) = EXTENDED
Unit of work events                        (MON_UOW_DATA) = NONE
   UOW events with package list         (MON_UOW_PKGLIST) = OFF
   UOW events with executable list     (MON_UOW_EXECLIST) = OFF
Lock timeout events                      (MON_LOCKTIMEOUT) = NONE
Deadlock events                            (MON_DEADLOCK) = WITHOUT_HIST
Lock wait events                           (MON_LOCKWAIT) = NONE
Lock wait event threshold                 (MON_LW_THRESH) = 5000000
Number of package list entries           (MON_PKGLIST_SZ) = 32
Lock event notification level           (MON_LCK_MSG_LVL) = 1
SMTP Server                               (SMTP_SERVER) =
SQL conditional compilation flags          (SQL_CCFLAGS) =
Section actuals setting                 (SECTION_ACTUALS) = NONE
Connect procedure                         (CONNECT_PROC) =
Adjust temporal SYSTEM_TIME period (SYSTIME_PERIOD_ADJ) = NO
Log DDL Statements                        (LOG_DDL_STMTS) = NO
Log Application Information               (LOG_APPL_INFO) = NO
Default data capture on new Schemas    (DFT_SCHEMAS_DCC) = NO
Database is in write suspend state                       = NO
```

<blockquote>

NOTE

If you are connected to a database, issuing the command `get db cfg` displays the contents of database configuration file; you don't need to specify the database name as part of the command.

</blockquote>

In this book, you learn some of the more important database configuration parameters. For a full treatment of all database configuration parameters, refer to the **DB2 Information Center > Database fundamentals > Configuring > Database Manager configuration parameters**.

To update one or more parameters in the database configuration file, issue the command `update db cfg for` *database_name*
      `using parameter_name value  parameter_name value...`

For example, to update the CHNGPGS_THRESH database configuration parameter in the *sample* database to a value of 20, issue the command

```
update db cfg for sample using CHNGPGS_THRESH 20
```

Issuing the `get db cfg for database_name` command after the `update db cfg` command shows the newly updated values. However, this does not mean the change will take effect right away. Several parameters in the database configuration file require all connections to be removed before the changes take effect on the first new connection to the database. In most production environments, this is the same as an outage as it is not possible to disconnect all users. For other parameters, the update is dynamic, and the new value takes effect immediately after executing the command; these are called **configurable online parameters**.

> **NOTE**
>
> Configurable online parameters of the database configuration file can be updated dynamically only if you first connect to the database. If a database connection has not been performed, the parameter is not changed immediately, but after all connections are removed.

IBM Data Studio provides the list of database configuration parameters. Parameters with a check mark under the column *Immediate* are configurable online. Refer to the "Configuring a Database" section from IBM Data Studio for details.

To get the current, effective setting for each configuration parameter along with the value of the parameter on the first new connection to the database after all connections are removed, use the `show detail` option of the `get db cfg` command.

This option requires a database connection. If you run this command after changing the CHNGPGS_THRESH configuration parameter as just shown, you see that the current value is 80, but the next effective or delayed value is 20. The related output from the `get db cfg show detail` command would look like the following:

```
C:\Program Files\SQLLIB\BIN>db2 get db cfg for sample show detail
Description                         Parameter              Current Value     Delayed Value
----------------------------------------------------------------------------------------

...

Changed pages threshold             (CHNGPGS_THRESH) =         80                 20
```

For parameters with value AUTOMATIC, the `get db cfg` command also shows the actual value of parameters. For example, when you issue the `get db cfg` command while connected to a database, you could see output like the following for the MAXAPPLS parameter:

```
C:\Program Files\SQLLIB\BIN>db2 get db cfg
...
Max number of active applications      (MAXAPPLS) =    AUTOMATIC(40)
```

To reset all the database configuration parameters to their default values, use the command reset db cfg for *database_name*.

Configuring a Database from IBM Data Studio

If you prefer a graphical tool to configure your database, IBM Data Studio is what you need. Right-click the database you want to configure, and a set of menus displays, as shown in Figure 5.14.

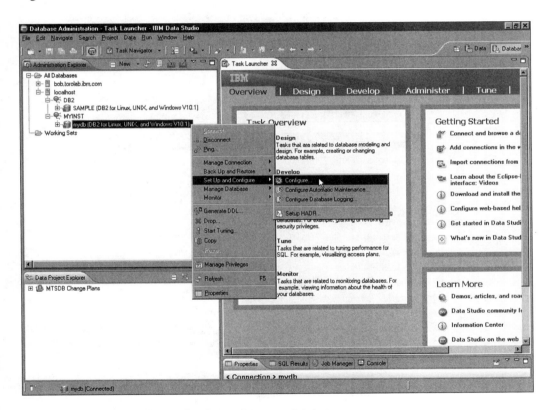

Figure 5.14   Using IBM Data Studio to manage a database

The menu options are self-explanatory: From the menu, you can connect and disconnect from the database, ping the database, backup and restore the database, monitor the database, manage data access privileges, and many other tasks.

To configure the database, select **Set Up and Configure > Configure**. On the **Configure Parameters** tab, in Figure 5.15, you see a list of parameters. They are organized into groups based on the purpose of the parameters. Notice that there is a *Deprecated* group, indicating that these parameters are deprecated and you should use the replacement parameters as soon as possible. Deprecated parameters might be discontinued in the next release.

If you are not familiar with the definition of a parameter, hover the mouse over the row of interest and get an information dialog. Same as modifying the database manager configuration parameter, double-click the row and enter the new value.

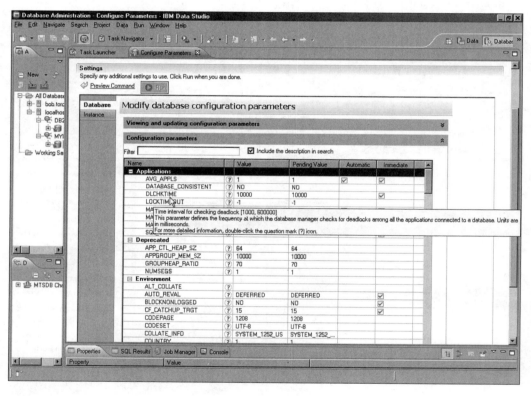

Figure 5.15   Using the Data Studio to configure a database

If you select the menu **Manage Database** as shown in Figure 5.16, you can **Start** and **Stop** the database. There are no explicit commands to stop and start a database. To "stop" a database, the `deactivate database` command is executed to stop all services or process needed by the database and release the memory. To "start" a database, it executes the `activate database` command. The command activates a database by allocating all the necessary database memory and services or processes required. The first connection to the database normally performs these operations; therefore, by using the `activate database` command before connecting to the database, the first connection no longer has to pay the price of this extra overhead.

A *Restart* option is also available under the *Manage Database* menu. The option maps to the `restart database` command, which you can use for recovery purposes when a database is left in an inconsistent state after a crash recovery. Don't use this command if you only want the new value of a database configuration parameter that is not dynamic to take effect. Instead, use the `force applications` command or ensure all applications disconnect from the database.

In Figure 5.16 you also see another two options: *Quiesce* and *Unquiesce*. In some situations, database administrators want to perform some administrative tasks that require exclusive use of the database. They want to avoid restarting the database. You might consider using the *Quiesce* function to force all users off the database and put it into a quiesced mode. While the database is in this mode, no new connections can be made to the database. You can perform administrative tasks on it. *Unquiesce* the database after the tasks are complete.

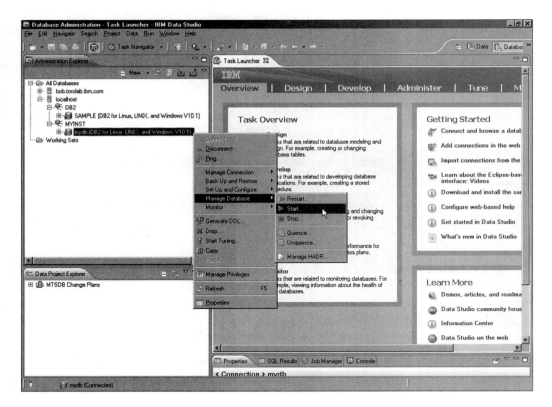

Figure 5.16   Manage database menu in Data Studio

> **NOTE**
>
> You can use the IBM InfoSphere Optim Configuration Manager to manage your database configurations. All configuration changes are recorded, which can be used to analyze activities on your database system.

Using the DB2 Commands at the Database Level

Table 5.4 summarizes the most common commands used to configure a database. For more information about database concepts, refer to Chapter 7, "Working with Database Objects."

> **NOTE**
>
> If a DB2 registry variable, Database Manager Configuration parameter, or database configuration parameter accepts only Boolean values, the values YES and ON and the values NO and OFF respectively are equivalent.

Table 5.4   The DB2 Database-Level Commands

Command	Explanation
get db cfg	Displays the database configuration file.
update db cfg	Updates the database configuration file.
reset db cfg	Resets the database configuration file to its default values.

Use of these commands are the same as that of the instance level (database manager configuration) commands. To update one or more parameters in the DB Configuration file, issue the command

```
update db cfg
      using parameter_name value parameter_name value ...
```

For example, to update the SORTHEAP DB Configuration parameter, issue the following command:

```
      update db cfg using SORTHEAP 5000
```

The Configuration Advisor

If you are new to DB2, it can be overwhelming to understand what each instance and database parameters are for and what value to set them to. Fortunately, DB2 has the Configuration Advisor tool to help DB2 tune itself. For better results, you need to provide the tool the characteristics of your system and workload.

You can invoke the Configuration Advisor using the command AUTOCONFIGURE, as shown in Listing 5.4.

Listing 5.4   The autoconfigure Command

```
>>-AUTOCONFIGURE--+-----------------------------------------+----->
                  |             .--------------------------. |
                  |             V                          | |
                  '-USING----input-keyword--param-value-+-'

>--+----------------------+-----------------------------------><
   |          .-DB ONLY----. |
   '-APPLY--+-DB AND DBM-+-'
            '-NONE------'
```

Table 5.5 lists and describes the input keywords.

Table 5.5   Autoconfigure Keywords

Keyword	Valid Values [Default]	Explanation
mem_percent	1–100 [80]	Percentage of memory to dedicate. If applications other than the operating system are running on this server, set this to less than 100.
Workload_type	simple, mixed, complex [mixed]	Simple workloads tend to be I/O intensive and mostly transactions, whereas complex workloads tend to be CPU-intensive and mostly queries.
num_stmts	1–1000000 [10]	Number of statements per unit of work.
Tpm	1–50000 [60]	Transactions per minute.
admin_priority	performance, recovery, both [both]	Optimize for better performance (more transactions per minute) or better recovery time.
is_populated	yes, no [yes]	Whether the database is populated with data.
num_local_apps	0–5000 [0]	Number of connected local applications.
num_remote_apps	0–5000 [10]	Number of connected remote applications.
Isolation	RR, RS, CS, UR [CS]	Isolation level of applications connecting to this database (Repeatable Read, Read Stability, Cursor Stability, Uncommitted Read).
bp_resizeable	yes, no [yes]	Whether the buffer pools are resizable.

The `autoconfigure` command enables you to apply the suggested changes to the database only (`DB ONLY`), the database and the database manager (`DB AND DBM`), or not apply the suggested changes at all (`NONE`).

The Configuration Advisor can be used to obtain an initial set of values for DB2 configuration parameters. Moreover, it is run automatically, with default values, when you invoke the `CREATE DATABASE` command. If you want to pass specific values to the tool when creating a database, invoke explicitly the `autoconfigure` command as an option of the `CREATE DATABASE` command:

```
CREATE DATABASE mydb
     AUTOCONFIGURE using mem_percent 75 APPLY DB AND DBM
```

The `autoconfigure` command can also be invoked using the `ADMIN_CMD` stored procedure so that the command can be programmed in an SQL script or called from another stored procedure.

You can enable or disable this feature by setting the following registry variable before creating a database.

```
db2set DB2_ENABLE_AUTOCONFIG_DEFAULT=YES
db2set DB2_ENABLE_AUTOCONFIG_DEFAULT=NO
```

Setting it to YES means the Configuration Advisor automatically runs when you create a database. If you set it to NO, you can still run the Configuration Advisor manually afterward.

Design Considerations for Instances and Databases

Now that you are familiar with the concepts of instances and how to configure instances and databases, you might be wondering about design issues. Is it better to have one instance or multiple instances per server? Is it better to have one database or multiple databases per instance?

You might want to have multiple instances per server for the following reasons.

- You want to separate your development and test environments, but you cannot afford to have different servers.

- For security reasons, you want to have different instances. As you see in Chapter 8, "Implementing Security," you can grant SYSADM authority to an operating system group by assigning the name of this group to the SYSADM_GROUP Database Manager Configuration parameter. For example, if not all system administrators should have access to the PAYROLL database, you can put this database in its own instance and create an operating system group with only authorized user IDs, which you would then assign to SYSADM_GROUP. The other instances would have another operating system group assigned to their own SYSADM_GROUP Database Manager Configuration parameters.

- You want to configure instances differently depending on your application. For example, the INTRA_PARALLEL Database Manager Configuration parameter should be set to NO when the workload is OLTP type but set to YES when the workload is OLAP (or DSS) type. Because this is an instance-level parameter, all the databases inside the instance use the same setting. Creating databases that will be used for either OLTP or OLAP in different instances allow you to set INTRA_PARALLEL correctly for each case.

If this does not apply to you, in a production environment, we recommend having one instance per server (physical or virtual) and one database per instance; this guarantees that all resources are allocated to that one database and instance. Because server virtualization is the typical environment these days, do take virtualization into account as you are doing server capacity planning.

> **NOTE**
>
> OLTP stands for online transaction processing. The OLTP type of workload implies short transactions performing simple `SELECT`, `INSERT`, `UPDATE`, and `DELETE` operations, affecting a small number of rows. In reality, there are few databases used only for pure OLTP workloads. Most databases are used for a mixed workload.
>
> OLAP stands for online analytical processing and DSS for decision support systems. OLAP and DSS have similar types of workload, and they imply complex `SELECT` statements, normally using several `JOIN` operations.

If you do decide to create multiple instances on a server, remember that an instance consumes some resources when started. When the instance is started and system resources for the database manager are reserved, the instance itself does not consume many more resources. However, databases inside the instances can consume a lot of memory depending, for example, on the size of their buffer pools. In other words, you need to find the right balance between the number of instances on a server and the number of databases within each instance.

Keep in mind that when you have many instances, each with many databases, the memory used by all the databases and instances when they are active should be less than the physical memory of the machine; otherwise paging or swapping occur, which affects the performance of the entire system. With 64-bit instances, these memory limitations are reduced.

Case Study

You have just returned from a DB2 training class and would like to practice what you have learned by changing some DB2 registry variables and configuration parameters. The test system you are working with has one instance called *DB2* and two databases, *mydb* and *testdb*.

In case you need to go back to the current configuration, you first save the contents of your configuration files by simply redirecting the output to files.

```
db2set -all > db2set.bk
db2 get dbm cfg > dbmcfg.bk
db2 get db cfg for mydb > dbcfg_mydb.bk
db2 get db cfg for testdb > dbcfg_testdb.bk
set > environmentVariables.bk
```

If you do need to go back to your current configuration, review the contents of these files and enter the appropriate commands to set your environment variables correctly (set/export), DBM Configuration file (update dbm cfg), database configuration file (update db cfg), and DB2 registry variables (db2set).

You are not sure which *DB2* instance is the current active one. Therefore you enter two commands:

```
db2ilist
```

and

```
db2 get instance
```

The first command lists all instances in your server; in this case, there is only one instance, *DB2*. The second command shows you that the *DB2* instance is the current active instance.

You like to reuse CLP commands that you have typed before, therefore you decide to increase the number of CLP commands that are kept as "history." You don't quite remember which DB2 registry variable has to be modified, so you issue the command

```
db2set -lr
```

This lists all the DB2 registry variables you can set. You review the list and recognize the registry variable you need: DB2_CLP_HISTSIZE (discussed in Chapter 4). You issue the command

```
db2set DB2_CLP_HISTSIZE=50
```

This command sets the DB2_CLP_HISTSIZE registry variable only for the active instance because the -i option is the default.

You decide to make this change globally, so you issue:

```
db2set DB2_CLP_HISTSIZE=50    -g
```

You make sure that there are no spaces before and after the equal (=) sign to avoid getting an error. You confirm that the registry variable is set by issuing the command

```
db2set -all
```

You notice the same variable is set twice: once at the instance level (denoted by [i]), the other at the global level (denoted by [g]). You change your mind and decide to set this registry variable only for the current instance, not globally. You unset the registry variable as follows:

```
db2set DB2_CLP_HISTSIZE=    -g
```

As indicated in Table 5.1, to unset the value of a DB2 registry variable, leave a blank after the equal sign.

You have to bring the instance down and then up by issuing the commands `db2stop` and `db2start` to ensure that the new registry variable value takes effect. Because you are planning to make other changes that might require an instance restart, you decide to wait until you finish all your changes.

After issuing the `get dbm cfg` command, you decide to change to the SHEAPTHRES parameter from 0 to 20005. You reverse the change afterward, as you are only testing what you have learned about instance commands for now. You issue the command

```
db2 update dbm cfg using SHEAPTHRES 20005
```

You want to see the current and delayed values for this parameter, so you issue

```
db2 get dbm cfg show detail
```

You want to make changes to your database configuration. You check your system with the `list applications` command. You know there are two databases in the instance, *mydb* and *testdb*. The output of the command shows that there are no connections to *mydb*, but *testdb* has 10 users connected to it.

Also, other users are working heavily on the test machine, which is running other software. Because you don't want to interfere with their work, you don't want to connect to the mydb database; this would allocate memory for the different database resources. Nonetheless, you do realize that making changes to a Database Configuration parameter does not require you to be connected to the database. After all, the database configuration is a binary file, so you are simply updating this file, and the database does not need to be active. You issue this command to increase the sort heap:

```
db2 update db cfg for mydb using SORTHEAP 1024
```

Because you are not connected to the database, you must specify the database name as part of the command. Given that the database is down, you don't really care whether the parameter SORTHEAP is configurable online or not. The next time there is a connection to the database, the new value will take effect. You do want to make sure the value has indeed been set to 1024, so you issue

```
db2 get db cfg for mydb
```

You feel you have done enough hands-on practice for the day. You revert the changes you didn't really want back to the way they were and then issue the `db2stop` and `db2start` commands so that other users can also use the test system.

Summary

This chapter discussed the DB2 environment and its environment variables and DB2 profile registry. It explained how to list the contents of environment variables and how to modify them either temporarily or permanently.

How to manipulate the DB2 profile registry variables with the `db2set` command was also covered. The different levels of the DB2 profile registry were explained, as well as the priority that DB2 takes into consideration when the same variable is set at different levels.

There was a detailed explanation of instances, and it showed how an instance can be created, dropped, started, stopped, and configured. For non-root Linux/UNIX installations, some of the instance administration was different, and this was pointed out. It also described the Database Administration Server (DAS), which is a background process that needs to be running at the database server to allow remote IBM Data Studio clients to graphically administer a database server. The chapter also discussed the similarity between configuring instance and database configuration parameters.

After reading this chapter, you should have a solid background on how to work and manage instances as well as how to configure a database.

Review Questions

1. Which environment variable determines the current active instance on your database server?

2. How can you set up your DB2 environment in Linux or UNIX?

3. Which command can you use to remove the DB2COMM registry variable from the DB2 Global-Level Profile Registry?

4. Which command can you use to list all the instances in your server?

5. What authority is required to create a *DB2* instance on Linux or UNIX?

6. What authority is required to create a *DB2* instance on Windows?

7. What command can be used to remove an unneeded instance from your server?

8. You want to perform the `get dbm cfg show detail` command. What command do you have to issue first?

9. What can you do to gain exclusive access to an instance?

10. What is the difference between an attachment and a connection?

11. Which of the following commands list all of the available registry variables in DB2?

    A.   db2set -a
    B.   db2set -all
    C.   db2set -lr
    D.   b2set -ltr

12. Which two of the following are not database configuration parameters?

    A.   SHEAPTHRES
    B.   SHEAPTHRES_SHR
    C.   BUFFPAGE
    D.   MAX_QUERYDEGREE
    E.   MAXLOCKS

13. You have three databases: one for development, one for testing, and one for production. To ensure that an error in an application in the development database will not affect the other databases, how would you configure these databases?

    A.   Combine them into one database using different schemas
    B.   Create all the databases in the same instance
    C.   Put each database on a different drive/file system on the server
    D.   Create each database in a different instance

14. Which of the following commands will show the current and delayed values for the Database Manager Configuration parameters?

    A.   `get dbm cfg`
    B.   `get dbm cfg show detail`
    C.   `get dbm cfg show all`
    D.   `get complete dbm cfg`

15. Which of the following commands updates the DAS configuration?

    A.   `das update cfg`
    B.   `db2 update dbm cfg for das`
    C.   `db2admin update cfg`
    D.   `db2 update admin cfg`

16. Which of the following commands changes the DAS configuration back to the default values?

    A.   `das reset cfg`
    B.   `db2 reset dbm cfg for das`
    C.   `db2admin reset cfg`
    D.   `db2 reset admin cfg`

17. Which of the following commands stops the *DB2* instance even if there are active connections to databases in the instance?

    A.   `db2 force applications all`
    B.   `db2 stop all applications`
    C.   `db2stop force`
    D.   `db2stop applications all`

18. Which of the following commands/statements requires an attachment to a remote instance?

A.   `db2 list applications`
B.   `db2 list db directory`
C.   `db2 select * from employee`
D.   `db2 create database mydb`

19. Which of the following commands can be used to review the contents of the Database Configuration file for the database to which you are currently connected?

A.   `db2 list database configuration`
B.   `db2 list db cfg`
C.   `db2 get dbm cfg`
D.   `db2 get db cfg`

20. Which two of the following commands do not set the value of the INTRA_PARALLEL parameter to YES?

A.   `db2 update database manager configuration using INTRA_PARALLEL YES`
B.   `db2 update dbm cfg using INTRA_PARALLEL 1`
C.   `db2 update dbm cfg using INTRA_PARALLEL ON`
D.   `db2 update database configuration using INTRA_PARALLEL YES`

Configuring Client and Server Connectivity

Before you can perform any work on a database, you first need to connect to it, either from the same system or from a remote client system. We call the system where your database resides a DB2 server and the system where you issue your commands to connect, the client. It is possible that the same system acts as both the DB2 server and the client. In this chapter, you learn what needs to be installed and what needs to be configured in your DB2 server and your client.

In this chapter, you learn about

- The DB2 directories used for connectivity
- How to configure database connections manually using DB2 commands
- How to connect from IBM Data Studio and other JDBC applications
- How to diagnose DB2 connectivity problems

NOTE

In this chapter, we only describe database connectivity using the TCPIP protocol. DB2 also supports named pipes. For discussion on named pipes connectivity and set up, refer to the **DB2 Information Center > Database fundamentals > Configuring > Configuring IBM data server client communications**.

Client and Server Connectivity: The Big Picture

Figure 6.1 provides the big picture of client and DB2 server connectivity. It shows the different parties and components involved.

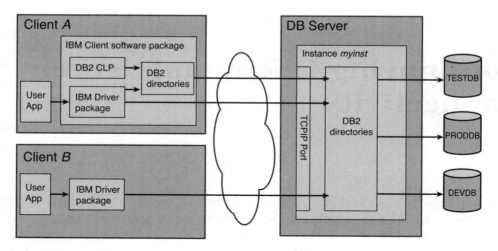

Figure 6.1   The big picture of client and server connectivity

On the right side of the figure, you see a DB2 server with three databases, TESTDB, PRODDB, and DEVDB associated to instance *myinst*. The database administrator must first configure the DB2 server so that TCPIP listeners are enabled and listening on the port reserved for the *myinst* instance. The database administrator also has to work with the system administrator to create operating system user IDs and passwords authorized to connect to the databases.

On the left side of the figure, there are two client systems: Client A and Client B. Client A has Data Server Client installed. The software includes tools such as the DB2 Command Line Processor (CLP) and also the Data Server Driver Package. Client B, on the other hand, only has the Data Server Driver Package installed or copied to the appropriate paths.

From Client A, the user enters the information he gets from the DB2 server database administrator into DB2 directories. DB2 directories are binary files that store information about which databases you can connect to from your client and how to connect to them. When the DB2 directory information is populated properly, you can connect to the desired database from the DB2 CLP.

If you want to connect from a user application, this application invokes the APIs of the driver package to connect to the DB2 server. Depending on the type of driver, the information might or might not access DB2 directories. For example, a JDBC Type 2 application needs to retrieve connectivity information from the DB2 directories; on the other hand, a JDBC Type 4 application does not retrieve information from the DB2 directories. Instead, the connection information is included in the connection string of the program itself. In fact, if you only want to run JDBC Type 4 applications from your client, you don't even have to install Data Server Client; you can simply install an Data Server Driver Package as shown for client B. Data Server Driver Packages have much smaller footprint than the Data Server Client.

All aspects required to connect from clients to DB2 servers are covered in the following sections. We show you how to populate the information into the DB2 directories using DB2 commands.

The DB2 Database Directories

This section describes the DB2 database directories (DB2 directories) and how they are related. Consider the following statement used to connect to the database with the name or alias *sample*:

```
CONNECT TO sample
```

Given only the database name or alias, how does DB2 know how to find the database *sample*? If *sample* resides on a remote server, how does the client know how to connect to that server?

All database and server information is stored in the DB2 directories. Table 6.1 lists these directories and the corresponding commands to view, insert, and delete their contents. More detailed information about the directories and commands is presented in the next sections.

Table 6.1   The Commands to View, Insert, and Delete the Contents of the DB2 Directories

Directory Name	Command to View Contents	Command to Insert Contents	Command to Delete Contents

System database	`list db directory`
	
	or
	
	`list database directory`
		`catalog db` (for remote and local databases)
		
		or
		
		`create database` (for local databases only)
			`uncatalog db` (for remote and local databases)
			
			or
			
			`drop database` (for local databases only)

Local database	`list db directory on path/drive`
	
	or
	
	`list database directory on path/drive`
		`create database` (for local databases only)	`drop database` (for local databases only)

Node	`list node directory`	`catalog TCPIP node`	`uncatalog node`
DCS	`list dcs directory`	`catalog DCS database`	`uncatalog DCS database`

Note that you cannot update an entry you entered with the `catalog` command. You have to delete the entry with the `uncatalog` command first and then insert the correct or updated entry using the `catalog` command.

The DB2 Database Directories: An Analogy Using a Book

To understand how the DB2 directories work let's use an analogy. Above the dotted line in Figure 6.2 is the table of contents for a book called *The World*. This table of contents shows that the book is divided into several parts. If you jump to any of these parts, you see a subset of the table of contents. The Resources section presents information about other books; with that information you can find a given book in a library or bookstore or on the Internet, and after you find the book, the process repeats itself where you first review the table of contents for that book and then look at its different parts.

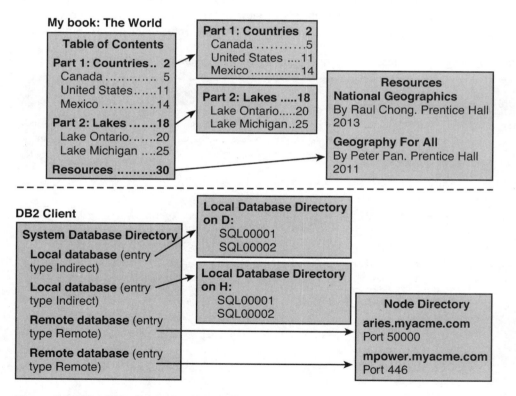

Figure 6.2   The DB2 directories: A book analogy

Similarly, with DB2 directories (shown below the dotted line), whenever you issue a CON-NECT TO <database> statement, DB2 looks for the information in the *system database directory*, which is equivalent to the table of contents: It shows all the databases available for you to connect (or attach) to from this machine. When an entry in this directory has the type *indirect*, it means the database is local (it resides in the current DB2 instance). To look for more information about this local database, you can view the *local database directory*, which is equivalent to the subset of the table of contents. When an entry in the system database directory is *remote*, it means that the database resides in a different instance than the current one, and this instance can be on a different server or the same server. Thus, you need to review the *node directory* for information about how to access this remote server or instance. This is similar to the Resources (or bibliography) section of a book, where information points to a different book with more information about a given topic.

The *Database Connection Services (DCS) directory* (not shown in Figure 6.2) contains extra information required when you connect to a host database server like DB2 for z/OS and DB2 for i.

NOTE

In this chapter, host database servers like DB2 for z/OS and DB2 for i are only used as database servers and not as clients.

The System Database Directory

As mentioned earlier, the system database directory is like a table of contents: It shows you all the databases you can connect to from your system. The system database directory is stored in a binary file with name SQLDBDIR and is in the following location.

In Windows 7, Windows 2008 R2, and Windows Server 2012 operating systems, the SQLDBDIR file for an instance called *DB2* that uses *DB2COPY1* can be found in the path C:\ProgramData\IBM\DB2\DB2COPY1\DB2\SQLDBDIR.

Note that the subdirectory SQLDBDIR in this path has the same name as the system database directory binary file (SQLDBDIR) inside it.

On Linux and UNIX, the SQLDBDIR file for an instance called *db2inst1* can be found in the path home/db2inst1/sqllib/sqldbdir.

You should not modify this file manually. To display the contents of the system database directory, use the list db directory command, as shown in Figure 6.3.

Figure 6.3   A sample DB2 system database directory

The system database directory shown in Figure 6.3 indicates that you can connect to three different databases from this system: MYHOSTDB, MYRMTDB (the alias for the database named RMTDB), and MYLOCDB. Let's examine each of these database entries in detail starting from the bottom (Database 3 entry) to the top (Database 1 entry).

The relevant fields in Database 3 entry are as follows:

- Database alias = MYLOCDB. This indicates the alias you need to use in the CONNECT statement. It must be a unique name within the system database directory.

- Database name = MYLOCDB. This is the actual database name. For this particular entry it is the same as the alias name.

- Directory entry type = Indirect. An entry type of Indirect means that the database is local; that is, it resides in the same instance where you are currently working.

- Database Drive = H:\MYINST2. From the previous field you know this database is local. This field tells where on the server this database is stored. Note that the example in Figure 6.3 is for a Windows system. For a Linux or UNIX system the field would be *Local database directory* instead of *Database Drive*.

- Database release level = a.00. This provides an internal code that indicates to IBM technical support the version and release of DB2 that can operate on the database. For example, if you created a database with DB2 10.5 and later move this database to a system running an old DB2 version (say DB2 8.1), then, the DB2 8.1 code may not be able to be used to work on this database.

- Comment. This displays any comment that was entered when the database was cataloged with the catalog command.

- Catalog database partition number = 0. This is only applicable to environments where a database partitioning environment is in place as discussed in Chapter 2, "DB2 at a Glance: The Big Picture."

- Alternate server hostname and alternate server port number are applicable in High Availability Disaster Recovery (HADR) environments, which are not discussed in this book.

The relevant fields in Database 2 entry that have not been described yet are

- Directory entry type = Remote. An entry type of *Remote* means that the database resides on a different instance or server than the one on which you are currently working.

- Node name = *MYNODE1*. From the previous field you know this database is remote. The node name field tells the name of the entry in the node directory where you can find the information about the server and instance that hosts the database.

The relevant field in the Database 1 entry that has not been described earlier is

- Authentication = SERVER. This entry indicates the authentication type cataloged at the client. It appears when specified in the catalog command and only for REMOTE databases. In this example, a value of SERVER means that security should be handled at the server where the instance is running. Other options are discussed in Chapter 8, "Implementing Security."

The Local Database Directory

The local database directory is also stored in a file called SQLDBDIR. However, this file is different from the SQLDBDIR file for the system database directory in that it resides on every *drive* (in Windows) or *path* (in Linux or UNIX) that contains, or at some time contained, a database. It contains information only for databases on that drive/path, and it is a subset of the system database directory.

On Windows, the local database directory file for an instance called *DB2* can be found at C:\DB2\NODE0000\SQLDBDIR.

On Linux and UNIX, the local database directory file for the *db2inst1* is located at home/db2inst1/db2inst1/NODE0000/sqldbdir.

You should not modify this file manually. Use the `list db directory` on drive/path command to display the local database directory, as shown in Figure 6.4.

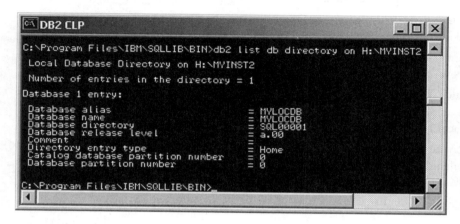

Figure 6.4   A sample DB2 local database directory

Figure 6.4 shows MYLOCDB is the only database stored in H:\MYINST2. Note that MYLOCDB also appeared in the system database directory in Figure 6.3 because the local database directory is a subset of the system database directory. In Windows, by default the `create database` command can only specify a drive, not a path, where a database is created; therefore, the command `list db directory on H:` should return the same output as `list db directory on H:\MYINST2`.

If the `DB2_CREATE_DB_ON_PATH` registry variable is set to YES, then a path can be specified. On Linux and UNIX, a path can be specified with the `create database` command; therefore, when using the `list db directory` command, specify the full path. Chapter 7, "Working with Database Objects," explains the `create database` command in detail.

The relevant information in the entry of Figure 6.4 is as follows:

Database directory = SQL00001. This is the subdirectory where the database is physically stored in your server.

The Node Directory

The node directory stores information about how to communicate to a remote instance where a given database resides. It is stored in a file called *SQLNODIR*.

On Windows 7, Windows 2008 R2, and Windows 2012 operating system, the SQLNODIR file for an instance called *DB2* that uses *DB2COPY1* can be found in the path C:\ProgramData\ IBM\DB2\DB2COPY1\DB2\SQLNODIR.

On Linux and UNIX, the SQLNODIR file for an instance called *db2inst1* can be found in the path home/db2inst1/sqllib/sqlnodir.

You should not modify this file manually. One important field in the node directory is the communication protocol used to communicate with the server, as several other fields are displayed depending on this entry. For example if the node directory contains a TCP/IP entry, the other fields provided are the IP address (or host name) of the server and the service name (or port number) of the instance where the database resides. Use the `list node directory` command as shown in Figure 6.5 to display the contents of the node directory.

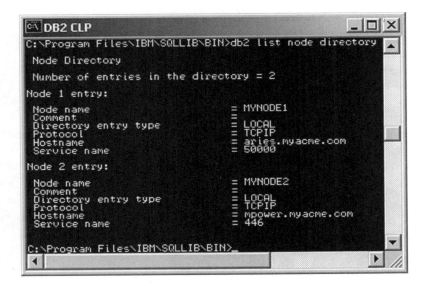

Figure 6.5 A sample DB2 node directory

There are two entries in Figure 6.5. We explain the first one in detail next (the second entry has a similar explanation and thus is not described). Node 1 entry has these relevant fields:

- Node name = *MYNODE1*. This is the name of this node entry. It was chosen arbitrarily.

- Directory entry type = LOCAL. This indicates the entry is found in the local node directory file as opposed to an LDAP server or LDAP cache, in which case the value of this field would be LDAP.

- Protocol = TCPIP. This is the communication protocol that is used to communicate with the remote system.

- Host name = aries.myacme.com. This is the host name of the remote database server. Alternatively, the IP address can be provided.

- Service Name = 50000. This is the TCP/IP port number used by the instance in the remote server to listen for connections.

> **NOTE**
>
> Because the node directory contains the information required to connect to an instance, it is not only used by the CONNECT statement but also by the attach command as described in Chapter 5, "Understanding the DB2 Environment, DB2 Instances, and Databases."

The Database Connection Services Directory

The DCS directory is required only when connecting to a host server like DB2 for z/OS and DB2 for i. This directory is available only when the DB2 Connect software is installed. Use the list dcs directory command as shown in Figure 6.6 to display the contents of the DCS directory.

Figure 6.6   A sample DCS directory

In Figure 6.6 the relevant fields are as follows:

- Local database name = MYHOSTDB. This name must match the corresponding entry in the system database directory.
- Target database name = HOSTPROD. Depending on the host, this entry corresponds to the following:

  For DB2 for z/OS: The location name of the DB2 subsystem

  For DB2 for i: The local RDB name

The Relationship Between the DB2 Directories

Now that you have a good understanding of the DB2 directories, let's see how all of them are related by using a few figures.

A Local Connection

Figure 6.7 illustrates the process of connecting to a local DB2 database. When a user issues the statement

```
CONNECT TO mylocdb USER raul USING mypsw
```

> **NOTE**
>
> You can also issue the CONNECT statement without specifying USING mypsw. DB2 prompts you for the password. That way, the password won't be shown in clear text.

DB2 follows these steps:

1. Looks for the system database directory.

2. Inside the system database directory, looks for the entry with a database alias of MYLOCDB.

3. Determines the database name that corresponds to the database alias (in Figure 6.7 the database alias and name are the same).

4. Determines if the database is local or remote by reviewing the *Directory entry type* field. In Figure 6.7, the entry type is *Indirect*, so the database is local.

5. Because the database is local, DB2 reviews the *Database drive* field, which indicates the location of the local database directory. In Figure 6.7, it is H:\MYINST2.

6. Looks for the local database directory.

7. Inside the local database directory, DB2 looks for the entry with a database alias that matches the database name of MYLOCDB.

8. Determines the physical location where the database resides by looking at the field *Database Directory*. In Figure 6.7, it is SQL00001.

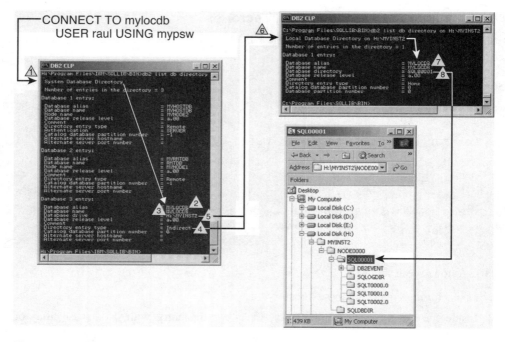

Figure 6.7   The local database connection process

A Remote Connection to a DB2 Database on Another Server

Figure 6.8 illustrates the process of connecting to a remote DB2 database. When a user issues the statement

        CONNECT TO myrmtdb USER raulrmt USING myrmtpsw

DB2 follows these steps:

1. Looks for the system database directory.

2. Inside the system database directory, looks for the entry with a database alias of MYR-MTDB.

3. Determines the database name that corresponds to the database alias. In Figure 6.8 the database name is RMTDB. This information is used later in step 8.

4. Determines if the database is local or remote by reviewing the *Directory entry type* field. In Figure 6.8, the entry type is *Remote*, so the database is remote.

5. Because the database is remote, DB2 reviews the Node name field, which indicates the entry name to look for in the node directory. In the figure, the node name is *MYNODE1*.

6. Looks for the node directory.

7. Inside the node directory, looks for the entry with a node name of *MYNODE1*.

8. Determines the physical location of the server or instance where the database resides. In this example, the TCP/IP protocol is used, so DB2 looks for the fields *Hostname* and *Service Name*. In Figure 6.8, their values are *aries.myacme.com* and *50000*, respectively. With this information and the database name obtained in step 3, DB2 initiates the connection.

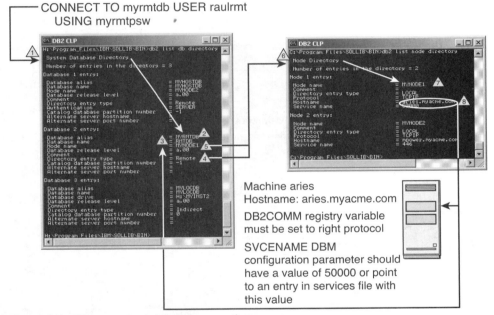

Figure 6.8 The remote database connection process

A Remote Connection to a Host DB2 Server

Figure 6.9 illustrates the process of connecting to a remote DB2 host server, which can be DB2 for z/OS or DB2 for i. When a user issues the statement

```
CONNECT TO myhostdb USER raulhost USING myhostpsw
```

DB2 follows these steps:

1. Looks for the system database directory.

2. Inside the system database directory, looks for the entry with a database alias of MYHOSTDB.

3. Determines the database name that corresponds to the database alias. (In Figure 6.9 the database name and alias are the same). This information is used later in step 9.

4. Determines if the database is local or remote by reviewing the *Directory entry type* field. In Figure 6.9, the entry type is *Remote*, so the database is remote.

5. Because the database is remote, DB2 reviews the *Node name* field, which indicates the entry name to look for in the node directory. In the figure, the node name is *MYNODE2*.

6. Looks for the node directory.

7. Inside the node directory, DB2 looks for the entry with a node name of *MYNODE2*.

8. Determines the physical location where the database resides. In this example, the TCP/IP protocol is used therefore DB2 looks for the fields *Hostname* and *Service Name*. In Figure 6.9, their values are *mpower.myacme.com* and *446*, respectively.

9. DB2 detects that this is a host database server and thus, with the database name obtained in step 3, it accesses the DCS directory.

10. Inside the DCS directory, DB2 looks for the entry with a local database name of MYHOSTDB.

11. Determines the target database name that corresponds to MYHOSTDB. In this example it is HOSTPROD. With this information and the connectivity information obtained in step 8, DB2 initiates the connection.

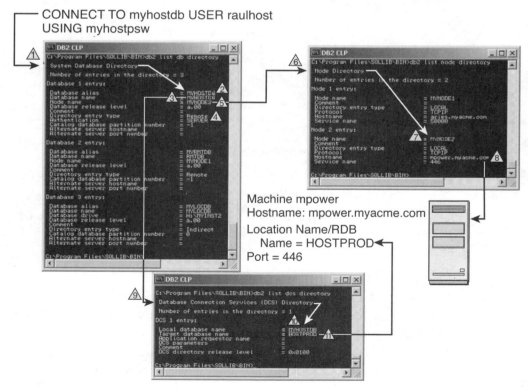

Figure 6.9   The remote host DB2 database connection process

Supported Connectivity Scenarios

In this section, we discuss the following connectivity scenarios in detail:

- **Scenario 1:** Local connection from a Data Server client to a DB2 server
- **Scenario 2:** Remote connection from a Data Server client to a DB2 server
- **Scenario 3:** Remote connection from a Data Server client to a DB2 host server
- **Scenario 4:** Remote connection from a Data Server client to a DB2 host server through a DB2 Connect gateway
- **Scenario 5:** Remote connection from an application to a DB2 server

A DB2 host server can be DB2 for z/OS or DB2 for i.

Scenario 1: Local Connection from a Data Server Client to a DB2 Server

Figure 6.10 illustrates a local connection.

Machine 1: 'Aries'
Hostname: aries.myacme.com
IP Address: 9.82.24.88
Operating System: Linux/UNIX/Windows
DB2 server installed

From the CLP issue:
CONNECT TO mylocdb
    USER myuser
    USING mypsw

Database name: MYLOCDB
User: myuser
Password: mypsw

Figure 6.10   The process of connecting locally from a Data Server client to a DB2 Server

Figure 6.10 shows one server, machine 1 *Aries*, which has a DB2 server installed. As part of the DB2 server, a Data Server client component is also installed. A local connection happens when a user connects from the Data Server client to a database in the DB2 server where both reside on the same machine.

In this configuration, the server can be any one of the DB2 server editions:

- DB2 Express-C
- DB2 Express
- DB2 Workgroup
- DB2 Enterprise
- DB2 Advanced Workgroup
- DB2 Advanced Enterprise

When you create a database with the `create database` command (or in Data Studio), an entry is automatically created in the system database directory and the local database directory.

You normally do not need to issue `catalog` commands for a local database. However, it is possible for a local database to get "lost" in the system database directory. For example, this can happen if someone issues the `uncatalog database` command to remove the database from the system database directory, or when the system database directory is reset when reinstalling DB2, or when the instance is dropped. In these cases, as long as the database was not dropped (either by the `drop database` command or using Data Studio), the database still physically exists on the system, and the entry in the system database directory is simply missing. To get the database back into the system database directory, use this command:

```
catalog db database_name [as database_alias] [on drive/path]
```

where

`drive` (Windows)/`path` (UNIX) is the location where the database files are physically stored.

When the database is cataloged, you can connect to it and use it just like before.

> **NOTE**
>
> If you drop an instance, the databases that belong to that instance are not dropped because the databases reside on different directories from that of the instance. To recover these databases, all you need to do is to create a new instance with the same name as the one dropped and catalog the databases back using the `catalog db` command.

A variation of this scenario occurs when a thin client is used. A thin client is another machine that does not have a Data Server client installed, but where a user invokes operating system commands or utilities like the Windows Terminal Service or Remote Desktop Connection (on Windows) or telnet (on Linux or UNIX) to reach the machine where a DB2 server is installed. Then any command you issue from the keyboard at the thin client is equivalent to issuing the command locally at the DB2 server, so when the `connect to` database statement is issued, the connection is also considered local.

Scenario 2: Remote Connection from a Data Server Client to a DB2 Server

In most cases, you do not have the authority to log on to the database server to perform a local database connection. Database servers are typically set up so that connections are performed through Data Server clients. In this scenario, Data Server client code is installed on a different machine from the database server machine. The connect statement is issued from the Data Server client machine. Figure 6.11 shows a connection from the machine *Libra* to a remote DB2 instance that resides on the server *Aries*.

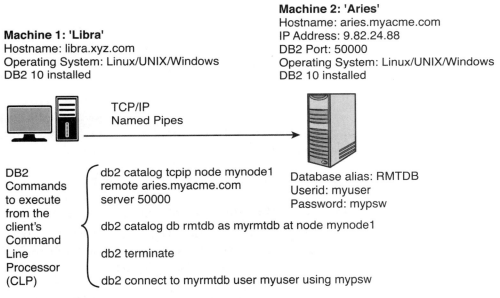

Machine 2: 'Aries'
Hostname: aries.myacme.com
IP Address: 9.82.24.88
DB2 Port: 50000
Operating System: Linux/UNIX/Windows
DB2 10 installed

Machine 1: 'Libra'
Hostname: libra.xyz.com
Operating System: Linux/UNIX/Windows
DB2 10 installed

TCP/IP
Named Pipes

DB2
Commands
to execute
from the
client's
Command
Line
Processor
(CLP)

db2 catalog tcpip node mynode1
remote aries.myacme.com
server 50000

db2 catalog db rmtdb as myrmtdb at node mynode1

db2 terminate

db2 connect to myrmtdb user myuser using mypsw

Database alias: RMTDB
Userid: myuser
Password: mypsw

Note: Named Pipes is a supported protocol if and only if client and server machines are using Windows.

Figure 6.11   The process of connecting remotely from a Data Server client to a DB2 server

In this configuration, the machine *Libra* is considered a client to database server *Aries*. The client must have one of the following installed:

- Data Server Client
- DB2 Express-C
- DB2 Express
- DB2 Workgroup
- DB2 Enterprise

- DB2 Advanced Workgroup
- DB2 Advanced Enterprise

The server must have one of the following installed:

- DB2 Express-C
- DB2 Express
- DB2 Workgroup
- DB2 Enterprise
- DB2 Advanced Workgroup
- DB2 Advanced Enterprise

The supported communication protocols are

- TCPIP
- Named Pipes (only if both the client and server are Windows)

To configure the connection shown in Figure 6.11, you need to enable the database server to accept client connections and catalog the node directory and the system database directory on the client.

The following sections describe these steps.

Enabling the Database Server to Accept Client Connections

Clients connect to the database server across the network using TCP/IP, or Named Pipes (Windows only). The server must have a process that is running to receive these connect requests. We call this process a **listener** because it "listens" to any request that comes in from the network and tells the database manager to serve it.

You need to perform the following steps on the database server to set up the listener if you are using the TCP/IP communication protocol.

1. Update the services file to reserve a TCP/IP port for the DB2 instance.

   On Linux and UNIX, the services file is located in /etc/services.

   On Windows, the services file is located in C:\Windows\System32\drivers\etc\services for 32-bit processors and C:\Windows\System64\drivers\etc\services for 64-bit processors.

The entry in the services file must look like this:

```
service_name        port_number        /tcp
```

where

`service_name` is an arbitrary name to associate with the port number.

`port_number` is the TCP/IP port number you are going to reserve for this DB2 instance. The port number must not already exist in the services file, and it should have a value of 1024 or higher for DB2 on LUW.

2. Update the SVCENAME parameter in the Database Manager Configuration file.

   Log on as the local administrator (Windows) or the instance owner (Linux or UNIX) and issue the following command from the Command Line Processor:

   ```
   update dbm cfg using svcename port_number/service_name
   ```

   You need to specify either a port number or the service name you defined in step 1.

3. Enable TCP/IP support for the instance. Issue the following command:

   ```
   db2set DB2COMM=TCPIP
   ```

4. Stop and restart the instance to make the changes you made in the previous steps effective. Issue `db2stop` and `db2start`.

> **NOTE**
>
> If you are working with the default instance created and configured by the DB2 Setup Wizard, the services file, SVCENAME, and the DB2COMM parameters are already correctly configured for you.

Cataloging the Node Directory and Database Directory on the Client

After enabling the server to accept client connections, you need to tell the client how to connect to the server. You do this by cataloging the node directory and the system database directory at the client.

DB2 has built-in support for Internet Protocol Version 6 (IPv6). IPv6 is a new version of the Internet Protocol, designed as a successor to IP version 4 (IPv4), which is what is widely in use. You can now connect to servers using either IPv4 or IPv6.

Use the information in Table 6.2 for completing the procedure in this section.

Table 6.2   TCP/IP Connectivity Worksheet

Parameter	Description	Sample Values
Host name	The host name of the remote server. Use the tcpip keyword if you want to specify the hostname instead of the IP address. You can specify the hostname regardless if the server is using an IPv4 or IPv6 address.	aries.myacme.com
IPv4 address	This is the standard 32bit IP address of the remote server specified in decimal format. You should not specify an IPv6 address with the tcpip4 keyword. The catalog command will not fail, but your subsequent connections will.	9.82.24.88
IPv6 address	This is the new 128bit IP address of the remote server specified in hexadecimal format. You should not specify the IPv4 address with the tcpip6 keyword. The catalog command will not fail, but your subsequent connections will.	1080:21DA:9C5A:2F3B:02A A:00FF:FE28:417A
Service name	The name that maps to the TCP/IP port number. The service name and port number are used interchangeably.	db2inst1
Port number	The TCP/IP port number where the instance is listening for incoming connections on the server. The service name and port number are used interchangeably.	50000
Node name	An arbitrary name used to identify the remote server. It must be unique in the client's node directory.	Mynode1
Database name	The database on the server. It is the database to which you want to connect.	RMTDB
Database alias (optional)	An alias for the database name. If specified, all connections must use this alias. If not specified, the database alias will be the same as the database name.	MYRMTDB

1. Catalog a TCP/IP node on the client:

   ```
   catalog tcpip/tcpip4/tcpip6 node nodename
   remote hostname/IPv4_address/IPv6_address
   server service_name/port_number_of_server
   ```

2. Catalog an entry in the database directory on the client:

   ```
   catalog db database_name [as database_alias] at node nodename
   ```

3. Issue a `terminate` command to flush the directory cache:

   ```
   Terminate
   ```

Table 6.3 demonstrates how to use these commands based on the examples shown in Figure 6.11 and Figure 6.12. Figure 6.11 and Figure 6.12 show the three node directory entries and three system database directory entries, respectively, for remote connection to their respective databases. The information in this table applies to all Linux, UNIX, and Windows platforms.

Table 6.3   Example of Configuring a Remote Connection to a DB2 Server Using TCP/IP

Information You Need to Obtain from Server Machine 2 (*Aries*) to Perform the Commands on Client Machine 1	Command to Run on Client Machine 1 (*Libra*)
Hostname1 = aries.myacme.com IP address = 9.82.24.87 Service name/port # in services file = db2inst 50000	```db2 catalog tcpip node mynode1 remote aries.myacme.com server 50000```
Hostname2 = aries2.myacme.com IP address = 9.82.24.88 Service name/port # in services file = db2inst1 50010	```db2 catalog tcpip4 node mynode2 remote 9.82.24.88 server db2inst1```
Hostname3 = aries.myacme.com IP address (IPv6) = 1080:21DA:9C5A:2F3B:02A A:00FF:FE28:417A Service name/port # in services file = db2inst2 50020	```db2 catalog tcpip6 node mynode3 remote 1080:21DA:9C5A:2F3B:02A A:00FF:FE28:417A server 50020```

Information You Need to Obtain from Server Machine 2 (*Aries*) to Perform the Commands on Client Machine 1	Command to Run on Client Machine 1 (*Libra*)

Database alias on Machine 2 = RMTDB
 	
Note: The database must exist in the system database directory of Machine 2. If the database alias and the database name are different, then the database alias should be used.
 	
Note: *MYRMTDBx* is an alias to the database *RMTDBx*, where x is either 1, 2, or 3. Specifying the alias is optional, but if specified, the alias is what you should use in the connect command. Otherwise, use the database name.
	`db2 catalog db rmtdb1`
	`    as myrmtdb1`
	`    at node mynode1`
	
	`db2 catalog db rmtdb2`
	`    as myrmtdb2`
	`    at node mynode2`
	
	`db2 catalog db rmtdb3`
	`    as myrmtdb3`
	`    at node mynode3`

No information needed.	`db2 terminate` Note: This command is needed to make the previous catalog commands effective.

A valid user ID and password that has CONNECT privileges to databases RMTDB1, RMTDB2 and RMTDB3. This user ID will be used from Machine 1 to connect to RMTDB.	`db2 connect to myrmtdb1`
	`    user userid using password`
	
	`db2 connect to myrmtdb2`
	`    user userid using password`
	
	`db2 connect to myrmtdb3`
	`    user userid using password`

After completing the `catalog` commands in Table 6.3, the client's database directory and node directory looks like Figures 6.12 and 6.13, respectively.

Figure 6.12 Sample client system database directory for remote connections to DB2 databases

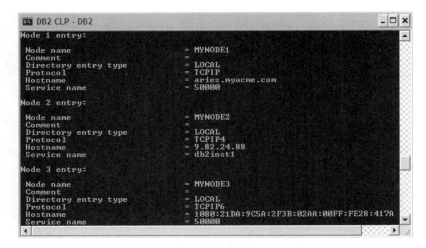

Figure 6.13 Sample client system node directory for remote connections to DB2 databases

Scenario 3: Remote Connection from a Data Server Client to a DB2 Host Server

Figure 6.14 illustrates the configuration used for this scenario. The machine *aries* is considered a client to the database server *mpower*.

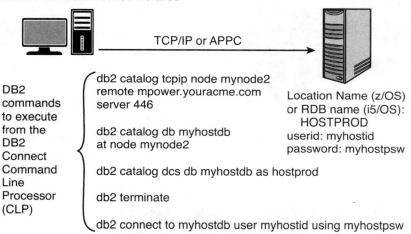

Machine 1: 'aries'
Hostname: aries.myacme.com
IP Address: 9.99.24.88
DB2 Port: 50000
Operating System: Linux/UNIX/Windows
DB2 10 Connect License installed

Machine 2: 'mpower'
Hostname: mpower.youracme.com
IP Address:158.228.20.3
DB2 Port: 446
Operating System: z/OS or i5/OS
DB2 for z/OS or DB2 for i installed

TCP/IP or APPC

DB2 commands to execute from the DB2 Connect Command Line Processor (CLP)

db2 catalog tcpip node mynode2
remote mpower.youracme.com
server 446

db2 catalog db myhostdb
at node mynode2

db2 catalog dcs db myhostdb as hostprod

db2 terminate

db2 connect to myhostdb user myhostid using myhostpsw

Location Name (z/OS)
or RDB name (i5/OS):
     HOSTPROD
userid: myhostid
password: myhostpsw

Figure 6.14   The process of connecting remotely from a Data Server client to a DB2 host server

The client must have a DB2 Connect license. The only communication protocol supported is TCP/IP.

Setting up a remote connection to a host DB2 database follows the same principle as setting up a connection to a DB2 for Linux, UNIX, and Windows database. You need to configure both the client and the server.

Enable the database server to accept client connections, and then catalog the node directory, system database directory, and DCS directory on the client.

Enabling the Database Server to Accept Client Connections

We do not go through the host database server configuration in this book. However, at a minimum, for DB2 for z/OS, make sure that the distributed data facility (DDF) is running on the mainframe. DDF is the facility in DB2 for z/OS that allows for remote communication support.

You can verify this by issuing the `-display ddf` command from the mainframe. To start DDF, issue the `-start ddf` command.

This is an example output of running the `-display ddf` (`-DIS DDF`) command:

```
DSNL080I  -DB2A DSNLTDDF DISPLAY DDF REPORT FOLLOWS:
DSNL081I STATUS=STARTD
DSNL082I LOCATION          LUNAME              GENERICLU
DSNL083I TORXLS            NETD.DB2ALU1        -NONE
DSNL084I TCPPORT=5001  SECPORT=5003  RESPORT=5002  IPNAME=-NONE
DSNL085I IPADDR=::192.168.0.61
DSNL086I SQL    DOMAIN=raul.chong.ca
DSNL105I CURRENT DDF OPTIONS ARE:
DSNL106I PKGREL = COMMIT
DSNL099I DSNLTDDF DISPLAY DDF REPORT COMPLETE
***
```

For DB2 for i, make sure the distributed data management (DDM) is started. DDM is the facility in DB2 for i that allows for remote communication support. To start DDM from the IBM i server or to verify that DDM is already started, issue

```
STRTTCPSVR SERVER(*DDM)
```

The TCPIP port 446 is usually the default value for DB2 for z/OS and DB2 for i.

Cataloging the Node Directory, Database Directory, and DCS Directory on the Client

After you have enabled the server to accept client connections, you need to tell the client how to connect to the server. You do this by cataloging the node directory, system database directory, and DCS directory on the client.

Use the information in Table 6.5 for completing the procedure in this section.

Table 6.5 TCP/IP Connectivity Worksheet for Data Server Client to DB2 Host Connection

Parameter	Description	Sample Values
Host name or IP address	The host name or IP address of the remote server.	mpower.youracme.com 158.228.10.3
Port number	The TCP/IP port number on which DB2 is listening for incoming connections on the server.	446
Node name	This is an arbitrary name and is used to identify the remote server. It must be unique in the client's node directory.	mynode2

Parameter	Description	Sample Values
Target database name	The database on the host server. For DB2 for z/OS and OS/ 390 servers, this is the *Location name*. For DB2 for i5/OS servers, this is the *RDB name*.	hostprod
Database name	An arbitrary name you would like to associate with the target database name.	myhostdb
Database alias (optional)	You can optionally specify a database alias for the database name. If specified, all connections must use this alias name; if not specified, the database alias is the same as the database name.	myhostdb

1. Catalog a TCP/IP node on the client.

   ```
   Catalog tcpip/tcpip4/tcpip6 node nodename
   remote hostname/IPv4_address/IPv6_address
       server service_name/port_number_of_server
   ```

2. Catalog a database directory on the client.

   ```
   catalog db database_name [as database_alias] at node nodename
   ```

3. Catalog a DCS database directory on the client by issuing the following command from the client's command window:

   ```
   catalog dcs db database_name as target_database_name
   ```

   The database_name field must match the database_name in the `catalog db` command in step 2.

4. Issue the `terminate` command to refresh the cache:

   ```
   terminate
   ```

Table 6.6 demonstrates how to use these commands based on the example shown in Figure 6.15.

After completing the three catalog commands in Table 6.6, the client machine's system database directory and node directory look as shown in Figure 6.15.

Table 6.6   Example of Configuring a Remote Connection to DB2 for z/OS or DB2 for i Database (Continued)

Information You Need to Obtain from Host Server Machine 2 (mpower) to Perform the Commands on Client Machine 1 (*Aries*)	Command to Run on Client Machine 1 (*Aries*)

Host name of Machine 2 = mpower.youracme.com
 	
The TCP/IP port DB2 uses = 446
	`db2 catalog tcpip node mynode2`
	`    remote mpower.youracme.com`
	`    server 446`

No information needed.	`db2 catalog db myhostdb`
	`    at node mynode2`
	
	Note: myhostdb is an arbitrary database name, but it must match the entry for the DCS directory here.

hostprod = The *Location name* if the server is DB2 for z/OS or *RDB name* if the server is DB2 for i.	`db2 catalog dcs db myhostdb` `    as hostprod`
No information needed.	`db2 terminate` Note: This command is needed to make the previous `catalog` commands effective.
A valid user ID and password that has connect privilege to the host database.	`db2 connect to myhostdb` `    user userid using password`

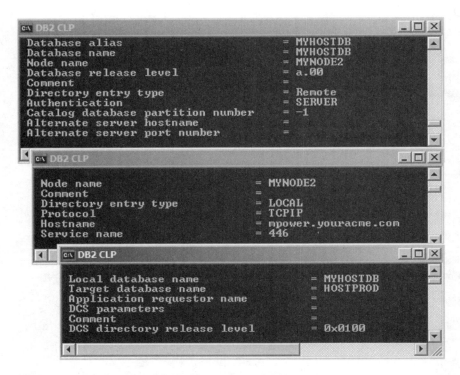

Figure 6.15 Sample client's system database directory, node directory, and DCS directory for remote connection to a DB2 host database

Scenario 4: Remote Connection from a Data Server Client to a DB2 Host Server via a DB2 Connect Gateway

Imagine you have 1,000 clients who need to connect to a host database. If you set up the connections from each client, you would need to have licenses for DB2 Connect Personal Edition for each client. This could be very costly; instead, install an appropriate DB2 Connect license such as DB2 Connect Enterprise, once on one machine, and use it as a gateway to service all connections from clients to the host database.

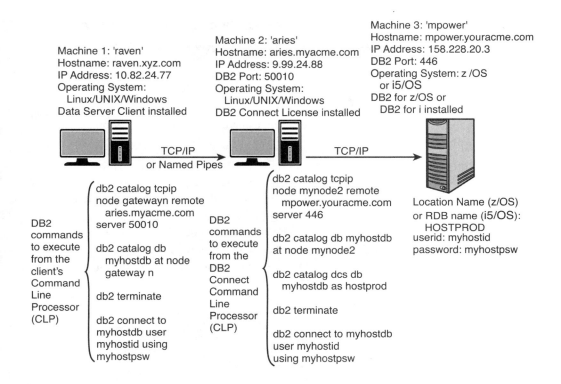

Figure 6.16 The process of connecting from a Data Server client to a DB2 server via a DB2 Connect gateway

In this configuration, Machine 1 is the client, Machine 2 is referred to as the DB2 Connect gateway, and Machine 3 is the host database server.

The DB2 Connect gateway is the only machine that needs to have DB2 Connect Enterprise edition license installed. Its task is to serve as a middleman between the clients and the host database server. The gateway machine can serve hundreds of clients.

When configuring this type of connection, you can break the three-tier connection into two parts:

- Part one is the gateway-to-host server connection. This is identical to what we discussed in "Scenario 3: Remote Connection from a Data Server Client to a DB2 Host Server." Follow the same steps Scenario 3 to configure the gateway. Make sure you can connect from the gateway to the host database before proceeding to the next step.

- Part two is the client-to-gateway connection. From the client's perspective, the gateway machine is the database server. (The client does not know anything about the host server mpower.) Thus, when configuring this part of the connection, treat the gateway as the server and follow the same steps described in "Scenario 2: Remote Connection from a Data Server Client to a DB2 Server."

Scenario 5: Remote Connection from an Application to a DB2 Server

In this section, we describe how an application can connect to a DB2 server. There are two methods under this scenario:

- The application connects to the DB2 server using connectivity information from the DB2 directories.
- The application connects to the DB2 server using connectivity information provided in the connection string.

Several programming languages such as Java or PHP allow you to connect to a DB2 database using either of these two methods. In this section we use Java to explain both methods. Java Database Connectivity (JDBC) is an API designed to work with relational databases. With JDBC there are two main types of drivers: JDBC type 2 (Native API driver) and JDBC type 4 (pure Java driver). Type 4 is the preferred option for most application developers. Because this is not an application development book, we do not explain in detail how you need to code your Java application; the main difference to note in the Java application is the connection string. Figure 6.17 illustrates the differences of both methods.

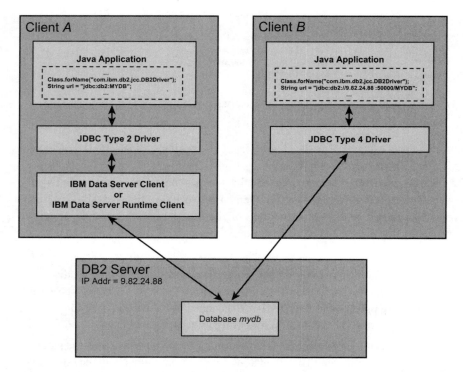

Figure 6.17   Connecting to DB2 server from applications using JDBC type 2 and JDBC type 4 connections

On the left side of Figure 6.17, Client A is running a Java application that uses JDBC Type 2. You can tell it is type 2 because of the URL in the connection string:

```
String url = "jdbc:db2:MYDB";
```

In this example, the connection string only provides the name of the database; so how will the application know where the database *mydb* is? It uses the information in the DB2 directories that come with an IBM Data Server Client, or an IBM Data Server Runtime Client.

On the right side of Figure 6.17, Client B is running another Java application, but it is using JDBC Type 4. You can tell it is type 4 because of the URL in the connection string:

```
String url = "jdbc:db2://9.82.24.88:50000/MYDB";
```

In this case, the connection string does include the IP address, the port, and the database name. There is no need to install an IBM Data Server Client or IBM Data Server Runtime Client. You can simply install or copy the JDBC drivers that come with any of these two packages:

- IBM Data Server Driver Package
- IBM Data Server Driver for JDBC and SQLJ

Alternatively, if you are not concerned about the footprint of the software you install, you can install one of the client packages, which also include the drivers.

> **NOTE**
>
> IBM Data Studio uses a JDBC Type 4 connection to DB2 servers.

DB2 Packages and the Bind Process

Some DB2 utilities are database programs with embedded SQL. These programs must be "bound" so that optimized data access plans are created for the SQL statements used in the programs. The packages reside on the database server. They are version and Fix Pack level -specific; therefore, a package created at the DB2 10, Fix Pack 1 level cannot be used by a client running at DB2 10, Fix Pack 2. If this client needs to use these utilities, it must create packages at its own DB2 level. (Refer to Chapter 7 for a more detailed explanation of packages.) Note that this might not be necessary for user applications in general.

After a client establishes a connection to a database server, it should be able to access the data in the database. If you try to run a CLI/ODBC application or issue the `import/export` commands and receive SQL0805N "Package not found" error, this is because these utilities or applications were not bound to the database server and packages were not found.

DB2 provides automatic binding of the utilities, which is performed as part of the process of applying a Fix Pack. Also for Linux and UNIX, the `db2iupdt` and `dasupdt` commands are automatically bound as part of the Fix Pack upgrade. However if, for some reason, you encounter this error, you can execute the BIND command to create the packages.

To create all of the packages for the DB2 utilities at once, run the following commands from an IBM Data Server Client's CLP window:

```
connect to database_alias user userid using password
bind @db2ubind.lst blocking all grant public
bind @db2cli.lst   blocking all grant public
```

If the database server is a host database, you must run one of the following commands on the DB2 Connect machine.

- If the host is DB2 for z/OS, use

  ```
  bind @ddcsmvs.lst blocking all grant public
  ```

- If the host is DB2 for i, use

  ```
  bind @ddcs400.lst blocking all grant public
  ```

You need to use the symbol @ when you specify a file that contains a list of bind files (with the .lst file extension), rather than a bind file (with the .bnd file extension) itself. The .lst files are in the *install_directory*\bnd directory on Windows and in the *instance_home*/sqllib/bnd directory on Linux or UNIX. Both contain a list of bind files the bind command runs against. A package is created for each of these bind files.

> **NOTE**
>
> The IBM Data Server Runtime Client does not include the required bind files, so you cannot run the bind command from a Runtime Client. You can use the IBM Data Server Client (also known as the "full" or "fat" client).

You must bind the utilities for each database you want to access. Binding only needs to be done once by a client. When a package is successfully bound to the database, all Data Server clients of the same DB2 version and Fix Pack level can use it. If you have different versions and Fix Packs of clients, you must bind the utilities for each client version and Fix Pack level.

> **NOTE**
>
> You must have BINDADD authority to create a new package in a database or BIND privilege if the package already exists.

Automatic Client Reroute Feature

What is the typical scenario for your connected client applications when there is an outage at the data server? Can your application logic handle a "SQL30081N A Communication error has been detected" error message when the application encounters a data server communication problem? Does your application simply return an application error to your user, or does it try to re-establish the connection? Even if it does, if the data server is still down, the attempt is in vain. This is where the automatic client reroute feature comes to the rescue. Automatic client reroute redirects database client application connections from a primary database server to an alternate database server if the primary database server fails or if there is a loss of communication between the client application and the primary server.

To enable the automatic client reroute feature, issue the UPDATE ALTERNATE SERVER command on the primary database.

Here is the syntax of the command:

```
UPDATE ALTERNATE SERVER FOR DATABASE database-alias
USING HOSTNAME alternate-server-hostname PORT port-number
```

To enable the client reroute feature on the TEST1 database on server1, so that all existing and new client connections will be rerouted to server2 following a takeover, issue the following command on server1:

```
UPDATE ALTERNATE SERVER FOR DATABASE test1 USING HOSTNAME
server2.torolab.ibm.com PORT 50000
```

NOTE

Port 50000 is the SVCENAME port for the database instance.

The alternate server information is stored in server1's database directory. If you issue a LIST DB DIRECTORY command, you see that the alternate server information (both the hostname and the port number) has been added:

```
Database alias                          = TEST1
Database name                           = TEST1
Local database directory                = C:
Database release level                  = b.00
Comment                                 =
Directory entry type                    = Indirect
Catalog database partition number       = 0
Alternate server hostname               = server2
Alternate server port number            = 50000
```

When a remote client application connects to this database, the alternate server information is retrieved and gets stored in the database directory of the client as well. Using this information, the client knows which server to connect to in case the primary server, *server1*, becomes unavailable.

Because the client does not get this alternate server information until it makes a connection to the primary server, the UPDATE ALTERNATE SERVER command must be issued before a takeover operation, and you must make sure that the client has at least made one successful connection to it prior to the takeover.

Application Connection Timeout Support

You can set a connection timeout value for DB2 database connections. A connection timeout value is a limit to the amount of time that an application should wait for a connection. Setting a connection timeout value is useful in case the database server is inaccessible; if not set, the client waits indefinitely for a reply from the server.

You can use the ConnectTimeout IBM Data Server Driver configuration keyword to enable connection timeout.

For example, update the *db2dsdriver.cfg* file so that all CLI /ODBC applications connecting to database MYDB22 time out after 10 seconds if a connection cannot be established:

```
<parameter name="ConnectionTimeout" value="10"/>
```

Alternatively, you can set the DB2TCP_CLIENT_CONTIMEOUT registry variable.

```
db2set DB2TCP_CLIENT_CONTIMEOUT=10
```

> **NOTE**
>
> You can configure the connect timeout support in conjunction with the automatic client reroute feature. In this case, after the connect timeouts on the primary server, client reroute takes over and re-establishes the connection on a secondary server.

TCP/IP Keepalive Timeout Support

If you are using the TCP/IP protocol to communicate between clients and servers, you can tune the IBM Data Server Driver `keepalivetimeout` parameter to timely detect whether the connection is still up and running or if it has broken.

Update the *db2dsdriver.cfg* file and use the following line to set the TCP/IP keepalive timeout to 20 seconds.

```
<parameter name="keepAliveTimeout" value="20"/>
```

Alternatively, you can set the DB2 registry variable:

```
db2set DB2TCP_CLIENT_KEEPALIVE_TIMEOUT=20
```

Diagnosing DB2 Connectivity Problems

Sometimes database connections fail. In this section, we look at some techniques to diagnose connectivity problems. Figure 6.18 illustrates what happens when you issue a CONNECT TO database statement. It also shows how the system database, node, and DCS directories are used during the process. For example, when the CONNECT TO SAMPLE statement is issued, DB2 first looks for the database *alias* SAMPLE in the system database directory. This is the alias used for the database with the name MYSAMPLE. If the alias is not found, you get an SQL1013N error. If it is found, DB2 checks whether this is a local or remote database. If it is a local database, DB2 initiates a connection to the database MYSAMPLE. If it is a remote database, DB2 checks the node directory to retrieve information about the remote server and then initiates a connection to the server.

The flowchart in Figure 6.18 shows what is involved to establish a database connection. Follow this chart to diagnose connection problems more easily.

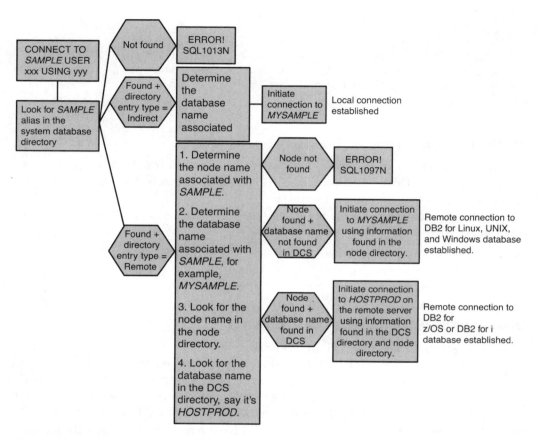

Figure 6.18   Database connection flowchart

Diagnosing Client-Server TCP/IP Connection Problems

SQL30081N Communication error and *SQL1013N Database not found* are the most common connection errors. If either of these errors occurs, you should verify the server and client configurations.

- On the server, verify that the DB2 instance is properly set up to accept client connections.

- On the client, verify that the node directory, database directory, and in the case of a host connection, the DCS directory, are set up correctly.

Verifying the Server Configuration

At the database server, follow this procedure to verify its configuration:

1. Verify that the database exists by issuing one of the following commands at the server:

   ```
   list db directory
   ```

   or

   ```
   list db directory show detail
   ```

   Figure 6.19 shows the output for the `list db directory` command.

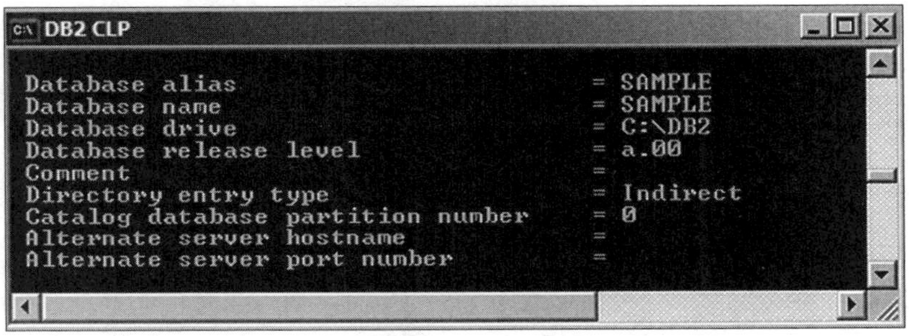

Figure 6.19 Verifying that a database exists on the server

Figure 6.19 confirms that the *sample* database resides locally on the server since the *Directory entry type* field has a value of *Indirect*. If the database resided on a different server, this field would have a value of *Remote*.

2. Check the DB2COMM registry variable to verify that the correct communication protocol is specified by using the `db2set -all` command (see Figure 6.20).

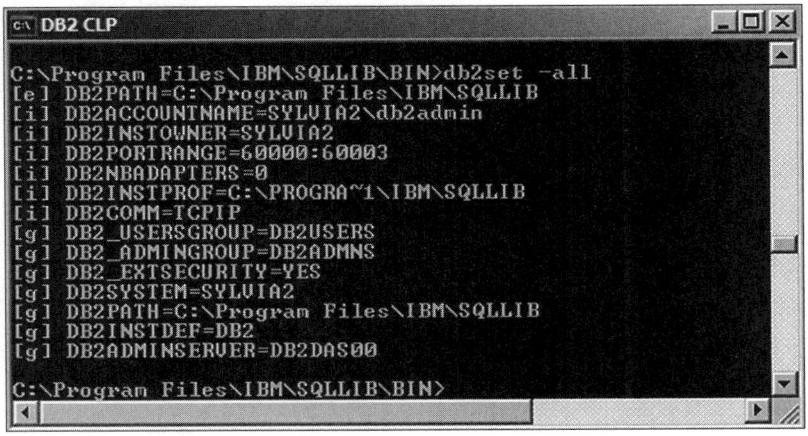

Figure 6.20 Checking the DB2COMM registry variable on the server

Figure 6.20 shows that DB2COMM is set to TCPIP; therefore, the server is ready to listen for TCP/IP requests.

3. Verify that the appropriate configuration parameters are set in the Database Manager Configuration file. Issue the `get dbm cfg` command and examine the following:

   • SVCENAME must be set to a port number or service name.

   In Figure 6.21, you can see that the SVCENAME is set to a service name, `db2c_DB2`.

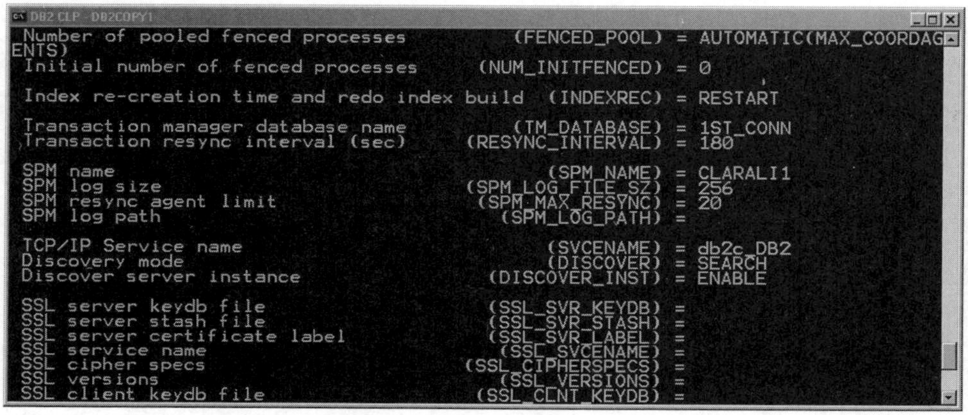

Figure 6.21   Verifying that SVCENAME is correctly set on the server

If SVCENAME is set to a service name instead of a port number, confirm that the value listed there is mapped to a unique port number in the operating system's services file. For example:

```
db2c_DB2        50000/tcp    # Connection port for DB2 instance
db2inst1
```

If this line does not exist in the services file, use a text editor to add it.

After you have made sure you can connect locally on the server and that the server is set up correctly to accept client connections, verify the client configuration.

Verifying the Client Configuration

At the client, follow these steps to verify its configuration:

1. Verify that the server connectivity information has been correctly entered in the node directory by using the `list node directory` command.

   The service name in the client's node directory is a port number that matches the port number referenced by the SVCENAME on the server. For example, the SVCENAME on the server is set to *db2c_DB2*, as shown in Figure 6.21, and as we saw, this mapped to port 50000 in the server's services file. Therefore, the client needs to specify port 50000 in the node directory, as shown in Figure 6.22.

Figure 6.22 Checking the node directory on a client

Alternatively, the client can specify a service name instead of the port number in the node directory. However, this service name needs to be defined in the client's services file, not the server's services file. For example, the node directory can have the service name *db2conn*. If this is the case, then in the client's services file, you must set *db2conn* to 50000:

```
db2conn    50000/tcp
```

2. Verify that you can ping the host name exactly as it appears in the node directory. If you cannot, that means there is a problem connecting to the server. Try to ping the IP address of the server. If that works, then recatalog the node using the IP address instead of the host name and try again.

   To recatalog the node directory, you need to first uncatalog the existing node:

   ```
   uncatalog node nodename
   ```

3. Even if the client can reach the server, it does not necessarily mean that the client can access the port to connect to databases on the server. Sometimes, for security reasons, the server port is not open to client connections, or the port is not enabled at all. To test if a port is accessible, you can telnet to the port as follows:

   ```
   telnet hostname or ip address 50000
   ```

   If DB2 is listening on that port on the server, you will see the Telnet window open, but it will hang, since DB2 is not configured to respond to the `telnet` command. This means that you have indeed reached that port on the server.

   If you get an immediate error, this means that either the server is not listening on this port (refer back to the section "Verifying the Server Configuration" to resolve this), or the port is behind a firewall and is not reachable by clients. Contact your network administrator for assistance.

4. Confirm that the correct database values appear in the database directory using the `list db directory` command. The database *name* in the client's database directory must match the database *alias* in the server's database directory (see Figure 6.23).

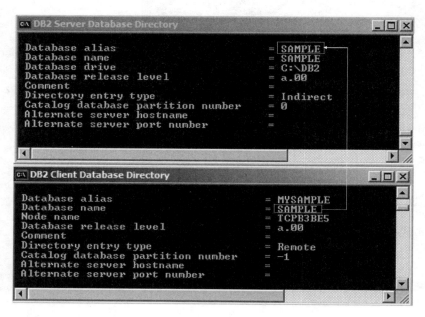

Figure 6.23   Verifying that the database name in the client database directory matches the database alias on the server

If the database resides on a host server, verify the DCS directory. Using the `list dcs directory` command, ensure that the database name in the database directory matches the database name in the DCS directory (see Figure 6.24). The target database name in the DCS directory must be the Location name if the host server is DB2 for z/OS, or the RDB name if the host server is DB2 for i.

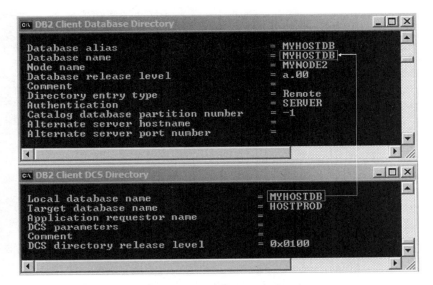

Figure 6.24 Verifying that the database name in the database directory matches the database name in the DCS directory

Figure 6.25 displays a flowchart for diagnosing client-server connectivity problems. It summarizes what we have discussed so far. The client is a Data Server client, and the server can be either a DB2 server or a DB2 Connect gateway.

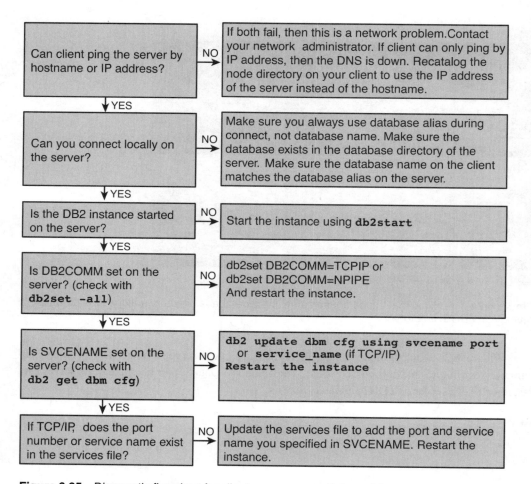

Figure 6.25   Diagnostic flowchart for client-server connectivity problems

Figure 6.26 displays a flowchart for diagnosing client-host connectivity problems.

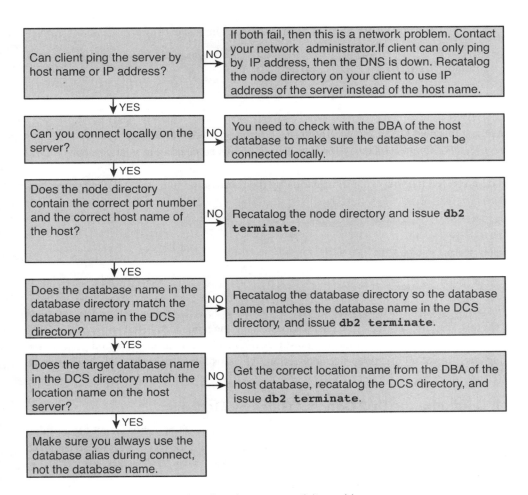

Can client ping the server by host name or IP address?	**NO** → If both fail, then this is a network problem. Contact your network administrator. If client can only ping by IP address, then the DNS is down. Recatalog the node directory on your client to use IP address of the server instead of the host name.

↓ YES

Can you connect locally on the server?	**NO** → You need to check with the DBA of the host database to make sure the database can be connected locally.

↓ YES

Does the node directory contain the correct port number and the correct host name of the host?	**NO** → Recatalog the node directory and issue **db2 terminate**.

↓ YES

Does the database name in the database directory match the database name in the DCS directory?	**NO** → Recatalog the database directory so the database name matches the database name in the DCS directory, and issue **db2 terminate**.

↓ YES

Does the target database name in the DCS directory match the location name on the host server?	**NO** → Get the correct location name from the DBA of the host database, recatalog the DCS directory, and issue **db2 terminate**.

↓ YES

Make sure you always use the database alias during connect, not the database name.

Figure 6.26   Diagnostic path for client-host connectivity problems

In Figure 6.26, the client has at least DB2 Connect Personal Edition license installed (review "Scenario 3").

For a three-tier configuration where a DB2 Connect gateway works as the middle tier, the diagnosing path splits into two parts. First, you need to make sure the connection is working from the Connect gateway to the host database. For this, use the flowchart in Figure 6.26. Second, for the client-gateway connection, use the flowchart in Figure 6.25.

In addition, the following diagnosis aids may also help:

- db2 ping tests the network response time of the underlying connectivity between a client and a database server.

- Changing the DIAGLEVEL parameter to 4 at the client side (this is discussed in Appendix D, "Diagnosing Problems")
- Running JDBC traces

Case Study

You have just installed DB2 Connect Enterprise Edition on an AIX machine. You are using this machine as a DB2 Connect gateway for Data Server clients connecting to your company's DB2 for z/OS server.

You are given the following information by the database administrator (DBA) of the host database:

```
Hostname        = jupiter.myacme.com
Port Number     = 446
Location Name   = OS390L1
User ID         = user1
Password        = userpwd
```

For security reasons, the DB2 for z/OS location name is not to be exposed to the Data Server clients. The clients refer to the host database using the name DB2PROD.

When you installed DB2 Connect, an instance *db2inst1* was created. Now you perform the following steps to set up this three-tier connection. All steps are performed while logged on as *db2inst1*.

Step 1: Configure the DB2 Connect Gateway Machine

Use the information given by the DB2 for z/OS database administrator (who can get most of this information by running the -DIS DDF command) to catalog the node directory, system database directory, and the DCS directory on the DB2 Connect gateway:

```
catalog tcpip node node1 remote jupiter.myacme.com server 446
catalog db db2prod at node node1
catalog dcs db db2prod as os390l1
terminate
```

Step 2: Test the Connection from the DB2 Connect Gateway Machine to the Host

Use the following DB2 command to connect to the host database:

```
CONNECT TO db2prod USER user1 USING userpwd
```

If the connection fails, the problem could be that

- The user ID or password is incorrect.
- There is a network problem.
- The host server is not set up properly to accept client connections.

As the problem is likely to be on the host side, contact your host's DBA first to investigate the problem before moving on to step 3.

Step 3: Enable the TCP/IP Listener on the Gateway Machine

To make this gateway machine capable of accepting client connections, you need to enable the TCP/IP listener for the *db2inst1* instance. If you created the *db2inst1* instance using the DB2 Setup Wizard during product installation, you do not need to perform this step because it has already been done for you. However, because you created *db2inst1* manually using the `db2icrt` command, you need to perform the following steps to enable the TCP/IP listener.

1. Manually add the following entry in the etc/services file:

   ```
   db2conn1 50000/tcp #DB2 connection port for db2inst1
   ```

2. Execute the following DB2 commands:

   ```
   update dbm cfg using svcename db2conn1
   db2set DB2COMM=TCPIP
   db2stop
   db2start
   ```

Step 4: Configure a Data Server Client to Connect to the Host via the Gateway

The Data Server client connects to the host database via the DB2 Connect gateway. On the client, perform the following commands to catalog the client's node directory and database directory to connect to the gateway. The host name of the gateway is *mercury.myacme.com*.

```
catalog tcpip node node1 remote mercury.myacme.com server 50000
catalog db db2prod at node node1
terminate
```

To connect to the host from the client, execute

```
CONNECT TO db2prod USER user1 USING userpwd
```

If the connection is successful, configure other clients in the same way.

Summary

In this chapter, you learned the how to configure connections from a Data Server client to a DB2 server. Five supported connection scenarios were discussed in detail:

- Local connection from a Data Server client to a DB2 server
- Remote connection from a Data Server client to a DB2 server
- Remote connection from a Data Server client to a DB2 host server
- Remote connection from a Data Server client to a DB2 host server via a DB2 Connect gateway
- Remote connection from an application to a DB2 server

A local connection occurs when a Data Server client and a DB2 server reside on the same server. A connection from a Data Server client to a DB2 server requires that at least the IBM Data Server Runtime Client be installed on the client machine. In some cases, not even an IBM Data Server Runtime Client is required; for example, if running a JDBC Type 4 application you only need the appropriate driver copied to the machine where the application is invoked. On the server machine, at least DB2 Express-C Edition is required. A connection from a Data Server client to a DB2 host server requires that at least the DB2 Connect Personal Edition software license be installed on the client machine. The supported host servers are DB2 for z/OS and DB2 for i.

TCP/IP is the supported communication protocol for all of the above connections. Named Pipes is supported if both the client and the server are on Windows. DB2 can connect to servers using IPv4 or IPv6 addresses. Commands have been added or enhanced to provide IPv6 support. For example, the existing `CATALOG TCPIP NODE` command has been supplemented with the additional commands, `CATALOG TCPIP4 NODE` and `CATALOG TCPIP6 NODE`, to enable you to request a particular type of connection.

Connectivity information is stored in four main directories: the system database directory, the local database directory, the node directory, and the DCS directory. The system database directory contains the names and aliases of both remote and local databases. The local database directory contains the names and aliases of databases that exist locally on a particular drive (on Windows) or path (on Linux or UNIX). The information about how to reach a remote server is stored in the client's node directory. For a TCP/IP connection, the remote server's host name or IP address and the DB2 port number are stored. To connect to a database residing on a host server, a DCS directory is also required. An entry in the DCS directory contains the actual database name known to the host server.

After configuring the connections, you need to bind database utilities, or else the client will not be able to use any of the database utilities such as import or export. Run the `bind` command on the *db2ubind.lst* file to bind database utilities. If the client is going to run CLI/ODBC applications, run the `bind` command on the *db2cli.lst* file as well to create CLI packages on the server. If the server is DB2 for z/OS, use the *ddcsmvs.lst* file in the `bind` command. If the server is DB2 for i, use the *ddcs400.lst* file.

The binding of utilities must be done for each database you want to access. When a package is successfully bound to the database, all Data Server clients of the same type and DB2 level can use it.

Step-by-step instructions were provided to help diagnose DB2 connectivity problems. Follow the flowcharts provided to pinpoint where the connectivity issue lies.

Review Questions

1. Which DB2 directory contains information about all the databases you can connect to from a Data Server client machine?

2. Which command is used to review the contents of the local database directory located in drive H: on a Windows machine?

3. If the system database directory contains an entry with a type of *indirect*, what does this say about the entry?

4. If the SVCENAME database manager parameter has a value of *db2_cDB2*, which port is being used?

5. Which communication protocols are supported when connecting from a DB2 Connect gateway to a DB2 for z/OS server?

6. Why is DB2 Connect Enterprise Edition the recommended DB2 Connect product to use to support 1,000 clients connecting to a DB2 for i server?

7. Which command can you use to remove an incorrect entry from the DCS directory?

8. Which command can you use to remove an incorrect entry from the node directory?

9. What should you check to verify that the correct communication protocol is specified?

10. After creating and updating database and node entries, why is it a good practice to issue a `terminate` command?

11. Given the following command:

    ```
    catalog tcpip node srv2 remote server2 server db2port
    ```

    Which of the following DB2 directories are updated?
    A.   DCS directory
    B.   System database directory
    C.   Local database directory
    D.   Node directory

12. You accidentally dropped your instance MYINST, which was associated to only one database called MYDB. Which of the following statements is true?

   A.   When the instance was dropped, your database was also dropped.

   B.   You can recover the database using the `restore <path where database resides>` command.

   C.   Issue this command from the CLP: `catalog instance MYINST database MYDB`.

   D.   After recreating the instance, issue this command from the CLP: `catalog db MYDB on <path where database resides>`

13. The following entry appears in the services file of a Data Server client machine

   ```
   db2c_DB2     60000
   ```

   whereas the SVCENAME value for the *DB2* instance at the server is 50005. Which of the following commands is the correct one to use?

   A.   `catalog tcpip node mynode remote aries server 60000`
   B.   `catalog tcpip node mynode remote aries server 50005`
   C.   `catalog tcpip node mynode remote aries server db2c_DB2`
   D.   `catalog tcpip node mynode remote aries server 50000`

14. Which of the following commands inserts an entry in the system database directory?

   A.   `catalog system database directory mydb at node mynode`
   B.   `insert into system db value (mydb)`
   C.   `create database mydb on F:`
   D.   `catalog dcs db mydb`

15. Which of the following commands are required to enable a DB2 server for TCPIP connectivity? (Choose all that apply.)

   A.   `update dbm cfg using SVCENAME 50000`
   B.   `db2set DB2COMM=TCPIP`
   C.   `connect to sample`
   D.   `ping myhost`

16. Which IBM data server(s) is supported by the IBM Data Server Client?

   A.   `DB2 for Linux, UNIX, and Windows`
   B.   `DB2 for i`
   C.   `solidDB`
   D.   `DB2 on z/OS`

17. Which communication protocols are supported when connecting from a DB2 on Windows client to a DB2 on Windows server?

   A.   Named Pipes
   B.   TCPIP
   C.   LDAP
   D.   All of the above

18. Which of the following commands properly catalog a remote DB2 instance accepting TCP/IP connections?

    A. `catalog tcpip4 node mynode1 remote 9.23.223.98 server 1032`

    B. `catalog tcpip6 node mynode1 remote 2001:0db8::1428:57ab server 50000`

    C. `catalog tcpip node mynode1 remote 9.23.223.98 server db2inst1`

    D. `catalog tcpip4 node mynode1 remote aries.acme.com server db2inst1`

19. You have a JDBC Type 4 application and would like to keep a small software footprint on your machine. Which of the following would you choose to connect to a remote DB2 server?

    A. IBM Data Server Driver Package
    B. IBM Data Server Driver for JDBC and SQLJ
    C. IBM Data Server Runtime Client
    D. IBM Data Server Client

20. You just joined the Human Resources team and need to connect to the HR database. What information would you need from the database administrator? TCPIP is the only protocol used in your company.

    A. IP address of the database server
    B. TCPIP port number reserved for the DB2 instance
    C. Database name
    D. User ID and password authorized to access the database.

## CHAPTER 7

Working with Database Objects

In this chapter, we discuss how to create and work with databases. First, we explain how DB2 stores database objects on disk and memory with an introduction to different concepts such as automatic storage, storage groups, table spaces, and buffer pools. Then we describe the various database objects that can be created in the database, such as tables, indexes, and views. The chapter assumes you have basic knowledge of the Structure Query Language (SQL); if not, refer to Appendix B, "Introduction to SQL."

In this chapter, you learn about

- The big picture of DB2 databases and database objects
- Database creation and structure
- The definitions of database partitions, partition groups, table spaces, buffer pools, storage groups, containers, pages, extents
- The DB2 data types
- How to work with tables, indexes, views, and schemas
- The definition of application-related objects like packages, modules, triggers, user-defined functions, stored procedures, and sequences

Database Objects: The Big Picture

A database is a collection of database objects. You can create a database on one or more database partitions. A **database partition**, as its name implies, is part of a database. We introduce you to the DB2 database objects in Figure 7.1 where these objects are illustrated in a database created in a single-partition environment (database partition 0).

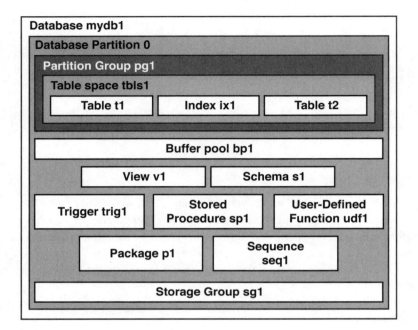

Figure 7.1   An overview of the DB2 database objects

- A **partition group** is a logical database object that represents a collection of database partitions. In a single-partition environment as shown in Figure 7.1, partition groups are not relevant; however, in multipartition environments, a partition group facilitates the work of a database administrator, as he or she is able to perform database operations on or within several partitions at a time. Partition groups can contain one or more table spaces. In Figure 7.1, partition group *pg1* contains table space *tbls1*.

V10 • A **storage group** is a logical object that defines a list of storage paths that point to containers where the data is actually stored. The containers can be files, directories, or devices. The storage paths should point to containers of similar characteristics, such as device read rate, size, disk seek, and latency times. Storage groups are only used when the **automatic storage** capability is enabled.

- A **table space** is a logical object that associates tables and indexes to the physical devices where these objects are stored, as well as to the physical memory where the data in these objects is cached when it is being accessed. Tables and indexes must be created inside a table space as illustrated in Figure 7.1, where tables *t1* and *t2* and index *ix1* are all created inside table space *tbls1*.

- A **table** consists of rows and columns, like spreadsheets. Data can be inserted, deleted, and updated within a table. Figure 7.1 has two tables, *t1* and *t2*.

- An **index** is an ordered set of keys each pointing to a row in a table. Indexes improve application performance when looking for specific rows. They can also be used to guarantee the uniqueness of rows. In Figure 7.1, index *ix1* is associated to table *t1*.

- A **buffer pool** is an area in physical memory that caches the database information most recently used. Without buffer pools, every single piece of data has to be retrieved from disk, which is very slow. Buffer pools are associated to tables and indexes through a table space. In Figure 7.1, table space *tbls1* is associated to buffer pool *bp1*, therefore tables *t1* and *t2* and index *ix1* use buffer pool *bp1*.

- A **view** is an alternate way of representing data that exists in one or more tables. A view can include some or all of the columns from one or more tables. It can also be based on other views. In Figure 7.1, view *v1* is based on table *t1*.

- Every object in the database is created with a two-part name separated by a dot:

  schema_name.object_name

  The first part of this two-part name is the schema name. A **schema** is an object that provides a logical grouping of other database objects. A schema can be owned by an individual who can control access to the objects within it. Schemas can be implicitly or explicitly specified when accessing an object.

- A **trigger** is an object that contains application logic that is triggered by specific actions like an update to a table. For example, in Figure 7.1, a trigger can be created so that after table *t1* is updated, table *t2* is also updated with some other information.

- A **stored procedure** is an object used to move application logic into your database. By keeping part of the application logic in the database, there are performance improvements as the amount of network traffic between the application and the database is considerably reduced.

- A **user-defined function** (UDF) enables database users to extend the SQL language by creating functions that can be used anywhere a DB2 built-in function is used. Similar to stored procedures, application logic can be moved to the database by using UDFs.

- A **package** is an object containing the compiled version of your SQL queries as well as the access path that the DB2 optimizer, the brain of DB2, has chosen to retrieve the data for those queries.

- A **sequence** object enables the generation of unique numbers in sequence. These numbers can be used across the database as a unique identifier for tables or for applications.

To create, modify, or delete database objects, you first need to connect to the database using the CONNECT statement (see Chapter 6, "Configuring Client and Server Connectivity") and then use Data Definition Language (DDL) SQL statements consisting of the following:

- CREATE
- DECLARE
- ALTER
- DROP

The following objects can be created and dropped using the CREATE and DROP statements, respectively:

- Tables
- Indexes
- Schemas
- Views
- User-defined functions
- User-defined types
- Buffer pools
- Table spaces
- Storage groups
- Stored procedures
- Triggers
- Servers (for federated databases)
- Wrappers (for federated databases)
- Nicknames (for federated databases)
- Sequences
- Modules

You use the DECLARE statement to create temporary tables, and the ALTER statement to change one or more attributes or characteristics of an existing database object. You can alter most, but not all, of the database objects created with the CREATE statement. The CREATE, DECLARE, ALTER, and DROP statements are used throughout this chapter.

Figure 7.2 illustrates the interaction between different database objects. It presents a combination of physical and logical views of the primary database objects.

Figure 7.2 illustrates a user retrieving some data from the table *t2*. From this user's perspective, the information he needs is stored in a table, and how and where it is stored on disk is irrelevant. When this user issues the SQL statement,

```
SELECT ProdId FROM t2 WHERE ProdName = 'Plum'
```

the column from the specified rows in the table is retrieved by DB2 and returned to the user. Behind the scenes, DB2 might need to read a number of pages of data from one or more physical disks or from memory to provide this information to the user.

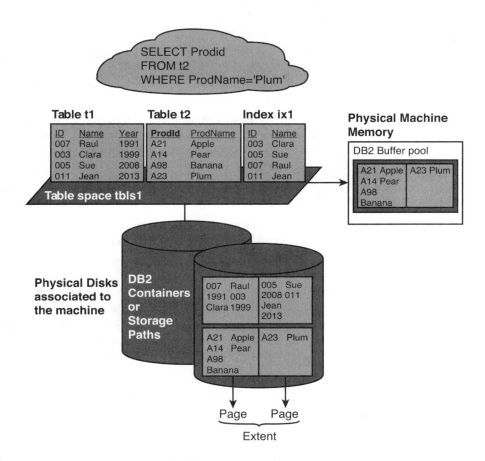

Figure 7.2 Interaction between different database objects

DB2 stores table and index data on **pages**, which are the smallest unit of storage in a DB2 database. Figure 7.2 shows four pages for the table *t2*, and each page contains one or more rows from the tables *t1* and *t2* and one or more key values for the index *ix1* on table *t1*.

When DB2 processes SQL statements such as a SELECT, it must access the data and/or index pages. DB2 attempts to access these pages from the buffer pools. If the desired pages are already in the buffer pool due to the prior processing of other SQL statements that needed those pages, DB2 can process the request immediately. If the page is not in the buffer pool, DB2 must read it from disk and place it in the buffer pool, as shown on the right side of Figure 7.2.

Rather than reading one page at a time, DB2 can group pages together into **extents** and read multiple pages with each I/O request. In Figure 7.2 you can see that pages are grouped together in extents of two pages. You can also see that the tables and indexes are stored in table spaces. Table spaces are a logical layer between your logical tables and your physical resources such as memory and disks. **Containers** are the physical storage for the table spaces, and **Storage Groups** are a group of storage paths to containers of similar characteristics, such as device read rate, size, disk seek, and latency times.

To optimize performance, DB2 lets you specify the table spaces in which you want your tables and indexes stored. You can also associate buffer pools with specific table spaces so that you can optimize the placement of tables and indexes within memory. Moreover, with automatic storage managed table spaces and the multitemperature data management feature, storage management has been greatly simplified and improved. The following sections describe some of these features in more detail.

Databases

A database is a collection of information organized into interrelated objects such as table spaces, partition groups, and tables. Each database is an independent unit containing its own system information, temporary space, transaction logs, and configuration files, as illustrated in Figure 7.3.

Figure 7.3 shows two databases, MYDB1 and MYDB2, inside the instance *DB2* in a single-partition environment (Database Partition 0). The box showing *Database Partition 0* is included for completeness; in a single-partition environment you can ignore this box. Because databases are independent units, object names from different databases can be the same. For example, the name of the table space *MyTablespace1* is used in both databases in the figure. As you see later in this chapter, you use table spaces to specify where the data will reside; if using automatic storage, they would be stored in storage groups assigned to the database. Other information such as configuration files (discussed in Chapter 5, "Understanding the DB2 Environment, DB2 Instances, and Databases"), the local database directory (also known as Local db Directory, discussed in Chapter 6), history files, log control files, and so on, can be stored separately.

Figure 7.3 also shows the three table spaces that DB2 creates by default when you create a database: SYSCATSPACE, TEMPSPACE1, and USERSPACE1. These table spaces are described in the "Table Spaces" section.

Other objects in the figure are discussed later in this chapter.

Database Partitions

You can create a single-partition or a multipartition database, depending on your needs.

In a multipartition environment, a **database partition** (or simply **partition**) is an independent part of a database containing its own data, indexes, configuration files, and transaction logs. Database functions are also distributed between all the database partitions. This provides for great scalability.

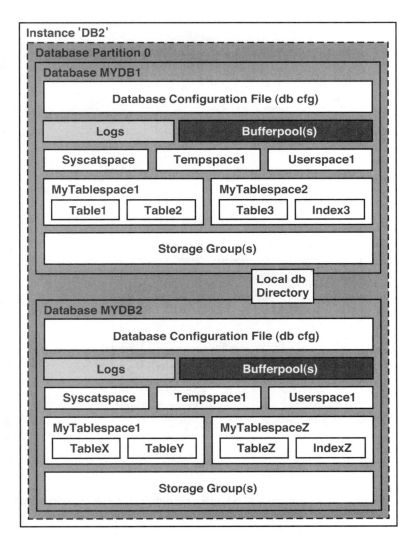

Figure 7.3 A database and its objects

Multiple database partitions can reside on one physical server; these are sometimes referred to as **logical partitions** sharing the resources of the machine. Database partitions can also reside on different physical servers. The collection of all of these partitions corresponds to one database.

NOTE

Multipartition database support capabilities are included in DB2 Advanced Enterprise Server Edition, DB2 Advanced Workgroup Server Edition, and DB2 Developer Edition. Prior DB2 versions offered these capabilities as a separate feature known as Database Partitioning Feature (DPF). Other data warehouse capabilities have also been included in these editions. Prior DB2 versions or releases included them in the InfoSphere Warehouse Enterprise Edition.

Figure 7.4 shows two databases, MYDB1 and MYDB2, in a multipartition environment with three database partitions.

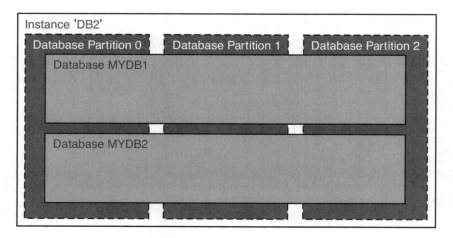

Figure 7.4   Database partitions

As mentioned in Chapter 2, "DB2 at a Glance: The Big Picture," an instance associates the DB2 binary code (also called the DB2 copy) to databases. Database partitions, on the other hand, are used to split your database into different parts. Therefore, an instance in a multipartition environment associates the DB2 binary code to the different database partitions. Figure 7.4 shows this association.

The Database Node Configuration File (db2nodes.cfg)

In a multipartition environment you define the database partitions that are part of your database by entering the appropriate information in the database node configuration file, *db2nodes.cfg*.

On Linux and UNIX platforms, the *db2nodes.cfg* file can contain up to five columns, as shown in Table 7.1.

Table 7.1   Columns of the *db2nodes.cfg* Configuration File for Linux and UNIX

	Partition Number	Hostname	Logical Port	Netname	Resource-setname
Is the Column Required?	Yes	Yes	Sometimes	Sometimes	Optional
Description	DB2 uses this column to identify the partition.	The TCP/IP host name of the server where the partition is created.	This column must be used if you want to create more than one partition on the same server. It specifies the logical port for the partition within the server and must be unique within a server.	Supports a host that has more than one active TCP/IP interface, each with its own host name. It is required if you are using a high speed interconnect for inter- partition communication or if the resourceset-name column is used.	It specifies the operating system resource that the partition should be started in.

On Windows there is also another column, *Computername*, which contains the computer name for the machine on which the partition resides. Table 7.2 shows the order of the columns on Windows systems and whether they are required.

Table 7.2   Columns of the *db2nodes.cfg* Configuration File for Windows

	Partition Number	Hostname	Computer-name	Logical Port	Net-name	Resource-setname
Is the Column Required?	Yes	Yes	Yes	Some-times	Some-times	Optional

When you create an instance in a DB2 edition that includes database partitioning support, a default *db2nodes.cfg* file is created with one row. On Linux and UNIX, the default file has three columns and looks like the following:

```
0    myserver    0
```

On Windows, the default file has four columns and looks like the following:

```
0    myserver    myserver    0
```

The *db2nodes.cfg* file is located

- Under the sqllib directory for the instance owner on Linux and UNIX
- Under the SQLLIB*Instance_name* directory on Windows

There is only one *db2nodes.cfg* file per instance, and all the databases you create under this instance are partitioned when the CREATE DATABASE command is executed based on the contents of this file. To create multiple partitions, edit the *db2nodes.cfg* file and add an entry for each database partition. For example, assume you have an eight-way SMP server (a server with eight CPUs or cores) running Linux as shown in Figure 7.5.

Server mypenguin

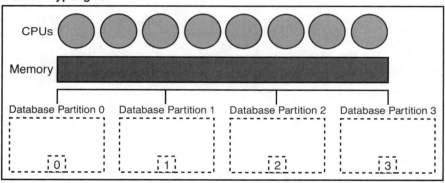

Figure 7.5   An eight-way SMP Linux server with four database partitions

You need to edit the *db2nodes.cfg* file to make it look like the following:

```
0    mypenguin    0
1    mypenguin    1
2    mypenguin    2
3    mypenguin    3
```

In another scenario, assume you are installing DB2 on a cluster of eight two-way SMP Linux servers, and you want to create one partition on each server as illustrated in Figure 7.6 (not all servers are shown).

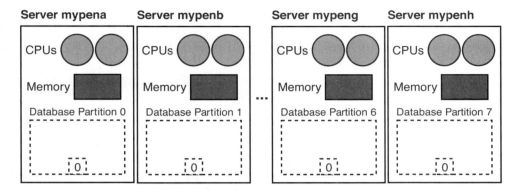

Figure 7.6 A cluster of eight two-way SMP Linux servers with eight partitions in total

You need to edit the *db2nodes.cfg* file to make it look like the following:

```
0    mypena    0
1    mypenb    0
2    mypenc    0
3    mypend    0
4    mypene    0
5    mypenf    0
6    mypeng    0
7    mypenh    0
```

In yet another scenario, assume you are installing DB2 on a cluster of four UNIX servers with four CPUs each and you want to create two partitions on each server as shown in Figure 7.7.

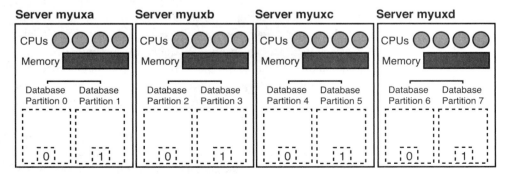

Figure 7.7 A cluster of four four-way SMP UNIX servers with eight database partitions in total

You need to edit the *db2nodes.cfg* file to make it look like the following:

```
0     myuxa     0
1     myuxa     1
2     myuxb     0
3     myuxb     1
4     myuxc     0
5     myuxc     1
6     myuxd     0
7     myuxd     1
```

On Linux and UNIX, you can edit the *db2nodes.cfg* file with any ASCII editor (for example, *vi*). On Windows, you should not edit the *db2nodes.cfg* file directly; instead, use the db2ncrt and db2ndrop commands to add and remove database partitions, respectively.

You can also use the db2start command to add and/or remove a database partition from the DB2 instance and the *db2nodes.cfg* file as follows:

- Use the db2start command with the add dbpartitionnum option to add a partition to the database and insert an entry for the partition into the *db2nodes.cfg* file.

- Use the db2start command with the drop dbpartitionnum option to remove a partition from the database and delete its entry from the *db2nodes.cfg* file.

You can also use the add dbpartitionnum command to add a partition to the database even if the partition already has an entry in the *db2nodes.cfg* file.

Automatic Storage

DB2 automatic storage greatly simplifies storage management. Using this capability, you can have DB2 automatically manage the space in your table spaces. The idea is to centralize storage management using another level of abstraction called a **storage group**. A storage group is a collection of **storage paths** that have similar characteristics, and a storage path is just a piece of storage, such as a drive, a path, or filesystem. Rather than assigning containers with explicit definitions to table spaces, you now assign them storage groups. By doing this, not only does DB2 take care of creating, extending and adding containers in the storage groups when needed, but you can also add or remove storage paths to the storage group easily and have DB2 rebalance the data so it is always striped across all storage paths. Storage groups are explained in more detail later in this chapter.

Automatic storage needs to be enabled at the database level first before it can be used at the table space level. This can be done using the AUTOMATIC STORAGE YES clause in the CREATE DATABASE command. Because this clause is the default, it doesn't need to be explicitly included in the command. Next, when you create or alter table spaces, you need to use the USING STOGROUP clause of the CREATE TABLESPACE or ALTER TABLESPACE statements to assign a storage group to the table space. If a database is created with the AUTOMATIC STORAGE NO clause, automatic storage managed table spaces cannot be used.

 NOTE

The AUTOMATIC STORAGE clause in the CREATE DATABASE command is deprecated given that automatic storage is the default behavior starting from DB2 10.1.

When you first create a database you can specify storage paths to use; these are assigned to the storage group you have designated as the default. If you have not designated a default storage group, IBMSTOGROUP is used, and it is created automatically as you are creating the database.

You can create more storage groups or alter existing ones and later tell DB2 to use them for your table spaces. You can also change the storage group to be used as default. The data inserted into the table spaces are automatically striped across all of the storage paths in the storage group assigned to the table space.

Automatic storage is also discussed in the "Automatic Storage Managed Table Spaces" section.

Creating a Database

Use the CREATE DATABASE command to create a database. The basic syntax of the command is shown in Figure 7.8.

At the top of Figure 7.8, rules for the database name are listed. At the bottom of the figure, for the ON and DBPATH ON parameters, other rules are listed depending on whether automatic storage has been enabled (AUTOMATIC STORAGE YES) or disabled (AUTOMATIC STORAGE NO). As mentioned in an earlier note, AUTOMATIC STORAGE is enabled by default. We recommend you keep this option enabled.

When a database is created, the database structure (referred to as *db structure* in Figure 7.8) can be stored in a different location than the database data (referred to as *db data* in Figure 7.8). The *db structure* consists of a hierarchical directory structure with database configuration information, history file information, log control files with information about active logs, and so on. The *db data* is the database data such as the contents of your tables.

In Figure 7.8, there is also reference to the DFTDBPATH db configuration parameter. The default value for this parameter on Windows is the drive where DB2 is installed and on Linux and UNIX is the instance owner's home directory. When you do specify the drives or the paths for the database or the database storage paths, keep the following in mind:

- They must exist ahead of time and be accessible.
- There must be sufficient space available on the drives or file systems to hold at least the system catalogs.

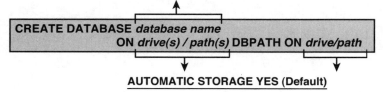

• Can be a maximum of eight characters long
• Cannot contain all numbers
• Cannot start with a number
• Cannot contain spaces
• Must be unique within the same DB2 instance

CREATE DATABASE *database name*
                    ON *drive(s) / path(s)* **DBPATH ON** *drive/path*

AUTOMATIC STORAGE YES (Default)

-Drive(s)/path(s) will be used to store db data

-Several drives/paths can be specified. These are
called storage paths. The storage paths will be part of
the default storage group

-If no default storage group is specified,
IBMSTOGROUP is automatically created and used
as the default storage group

-Storage group is used with table spaces managed
by automatic storage to store db data

- If ON drive(s)/path(s) is not specified, value of db
cfg parameter dftdbpath is used for path

-Drive/path will be used to store db structure

-If not specified, use first storage path listed in
the ON parameter. If ON parameter not
specified, use value of db cfg parameter
dftdbpath for path

- On Windows, only a drive can be specified
unless this DB2 registry variable is set:
DB2_CREATE_DB_ON_PATH=YES

AUTOMATIC STORAGE NO

- Only one drive/path can be specified

- Will be used to store db structure and db data

- If not specified, value of db cfg parameter
dftdbpath is used for path

- DBPATH ON is not applicable

Figure 7.8   The CREATE DATABASE command basic syntax

In addition, in the CREATE DATABASE command, you can optionally specify

• The database partition number for the catalog table space (for multipartition environments).

• The definition of the temporary and default user table spaces if you do not want to use
the default locations.

• The code set and territory allow you to specify the character set that you want DB2 to
use to store your data and return result sets.

• The collating sequence lets you specify how DB2 should sort data when you create
indexes or use the SORT or ORDER BY clauses in SELECT statements.

Default Database Objects Created

When a database is created using the default syntax of the CREATE DATABASE command, several objects are created:

- The partition group IBMCATGROUP, which contains the table space SYSCATSPACE (catalog table space), that stores the DB2 catalog tables and views
- The partition group IBMTEMPGROUP, which contains the table space TEMPSPACE1 (system temporary table space)
- The partition group IBMDEFAULTGROUP, which contains the table space USERSPACE1 (user table space)
- The buffer pool IBMDEFAULTBP
- The storage group IBMSTOGROUP
- A database configuration file

Figure 7.9 shows these default objects that are created when you create a database. For illustration purposes, we arbitrarily chose a multipartition database with three partitions, but any number of partitions could have been used.

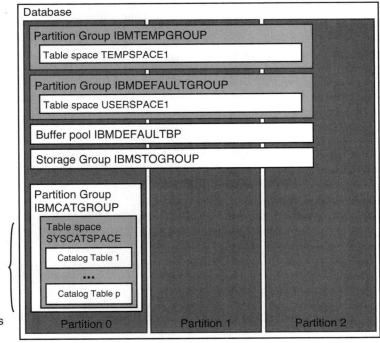

All object definitions are in Catalog tables:
- Partition Groups
- Buffer pools
- Storage Groups
- Table spaces
- Tables
- Indexes
- Views
- Packages
- Triggers
- Stored Procedures
- Sequences

Figure 7.9 A database with default database objects created

The CREATE DATABASE command in a multipartition environment automatically takes the contents of the database partition configuration file (*db2nodes.cfg*) into consideration. The partition where you issue the CREATE DATABASE command becomes the catalog partition for the database, and the system catalog tables for this database are created on that partition. If you do not explicitly connect to a database partition or server, the database is created with the system catalogs on the first partition in the *db2nodes.cfg* file.

Listing Databases

When you create a database with the CREATE DATABASE command, entries in the system database directory and local database directory are automatically entered. To list the system database directory contents, issue the command

```
list db directory
```

To list the local database directory contents, issue the command

```
list db directory on drive/path
```

Chapter 6 discusses the system and local database directories in detail.

Dropping Databases

If you no longer need the data in a database, you can drop the database from the system using the DROP DATABASE command. This command removes the database from the local and system database directories and deletes all table spaces, tables, logs, and directory structure supporting the database. After dropping a database, the space is immediately available for reuse.

For example, if you run the command

```
DROP DATABASE sales
```

the entries in the system and local database directories for this database are removed, and the database's SQL*xxxxx* and SALES directories are also removed. The local database directory (SQLDBDIR) is *not* removed when you drop a database because there might be other databases in the same path or on the same drive.

> **NOTE**
>
> The only supported way to remove a database is to use the DROP DATABASE command. Manually deleting the SQL*xxxxx* directory for the database is not supported because it leaves the database entries in both the local and system database directories.

Database Creation Examples

In this section, we provide a few examples of how to create a database with different parameters.

Creating a Database in a Single-Partition Environment

Let's say you are working on a single-partition DB2 environment running on a Windows server and the DB2 instance name you created is *myinst*. If you issue the command

```
CREATE DATABASE sales ON D:
```

several directories are created on the D: drive as shown in Figure 7.10.

Figure 7.10   Directories created when a database is created

Continuing with the example, you can create two additional databases, *test* and *prod,* using the following commands:

```
CREATE DATABASE test ON D:
CREATE DATABASE prod ON D:
```

Figure 7.11 shows the additional directories these commands create.

Table 7.3 shows the database name and the directories that DB2 created when the database was created.

Table 7.3   Directory Names for Databases

Database Name	Directory Names
Sales	SQL00001 and SALES
Test	SQL00002 and TEST
Prod	SQL00003 and PROD

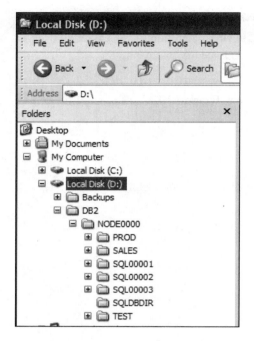

Figure 7.11   Directories created for the database sales, test, and prod

Using the `LIST DB DIRECTORY ON drive/path` enables you to map the SQL*xxxxx* directory to the actual database name, where *xxxxx* in SQL*xxxxx* represent digits. In this case if you issue the command

```
LIST DB DIRECTORY ON D:
```

you get the output shown in Figure 7.12.

If you drop one of these databases, its SQL*xxxxx* directory and the directory with the database's name are deleted. If you create a new database at a later time, the SQL*xxxxx* directory name is reused. For example, if you drop the database *test*, the directories SQL00002 and TEST are deleted. If you then create a new database called QA, the directory SQL00002 is re-created (along with the QA directory used for the QA database).

Creating a Database in a Multipartition Environment

Let's say you are working on a DB2 multipartition environment running on a single SMP Linux server with the following *db2nodes.cfg* file:

```
0       mylinx1       0
1       mylinx1       1
2       mylinx1       2
```

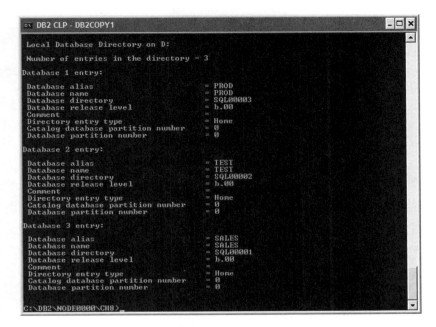

```
 DB2 CLP - DB2COPY1                                         _ □ ×

Local Database Directory on D:

Number of entries in the directory = 3

Database 1 entry:

  Database alias                      = PROD
  Database name                       = PROD
  Database directory                  = SQL00003
  Database release level              = b.00
  Comment                             =
  Directory entry type                = Home
  Catalog database partition number   = 0
  Database partition number           = 0

Database 2 entry:

  Database alias                      = TEST
  Database name                       = TEST
  Database directory                  = SQL00002
  Database release level              = b.00
  Comment                             =
  Directory entry type                = Home
  Catalog database partition number   = 0
  Database partition number           = 0

Database 3 entry:

  Database alias                      = SALES
  Database name                       = SALES
  Database directory                  = SQL00001
  Database release level              = b.00
  Comment                             =
  Directory entry type                = Home
  Catalog database partition number   = 0
  Database partition number           = 0

C:\DB2\NODE0000\CH8>
```

Figure 7.12 Output from the command list db directory on D:

If you log in as the instance owner *db2inst1* on this server and create a database with this command

```
create database sales on /data
```

the directory structure shown in Figure 7.13 is created.

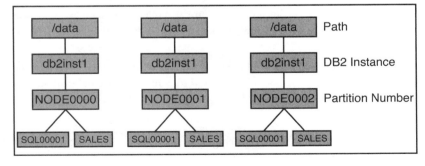

Figure 7.13 Directory structure for a three-partition database

As Figure 7.13 illustrates, there are three NODE*xxxx* directories, one for each database partition. The NODE*xxxx* directory is named based on the database instance's expanded four-digit partition number designated in the first column in the *db2nodes.cfg* file. Because the partition numbers used in the *db2nodes.cfg* file are 0, 1, and 2, these directories are NODE0000, NODE0001, and NODE0002.

Creating a Database with a Separate Table Space for Temporary Data and User Data

When you create a database you can specify different locations and table space types for the temporary and user table spaces. For example

```
CREATE DATABASE sales ON /data1, /data2, /data3
    TEMPORARY TABLESPACE MANAGED BY SYSTEM USING ('/temp')
```

The preceding statement lets the catalog and user table spaces default to the database storage paths (/data1, /data2, and /data3). You are also specifying to use an SMS (System Managed Space) table space for the temporary table space, and this temporary table space uses the file system /temp.

You can also create the user table space as a DMS (Database Managed Space) table space as shown here:

```
CREATE DATABASE sales ON /data1, /data2, /data3
    TEMPORARY TABLESPACE MANAGED BY SYSTEM USING ('/temp')
USER TABLESPACE MANAGED BY DATABASE USING (file '/userspc/cont1' 40M)
```

SMS and DMS table spaces are discussed in detail in section, "Table Spaces."

The SAMPLE Database

DB2 contains a program to create a sample database that can be used for testing or for learning purposes. This database called SAMPLE, can be created from the First Steps GUI tool (which can be started with the command db2fs). Alternatively, you can create this database with the command db2sampl. The SAMPLE database contains some tables with a few rows of data in each.

Use the command's -k option if you would like the SAMPLE database to be created with primary keys. In addition, you can specify the path if you would like this database to be created in a different location. For example, the command

```
db2sampl /data -k
```

creates the SAMPLE database in the */data* path, and the tables in the database have primary keys associated with them.

You can also create a sample database with XML data using the command

```
db2sampl /data -xml
```

Partition Groups

In a multipartition environment, a database partition is an independent subset of a database that contains its own data, indexes, configuration files, and transaction logs. A database **partition group** is a logical grouping of one or more database partitions for a database. By grouping database partitions, you can perform database operations at the partition group level rather than individually on each partition. This allows for database administration flexibility. For example, let's say you want to create a buffer pool with the same definition in three partitions. If you first create a partition group *pgall* that consists of the three partitions, you can associate the buffer pool *bp1* you are about to create with this partition group. This lets you use the same buffer pool definition on each partition.

Partition groups also enable you to associate table spaces to database partitions. For example, if you would like table space *tbls1* to use only database partitions 1 and 2, you can create a partition group *pg12* with these two partitions and then associate the table space *tbls1* to *pg12*.

Figure 7.14 illustrates the objects discussed in the preceding examples.

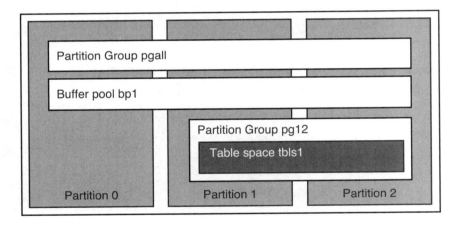

Figure 7.14   Partition groups

In Figure 7.14, the buffer pool definition is repeated across all the partitions. If you create the buffer pool with 20,000 4K pages, each partition allocates 20,000 4K pages. Note that the 20,000 4K pages are *not* split across all three partitions as the figure might suggest.

Database Partition Group Classifications

Partition groups are classified based on the number of database partitions they contain:

- Single-partition partition groups contain only one database partition.
- Multipartition partition groups contain more than one database partition.

Figure 7.15 shows four database partition groups.

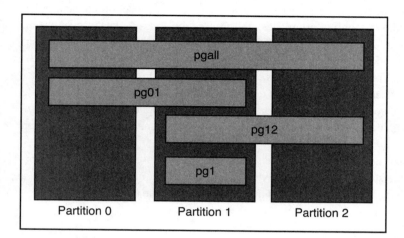

Figure 7.15   Database partition groups

- *pgall* is a multipartition partition group that spreads across all the database partitions.
- *pg01* is a multipartition partition group that spreads across partitions 0 and 1.
- *pg12* is a multipartition partition group that spreads across partitions 1 and 2.
- *pg1* is a single-partition partition group that resides on database partition 1.

NOTE

Database partitions can belong to more than one partition group. For example, in Figure 7.15 database partition 1 is part of all four partition groups.

Default Partition Groups

When you create a database, DB2 automatically creates three partition groups within that database. Table 7.4 describes these partition groups.

Table 7.4   Default Partition Groups

Partition Group Name	Description
IBMDEFAULTGROUP	This is the partition group where the user table space (USERSPACE1) resides and the default partition group for any tables that you create. By default, it spans all database partitions that you have defined in the *db2nodes.cfg* file. You can alter this partition group to either add or remove database partitions. This partition group cannot be dropped.
IBMTEMPGROUP	This partition group is where the system temporary table space (TEMPSPACE1) and all temporary tables created during database processing are placed. It spans all database partitions that you have defined in the *db2nodes.cfg* file. This partition group cannot be dropped.
IBMCATGROUP	This partition group is where the DB2 catalog table space (SYSCATSPACE) and the system catalog tables reside. It consists of only one partition, the database's catalog partition. The catalog partition is the partition where you executed the CREATE DATABASE command. This partition group cannot be altered to either add or remove database partitions. This partition group cannot be dropped.

NOTE

If you create a user temporary table space, you must create it in the IBMDEFAULTGROUP or any other partition group that you have created. DB2 does not allow you to create a user temporary table in the IBMTEMPGROUP. User temporary table spaces are described later in this chapter.

Creating Database Partition Groups

You create a database partition group with the statement CREATE DATABASE PARTITION GROUP. The statement also records the partition group definition in the database system catalog tables.

The following commands show how to create the partition groups you see in Figure 7.15. For this example assume that the *db2nodes.cfg* file contains the following entries for the database partitions numbered 0, 1, and 2:

```
0      mylinx1      0
1      mylinx1      1
2      mylinx1      2
```

Starting with *pgall*, there are two ways to create this partition group using the CREATE
DATABASE PARTITION GROUP statement:

```
create database partition group pgall on dbpartitionnums (0,1,2)
```

or

```
create database partition group pgall on all dbpartitionnums
```

You would create the other partition groups in Figure 7.15 as follows:

```
create database partition group pg01 on dbpartitionnums (0,1)
create database partition group pg12 on dbpartitionnums (1,2)
create database partition group pg1  on dbpartitionnums (1)
```

Modifying a Database Partition Group

You can modify a partition group with the ALTER DATABASE PARTITION GROUP statement.
This statement changes the definition of an existing partition group by adding or removing partitions. If you want to add a new partition to the partition group, that partition must already be
defined in the *db2nodes.cfg* file.

Continuing with the example from the previous section, you can add a new database partition to the instance by editing the *db2nodes.cfg* file and adding a fourth line:

```
0      mylinx1              0
1      mylinx1              1
2      mylinx1              2
3      mylinx1              3
```

If you now want to alter the partition group *pgall* to add partition number 3, issue this
statement:

```
alter database partition group pgall add dbpartitionnum (3)
```

Notice that partition number 1 in this example is one part of all partitions groups. To reduce
some of the load on that partition, you can remove it from partition group *pgall*, as follows:

```
alter database partition group pgall drop dbpartitionnum (1)
```

Listing Database Partition Groups

You can list all partition groups in your database with the LIST DATABASE PARTITION GROUP
statement. This lists all the partition groups that are defined in the database, regardless of which

database partition you are currently connected to. The following is the output of this statement for the example we have been discussing:

```
DATABASE PARTITION GROUP
------------------------------------------------
IBMCATGROUP
IBMDEFAULTGROUP
PGALL
PG01
PG1
PG12
```

To see which partitions are included in each partition group, use the SHOW DETAIL option with the LIST DATABASE PARTITION GROUP statement. This option provides additional information, including

- **PMAP_ID**: The partitioning map associated with the partition group.
- **DATABASE PARTITION NUMBER**: The database partition number as defined in the *db2nodes.cfg* file.
- **IN_USE**: The status of the database partition.

The output of this command contains three columns and one row for each database partition that is part of the partition group, with the exception of the IBMTEMPGROUP.

```
DATABASE PARTITION   DATABASE PARTITION    IN_USE
       GROUP                 NUMBER
------------------   -------------------   -------
IBMCATGROUP                   0               Y
IBMDEFAULTGROUP               0               Y
IBMDEFAULTGROUP               1               Y
IBMDEFAULTGROUP               2               Y
IBMDEFAULTGROUP               3               Y
PGALL                         0               Y
PGALL                         1               Y
PGALL                         2               Y
PGALL                         3               Y
PG01                          2               Y
PG01                          3               Y
PG12                          2               Y
PG12                          3               Y
PG1                           2               Y
```

> **NOTE**
>
> This information is also available in the system catalog view SYSCAT.NODEGROUPDEF.

Dropping a Database Partition Group

A partition group does not consume any system resources, but if a partition group is not being used, you can drop it using the DROP DATABASE PARTITION GROUP statement. If the partition group is being used, you would not be allowed to drop it, and an error message would be returned. If you wanted to drop the partition group *pg12* from this example, use the statement

```
DROP DATABASE PARTITION GROUP pg12
```

Table Spaces

A table space is a logical object in your database. It is used to associate your logical tables and indexes to their physical storage devices (containers or storage groups) and physical memory (buffer pools). All tables and indexes must reside in table spaces. A table can span table spaces as we discuss in the "Partitioned Tables" section.

Table Space Classification

Table spaces can be classified based on how the table space is managed and on what type of data they contain.

Based on how the table space is managed, a table space can be one of the following types:

- **System-managed space (SMS):** This type of table space is managed by the operating system and requires minimal administration. Data is stored in operating system files, and space for tables is allocated on-demand.

- **Database-managed space (DMS):** This type of table space is managed by the DB2 database manager and requires some administration. You provide a list of devices or files and their sizes when defining the DMS table space, and DB2 then allocates the defined amount of space.

- **Automatic storage:** This type of table space is managed by the DB2 database manager and requires minimal administration. The database manager determines which type of table space (SMS or DMS) is used and which containers are assigned to the table space based on the storage groups that are associated with the database.

NOTE

With DB2 10, SMS and DMS table space types have been deprecated except when used for temporary and catalog table spaces.

Based on the type of data it contains, a table space can be one of the following types:

- **Regular:** Use this type of table space to store any kind of data (including indexes) except temporary data. This type is allowed in both, SMS, and DMS table spaces.
- **Large:** Use this type of table space to store any kind of data (including indexes) except temporary data. This type is only allowed on DMS table spaces. Large table spaces can hold tables larger than regular table spaces can, and these tables can support more than 255 rows per data page.
- **Temporary:** Use this type of table space to hold temporary data. In turn, temporary table spaces can be further classified as two types:
  - **System:** These table spaces hold temporary data required by DB2 to perform operations such as sorts or joins, which cannot be completed in memory and require space for processing the result set.
  - **User:** These table spaces hold temporary data from tables created with the DECLARE GLOBAL TEMPORARY TABLE statement or the CREATE GLOBAL TEMPORARY TABLE statement. This type of table is explained in the section titled "Temporary Tables."

NOTE

System temporary table spaces and user temporary table spaces are commonly confused. Remember that system temporary table spaces are used by DB2, but user temporary table spaces are used by users when they declare or create global temporary tables.

Default Table Spaces

When a database is created, the following table spaces are created in the database by default:

- **SYSCATSPACE** contains the DB2 system catalog tables and views. This set of tables and views contains system information about all the objects in the database.
- **TEMPSPACE1** is used for system temporary data when DB2 needs temporary tables to process large sort or join operations.

- **USERSPACE1** is the table space where tables and indexes are initially created by default if a table space name has not been explicitly indicated in the CREATE TABLE statement. The section "User Tables" describes in detail the rules followed when a table space is implicitly assigned to a table.

Before we can continue discussing table spaces, it is important to explain how a table space's containers work and how data is striped across the containers in a table space based on extents.

Containers

When you create a table space that is not using automatic storage, you define the **container**(s) for the table space to define the physical storage of the table space. How you define the container depends on the type of table space you are creating. For SMS table spaces, a container can only be a directory. For DMS table spaces, a container can either be a file or a logical device or drive name.

When you create the table space, you have to define at least one container. A table space can have a number of containers associated with it, but after it has been defined, a container can belong to one and only one table space. Figure 7.16 illustrates this.

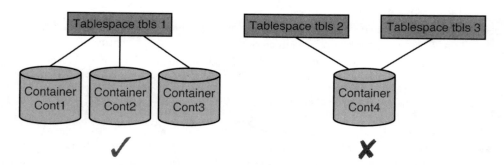

Figure 7.16   One table space can contain multiple containers, but a container can be associated with only one table space.

Storage Groups

A storage group is a collection of storage paths where data can be stored. The storage paths should have similar characteristics; for example, all the devices pointed to by the storage path should have similar sizes, read rates, and latency times. You can create storage groups to represent different classes of storage available to your database system and assign table spaces to the storage group that best suits the data. Storage groups are only applicable to table spaces managed by automatic storage.

If you create a database using automatic storage, you need to specify at least one storage path for the database; this storage path is assigned to the default storage group you've designated or to IBMSTOGROUP if you didn't designate one ahead of time. When you create a table space managed by automatic storage, you can assign to it a storage group; if you don't, the default storage group is used (the default storage group can be changed if desired). When you create tables and indexes in the table space, they are striped across the storage paths of the associated storage group in the same manner as with containers.

A table space can be associated with only one storage group, but a storage group can be used by multiple table spaces. Figure 7.17 illustrates this.

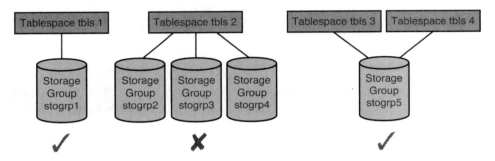

Figure 7.17   One table space uses only one storage group, but a storage group can be associated to many table spaces.

You create storage groups with the CREATE STOGROUP statement. The syntax for this command is shown here:

```
>>-CREATE--STOGROUP--storagegroup-name----------------------->

     .-,--------------.
     V                |
>--ON---'storage-path'-+--•---------------------------------->
>--+------------------------------------------+--•----------->
   '-OVERHEAD--number-of-milliseconds-'
>--+------------------------------------------------+--•-------->
   '-DEVICE READ RATE--number-megabytes-per-second-'
>--+-----------------------------------------+--•--------------------->
   '-DATA TAG--+-integer-constant-+-'
               '-NONE------------'
>--+-----------------+--•-------------------------------------------->< 
   '-SET AS DEFAULT-'
```

The OVERHEAD and DEVICE READ RATE are attributes of your media. If your media consists of devices with different values for these parameters respectively, use an average. These parameters are helpful for DB2 to calculate and optimize access to your data.

The DATA TAG parameter is used with the multitemperature data management feature as you see in the next section.

The SET AS DEFAULT clause can be used if you want the storage group you are creating to be the default one. This default storage group would be used when an automatic storage managed table space is created without specifying the storage group.

Let's take a look at a simple example. To create the storage group *mystogroup* using storage paths */fs1*, */fs2*, */fs3*, where the overhead rate is 0.75 and the device read rate is 500, issue this statement:

```
CREATE STOGROUP mystogroup
   ON '/fs1', '/fs2', '/fs3'
   OVERHEAD 0.75 DEVICE READ RATE 500
```

Use ALTER STOGROUP to alter the definition of a storage group. You can also add and remove storage paths from a storage group. If this is the case, you should also run the ALTER TABLESPACE statement with the REBALANCE option for each table space that is associated with that storage group. In case you were adding storage paths, this rebalance would allow striping across all storage paths, including the recently added ones. If you were dropping storage paths, this would move allocated extents off the storage paths dropped.

Following is a simple example of dropping storage paths /db2/fs1 and /db2/fs2 from storage group TESTGRP:

```
ALTER STOGROUP TESTGRP DROP '/db2/fs1', '/db2/fs2'
```

You drop a storage group using DROP STOGROUP <storage group name>. You can only use this statement if there are no table spaces using the storage group you want to drop.

Multitemperature Data Management

When working with data, it is common to classify it as "hot" if it is frequently accessed, or "cold" if it is rarely used. With this in mind, when we talk about multitemperature data management, we refer to the ability of DB2 to manage the storage and access of data depending on its "temperature," or how often the data is used.

Using storage groups, DB2 can easily and efficiently manage multitemperature data by enabling users to assign suitable storage groups, which in effect means that data is physically separated to faster or slower storage devices. For example, more frequently accessed (hot) data can be assigned to a storage group with fast storage devices, and older and less frequently accessed (warm or cold) data can be assigned to a storage group with slower storage devices.

This can reduce storage costs because not all data needs fast and expensive storage devices; only part of the data does. In fact, hot data typically represents a small fraction of the total amount of data in a typical data warehouse; therefore, savings can be substantial. In a data warehouse, it is also common to see hot data cooling down as time goes by. With multitemperature data management, you can easily move the data online and in the background. If there is an important workload that requires more processing power at a given point in time, this data movement can be suspended and later resumed after the important workload ends.

This feature also utilizes DB2 workload management, which enables users to prioritize queries based on the data they access. You can assign a data tag attribute to a storage group or table space, which is used to determine how many system resources a specific workload can use. A data tag is simply a value from 0 to 9. With these capabilities, you can reserve system resources to process "hot" data while throttling resources to process "cold" data.

Pages

DB2 stores table and index data on a page, which is the smallest unit of storage in a DB2 database. DB2 creates and manages the pages in the table space automatically, but you can control the page size for your table spaces. If you do not explicitly specify the page size when you create the table space, DB2 uses the default size used when the database was created. The database configuration parameter `pagesize` (*Database page size*) tells you the default page size for the database. If no page size was specified when creating the database, the default is 4K (K stands for a kilobyte). DB2 supports four different page sizes: 4K, 8K, 16K, and 32K.

It is important to note that a row within a table cannot span pages (that is, the entire row must fit on a single page). The page size for the table must be large enough to hold all of the columns in the table. For example, if a table is created as follows,

```
CREATE TABLE mytable (lastname    CHAR(100),
                      firstname   CHAR(100),
                      address     CHAR(4000)
                     )
```

the total space required to store a row is the sum of the column sizes, and this exceeds the size of a 4K page. Therefore, this table must be created in a table space with a page size is of at least 8K. Tables are described in detail later in this chapter.

> **NOTE**
> After you have created a table space with a given page size, you cannot alter that size. The only option is to drop and re-create the table space using a different page size.

Extents

An extent is a collection of consecutive pages in a table space. For performance reasons, DB2 reads and writes extents of pages rather than single pages to optimize I/O. An extent can only contain pages for one object. For example, DB2 does not allow one page within an extent to belong to table A and another one to index A or table B.

If you are familiar with RAID (redundant array of inexpensive disks) or striped file systems, you understand the concept of **striping**—where data is written to the various underlying disks in pieces. DB2 does the same basic operation within its table spaces. When you create a table space with more than one container, DB2 writes the data to the containers in a round-robin fashion. DB2 fills an extent in one container and then fills an extent in the next container and so on until it has written an extent in all of the containers in the table space. DB2 then fills the second extent in each of the containers—and so on.

For example, if you create a table space with four containers (or the storage group in an automatic storage managed table space has four storage paths) and create a table in that table space, as you add data to the table, the data is striped across the table space containers as follows: The first extent of pages for the table is placed in the first container or storage path (for example, Container 0 or storage path A). Next, extent 1 is written to Container 1 or storage path B, extent 2 is written to Container 2 or storage path C, and extent 3 is written to Container 3 or storage path D. At this point, there is one extent in each of the four containers or storage paths, so DB2 starts striping the data back at the first container or storage path. Therefore, extent 4 is written to Container 0 or storage path A, extent 5 will be written to Container 1 or storage path B, and so on as more data is added to the table. Figure 7.18 illustrates this.

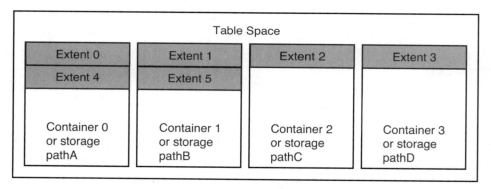

Figure 7.18   Table spaces, containers, storage paths, and extents

NOTE

The first extent (extent 0) for each object can start in any of the defined containers or storage paths. Not all objects start in the first Container 0 or storage path A.

You can control the extent size when you create a table space with the EXTENTSIZE clause of the CREATE TABLESPACE statement. If you do not explicitly specify the extent size when you create the table space, DB2 uses the default extent size based on the database configuration parameter DFT_EXTENT_SZ.

> **NOTE**
>
> After you have created a table space with a given extent size, you cannot alter that size. The only option is to drop and re-create the table space to use a different extent size.

Creating Table Spaces

You create a table space with the CREATE TABLESPACE statement. When you create a table space, you can define the following:

To indicate the type of data that the table space stores, include one of these keywords:

- REGULAR
- LARGE
- SYSTEM TEMPORARY
- USER TEMPORARY

To indicate the type of table space based on how it is managed, you can use these keywords:

- AUTOMATIC STORAGE
- SYSTEM (for SMS table spaces)
- DATABASE (for DMS table spaces)

Although each of these options for specifying the table space storage type are mutually exclusive, if your table space is MANAGED BY AUTOMATIC STORAGE, DB2 determines what type of storage to use under the covers.

- To indicate the page size to use for all tables and indexes in the table space, use PAGESIZE *integer* (the page size specified when creating the database is the default).
- To indicate the extent size for the table space, use EXTENTSIZE *number of pages* (the default is determined by the database configuration file parameter DFT_EXTENT_SZ).
- To indicate the name of the buffer pool associated to this table space, use BUFFER-POOL *buffer pool name*. This buffer pool must exist before you create the table space and must have the same page size as you specify for the table space. By default, the table space is associated with the IBMDEFAULTBP buffer pool. You can change this when you create the table space because the page size of the table space must match the page size of the associated buffer pool. If you are using a multipartitioned database, you also need to tell DB2 in which partition group to create the table space.

- To indicate the storage group where the table space data is stored, use STOGROUP *storage group name*. This is only applicable to automatic storage table spaces. If not specified, the default storage group is used. The storage group must exist before you create the table space. The storage group name is a one-part name; that is, it does not have a schema name.

In addition, you can optionally specify the following I/O characteristics of the table spaces and its containers:

- The overhead, which is the same as the seek time for the disks. If you have one kind of disk, then you can usually find this value on the disks or from the manufacturer. If you have a mixture of disks in the table space, you need to calculate the average overhead, seek time, and latency for the disks.

- The transfer rate for the disks specifies the amount of time (in milliseconds) required for the I/O subsystem to read one page from disk into memory. As with the overhead, if you are using a mixture of disk types, calculate an average value for this parameter.

- The prefetch size for the table space, which indicates the number of pages fetched ahead of time to improve performance. DB2 uses the database configuration file parameter `DFT_PREFTECH_SZ` if you do not specify this value.

- The database partition group where the table space is created.

- Allow dropped table recovery. If you accidentally drop a table and this option is enabled, you can specify the `RECOVER TABLE ON` option when you are rolling forward so that the table is not deleted and you can recover the table's data.

SMS Table Spaces

System-managed space (SMS) table spaces use the file system manager to manage the tables and indexes stored within the table space. The only type of container allowed for an SMS table space is a directory, which you specify in the `CREATE TABLESPACE` statement. When you create tables and indexes, DB2 creates a file for every object within the table space inside the directory containers.

Because you cannot add containers to an SMS table space using the `ALTER TABLESPACE` statement, it is important for you to create the table space on a file system with enough space.

> **NOTE**
>
> Although you cannot normally add containers to an SMS table space directly, you can increase the size of the existing file system containers using operating system commands. You can add a container to an SMS table space on a partition where there are no existing containers for the table space using the `SYSTEM CONTAINER` clause. You can also add a container indirectly by backing up the database and performing a redirected restore.

Creating SMS Table Spaces

You need to use the CREATE TABLESPACE statement with the MANAGED BY SYSTEM clause to create an SMS table space. You also specify the path for the containers for the table space. For example, the following statement creates an SMS table space *space1* using one directory container 'c:\space1':

```
CREATE TABLESPACE space1
   MANAGED BY SYSTEM USING ('c:\space1')
```

Note that the path is included with the USING keyword. You can specify this as an absolute or a relative path. The given example uses an absolute path (it completely specifies the location of the directory). Following is the same example, but it uses a relative path:

```
CREATE TABLESPACE space1
   MANAGED BY SYSTEM USING ('space1')
```

A relative path is relative to the database directory (for example, the SQL*xxxxx* directory) where the database was created. The statement just shown creates the following directory assuming the current instance is DB2 and there is only one database created on the C: drive on Windows:

C:\DB2\NODE0000\SQL00001\SPACE1

For the instance *db2inst1* with only one database created on /mydata file system on Linux or UNIX, the command creates the directory

/mydata/db2inst1/NODE0000/SQL00001/space1

> **NOTE**
>
> If the directory you specify does not exist, DB2 creates it. If the directory does exist, it cannot contain any files or subdirectories.

You can create more than one container for the table space as follows:

```
create tablespace space1
managed by system using
('c:\space1',  'd:\space1')
```

or

```
create tablespace space1
managed by system using
('/data1/space1', '/data1/space2')
```

> **NOTE**
>
> In the preceding examples, you created the containers on the same drive and file system. In practice, you should not do this, as this is not an optimal configuration and could cause I/O contention.

If you create a table in an SMS table space, DB2 creates a file for each object and stores the information for the object in that file. Whenever you create a table it is assigned an object ID. Each of the files that is created for an object associated with the same table is assigned the same object ID by DB2 if the table is in an SMS table space. This object ID is then used in the file name for the objects in an SMS table space.

If you look inside an SMS table space directory container, you see several files named SQL*xxxxx*.DAT, SQL*xxxxx*.INX, SQL*xxxxx*.LB, SQL*xxxxx*.LBA, and SQL*xxxxx*.LF. If the table space has more than one container, DB2 creates the same files in all of the table space's containers.

DMS Table Spaces

DB2 manages the storage and retrieval of database objects from within the table space with database-managed space (DMS) table spaces. When you create a DMS table space, the only type of containers that can be specified are files, logical drives, or logical devices (raw devices). With DMS table spaces, when you create tables and indexes, DB2 places the pages for these objects in the table space and keeps track of where things are located.

Creating DMS Table Spaces

To create a DMS table space, specify MANAGED BY DATABASE with the CREATE TABLESPACE statement. You then specify the path for the containers as follows:

```
CREATE TABLESPACE tablespace_name
    MANAGED BY DATABASE USING
        (FILE 'file_name' size)
```

   or

```
CREATE TABLESPACE tablespace_name
    MANAGED BY DATABASE USING
        (DEVICE 'device_name' size)
```

> **NOTE**
>
> If the file already exists, DB2 checks to make sure it is not used as a container for another tablespace. If it is not already used, DB2 uses the file. If you are using a logical drive or raw logical device, you must first create the drive or device using operating system commands.

Using Device Containers

If you are building a table space on Linux or UNIX and want to use a raw device, you must first create a logical volume using the tools provided by your operating system. If you are using Windows, create a disk partition that can be used as the container, but you need to remember *not* to format the partition to create a file system.

It is important to note the size of these volumes or partitions so that when you are creating the table space and assigning the containers to the devices you do not waste space. Because the volume/partition cannot be used for any other purpose, you might as well size the container to use the whole device/partition.

> **NOTE**
>
> You can extend or resize the container later to use up the free space if you do leave some space on the logical volumes/disk partitions.

When you create the table space, you can specify the size of the containers by either

- Number of pages based on the page size for the table space (the default)
- Actual size in KB, MB, or GB

The following are two examples of creating DMS table spaces with device containers:

```
CREATE TABLESPACE ts1 MANAGED BY DATABASE USING
    (DEVICE '/dev/rmydisk1' 20000)

CREATE TABLESPACE ts2 MANAGED BY DATABASE USING
    (DEVICE '\\.\G:' 200MB)
```

Using File Containers

As with SMS containers, when you specify the name for a file container, you can use either a relative file name or the absolute file name. When you issue the CREATE TABLESPACE statement, you specify the container name(s) and size(s). If the file exists, DB2 checks to see if the file is the right size and if it is used for any other purpose. If it is the right size and not used for another purpose, DB2 uses the file. If it is not the right size but is not used for any other purpose, DB2 either expands or shrinks the file to make it the right size. If the file does not exist, DB2 creates it with the size that you specified.

In the same manner as with device containers, you can specify the size of the containers in either

- Number of pages based on the page size for the table space (the default)
- Actual size in KB, MB, or GB

The following are two examples of creating DMS table spaces with file containers:

```
CREATE TABLESPACE ts1 MANAGED BY DATABASE USING
      (file '/myfile1' 2GB)

CREATE TABLESPACE ts2 MANAGED BY DATABASE USING
      (file 'C:\dbfiles\ts2' 20000)
```

Automatic Storage Managed Table Spaces

Automatic storage table spaces use space in the storage group defined for the database or table space and can grow automatically as the table space is getting close to being full. DB2 chooses whether to use SMS or DMS for the underlying storage for the table space depending on the type of data it stores (for example, temp or regular).

When you create a table space using automatic storage, you define its initial size, maximum size, and growth increment. As the table space begins to fill up, DB2 automatically grows the table space by the specified increment.

You can add storage paths to the storage group used by an automatic storage managed table space, and these storage paths are used for new data that is added. An ALTER TABLESPACE with the REBALANCE clause should be run to ensure striping across all storage paths in the storage group occurs.

Creating Automatic Storage Table Spaces

Use the CREATE TABLESPACE statement with the MANAGED BY AUTOMATIC STORAGE clause to create an automatic storage managed table space. This clause is the default, so it does not need to be explicitly specified. You can also include the USING STOGROUP *storage-group-name* clause to assign a storage group to the table space. Only one storage group can be assigned. If this clause is not specified, the default storage group is used.

Let's take a look at some examples. The following statement creates a table space named *auto1* managed by automatic storage and using the default storage group

```
      CREATE TABLESPACE auto1
```

To create a table space using automatic storage that starts at 100MB and grows up to a maximum of 750MB in increments of 50MB in the default storage group, use the following statement:

```
CREATE TABLESPACE auto1
    initialsize 100M
    increasesize 50M
    maxsize 750M
```

Comparing SMS, DMS, and Automatic Storage Table Spaces

Table 7.5 summarizes the differences between SMS, DMS, and automatic storage table spaces. As you can see, all table space types stripe the extents in a round-robin fashion across the containers or, in the case of automatic storage, across the storage paths in a storage group. SMS and automatic storage table spaces grow and shrink as data is added or deleted, while DMS table spaces are preallocated when the table space is created. All types of table spaces provide very good performance.

For automatic storage table spaces, behind the scenes DB2 is actually choosing automatically the optimal underlying table space for the type of data that will be stored in the table space. For example, for a temporary table space, it will likely choose SMS, but for a regular or large table space. it will likely choose DMS.

Table 7.5   Comparing SMS and DMS Characteristics

Characteristic	SMS	DMS	Automatic Storage
Striping	Yes	Yes	Yes (using storage groups)
Object management	Operating system using unique file names	DB2	DB2
Space allocation	Grows/shrinks on demand	Preallocated	Grows/shrinks on-demand
Ease of administration	Easy	Average	Very easy
Performance	Good	Very good Can achieve up to 5 to 10 percent advantage with raw containers. Index, LOBs, and data for a single table can be spread across table spaces.	Very good

Table 7.6 summarizes the differences of managing nonautomatic storage and automatic storage table spaces.

Table 7.6   Differences Managing Nonautomatic Storage and Automatic Storage

Nonautomatic Storage	Automatic Storage
Containers must be explicitly specified when the table space is created.	Containers are assigned and allocated automatically by the DB2. They cannot be explicitly specified.
The initial size for the table space cannot be specified using the INITIALSIZE clause.	The initial size for the table space can be specified using the INITIALSIZE clause.
Automatic resizing of table spaces is off (AUTORESIZE NO) by default.	Automatic resizing of table spaces is on (AUTORESIZE YES) by default.
Container operations can be performed using the ALTER TABLESPACE statement (ADD, DROP, BEGIN NEW STRIPE SET, and so on).	Container operations cannot be performed because DB2 manages the space.
A redirected restore operation can be used to redefine the containers associated with the table space.	A redirected restore operation cannot be used to redefine the containers associated with the table space because DB2 manages the space.

Listing Table Spaces

You can get a list and details of table spaces in your database using the MON_GET_TABLESPACE table function. The syntax of the function is

```
>>-MON_GET_TABLESPACE--(--tbsp_name--,--member--)-------------><
```

- tbsp_name is the name of the table space. If not specified, all table spaces in the database you are connected to are displayed.
- member is an integer used to specify the member of the database. Use -2 to retrieve all members.

Functions and how to use them are discussed later in this chapter; however, following is an example of how you would typically invoke this particular table function:

```
SELECT varchar(tbsp_name, 30) as tbsp_name, tbsp_type
  FROM TABLE(MON_GET_TABLESPACE('',-2)) AS t
```

Table functions return a table as output; therefore you invoke them after the FROM clause, and need to use the TABLE (...) AS <alias> clause. In the example, t is the name of the alias.

This is the sample output you would receive:

```
TBSP_NAME         TBSP_TYPE
----------------  ----------
SYSCATSPACE       DMS
USERSPACE1        DMS
TEMPSPACE1        SMS
```

Another related table function you can use is `MON_GET_CONTAINER` to obtain information about table space containers. Refer to the DB2 Information Center for more details about these functions.

> **NOTE**
>
> The command `LIST TABLESPACES` can also be used to obtain information about table spaces; however, this is a deprecated command.

Altering a Table Space

You can change the type, size and other characteristics—such as the prefetch size, overhead, and transfer rate—of the tables spaces in your databases using the `ALTER TABLESPACE` statement.

You can only change the type of a table space from DMS to AUTOMATIC STORAGE. This is achieved using the `ALTER TABLESPACE` statement with the `USING STOGROUP` clause. Prior to doing this, if the table space had been part of a database created with `AUTOMATIC STORAGE NO`, enable the database to use automatic storage simply by creating a storage group in the database.

You can also change buffer pool and storage group assignments and bring an offline table space back online. The storage characteristics can only be modified for automatic storage and DMS table spaces.

To change the I/O characteristics for your table spaces, you must first connect to the database and then use the `ALTER TABLESPACE` statement with the parameter you want to change. For example

```
ALTER TABLESPACE   ts2     PREFETCHSIZE 128
ALTER TABLESPACE   ts1     OVERHEAD      10
ALTER TABLESPACE   mytspc  TRANSFERRATE 100
```

Dropping a Table Space

Although an SMS table space does not consume any space unless there are objects (such as tables and indexes) in the table space, a DMS table space continues to hold all of its allocated space. If you create a table space and find that you did not create any objects in the table space, it is good practice to drop the table space.

Dropping a table space can also be a fast and efficient method for dropping tables. If you drop a table space and there are tables in the table space, then DB2 drops the tables as well, as long as there are no objects for the tables in other table spaces (that is, the data object for the table is in one table space, and the index object is in another table space). When you drop a table space this way, DB2 does not log all the row and page deletions as it does for a drop table operation;

therefore, this can be a much more efficient method to drop a table, especially if you have only that table defined in the table space.

To drop a table space you use the DROP TABLESPACE statement:

```
DROP TABLESPACE myts
```

This removes all entries for the table space from the system catalogs as well as its entries in the table spaces file, and it drops all objects defined wholly within the table space.

Buffer Pools

DB2 buffer pools are an area in real memory where all database work really happens. Buffer pools temporarily store (cache) regular data and index pages when they are read from disk to be scanned, updated, inserted, or deleted. The buffer pool area improves the performance of the database because the pages can be accessed much more quickly from memory than from disk.

When you connect to a database, the database buffer pools (along with the lock list, database heap, and so on) are allocated in memory. When you (or anyone else using the database) disconnect all applications from the database, this memory is freed back to the operating system.

> **NOTE**
>
> If your applications frequently connect to and disconnect from the database, you should consider activating the database (using the ACTIVATE DATABASE command) so that the buffer pools and all database-related memory remain allocated. This eliminates the overhead of allocating all of this memory each time an application connects to the database. When you then want to "close" the database, use the DEACTIVATE DATABASE command.

When you create a database, a default buffer pool, IBMDEFAULTBP, is automatically created. This buffer pool is associated with the default table spaces SYSCATSPACE, TEMPSPACE1, and USERSPACE1, and you cannot drop it, but you can change its size using the ALTER BUFFERPOOL statement. On Linux and Windows, the default buffer pool is 250 pages or 1MB; on UNIX, the default buffer pool is 1,000 pages or 4MB.

The database manager also allocates the hidden system buffer pools IBMSYSTEMBP4K, IBMSYSTEMBP8K, IBMSYSTEMBP16K, and IBMSYSTEMBP32K. These buffer pools have a page size of 4KB, 8KB, 16KB, and 32KB, respectively, and have a size of 16 pages. You cannot use or alter these buffer pools directly; they are used internally by DB2 for system tables.

Creating Buffer Pools

To create a buffer pool, use the CREATE BUFFERPOOL statement. This statement enables you to define, among other things

- **The name of the buffer pool:** This name cannot already be used within the database and cannot begin with the characters SYS or IBM.
- **Whether to create the buffer pool immediately or wait until the database is stopped and restarted:** If you tell DB2 to create the buffer pool immediately but there is not enough memory available, DB2 instead creates it deferred. The default option is IMMEDIATE.
- **The database partition group on which to create the buffer pool.** If you do not specify a database partition group, the buffer pool is created on all partitions.
- **The page size used for the buffer pool.** The default page size is 4K, or 4096 bytes.
- **The size of the buffer pool, specified in the number of pages.** In a partitioned database, this is the default size for all database partitions where the buffer pool exists. The EXCEPT ON DBPARTITIONNUMS clause allows the buffer pool to have different sizes on the different database partitions.
- **The number of pages to be created in the block-based area of the buffer pool.** This area cannot be more than 98 percent of the total buffer pool size. Specifying a value of 0 disables block I/O for the buffer pool. Enabling block-based I/O by setting NUMBLOCK-PAGES to a value greater than zero can help performance for applications that perform a lot of sequential prefetching.
- **The number of pages within a given block in the block-based area of the buffer pool.** The block size must be between 2 and 256 pages; the default value is 32 pages.

> **NOTE**
>
> The page size and buffer pool name cannot be altered after they are defined for a buffer pool.

To examine buffer pools in more detail, let's look at a few examples. Consider a database that is used for a web-based ordering application. Performance is fine most of the time, but once a week management runs some reports that cause the system to slow down. In examining the reports you notice that there are large, multiple joins that create a large temporary table. To isolate the creation of the temporary table from overwhelming the buffer pool, you can create a 10,000-page buffer pool dedicated to the temporary table space as follows:

```
CREATE BUFFERPOOL tempbp SIZE 10000
```

You then need to tell the table space to use the buffer pool:

```
ALTER TABLESPACE tempspace1 BUFFERPOOL tempbp
```

As mentioned earlier, the default page size for a database is 4K. If you want to create a table that is more than 4005 bytes, you need to create a table space with a larger page size. But before you can create this table space, you need to create a buffer pool with the same page size. For this example, assume that a 16K page size is best for this table:

```
CREATE BUFFERPOOL mybp16k SIZE 100000 PAGESIZE 16K
```

You can then create the table space as follows:

```
CREATE TABLESPACE tspc16k PAGESIZE 16K BUFFERPOOL mybp16k
```

If you know that this table will be scanned a lot and that it would benefit from sequential prefetch, you could set aside a portion of the buffer pool for block-based I/O as follows:

```
CREATE BUFFERPOOL mybp16k
    SIZE 100000
    PAGESIZE 16K
    NUMBLOCKPAGES 24000
    BLOCKSIZE 256
```

If you specify a block size that is larger than 98 percent of the buffer pool size, you get the following error:

```
SQL20150N The number of block pages for a buffer pool is too
large for the size of the buffer pool. SQLSTATE=54052
```

> **NOTE**
>
> If you are using block-based I/O, you should ensure that the block size you set is based on the table space's extent size.

If you are creating a buffer pool in a multipartition database, and the table space you are creating the buffer pool for is in a database partition group that is not defined on all database partitions, you can specify in which partition group the buffer pool is created:

```
CREATE BUFFERPOOL mybp16k
    SIZE 100000
    PAGESIZE 16K
    NUMBLOCKPAGES 24000
    BLOCKSIZE 256
    DATABASEPARTITIONGROUP pg16k
```

If you are creating a buffer pool in a multipartition database and you want the buffer pool to be sized larger on some database partitions, you can specify these partitions and their sizes as follows:

```
CREATE BUFFERPOOL mybp16k
    SIZE 100000
    PAGESIZE 16K
    NUMBLOCKPAGES 24000
    BLOCKSIZE 256
    EXCEPT ON DBPARTITIONNUMS 1,2,3 SIZE 200000
```

In this case you can also use the commands

```
CREATE BUFFERPOOL mybp16k
    SIZE 100000
    PAGESIZE 16K
    NUMBLOCKPAGES 24000
    BLOCKSIZE 256
    EXCEPT ON DBPARTITIONNUMS 1 TO 3 SIZE 200000
```

or

```
CREATE BUFFERPOOL mybp16k
    SIZE 100000
    PAGESIZE 16K
    NUMBLOCKPAGES 24000
    BLOCKSIZE 256
    EXCEPT ON DBPARTITIONNUM 1 SIZE 200000
    EXCEPT ON DBPARTITIONNUM 2 SIZE 200000
    EXCEPT ON DBPARTITIONNUM 3 SIZE 200000
```

Altering Buffer Pools

You can change some of the attributes of a buffer pool using the ALTER BUFFERPOOL statement. DB2 enables you to change the following:

- Size
- Database partition group
- Block-based area
- Block size
- Enabling or disabling extended storage

Given a buffer pool created with the statement

```
CREATE BUFFERPOOL mybp16k
    SIZE 100000
    PAGESIZE 16K
    NUMBLOCKPAGES 24000
```

```
BLOCKSIZE 256
DATABASEPARTITIONGROUP PG16K
```

to make the buffer pool twice as large, you would use the statement:

```
ALTER BUFFERPOOL mybp16k
   SIZE 200000
```

Notice that because you did not want to change the block-based area size or the block size, you did not specify these options in the `ALTER BUFFERPOOL` statement.

To make the size of the block-based area 32,000 pages instead of 24,000 pages, you would use the statement:

```
ALTER BUFFERPOOL mybp16k
   NUMBLOCKPAGES 32000
```

To allocate this buffer pool also on the partitions in the database partition group *pg1234*, use the statement

```
ALTER BUFFERPOOL mybp16k
   DATABASEPARTITIONGROUP pg1234
```

Dropping Buffer Pools

You cannot drop any buffer pools that are associated with a table space. Before you can drop the buffer pool, you need to associate the table space with a different buffer pool using the `ALTER TABLESPACE` statement.

When there are no longer any table spaces associated with the buffer pool, you can drop it using the `DROP BUFFERPOOL` statement. This releases the memory back to the operating system for use by other DB2-related buffers and heaps or for other application memory requests.

To drop the buffer pool MYBP16K, use the statement

```
DROP BUFFERPOOL mybp16k
```

Schemas

A schema is a database object used to logically group other database objects together. Every database object name has two parts:

```
schema_name.object_name
```

This two-part name (also known as the fully qualified name) must be unique within the database. Here are some examples:

```
db2admin.tab1
mary.idx1
sales.tblspace1
```

When you create an object, it is always created within a schema, even if you do not explicitly specify the schema name. When you do not specify the schema name, DB2 uses your **authorization ID** (the ID used to connect to the database) as the object's schema. If you connect to a database as *peter* and in a query specify a table simply as *tab1*, DB2 interprets this as *peter.tab1*.

> **NOTE**
>
> A schema does *not* need to map to a user ID. Any user with the appropriate authorization can create a schema. For example, assuming user *peter* has the correct authorizations, he can create the schema *foo*, where *foo* does not map to any user.

To create the schema *user1*, use the `CREATE SCHEMA` statement as follows:

```
CREATE SCHEMA user1
```

Or if you are connected to the database as *user1*, when you create the first new object using this connection without explicitly typing the schema name, DB2 automatically creates the schema *user1* and then the object. This assumes you have the appropriate authorization, in this case, the IMPLICIT_SCHEMA privilege. Assuming you have the privilege to create tables, the following statement creates the schema *user1*, followed by the table *table1*.

```
CREATE TABLE table1 (mycol int)
```

If you are connected to the database as *user1*, you can also create objects under a different schema. In this case, explicitly indicate the schema name, for example

```
CREATE TABLE newuser.table1 (mycol int)
```

This statement creates a table called *table1* in the schema *newuser*. If the schema doesn't already exist, it is created. Although running both of these `CREATE TABLE` statements results in two tables in the database called *table1*, they are different tables because one is in the schema *user1,* and the other is in the schema *newuser*.

> **NOTE**
>
> Creating schemas implicitly or explicitly requires the user to have the appropriate authorizations or privileges. Refer to Chapter 8, "Implementing Security," for more details.

When you access a database object, you can omit the schema name. Let's say you are connected to the database as *user1* and you issue the following statement:

```
SELECT * FROM table1
```

This statement references table *user1.table1*.

If the table you want to access is *newuser.table1*, you must explicitly include the schema name:

```
SELECT * FROM newuser.table1
```

Alternatively, you can use the SET SCHEMA command to set the schema to use for the session. For example, while connected to the database as *user1*, you could do

```
set schema newuser
```

Then when issuing this statement

```
SELECT * FROM table1
```

the table referenced would be *newuser.table1*.

You cannot alter a schema, but you can drop it (as long as no objects exist within the schema) and re-create it with the new definition. Use the DROP SCHEMA statement to drop a schema:

```
DROP SCHEMA newuser RESTRICT
```

You must specify the RESTRICT keyword; it is part of the DROP SCHEMA syntax and serves as a reminder that you cannot drop a schema unless it is unused.

Data Types

Before continuing with our discussion of database objects, you need to understand the data types supported by DB2. A data type indicates what type of data can be saved in a column or variable and how large it can be. DB2 data types are either

- Built-in data types
- User-defined types (UDTs)

DB2 Built-in Data Types

DB2 provides several built-in data types, which can be classified into the following categories:

- Numeric
- Boolean
- String
- Datetime
- Extensible Markup Language

Figure 7.19 summarizes the built-in data types supported in DB2.

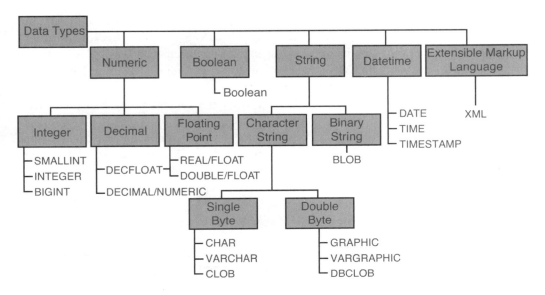

Figure 7.19 The DB2 built-in data types

Numeric Data Types

The numeric data types include the following:

- Small integer (SMALLINT)
- Integer (INT or INTEGER)
- Big integer (BIGINT)
- DECIMAL/NUMERIC
- REAL/FLOAT
- DOUBLE/FLOAT
- Decimal floating-point (DECFLOAT)

A SMALLINT uses the least amount of storage in the database for each value. The data value range for a SMALLINT is –32768 to 32767. The precision for a SMALLINT is five digits to the left of the decimal. Each SMALLINT column value uses 2 bytes of database storage.

An INTEGER uses twice as much storage as a SMALLINT but has a greater range of possible values. The data value range for an INTEGER data type is –2,147,483,648 to 2,147,483,647. The precision for an INTEGER is 10 digits to the left of the decimal. Each INTEGER column value uses 4 bytes of database storage.

The BIGINT data type is available for supporting 64-bit integers. The value range for BIGINT is −9,223,372,036,854,775,808 to 9,223,372,036,854,775,807. Because platforms include native support for 64-bit integers, processing large numbers with BIGINT is more efficient than processing with DECIMAL and more precise than using DOUBLE or REAL. Each BIGINT column value uses 8 bytes of database storage.

The SMALLINT, INTEGER, and BIGINT data types do not allow any digits to the right of the decimal.

A DECIMAL or NUMERIC data type is used for numbers with fractional and whole parts. The DECIMAL data is stored in a packed format. You must provide the precision and scale when using a DECIMAL data type. The **precision** is the total number of digits (ranging from 1 to 31 digits), and the **scale** is the number of digits in the fractional part of the number.

> **NOTE**
>
> If you do not explicitly specify the precision and scale, DB2 will use a default value of DECIMAL(5,0), that is, a precision of 5 digits and a scale of 0 digits.

A REAL data type is an approximation of a number. The approximation requires 32 bits or 4 bytes of storage. To specify a single-precision number using the REAL data type, you must define its length between 1 and 24.

A DOUBLE or FLOAT data type is also an approximation of a number. The approximation requires 64 bits or 8 bytes of storage. To specify a double-precision number using the FLOAT data type, you must define its length between 25 and 53.

The DECFLOAT data type is useful in business applications that deal with exact decimal values such as financial applications where monetary values are manipulated. It supports the 16-digit and 34-digit decimal floating-point encodings, corresponding to 8 bytes and 16 bytes of storages, respectively. Although the FLOAT data type provides binary approximations to decimal data, DECFLOAT provides exact decimal values. DECFLOAT provides the accuracy of DECIMAL with some of the performance advantages of FLOAT.

Boolean Data Types

The BOOLEAN data type is used mainly when working with the SQL Procedural Language (SQL PL). It can only be used for local variables, global variables, parameters, or return types in compound SQL statements. A Boolean value represents a truth value of TRUE or FALSE. A Boolean expression or predicate resulting in a value of unknown is represented as the NULL value.

String Data Types

You can define string or character columns as either fixed-length or variable-length. The character string data types include the following:

- Character (CHAR)
- Variable character (VARCHAR)
- Character large object (CLOB)
- GRAPHIC
- VARGRAPHIC
- Double-byte character large object (DBCLOB)

A CHAR column is stored as a fixed-length field in the database; if the string you enter is shorter than the defined length of the column, the string is padded with blanks. This wastes space within the database if you tend to store strings that are a lot shorter than the length of the column. A fixed-length character column can have a maximum length of 254 characters. If no length is specified, DB2 uses the default length of 1 character.

A VARCHAR column stores only the characters entered for the string, and its maximum size closely corresponds to the page size for the table. For example, for a table created in a table space with a 32K page size, the maximum length of a VARCHAR string is 32,672 characters.

NOTE

You can use the FOR BIT DATA clause of CHAR and VARCHAR data types to indicate the data will be stored as a sequence of bytes (binary data). The clause can be used for nontraditional data such as video and audio. Code page conversions do not occur because data is compared bit by bit.

GRAPHIC data types use 2 bytes of storage to represent a single character. There are two types:

- **GRAPHIC**: Fixed-length with a maximum of 127 characters
- **VARGRAPHIC**: Variable-length with a maximum of 16,336 characters

When a VARCHAR data type's maximum size of 32,672 bytes is not enough to hold your data, use large objects. Large objects (LOBs) can store data greater than 32K up to 2GB in size. They are typically used to store information such as an audio file, or a picture. Though XML documents can also be stored as LOBs, we recommend you to use the XML data type instead to take advantage of pureXML technology.

Three kinds of LOB data types are provided with DB2:

- Binary large object (BLOB)
- Single-byte character large object (CLOB)
- Double-byte character large object (DBCLOB)

BLOBs store variable-length data in binary format and are ideal for storing video or audio information in your database. This data type has some restrictions; for example, you cannot sort by this type of column.

CLOBs store large amounts of variable-length, single-byte character set (SBCS) or multi-byte character set (MBCS) character strings—for example, large amounts of text such as white papers or long documents.

DBCLOBs store large amounts of variable-length, double-byte character set (DBCS) character strings, such as large amounts of text in Chinese.

LOBs are accessed directly from disk without going through the buffer pool, so using LOBs is slower than using other data types. In addition, because changes to a database are logged in transaction log files, these files might get filled quickly when modifying a LOB column. To prevent this from happening, the CREATE TABLE statement has the NOT LOGGED option for LOB columns. For LOB columns defined as more than 1GB in size, NOT LOGGED is required.

The CREATE TABLE statement also has the COMPACT option for LOBs to allocate just the necessary disk space. However, if you perform an update to the LOB column that would increase the size of the LOB, DB2 would need to allocate more space at that time, which incurs a performance penalty. Note that this option does not compress the LOBs.

> **NOTE**
>
> Do not use LOBs to store data less than 32K in size. Instead, use VARCHAR or VARCHAR FOR BIT DATA, which can hold a maximum of 32,672 bytes. This helps with database performance.

Datetime Data Types

Date and time data types are special character data types used to store date and/or time values in specific formats. These data types are stored in an internal format by DB2 and use an external format for the users. DB2 supports three datetime data types: DATE, TIME, and TIMESTAMP.

- The DATE type stores a date value (month, day, and year). Its external format is MM-DD-YYYY or MM/DD/YYYY.

- The TIME type stores a time value (hour, minute, and second). Its external format is HH:MM:SS or HH.MM.SS.

- The TIMESTAMP type combines the DATE and TIME types but also stores the time down to the nanosecond. Its external format is MM-DD-YYYY-HH.MM.SS. NNNNNN.

Extensible Markup Language Data Type

The Extensible Markup Language data type, XML, is a data type that is part of the SQL standard with XML extensions (SQL/XML). This data type allows for storing well-formed XML documents natively (in a parsed-hierarchical manner) internally in a DB2 database. The XML data type can be transformed to a serialized string value using the XMLSERIALIZE function, and a serialized string value can be transformed into an XML value using the XMLPARSE function.

User-Defined Types (UDTs)

User-defined types (UDTs) enable database users to create or extend the use of data types for their own needs. UDTs can be classified as DISTINCT, STRUCTURE, ROW, ORDINARY ARRAY, ASSOCIATIVE ARRAY, and CURSOR. This section discusses only DISTINCT types. Refer to the DB2 Information Center for the other kinds of UDTs.

A DISTINCT UDT can enforce business rules and prevent data from being used improperly. UDTs are built on top of existing DB2 built-in data types.

To create a UDT, use the CREATE TYPE statement:

```
CREATE TYPE type_name AS built-in_datatype WITH COMPARISONS
```

The WITH COMPARISONS clause is required only for compatibility with earlier versions of products in the DB2 family. It can be used for all data types, except BLOB, CLOB, and DBCLOB data types. This clause causes DB2 to create system-generated SQL functions that perform casting between the types; these are known as *casting functions*.

For example, let's say you create two UDTs, *celsius* and *fahrenheit*:

```
CREATE TYPE  celsius   AS integer WITH COMPARISONS
CREATE TYPE fahrenheit AS integer WITH COMPARISONS
```

The first statement creates a casting function named celsius, and the second statement creates a casting function named fahrenheit.

Now, let's say you create a table using the newly created UDTs:

```
CREATE TABLE temperature
      (country          varchar(100),
       average_temp_c   celsius,
       average_temp_f   fahrenheit
      )
```

Table *TEMPERATURE* keeps track of the average temperature of each country in the world in both Celsius and Fahrenheit. If you would like to know which countries have an average temperature higher than 35 degrees Celsius, you can issue this query:

```
SELECT country FROM temperature WHERE average_temp_c > 35
```

Would this query work? At first, you might think it will, but remember that average_temp_c has data type *celsius*, and 35 is an INTEGER. Even though *celsius* was created based on the INTEGER built-in data type, this comparison cannot be performed as is. To resolve this problem, use the casting function generated with the creation of the *celsius* UDT as shown here:

```
SELECT country FROM temperature WHERE average_temp_c > celsius(35)
```

UDTs enforce business rules by preventing illegitimate operations. For example, the following query will not work:

```
SELECT country FROM temperature WHERE average_temp_c = average_temp_f
```

Because column `average_temp_c` and `average_temp_f` are of different data types, this query results in an error. If UDTs had not been created and the INTEGER built-in data type had been used instead for both columns, the query would have worked—but what meaning in real life would that have?

To drop a UDT, use the statement `DROP TYPE type_name`. This also drops the casting functions associated with the UDT.

Choosing the Proper Data Type

It is important to choose the proper data type because this affects performance and disk space. To choose the correct data type, you need to understand how your data will be used and its possible values. Table 7.6 summarizes what you should consider.

Table 7.6   Choosing the Proper Data Types

Question	Data Type
Is your data variable in length, with a maximum length of fewer than 10 characters?	CHAR
Is your data variable in length, with a minimum length of 10 characters?	VARCHAR
Is your data fixed in length?	CHAR
Is your data going to be used in sort operations?	CHAR, VARCHAR, DECIMAL, INTEGER
Is your data going to be used in arithmetic operations?	DECIMAL, REAL, DOUBLE, BIGINT, INTEGER, SMALLINT
Does your data require decimals?	DECIMAL, REAL, DOUBLE, FLOAT
Do you need to store very small amounts of nontraditional data such as audio or video?	CHAR FOR BIT DATA, VARCHAR FOR BIT DATA
Do you need to store nontraditional data such as audio or video or data larger than a character string can store?	CLOB, BLOB, DBCLOB
Does the data contain timestamp information?	TIMESTAMP
Does the data contain time information?	TIME

Question	Data Type
Does the data contain date information?	DATE
Do you need a data type to enforce your business rules that have a specific meaning (beyond DB2 built-in data types)?	User-defined type
Will you work with XML documents in your database?	XML

> **NOTE**
>
> For the first two rows of Table 7.6, we chose CHAR versus VARCHAR depending on the length of the data. If the maximum length is fewer than 10 characters, we suggest using a CHAR data type; otherwise, we recommend VARCHAR. Normally for small variable-length columns, a CHAR column provides better performance. We chose the value of 10 characters based on our experience, but it can vary depending on your data.

Tables

A table is an unordered set of records, consisting of rows and columns. Each column has a defined data type, and each row represents an entry in the table. Figure 7.20 shows an example of a table with n rows and m columns. The *sales_person* column with a VARCHAR data type is the first column in the table, followed by the *region* column with a CHAR data type, and the *year* column with an INTEGER data type. The *info* column is the mth column in the table and has an XML data type.

Table Classification

One main classification of tables is based on how the data is organized in the data pages:

- **Row-organized tables:** The data is stored by rows in the data pages, and a data page can hold data of one or more rows. For example, using the information from Figure 7.20, all of row 1, row 2, and so on could be store in a data page.
- **Column-organized tables:** The data is stored by columns in the data pages, and a data page can hold data of only one column. For example, using the information from Figure 7.20, column 1 would be stored in a data page, column 2 would be stored in another data page, and so on. Column-organized tables is a new feature introduced in DB2 10.5 and is also known as BLU Acceleration.

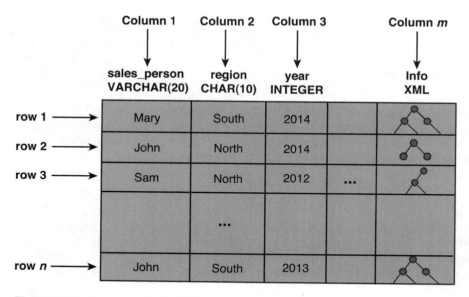

Figure 7.20   An example of a table

Row-organized tables are the traditional type of tables that have been used with DB2, and all of the sections that follow up to section "Temporal Tables and Time Travel Query" mainly apply to this type of tables. Column-organized tables are discussed in more detail in section "Column-organized Tables (aka DB2 BLU Acceleration)."

Row-organized tables can be classified as illustrated in Figure 7.21. You learn more about each of these tables in the next sections.

System Catalog Tables

DB2 automatically creates system catalog tables when a database is created. They always reside in the SYSCATSPACE table space. System catalog tables contain information about all the objects in the database. For example, when you create a table space, its information is loaded into one or more system catalog tables. When this table space is referenced during a later operation, DB2 checks the corresponding system catalog tables to see whether the table space exists and whether the operation is allowed. Without the system catalog tables, DB2 cannot function.

Some of the information contained in system catalog tables includes the following:

- Definitions of all database objects
- Column data types of the tables and views
- Defined constraints
- Object privileges
- Object dependencies

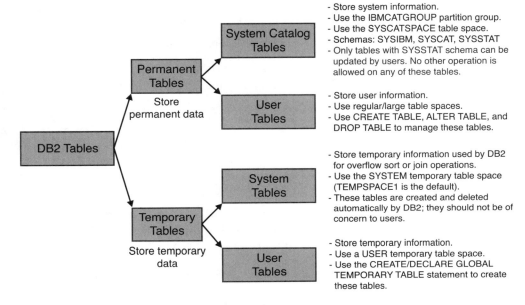

Figure 7.21 Classification of row-organized tables in DB2

System catalog tables or views use the SYSIBM, SYSCAT, or SYSSTAT schemas:

- The **SYSIBM schema** is used for the base system catalog tables.

- The **SYSCAT schema** is used for views defined on the system catalog tables. DB2 users should normally query the SYSCAT views rather than the SYSIBM tables for information.

- The **SYSSTAT schema** is used for views containing information about database statistics and is also based on the system catalog tables.

Although you cannot update the tables and views residing under the SYSIBM and SYSCAT schemas, you can update the views under the SYSSTAT schema. Updating these views can sometimes influence the DB2 optimizer to choose a different access path.

User Tables

User tables are used to store a user's data. A user can create, alter, drop, and manipulate user tables.

To create a user table, use the CREATE TABLE statement. You can specify the following:

- The name of the table
- The columns of the table and their data types

- The table spaces where you want the table, index, and long objects to be stored within the database
- The constraints you want DB2 to build and maintain on the table, such as referential constraints and unique constraints

The following example illustrates the creation of the table *MYEMPLOYEES* with four columns:

```
CREATE TABLE myemployees (
        empID    INT          NOT NULL PRIMARY KEY,
        empname  VARCHAR(30)  NOT NULL,
        info     XML,
        history  CLOB)
```

In which table space would the table *MYEMPLOYEES* be created? In cases where a table space is not specified, as in this example, follow the flow chart shown in Figure 7.22 to determine what table space would be used.

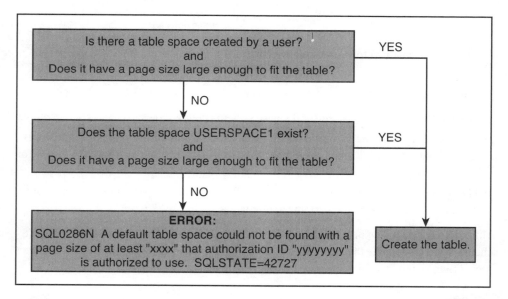

Figure 7.22 Guidelines for determining how the default table space is chosen for a table

This next example uses the same CREATE TABLE situation, but it indicates the table spaces to be used for the table data, index, and long objects:

```
CREATE TABLE myemployees (
            empID    INT            NOT NULL PRIMARY KEY,
            empname  VARCHAR(30)    NOT NULL,
            info     XML,
            history  CLOB)
            IN datadms
      INDEX IN indexdms
      LONG  IN largedms
```

Use the IN clause to specify the table space where the table data will reside. Use the INDEX IN clause to specify where all indexes for the table will reside. Use the LONG IN clause to indicate where the XML or LOB objects will reside.

NOTE

If different table spaces are used for the table, index, and long data, all of these table spaces must be DMS. In addition, the table space where the long data is to be stored must be defined as a *large* table space.

NOTE

In previous versions of DB2, *large* table spaces were known as *long* table spaces. Though the syntax of the CREATE TABLESPACE statement uses the LARGE clause, the syntax of the CREATE TABLE statement still uses LONG.

Figure 7.23 shows the command used to create the table *MYEMPLOYEES* and also the corresponding table space commands to create the required table spaces. Note that all of the statements are creating LARGE table spaces, even for the first two statements where LARGE is not explicitly provided given that this is the default for DMS table spaces.

You can also create a table based on the definition of another table, for example:

```
CREATE TABLE myclone LIKE myemployees
```

The table *MYCLONE* has the same definition as the table *MYEMPLOYEES*; however, other objects like constraints, indexes, or triggers associated with the table are not copied. Table data is not copied either.

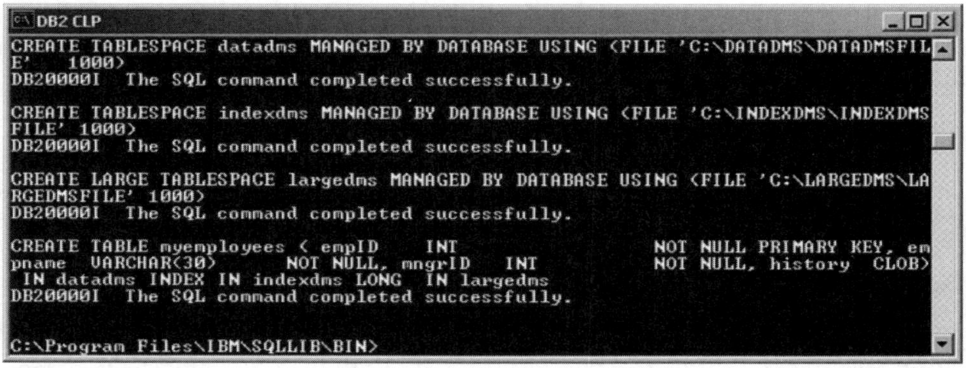

Figure 7.23   Creating a table where table, index, and long data are stored in different DMS table spaces

Another alternative is to create the table structure based on the result of a query, as shown next:

```
CREATE TABLE myclone2 AS (SELECT * FROM myemployees) WITH NO
DATA
```

The WITH NO DATA clause (or the equivalent DEFINITION ONLY clause) is required so that only the structure of the table is copied; otherwise, you would be creating a materialized query table (MQT), which is described in the section, "Materialized Query Tables and Summary Tables."

After you have created a table, you can make changes using the ALTER TABLE statement. For example, to add the column *address* to the table *MYEMPLOYEES*, use this statement:

```
ALTER TABLE myemployees ADD COLUMN address CHAR(45)
```

To drop a table and all its contents, use the DROP TABLE statement, for example:

```
DROP TABLE myemployees
```

Default Values

In the CREATE TABLE statement, you can use the DEFAULT clause for a given column to provide a default value for the column. This means that when you use an INSERT statement to insert a row that does not provide a value for the column, the default value specified in the DEFAULT clause is used. For example, let's say you create the table *COMPANY* with this statement:

```
CREATE TABLE company (
        companyID       INTEGER,
        companyName     VARCHAR(30),
        city            VARCHAR(20) DEFAULT 'TORONTO'
        )
```

Inserting a record with either of the following two statements provides the same result.

```
(1)    INSERT INTO company  (companyID, companyName,  city)
                   VALUES (   111   ,  'cityOne' , DEFAULT)
(2)    INSERT INTO company  (companyID, companyName)
                   VALUES (   111,      'cityOne' )
```

The following row would be inserted.

```
COMPANYID    COMPANYNAME                            CITY
----------- ----------------------------- --------------------
        111 cityOne                                TORONTO
```

In the first INSERT statement, the DEFAULT keyword is used. In the second INSERT state-ment, the third column (*city*) is not included in the statement. In both cases, this means that the default value as defined in the table is inserted for that column.

What about the table columns that do not have a DEFAULT clause? What is inserted when test columns are omitted from the INSERT statement? In such scenarios, DB2 inserts a NULL, assuming the column accepts NULL values. If the column does not accept NULL values, you receive an error. (We describe NULLs in the next section.) For example, the result of this statement

```
INSERT INTO company  (city)
            VALUES ('ATLANTA')
```

is

```
COMPANYID    COMPANYNAME                            CITY
----------- ----------------------------- --------------------
         -  -                                       ATLANTA
```

The dash (-) represents a NULL value.

The columns of a table can also be defined with the DEFAULT keyword just by itself. In such a scenario, DB2 uses default values depending on the data type of the column. Typically, DB2 chooses a zero for numeric data types and a blank for character strings. For example, let's re-create the table *COMPANY* as follows:

```
CREATE TABLE company  (
        companyID          INTEGER      DEFAULT,
        companyName        VARCHAR(30)  DEFAULT,
        city               VARCHAR(20)  DEFAULT 'TORONTO'
        )
```

Issuing the following statement

```
INSERT INTO company  (city)
            VALUES (DEFAULT)
```

returns

```
COMPANYID   COMPANYNAME                              CITY
----------- ------------------------------ ------------
          0                                          TORONTO
```

This example shows that because the columns *companyID* and *companyName* are both defined with the DEFAULT clause just by itself, DB2 chose a default value of zero for column *companyID*, which is an INTEGER, and a blank for column *companyName*, which is a VARCHAR.

Using NULL Values

NULL values represent an unknown state. For example, let's review the contents of the table *STUDENT*, which contains NULL values:

```
NAME                 MARK
-------------------- -----------
Peter                        100
Mary                          60
John                           -
Raul                          80
Tom                            -
```

John and Tom were sick the day of the exam; therefore, the teacher put NULL values for their marks. This is different than giving them a mark of zero. If you issue this statement

```
SELECT avg(mark) as average FROM student
```

The result is:

```
AVERAGE
-----------
         80
```

Note that the average was calculated as follows: (100 + 60 + 80) / 3. The total number of students considered in the calculation was three, not five, because NULL values were not taken into consideration in the calculation.

Your business requirements dictate when NULL values are allowed in your columns. Let's review another example to illustrate when using NOT NULL is appropriate. The following statement creates a table that stores a company phone directory.

```
CREATE TABLE telephoneDirectory (
    empID       CHAR(3)         NOT NULL PRIMARY KEY,
    phone_no    VARCHAR(15)     NOT NULL,
    deptname    VARCHAR(20)     NOT NULL DEFAULT 'Marketing',
    position    VARCHAR(30)     DEFAULT 'Clerk'
)
```

In the example, let's assume the business requirements indicate that the column *empID* must uniquely identify a row. Thus, *empID* should be created as NOT NULL so that NULL values are not accepted; otherwise, several rows might have NULLs, which would not make the rows unique.

Next, the column *phone_no* is also defined as NOT NULL per the business requirements. If the purpose of this table is to store telephone numbers, it's understandable that this column does not accept NULLs.

The third column, *deptname*, is defined as NOT NULL with a DEFAULT value of Marketing. This means that a NULL value is not accepted, and when the column is omitted in an INSERT statement, the default value of Marketing is used. For example, if you issue this statement:

```
INSERT INTO telephoneDirectory (empID, phone_no)
                VALUES ('111', '905-123-4567')
```

The result is:

```
EMPID PHONE_NO          DEPTNAME              POSITION
----- ---------------   --------------------  --------------------
111   905-123-4567      Marketing             Clerk
```

The fourth column, *position*, allows NULL values and has a default value of Clerk. This case was explained in the section "Default Values." The NOT NULL DEFAULT *value* clause works the same as the DEFAULT *value* clause only in that NULL values are not allowed.

Identity Columns

An identity column is a numeric column in a table that automatically generates a unique numeric value in sequence for each row inserted. A unique identifier is often used in applications to identify a specific row. Unlike sequence objects, which we discuss in the section entitled, "Sequences," identity columns are bound to the table they are defined on. There can be only one identity column per table. DB2 can generate the identity column values in two ways.

- **Generated always**: The values are always generated by DB2. Applications are not allowed to provide an explicit value.

- **Generated by default**: The values can be explicitly provided by an application; if no value is given, DB2 generates one. In this case, however, DB2 cannot guarantee the uniqueness of the value generated.

To create an identity column, use the CREATE TABLE statement with the GENERATED clause and make sure it contains the IDENTITY keyword because GENERATED can also be used to generate other values automatically that are not identity columns. Here is an example:

```
CREATE TABLE product (
       productno   INTEGER GENERATED ALWAYS AS
                            IDENTITY (START WITH 200 INCREMENT BY 1),
       description VARCHAR(50) )
```

The column *productno* is an INTEGER defined as an identity column that is always generated. The value generated starts from 200, and it is incremented by 1. Let's perform a few INSERT statements and see the results obtained.

```
INSERT INTO product VALUES (DEFAULT,'banana');          --->inserts 200,banana
INSERT INTO product (description) VALUES ('apple');     --->inserts 201,apple
INSERT INTO product VALUES (300,'pear');                --->error SQL0798N
COMMIT;

INSERT INTO product (description) VALUES ('orange');    --->inserts 202,orange
ROLLBACK;
INSERT INTO product (description) VALUES ('plum');      --->inserts 203,plum
COMMIT;
```

The following query shows the final result:

```
SELECT * FROM product;
PRODUCTNO    DESCRIPTION
----------- ------------
        200 banana
        201 apple
        203 plum
```

The first two INSERT statements show that two identity column values were generated: 200 and 201. The third INSERT statement returns an error because you cannot explicitly insert a value for an identity column generated as ALWAYS. After the third INSERT statement, we issue a COMMIT to guarantee these rows are stored in the database. The fourth INSERT statement causes another identity column value, 202, to be generated; however, we issue a ROLLBACK statement right after, so this row is not stored in the database. Note that the final INSERT statement, which inserts the product plum, generates a value of 203, not 202 since 202 was generated and assigned to the previous statement.

> **NOTE**
>
> An identity column value is generated only once. After the value has been generated, even if a ROLLBACK statement is performed, it will not be generated again.

Now let's review another example, this time creating the same table *PRODUCT* with the GENERATED BY DEFAULT clause.

```
CREATE TABLE product (
        productno   INTEGER GENERATED BY DEFAULT AS
                           IDENTITY (START WITH 200 INCREMENT BY 1),
        description VARCHAR(50) )
```

Next, to insert a few rows

```
INSERT INTO product VALUES (DEFAULT,'banana');        --->inserts 200,banana
INSERT INTO product (description) VALUES ('apple');   --->inserts 201,apple
INSERT INTO product VALUES (300,'pear');              --->inserts 300,pear
INSERT INTO product VALUES (201,'orange');            --->inserts 201,orange
COMMIT;
INSERT INTO product (description) VALUES ('papaya');  --->inserts 202,papaya
ROLLBACK;
INSERT INTO product (description) VALUES ('plum');    --->inserts 203,plum
COMMIT;
```

The following query shows the final result:

```
SELECT * FROM product
PRODUCTNO    DESCRIPTION
-----------  --------------------
        200  banana
        201  apple
        300  pear
        201  orange
        203  plum
```

The first two INSERT statements show that two identity column values were generated: 200 and 201. For the third and fourth INSERT statements, we explicitly provided the values 300 and 201, respectively, for the identity column. Note that DB2 did not return an error as in the previous example because we defined the identity column as GENERATED BY DEFAULT. After the fourth INSERT statement, we issue a COMMIT to guarantee these rows are stored in the database.

The fifth INSERT statement causes another identity column value, 202, to be generated; however, we issue a ROLLBACK statement right after, so this row is not stored in the database. Note that the final INSERT statement, which inserts the product plum, generates a value of 203, not 202.

We recommend that you create an unique index on the column that makes up the identity column or define it as a primary key if you need to guarantee uniqueness. You receive an error message if the identity column tries to generate a value that already exists. One way to get past this error would be to reset the identity column to restart at a given value. You can do this with the ALTER TABLE statement with the RESTART clause.

The following final example illustrates a GENERATED value, which is not an identity column. The example uses GENERATED ALWAYS, but you can also use GENERATED BY DEFAULT.

```
CREATE TABLE income (
  empno     INTEGER,
  salary    INTEGER,
  taxRate   DECIMAL(5,2),
  netSalary DECIMAL(7,2) GENERATED ALWAYS AS (salary * (1 - taxRate))
)
```

If you insert the following row

```
  INSERT INTO income (empno, salary, taxRate) VALUES (111, 50000, 0.3)
```

the result is

```
EMPNO        SALARY      TAXRATE NETSALARY
----------- ----------- ------- ---------
        111       50000    0.30  35000.00
```

DB2 generates the value of the last column *NETSALARY* based on the *SALARY* and *TAXRATE* columns.

Constraints

Constraints allow you to create rules for the data in your tables. You can define four types of constraints on a table.

- A **unique** constraint ensures that no duplicate key values can be entered in the table.
- A **referential** constraint ensures that a value in one table must have a corresponding entry in a related table.
- A **check** constraint ensures that the values you enter into the column are within the rules specified when the table was defined.
- An **informational** constraint enables you to enforce or not enforce a constraint.

These constraints are discussed further in the following sections.

Unique Constraints

A unique constraint indicates that the values for a given column must all be unique. A unique constraint is defined in the CREATE TABLE or ALTER TABLE statements using the UNIQUE clause or the PRIMARY KEY clause. A primary key, as you see in the next section, is also a unique constraint.

All the columns that make up a unique constraint must be defined as NOT NULL. For the following example, the column *empID* must be defined as NOT NULL because it is the primary key. The column *deptID* must also be defined as NOT NULL because it is a unique constraint.

```
CREATE TABLE employ (
      empID   INT        NOT NULL PRIMARY KEY,
      name    CHAR(30)   ,
      deptID  INT        NOT NULL UNIQUE
      )
```

Now, let's perform a few INSERT statements in sequence.

INSERT INTO employ VALUES (111, 'Peter', 999)   **---> inserts 111, Peter, 999**
INSERT INTO employ VALUES (111, 'Peter', 123)   **---> SQL0803N error, duplicate ➡primary key 111**
INSERT INTO employ VALUES (789, 'Peter', 999)   **---> SQL0803N error, duplicate ➡unique key 999**

This example illustrates that an error (SQL0803N) occurs if the value you attempt to insert for a unique or primary key column is not unique (it already exists in the table).

Unique constraints are implemented using unique indexes. When a CREATE TABLE statement has the UNIQUE or PRIMARY KEY keywords, DB2 automatically creates a corresponding unique index. The name of this system-generated index starts with SQL followed by a timestamp. For the example just shown, two unique indexes were generated with these names:

```
SQL130922135806320
SQL130922135806460
```

Both indexes were created on September 22, 2013, at 1:58 p.m.

Though you would normally not refer to an index name directly in an application, a good index name can be helpful when analyzing an **explain** output. An explain output displays the access path DB2 chooses to access your data for a given query. Therefore, rather than letting DB2 generate system names for your indexes, we recommend using the ALTER TABLE statement in the case of primary key columns and the CONSTRAINT clause to explicitly give names to the indexes. For example, let's rewrite the CREATE TABLE statement used in the previous example as follows:

```
CREATE TABLE employ (
     empID    INT       NOT NULL,
     name     CHAR(30)  ,
     deptID   INT       NOT NULL CONSTRAINT unique_dept_const UNIQUE
     )
```

```
ALTER TABLE employ ADD CONSTRAINT employ_pk PRIMARY KEY (empID)
```

In this example, we removed the PRIMARY KEY clause of the CREATE TABLE statement and added an ALTER TABLE statement. The ALTER TABLE statement enabled us to put in a name for the constraint (employ_pk), which also becomes the name of the corresponding unique index.

Instead of the ALTER TABLE statement, you can also use the following two statements with the same result:

```
CREATE UNIQUE INDEX employ_pk ON employ (empID)
ALTER TABLE employ ADD PRIMARY KEY (empID)
```

In this case, the CREATE UNIQUE statement explicitly creates the unique index and specifies the desired name for the index. Next, the ALTER TABLE statement indicates that the same column used for the unique index is also used as the primary key. After executing the ALTER TABLE statement, you receive this warning message:

```
SQL0598W  Existing index "EMPLOY_PK" is used as the index for the
primary key or a unique key. SQLSTATE=01550
```

This warning is acceptable because this is in fact what is desired.

In the previous CREATE TABLE statement, we also added a unique constraint using the clause CONSTRAINT unique_dept_const UNIQUE. With this clause, DB2 generates a corresponding unique index with the name unique_dept_const.

You can also use the ALTER TABLE statement to add a unique constraint, as shown in this example:

```
ALTER TABLE employ ADD CONSTRAINT unique_dept_const UNIQUE (deptID)
```

Referential Constraints

Referential constraints are used to support *referential integrity*. Referential integrity enables your database to manage relationships between tables.

Using Primary, Unique, and Foreign Keys to Establish Referential Integrity

Referential integrity can be better explained with examples. Assume you have two tables, as illustrated in Figure 7.24.

COUNTRY table (Parent table)

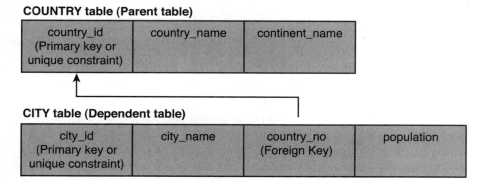

CITY table (Dependent table)

Figure 7.24   Referential integrity between two tables

The figure shows the tables *COUNTRY* and *CITY,* where *COUNTRY* is the parent table containing information about all the countries in the world, and *CITY* is the dependent table containing information about a particular city for a given country. Note that the column *country_ID* and the column *country_no* are used to establish a relationship between the two tables.

The *country_ID* column is a primary key column. A primary key consists of one or more columns; it is a special case of a unique constraint. Although there can be many unique constraints in a table, there can be only one primary key. A primary key is used to establish a referential integrity relationship with another table.

The *country_no* column, known as the foreign key column, references the primary key column of the parent table. Because of this relationship, the *country_no* column cannot have a value that does not exist in the *country_ID* column. The data type for this column must be compatible with the primary key column of the parent table. For the example illustrated in Figure 7.26, if the parent key column is defined as type INTEGER, the foreign key column can be defined as type DECIMAL because it is a numeric data type for which conversion is allowed; however, it cannot be defined as type CHAR. Other than this restriction, the foreign key can be treated like any other column. It can use the NOT NULL, UNIQUE, and even PRIMARY KEY clauses.

To establish the referential integrity relationship between the two tables, let's look at the corresponding CREATE TABLE statements for both tables.

```
CREATE TABLE country (
      country_ID       INT             NOT NULL PRIMARY KEY,
      country_Name     VARCHAR(30)     NOT NULL,
      continent_Name   CHAR(15)
      )
CREATE TABLE city (
      city_ID          INT             NOT NULL PRIMARY KEY,
      city_name        VARCHAR(30)     NOT NULL,
```

```
country_no      INT              REFERENCES country,
population      INT
)
```

Note that the CREATE TABLE statement for the *city* table includes the REFERENCES clause and that it does not need to specify any column of the parent table *COUNTRY*. DB2 automatically looks for the primary key column of the parent table to establish the relationship.

What if there is no primary key column for the parent table but a unique constraint instead? What if the parent table contains more than one unique constraint? In such cases, use the REFER-ENCES clause followed by the correct column name(s). For example, let's say we actually created the *COUNTRY* table in Figure 7.24 with no primary key but two unique constraints, as follows:

```
CREATE TABLE country (
        country_ID      INT              NOT NULL UNIQUE,
        country_Name    VARCHAR(30)      NOT NULL,
        continent_Name  CHAR(15)         NOT NULL UNIQUE
        )
```

To establish referential integrity using the column *country_ID*, this column must be speci-fied in the CREATE TABLE statement for the *CITY* table, as shown next:

```
CREATE TABLE city (
        city_ID         INT              NOT NULL PRIMARY KEY,
        city_name       VARCHAR(30)      NOT NULL,
        country_no      INT              REFERENCES country(country_ID),
        population      INT
        )
```

NOTE

A unique constraint on a column that has been defined as NOT NULL can also be referenced by a foreign key clause because a primary key is basically the same as a unique constraint.

You can also use the ALTER TABLE statement to add a foreign key, for example

```
ALTER TABLE city
    ADD FOREIGN KEY (country_no) REFERENCES country (country_ID)
```

This statement would add to the table *CITY* the foreign key using column *country_no*, which would reference column *country_ID* in table *COUNTRY*.

Referential Integrity Implications on SQL Operations

The enforcement of referential integrity has implications on INSERT, UPDATE, and DELETE operations, which must follow certain rules. To explain these rules, let's look at the following example using Figure 7.25.

We used the first two tables, *COUNTRY* and *CITY*, in previous examples. In this particular example, we inserted a few records in each of these tables. A new table, *DISTRICT*, which is dependent on table *CITY*, is also illustrated. Here is the CREATE TABLE statement for the table *DISTRICT*.

```
CREATE TABLE district (
        district_ID      INT              NOT NULL PRIMARY KEY,
        district_name    VARCHAR(30)      NOT NULL,
        city_no          INT              REFERENCES city,
        registrations    INT
        )
```

When inserting values into tables under referential integrity, the order of the INSERTs is important (as you see in the next sections). The following cases are examined:

- **Inserting to a Parent Table**

  What would happen if the following record were inserted in table *COUNTRY*?

  ```
  INSERT INTO country  VALUES (2,'Spain',4)
  ```

  Because *COUNTRY* is the parent table at the top of Figure 7.25, any value can be inserted into this table without a need to worry about the dependent tables.

- **Inserting to a Dependent Table**

  What would happen if the following record were inserted in table *CITY*?

  ```
  INSERT INTO city     VALUES (44,'Vancouver',3,4000000)
  ```

COUNTRY table (Parent table)

country_ID (Primary key or unique constraint)	country_name	continent_name
1	Canada	North America

CITY table (Dependent table)

city_id (Primary key or unique constraint)	city_name	country_no (Foreign Key)	population
11	Toronto	1	8,000,000
22	Montreal	1	6,000,000
33	Calgary	1	5,000,000

DISTRICT table (Dependent table)

district_id (Primary key or unique constraint)	district_name	city_no (Foreign Key)	registrations
111	North York	11	300
222	Markham	11	900

Figure 7.25   An example to illustrate SQL operations under referential integrity

Table *CITY* is dependent on table *COUNTRY* based on column *country_no* (the third column in the *CITY* table). This INSERT statement is trying to insert a record with a value of 3 for the *country_no* column. From Figure 7.14, you can see this value is not present in table *COUNTRY*; therefore, this record cannot be inserted and an error would be returned.

- **Deleting a Row from the Parent Table**

What would happen if the following record were deleted from table *COUNTRY*?

```
DELETE FROM country WHERE country_name = 'Canada'
```

This DELETE statement would fail with an error SQL0532N because there are related dependent rows. This is the default behavior, also called the NO ACTION delete rule.

You can specify DELETE rules in the CREATE TABLE statement of the dependent table. In addition to NO ACTION, you can use the following rules:

- **RESTRICT:** The behavior is exactly the same as the NO ACTION rule. The difference is when this constraint is enforced. For more details, refer to the *DB2 SQL Reference* manual.

- **CASCADE:** All the dependent rows are deleted when the parent table row is deleted.

- **SET NULL:** All the dependent rows have the value of the foreign key column set to NULL if NULLs are allowed; otherwise, an error is returned. All the other columns remain unchanged.

For example, let's say we actually created the table *CITY* as follows:

```
CREATE TABLE city (
    city_ID         INT             NOT NULL PRIMARY KEY,
    city_name       VARCHAR(30)     NOT NULL,
    country_no      INT             REFERENCES country(country_ID)
                                        ON DELETE CASCADE,
    population      INT
    )
```

Note that we added the clause ON DELETE CASCADE to the foreign key column *country_no*.

If we execute the following statement again, will it work this time?

```
DELETE FROM country WHERE country_name = 'Canada'
```

The answer is no. Though we defined the CASCADE rule correctly in the *CITY* table, we did not define it in the *DISTRICT* table. All dependent tables need to be defined using CASCADE if you want all the dependent rows to be deleted. In this example, if we had defined the *DISTRICT* table correctly, all the rows of all the tables would have been deleted. Because we did not, no rows were deleted.

- **Deleting a Row from a Dependent Table**

You can delete a row from a dependent table with no implications unless the dependent table is the parent of another table.

- **Updating a Row from the Parent Table**

You cannot update the primary key of the parent table. To ensure you don't duplicate an existing value, DB2 does not allow this operation.

- **Updating a Row from a Dependent Table**

You can update the foreign key of a dependent table only if the new value already exists in the parent table and the foreign key is defined as NOT NULL. This is the default behavior, which corresponds to the NO ACTION update rule.

For example, issuing this statement

```
UPDATE city SET country_no = 7 WHERE city_name = 'Montreal'
```

would return error SQL0530N, which indicates the value of 7 does not exist in the parent table.

The other UPDATE rule possible is RESTRICT, which behaves similarly to the NO ACTION rule. The difference is when the rule enforcement takes place. For details about this rule, review the *DB2 Information Center*.

You can specify UPDATE rules on the CREATE TABLE statement of a dependent table. For example, we could have created the *CITY* table as follows (on top of the DELETE rules of the previous example).

```
CREATE TABLE city (
      city_ID        INT              NOT NULL PRIMARY KEY,
      city_name      VARCHAR(30)      NOT NULL,
      country_no     INT              REFERENCES country(country_ID)
                                           ON DELETE CASCADE
                                           ON UPDATE RESTRICT,
      population     INT
)
```

Check Constraints

Check constraints are used to enforce data integrity at the table level. When the check constraint is defined, every INSERT or UPDATE operation must satisfy the constraint; otherwise, you receive an error. For example, let's create the table *STUDENT*:

```
CREATE TABLE student (
      student_ID     INT              NOT NULL PRIMARY KEY,
      name           VARCHAR(30)      NOT NULL,
      sex            CHAR(1)          NOT NULL
      CONSTRAINT sex_check_const CHECK (sex in ('M', 'F'))
      )
```

This table has the check constraint *sex_check_const* defined, which verifies that the column *sex* has the values of M or F. Now let's attempt the following statement:

```
INSERT INTO student VALUES (1, 'Tom', 'Z')
```

This produces an error SQL0545N because the value Z does not satisfy the check constraint. You can also add a check constraint with the ALTER TABLE statement, as shown:

```
ALTER TABLE student
      ADD CONSTRAINT sex_check_const CHECK (sex in ('M', 'F'))
```

If you are adding a check constraint with the ALTER TABLE statement to a table that already has data, DB2 checks the entire table to make sure the existing data satisfies the check constraint. If it doesn't, the ALTER TABLE statement fails with error SQL0544N.

If you do not want DB2 to check the table when a check constraint is added, you can use the SET INTEGRITY statement. This statement turns off check constraint and referential constraint checking. For example, let's say you create the *STUDENT* table without a check constraint and insert some rows that will later be invalid for the check constraint.

```
CREATE TABLE student (
        student_ID      INT             NOT NULL PRIMARY KEY,
        name            VARCHAR(30)     NOT NULL,
        sex             CHAR(1)         NOT NULL
        )
INSERT INTO student VALUES (1, 'Tom',  'Z')
INSERT INTO student VALUES (2, 'Mary', 'A')
```

Now you attempt to add the following check constraint:

```
ALTER TABLE student
    ADD CONSTRAINT sex_check_const CHECK (sex in ('M', 'F'))
```

You receive error SQL0544N, as indicated earlier. Thus, use the SET INTEGRITY command to turn off constraint checking so that you can add the constraint

```
    SET INTEGRITY FOR student OFF
```

At this point, the *STUDENT* table is put in CHECK PENDING state, a state that allows only a few operations on the table, like ALTER TABLE. Other operations such as SELECT, INSERT, UPDATE, and DELETE are disallowed.

After turning off constraint checking, you can repeat the ALTER TABLE statement, which this time should be successful. Use the SET INTEGRITY statement again to turn constraint checking on as follows:

```
    SET INTEGRITY FOR student CHECK IMMEDIATE UNCHECKED
```

The IMMEDIATE UNCHECKED option turns on check constraints again but does not check the existing table data. Alternatively, you can also issue

```
    SET INTEGRITY FOR student IMMEDIATE CHECKED
```

In this case, the IMMEDIATE CHECKED option turns on check constraints again and also checks the existing table data. If a violation is encountered, the table remains in CHECK PENDING state. The SET INTEGRITY statement has an option to move the violating records to an exception table.

```
SET INTEGRITY FOR student IMMEDIATE CHECKED
    FOR EXCEPTION IN student USE my_exception_table
```

The name of the exception table in this example is *my_exception_table*. This table must exist with at least the same columns as the original source table, in this case, the *STUDENT* table. After this `SET INTEGRITY` statement is executed, the violating rows would be moved to the exception table, and the `CHECK PENDING` status would be removed. For more details about the `SET INTEGRITY` statement, refer to the DB2 Information Center.

Informational Constraints

As discussed earlier, you have the ability to turn constraint checking off with the `SET INTEGRITY` statement; however, this is mainly used to perform table alterations to add new constraints to existing tables. In addition, using the `SET INTEGRITY` statement puts your table in `CHECK PENDING` status, which prevents you from performing many operations on your table. What if your application already performs constraint checking, and thus there is no need for DB2 to check the data again?

For example, large applications such as SAP, PeopleSoft, and Siebel are written to check the constraints before they insert the data into DB2. In this case, defining the constraint in DB2 would cause extra overhead if DB2 is also enforcing the rule and revalidating the constraint. However, if you do not define these constraints, the DB2 optimizer cannot use them to its advantage in choosing the most optimal access plans, which directly affects performance.

Informational constraints enable you to specify whether or not DB2 should enforce the constraint and whether or not it can be used by the optimizer to choose the best access plan for the application statements.

The default operation when you create a constraint is that it is always enforced and can be used by the optimizer. You can change this default behavior by using informational constraints, which are implemented by using the following clauses of the `CREATE TABLE` statement.

- **ENFORCED**: This is the default option. Use this clause if you want DB2 to check the constraints for every operation on the table.
- **NOT ENFORCED**: Use this clause if you do not want DB2 to check the constraints for every operation on the table.
- **ENABLE QUERY OPTIMIZATION**: Use this clause so that the DB2 optimizer can use the knowledge of the constraint when building the plan for accessing the table or referenced tables.
- **DISABLE QUERY OPTIMIZATION**: Use this clause if you want the DB2 optimizer to ignore the constraints defined on your table.

The following example illustrates how informational constraints work:

```
CREATE TABLE student (
        student_ID      INT             NOT NULL PRIMARY KEY,
        name            VARCHAR(30)     NOT NULL,
        sex             CHAR(1)         NOT NULL
```

```
CONSTRAINT sex_check_const CHECK (sex in ('M', 'F'))
NOT ENFORCED
ENABLE QUERY OPTIMIZATION
)
```

Note that the constraint for table *STUDENT* is not enforced, but the constraint is used for query optimization. Now let's issue the following statements:

```
(1)   INSERT INTO student VALUES (5, 'John', 'T')
(2)   SELECT * FROM student WHERE sex = 'T'
```

The first statement executes successfully—a T can be inserted for the *sex* column because the constraint *sex_check_const* is not enforced.

The second statement returns zero records because query optimization is enabled. Therefore, the optimizer does not scan the table but checks the constraints defined for the *sex* column in the DB2 catalog tables and assumes it has only values of M or F, quickly returning a result of zero records. Of course, this result is incorrect. If you want to obtain the correct result, disable query optimization. You can do this with the ALTER TABLE statement:

```
ALTER TABLE student
      ALTER CHECK sex_check_const DISABLE QUERY OPTIMIZATION
```

If you perform the second statement again, this time you should get one record.

```
SELECT * FROM student WHERE sex = 'T'
STUDENT_ID  NAME                           SEX
----------- ------------------------------ ---
          5 John                           T
```

> **NOTE**
>
> After issuing the ALTER TABLE statement to enable or disable query optimization, make sure to issue a terminate command if working from the CLP so the change takes effect.

> **NOTE**
>
> Use informational constraints only if you are certain the data to be inserted or updated has been correctly checked by your application. Normally you want to use the options NOT ENFORCED and ENABLE QUERY OPTIMIZATION together because you want DB2 to reduce overhead by not performing constraint checking, but having the DB2 optimizer take into account the constraint definition.

Not Logged Initially Tables

The NOT LOGGED INITIALLY clause of the CREATE TABLE statement enables you to create a table that is not logged when an INSERT, UPDATE, DELETE, CREATE INDEX, ALTER TABLE, or DROP INDEX operation is performed in the same unit of work in which the CREATE TABLE statement was issued. For example, let's say you execute the following statements in a script:

```
CREATE TABLE products (
       productID     INT,
       product_Name VARCHAR(30)
       )
       NOT LOGGED INITIALLY;
INSERT INTO products VALUES (1,'door');
INSERT INTO products VALUES (2,'window');
. . .
INSERT INTO products VALUES (999999,'telephone');
COMMIT;
INSERT INTO products VALUES (1000000,'television');
UPDATE products SET product_name = 'radio' where productID = 3456;
ALTER TABLE products ACTIVATE NOT LOGGED INITIALLY;
INSERT INTO products VALUES (1000001,'desk');
INSERT INTO products VALUES (1000002,'table');
. . .
INSERT INTO products VALUES (1999999,'chair');
COMMIT;
```

Any operation from the CREATE TABLE statement until the first COMMIT is not logged. After the COMMIT is issued, any subsequent operation is logged. For this example, the INSERT and UPDATE statements after the first COMMIT are logged.

> **NOTE**
>
> Using ACTIVATE NOT LOGGED INITIALLY means that operations are not logged until the first COMMIT. Should you experience a crash in your system while this operation is taking place, DB2 cannot recover this data. Typically, you use this option when you have the source data safe and stored in another system and all you want is to load data quickly into DB2. Because operations are not logged, performance is improved.

After creating the table as NOT LOGGED INITIALLY, if you would like to turn off logging temporarily again, you can use the ALTER TABLE statement with the ACTIVATE NOT LOGGED INITIALLY clause, as shown in the example. Any operations between the ALTER TABLE and the second COMMIT are not logged.

> **NOTE**
>
> You can use the statement `ALTER TABLE table_name ACTIVATE NOT LOGGED INI-TIALLY` only for tables that were originally created with the `NOT LOGGED INITALLY` clause.

You can also use the `WITH EMPTY TABLE` clause as part of the `ALTER TABLE table_name ACTIVATE NOT LOGGED INITIALLY` statement or the `TRUNCATE` statement to remove all the data of the table. These two methods are faster than using a `DELETE FROM table_name` statement. For example, to remove all the rows of the table *PRODUCTS*, issue

```
ALTER TABLE products ACTIVATE NOT LOGGED INITIALLY WITH EMPTY TABLE
```

or

```
TRUNCATE products
```

Partitioned Tables

The table partitioning feature, also known as range partitioning, enables you to create partitioned tables. With partitioned tables you can create a table that can span multiple table spaces. Performance can be improved for queries using this table because they can be directed automatically only to the partitions where the data required resides. For example, if you partition a table based on the month, and a user runs a query that calculates the total sales for March, the query need only access the data for March, not the data for any other month.

There are two forms of the create table syntax that can be used to create a partitioned table, the short form and the long form. For example, the two statements that follow create a table with the same table partitioning scheme:

```
CREATE TABLE t1(c1 INT)
     IN tbsp1, tbsp2, tbsp3, tbsp4
     PARTITION BY RANGE(c1)
     (STARTING FROM (1) ENDING (200) EVERY (50))

CREATE TABLE t1(c1 INT)
     PARTITION BY RANGE(t1)
     (STARTING FROM (1) ENDING(50)  IN tbsp1,
                        ENDING(100) IN tbsp2,
                        ENDING(150) IN tbsp3,
                        ENDING(200) IN tbsp4)
```

In both cases, the first table partition (numbers from 1 to 50) are placed in table space *tbsp1*, the second table partition in *tbsp2*, the third table partition in *tbsp3*, and the fourth table partition in *tbsp4,* as shown in Figure 7.26.

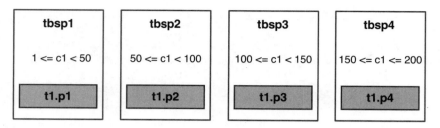

Figure 7.26   An example to illustrate partitioned tables

For a table that has date ranges, you can specify either explicit start and stop values for the ranges, or you can leave it open-ended, using the special registers MINVALUES and MAXVALUES.

The table defined as

```
CREATE TABLE sales(sdate DATE, customer INT)
     PARTITION BY RANGE(sdate)
      (STARTING '1/1/2013'  ENDING '3/31/2013',
       STARTING '4/1/2013'  ENDING '6/30/2013',
       STARTING '7/1/2013'  ENDING '9/30/2013',
       STARTING '10/1/2013' ENDING '12/31/2013')
```

would look like what you see in Figure 7.27.

Figure 7.27   Table partitioned by date every three months

If you attempt to enter a row with a date in 2012, you get the following error:

```
DB21034E  The command was processed as an SQL statement because it was
not a valid Command Line Processor command.  During SQL processing it
returned:
SQL0327N  The row cannot be inserted into table "RFCHONG.SALES"
because it is outside the bounds of the defined data partition ranges.
SQLSTATE=22525
```

However, you can also define the table so that the first range accepts all dates up to March 31, 2013, as follows:

```
CREATE TABLE sales(sdate DATE, customer INT)
     PARTITION BY RANGE(sdate)
     (STARTING MINVALUE     ENDING '3/31/2013',
      STARTING '4/1/2013'   ENDING '6/30/2013',
      STARTING '7/1/2013'   ENDING '9/30/2013',
      STARTING '10/1/2013'  ENDING '12/31/2013')
```

By default, the range boundaries are inclusive, so to avoid leaving holes in the table, you can create the ranges using the EXCLUSIVE option for the ending boundary as follows:

```
CREATE TABLE sales(sdate DATE, customer INT)
     IN tbsp1, tbsp2, tbsp3, tbsp4
     PARTITION BY RANGE(sdate)
     (STARTING MINVALUE     ENDING '3/31/2013' EXCLUSIVE,
      STARTING '3/31/2013'  ENDING '6/30/2013' EXCLUSIVE,
      STARTING '6/30/2013'  ENDING '9/30/2013' EXCLUSIVE,
      STARTING '9/30/2013'  ENDING '12/31/2013')
```

This table looks the same as what's shown in Figure 7.27.

As you add new data to the table, you can create a new stand-alone table, load data into the table, and then attach the table to the range partitioned table as follows:

```
CREATE TABLE sales1Q14(sdate DATE, customer INT) in tbsp5

LOAD FROM sales.del OF DEL REPLACE INTO sales1Q14

ALTER TABLE sales ATTACH PARTITION
  STARTING ('1/1/2014')
  ENDING ('3/31/2014')  FROM sales1Q14

SET INTEGRITY FOR TABLE sales OFF
```

Now the table looks like what you see in Figure 7.28.

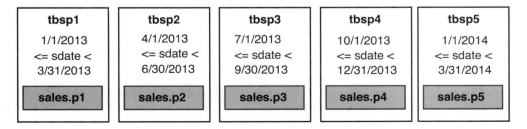

Figure 7.28 Partitioned table after attaching a partition

Detaching Partitions

You can remove the old table partitions using the DETACH command, but you must know the name of the table partition to do this. You can look up the table partition name using the DESCRIBE DATA PARTITIONS SHOW DETAIL command or name the table partitions when you are creating the table as follows:

```
CREATE TABLE carsales(sale_date DATE, VIN char(30))
  PARTITION BY RANGE(sale_date)
  (part q113 STARTING MINVALUE    ENDING '3/31/2013' EXCLUSIVE,
   part q213 STARTING '3/31/2013' ENDING '6/30/2013' EXCLUSIVE,
   part q313 STARTING '6/30/2013' ENDING '9/30/2013' EXCLUSIVE,
   part q413 STARTING '9/30/2013' ENDING '12/31/2013')
```

You can then detach the table partition for the first quarter of 2013 into the table *tblq113* as follows:

```
    alter table carsales detach partition q113 into tblq113
```

Combine the use of range partitioning with the multitemperature data management feature for an efficient way to manage your data as it "cools off." Hot data that has turned into warm data can be moved to storage groups with slower media. This can be done easily by altering the corresponding table spaces of the partitioned table to use a different storage group.

Row Compression

DB2 makes it easy to compress the data in your tables using row compression. Row compression provides a number of advantages such as

- Decreased disk storage costs, given that the data and corresponding logs are compressed on disk
- Decreased I/O bandwidth consumption because there is less data being sent across the I/O channels
- Increased memory efficiency because the data is compressed in the buffer pools

Compression also presents a disadvantage; it can lead to CPU overhead associated with compression and decompression of the data.

Depending on whether your system is I/O-bound (limited by I/O resources) or CPU-bound (limited by CPU resources), you should decide about using compression or not. If your system is I/O-bound, compression is recommended and if CPU-bound, try compression on a test system and monitor performance.

Compression Dictionary

DB2 utilizes a dictionary-based compression, which is built automatically when compression is enabled. The dictionary is built by scanning the data (or a representative sample of the data), and then any further data added to the table or updated within the table also examines the dictionary to determine if data within that row can be compressed.

Compression works by replacing repeating strings within a row of data with a much smaller symbol. For example, if you have a table that includes customer addresses, you are likely to find repeated information because there are a number of people living in the same city. For these customers DB2 can replace common strings such as "Dallas, TX, 23456" with a short 12-bit symbol. Because DB2 can do this for the most common, most repeated cities (or any other series of bytes) in the table, you can see how compression results in significant savings.

Consider an example with the following three rows of data in a table:

Fred	Smith	500	1000	Plano	Texas	24355
John	Smith	500	2000	Plano	Texas	24355
Sam	Smith	600	8000	Plano	Texas	24355

You can see that there are a number of repeating strings in these rows. But DB2 not only looks for repeating strings in columns, it can also look for these repeating strings across columns or within a column. So let's take the example here and examine the compression dictionary that DB2 would build for these rows.

Notice that the name Smith is repeated in all three rows, so that would be the first entry in the dictionary. The department 500 is also repeated (but only in two rows), as is the address Plano, Texas, 24355. But look closer; if you look at the fourth column, you see that all rows end in 000, so really the string 000 Plano Texas 24355 is repeated, and you can replace this entire string with a symbol. So for this data, the dictionary would contain three values, as shown here:

01	Smith
02	500
03	000 Plano Texas 24355

Now, DB2 can store the first two rows on disk as follows:

```
Fred 01 02 1 03
John 01 02 2 03
```

Types of Row Compression

There are two types of row compression:

- Classic row compression, also known as static compression
- Adaptive compression

Classic row compression works using a table-level dictionary that is created and behaves as described earlier. This dictionary is static, which means that as new data is inserted, or as data is changed, the dictionary is not automatically updated; therefore the compression ratio decreases over time. To improve the compression ratios, the REORG utility with the RESETDICTIONARY option should be used to build a new dictionary and compress the data using this new dictionary.

With adaptive compression, not only a table-level dictionary is automatically built in the same fashion as classic row compression, but data page-level dictionaries are also automatically built. If changes in a given page are considerable, the corresponding page-level dictionary is recreated automatically. Therefore, high compression ratios are maintained without the need for an explicit REORG operation.

The functionality of adaptive compression is a superset of the functionality of classic row compression. Data that is stored within data rows, including inlined LOB or XML values, can be compressed with both adaptive and classic row compression.

> **NOTE**
>
> Adaptive compression is available as part of the Advanced Enterprise Server Edition and the Advanced Workgroup Server Edition.

Enabling Row Compression

Compression is enabled at the table level either when the table is created or by altering an existing table using the CREATE or ALTER TABLE statements. The syntax of these statements is as follows:

```
CREATE TABLE---<table-name>------------>
       .-COMPRESS NO--------------.
>--●--+--------------------------+----->
      |                 .-ADAPTIVE-. |
      '-COMPRESS YES-+----------+-'
                     '-STATIC---'


ALTER TABLE---<table-name>------------>
                        .-ADAPTIVE-.
>--●--+-COMPRESS--+-YES-+----------+-+
      |           '-STATIC---' |
      '-NO---------------'
```

For example, if user *RFCHONG* wants to create the table *MYEMP* using adaptive row compression, he can issue this command:

```
create table myemp (
    EMP_ID integer not null,
    EMP_LAST_NAME varchar(20) not null,
    EMP_FIRST_NAME varchar(20) not null
)COMPRESS YES ADAPTIVE;
```

The ADAPTIVE keyword in this example is optional as it is the default.

Table Compression

You can compress tables to a certain extent by using the VALUE COMPRESSION clause of the CREATE TABLE statement. This clause tells DB2 that it can use a different internal format for the table rows so that they occupy less space. In a sense, this clause turns on compression for the table; however, you need to specify another clause, COMPRESS SYSTEM DEFAULT, for each column you want to compress. Only the columns whose values are normally NULL or the system default value of 0 can be compressed. Also, the data type must not be DATE, TIME, or TIME-STAMP. If the data type is a varying-length string, this clause is ignored. Here's an example:

```
CREATE TABLE company (
        company_ID      INTEGER     NOT NULL PRIMARY KEY,
        name            CHAR(10),
        address         VARCHAR(30)             COMPRESS SYSTEM DEFAULT,
        no_employees    INTEGER     NOT NULL COMPRESS SYSTEM DEFAULT
    )
        VALUE COMPRESSION
```

The column *address* is ignored because it's a VARCHAR column, and the column *no_employees* is compressed. Table compression saves space especially for tables used in data warehousing applications where many rows contain NULLs or the system default value of 0. However, UPDATE operations can be impacted when changing to a different value than the default of 0 because the compressed value would first have to be expanded and then updated.

For an existing table containing data, you can enable table compression using the ALTER TABLE statement, as shown in this example:

```
ALTER TABLE city ACTIVATE VALUE COMPRESSION
ALTER TABLE city
    ALTER COLUMN population COMPRESS SYSTEM DEFAULT
```

In this example, you are enabling compression by using the first statement and then specifying which column to compress by using the second statement. In addition, if the table *CITY* were populated, the REORG utility would have to be executed on the table for the compression to take effect on the existing rows.

Materialized Query Tables and Summary Tables

Materialized query tables (MQTs) allow users to create tables with data based on the results of a query. The DB2 optimizer can later use these tables to determine whether a query can best be served by accessing an MQT instead of the base tables. Here is an example of an MQT:

```
CREATE SUMMARY TABLE my_summary
          AS  (SELECT  city_name, population
                 FROM country A, city B
               WHERE  A.country_id = B.country_no)
          DATA INITIALLY DEFERRED
          REFRESH DEFERRED
```

The SUMMARY keyword is optional. The DATA INITIALLY DEFERRED clause indicates that DB2 is not immediately populating the *my_summary* MQT table after creation, but it will populate it following the REFRESH TABLE statement:

```
    REFRESH TABLE my_summary
```

The REFRESH DEFERRED clause in the CREATE SUMMARY TABLE statement indicates that the data in the table is refreshed only when you explicitly issue a REFRESH TABLE statement. Alternatively, you can create the MQT with the REFRESH IMMEDIATE clause, which means DB2 immediately refreshes the data when the base tables are changed.

DB2 checks the registry variable *CURRENT REFRESH AGE* to determine whether or not the MQT contains up-to-date information. This registry can have a value from 0 up to 99999999999999 (9,999 years, 99 months, 99 days, 99 hours, 99 minutes, and 99 seconds), which indicates the maximum duration the DB2 optimizer can wait since the last REFRESH TABLE statement was issued on an MQT to consider MQT tables in its calculations. For example, if an MQT were refreshed today, and the *CURRENT REFRESH AGE* has a value of 5 days, then the DB2 optimizer can consider the MQT in its calculations for the next 5 days. If the value of this register is 0, only the tables created with the REFRESH IMMEDIATE clause can be used for optimization.

Temporary Tables

Temporary tables can be classified as system or user tables. DB2 manages system temporary tables in the system temporary table space. DB2 creates and drops these tables automatically, which it uses when it needs more space than the memory it has available for operations like sort or join. Because users don't have control over system temporary tables, we don't discuss them any further in this section.

With respect to user temporary tables, you can use them in situations where you need to perform a temporary operation. For example, say you have a file with contents you want to join to an existing table. First, you can load the file data into the temporary table and then perform the join operation.

You create user temporary tables inside a user temporary table space. For example, the following statement creates a user temporary table space called *usrtmp4k*.

```
CREATE USER TEMPORARY TABLESPACE usrtmp4k
     MANAGED BY SYSTEM USING ('C:\usrtmp')
```

User temporary tables, referred to as temporary tables from here on, store temporary data, that is, data that will be destroyed after a session or when a connection ends. Temporary tables are typically used in situations where you need to compute a large result set from an operation and you need to store the result set temporarily to continue with further processing.

Though transaction logging is allowed with temporary tables, most users don't need to log temporary data. In fact, not having transaction logging for this type of table improves performance.

Temporary tables exist only for one connection; therefore, there are no concurrency or locking issues.

Temporary tables are of two kinds:

- Declare Global Temporary Tables (DGTTs)
- Create Global Temporary Tables (CGTTs)

The main difference between the two types is that with DGTTs, the table definition is also deleted after the session ends, but with CGTTs, the table definition remains. In fact CGTT table definitions are permanently stored in the DB2 catalog, and thus the CGTT could simply be used in other sessions without having to create it again. As with DGTTs, the data of CGTTs is independent from each other from connection to connection and disappears after the connection closes.

CGTT is probably the preferred type of temporary table to use. CGTT behaves more like a regular table for SQL programmers. If you work with other non-DB2 databases, CGTT behaves similarly to temporary tables of those other products, so they are easy to migrate to DB2.

To create a DGTT, use the DECLARE statement. Here's an example:

```
DECLARE GLOBAL TEMPORARY TABLE temp_dgtt1 (col1 int, col2 int.)
ON COMMIT PRESERVE ROWS
IN  usrtmp4k
```

Table *temp_dgtt1* is created in *usrtmp4k*, the user temporary table space we created earlier.

DB2 uses the schema *session* for all temporary tables regardless of the user ID connected to the database. After you create a temporary table, you can access it just like any regular table. The following statement inserts a row into table *temp_dgtt1:*

```
INSERT INTO session.temp_dgtt1 (1,2)
```

The following statement selects all the rows in table *temp_dgtt1:*

```
SELECT * FROM session.temp_dgtt1
```

You can drop and alter temporary tables, but you cannot create views or triggers against them. Indexes are allowed.

To create a CGTT, use the CREATE statement. Here's an example:

```
CREATE GLOBAL TEMPORARY TABLE temp_cgtt1 (col1 int, col2 int)
  ON COMMIT PRESERVE ROWS
  IN  usrtmp4k
```

Insert and query the CGTT table as follows:

```
INSERT INTO session.temp_cgtt1 (1,2)
SELECT * FROM session.temp_cgtt1
```

> **NOTE**
>
> When working with temporary tables, make sure to explicitly specify the schema *session*. If you work with objects without specifying the schema, DB2 defaults to the authorization ID or connection ID.

You can create indexes on temporary tables to improve performance. For CGTT, an index added in one session is visible to other sessions. However, if the session data conflicts with a new index, (such as duplicate rows conflicting with a unique index), the index is not materialized for that session until the data is corrected. It is best to have all the indexes defined right after creating the CGTT.

V10 Temporal Tables and Time Travel Query

Time travel queries are introduced in DB2 10 to retrieve information from the past, the present, or the future. To implement this feature, temporal tables are used. Temporal tables are not the same as temporary tables discussed earlier. Let's take a look at an example to illustrate how they work.

Let's say your company provides benefits to its employees through an insurance company called ACME. During the benefit enrollment period, you sign up for the benefits you want for you and your family, and the information is stored in the table *BENEFITS* shown next. Say your policy ID is 111. For simplicity, we only show the records for your policy in the table.

Table BENEFITS

PolicyID	Coverage	Smoker	Dependents
111	50,000	N	0

ACME insurance company wants to keep track of changes in your policy through the years. There may be situations when a policy holder may dispute a claim reimbursement from a time period that has already passed. If this information is not recorded, ACME would not be able to investigate the claim. If ACME were tracking this information manually, they would probably add two columns to the table *BENEFITS* to indicate the time period when the given values for the policy are in effect. For this example, the table could look like this assuming your very first enrollment day happened on June 1, 2007. The date of December 30, 9999 indicates the record is current.

Table BENEFITS

PolicyID	Coverage	Smoker	Dependents	sys_start	sys_end
111	50,000	N	0	Jun 1, 2007	Dec 30, 9999

For ease of understanding, dates in all tables in this section are displayed in MMM DD, YYYY format. Now, assume that on December 10, 2008, your daughter is born. You inform ACME that same day and ask them to increase coverage to 75,000. Therefore, the table *BENEFITS* would look like this:

Table BENEFITS

PolicyID	Coverage	Smoker	Dependents	sys_start	sys_end
111	75,000	N	1	Dec 10, 2008	Dec 30, 9999

Where will the previous "old" row be stored? ACME would probably need to create a history table, call it *BENEFITS_HISTORY* as shown next. The *sys_start* column would have a value of June 1, 2007, and the *sys_end* column will have a date of Dec 10, 2008. By convention, the *sys_start* column is inclusive, and the *sys_end* column would be exclusive, that is Dec 10, 2008, is not included in the period, but it ends on Dec 9, 2008, at 11:59pm:

Table BENEFITS_HISTORY

PolicyID	Coverage	Smoker	Dependents	sys_start	sys_end
111	50,000	N	0	June 1, 2007	Dec 10, 2008

Now, assume on May 26, 2013, your second daughter is born. As last time, you inform ACME about it that same day and request an increase of coverage to 100,000. The *BENEFITS* and *BENEFITS_HISTORY* tables would look as follows:

Table BENEFITS

PolicyID	Coverage	Smoker	Dependents	sys_start	sys_end
111	100,000	N	2	May 26, 2013	Dec 30, 9999

Table BENEFITS_HISTORY

PolicyID	Coverage	Smoker	Dependents	sys_start	sys_end
111	50,000	N	0	June 1, 2007	Dec 10, 2008
111	75,000	N	1	Dec 10, 2008	May 26, 2013

Now that you've seen this example, the information needed by ACME, let's show you how this can be implemented in DB2 using temporal tables. The *BENEFITS* table can be created as follows:

```
CREATE TABLE benefits (
    PolicyID      INT primary key not null,
    coverage      INT,
    smoker        CHAR(1),
    sys_start     TIMESTAMP(12) GENERATED ALWAYS AS ROW BEGIN NOT NULL,    ---- (1)
    sys_end       TIMESTAMP(12) GENERATED ALWAYS AS ROW END   NOT NULL,    ---- (2)
    trans_start   TIMESTAMP(12) GENERATED ALWAYS
                        AS TRANSACTION START PolicyID IMPLICITLY HIDDEN,   ---- (3)
    PERIOD SYSTEM TIME (sys_start, sys_end)                                ---- (4)
);
```

Let's review this statement in detail:

In (1), the column *sys_start* was created as timestamp using `GENERATED ALWAYS AS ROW BEGIN`. This means DB2 automatically generates the value when a new row is inserted, updated, or deleted. Because it says `BEGIN`, it means it is the beginning of the period.

In (2), for column *sys_end*, a similar timestamp column as *sys_start* is created, but this time it uses `ROW END` in the clause. DB2 automatically generates the value when a new row is inserted, updated, or deleted, but this time the value represents the end of the period.

Both (1) and (2) could include the clause IMPLICITLY HIDDEN, which would hide the columns so they don't appear when issuing SELECT statements.

In (3), there is a third column *trans_start* that is specified with the clause GENERATED ALWAYS AS TRANSACTION START <*column name*>. In this case, the column PolicyID is used to indicate this is the column to keep track when the transaction first executes a statement that changes the table's data. You can hide this column, so the IMPLICITLY HIDDEN clause is included in the statement.

In (4), the clause PERIOD SYSTEM_TIME (<*column name*>, <*column name*>) indicates which columns are used to track the system time. In this case the beginning system time is recorded in column *sys_start*, and the ending system time is recorded in column *sys_end*. **System time** means the time the "system" recorded the transaction. So if you execute an INSERT statement on December 10, 2008, this is the date DB2—the system—records. Another type of time known as **business time** or **application time** is discuss later in this section.

Next, you need to create the *BENEFITS_HISTORY* table using a simple CREATE TABLE ... LIKE statement as follows:

```
CREATE TABLE benefits_history like benefits
```

The last step to enable time travel query using system time is to establish the relationship between the *BENEFITS* and *BENEFITS_HISTORY* tables using the ALTER TABLE ... ADD VERSIONING USE HISTORY TABLE clause as shown below:

```
ALTER TABLE benefits ADD VERSIONING USE HISTORY TABLE benefits_history;
```

When the *BENEFITS* and *BENEFITS_HISTORY* tables have been created, and "versioning" has been enabled, you can insert rows into the *BENEFITS* table. You do not need to do anything with the *BENEFITS_HISTORY* table; DB2 takes care of updating it appropriately. For example, you can issue the following INSERT statement to enter the first row into table *BENEFITS*:

```
INSERT INTO benefits VALUES (111, 50000, 'N')
```

When you want to retrieve information about benefits for policy 111 for a given period, you can issue a SELECT statement using the *BENEFITS* table. There are three period specifications in the FROM clause you can use:

- **FOR SYSTEM_TIME AS OF ...:** Enables you to query data as of a certain point in time.
- **FOR SYSTEM_TIME FROM ... TO ...:** Enables you to query data from a certain time to a certain time.
- **FOR SYSTEM_TIME BETWEEN ... AND ...:** Enables you to query data between a range of start/end times.

Let's take a look at an example with one of these clauses:

```
SELECT coverage
FROM benefits FOR SYSTEM_TIME AS OF '2009-12-01'
WHERE policyid = 111;
```

Using the tables shown earlier, the output of this statement would be 75,000. DB2 obtains the information from the *BENEFITS_HISTORY* table even though the query makes no mention of this table at all, just the *BENEFITS* table.

Let's now provide another scenario where time travel query is used. Let's say a bank is running a promotion where it is offering its credit card with a promotional interest rate of 1% from Jan 1, 2014, until July 1, 2014. After that period, interest rates would go up to 19% on any balance outstanding. The time period in this example is driven by the business that is setting up this promotion, so this is an example of business time. To implement the time query travel feature in this case, there is no need to create a history table as in the previous case; instead, two TIMESTAMP or DATE columns are needed in addition to the clause PERIOD BUSINESS_TIME (*<column name>, <column name>*). Let's take a look at the CREATE TABLE statement for this example:

```
CREATE TABLE promotions (
    promotionID     INT NOT NULL,
    rate            INT,
    bus_start       DATE NOT NULL,                              ---- (1)
    bus_end         DATE NOT NULL,                              ---- (2)
    PERIOD BUSINESS_TIME(bus_start, bus_end),                   ---- (3)
    PRIMARY KEY(promotionID, BUSINESS_TIME WITHOUT OVERLAPS) ); ---- (4)
```

In (1) and (2), we have defined two DATE columns to store the business start date (*bus_start*) and business end date (*bus_end*). In (3), the clause PERIOD BUSINESS_TIME (bus_start, bus_end) established the period as business time and specifies which columns are to be used for the start and end of the period. Like for system time, with business time, the start date would be inclusive, and the end date would be exclusive. In (4), the optional clause BUSINESS_TIME WITHOUT OVERLAPS is used to ensure that if an insert of a record that has overlapping business dates is attempted, an error is reported.

The following INSERT statements can be used for this example:

```
INSERT INTO promotions VALUES (1, 1,'2014-01-01','2014-07-01')
INSERT INTO promotions VALUES (1,19,'2014-07-01','9999-12-30')
```

Table *PROMOTIONS* would look as follows:

Table PROMOTIONS

promotionID	Rate	bus_start	bus_end
1	1	Jan 1, 2014	Jul 1, 2014
1	19	Jul 1, 2014	Dec 30, 9999

Though you can directly query the *PROMOTIONS* table like any regular table, when you want to consider temporal conditions, you must include one of these period specifications in the FROM clause:

```
FOR BUSINESS_TIME AS OF ...
FOR BUSINESS_TIME FROM ... TO ...
FOR BUSINESS_TIME BETWEEN ... AND ...
```

Let's take a look at an example with one of these clauses:

```
SELECT rate
   FROM promotions FOR BUSINESS_TIME FROM '2014-03-01' TO '2014-08-01'
   WHERE promotionID = 1;
```

Using the table shown earlier, the output of this statement would be two rows because the query is using a business time that expands two periods:

```
RATE
-----
1
19
```

A more advanced case of temporal tables can combine both, system time and business time. In this case, the tables that are used are called bitemporal tables. Refer to the DB2 Information Center for more details about bitemporal tables and other features of time travel queries.

V10 Column-Organized Tables (aka DB2 BLU Acceleration)

Column-organized table support is heralded as a breakthrough technology introduced in DB2 10.5. It provides columnar storage capabilities to the DB2 data server. A column-organized table is a table where the data pages contain column data instead of row data. This is very different from the traditional row-organized table. Systems that support analytic workloads with complex queries involving star schema data marts, table scans, multitable joins, and aggregation benefit from this new table format; it can provide significant improvements to storage, query performance, and simplify database schema design. Traditional row-organized tables with index access are still more appropriate for short transactional workloads.

There are four innovations by IBM Research behind BLU Acceleration technology:

- In-memory columnar processing with dynamic movement of data from storage
- Actionable compression, a technique that preserves order so that data can be used with decompression
- Parallel Vector Processing, a technique to utilize today's most commodity CPU's multi-core and SIMD (Single Instruction Multiple Data) parallelism architecture
- Data skipping, a technique to avoid processing irrelevant data

With column-organized tables, typical performance tuning objects or activities such as indexes, materialized views, optimizer hints, or statistics collection, are no longer needed. There are also no schema changes and no SQL changes necessary. Hence column-organized tables are super-fast and super easy to use. Simply create the table, load it, and use it!

If you are creating a brand new database and you intend to use column-organized tables for most of your tables, it is recommended to set the DB2_WORKLOAD registry variable to ANALYTICS prior to creating the database. The setting helps tune the database to optimize column-organized tables.

To create a column-organized table, specify the ORGANIZE BY COLUMN clause in the CREATE TABLE statement.

```
CREATE TABLE myemployees (
        empID    INT           NOT NULL PRIMARY KEY,
        empname  VARCHAR(30)   NOT NULL,
        rank  VARCHAR(10)  NOT NULL,
        startDate DATE        NOT NULL,
        salary   INTEGER      NOT NULL)
  ORGANIZE BY COLUMN
```

The statement syntax is the same as the row-organized table with some restrictions. The following data types are supported in a column-organized table:

- SMALLINT
- INTEGER
- BIGINT
- DECIMAL
- REAL
- DOUBLE
- CHAR (including FOR BIT DATA)
- VARCHAR (including FOR BIT DATA)
- GRAPHIC

- VARGRAPHIC
- DATE
- TIME
- TIMESTAMP
- Distinct type of a supported type

After creating the table, you can populate the table with the LOAD command. The LOAD utility is discussed in Chapter 10, "Maintaining, Backing Up, and Recovering Data." It is recommended that the majority of data be added by using a single LOAD command so that the column compression dictionaries are created. Note that column-organized tables use actionable compression; therefore, static and adaptive compression are not supported nor needed.

If you want to convert some or all of your row-organized tables to column-organized tables, use the db2convert command. Here are two examples (it is recommended a full database backup is performed in case you want to revert any changes). Database backup is discussed in Chapter 10 as well:

Convert all tables in the TESTDB database into column-organized tables:

```
db2convert -d TESTDB
```

Convert just the empProfile table under the schema john in the TESTDB database:

```
db2convert -d TESTDB -z john -t empProfile
```

Note that you can have both row and column organized tables in a database.

Indexes

Indexes are database objects built based on one or more columns of a table. They are used for two main reasons:

- To improve query performance. Indexes can be used to access the data faster using direct access to rows based on the index key values.
- To guarantee uniqueness when they are defined as unique indexes.

Working with Indexes

To create an index, use the CREATE INDEX statement. This statement requires at a minimum

- The name of the index
- The name of the associated table
- The columns that make up the index (also known as index keys)

In addition, you can specify the following:

- Whether the index is unique (enforce uniqueness for the key values) or nonunique (allow duplicates)
- Which order DB2 should use to build and maintain the key values: ascending (ASC, the default) or descending (DESC) order
- Whether to create INCLUDE columns that are not part of the index key but are columns often retrieved by your queries

For example, let's consider the following statement:

```
CREATE UNIQUE INDEX company_ix
     ON company (company_ID ASC, name DESC)
     INCLUDE (no_employees)
```

This statement creates a unique index *company_ix*. This index is associated with the table *COMPANY* based on the columns *company_ID* in ascending order and *name* in descending order. Bi-directional scans are allowed by default in indexes, primary keys, and unique keys, which means that an index can be traversed in both directions.

In addition, an INCLUDE column *no_employees* was added to the index definition. This column does not belong to the index key; that is, the index is not built and maintained taking this column into consideration. Instead, an INCLUDE column is useful for performance reasons. Assuming the users of table *COMPANY* often retrieve the *no_employees* column, without the INCLUDE column, DB2 would first have to access the index page and then the data page. Rather than performing two access operations, why not add the desired column in the index?

NOTE

INCLUDE columns in an index can improve performance at the cost of having a larger index. The effect of adding an INCLUDE column versus including the column as part of the index key is the same; however, the maintenance cost of updating INCLUDE columns is less than that of updating key columns.

Now let's consider another example that shows how an index looks. The following statement was used to create a table containing the sales records of a company:

```
CREATE TABLE sales (
     sales_person      VARCHAR(30)   NOT NULL,
     region            CHAR(5)       NOT NULL,
     number_of_sales   INT           NOT NULL,
     year              INT
     )
```

Figure 7.29 illustrates the contents of this table.

sales_person	region	number_of_ sales	year
Mary	South	10	2002
John	North	9	2000
Sam	North	8	2000
Mary	East	12	2001
John	West	13	2001
Sam	South	12	2001
Mary	West	15	2002
Sam	South	15	2002
Mary	East	12	2002
John	West	12	2000
Sam	North	14	2001
John	South	21	2002

Figure 7.29   The sales table

Let's define an index on the *sales_person* column of the *SALES* table using the following CREATE INDEX statement:

```
CREATE INDEX index1 ON sales (sales_person)
```

When DB2 builds the index *index1*, it creates pointers to the data pages of each record in the table. Each record is identified by a record ID (RID). An index on the *sales_person* column is shown in Figure 7.30.

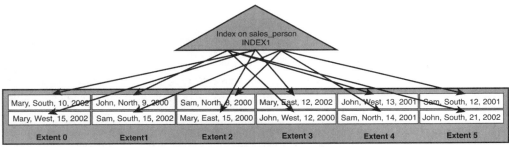

Figure 7.30   An index defined on the sales_person column

Rows are stored on physical disks, and disks are divided into extents. An extent contains a fixed number of pages. We discussed about pages and extents earlier in the chapter.

Let's say you issue the following query:

```
SELECT * FROM sales WHERE sales_person = 'Sam'
```

For this query, DB2 would use index *index1*, and as you can see from Figure 7.30, it would follow the pointers to extents 1, 2, 4, and 5; all of these extents have a data page with a record where the salesperson is Sam. An index gives you a direct access to the records you are looking for. Without an index, DB2 can scan all the data pages in all the extents for the table. This operation is known as a **table scan**, and for very large tables, it can be an expensive operation.

After an index has been created, it cannot be modified. To add or remove a key column from the index, you must drop and recreate the index. To drop an index, use the DROP INDEX statement. For example:

```
DROP INDEX index1
```

> **NOTE**
>
> An index automatically created by the database manager when a primary key or unique constraint was defined cannot be dropped with the DROP INDEX statement. To drop these indexes, use the ALTER TABLE statement with the DROP PRIMARY KEY or DROP UNIQUE constraint_name clauses, respectively.

Indexes can improve query performance considerably; however, the more indexes you define on a table, the more the cost incurred when updating the table because the indexes also need to be updated. The larger you define the size of an index (based on the number of key columns and their columns sizes), the more the cost to update the index. Choose your indexes wisely.

The Index Advisor, part of the Design Advisor tool, can recommend indexes for you based on a specific query or a set of queries. You can launch the Design Advisor from the command line by using the db2advis command.

Clustering Indexes

In the example in the section, "Working with Indexes," you saw that index *index1* (based on the *sales_person* column) improved query performance over table scans. However, because the data pages for the corresponding records were spread across different extents, several I/O requests to the disk were required. Would it not be more efficient to keep all of the desired data pages clustered together on the same extent?

You can achieve this by using a clustering index. A **clustering index** is created so that the index pages physically map to the data pages. That is, all the records that have the same index key are physically close together. Figure 7.31 illustrates how *index1* works when created as a clustering index using the CLUSTER clause as follows.

        CREATE INDEX index1 ON sales (sales_person) CLUSTER

   In the figure, when you issue this query

        SELECT * FROM sales WHERE sales_person = 'Sam'

DB2 still uses index *index1*, but it requires less I/O access to the disk because the desired data pages are clustered together on extents 4 and 5.

> **NOTE**
>
> There can be only one clustering index per table.

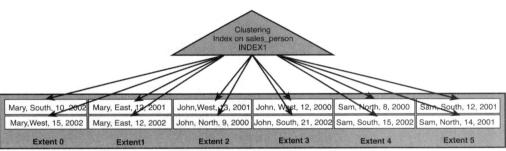

Figure 7.31   A clustering index on the sales_person column

Multidimensional Clustering (MDC) Tables and Block Indexes

Multidimensional clustering (MDC), as its name implies, allows for clustering of the physical data pages in multiple dimensions. For example, using the *SALES* table illustrated previously in Figure 7.29, you can cluster the data based on two dimensions: *sales_person* and *year* columns. This method of clustering has several benefits over clustering indexes:

- With MDC, the data pages are physically clustered by several dimensions simultaneously. With clustering indexes, only one cluster index is allowed per table; the other indexes in the table are unclustered.

- MDC guarantees clustering over time even though frequent INSERT operations are performed. Thus, less maintenance and overhead is required. With clustering indexes, this is not the case. As data pages are filled up, a clustered INSERT operation can encounter the situation where the row to insert does not fit into the right page to maintain the clustering of the data. In such cases, the row can end up on a page that is not close to the other related rows. Clustering indexes require an administrator to perform periodic table reorganizations to recluster the table and set up pages with additional free space to accommodate future clustered INSERT requests.

- MDC uses **block indexes**, indexes that point to an entire block of pages. These are smaller indexes than regular and clustering indexes, which point to a single record.

> **NOTE**
>
> MDC is primarily intended for data warehousing environments; however, it can also work in online transaction processing (OLTP) environments.

MDC Tables

Let's redefine our *SALES* table as an MDC table, using dimensions *sales_person* and *year*.

```
CREATE TABLE sales (
        sales_person      VARCHAR(30)     NOT NULL,
        region            CHAR(5)         NOT NULL,
        number_of_sales   INT             NOT NULL,
        year              INT
        )
ORGANIZE BY DIMENSIONS (sales_person, year)
```

DB2 places records that have the same *sales_person* and *year* values in physical locations that are close together as they are inserted into the table. These locations are called **blocks**. A block can be treated as an extent. The size of an extent can be defined in the CREATE TABLESPACE statement. The minimum size for a block is two pages, like extents.

Figure 7.32 illustrates the contents of the *sales* table using the new MDC definition. For simplicity, in this example a block can hold only two records.

The figure shows this MDC table is physically organized such that records having the same *year* and *sales_person* values are grouped together into separate blocks. For example, all records in block 0 have *sales_person* = John and *year* = 2000. All records in block 4 have *sales_person* = Mary and *year* = 2002.

When a block is filled, DB2 allocates a new block or reuses an old block for the new records inserted. In Figure 7.32, block 4 was filled, and thus block 5 had to be created.

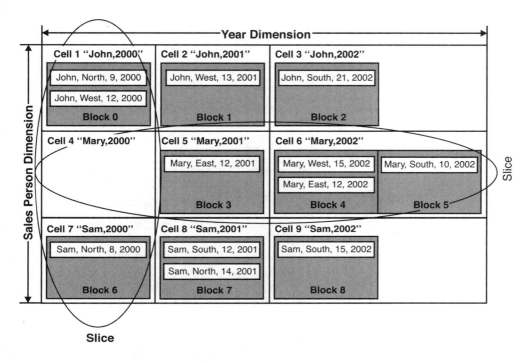

Figure 7.32   The sales table defined as an MDC table

Blocks that have the same dimension values are grouped into **cells**. Each cell represents a unique combination of the dimension values. If there are X different values for *sales_person* and Y different values for *year*, there are X*Y number of cells. In Figure 7.32, you see the table *SALES* has three values for dimension *sales_person*, namely, John, Mary, and Sam. It also has three values for dimension *year*, namely, 2000, 2001, and 2002. Therefore, nine cells are illustrated, one for each combination.

A cell contains only the necessary blocks to store the records that have the dimension values of that cell. If there are no records (as in the case of cell 4 in Figure 7.32), no blocks are allocated.

In Figure 7.32, we also illustrate the concept of a slice. A **slice** consists of all the cells that belong to a specific value of a dimension. The figure highlights two out of six slices, one for dimension *year* with a value of 2000 and the other for dimension *sales_person* with a value of Mary.

Block Indexes

Block indexes are pointers to a block, not a single record. A block index points to the beginning of each block, which has a unique block ID (BID). MDC tables use only block indexes. Figure 7.33 shows a comparison between a regular index and a block index.

Regular Index   Block Index

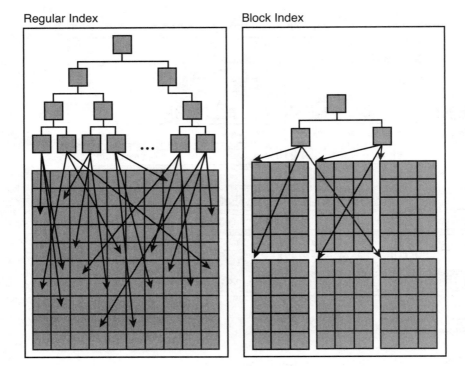

Figure 7.33   A regular (RID) index versus a block index

A block index has the following advantages over a regular index:

- Block indexes are significantly smaller than regular indexes because they point to a block rather than a record. The reduced size makes index scans much faster.

- Less maintenance overhead is associated with block indexes. They only need to be updated when adding the first record to a block and removing the last record from a block.

- Prefetching is done in blocks, thus the amount of I/O is reduced.

An MDC table defined with even a single dimension can benefit from block indexes and can be a viable alternative to a regular table using a clustering index.

When an MDC table is created, a **dimension block index** is created for each specified dimension. For our *SALES* table, two dimension block indexes are created, one for the *sales_ person* dimension and one for the *year* dimension, as illustrated in Figure 7.34.

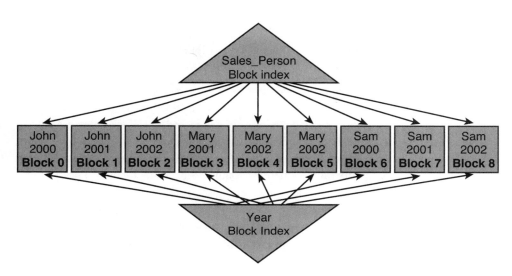

Figure 7.34 Block indexes for sales_person and year

A query requesting records that have *sales_person* = John can use the *sales_person* block index to quickly access all three blocks (block 0, 1, and 2) that satisfy this criteria. Another query can use the *year* block index to independently access all blocks that have *year* = 2002 (blocks 2, 4, 5, and 8).

In addition to the dimension block indexes, a **composite block index** is also created during MDC table creation. A composite block index contains all columns across all dimensions and is used to maintain the clustering of data over INSERT and UPDATE activity. If a single dimension block index already contains all the dimension key columns, a composite block index is not created.

The Block Map

A block map is an array containing an entry for each block of an MDC table. The entry indicates whether or not a block is in use. Each block has a unique identifier (BID) and also an IN_USE status bit. When a DELETE operation removes the last record in a block, DB2 frees the block by changing its IN_USE status bit and removing its BID from all block indexes. When new records are inserted and they can no longer fit into existing blocks, DB2 first scans for free blocks, looking for ones without the IN_USE bit set. If a free block is found, DB2 reuses it, updates its IN_USE bit, and adds its BID to block indexes.

Reusing free blocks greatly reduces fragmentation and in turn minimizes the need to reorganize the MDC table even though pages within the blocks might be fragmented.

Choosing Dimensions for MDC Tables

Choosing the right dimensions for an MDC table is crucial for obtaining the maximum advantages MDC can provide. You should consider the following:

- **Choose columns with the lowest cardinality:** One of the advantages of using block indexes is that they point to a block rather than a record; therefore, there are fewer pointers to traverse. If each block contains only one record, the block index essentially becomes a regular index. You should try to minimize the number of blocks by increasing the number of records they can contain. You can achieve this by choosing columns with the lowest cardinality, that is, the lowest number of distinct values. For example, a column like *region*, with possible values of North, South, East, and West, is a good choice. A column like *employee_id*, which uniquely identifies each employee of a company that has 100,000 employees, is definitely a bad choice.

- **Choose the correct block size (extent size):** MDC tables allocate space in blocks. The entire block is allocated even if only one record is inserted. For example, if your block can hold 100 pages, and on average only 10 records are inserted per block (assuming only one record can fit in a page), then 90% of the space is wasted. Thus, make sure you choose the correct block size.

- **Choose the right number of dimensions:** The higher the number of dimensions, the more possible combinations you can have, and therefore the higher the number of possible cells. If there are many cells, each cell will likely contain only a few records, and if that is the case, the block size needs to be set to a small number.

> **NOTE**
>
> The Design Advisor tool can make recommendations on what dimensions to choose for a given table.

Combining Database Partitioning, Table Partitioning, and MDC

For ultimate flexibility and maximum performance, you can combine database partitioning, table partitioning, and MDC. Database partitioning parallelizes everything across all data partitions, and table partitioning and MDC drastically reduce the I/O required to scan the data and build the result set.

The following statement illustrates how to combine the three types of partitioning:

```
CREATE TABLE carsales
 (custID INT, sales date, make char(30), model char(30), color
➥char(30))
```

```
DISTRIBUTE BY HASH (custID)
PARTITION BY RANGE (sales)
    STARTING FROM ('01/01/2013')  ENDING ('12/31/2013')  EVERY 1
➥months)
    ORGANIZE BY DIMENSIONS (make, model, color)
```

In the preceding example, consider a query looking only for a specific make, model, and color of car sold in a specific month—for example all red, Ford, Mustangs sold in February, 2013. In this case the query runs automatically and in parallel, across all database partitions; within each database partition only the data in the February table partition is accessed, and then only the data block(s) containing *red*, *Ford* and, *Mustangs*. No data blocks for other makes, models, or colors of cars need be read.

Figure 7.35 shows how these partitioning schemes work together to optimize data access.

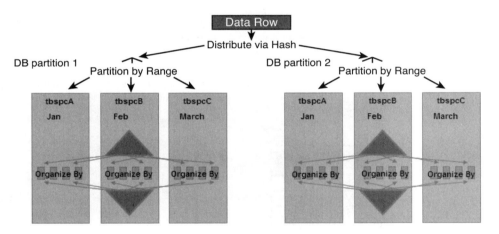

Figure 7.35 Combining database partitioning, table partitioning, and MDC

Views

A view is a virtual table derived from one or more tables or other views. It is virtual because it does not contain any data, but a definition of a table based on the result of a SELECT statement. Figure 7.36 illustrates view *view1* derived from table *table1*.

A view does not need to contain all the columns of the base table. Its columns do not need to have the same names as the base table, either. This is illustrated in Figure 7.36, where the view consists of only two columns, and the first column of the view has a different name than the corresponding column in the base table. This is particularly useful for hiding confidential information from users.

View1   **Table1**

ID	Name
001	John
002	Mary
003	Sam
004	Julie

Employee_ID	Name	Salary	Deptno
001	John	60000	101
002	Mary	60000	101
003	Sam	65000	111
004	Julie	70000	112

Figure 7.36 A view derived from a table

You can create a view using the CREATE VIEW statement. For example, to create the view *view1* shown in Figure 7.36, issue this statement.

```
CREATE VIEW view1 (id, name)
     AS SELECT employee_id, name FROM table1
```

To display the contents of *view1*, use the following statement.

```
SELECT * FROM view1
```

You can also create views based on multiple tables. Figure 7.37 shows a view created from two tables.

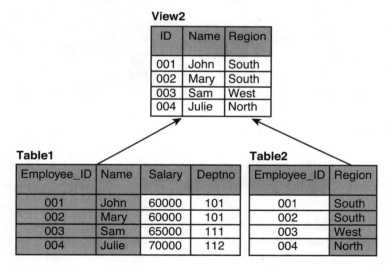

View2

ID	Name	Region
001	John	South
002	Mary	South
003	Sam	West
004	Julie	North

Table1

Employee_ID	Name	Salary	Deptno
001	John	60000	101
002	Mary	60000	101
003	Sam	65000	111
004	Julie	70000	112

Table2

Employee_ID	Region
001	South
002	South
003	West
004	North

Figure 7.37 A view derived from two tables

Here is the corresponding CREATE VIEW statement for Figure 7.37:

```
CREATE VIEW view2 (id, name, region)
AS SELECT table1.employee_id, table1.name, table2.region
    FROM table1,table2
   WHERE table1.employee_id = table2.employee_id
```

With this statement, we have combined the information of *table1* and *table2* into *view2*, while limiting access to the salary information.

When you create a view, its definition is stored in the system catalog table *SYSCAT.VIEWS*. This table contains information about each view such as its name, schema, whether or not it is read-only, and the SQL statement used to create the view. For example, in Figure 7.38 we show part of the information for views *view1* and *view2* in *SYSCAT.VIEWS*.

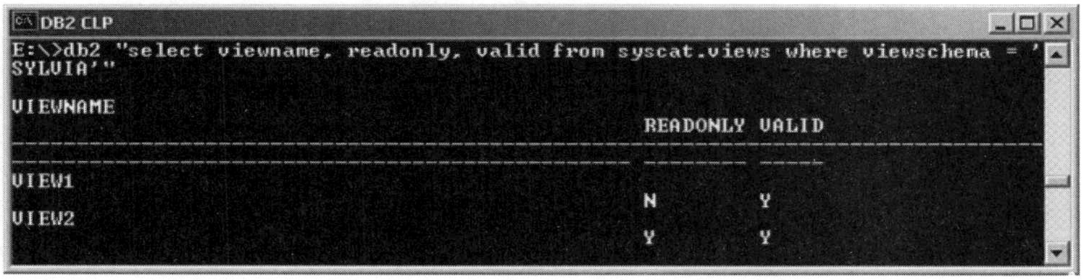

Figure 7.38   View definitions stored in the SYSCAT.VIEWS table

When a view is referenced in a query, DB2 reads and executes the view definition from the *SYSCAT.VIEWS* table, pulls the data from the base table, and presents it to the users.

To remove a view, use the DROP VIEW statement. For example, to remove the view *view1*, use

```
DROP VIEW view1
```

If any of the base tables or views is dropped, the views that are dependent on them are marked invalid, and the value in the *VALID* column shown in Figure 7.38 is set to X instead of Y. When this happens, you cannot use these views. This is true even if you have recreated the base table or view afterward.

View Classification

Views are classified by the operations they allow. There are four classes of views:

- Deleteable views
- Updatable views
- Insertable views
- Read-only views

In the *SYSCAT.VIEWS* catalog table, when the value of the column *READ-ONLY* is Y, this indicates that the view is read-only; otherwise, it is either a deleteable, updatable, or insertable view. Figure 7.39 shows *view2* is a read-only view, but *view1* is not.

Figure 7.39 illustrates the relationship between the different types of views. The views are discussed further in the next sections.

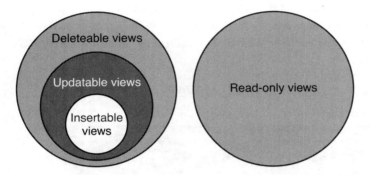

Figure 7.39   View classifications and relationships

Deleteable Views

A deleteable view enables you to execute the DELETE statement against it. All of the following must be true:

- Each FROM clause of the outer fullselect identifies only one base table (with no OUTER clause), a deleteable view (with no OUTER clause), a deleteable nested table expression, or a deleteable common table expression (cannot identify a NICKNAME used with federated support).
- The outer fullselect does not include a VALUES clause.
- The outer fullselect does not include a GROUP BY clause or a HAVING clause.
- The outer fullselect does not include column functions in the SELECT list.
- The outer fullselect does not include SET operations (UNION, EXCEPT, or INTERSECT), with the exception of UNION ALL.
- The base tables in the operands of a UNION ALL must not be the same table, and each operand must be deleteable.
- The select list of the outer fullselect does not include DISTINCT.

For further detail, refer to the DB2 Information Center. In the previous example, *view1* is a deleteable view. However, *view2* is not because it does not follow the first rule. In *view2*'s definition, the SELECT statement contains two base tables in the FROM clause.

Updatable Views

An updatable view is a special case of a deleteable view. A view is updatable when at least one of its columns is updatable. All of the following must be true:

- The view is deleteable.
- The column resolves to a column of a base table (not using a dereference operation), and the READ ONLY option is not specified.
- All the corresponding columns of the operands of a UNION ALL have exactly matching data types (including length or precision and scale) and matching default values if the fullselect of the view includes a UNION ALL.

In the previous example, *view1* is an updatable view. However, *view2* is not because it is not deleteable.

You can update *view1* using the UPDATE statement, and the changes are applied to its base table. For example, the following statement changes the value of column *employee_id* to 100 for records with the *name* value of Mary in *table1*.

```
UPDATE view1 SET id='100' WHERE name = 'Mary';
```

Insertable Views

An insertable view enables you to execute the INSERT statement against it. A view is insertable when all of its columns are updatable. For example, *view1* fits this rule. The following statement inserts a row into *table1*, which is the base table of *view1*.

```
INSERT INTO view1 VALUES ('200', 'Ben');
```

Figure 7.40 displays the contents of *table1* after executing the INSERT statement on *view1*. Note that the *salary* and *deptno* columns for Ben contain NULL values because these two columns are not contained in *view1*.

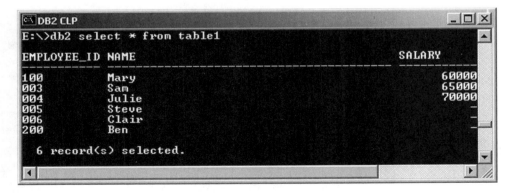

Figure 7.40 Contents of table1 after inserting a row into view1

If *table1* were defined such that NULL values were not allowed in one of the *salary* or *deptno* columns, the INSERT statement would fail, and *view1* would not be an insertable view.

Read-Only Views

A read-only view is not deleteable. In Figure 7.37, shown earlier, *view2* is a read-only view. Its read-only property is also stored in the *SYSCAT.VIEWS* table, which is shown in Figure 7.38.

> **NOTE**
>
> Even if a view is read-only, INSERT, UPDATE, and DELETE operations are still possible by using an INSTEAD OF trigger. For more information, see the section about triggers later in this chapter.

Using the WITH CHECK OPTION

You can define a view to selectively display a subset of rows of its base table by using the WHERE clause in the CREATE VIEW statement. To ensure that all the INSERT and UPDATE operations conform to the criteria specified in the WHERE clause of the view, you can use the WITH CHECK OPTION clause. For example, let's create the view *view3* derived from table *table1* (see Figure 7.36) as follows:

```
CREATE VIEW view3 (id, name,deptno)
     AS SELECT employee_id, name, deptno
        FROM table1
        WHERE deptno = 101
     WITH CHECK OPTION
```

If you issue a SELECT * FROM view3 statement, you obtain the following result:

```
ID  NAME                  DEPTNO
--- --------------------- -----------
001 John                     101
002 Mary                     101
```

Only two rows are retrieved because these are the only rows that satisfy the WHERE clause. What happens if you issue the following statement?

```
INSERT INTO view3 VALUES ('007','Shawn',201)
```

This statement fails because 201 does not conform to the criteria of the WHERE clause used in the CREATE VIEW definition, which is enforced because of WITH CHECK OPTION. If *view3* had not been defined with this clause, the INSERT statement would have succeeded.

Nested Views

Nested views are ones based on other views, for example

```
CREATE VIEW view4
      AS SELECT * FROM view3
```

In this example, *view4* has been created based on *view3*, which was used in earlier examples. The `WITH CHECK OPTION` clause specified in *view3* is still in effect for *view4*; therefore, the following `INSERT` statement fails for the same reason it fails when inserting into *view3*.

```
INSERT INTO view4 VALUES ('007','Shawn',201)
```

When a view is defined with the `WITH CHECK OPTION` clause, the search condition is propagated through all the views that depend on it.

Packages

A package is a database object containing executable SQL (or placeholders to executable SQL), including the access path the DB2 optimizer takes to perform the SQL operation. Packages are stored in the database system catalog tables.

To explain how a package works, let's review with Figure 7.41, which illustrates the preparation of a C application program with embedded SQL.

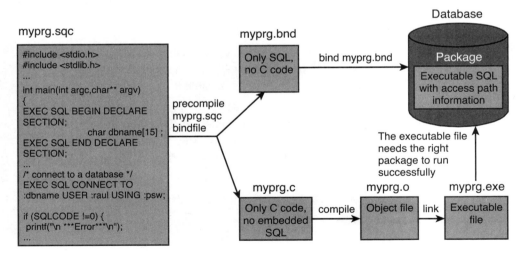

Figure 7.41 How a package is obtained

In the figure, the C program myprg.sqc contains embedded SQL. Issuing the `precompile` command (also known as the `prep` command) with the `bindfile` option generates two files, the myprg.bnd bind file containing only SQL information and the myprg.c file containing only C code.

The bind file is compiled using the `bind` command to obtain a package that is stored in the database. To issue the `bind` command, a connection to the database must exist.

The myprg.c file is compiled and linked like any regular C program. The resulting executable file myprg.exe has to be in sync with the package stored in the database to successfully execute; otherwise, if for example the bnd file was not bound, you receive error SQL0805N.

Triggers

A trigger is a database object associated to a table or a view that contains some application logic, which is executed automatically on an INSERT, UPDATE, or DELETE operation on the table or view. For example, you can use a trigger:

- To validate the input in an INSERT statement
- To compare the new value of a row being updated to an old value
- To insert logging information to another table for audit trail purposes when a row is deleted

Triggers can be classified as BEFORE, AFTER, or INSTEAD OF triggers.

- BEFORE triggers are activated before any table data is affected by the triggering SQL statement. For example, if you are inserting a row into a table, the BEFORE trigger is activated first before the INSERT is completed.
- AFTER triggers are activated after the triggering SQL statement has successfully completed. For example, if a DELETE operation on table *A* completed successfully, an AFTER trigger could be invoked to perform an INSERT on table *B*.
- INSTEAD OF triggers are used to perform INSERT, UPDATE, or DELETE operations on views where these operations are otherwise not allowed. Though read-only views cannot be modified, the underlying tables can; thus, by using an INSTEAD OF trigger, you can make sure that logic is triggered when the view is affected, but the action is performed on the tables themselves.

To create a trigger, use the CREATE TRIGGER statement as demonstrated here:

```
CREATE TRIGGER default_time
      NO CASCADE BEFORE INSERT ON schedule
      REFERENCING NEW AS n
      FOR EACH ROW
      MODE DB2SQL
      WHEN (n.start_time IS NULL)
            SET n.start_time = '12:00'
```

This example shows a BEFORE trigger that is activated when an INSERT statement is performed on table *SCHEDULE*. If the row being inserted has a value of NULL for column *start_time*, the code assigns a value of 12:00 and then continues with the INSERT operation. The REFERENCING NEW clause simply indicates a way to identify the new value of a column.

Here is another example, this time for an AFTER trigger:

```
CREATE TRIGGER audit_qty
     AFTER UPDATE OF quantity ON inventory
     REFERENCING OLD AS o NEW AS n
     FOR EACH ROW
     MODE DB2SQL
     INSERT INTO sold
        VALUES (n.product_ID, n.daysold, o.quantity - n.quantity)
```

This AFTER trigger can be used in the following scenario. Let's say you administer a convenience store. You would like to know how many items of each product are sold per day; therefore, you perform a count every night and update your database with the new count. With the help of this AFTER trigger, you can easily query the *SOLD* table, which is automatically updated when you update the column *quantity* of table *INVENTORY*. The number of items sold for the day is obtained by subtracting the old quantity value minus the new quantity value.

Next is an example of an INSTEAD OF trigger:

```
CREATE TRIGGER update_view2
     INSTEAD OF UPDATE
     ON view2
     REFERENCING OLD AS o NEW AS n
     FOR EACH ROW
     MODE DB2SQL
     BEGIN ATOMIC
        UPDATE table2
        SET region = n.region
        WHERE region = o.region;
     END
```

This example demonstrates how a read-only view can still be updated by using INSTEAD OF triggers. In the example, the trigger updates the *region* column of table *table2* when the view *view2* (a read-only view) is updated.

Stored Procedures

Stored procedures are programs whose executable binaries reside at the database server. They serve as subroutines to calling applications, and they normally wrap multiple SQL statements with flow logic. Figure 7.42 depicts a situation in which stored procedures are useful.

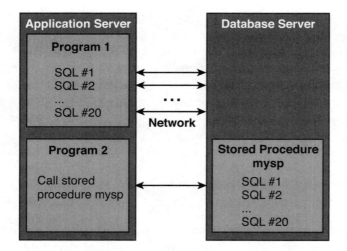

Figure 7.42   Reducing network traffic by using stored procedures

In the figure, *Program 1* and stored procedure *mysp* execute the same set of SQL statements. *Program 1*, however, does not perform as well as *Program 2* because of the extra overhead of sending each SQL statement through the network and waiting for its return. On the other hand, *Program 2* only needs to call the stored procedure *mysp* once and then wait for its return. Because *mysp* performs all the SQL statements within the database server, there is minimal network overhead.

Besides improving response time for applications running on a different server than the database server, stored procedures also provide a central location to store database application logic. This allows for a single place to maintain your code. Stored procedures also provide security advantages. For example, an administrator can limit the operations a user can perform by only letting the user access "secure" tables through stored procedures he created.

You can write stored procedures in several languages, such as C, Java, and SQL PL. SQL PL procedures are the most popular ones because they are easy to learn, provide very good performance, and are compatible across the DB2 platforms, including DB2 for z/OS and DB2 for i5/OS.

To create a stored procedure in the database, use the CREATE PROCEDURE statement. Stored procedures that do not use the SQL PL language are known as **external procedures**. For this type of procedure, the CREATE PROCEDURE statement simply registers the procedure to DB2. The executable code is normally kept under the sqllib\function\routine subdirectory.

In the case of SQL PL stored procedures, the source code is included with the CREATE PROCEDURE statement. Moreover, executing the CREATE PROCEDURE statement compiles the code, binds the SQL statements, and creates the necessary packages.

The following is an example of an SQL PL stored procedure created in the database SAM-PLE (which is provided with DB2):

```
CREATE PROCEDURE CSMMGR.NEW_SALARY (IN  p_empno   CHAR(6),
                                    OUT p_empName VARCHAR(30) )
        LANGUAGE SQL
-------------------------------------------------------------------
-- SQL Stored Procedure used to update the salary of an employee
-------------------------------------------------------------------
P1: BEGIN
  DECLARE v_firstName VARCHAR(12);
  DECLARE v_lastName  VARCHAR(15);
  UPDATE employee SET salary = salary * 1.05
        WHERE empno = p_empno;
  SELECT lastname, firstnme INTO v_lastName, v_firstName
    FROM employee WHERE empno = p_empno;
  SET p_empName = v_lastName || ', ' || v_firstName;
END P1
```

In this example, the procedure name is *CSMMGR.NEW_SALARY*. This procedure takes an input parameter *p_empno* and an output parameter *p_empName*. The procedure increases by 5% the value in the *salary* column of table *EMPLOYEE* for the employee with employee number *p_empno*. It then returns the name of the employee who received the increase in the format *last-name, firstname*.

> **NOTE**
>
> We recommend using the IBM Data Studio tool to develop, debug, and test your SQL PL stored procedures. IBM Data Studio is discussed in Chapter 4, Using Database Tools and Utilities

To change the properties of your stored procedures, you can use the ALTER PROCEDURE statement. To drop a stored procedure, use the DROP PROCEDURE statement.

Stored procedures are also classified as fenced or unfenced. A **fenced stored procedure** runs in a different address space than the DB2 engine. This guarantees that a failure from the procedure does not corrupt the DB2 engine itself. In Linux and UNIX, a fenced user needs to be created to work with fenced stored procedures. Refer to Chapter 5, "Understanding the DB2 Environment, DB2 Instances, and Databases," for details.

An **unfenced stored procedure** runs in the same address space as the DB2 engine. In terms of performance, unfenced stored procedures run faster than fenced ones; however, there is a risk that unfenced procedures can corrupt DB2 information, so you should make sure to test these procedures thoroughly.

User-Defined Functions

Although stored procedures enable you to centralize code in your database, they cannot be directly called within a SQL statement. Functions, on the other hand, can be directly invoked from a SQL statement.

DB2 provides built-in functions that allow you to manipulate your data within a SQL statement. For example, the `year` function can retrieve the year of a timestamp column, as shown here:

```
db2 select year(current timestamp) from sysibm.sysdummy1
1
-----------
        2013
```

In addition to built-in functions, DB2 enables you to create your own functions. These user-defined functions (UDFs) enable you to simplify database application development by moving some of the logic to the database. It also gives users the capability to "extend" the SQL language to their own needs. A UDF takes zero to many input parameters and returns a value, a row, or a table. To create a UDF, use the `CREATE FUNCTION` statement.

UDFs can be classified as follows:

- **Sourced functions:** These functions are created on top of DB2 built-in functions. Here's an example:

  ```
  CREATE FUNCTION trim (p_var1 VARCHAR(50))
        RETURNS VARCHAR(50)
        RETURN RTRIM(LTRIM(p_var1))
  ```

  In this example, `RTRIM` is a DB2 built-in function that removes all the blanks at the end of a string. `LTRIM` is a DB2 built-in function that removes all the blanks at the beginning of a string. The UDF `trim` is created to remove blanks at the beginning and the end of a string by using these two built-in functions. To test the function, you can use the `VALUES` statement as follows:

  ```
  VALUES (trim('       hello    '))
  which returns:
  1
  --------------------------------------------------
  hello
  ```

- **SQL functions:** These functions are written in SQL PL language. They can return a scalar value, a single row, or a table of data. The following code shows an example of an SQL UDF returning a scalar value: the rounded salary of an employee.

```
CREATE FUNCTION csmmgr.salary_round(p_empno CHAR(6))
     RETURNS INTEGER
     LANGUAGE SQL
F1: BEGIN ATOMIC
     DECLARE v_salary INTEGER;
     SET v_salary = (SELECT ceiling(salary) FROM employee
                     WHERE empno = p_empno);
     RETURN v_salary;
END
```

This function takes an employee number as input and returns the salary rounded to the highest integer value. SQL functions can be developed with IBM Data Studio.

- **External functions:** These functions are defined in the database with references to object code libraries that are written in C, Java, or OLE. Consider this example:

```
CREATE FUNCTION csmmgr.db2killapp(INT)
     RETURNS INT
     EXTERNAL NAME 'db2killapplib!db2killapp'
     LANGUAGE C
     PARAMETER STYLE SQL
     NOT FENCED
     RETURNS NULL ON NULL INPUT
     NOT DETERMINISTIC
     NO SQL
     NO EXTERNAL ACTION
```

This statement registers the UDF csmmgr.db2killapp to DB2. It is an external function written in C. The C executable code is stored in the *db2killapplib* library, which is stored under the sqllib\function subdirectory.

Sequences

A sequence is a database object that allows automatic generation of values. Unlike identity columns, this object does not depend on any table—the same sequence object can be used across the database.

To create a sequence, use the CREATE SEQUENCE statement as demonstrated here:

```
CREATE SEQUENCE myseq AS INTEGER
     START WITH 1 INCREMENT BY 1
```

```
NO MAXVALUE
NO CYCLE
CACHE 5
```

This statement creates the sequence *myseq*, which is of type INTEGER. The sequence starts with a value of 1 and then increases by 1 each time it's invoked for the next value.

The `NO MAXVALUE` clause indicates there is no explicit maximum value in which the sequence stops; therefore, it is bound by the limit of the data type, in this case, INTEGER.

The `NO CYCLE` clause indicates the sequence does not start over from the beginning once the limit is reached.

`CACHE 5` indicates five sequence numbers are cached in memory, and the sixth number in the sequence is stored in a catalog table. Sequence numbers are cached in memory for performance reasons; otherwise, DB2 needs to access the catalog tables constantly to retrieve the next value in line. What would happen if your computer crashed and the following numbers were in the cache: 5, 6, 7, 8, and 9? These numbers would be lost, and the next time DB2 needed to retrieve a number, it would obtain the number from the catalog tables. In this example, 10 is the next number to be generated. If you are using the sequence number to generate unique identifiers, which must be in sequence with no gaps allowed, this would not work for you. The partial solution would be to use the `NO CACHE` clause to guarantee sequentially generated numbers with no gaps, but you pay a performance cost, and you might still have gaps if `ROLLBACK` operations are performed.

For the sequence value, you can use any exact numeric data type with a scale of zero, including SMALLINT, INTEGER, BIGINT, and DECIMAL. In addition, any user-defined distinct type based on these data types can hold sequence values.

NOTE

The options supported for sequence objects are the same as the ones for identity columns.

Table 7.7 shows other statements you can use with sequences.

Table 7.7   Other Statements Used with Sequences

Statement	Explanation
ALTER SEQUENCE	Alters the characteristics of a sequence, like the increment value.
DROP SEQUENCE	Drops the sequence.
NEXTVAL FOR *sequence_name* or NEXT VALUE FOR *sequence_name*	Retrieves the next value generated in the sequence.

Statement	Explanation
PREVVAL FOR *sequence_name* or PREVIOUS VALUE FOR *sequence_name*	Retrieves the previous value generated in the sequence.

Modules

A module is a database object that is a collection of other database objects such as functions, procedures, types, and variables. Modules are like schemas, which allow you to group database objects together in a named set. It defines a namespace to the database objects within the module. The database objects can refer to other objects defined in the module without providing an explicit qualifier.

Modules are particularly useful in situations where you need to define a routine that references to another routine that is not yet defined or if the routines have circular references. You can define a routine prototype first with name and parameters of the routine; the full routine definition can be done later.

The statement to create a module is as simple as shown here:

```
CREATE MODULE empProfile
```

Next, you can add routine definitions to the module with the ALTER MODULE statement. The following example shows that you can provide only the routine prototype:

```
ALTER MODULE empProfile
   PUBLISH PROCEDURE NEW_SALARY (IN p_empno CHAR(6), OUT p_empName
VARCHAR(30))
```

Later when you are ready to provide the routine definition, use the ADD clause as follows:

```
ALTER MODULE empProfile
   ADD PROCEDURE NEW_SALARY (IN p_empno CHAR(6), OUT p_empName
VARCHAR(30))
LANGUAGE SQL
P1: BEGIN
  DECLARE v_firstName VARCHAR(12);
  DECLARE v_lastName  VARCHAR(15);
  UPDATE employee SET salary = salary * 1.05
        WHERE empno = p_empno;
  SELECT lastname, firstnme INTO v_lastName, v_firstName
    FROM employee WHERE empno = p_empno;
  SET p_empName = v_lastName || ', ' || v_firstName;
END P1
```

There are few restrictions when defining database objects in the modules. Only the following database objects are allowed:

- SQL procedures
- SQL functions
- External procedures
- External functions
- Created conditions
- User-defined data type definitions
- Global variables of all data types
- A module initialization procedure for implicit execution upon module initialization

Case Study 1

Your company is evaluating switching from a database product to DB2. You have been given the task of creating several DB2 database objects as a proof-of-concept exercise on a single-partition environment. You've been reading DB2 documentation and are ready to give DB2 a try. You start by creating the database *testdb* using automatic storage (default) on your Windows server using as storage paths the drives E:, F:, G:, and H:. The command you use is:

```
CREATE DATABASE testdb ON E:, F:, G:, H:
```

This command takes a few minutes to complete as it creates several default database objects, including the default table spaces (SYSCATSPACE, TEMPSPACE1, and USER-SPACE1), the default buffer pool (IBMDEFAULTBP), and the default storage group (IBMS-TOGROUP) which consist of the storage paths E:, F:, G:, and H: as specified in the CREATE DATABASE command. Next, you create an automatic storage table space to use for your tables. The storage group and buffer pool being used are the default ones respectively:

```
CREATE TABLESPACE myts
```

To optimize access to data in this table space, you can add a new buffer pool and then assign the *myts* table space to use the buffer pool:

```
CREATE BUFFERPOOL mytsbp SIZE 50000
ALTER TABLESPACE myts BUFFERPOOL mytsbp
```

After the database is created, before you can create any object, you need to connect to the database; thus you perform this operation:

```
CONNECT TO testdb
```

Given that this is a single-partition environment, you don't have to bother with creating partition groups. Therefore, you start with the creation of your tables. The requirements for this proof-of-concept exercise indicate that you need to create a table for the departments in your organization. Every department must have a department ID, which must be unique within the organization. Every department must also have a name and a manager ID. Because all three of these columns are required, you need to define them as NOT NULL. To ensure that the department ID is unique, you have two options: create a unique index or define the column as the primary key for the table. You decide to create a primary key because you want to define relationships between the department ID in this table and other tables later.

Therefore, you create the table as follows:

```
CREATE TABLE dept (
        deptID    INT         NOT NULL PRIMARY KEY,
        deptname  CHAR(30)    NOT NULL,
        mngrID    INT         NOT NULL
        ) using myts
```

You also could have created the table in two steps as follows:

```
CREATE TABLE dept (
        deptID    INT         NOT NULL,
        deptname  CHAR(30)    NOT NULL,
        mngrID    INT         NOT NULL
        ) using myts
ALTER TABLE dept ADD PRIMARY KEY (deptID)
```

Next, because your applications tend to scan the table looking for department names on a regular basis, you create an index on the *deptname* column in the *DEPT* table as follows:

```
    CREATE INDEX deptnmx ON dept (deptname)
```

Next, you create the table of employees for your organization. Every employee has an employee ID, first and last names, and a salary. In addition, every employee belongs to a department. You issue the following statement to create the *EMP* table:

```
CREATE TABLE emp (
        empID    INT          NOT NULL PRIMARY KEY,
        fname    CHAR(30)     NOT NULL,
        lname    CHAR(30)     NOT NULL,
        deptID   INT          NOT NULL,
        salary   DECIMAL (12,2)
        ) using myts
```

Because your applications scan the table looking for employees' names on a regular basis, you also create an index on the first and last name columns in the table as follows:

```
    CREATE INDEX empnmx ON emp (lname, fname)
```

The employee and department tables are related: The department table is the parent table, and the employee table is the dependent table; therefore, any department ID in the employee table must exist in the department table. To establish this relationship, you create a referential constraint as follows:

```
ALTER TABLE emp ADD FOREIGN KEY (deptID) REFERENCES dept
```

Alternatively, you could have set up the same referential constraint by using a unique constraint in the dept table instead of the primary key as follows:

```
CREATE TABLE dept (
        deptID    INT        NOT NULL,
        deptname  CHAR(30)   NOT NULL,
        mngrID    INT        NOT NULL
        ) using myts
ALTER TABLE dept ADD CONSTRAINT deptun UNIQUE (deptID)
ALTER TABLE emp  ADD FOREIGN KEY (deptID) REFERENCES dept (deptID)
```

This is important because you might want to have more than one referential constraint for the same base table, and this allows you to reference different keys in the parent table.

There is also a requirement to enforce a rule that no employee can have a salary greater than $100,000.00; therefore, you create a check constraint as follows:

```
ALTER TABLE emp ADD CONSTRAINT salary CHECK (salary <= 100000.00)
```

After the alter table successfully completes, you test the CHECK constraint with the following statement:

```
INSERT INTO emp VALUES (123, 'Sam ', 'Johnson ', 345, 100005)
```

This INSERT statement fails as expected and reports this message:

```
SQL0545N  The requested operation is not allowed because a row
does not satisfy the check constraint "MYSCHEMA.EMP.SALARY".
SQLSTATE=23513
```

You know your applications already perform the salary check constraint before the data is entered into DB2, so you wonder if you can remove this constraint in DB2. However, when you ask your manager, he says the problem with that approach is that DB2 would not know that those rules exist and might therefore need to do extra checks that could cause inefficient access. To overcome this, you create informational constraints so that the DB2 optimizer knows about the rules when building the optimal access plan, but DB2 does not enforce the rules when the data is being manipulated. Therefore, you change the constraint you created earlier.

First, you drop the constraint:

```
ALTER TABLE emp DROP CONSTRAINT salary
```

Then you recreate it again as follows:

```
ALTER TABLE emp ADD CONSTRAINT salary
      CHECK (salary < 100000.00)
      NOT ENFORCED ENABLE QUERY OPTIMIZATION
```

You save all of these commands in a script file. Next, because several developers in your company will use this *testdb* database to test different things, you decide to create the objects again, but this time using a different schema. Because you have SYSADM authority, you can issue the following commands:

```
CREATE SCHEMA developer1
SET CURRENT SCHEMA developer1
```

You then execute the script file, which creates all the objects again, but in a different schema.

And that's it for your proof-of-concept exercise!

Case Study 2

In this second case study, assume that you are building a new table that will be quite large, and will likely contain a lot of repeated values. Start off by connecting to the SAMPLE database. If you have not previously created the SAMPLE database, you can create it with the db2sampl command:

1. Create a copy of the staff table that is part of the SAMPLE database as follows:

   ```
   create table stf like staff
   ```

2. Enable adaptive compression for the table:

   ```
   alter table stf compress yes
   ```

3. Next load a representative sample of the data into the table:

   ```
   insert into stf select * from staff
   ```

4. Load the table with "all" of the data by running the following statement ten times:

   ```
   insert into stf select * from staff
   ```

5. Create a table to store the car sales for the year 2013 and partition the table by month:

   ```
   CREATE TABLE carsales(sale_date DATE,
   make char(30),
   model char(30),
   color char(30))
   PARTITION BY RANGE(sale_date)
   ```

```
( STARTING '1/1/2013'
  ENDING '12/31/2013'
  EVERY 1 MONTH )
```

6. Create a table and add a new partition for January 2014:

```
create table jansales (sale_date DATE,
        make char(30),
        model char(30),
        color char(30))
alter table carsales attach partition
        starting ('2014-01-01')
        ending ('2014-03-31')   FROM jansales
```

And that's it! This second case study showed you how to work with row compression and table partitioning.

Summary

This chapter discussed the concept of databases, database partitions, and the DB2 database objects. It explained how to work with various DB2 database objects such as partition groups, table spaces, buffer pools, tables, views, indexes, schemas, stored procedures, and so on. It also discussed the automatic storage feature and how it can be used to simplify storage management.

The chapter also covered the DB2 data types (DB2 built-in and user-defined types), which are used as ways to define the columns of a table or as parameters to stored procedures and functions.

Table objects were discussed in detail because there are many topics associated with tables, such as constraints, referential integrity, the use of NULLs, identity columns, table compression, and row compression.

This chapter also described indexes and the different clauses of the CREATE INDEX statement such as INCLUDE. More complex subjects such as range partitioning or multidimensional clustering (MDC) tables, were also discussed. MDC tables allow for greater flexibility to cluster your data by several dimensions.

Views and their classification (deleteable, updatable, insertable, and read-only) were also explored.

The chapter also introduced application-related objects such as packages, triggers, stored procedures, user-defined functions, and sequences. Although this is not a DB2 application development book, this chapter provided you with the foundation to understand these objects.

Referring to the figures presented in the chapter should help you remember all the concepts introduced.

Review Questions

1. Consider the following instructions/commands/statements:

   Login to your Linux server as user JDOE
   ```
   su db2inst1 (switch user to db2inst1)
   CONNECT TO sample USER foo USING bar
   SELECT * FROM t1
   ```

   Which table will you select data from?

   A. JDOE.t1

   B. db2inst1.t1

   C. foo.t1

   D. bar.t1

2. Which of the following is not created when you create a database?

   A. IBMDEFAULTBP

   B. IBMDEFAULTSPACE

   C. IBMDEFAULTGROUP

   D. SYSCATSPACE

   E. IBMTEMPGROUP

3. Which of the following objects ensure rows are assigned a uniquely generated value across multiple tables?

   A. Identity column-defined as a primary key

   B. Unique index

   C. Sequence

   D. Row ID

4. Which of the following commands delete all rows from the table *t1* without logging?

   A. `Trunk table`

   B. `Delete * from t1 no log`

   C. `Alter table t1 activate not logged initially with truncate`

   D. `Alter table t1 activate not logged initially with empty table`

5. To ensure that a column can contain only the values T or F, which option should you choose?

   A. Create a unique index on the column.

   B. Create a check constraint on the column.

   C. Specify the column as NOT NULL.

   D. Create a view on the table.

6. When deleting a row from a table that has a primary key defined, which of the following options on a foreign key clause deletes all rows with the same value in the foreign key table?

   A. Restrict

   B. Cascade

   C. Drop

   D. Set NULL

7. Which two of the following can be referenced by a foreign key constraint?

   A. Unique index

   B. Unique constraint

   C. Check constraint

   D. Primary key

   E. Identity column

8. Given the table created as follows:
```
CREATE TABLE product (
        productno   INTEGER GENERATED ALWAYS AS
                        IDENTITY (START WITH 0 INCREMENT BY 5),
        description VARCHAR(50) )
```
And these statements:
```
INSERT INTO product VALUES (DEFAULT,'banana')
INSERT INTO product (description) VALUES ('apple')
INSERT INTO product VALUES (300,'pear');
```
   How many rows will be in the table?

   A. 0

   B. 1

   C. 2

   D. 3

9. Consider the following statement:

    `CREATE TABLE wqwq (c1 DECIMAL)`

    What will the precision and scale be for column c1?

    A. Precision = 15, scale = 0

    B. Precision = 15, scale =15

    C. Precision = 5, scale = 0

    D. Precision = 5, scale = 10

10. Which of the following is not a supported type of trigger?

    A. INBETWEEN

    B. AFTER

    C. INSTEAD OF

    D. BEFORE

11. Which of the following does not belong to a database?

    A. Schema

    B. Logs

    C. Registry variables

    D. System catalogs

12. Consider the following statement:

    `CREATE TABLE foo (c1 INT NOT NULL PRIMARY KEY, c2 INT)`

    How many database objects are created?

    A. 1

    B. 2

    C. 3

    D. 4

13.   Consider the following *db2nodes.cfg* file.

```
0 mysrv1 0
1 mysrv1 1
2 mysrv2 0
3 mysrv2 1
```

How many servers are the partitions running on?

A. 1

B. 2

C. 3

D. 4

14.   To create the table space *ts1* successfully using buffer pool *bp1* in the database sample, place the following steps in the correct order.

1. CREATE TABLESPACE ts1 PAGESIZE 16K BUFFERPOOL bp1
2. CONNECT TO sample
3. CREATE BUFFERPOOL bp1 SIZE 100000 PAGESIZE 16K

A. 1, 2, 3

B. 3, 2, 1

C. 2, 1, 3

D. 2, 3, 1

15.   A package contains which of the following? (Choose all that apply.)

A. Executable SQL statements

B. The access path that the DB2 optimizer chooses to retrieve the data

C. A collection of stored procedures and functions

D. A list of bind files

16.   Tables with the same name can be created within the same database by creating them in which of the following?

A. Different partitions

B. Different partition groups

C. Different table spaces

D. Different schemas

17. Which of the following can be used to obtain the next value of the sequence *seq1*? (Choose all that apply.)

    A. `seq1.nextValue`

    B. `NEXTVAL FOR seq1`

    C. `NEXT VALUE FOR seq1`

    D. `seq1.next`

18. Which of the following statements is true?

    A. A user temporary table space is created with the create temporary table statement.

    B. The creation of a user temporary table space fails if no system temporary table space is available.

    C. A user temporary table is created in TEMPSPACE1.

    D. A user temporary table space is needed so that declared global temporary tables can be declared.

19. Which of the following commands or statements enable compression for a table?

    A. `REORG`

    B. `RUNSTATS`

    C. `INSPECT`

    D. `CREATE`

    E. `ALTER`

20. Which of the following commands remove an existing range from a table and create a new table with the data from that range?

    A. `DETACH`

    B. `ALTER`

    C. `CREATE`

    D. `REORG`

21. Which of the following options can be used to partition data across multiple servers?

    A. Organize by

    B. Partition by

    C. Spread by

    D. Distribute by

22.   Which of the following page sizes is not supported by DB2?

     A. 2K

     B. 4K

     C. 8K

     D. 16K

CHAPTER **8**

Implementing Security

All tasks and concepts presented in the previous chapters assumed you had the administrative rights, or privileges, to set up client and server connectivity, execute SQL statements, create database objects, and so on. In the real world, administrative rights are typically given only to selected individuals. In addition, the privileges for users to access data must be controlled to comply with business and regulatory requirements. DB2 uses a number of components to support various security schemes. This chapter discusses each of the security components and provides examples to illustrate different implementation scenarios.

In this chapter, you learn about

- DB2 authentication methods
- Administrative authorities, database object privileges, and roles
- Database objects access control
- Data encryption
- Label-Based Access Control (LBAC)
- Row and Column Access Control (RCAC)
- Trusted contexts
- Windows security considerations

DB2 Security Model: The Big Picture

The DB2 security model consists of four major components:

- Authentication
- Authorization
- Database object security (also known as database object privileges)
- Content-based authorization consisting of Label-Based Access Control (LBAC) and Row and Column Access Control (RCAC).

415

Figure 8.1 illustrates these components.

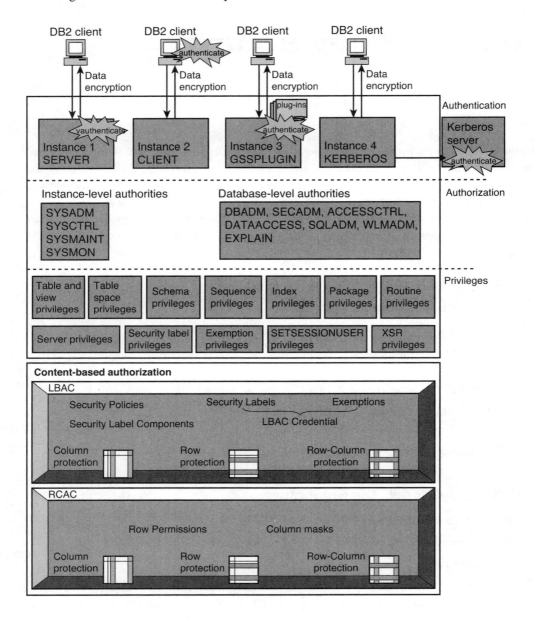

Figure 8.1   The big picture of the DB2 security model

A combination of external security services and internal DB2 privilege mechanisms handle DB2 security. As shown in Figure 8.1, a user goes through the **authentication** process (not performed by DB2) before he is allowed to connect to the database. After the user ID and password have been verified (either on the server or the client), an internal **authorization** process (performed by DB2) takes over and makes sure that the user has the privileges to perform the requested operations and access the requested data. This is represented by the Authorization and Privileges components in Figure 8.1. LBAC and RCAC are optional additional security mechanisms you can implement that allow for granular control of your data at the row and column levels. The following sections discuss all of these concepts in more detail.

Authentication Methods

Authentication is the process of validating the supplied user ID and password with a security facility. This authentication occurs when you try to connect to a database or attach to an instance. The security facility is external to DB2; user IDs and passwords are not stored in a DB2 instance or database. Authentication can occur at any of the following:

- At a DB2 server using Operating system authentication (Figure 8.1, Instance 1)
- At a DB2 client using Operating system authentication (Figure 8.1, Instance 2)
- Using a customized loadable library via Generic Security Service (GSS) (Figure 8.1, Instance 3)
- Using a Kerberos security service (Figure 8.1, Instance 4)

The authentication process also determines which operating system groups the user belongs to while not using GSS or Kerberos. Group membership lookup is essential because it lets users inherit certain authorities or privileges through the groups they belong to.

The following sections describe how to configure the authentication type at the DB2 server and at the client, respectively. The combination of the client and server authentication configurations determines where and how the authentication takes place (the authentication method).

Configuring the Authentication Type at a DB2 Server

To configure the authentication type at a DB2 server, you use the Database Manager (DBM) Configuration parameter AUTHENTICATION. If you are not already familiar with DBM Configuration parameters, refer to Chapter 5, "Understanding the DB2 Environment, DB2 Instances, and Databases." For completeness, we are including the command here to display the current DBM parameter settings:

```
get dbm cfg
```

From the output, locate the following line where the authentication type is specified:

```
Database manager authentication        (AUTHENTICATION) = SERVER
```

SERVER is the default authentication type of an instance. Figure 8.2 shows this authentication type.

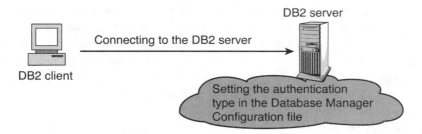

Figure 8.2   Configuring the authentication type at a DB2 server

To change the value to the KERBEROS authentication type, for example, use this DB2 command

```
update dbm cfg using authentication KERBEROS
```

Alternatively, you can use IBM Data Studio to make this change. Chapter 4, "Using Database Tools and Utilities," describes IBM Data Studio in detail.

Table 8.1 summarizes the values the AUTHENTICATION parameter accepts.

Table 8.1   Description of the Authentication Types

Authentication Type	Description
SERVER	Authenticates users at the DB2 server. This is the default value.
SERVER_ENCRYPT	Authenticates users at the DB2 server. When the user ID and password are sent to the server, they are both encrypted.
DATA_ENCRYPT	Authenticates users at the DB2 server; userID, password, and user data are all encrypted.
DATA_ENCRYPT_CMP	Authenticates users at the DB2 server; userID, password, and user data are all encrypted if both the DB2 server and client support data encryption. SERVER_ENCRYPT will be used instead if the client does not support data encryption.
KERBEROS	Authenticates users at a Kerberos server.

Authentication Type	Description
KRB_SERVER_ENCRYPT	Authenticates users at a Kerberos server if both the DB2 server and client support Kerberos security service. SERVER_ENCRYPT is used instead if the client does not support Kerberos security service.
GSSPLUGIN	Authenticates users using an external GSS Application Programming Interface (GSSAPI)-based security mechanism.
GSS_SERVER_ENCRYPT	Authenticates users using an external GSSAPI-based security mechanism if both the DB2 server and client support GSS. Use SERVER_ENCRYPT instead if the client does not support GSS.
CLIENT	Authenticates users at the DB2 client depending on the settings of two other configuration parameters: TRUST_CLNTAUTH and TRUST_ALLCLNTS.

The output of the `get dbm cfg` command includes another authentication-related parameter, called server connection authentication (SRVCON_AUTH):

```
Server Connection Authentication        (SRVCON_AUTH) = NOT_SPECIFIED
```

This parameter sets the authentication type at the DB2 server for incoming database connections. Note that only database connections evaluate the value of this parameter. Explicit instance attachment and operations that require implicit instance attachment still use AUTHENTICATION to resolve the authentication type.

By default, SRVCON_AUTH has a value of NOT_SPECIFIED. In this case, the value of AUTHENTICATION is used instead.

Configuring the Authentication Type at a DB2 Client

When a client is configured to connect to a database, you need to catalog the node and the database. The `catalog database` command discussed in Chapter 6, "Configuring Client and Server Connectivity," has an option called AUTHENTICATION that enables you to indicate the authentication type to be used when connecting to the specified database from a DB2 client as shown in Figure 8.3.

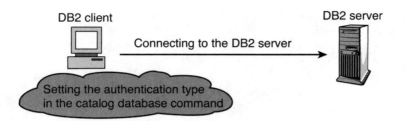

Figure 8.3   Setting the authentication type at a DB2 client

Listing 8.1 illustrates the syntax of the `catalog database` command. To execute this command, you need to have either SYSADM or SYSCTRL authority, or the database manager configuration parameter `CATALOG_NOAUTH` must be set to ON (or YES). Setting `CATALOG_NOAUTH` to ON means database cataloging is allowed without authority; this is the default setting for clients. For DB2 servers the default is OFF (or NO). Administrative authorities are discussed in section "Administrative Authorities" later in this chapter.

Listing 8.1   Syntax of the CATALOG DATABASE Command

```
>>-CATALOG--+-DATABASE-+---database-name--+-----------+---------->
            '-DB-------'                   '-AS--alias-'


>--+------------------+---------------------------------------->
   +-ON--+-path--+-----+
   |     '-drive-'     |
   '-AT NODE--nodename-'


>--+-----------------------------------------------------------+-->
   '-AUTHENTICATION--+-SERVER----------------------------------+-'
                     +-CLIENT--------------------------------+
                     +-SERVER_ENCRYPT-----------------------+
                     +-KERBEROS TARGET PRINCIPAL--principalname-+
                     +-DATA_ENCRYPT-------------------------+
                     '-GSSPLUGIN---------------------------'


>--+----------------------+-------------------------------><
   '-WITH--"comment-string"-'
```

If authentication type is not specified in the `catalog database` command, it defaults to the authentication type specified on the server.

To change this setting, explicitly specify the AUTHENTICATION keyword along with one of the supported values shown in Table 8.2. The following is an example of using GSSPLU-GIN authentication.

```
catalog db sample at node dbsrv authentication gssplugin
```

Table 8.2   Authentication Types Supported at DB2 Clients

Supported Authentication Values	Description
SERVER	Authenticates users at the DB2 server where the database resides.
SERVER_ENCRYPT	Authenticates users at the DB2 server where the database resides. When the user ID and password are sent to the server, they are both encrypted.

KERBEROS
TARGET PRINCIPAL *principalname*
	Authenticates users at a Kerberos server.
	Fully qualify the Kerberos principal name for the target server.
	For UNIX and Linux systems, use a name such as name/instance@REALM.
	For Windows, *principalname* is the logon account of the DB2 server service, which might look like one of the following:
	    userid@DOMAIN
	    userid@xxx.xxx.xxx.com
	    domain\userid

DATA_ENCRYPT	Authenticates users at the DB2 server. In addition, data encryption must be used for the connections.
GSSPLUGIN	Authenticates users with an external GSSAPI-based security mechanism.
CLIENT	Authenticates users at the DB2 client depending on the settings of two other configuration parameters: TRUST_CLNTAUTH and TRUST_ALLCLNTS

Authenticating Users at the DB2 Server

As mentioned earlier, authenticating a user and the associated password at the DB2 server is the default behavior. The DBM configuration parameter at the server and the authentication option in the database directory entry are both set to SERVER. DB2 does not maintain any user and password information. This implies that the user ID and password pair must be defined in the security facility built in the operating system of the server. Figure 8.4 demonstrates a few scenarios of server authentication.

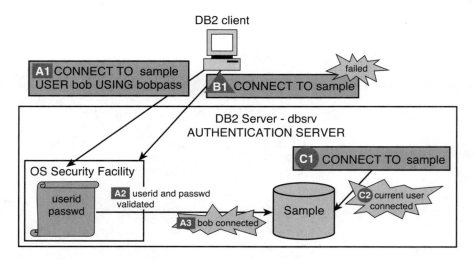

Figure 8.4   Example of SERVER authentication

> **NOTE**
>
> As long as the database server authentication type is set to SERVER, authentication always takes place at the server, even if the authentication type used in the CATALOG DB command and the client has a value other than SERVER.

In Scenario A, a user issues a CONNECT statement to connect to the SAMPLE database that is remotely located in the *dbsrv* DB2 server (A1). The user ID *bob* and the password *bobpass* are also provided. These pieces of information are validated by the DB2 server security facility, typically the operating system's security facility (A2). When validated, *bob* is connected to the SAMPLE database, provided he has the appropriate CONNECT privilege (A3) (privileges are discussed in section "Database Object Privileges" later in this chapter).

Scenario B uses the same environment except that no user ID and password are provided in the CONNECT statement (B1). When a remote database connection is requested, it is mandatory to supply a user ID and password. Therefore, the CONNECT statement specified in B1 fails.

Scenarios A and B are both remote requests. It is also common to make local database connections from the DB2 server itself. Scenario C demonstrates such a request. Because you must have already logged into the server console with a valid user ID and password, it is not necessary to supply a user ID and password in the CONNECT statement (C1). If you choose to connect to the database with a different user ID, then you need to issue the CONNECT statement with the user ID and password you wish as shown in A1.

The SERVER_ENCRYPT authentication type behaves exactly the same as SERVER authentication except that both the user ID and password are encrypted.

If you need to fine-tune the behavior of user authentication, you can also set different values for the DB2 global level registry variable DB2AUTH. Refer to the DB2 Information Center for more details about this variable.

Authenticating Users Using the Kerberos Security Service

Kerberos is a network authentication protocol that employs key cryptography to provide strong authentication for client/server applications. By using an encrypted key, Kerberos makes single sign-on to a remote DB2 server possible. Refer to Figure 8.5 to see how Kerberos authentication works with DB2.

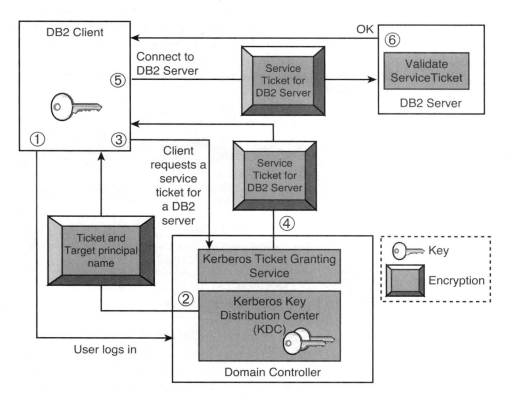

Figure 8.5   Example of Kerberos authentication

In Figure 8.5

1. A user logs in to the Kerberos system.

2. The Kerberos key distribution center generates a ticket and target principal name.

3. The DB2 client requests a service ticket for a DB2 server.

4. The Kerberos Key Distribution Center (KDC) grants a service ticket for the DB2 server.

5. The DB2 client connects to the DB2 server using the service ticket.

6. The DB2 server validates the service ticket and accepts the DB2 client connection request.

The AUTHENTICATION type KERBEROS allows Kerberos-enabled clients to be authenticated at the Kerberos server. Although Kerberos is gaining popularity, there will be clients that do not have Kerberos support enabled. To accommodate these clients and at the same time ensure all clients are able to connect securely, you can set the authentication type at the DB2 server as KRB_SERVER_ENCRYPT. This option allows all Kerberos-enabled clients to be authenticated with Kerberos security service, while other clients use SERVER_ENCRYPT authentication instead.

Table 8.3 summarizes the resolved authentication types based on different client and server authentication settings related to Kerberos.

Table 8.3   Summary of Kerberos-Related Client/Server Authentication Types

Client Specification	Server Specification	Client/Server Resolution
KERBEROS	KRB_SERVER_ENCRYPT	KERBEROS
Any other setting	KRB_SERVER_ENCRYPT	SERVER_ENCRYPT

Authenticating Users with Generic Security Service Plug-ins

You can write authentication mechanisms to implement your own security model. These authentication modules follow the Generic Security Service (GSS) Application Programming Interface (GSSAPI) standard as documented in the Internet's Requests for Comments (RFC) (see www. rfc-editor.org/rfc.html).

To employ the authentication plug-in, set the AUTHENTICATION type to GSSPLUGIN or GSS_SERVER_ENCRYPT so that the specified library modules are loaded at instance start time. DB2 clients then load an appropriate plug-in based on the security mechanism negotiated with the server during CONNECT or attach. You use the LOCAL_GSSPLUGIN Database Manager Configuration parameter to specify the name of the plug-in and must include the library name when using GSSPLUGIN or GSS_SERVER_ENCRYPT. Figure 8.6 illustrates an example of GSS.

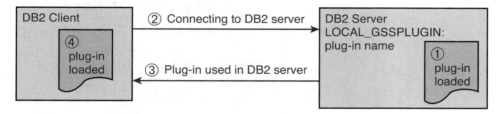

Figure 8.6 Example of GSS authentication

When clients do not support the GSSPLUGIN security mechanism, you can use the GSS_SERVER_ENCRYPT authentication type, which allows those clients to establish database connections with behavior equivalent to SERVER_ENCRYPT.

The DB2 authentication scheme requires plug-ins to manage the following:

- Group membership
- Authentication at the client
- Authentication at the server

If you do not specify the loadable libraries, DB2-supplied plug-ins are used instead. A few Database Manager Configuration parameters are used to support authentication plug-ins, which are listed in Table 8.4.

Table 8.4 Database Manager Parameters for Authentication Plug-Ins

Database Manager Parameter	Description
GROUP_PLUGIN	The name of the group management plug-in library.
CLNT_PW_PLUGIN	The name of the client-side password authentication plug-in. The functions in the named plug-in are also used for local instance-level actions if the AUTHENTICATION parameter is set to SERVER, CLIENT, SERVER_ENCRYPT, DATAENC, or DATAENC_COMP.
CLNT_KRB_PLUGIN	The name of the client-side Kerberos plug-in. This plug-in is used for local instance-level actions, that is, when the AUTHENTICATION parameter is set to KERBEROS or KRB_SERVER_ENCRYPT.
SRVCON_PW_PLUGIN	The name of the server-side password authentication module.

Database Manager Parameter	Description
SRVCON_GSSPLUGIN_LIST	The list of names of all GSSAPI plug-ins separated by commas. The number of plug-ins supported by the server is unlimited; however, the maximum length of the list of plug-in names is 256 characters, and each plug-in name must be fewer than 32 characters. This list should be stated with the most preferred plug-in first.
SRV_PLUGIN_MODE	Indicates if the plug-in is to be run in fenced or unfenced mode. (**Fenced** means that the plug-ins run in a different address space from the DB2 system controller process, and **unfenced** means executing the plug-ins in the same address space.) It is recommended to run user-defined modules in fenced mode to protect the system controller. Because this is an instance-level parameter, it applies to all plug-ins within the same instance. The default value is FENCED.

DB2 provides sample plug-ins so you can develop your own plug-ins more easily. You must place the library files in the designated directory where DB2 looks for

- Client-side user authentication plug-ins in the directory:

  $DB2PATH/security32/plugin/client (for Linux/UNIX 32-bit)

  $DB2PATH/security64/plugin/client (for Linux/UNIX 64-bit)

  $DB2PATH\security\plugin\instance-name\client (for Windows)

- Server-side user authentication plug-ins in the directory:

  $DB2PATH/security32/plugin/server (for Linux/UNIX 32-bit)

  $DB2PATH/security64/plugin/server (for Linux/UNIX 64-bit)

  $DB2PATH\security\plugin\instance-name\server (for Windows)

- Group plug-ins in the directory:

  $DB2PATH/security32/plugin/group (for Linux/UNIX 32-bit)

  $DB2PATH/security64/plugin/group (for Linux/UNIX 64-bit)

  $DB2PATH\security\plugin\instance-name\group (for Windows)

You specify the name of the plug-in as a Database Manager Configuration parameter. Use the full name of the library file but do not include the file extension or the path. For example, to configure the group plug-in, issue

```
update dbm cfg using group_plugin mygrplib
```

Authenticating Users at the Data Server Client

When you want to allow Data Server clients to perform their own authentication, set the server authentication type to CLIENT. This setting does not mean that client authentication applies to every client; qualified clients are determined by two other DBM Configuration parameters—TRUST_ALLCLNTS and TRUST_CLNTAUTH.

TRUST_ALLCLNTS (as you can tell from the name) specifies whether DB2 is going to trust all clients. DB2 categorizes clients into these types:

- **Untrusted** clients do not have a reliable security facility.
- **Trusted** clients have reliable security facilities like Windows Server, AIX, z/OS, and Linux.
- **Distributed Relational Database Architecture** (DRDA) clients are on host legacy systems with reliable security facilities, including DB2 for z/OS, and DB2 for i.

> **NOTE**
>
> Even though all DB2 clients use the DRDA database communication protocol to communicate with DB2 servers, only clients running on mainframe legacy systems are considered as DRDA clients for historical and backward-compatibility reasons.

TRUST_ALLCLNTS accepts any of the values summarized in Table 8.5.

Table 8.5   Values Allowed for TRUST_ALLCLNTS

TRUST_ALLCLNTS value	Description
YES	Trusts all clients. This is the default setting. Authentication takes place at the client.
NO	Trusts only clients with reliable security facilities (trusted clients, for example). Untrusted clients must provide user ID and password for authentication to take place at the server.
DRDAONLY	Trusts only clients that are running on IBM i or z/OS platforms. All other clients must provide user IDs and passwords.

You can specify a more granular security scheme with TRUST_ALLCLNTS. For example, you can let trusted clients perform authentication on their own and, at the same time, force untrusted clients to be authenticated at the server.

Consider a scenario in which you log into a Windows machine as *localuser* and connect to the remote database without specifying a user ID and password. *localuser* is the connected authorization ID at the database. What if you want to connect to the database with a different user ID, for example, *poweruser*, who has the authority to perform a database backup? To allow such behavior, use TRUST_CLNTAUTH to specify where authentication takes place if a user ID and password are supplied in a CONNECT statement or `attach` command. Table 8.6 presents the values for TRUST_CLNTAUTH.

Table 8.6   Values Allowed for TRUST_CLNTAUTH

TRUST_CLNTAUTH Value	Description
CLIENT	Authentication is performed at the client; user ID and password are not required.
SERVER	Authentication is done at the server only if the user ID and password are supplied.

DB2 evaluates TRUST_ALLCLNTS and TRUST_CLNTAUTH only if you set AUTHENTICATION to CLIENT on the DB2 server. Figures 8.8, 8.9, and 8.10 illustrate how to use these parameters.

In Figure 8.7, TRUST_ALLCLNTS is set to YES, so all clients are considered trusted and can perform their own authentication.

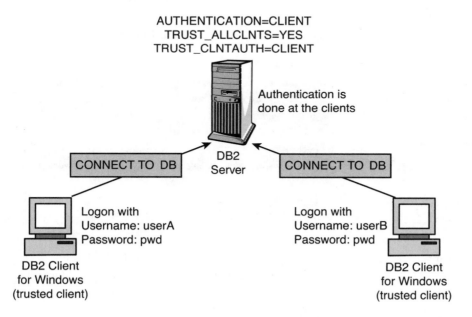

Figure 8.7   Example 1: TRUST_ALLCLNTS and TRUST_CLNTAUTH

In Figure 8.8, TRUST_ALLCLNTS is set to NO, so only trusted clients perform their own authentication. Authentication for untrusted clients is done at the server.

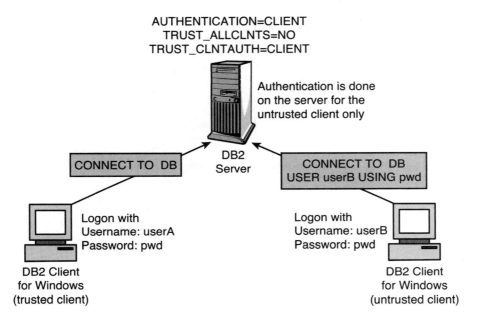

AUTHENTICATION=CLIENT
TRUST_ALLCLNTS=NO
TRUST_CLNTAUTH=CLIENT

Authentication is done
on the server for the
untrusted client only

DB2
Server

CONNECT TO DB

CONNECT TO DB
USER userB USING pwd

Logon with
Username: userA
Password: pwd

Logon with
Username: userB
Password: pwd

DB2 Client
for Windows
(trusted client)

DB2 Client
for Windows
(untrusted client)

Figure 8.8   Example 2: TRUST_ALLCLNTS and TRUST_CLNTAUTH

In Figure 8.9, TRUST_CLNAUTH is set to SERVER. When user ID and password are specified in the CONNECT statement, authentication is performed at the server.

In Figure 8.10, TRUST_CLNTAUTH is set to SERVER and both clients provide user ID and password in the CONNECT statement. Hence, authentication is performed at the server for both clients.

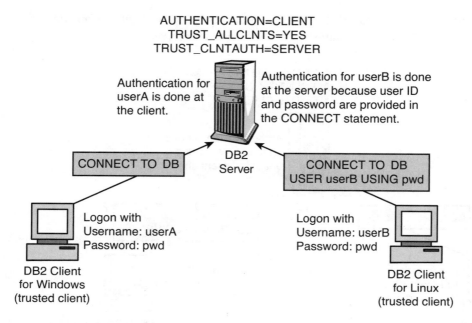

Figure 8.9   Example 3: TRUST_ALLCLNTS and TRUST_CLNTAUTH

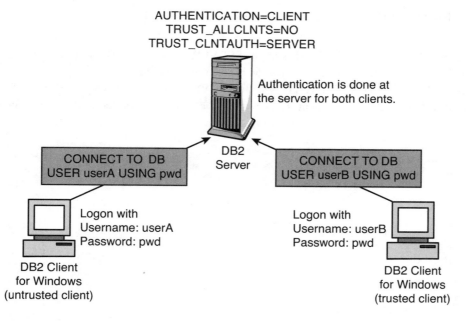

Figure 8.10   Example 4: TRUST_ALLCLNTS and TRUST_CLNTAUTH

Administrative Authorities

After the user has been successfully authenticated, DB2 checks to see if the user has the proper authority for the requested operations, such as performing database manager maintenance operations and managing databases and database objects.

Tables 8.7 and 8.8 describe each of the authorities supported in DB2.

Table 8.7   Instance-level Administrative Authorities

Authority	Description
SYSADM	These users have the highest authority level and full privileges for managing the instance; however, they do not necessarily have access to the data in the underlying databases. When a user with SYSADM authority creates a database, that user is automatically granted ACCESSCTRL, DATAACCESS, DBADM, and SECADM authority on the database; therefore he would have access to the data. On the other hand, if the database was not created by the SYSADM, in order to gain access to the data, a SECADM must grant the SYSADM with DBADM authority using the GRANT DBADM ON DATABASE statement with the WITH DATAACCESS and WITH ACCESSCTRL options. These are the default options.
SYSCTRL	These users have certain privileges in managing the instance, its databases, storage groups, and database objects. They can create new databases but do not have access to the data. For example, they cannot issue statements such as DELETE FROM employee or SELECT * FROM employee.
SYSMAINT	Similar to SYSCTRL, SYSMAINT users have certain privileges in managing the instance, its databases, and database objects. However, they cannot create new databases and do not have access to the data. For example, these users cannot issue statements such as DELETE FROM employee or SELECT * FROM employee.
SYSMON	These users can turn snapshot monitor switches on, collect snapshot data, and access other database system monitor data. No other task can be performed unless the required authority or privileges are granted to the same user by other means.

Table 8.8   Database-level Administrative Authorities

Authority	Description
SECADM	This authority can only be granted to a user by a user with SYSADM authority. Only the user who is granted SECADM (not even SYSADM) can create, drop, grant, and revoke security objects such as security labels, security label components, security policies, trusted contexts, and roles. SECADM can also transfer ownership on objects from one user to another.
ACCESSCTRL	Enables users to grant and revoke authorities and privileges (Other than SECADM, DBADM, ACCESSCTRL, and DATACCESS authorities) in a database.
DATAACCESS	Enables users to access data in a database.
DBADM	Enables users to perform administrative tasks on the specified database. By default they also have full data access to the database; however, a SECADM can revoke DATAACCESS authority, preventing a DBADM to access the data.
SQLADM	Enables users to monitor and tune SQL queries.
EXPLAIN	Enables users to explain query plans (but does not give access to the data itself).
WLMADM	Enables users to manage workloads.

Figures 8.11 and 8.12, extracted from the DB2 manuals, show the hierarchy of authorities and summarize what each authority can perform.

DB2's authorization model separates the duties of the system administrator (SYSADM), the database administrator (DBADM), and the security administrator (SECADM). This provides for better data privacy and governance compliance. In addition, the existence of more granular authorities allows for better control and helps minimize the risk of data exposure by not granting users more than what they need to do their jobs.

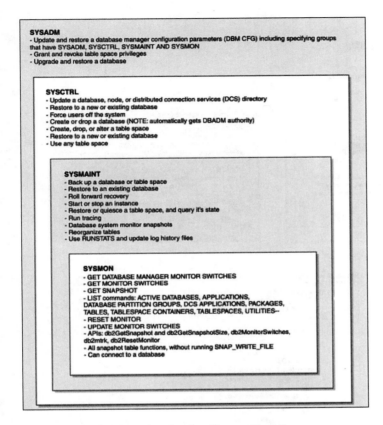

SYSADM
- Update and restore a database manager configuration parameters (DBM CFG) including specifying groups that have SYSADM, SYSCTRL, SYSMAINT AND SYSMON
- Grant and revoke table space privileges
- Upgrade and restore a database

SYSCTRL
- Update a database, node, or distributed connection services (DCS) directory
- Restore to a new or existing database
- Force users off the system
- Create or drop a database (NOTE: automatically gets DBADM authority)
- Create, drop, or alter a table space
- Restore to a new or existing database
- Use any table space

SYSMAINT
- Back up a database or table space
- Restore to an existing database
- Roll forward recovery
- Start or stop an instance
- Restore or quiesce a table space, and query it's state
- Run tracing
- Database system monitor snapshots
- Reorganize tables
- Use RUNSTATS and update log history files

SYSMON
- GET DATABASE MANAGER MONITOR SWITCHES
- GET MONITOR SWITCHES
- GET SNAPSHOT
- LIST commands: ACTIVE DATABASES, APPLICATIONS, DATABASE PARTITION GROUPS, DCS APPLICATIONS, PACKAGES, TABLES, TABLESPACE CONTAINERS, TABLESPACES, UTILITIES--
- RESET MONITOR
- UPDATE MONITOR SWITCHES
- APIs: db2GetSnapshot and db2GetSnapshotSize, db2MonitorSwitches, db2mtrk, db2ResetMonitor
- All snapshot table functions, without running SNAP_WRITE_FILE
- Can connect to a database

Figure 8.12 Instance-level authorities and functions

Managing Administrative Authorities

Now that you understand the roles of different authorities in DB2, it's time to show you how to give a user or a group of users an authority. A user receives the instance and database authorities through different commands and statements.

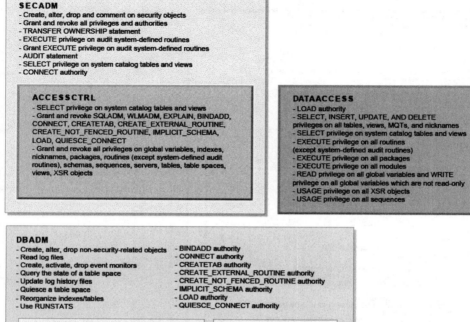

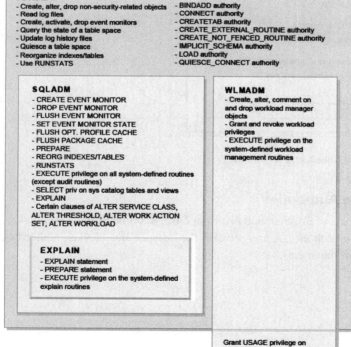

Figure 8.12   Database-level authorities and functions

For instance-level authorities such as SYSADM, SYSCTRL, SYSMAINT, and SYSMON, you assign operating system or security facility groups to have these authorities using the following Database Manager Configuration parameters:

```
SYSADM group name       (SYSADM_GROUP) =
SYSCTRL group name      (SYSCTRL_GROUP) =
SYSMAINT group name     (SYSMAINT_GROUP) =
SYSMON group name       (SYSMON_GROUP) =
```

These parameters are set to NULL (appearing as blank here) by default. On Windows, a NULL value for these parameters indicates that the members of the Windows **local administrators** group have these authorities. If Extended Security is enabled, as you see later in this chapter, members of the DB2ADMNS group would be the group having these authorities. On Linux and UNIX, a NULL value for these parameters indicates that the members of the primary group of the instance owner have these authorities.

To set any of the system groups, you use the `update dbm cfg` command. For example, if *admgrp* and *maintgrp* are valid groups, the following command configures the SYSADM_GROUP and SYSMAINT_GROUP:

```
update dbm cfg using sysadm_group admgrp sysmaint_group maintgrp
```

This command does not validate the existence of the group. It is your responsibility to enter a valid group name. To reset them to the default value of NULL, specify

```
update dbm cfg using sysadm_group NULL
```

NOTE

In resetting DBM and DB configuration parameters to the default value, you must use NULL in uppercase. DB2 treats the lowercase *null* as an input value.

Because the system group parameters are not configurable online, you need to stop and restart the instance for the changes to take effect.

With respect to database authorities, you grant and revoke them with the GRANT and REVOKE statements to a user, a role, or group of users. Listings 8.2 and 8.3 show the syntax of these statements, and Listing 8.4 illustrates how to use them.

Listing 8.2   GRANT Statement for Database Authorities

```
        .-,----------------------------.
        V                              |
>>-GRANT----+-BINDADD-------------------+-+--ON DATABASE-------->
            +-CONNECT-------------------+
```

```
                 +-CREATETAB-----------------+
                 +-CREATE_EXTERNAL_ROUTINE---+
                 +-CREATE_NOT_FENCED_ROUTINE-+
                 +-IMPLICIT_SCHEMA-----------+
                 +-DBADM---------------------+
                 +-LOAD----------------------+
                 +-QUIESCE_CONNECT-----------+
                 '-SECADM-------------------'


          .-,-------------------------------.
          V                                 |
>--TO----+-+-------+--authorization-name-+-+------------------><
          | +-USER--+                     |
          | +-GROUP-+                     |
          | '-ROLE--'                     |
          '-PUBLIC-----------------------'
```

Listing 8.3   REVOKE Statement for Database Authorities

```
             .-,-----------------------------.
             V                               |
>>-REVOKE----+-BINDADD-------------------+-+--ON DATABASE------->
             +-CONNECT-------------------+
             +-CREATETAB-----------------+
             +-CREATE_EXTERNAL_ROUTINE---+
             +-CREATE_NOT_FENCED_ROUTINE-+
             +-IMPLICIT_SCHEMA-----------+
             +-DBADM---------------------+
             +-LOAD----------------------+
             +-QUIESCE_CONNECT-----------+
             '-SECADM-------------------'


          .-,--------------------------------.
          V                                  |       .-BY ALL-.
>--FROM----+-+-------+--authorization-name-+-+--+--------+-----><
          | +-USER--+                      |
          | +-GROUP-+                      |
          | '-ROLE--'                      |
          '-PUBLIC-----------------------'
```

Listing 8.4 Examples of Granting and Revoking Database Authorities

```
CONNECT TO sample;
GRANT IMPLICIT_SCHEMA, CREATETAB ON DATABASE TO USER john;
GRANT LOAD ON DATABASE TO GROUP loadgrp, USER john;
GRANT BINDADD ON DATABASE TO PUBLIC;
GRANT SECADM ON DATABASE TO USER peter;

REVOKE LOAD ON DATABASE FROM GROUP loadgrp;
REVOKE CREATETAB ON DATABASE FROM PUBLIC;
```

As shown in Listing 8.4, you must first connect to the target database before you can use the GRANT or REVOKE statements.

The keywords USER, GROUP, and ROLE are optional for both GRANT and REVOKE statements. However, if you have a user ID, group name, or role name defined with the same name, you must specify USER, GROUP, or ROLE explicitly; otherwise you receive an error message.

Notice that the last example of Listing 8.4 uses the keyword PUBLIC. PUBLIC is not the name of a group defined in the operating system or in the external security facility; it is a special group to which everyone belongs. PUBLIC is automatically granted the following database privileges: CREATETAB, BINDADD, CONNECT, IMPLICIT_SCHEMA, and SELECT on the system catalog views. Use the RESTRICTIVE option of the CREATE DATABASE command if you do not want any privileges automatically granted to PUBLIC. For existing databases you can look in the database configuration (*db cfg*) file for the *Restrict access* field to verify if the RESTRICTIVE keyword was used when the database was created. If set to YES, then it was used; otherwise, it was not, in which case you would have to revoke one by one each of these database privileges if you don't want PUBLIC to have any access on your database. Granting and revoking database object privileges is discussed in the next section.

To grant or revoke ACCESSCTRL, DATAACCESS, DBADM, or SECADM authority, you must have SECADM authority. SECADM must be granted to a user explicitly; any attempt to grant SECADM to a group, a role, or to PUBLIC results in an error. Refer back to Figure 8.12—notice that operations that can be performed by SECADM cannot be performed by another user, not even SYSADM. The following query might be useful to check if a user has SECADM authority:

```
c:\>db2 select grantee, securityadmauth from syscat.dbauth

GRANTEE                                          SECURITYADMAUTH
------------------------------------------------ ---------------
RFCHONG                                                 Y
PUBLIC                                                  N

  2 record(s) selected.
```

The REVOKE statement uses the BY ALL option as its default. This means that this command revokes each named authority (as well as privileges—discussed later in this chapter) from all named users and/or groups who were explicitly granted those authorities (and privileges). However, there is no cascade effect to also revoke authorities (and privileges) that were implicitly granted. Stay tuned for the implicit privileges discussion in the following section.

> **NOTE**
>
> Connect privileges are granted to PUBLIC by default after the database is created. You can explicitly revoke this privilege after database creation. Alternatively, the RESTRICTIVE option of CREATE DATABASE can be used to restrict all privileges granted to PUBLIC.

Database Object Privileges

Controlling access to database objects is as important as authenticating users and managing administrative authorities. Privileges give users the right to access each individual database object in a specific way. Privileges can be granted explicitly and implicitly.

To grant privileges on database objects use the GRANT statement. For most database objects, you must have ACCESSCTRL authority, SECADM authority, or CONTROL privilege on that object, or you must hold the privilege WITH GRANT OPTION (as we discuss later on in this section). Additionally, users with SYSADM or SYSCTRL authority can grant table space privileges.

To revoke privileges on database objects, use the REVOKE statement. You must have ACCESSCTRL authority, SECADM authority, or CONTROL privilege on that object. Note that holding a privilege WITH GRANT OPTION is not sufficient to revoke that privilege. Additionally, only users with SYSADM or SYSCTRL authority can revoke table space privileges.

The following sections list all the supported privileges for each database object and discuss implicit privileges.

If you are not familiar with any database objects discussed in the following sections, see Chapter 7, "Working with Database Objects."

Schema Privileges

There are three schema privileges:

- CREATEIN enables users to create objects within the schema.
- ALTERIN enables users to alter objects within the schema.
- DROPIN enables users to drop objects within the schema.

For example, you can specify the GRANT and REVOKE statements against a given schema, as shown in the syntax diagrams in Listings 8.5 and 8.6.

Listing 8.5   GRANT Syntax Diagram for Schema Privileges

```
              .-,------------.
              V              |
>>-GRANT----+-ALTERIN--+-+--ON SCHEMA--schema-name------------->
            +-CREATEIN-+
            '-DROPIN---'


          .-,--------------------------------.
          V                                  |
>--TO----+-+-------+--authorization-name-+-+-------------------->
         | +-USER--+                       |
         | +-GROUP-+                       |
         | '-ROLE--'                       |
         '-PUBLIC-----------------------'


>--+------------------+----------------------------------------><
   '-WITH GRANT OPTION-'
```

The WITH GRANT OPTION in the GRANT statement in Listing 8.5 enables the named authorized user to grant the named privileges to other users.

Listing 8.6   REVOKE Syntax Diagram for Schema Privileges

```
              .-,------------.
              V              |
>>-REVOKE----+-ALTERIN--+-+--ON SCHEMA--schema-name------------->
            +-CREATEIN-+
            '-DROPIN---'


          .-,--------------------------------.
          V                                  |    .-BY ALL-.
>--FROM----+-+-------+--authorization-name-+-+--+--------+------><
           | +-USER--+                       |
           | +-GROUP-+                       |
           | '-ROLE--'                       |
           '-PUBLIC-----------------------'
```

Previously, we introduced the IMPLICIT_SCHEMA database authority, which enables the grantee to create a schema via the creation of database objects. You simply fully qualify the object name with the schema name when creating the object. For example, in Listing 8.7, the table *dairyprod* and index *prodindx* are created in the schema of *grocery*. Schema *grocery* is automatically created if it does not already exist.

Listing 8.7   Example of a Schema Created Implicitly

```
CREATE TABLE grocery.dairyprod
    ( prodno SMALLINT NOT NULL
    , desc VARCHAR(100)
    , qty INTEGER );

CREATE INDEX grocery.prodindx ON grocery.dairyprod (prodno);
```

You can also create a new schema explicitly using the CREATE SCHEMA statement, for example

```
CONNECT TO sample USER dbowner;
CREATE SCHEMA dev AUTHORIZATION devuser;
```

In the example, the CREATE SCHEMA statement requires that user *dbowner* has the DBADM authority. This creates a schema called dev where devuser is the schema owner. If the optional AUTHORIZATION clause of CREATE SCHEMA was not specified, then the authorization ID of the person issuing the statement would be the owner of the schema; in this example, it would be *dbowner*. In addition, if *dbowner* did not hold DBADM authority, then he could only create a schema with schema name *dbowner*.

Table Space Privileges

Tables and table spaces are logical objects, as discussed in Chapter 7, "Working with Database Objects." Tables are logically stored in table spaces, and table spaces are associated to physical storage devices. You need some USE privileges to be able to define tables in a table space. Listings 8.8 and 8.9 show the GRANT and REVOKE syntax diagrams with the USE privilege available for a specific table space. When a table space is created, its USE privilege is granted to PUBLIC by default. If you want to restrict usage of the table space, you should revoke the USE privilege from PUBLIC and grant it to selected users or groups individually.

Listing 8.8   GRANT Syntax Diagram for Table Space Privileges

```
>>-GRANT--USE--OF TABLESPACE--tablespace-name--TO--------------->


   .-,--------------------------------.
   V                                  |
>----+-+-------+--authorization-name-+-+---------------------->
     | +-USER--+                     |
```

```
| '-GROUP-'                           |
'-PUBLIC----------------------'


>--+-----------------+-----------------------------------------><
   '-WITH GRANT OPTION-'
```

Listing 8.9   REVOKE Syntax Diagram for Table Space Privileges

```
>>-REVOKE USE OF TABLESPACE--tablespace-name--FROM------------->


   .-,--------------------------------.
   V                                  |   .-BY ALL-.
>----+-+-------+--authorization-name-+-+---+-------+----------><
     | +-USER--+                      |
     | | +-GROUP-+                    |
     | '-ROLE--'                      |
     '-PUBLIC----------------------'
```

The following examples show how to grant and revoke the table space privileges.

```
GRANT USE OF TABLESPACE userspace1 TO USER db2admin;
REVOKE USE OF TABLESPACE userspace1 FROM PUBLIC;
```

Table and View Privileges

There are quite a number of privileges you can control for tables and views. Table 8.9 describes these privileges.

Table 8.9   Summary of Table and View Privileges

Table and View Privileges	Descriptions
CONTROL	Provides users with all privileges for a table or view as well as the ability to grant those privileges (except CONTROL) to others.
ALTER	Enables users to alter a table or view.
DELETE	Enables users to delete records from a table or view.
INDEX	Enables users to create an index on a table. This privilege does not apply to views.
INSERT	Enables users to insert an entry into a table or view.

Table and View Privileges	Descriptions
REFERENCES	Enables users to create and drop a foreign key, specifying the table as the parent in a relationship.
SELECT	Enables users to retrieve data from a table or view.
UPDATE	Enables users to update entries in a table or view. This privilege can also limit users to update specific columns only.
ALL PRIVILEGES	Grants all of these privileges except CONTROL on a table or view.

Listings 8.10 and 8.11 show the GRANT and REVOKE syntax diagrams for table and view privileges respectively.

Listing 8.10   GRANT Syntax Diagram for Table and View Privileges

```
                   .-PRIVILEGES-.
>>-GRANT--+-ALL--+------------+---------------------------+---->
          | .-,------------------------------------------. |
          | V                                            | |
          '---+-ALTER-------------------------------+-+-'
              +-CONTROL------------------------------+
              +-DELETE-------------------------------+
              +-INDEX--------------------------------+
              +-INSERT-------------------------------+
              +-REFERENCES--+-----------------------+-+
              |             |      .-,-----------.   | |
              |             |      V             |   | |
              |             '-(----column-name-+--)-'  |
              +-SELECT-------------------------------+
              '-UPDATE--+-----------------------+-----'
                        |     .-,-----------.    |
                        |     V             |    |
                        '-(----column-name-+--)-'


        .-TABLE-.
>--ON--+-------+---+-table-name-----+------------------------->
                   +-view-name------+
                   '-nickname-------'
```

```
        .-,--------------------------------.
        V                                  |
>--TO----+-+-------+--authorization-name-+-+------------------>
         | +-USER--+                      |
         | +-GROUP-+                      |
         | '-ROLE--'                      |
         '-PUBLIC----------------------'


>--+-----------------+------------------------------------><
   '-WITH GRANT OPTION-'
```

Listing 8.11 REVOKE Syntax Diagram for Table and View Privileges

```
                  .-PRIVILEGES-.        .-TABLE-.
>>-REVOKE--+-ALL--+------------+-+--ON--+-------+-------------->
           | .-,--------------. |
           | V                | |
           '---+-ALTER------+-+--'
                +-CONTROL----+
                +-DELETE-----+
                +-INDEX------+
                +-INSERT-----+
                +-REFERENCES-+
                +-SELECT-----+
                '-UPDATE-----'


>--+-table-name-+-------------------------------------------->
   +-view-name--+
   '-nickname---'
        .-,--------------------------------.
        V                                  |   .-BY ALL-.
>--FROM----+-+-------+--authorization-name-+-+--+--------+----><
           | +-USER--+                      |
           | +-GROUP-+                      |
           | '-ROLE--'                      |
           '-PUBLIC----------------------'
```

The following examples show how to grant and revoke some table and view privileges.

```
GRANT ALL PRIVILEGES ON TABLE employee TO USER db2admin WITH GRANT
OPTION;
GRANT UPDATE ON TABLE employee (salary, comm) TO GROUP db2users;
REVOKE CONTROL ON TABLE employee FROM PUBLIC;
```

The GRANT and REVOKE statements discussed here also apply to **nicknames** (database objects that represent remote tables and views residing in different databases). The remote databases can be databases in the DB2 family or non-DB2 databases. This feature is known as **federated database support**.

Index Privileges

Privileges for managing indexes is fairly straightforward: The only operation you can perform on an index after it has been created is to drop it. To change an index key, for example, you need to drop the index and re-create it. The CONTROL privilege enables the grantee to drop the index. Listings 8.12 and 8.13 demonstrate GRANT and REVOKE statements with index privileges.

Listing 8.12   GRANT Syntax Diagram for Index Privileges

```
>>-GRANT--CONTROL--ON INDEX--index-name------------------------->


         .-,-------------------------------.
         V                                 |
>--TO----+-+-------+--authorization-name-+-+------------------><
           | +-USER--+                    |
           | +-GROUP-+                    |
           | '-ROLE--'                    |
           '-PUBLIC-----------------------'
```

Listing 8.13   REVOKE Syntax Diagram for Index Privileges

```
>>-REVOKE CONTROL ON INDEX--index-name-------------------------->


         .-,-------------------------------.
         V                                 |   .-BY ALL-.
>--FROM----+-+-------+--authorization-name-+-+--+--------+----><
             | +-USER--+                    |
             | +-GROUP-+                    |
             | '-ROLE--'                    |
             '-PUBLIC-----------------------'
```

The following examples show how to grant and revoke index privileges:

```
GRANT CONTROL ON INDEX empind TO USER db2admin;
REVOKE CONTROL ON INDEX empind FROM db2admin;
```

Package Privileges

A **package** is a database object that contains the data access plan of how static SQL statements are executed. A package needs to be bound to a database before its associated program can execute it. The following are the privileges you use to manage packages:

- BIND allows users to rebind an existing package.
- EXECUTE allows users to execute a package.
- CONTROL provides users the ability to rebind, drop, or execute a package as well as the ability to grant the above privileges to other users and/or groups.

Listings 8.14 and 8.15 show the GRANT and REVOKE statements for package privileges, respectively.

Listing 8.14   GRANT Syntax Diagram for Package Privileges

```
            . - , - - - - - - - - - - - - - - - .
            V                         |
>>-GRANT----+-BIND---------+-+-------------------------------->
            +-CONTROL------+
            '-EXECUTE------'

>--ON--PACKAGE-------+--------------+--package-id-------------->
                     '-schema-name.-'


        . - , - - - - - - - - - - - - - - - - - - - - - - - - .
          V                                   |
>--TO----+-+-------+--authorization-name-+-+------------------->
         | +-USER--+                      |
         | +-GROUP-+                      |
         | '-ROLE--'                      |
         '-PUBLIC----------------------'


>--+------------------+---------------------------------->< 
   '-WITH GRANT OPTION-'
```

Listing 8.15   REVOKE Syntax Diagram for Package Privileges

```
            .-,----------------.
            V                  |
>>-REVOKE----+-BIND---------+-+-----------------------------------> 
             +-CONTROL------+
             '-EXECUTE------'


>--ON--PACKAGE-------+--------------+--package-id--------------->
                     '-schema-name.-'
     .-,------------------------------.
     V                                |    .-BY ALL-.
>--FROM----+-+-------+--authorization-name-+--+--+--------+----><
           | +-USER--+                        |
           | +-GROUP-+                        |
           | '-ROLE--'                        |
           '-PUBLIC-----------------------'
```

The following examples show how to grant and revoke package privileges:

```
GRANT EXECUTE, BIND ON PACKAGE emppack1 TO GROUP db2grp WITH GRANT
OPTION;
REVOKE BIND ON PACKAGE emppack1 FROM USER db2dev;
```

Routine Privileges

To be able to use a routine, a user must be granted with its associated EXECUTE privilege. As illustrated in Listings 8.16 and 8.17, EXECUTE is the only routine privilege, but it applies to all types of routines: functions, methods, and stored procedures.

Listing 8.16   GRANT Syntax Diagram for Routine Privileges

```
>>-GRANT EXECUTE ON--+-| function-designator |----------+------>
                     +-FUNCTION--+---------+--*---------+
                     |           '-schema.-'            |
                     +-| method-designator |------------+
                     +-METHOD * FOR--+-type-name------+-+
                     |               '-+---------+--*-' |
                     |                 '-schema.-'      |
                     +-| procedure-designator |---------+
                     '-PROCEDURE--+---------+--*--------'
                                  '-schema.-'
```

```
          .-,--------------------------------.
          V                                  |
>--TO----+-+-------+--authorization-name-+-+-------------------->
         | +-USER--+                      |
         | +-GROUP-+                      |
         | '-ROLE--'                      |
         '-PUBLIC----------------------'


>--+-----------------+----------------------------------------><
   '-WITH GRANT OPTION-'
```

Listing 8.17   REVOKE Syntax Diagram for Routine Privileges

```
>>-REVOKE EXECUTE ON--+-| function-designator |----------+----->
                      +-FUNCTION--+---------+--*---------+
                      |           '-schema.-'           |
                      +-| method-designator |-----------+
                      +-METHOD * FOR--+-type-name------+-+
                      |               '-+---------+--*-' |
                      |                 '-schema.-'      |
                      +-| procedure-designator |---------+
                      '-PROCEDURE--+---------+--*--------'
                                   '-schema.-'


          .-,--------------------------------.
          V                                  |
>--FROM----+-+-------+--authorization-name-+-+---------------->
           | +-USER--+                      |
           | +-GROUP-+                      |
           | '-ROLE--'                      |
           '-PUBLIC----------------------'


   .-BY ALL-.
>--+--------+--RESTRICT---------------------------------------><
```

The following examples show how to grant and revoke routine privileges:

```
GRANT EXECUTE ON PROCEDURE salary_increase TO USER db2admin WITH GRANT
OPTION;
REVOKE EXECUTE ON PROCEDURE salary_increase FROM USER db2admin;
```

Sequence Privileges

A sequence object generates unique, sequential numeric values. By default, the group PUBLIC can use any sequence object unless it is controlled by the USAGE privilege, as shown in Listing 8.18. You can restrict usage of certain sequence objects by revoking USAGE from PUBLIC.

There might also be cases where you want to change the sequence object definition, such as the minimum, maximum, and incremental values. You probably want to limit the ability to alter a sequence object to only a few users. Use the ALTER privilege (shown in Listing 8.19) to do that. RESTRICT is the default behavior that prevents the sequence from being dropped if dependencies exist.

Listing 8.18   GRANT Syntax Diagram for Sequence Privileges

```
          .-,----------.
          V           |
>>-GRANT----+-USAGE-+-+--ON SEQUENCE--sequence-name------------->
            '-ALTER-'


        .-,--------------------------------.
        V                                  |
>--TO----+-+-------+--authorization-name-+-+------------------->
         | +-USER--+                      |
         | +-GROUP-+                      |
         | '-ROLE--'                      |
         '-PUBLIC-----------------------'


>--+------------------+-----------------------------------------><
   '-WITH GRANT OPTION-'
```

Listing 8.19   REVOKE Syntax Diagram for Sequence Privileges

```
          .-,---------.
          V          |
>>-REVOKE----+-ALTER-+-+--ON SEQUENCE--sequence-name------------>
             '-USAGE-'


        .-,---------------------------------.
        V                                   |   .-RESTRICT-.
```

```
>--FROM----+-+-------+--authorization-name-+-+--+----------+---><
          | +-USER--+                      |
          | +-GROUP-+                      |
          | '-ROLE--'                      |
          '-PUBLIC----------------------'
```

The following examples show how to grant and revoke sequence privileges:

```
GRANT USAGE, ALTER ON SEQUENCE empseq TO USER d2admin WITH GRANT OPTION;
REVOKE ALTER ON SEQUENCE empseq FROM db2admin RESTRICT;
```

Security Label Privileges

Security labels are database objects used in a Label Based Access Control (LBAC) system to define a certain set of security rules. Data is considered protected when a security label is applied to it. To access protected data, you need to receive proper access for the associated security labels. LBAC and security labels are discussed in more detail in the section, "Label Based Access Control." Here, we introduce the GRANT and REVOKE commands for security labels as shown in Listings 8.20 and 8.21, respectively. You must have SECADM authority to issue these statements.

Listing 8.20 GRANT Syntax Diagram for Security Label Privileges

```
>>-GRANT SECURITY LABEL--security-label-name------------------>

                                   .-FOR ALL ACCESS---.
>--TO USER--authorization-name--+-----------------+---------><
                                +-FOR READ ACCESS--+
                                '-FOR WRITE ACCESS-'
```

Listing 8.21 REVOKE Syntax Diagram for Security Label Privileges

```
>>-REVOKE SECURITY LABEL--security-label-name--FROM USER--authorization-
name-><
```

Note that you can grant all, read-only, or write-only access to any user with a security label. This is an important step to limit access to protected data from every user. The statements themselves are quite straightforward. The security label must already be defined in the database catalogs, and it must be qualified with a security policy.

```
GRANT SECURITY LABEL SALES_POLICY.EAST_COAST TO USER bobby
GRANT SECURITY LABEL SALES_POLICY.ASIA TO USER wong FOR READ ACCESS
GRANT SECURITY LABEL SALES_POLICY.ASIA TO USER betty FOR WRITE ACCESS
REVOKE SECURITY LABEL SALES_POLICY.ASIA FROM user wong
```

SET SESSION AUTHORIZATION Statement and SETSESSIONUSER Privilege

DB2 special registers such as USER, CURRENT USER, SYSTEM_USER, and SESSION_ USER are introduced in Appendix B, "Introduction to SQL." Inside an application program or on the CLP, you can change the value of the SESSION_USER special register with the SET SESSION AUTHORIZATION statement. The syntax diagram of the statement is shown in Listing 8.22.

Listing 8.22 Syntax Diagram of the SET SESSION AUTHORIZATION Statement

```
                                 .-=-.
>>-SET--+-SESSION AUTHORIZATION-+---+---+------------------------>
        '-SESSION_USER----------'

>--+-authorization-name-+---+---------------------+-----------><
   +-USER--------------+   '-ALLOW ADMINISTRATION-'
   +-CURRENT_USER------+
   +-SYSTEM_USER-------+
   +-host-variable-----+
   '-string-constant---'
```

You can explicitly specify an authorization name in the statement like the following. It sets the SESSION_USER special register to *bobby*:

```
SET SESSION AUTHORIZATION = bobby
```

Alternatively, you can use the value stored in another special register. The example that follows sets SESSION_USER to the SYSTEM_USER special register:

```
SET SESSION_USER = SYSTEM_USER
```

The ALLOW ADMINISTRATION means that certain administration operations can be specified prior to this statement within the same unit of work. The administration operations include

- Data definition language (DDL)
- GRANT and REVOKE statements
- LOCK TABLE statement

- `COMMIT` and `ROLLBACK` statements
- Special registers `SET` statements

To invoke the `SET SESSION AUTHORIZATION` or the equivalent `SET SESSION_USER` statement, you need the SETSESSIONUSER privilege on an authorization ID. Listings 8.23 and 8.24 introduce the `GRANT` and `REVOKE` commands for the SETSESSIONUSER privilege on an authorization ID.

Listing 8.23   GRANT Syntax Diagram of the SETSESSIONUSER Privilege

```
                             .-,-------------------------------------.
                             V                                       |
>>-GRANT SETSESSIONUSER ON----+-USER--session-authorization-name-+-+->
                              '-PUBLIC--------------------------'


          .-,----------------------------.
          V                              |
>---TO----+-USER--+--authorization-name-+-><
          +-GROUP-+
          '-ROLE--'
```

Listing 8.24   REVOKE Syntax Diagram of the SETSESSIONUSER Privilege

```
                              .-,-------------------------------------.
                              V                                       |
>>-REVOKE SETSESSIONUSER ON----+-USER--session-authorization-name-+-+->
                               '-PUBLIC--------------------------'


          .-,----------------------------.
          V                              |
>---FROM----+-USER--+--authorization-name-+-><
            +-GROUP-+
            '-ROLE--'
```

The following examples show how to grant and revoke the SETSESSIONUSER privilege.

```
GRANT SETSESSIONUSER ON USER kevin, USER bobby TO GROUP devadmin
REVOKE SETSESSIONUSER ON USER bobby FROM GROUP devadmin.
```

The first example enables users in group *devadmin* to set the session authorization ID as users *kevin*, and *bobby*.

The second example revokes *devadmin's* ability to set session authorization ID as *bobby*.

Implicit Privileges

As discussed previously, DB2 privileges usually are granted explicitly with GRANT statements. In some cases users might also obtain privileges implicitly or indirectly by performing certain operations. You should pay attention to these privileges and determine whether they are valid per the security policies in your company.

- A user who is granted DBADM authority is also implicitly granted BINDADD, CONNECT, CREATETAB, CREATE_EXTERNAL_ROUTINE, CREATE_NOT_ FENCED_ROUTINE, IMPLICIT_SCHEMA, QUIESCE_CONNECT, and LOAD privileges.

- When a user creates a database with the RESTRICTIVE option, DBADM authority is granted to the database creator.

- When a user creates a database without the RESTRICTIVE option (this is the default behavior), the following authorities and privileges are also granted implicitly:

  - DBADM authority is granted to the database creator.

  - CONNECT, CREATETAB, BINADD, IMPLICIT_SCHEMA, privileges are granted to PUBLIC.

  - USE OF TABLESPACE privilege on the table space USERSPACE1 is granted to PUBLIC.

  - EXECUTE with GRANT privileges on all procedures in schema SQLJ and on all functions and procedures in schema SYSPROC are granted to PUBLIC.

  - BIND and EXECUTE privileges on all packages in schema NULLID are granted to PUBLIC.

  - CREATEIN privileges on schema SQLJ and NULLID are granted to PUBLIC.

  - SELECT privileges to the SYSIBM, SYSCAT, SYSSTAT catalog views are granted to PUBLIC.

  - UPDATE privilege to the SYSSTAT catalog views are granted to PUBLIC.

  - A user who creates a table, view, index, schema, or package automatically receives CONTROL privilege on the database object he or she creates.

If a program is coded with static SQL statements, packages that contain data access plans are generated and bound to the database at compile time. When a user executes the package, explicit privileges for database objects referenced in the statements are not required. The user only needs EXECUTE privilege on the package to execute the statements. However, this does not mean that the user has direct access to the underlying database objects.

Consider the example illustrated in Figure 8.13. A package *dev.pkg1* containing UPDATE, SELECT, and INSERT statements is bound to the database. A user who only has EXECUTE privilege on *dev.pkg1* can only manipulate table *t1* through the package. He cannot issue SELECT, UPDATE, and INSERT statements directly to *t1*.

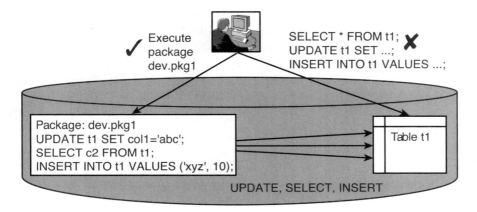

Figure 8.13   Example of controlling database object access via packages

As mentioned earlier in this chapter, implicit privileges remain even after the initial privilege is revoked. For example, if user *bob* is granted DBADM authority, he also implicitly receives the privileges BINDADD, CONNECT, CREATETAB, CREATE_NOT_ FENCED, and IMPLICIT_SCHEMA. Assuming, for some reason, DBADM is revoked from *bob* with this statement:

```
REVOKE dbadm FROM USER bob
```

bob no longer has DBADM authority, but he still has BINDADD, CONNECT, CREA-TETAB, CREATE_NOT_FENCED, and IMPLICIT_SCHEMA authorities. Each of them must be explicitly revoked if you want to remove all authorities from *bob*.

Roles and Privileges

In the last decade Role-Based Access Control (RBAC) has emerged as an access control model, which has been quickly adopted by a large number of software products, and in particular by Relational Database Management Systems (RDBMS). The central notion of RBAC is that users do not have discretionary access to enterprise objects. Instead, access permissions are associated with roles, and users are made members of appropriate roles. RBAC greatly simplifies management of authorization while providing an opportunity for system administrators to control access to enterprise objects at a level of abstraction that is close to the structure of their enterprise.

When roles are used, the assignment and update of privileges are much simplified. After the privileges are assigned or updated at the role level, you no longer need to perform the same operations to each user granted that role. Moreover, the privileges that you as a user gained through membership in one or more roles are considered for authorization when you create views, triggers, materialized query tables (MQTs), static SQL, and SQL routines.

After creating a role, the security administrator (who holds SECADM authority) can grant or revoke a role to or from a user, group, or another role as shown in Listings 8.25 and 8.26. In addition, the security administrator can delegate the management of membership in a role to an authorization ID by granting the authorization ID membership in the role with the WITH ADMIN OPTION.

Listing 8.25 GRANT ROLE Syntax Diagram

```
                             .-,-----------.
            .-ROLE-.         V             |
>>-GRANT--+------+------role-name-+-+--------------------------->


          .-,--------------------------------.
          V                                  |
>---TO----+-+-------+--authorization-name-+-+-------------------->
          | +-USER--+                      |
          | +-GROUP-+                      |
          | '-ROLE--'                      |
          '-PUBLIC----------------------'

>--+-----------------+---------------------------------------->< 
   '-WITH ADMIN OPTION-'
```

Listing 8.26 REVOKE ROLE Syntax Diagram

```
                                    .-,---------.
                          .-ROLE-.  V           |
>>-REVOKE--+-----------------+--+------+----role-name-+-------->
           '-ADMIN OPTION FOR-'
           .-,--------------------------------.
           V                                  |   .-BY ALL-.
```

```
>--FROM----+-+-------+--authorization-name-+-+--+--------+------><
           | +-USER--+                      |
           | +-GROUP-+                      |
           | '-ROLE--'                      |
           '-PUBLIC----------------------'
```

The following example illustrates how roles simplify the administration and management of privileges:

Usage Scenario

Alice is a teller at a bank and has the privilege to SELECT from tables *CUSTOMER, CHECKING*, and *SAVINGS*. One day Alice changes her job, and the database administrator has to revoke her privileges on those tables. The bank later hires two new tellers, Lisa and Tom. The database administrator again has to grant SELECT privilege on the tables to the new tellers.

Without database roles, the DBA has to execute

```
CONNECT TO sample;
GRANT SELECT ON TABLE customer TO USER alice;
GRANT SELECT ON TABLE checking TO USER alice;
GRANT SELECT ON TABLE savings TO USER alice;
REVOKE SELECT ON TABLE customer FROM USER alice;
REVOKE SELECT ON TABLE checking FROM USER alice;
REVOKE SELECT ON TABLE savings FROM USER alice;
GRANT SELECT ON TABLE customer TO USER lisa;
GRANT SELECT ON TABLE checking to USER lisa;
GRANT SELECT ON TABLE savings to USER lisa;
GRANT SELECT ON TABLE customer TO USER tom;
GRANT SELECT ON TABLE checking to USER tom;
GRANT SELECT ON TABLE savings to USER tom;
```

With database roles, the DBA can execute

```
CONNECT TO sample;
CREATE ROLE teller;
GRANT SELECT ON TABLE customer TO ROLE teller;
GRANT SELECT ON TABLE checking TO ROLE teller;
GRANT SELECT ON TABLE customer TO ROLE teller;
GRANT ROLE teller TO USER alice;
REVOKE ROLE teller FROM USER alice;
GRANT ROLE teller TO USER lisa;
GRANT ROLE teller TO USER tom;
```

There are more examples in DB2 manuals that demonstrate the advantages of using database roles.

This can also be implemented using operating system groups instead of roles. The main difference is that roles are defined within the database, and thus a DB2 user with appropriate privileges or authorities can manage the roles while groups are defined at the operating system level where you might need to be a system administrator at the operating system level to create groups.

TRANSFER OWNERSHIP Statement

When a database object is created, the authorization ID that was used to create the object was registered as the owner of that database object by default in the system catalogs. For example in the SYSCAT.TABLES catalog view, the *Owner* column captures the authorization ID under which the table, view, or alias was created. If this authorization ID is no longer applicable (for example, if the person leaves the team or company), the TRANSFER OWNERSHIP SQL statement is handy to change the ownership of a database object to another authorization ID. The *Owner* column for that database object is replaced by the new owner in the associated system catalog tables or views.

This SQL statement can only be executed by the original owner of the object or a user with the SECADM authority; it can work with many database objects. The new owner must be a user. Here are a couple of examples:

```
TRANSFER OWNERSHIP OF TABLE acct.employee TO USER roger PRESERVE PRIVILEGES
```

The preceding example changes the OWNER value from *acct* to *roger* for table *acct. employee* in the SYSCAT.TABLES view. The PRESERVE PRIVILEGES is a mandatory clause that keeps all existing privileges presently held by the current owner of the object, even after the transfer. If you want to remove access on any specific database objects from this current owner, you need to execute the respective REVOKE statements accordingly.

Assume the following view *acct.payroll* has SELECT and INSERT dependencies on an underlying table *acct.employee*:

```
TRANSFER OWNERSHIP OF VIEW acct.payroll TO USER ed PRESERVE PRIVILEGES
```

If the database object you are trying to transfer has dependent objects as it does in this case, then the new owner must have the same privileges on the dependent object. In the given example, the new owner *ed* must also have SELECT and INSERT privileges on *acct.employee*.

Data Encryption

DB2 can encrypt data while "at rest" (stored on disk) or while the data is in transit through the network.

To encrypt data while at rest, you can use the encryption and decryption built-in functions ENCRYPT, DECRYPT_BIN, DECRYPT_CHAR, and GETHINT. Table 8.10 provides more detail about these functions. Only CHAR, VARCHAR, and FOR BIT DATA can be encrypted.

Table 8.10   Description of Encryption and Decryption DB2 Built-in Functions

Function Name	Description
ENCRYPT	This function uses a password-based encryption method. It accepts a password and a password hint as arguments. Both are embedded in the encrypted data. A password hint is a phrase that helps a user remember passwords. When encrypted, the only way to decrypt the data is by using the correct password.
DECRYPT_BIN	Use this function to decrypt data that was encrypted with the ENCRYPT function. DECRYPT_BIN returns VARCHAR FOR BIT DATA
DECRYPT_CHAR	Same as DECRYPT_BIN but returns VARCHAR
GETHINT	If you forget your password, the data cannot be decrypted and may become unusable. Using the GETHINT function, you can return the password hint that is embedded in the encrypted data, and that might help you remember the password.

To encrypt data in transit, both the DB2 client and server must support it. There are two methods to encrypt data in transit:

- Using Secured Socket Layer (SSL)
- Using DATA_ENCRYPT authentication value

For the first method, applications using the IBM Data Server Driver for JDBC and SQLJ (type 4 connections), CLI, the .Net Data Provider, or the CLP support SSL and can connect to a DB2 database using an SSL socket. To configure SSL support, first, you create a key database to manage your digital certificates. Second, the DB2 instance owner must configure the DB2 instance for SSL support. For more details, refer to the DB2 manuals.

For the second method, first, you need to configure the authentication type at the DB2 server to DATA_ENCRYPT or DATA_ENCRYPT_CMP.

Second, specify the authentication value DATA_ENCRYPT in the catalog database command. It enforces SERVER_ENCRYPT authentication as well as encryption for user data. Here is an example of configuring the DB2 server and client to support data encryption.

On the DB2 server

```
db2 update dbm cfg using authentication DATA_ENCRYPT
```

On the DB2 client

```
db2 catalog database bankdb at node server1 authentication DATA_ENCRYPT
```

> **NOTE**
>
> Authentication type DATA_ENCRYPT_CMP is not valid in the catalog database command. If DATA_ENCRYPT is used in the command, make sure the DB2 server supports data encryption.

Label-Based Access Control (LBAC)

Label-Based Access Control (LBAC) uses labels to give you complete control over who can access the data in your tables and views at the row and column levels. A label is a database object that describes a set of security criteria. LBAC works much like combining predicates, views, and privileges into one powerful, easy to administer package. You do not need to define and manage hundreds of views to define fine-grained access to your data. Figure 8.14 provides a simplistic overview of how LBAC works.

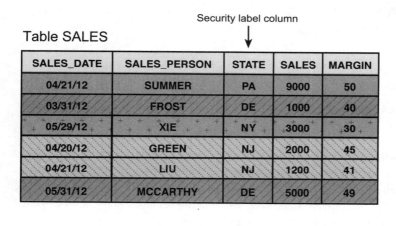

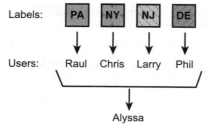

Figure 8.14 A simplistic overview of how LBAC works

In Figure 8.14, first, the SECADM designates a given column as the security label column for the table. In this example, it is the *State* column. Next, the SECADM creates labels for the different possible values of the label column and grants this label to a user. In the example, *PA*, *NY*, *NJ*, and *DE* are labels assigned to Raul, Chris, Larry, and Phil, respectively. This means that if for example, Larry runs a query on this table to retrieve all rows, he is only be able to see the fourth and fifth rows (don't count the header column) because Larry has a label of NJ, which authorizes him to only see rows that have NJ in the *State* column. On the other hand, if Alyssa runs the same query, she sees all the rows because she has a label that includes all the states and is authorized to see everything.

We describe in more detail how LBAC works in the next sections. Let's start reviewing the components of LBAC in Figure 8.15.

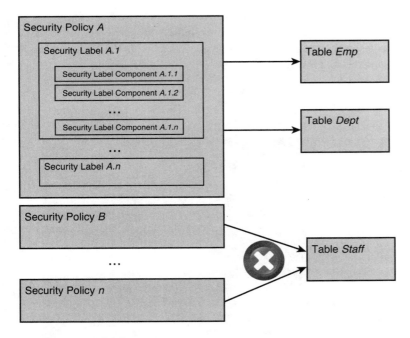

Figure 8.15 LBAC components

A security policy describes the criteria used to decide what data each user can see in a table or view. A security administrator (SECADM) performs all LBAC configuration required, which defines the security policy. Only one policy can be defined per table, but each table can have its own security policy. For example, as shown in Figure 8.15, you can have a table *Emp*, and a table *Dept*, both using the same security policy A; however you cannot have a table Staff use two different security policies (security policy *B* and *n*) at the same time.

The security policy is made up of at least one (but usually more) security label. For example, in Figure 8.15, security policy *A* is made up of security label *A.1*, *A.2*, up to *A.n*. Users who wish to access data in the table or view need to have the appropriate security label granted to them. When there's a match, access is permitted. There are three types of security labels:

- **Row security labels:** A security label associated with a row in a database table.
- **Column security labels:** A security label associated with a column in a database table.
- **User security labels:** A security label granted to a database user.

A security label is composed of security label components. For example, in Figure 8.15, security label *A.1* is composed of security label components *A.1.1*, *A.1.2*, up to *A.1.n*. There are three types of components that you can use to build your security labels:

- **Sets:** A set is a collection of elements where the order in which those elements appear is not important. All elements are deemed equal. For example, in Figure 8.16, the set indicates whether or not a specific drug is available for sale in a state. In this example, the X indicates a drug cannot be sold in that state.

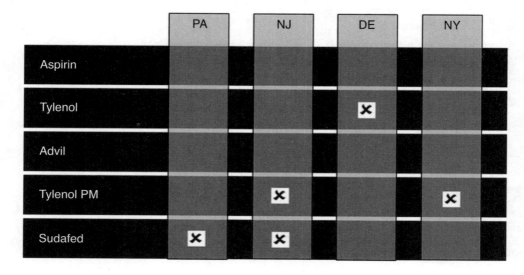

Figure 8.16   Security set

- **Arrays:** An array is an ordered set that can be used to represent a simple hierarchy. In an array, the order in which the elements appear is important. For example, the first element ranks higher than the second element and the second higher than the third. This is illustrated in Figure 8.17 where Confidential is first, then Private, and then Public. We also see that the scope of data that can be accessed decreases as the ranking decreases. In this example, each ranking can see the data in its level, as well as all data below that level.

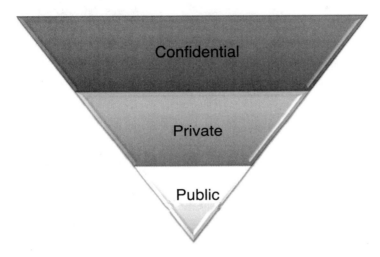

Figure 8.17   Security array

- **Trees:** A tree represents a more complex hierarchy that can have multiple nodes and branches. For example, trees can be used to represent organizational charts. You use a security policy to define the security label components that make up a particular security label. In Figure 8.18, a General can see all data and has the highest security classification. As you go down through the ranks, each lower level has a lower classification level and can see less data. At the bottom is the enlisted person, who can see almost nothing.

If you try to access rows that your LBAC credentials do not allow you to access, DB2 acts as if those rows do not exist. The rows are not returned to you if you select them, and you cannot delete or update them. Even aggregate functions ignore rows that your LBAC credentials do not allow you to access. The COUNT(*) function, for example, returns a count of only the rows you have read access to.

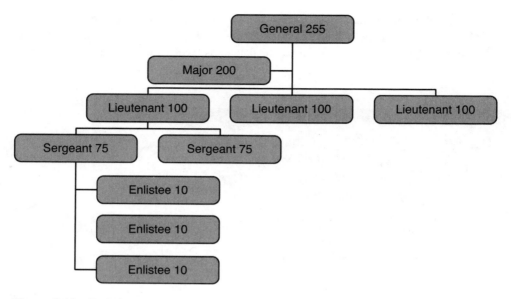

Figure 8.18   Security tree

Views and LBAC

You can define a view on a protected table the same way you can define one on a nonprotected table. When the view is accessed, the LBAC protection on the underlying table is enforced on top of any row or column restrictions enforced by the view. Because the LBAC credentials that are used to determine what rows to return are based on the authorization ID, two users accessing the same view might see different rows even when running the same query.

Implementing an LBAC Security Solution

The following sections provide an overview of how you would go about setting up LBAC protection on a specific table. Let's say you work in the Pharmaceutical industry and your company has sales operations in different states in the United States. We discuss how to implement security on your corporate *SALES* table. The *SALES* table is used to track every item sold by your sales force, and you want to be sure that people are not claiming other people's sales or poaching sales opportunities, given that there are large bonuses at stake for the sales force and their managers.

You want the following rules in place:

- VP of Sales (Alyssa) should be able to see all identified opportunities (all rows for all states).

- State Sales Executives should only see the opportunities in their states.

To build the security policy, you need to

- Determine what type of security label component is appropriate: Set, array, or tree.
- Identify the security labels and what components are part of the labels.
- Define the rules that should be used when comparing security labels and components.
- Determine any optional behaviors that you want to be applied when users access data—for example, exemptions on rules.

After you have developed your security policy, you can create the table (with the security label column defined) or alter an existing table and add the security label column. Then you attach the security policy to the table and grant users the appropriate security labels to allow or prevent them from accessing the protected data.

Let's take a look at these steps in more detail.

Step 1a: Determine the Type of the Security Label Components and Then Create Them

From your analysis, you have decided that a tree-type security label component can be used with each individual state as the element shown in Figure 8.19.

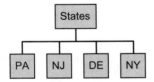

Figure 8.19   The tree security label component to use in this example

A security label component with a name SALESSTATE with the states as shown in Figure 8.19 can be created using the following command:

```
CREATE SECURITY LABEL COMPONENT SALESSTATE
        TREE ('STATES' ROOT,
              'PA' UNDER 'STATES',
              'NJ' UNDER 'STATES ',
              'NY' UNDER 'STATES ',
              'DE' UNDER 'STATES ' )
```

Step 1b: Define the Security Policy

After the security label component has been created, you then need to create the security policy. A security policy with a name SALESPOLICY that uses SALESSTATE can be created as follows:

```
CREATE SECURITY POLICY SALESPOLICY
    COMPONENTS SALESSTATE
    WITH DB2LBACRULES
    RESTRICT NOT AUTHORIZED WRITE SECURITY LABEL
```

Step 1c: Define the Security Labels

Because each state's sales executive need only see the sales and opportunities in their state, you should define a security label for each state, each state's sales executive, and the VP of sales. The security labels are based on the overall SALESPOLICY created previously. The security labels should be created as follows:

```
CREATE SECURITY LABEL SALESPOLICY.PA
    COMPONENT SALESSTATE 'PA'
CREATE SECURITY LABEL SALESPOLICY.NJ
    COMPONENT SALESSTATE 'NJ'
CREATE SECURITY LABEL SALESPOLICY.NY
    COMPONENT SALESSTATE 'NY'

CREATE SECURITY LABEL SALESPOLICY.DE
    COMPONENT SALESSTATE 'DE'

CREATE SECURITY LABEL SALESPOLICY.STATES
    COMPONENT SALESSTATE 'STATES'
```

Step 2: Create and Protect the SALES Table

```
CREATE TABLE SALES
   (SALES_DATE DATE,
    SALES_PERSON VARCHAR (15),
    STATE CHAR (2),
    SALES INTEGER,
    MARGIN INTEGER,
    STATETAG DB2SECURITYLABEL)
    SECURITY POLICY SALESPOLICY
```

In the preceding example, the *State* column (the state where the sale happens) and the *Statetag* column (the security tag) contain the same information, but because you normally don't query the security tag separately, you still need to have a column for the state.

Step 3: Load the Data

The following data is loaded into the table for this example:

SALES_DATE	SALES_PERSON	STATE	SALES	MARGIN	STATETAG
04/21/2012	SUMMER	PA	9000	50	PA
03/31/2012	FROST	DE	1000	40	DE
05/29/2012	XIE	NY	3000	30	NY
04/20/2012	GREEN	NJ	2000	45	NJ

Step 4: Grant Security Labels to the Users

After the *SALES* table has been created and protected, no users can access the table until security labels have been granted. To allow each state's sales executive access to his state's data, grant each of them the security label that corresponds to his state. If you only want them to read the data, you can grant only read authority, but because they also might want to change the data, this example grants read and write access. Note that in the last statement, user Alyssa is granted read and write access on all states.

```
GRANT SECURITY LABEL SALESPOLICY.PA
     TO USER Raul FOR ALL ACCESS

GRANT SECURITY LABEL SALESPOLICY.NY
     TO USER Chris FOR ALL ACCESS

GRANT SECURITY LABEL SALESPOLICY.NJ
     TO USER Larry FOR ALL ACCESS

GRANT SECURITY LABEL SALESPOLICY.DE
     TO USER Phil FOR ALL ACCESS

GRANT SECURITY LABEL SALESPOLICY.STATES
     TO USER Alyssa FOR ALL ACCESS
```

Step 5: Apply Rule Exemptions

A SECADM can grant or revoke an exemption to LBAC access rules to a given user. This means the indicated rule is enforced for that user. For example, to grant an exemption for write access for the SALES_POLICY to user Mary, issue `GRANT EXEMPTION ON RULE DB2LBACWRITET-REE FOR SALES_POLICY TO USER mary`

To revoke the exemptions on all of the predefined rules for SALES_POLICY from user Bobby, issue `REVOKE EXEMPTION ON RULE ALL FOR SALES_POLICY FROM USER bobby`

LBAC in Action

This next section examines how users access the table and what data they will see.

Example 1

If Alyssa, the VP of Sales attempts to insert some data into the *SALES* table, it is successful because she has read and write permission on all states.

```
INSERT into SALES VALUES (
    '06/02/2012',
    'LUCAS',
    'NY',
    1400,
    20,
    SECLABEL_BY_NAME('SALESPOLICY', 'NY'));
```

If Larry tries to insert a sale for Phil, the insert fails because Larry works in NJ, not in DE.

```
INSERT into  SALES VALUES (
    '06/02/2012',
    'SMITH',
    'DE',
    1500,
    12,
    SECLABEL_BY_NAME ('SALESPOLICY', 'DE'))
```

Example 2

If Larry tries to read the sales information for NY so that he can "scoop" some sales, he does not get any data.

```
SELECT sales_date, sales_person, state, sales, margin
     from  SALES where state='NY'
```

In this case no row is returned since the row in the table for this state is protected by security label SALESPOLICY.NY, and the security label that Larry holds is not authorized to read that row.

Example 3

Larry tries to read all of the sales data from the *SALES* table by issuing the command:

```
SELECT sales_date, sales_person, state, sales, margin
  FROM SALES;
```

In this case, only the rows with the sales policy NJ in the STATETAG are returned.

Column Level Security and Referential Integrity

You can use LBAC to protect columns in the same manner as shown for protecting rows.

With respect to referential integrity and LBAC, LBAC can work on tables with referential constraints defined on them; however, you need to consider the following:

- LBAC read access rules are *not* applied for internally generated scans of child tables. This is to avoid having orphan children.

- LBAC read access rules are *not* applied for internally generated scans of parent tables.

- LBAC write rules are applied when a CASCADE operation is performed on child tables.

LBAC provides a mechanism for protecting rows and/or columns in your tables and ensuring that only the people with permission can see or alter the data in the tables.

V10 Row and Column Access Control (RCAC)

Row and Column Access Control (RCAC) is another method to provide fine-grained access to your data at the row and column levels. Although LBAC uses labels to control access, RCAC uses row permissions and column masks. Row permission and column masks are database objects that define the rules that need to be followed to access rows and columns, respectively.

Figure 8.20 provides a simplistic overview of how RCAC works. It is similar to Figure 8.14, which provided a simplistic overview of LBAC. This helps you understand the difference between both methods.

Table SALES

SALES_DATE	SALES_PERSON	STATE	SALES	MARGIN
04/21/12	SUMMER	PA	9000	50
03/31/12	FROST	DE	1000	40
05/29/12	XIE	NY	3000	30
04/20/12	GREEN	NJ	2000	45
04/21/12	LIU	NJ	1200	41
05/31/12	MCCARTHY	DE	5000	49

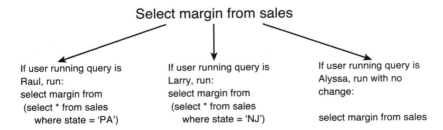

Users: Raul   . . .   Larry   Alyssa

Select margin from sales

If user running query is
Raul, run:
select margin from
(select * from sales
    where state = 'PA')

If user running query is
Larry, run:
select margin from
(select * from sales
    where state = 'NJ')

If user running query is
Alyssa, run with no
change:

select margin from sales

Figure 8.20   A simplistic overview of how RCAC works

In Figure 8.20 we only illustrate how row permissions work; a similar approach is used for column masks. In the example, say a user issues the query

```
select margin from sales
```

When you create the row permission, you can add logic to test which user is executing the query, using built-in functions or the special register CURRENT USER. If the user is *Raul* as in this example, then intercept the query and execute first the logic that determines which rows *Raul* can access. For this example, the logic that was coded is that *Raul* can only see rows that list the state PA. After this has been determined, DB2 proceeds executing the original query over the subset of rows. In Figure 8.20 we represent this with the query

```
select margin from (select * from sales where state = 'PA')
```

This can obviously be written as

```
select margin from sales where state = 'PA'
```

but we wanted to give you an idea of how the query would be processed. In a sense, it's similar to how views are handled. For example, if you issue

```
create view mysales as
   select * from sales where state = 'PA'


select margin from mysales
```

DB2 would first resolve the view by running its definition at runtime, and then it would apply the SELECT statement. Thus, it would look like

```
select margin from (select * from sales where state = 'PA')
```

which is exactly the same as what is shown in the Figure 8.20 for user *Raul*.

This is a simplistic overview of RCAC so you understand how it works. We cover the details in the next sections. For column masks the idea is similar: You use built-in functions to determine which user is executing the query and then run a CASE statement to return a column or not or to mask part of it.

Built-In SQL Functions and Session Variables Supporting RCAC

Table 8.11 describes built-in SQL functions to verify the membership of a user in a given group or role. These functions can later be used in your logic when creating a row permission or column mask.

Table 8.11 Built-In SQL Functions Supporting RCAC

Function name	Description
VERIFY_ROLE_FOR_USER	Use this function to verify if a user has a given database role.
VERIFY_GROUP_FOR_USER	Use this function to verify if a user is member of a given external group.
VERIFY_TRUSTED_CONTEXT_ROLE_FOR_USER	Use this function to verify if a user has a given database role acquired through a trusted context.

Table 8.12 lists several session variables you can use that can help in your logic when working with RCAC.

Table 8.12 Session Variables Supporting RCAC

Session Variable Name	Description
SYSIBM.TRUSTED_CONTEXT	This variable stores the name of the trusted context associated with the current trusted connection.
SYSIBM.CLIENT_IPADDR	This variable stores the current client IP address.
SYSIBM.CLIENT_HOST	This variable stores the current client host name.
SYSIBM.ROUTINE_SCHEMA	This variable stores the schema name of the currently executing routine.
SYSIBM.ROUTINE_SPECIFIC_NAME	This variable stores the specific name of the currently executing routine.
SYSIBM.ROUTINE_TYPE	This variable stores the type of the currently executing routine (P = Stored procedure, F = Function).
SYSIBM.ROUTINE_MODULE	This variable stores the module name of the currently executing routine.
SYSIBM.PACKAGE_NAME	This variable stores the name of the currently executing package.
SYSIBM.PACKAGE_SCHEMA	This variable stores the schema of the currently executing package.
SYSIBM.PACKAGE_VERSION	This variable stores the version of the currently executing package.

Creating Row Permissions

Listing 8.27 shows the syntax of the CREATE PERMISSION statement

Listing 8.27   CREATE PERMISSION Syntax Diagram

```
>>-CREATE-+------------+-PERMISSION--permission-name--ON--table-name-------->
          '-OR REPLACE-'

>----+----------------------------+---------------------------------------->
     |  .--AS--.                   |
     '--+------+--correlation-name--'

                                                           .-DISABLE-.
>----FOR ROWS WHERE--search-condition--ENFORCED FOR ALL ACCESS-+---------+-><
                                                           '-ENABLE--'
```

Following are some examples showing you how to use this statement.
To only allow user *Mary* to see all rows in table EMPLOYEE, issue

```
CREATE PERMISSION user_permission
       ON EMPLOYEE
       FOR ROWS WHERE CURRENT USER = 'MARY'
ENFORCED FOR ALL ACCESS ENABLE;
```

To allow users who are members of the PA group access to rows with sales information only in the state of Pennsylvania (PA), issue

```
CREATE PERMISSION sales_permission
ON SALES
FOR ROWS WHERE
    VERIFY_GROUP_FOR_USER (USER, 'PA')= 1
AND STATE = 'PA'
ENFORCED FOR ALL ACCESS ENABLE;
```

To allow members of the HR department (with role 'HR') access to table PAYROLL only through the stored procedure HRPROC.MYPROC, issue

```
CREATE PERMISSION salary_permission
ON PAYROLL
FOR ROWS WHERE
        VERIFY_ROLE_FOR_USER(USER, 'HR')= 1
AND ROUTINE_SPECIFIC_NAME = 'MYPROC'
AND ROUTINE_SCHEMA = 'HRPROC'
AND ROUTINE_TYPE = 'P'
ENFORCED FOR ALL ACCESS ENABLE;
```

Creating Column Masks

Listing 8.28 shows the syntax of the CREATE MASK statement

Listing 8.28　CREATE MASK Syntax Diagram

```
>>-CREATE-+------------+-MASK--mask-name--ON--table-name---------------->
          '-OR REPLACE-'
>----+----------------------------+---------------------------------->
     |    .--AS--.                |
     '--+------+--correlation-name--'
                                      .-DISABLE-.
>----FOR COLUMN--column-name--RETURN—cases-expression--+---------+----><
                                                       '-ENABLE--'
```

Following are some examples showing you how to use this statement.
To only allow users with the HR role see the *Salary* column in the *EMPLOYEE* table, issue

```
CREATE MASK salary_mask
     ON EMPLOYEE
     FOR COLUMN salary RETURN
  CASE WHEN VERIFY_ROLE_FOR_USER(SESSION_USER, 'HR')= 1
         THEN salary
       ELSE
         NULL
END
ENABLE;
```

To mask the first 12 digits of credit card numbers from all users that are not part of the billing department (with role BL), issue

```
CREATE MASK creditcard_mask
     ON INVOICE
     FOR COLUMN creditcard RETURN
  CASE WHEN VERIFY_ROLE_FOR_USER(SESSION_USER, 'BL')= 1
         THEN creditcard
       ELSE
         'XXXX-XXXX-XXXX-' || SUBSTR(creditcard,13,4)
END
ENABLE;
```

Enforcing Row Permissions and Column Masks

Figure 8.21 lists the different statements used to enforce row permissions.

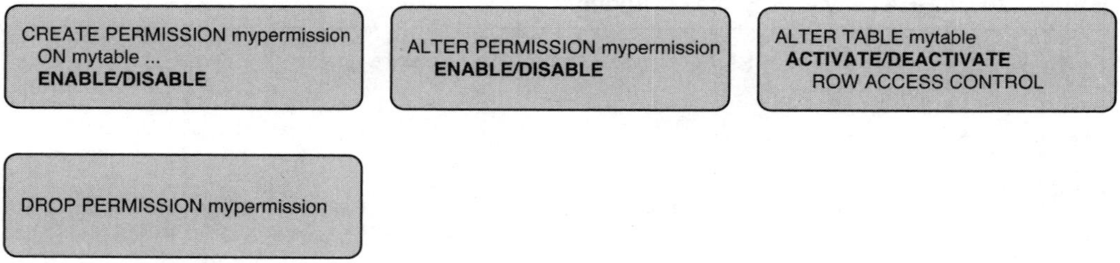

Figure 8.21   Statements used to work with row permissions

When you create a permission with the CREATE PERMISSION statement explained in an earlier section, you can indicate whether the permission is enabled or disabled. If the permission is disabled, you can enable it with the statement

```
ALTER PERMISSION mypermission ENABLE
```

If at a later time you want to disable it, issue

```
ALTER PERMISSION mypermission DISABLE
```

When the permission is enabled, it is not enforced until you activate RCAC at the row level with this statement:

```
ALTER TABLE mytable ACTIVATE ROW ACCESS CONTROL
```

If you later on want to deactivate RCAC at the row level, issue

```
ALTER TABLE mytable DEACTIVATE ROW ACCESS CONTROL
```

To delete a permission, issue

```
DROP PERMISSION mypermission
```

Figure 8.22 lists the different statements used to enforce column masks.

Figure 8.22   Statements used to work with column masks

When you create a mask with the CREATE MASK statement, explained in section "Creating Column Masks," you can indicate whether the mask is enabled or disabled. If the mask was created disabled, you can enable it with the statement

```
ALTER MASK mymask ENABLE
```

If at a later time you want to disable it, issue:

```
ALTER MASK mymask DISABLE
```

When the mask is enabled, it is not enforced until you activate RCAC at the column level with this statement:

```
ALTER TABLE mytable ACTIVATE COLUMN ACCESS CONTROL
```

If you later on want to deactivate RCAC at the column level, issue

```
ALTER TABLE mytable DEACTIVATE COLUMN ACCESS CONTROL
```

To delete a mask, issue

```
DROP MASK mymask
```

Behavior of INSERT, DELETE, and UPDATE Under RCAC

The following sentences explain how an INSERT, DELETE, or UPDATE operation works under RCAC:

- You cannot insert a row that you cannot select.
- You cannot update a row that you cannot select.
- You cannot delete a row that you cannot select

For example, if you want to insert, update, or delete a row with sales information for the state of Pennsylvania, but there is a row permission that indicates that you cannot select rows for the state of Pennsylvania, then you cannot proceed with the operation on the row.

Implementing a RCAC Security Solution

Let's use the same scenario explained in the section, "Implementing an LBAC Security Solution," but this time we implement it using RCAC. We also expand the scenario to highlight features of RCAC.

As discussed earlier, say you work in the pharmaceutical industry, and your company has sales operations in different states in the U.S. The *SALES* table is used to track every item sold by your sales force, and you want the following rules in place:

- VP of Sales (Alyssa) should be able to see all identified opportunities (all rows for all states).
- State Sales Executives should only see the opportunities in their states.

Follow these steps:

Step 1: Create the Table Sales

Create the table *SALES* as shown here. Say user *peter*, who is a SECADM and DBADM, is issuing these statements.

```
CREATE TABLE SALES
   (SALES_DATE DATE,
    SALES_PERSON_ID CHAR(3),
    SALES_PERSON VARCHAR (15),
    STATE CHAR (2),
    SALES INTEGER,
    MARGIN INTEGER)
```

Step 2: Load the Data

The following data is loaded into the table for this example using this INSERT statement:

```
INSERT INTO SALES
     VALUES ('04/21/2012','111','SUMMER','PA',9000,50),
            ('03/31/2012','222','FROST','DE',1000,40),
            ('05/29/2012','333','XIE', 'NY',3000,30),
            ('04/20/2012','444','GREEN', 'NJ',2000,45)
```

The table would look like this after being loaded:

SALES_DATE	SALES_PERSON_ID	SALES_PERSON	STATE	SALES	MARGIN
04/21/2012	111	SUMMER	PA	9000	50
03/31/2012	222	FROST	DE	1000	40
05/29/2012	333	XIE	NY	3000	30
04/20/2012	444	GREEN	NJ	2000	45

Step 3: Create Roles and Row Permissions

As a SECADM, create the following roles and row permissions to meet the rules specified earlier:

```
CREATE ROLE PA;
GRANT SELECT, UPDATE, INSERT ON SALES TO ROLE PA;
GRANT ROLE PA TO USER Raul;
CREATE PERMISSION SALESPOLICY_PA_permission
   ON SALES
   FOR ROWS WHERE
      VERIFY_ROLE_FOR_USER(USER, 'PA')= 1
```

```
        AND STATE = 'PA'
        ENFORCED FOR ALL ACCESS ENABLE;


CREATE ROLE NY;
GRANT SELECT, UPDATE, INSERT ON SALES TO ROLE NY;
GRANT ROLE NY TO USER Chris;
CREATE PERMISSION SALESPOLICY_NY_permission
    ON SALES
    FOR ROWS WHERE
        VERIFY_ROLE_FOR_USER(USER, 'NY')= 1
        AND STATE = 'NY'
        ENFORCED FOR ALL ACCESS ENABLE;


... (repeat similar steps for NJ and DE)


CREATE ROLE VP;
GRANT SELECT, UPDATE, INSERT ON SALES TO ROLE VP;
GRANT ROLE VP TO USER Alyssa;
CREATE PERMISSION SALESPOLICY_VP_permission
    ON SALES
    FOR ROWS WHERE
        VERIFY_ROLE_FOR_USER(USER, 'VP')= 1
        ENFORCED FOR ALL ACCESS ENABLE;
```

Step 4: Activate RCAC at Row and Column Levels

As a SECADM (and DBADM), issue these commands

```
ALTER TABLE sales ACTIVATE ROW ACCESS CONTROL;
ALTER TABLE sales ACTIVATE COLUMN ACCESS CONTROL;
```

RCAC in Action

This section examines how users access the table and what data they will see.

Example 1

If Alyssa, the VP of Sales attempts to insert some data into the *SALES* table, it is successful because she has access to all rows for all states.

```
INSERT into SALES VALUES (
    '06/02/2012',
    'LUCAS',
```

```
    'NY',
    1400,
    20);
```

If Larry tries to insert a sale for Phil with the following INSERT statement

```
INSERT into  SALES VALUES (
    '06/02/2012',
    'SMITH',
    'DE',
    1500,
    12);
```

the insert will fail with the following error message because Larry works in NJ, not in DE.

```
    SQL20471N   The INSERT or UPDATE statement failed because a
    resulting row did not satisfy row permissions.   SQLSTATE=22542
```

Example 2

If Larry tries to read the sales information for NY so that he can "scoop" some sales, he does not get any data:

```
SELECT sales_date, sales_person, state, sales, margin
  from  SALES where state='NY';
```

In this case, no row is returned because the row permission SALESPOLICY_NY_permission indicates that only users with the NY role can access this row, and Larry does not hold the NY role.

Example 3

Larry tries to read all of the sales data from the *SALES* table by issuing this command:

```
SELECT sales_date, sales_person, state, sales, margin
  from  SALES;
```

In this case, only the rows with the sales policy NJ are returned.

Extending the Case Scenario

Now let's extend the scenario by first creating another table called *SELLER* with this statement:

```
CREATE TABLE SELLER
        (ID CHAR(3),
         SALES_PERSON_NAME VARCHAR (15),
         SSN VARCHAR (15),
```

```
STATE CHAR (2),
PHONE VARCHAR(12),
RATING CHAR(2),
SALARY INTEGER)
```

and let's load the table using this INSERT statement:

```
INSERT INTO SELLER VALUES
('111','SUMMER','111111111','PA','9991119999','1',70000),
('222','FROST','222222222','DE','8882228888','4',30000),
('333','XIE','333333333','NY','7773337777','2',35000),
('444','GREEN','444444444','NJ','6664446666','2',90000);
```

Now let's add the following rules:

- VPs compensate excellent performers based on their sales achievements. To get a good assessment of how much of a raise a given sales person will get or how much commission he is entitled to, they would like to see the seller's current base salary and the rating they have so far as a seller. For example, a rating of 1 is excellent, and a rating of 5 is poor. This means that VPs should have access to all the information in the *SELLER* table except the social security number (SSN), which can be masked.

- Individual sellers should see only the sales they are or were involved in.

For the first rule, the following column mask can be created:

```
CREATE MASK ssn_mask
   ON SELLER
   FOR COLUMN SSN RETURN
   CASE WHEN VERIFY_ROLE_FOR_USER(SESSION_USER, 'VP')= 1
        THEN SSN
        ELSE 'XXX-XX-' || SUBSTR(SSN,6,4)
   END
ENABLE;
```

Make sure to grant SELECT on the table to the role VP and to enable RCAC for column access control for this table as follows:

```
GRANT SELECT ON TABLE SELLER TO VP;
ALTER TABLE seller ACTIVATE COLUMN ACCESS CONTROL;
```

When Alyssa issues a SELECT * FROM SELLER, she gets the following. Note the column SSN is masked.

```
SELECT * from  seller;
```

ID	SALES_PERSON_NAME	SSN	STATE	PHONE	RATING	SALARY
111	SUMMER	XXX-XX-1111	PA	9991119999	1	70000
222	FROST	XXX-XX-2222	DE	8882228888	4	30000
333	XIE	XXX-XX-3333	NY	7773337777	2	35000
444	GREEN	XXX-XX-4444	NJ	6664446666	2	90000

For the second rule, we create a row permission on table *SALES* using information from table *SELLER*. First we need to create the SELLER role and grant the appropriate privileges on table *SALES*.

```
CREATE ROLE SELLER;
GRANT SELECT ON TABLE SALES TO SELLER;
GRANT ROLE SELLER TO SUMMER, FROST, XIE, GREEN;

CREATE PERMISSION SELLER_PERMISSION
  ON SALES
  FOR ROWS WHERE
    VERIFY_ROLE_FOR_USER (USER, 'SELLER') = 1
AND STATE =
  (SELECT STATE FROM SELLER WHERE SALES_PERSON_NAME = USER)
  ENFORCED FOR ALL ACCESS
  ENABLE;


ALTER TABLE sales ACTIVATE ROW ACCESS CONTROL;
```

Following is what seller FROST would see when he queries the *SALES* table:

```
SELECT * FROM SALES
```

SALES_DATE	SALES_PERSON_ID	SALES_PERSON	STATE	SALES	MARGIN
03/31/2012	222	FROST	DE	1000	40

As expected, he only sees the row showing only him and his sales.

Benefits of Using RCAC

DB2's direction for the past few versions has been on enhancing its security mechanisms so that users are not given more access than what is needed to perform their jobs. This is in tune with what the industry and government is expecting in terms of regulatory compliance with several acts enacted in the United States such as the Health Insurance Portability and Accountability Act (HIPAA), Federal Information Security Management Act (FISMA), Sarbanes-Oxley Act, and more.

With this in mind, SECADM, ACCESSCTRL, and DATAACCESS authorities were created. Continuing in this direction, RCAC allows security administrators to further control access to data at the row and column levels. Prior to RCAC, a user with DATAACCESS authority could access all the data in the database; it was not possible to just revoke SELECT for a given table, for example. With RCAC, every user is affected, including those with DATAACCESS authority. The SECADM is the only authority required to set up RCAC.

Moreover, no matter how data is accessed, whether via SQL, an application, or a tool, data is protected the same way at the table level. Even if a view is created based on a table protected using RCAC, the view has the same constraints. This is because RCAC is built on top of the regular authority and privileges security model.

Prior to RCAC, administrators and programmers had to implement similar mechanisms using views, stored procedures, or application logic. Most of the time, the application server had to handle the security rules. With RCAC this is all handled now by the DB2 database server in a more efficient and flexible way. No application changes are required to work with RCAC, and it is easy to set up rules because row permissions and column masks are based on SQL expressions.

Another benefit of RCAC is that it facilitates multi-tenancy. With Cloud Computing gaining more popularity every day, Software as a Service (SaaS) providers need to reuse its resources as efficiently as possible. RCAC enables SaaS vendors to share tables among several independent tenants who would access their data without being aware of one another.

Just as in the case of LBAC, database administrators need to be aware that queries run by different users can return different results. This is by design because data is protected based on who is querying the data. They should also be aware that because row permissions and column masks apply to SQL operations only, they would not apply to non-SQL utilities such as LOAD, REORG, and RUNSTATS.

Trusted Contexts

In a three-tiered application model, where you have a web server, an application server, and a database server, the middle tier (the application server) is responsible for authenticating the users running the client applications and for managing the interactions with the database server.

Although the three-tiered application model has many benefits, all interactions with the database server occur under the middle tier's authorization ID. This raises some security concerns. For example, let's take a look at Figure 8.23.

The figure shows that although many users coming from the web server to the application server have their own user IDs (for example, Mary, Tom, Sue), the connection from the application server to the database server is normally performed by one or few connections with fixed user IDs (Smith in the example). This is done for performance reasons because connecting and disconnecting often from the database can be costly. However, this raises a security problem of not being able to map one to one which user performed what action on the database server. For example, was it user Mary who deleted a given record? At the database server, you cannot determine this because all auditing will point to user Smith.

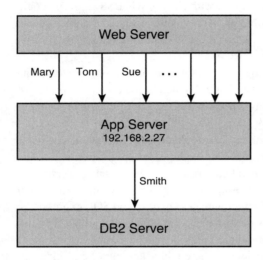

Figure 8.23   Trusted context

Trusted context tries to solve the problem of identifying who is doing what at the database server. Using trusted contexts, you do not break the application server to database server connection per user; you keep using the same fixed connections. However, you can identify through trusted contexts (based on IP address, domain name, and so on) the user performing the operation. For the example in Figure 8.23, a SECADM can create the following trusted context at the DB2 server by issuing this statement:

```
CREATE TRUSTED CONTEXT ctxt
  BASED UPON CONNECTION USING SYSTEM AUTHID smith
  ATTRIBUTES (ADDRESS '192.168.2.27')
  DEFAULT ROLE managerRole ENABLE
```

In the preceding statement, the trusted context is created between the application server located at IP address 192.168.2.27 using authorization Smith to connect from the application server to the DB2 server. So when there is a connection coming from user Smith from this IP address, the trusted context takes place, and this connection has the role of *managerRole*. Now that this context is "trusted" at the application server, you can code a way to switch users at the application server level. DB2 provides APIs that help you do this. So say from the web server you access the application server as Mary, and then at the application server you code some logic that if it's Mary (who happens to be a manager), switch user ID Smith to be Mary for the trusted context ctxt—so from the DB2 server, Mary is now the user performing operations.

Windows Security Considerations

In most production environments, database administrators usually group users together and grant certain privileges or database authorities to those groups. As you can imagine, this is more efficient than maintaining privileges for each individual user. So it is important to understand how the groups are being looked up for the users by DB2.

Windows Domain Considerations

Windows domain environments have different types of user groups: Local Groups and Global Groups. A local group can be defined on your DB2 server, which is part of a Windows domain, say domain MMDOM. In a domain, a domain controller is a server that maintains a master database of all the domain users' credentials. It is also used to authenticate domain logons. A Global group can be defined on this domain controller.

In Figure 8.24, you can see that a user ID db2admin is a member of global group *mmdba* in the domain *mmdom*. To use global groups, you must include them inside a local group on the DB2 server. When DB2 enumerates all the groups that a person is a member of, it also lists the local groups the user is a member of indirectly. Permission to access the database and/or object must be granted to this local group.

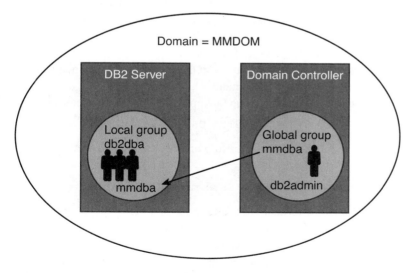

Figure 8.24 Support of global groups in DB2

Figure 8.25 shows a second scenario, where the same user ID, db2admin, is also defined locally at the DB2 server and is a member of a local group called *db2dba*.

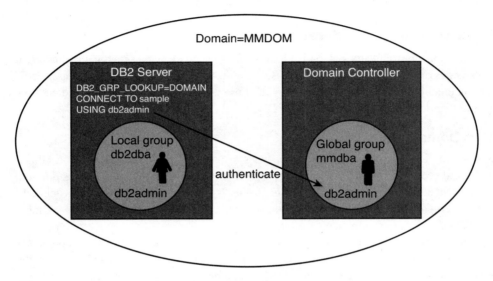

Figure 8.25   Support of LOCAL or DOMAIN group lookup

A user connects to the database as db2admin and tries to drop a table. Which group do you want DB2 to enumerate for db2admin? It is important for DB2 to enumerate the right group because local group DB2DBA might only hold SELECT privileges on the table, whereas the global group MMDBA has DBADM with DATAACCESS authority.

The first option is to include the Windows domain with the user ID during authentication, such as in the CONNECT statement or the ATTACH command. The fully qualified DB2 authentication ID can be as long as 30 characters. This makes group lookup on Windows more deterministic.

```
CONNECT TO sample USER mmdba/db2admin USING password
```

Note that the fully qualified authentication ID also works in GRANT and REVOKE statements. For example:

```
GRANT SELECT ON TABLE employee TO USER mmdba/db2admin
```

Alternatively, use the DB2 registry variable DB2_GRP_LOOKUP to tell DB2 where to validate user accounts and perform group member lookup. Set the variable to LOCAL to force DB2 to always enumerate groups and validate user accounts locally on the DB2 server. Set the variable to DOMAIN to force DB2 to always enumerate groups and validate user accounts on the Windows domain to which the user account belongs. For example

```
db2set DB2_GRP_LOOKUP = DOMAIN
```

If a user wants to log onto his or her laptop as a domain user in a disconnected environment, Windows supports this via cached credentials. When a credential is cached, information kept from the last logon is referenced if the machine cannot contact the domain controller. DB2 supports this behavior by using an access token.

An access token is created after a user has successfully logged on to the system. The token is an object that describes the security context of a process or thread. The information in an access token includes the identity, all of the groups the user belongs to, and privileges of the user account associated with the process or thread.

You can also use the DB2_GRP_LOOKUP registry variable to enable access token support. Besides LOCAL and DOMAIN, there are three other valid values: TOKEN, TOKENLOCAL, and TOKENDOMAIN. These values can be used with LOCAL or DOMAIN to determine where to look up groups if an access token is not available. Table 8.13 highlights the behavior of these values.

Table 8.13   DB2_GRP_LOOKUP Registry Variable Settings

DB2_GRP_LOOKUP Setting	Description
TOKEN	Enables access token support to look up all groups that the user belongs to at the location where the user account is defined.
LOCAL, TOKENLOCAL	Enables access token support to look up local groups or to fallback to use LOCAL group lookup if an access token is not available.
DOMAIN, TOKENDOMAIN	Enables access token support to look up domain groups or to fall back to DOMAIN group lookup if an access token is not available.

Windows Extended Security

DB2 enables by default the DB2 Windows Extended Security feature at installation time. Extended security is used to provide more security for DB2 at the operating system level. For example, when enabled, it can prevent access through the Windows operating system to DB2 files and directories, such as the ones where DB2 stores instance information. With extended security, two Windows groups are created:

- **DB2ADMNS:** Members of this group have complete access to all DB2 objects through the operating system.
- **DB2USERS:** Members of this group have read and execute access for all DB2 objects located in the installation and instance directories through the operating system.

As mentioned in an earlier section, when SYSADM_GROUP dbm cfg parameter is left with its default NULL value, the members of the DB2ADMNS group are SYSADM.

You can specify the DB2ADMNS and the DB2USERS groups either as local groups or as domain groups. Both groups must be of the same type—either both local or both domain.

Authority and Privilege Metadata

Up to this point, we have introduced different authorities and privileges. Now we show you where all this security information is stored and how to easily retrieve it.

Just like most of the information about a database, authorities and privileges metadata is stored in the catalog tables and views, listed in Table 8.14. For a complete list of all DB2 catalog tables and descriptions, refer to the DB2 Information Center.

Table 8.14   System Catalog Views Containing Authority and Privilege Metadata

Catalog View	Description
SYSCAT.COLAUTH	Stores column privileges for each grantee. Column privileges are granted through table and view privileges. The two privilege types are Update and Reference.
SYSCAT.DBAUTH	Stores database authorities for each grantee.
SYSCAT.INDEXAUTH	Stores index privileges for each grantee.
SYSCAT.PACKAGEAUTH	Stores package privileges for each grantee.
SYSCAT.PASSTHRUAUTH	Stores information about authorizations to query data sources in pass-through sessions. Pass-through sessions (not discussed in this book) are used in federated database environments.
SYSCAT.ROLEAUTH	Stores database roles granted to users, groups, roles or PUBLIC.
SYSCAT.ROUTINEAUTH	Stores routine privileges for each grantee.
SYSCAT.SCHEMAAUTH	Stores schema privileges for each grantee.
SYSCAT.SEQUENCEAUTH	Stores sequence privileges for each grantee.
SYSCAT.TABAUTH	Stores table privileges for each grantee.
SYSCAT.TBSPACEAUTH	Stores table space privileges for each grantee.
SYSCAT.XSROBJECTAUTH	Stores XSR object USAGE privileges for each grantee.
SYSCAT.SECURITYLABELS	Stores information of security labels.
SYSCAT.SECURITYLABELACCESS	Stores database authorization IDs and types of access to security labels defined in the database.
SYSCAT.SECURITYLABELCOMPONENTS	Stores information of security label components.

Catalog View	Description
SYSCAT.SECURITYLABELCOMPO-NENTELEMENTS	Stores element value for each security label component.
SYSCAT.SECURITYPOLICY	Stores information of security policies.
SYSCAT.SECURITYPOLICYCOMPO-NENTRULES	Stores read and write access rules for each security label component of its associated security policy.
SYSCAT. SECURITYPOLICYEXEMPTIONS	Stores information of security policy exemptions.

Although querying the catalog views can give you everything (and sometimes more than) you want to know, the following are a few commands, statements, and tools you will find handy.

From the DB2 CLP, you can obtain the authorities of users by running these statements:

```
connect to <dbname>
select * from table(AUTH_LIST_AUTHORITIES_FOR_AUTHID (<authID>,
<authIDType>)
```

where authIDType can be *G* for group, *R* for a role, and *U* for user.

For example, to review the authorities for a user with authorization ID rfchong in database SAMPLE, issue

```
connect to SAMPLE
select * from table(AUTH_LIST_AUTHORITIES_FOR_AUTHID ('rfchong','U'))
```

You can also retrieve similar information from IBM Data Studio. Right-click the desired database and select **Manage Privileges**. This displays the Properties tab (see Figure 8.26), where you can manage database-level authorities for existing users and groups.

NOTE

The user IDs and user groups shown in IBM Data Studio refer to existing users and groups created outside of DB2, typically using operating system commands. Even though Data Studio has an option to create users and groups (under the Users and Groups folder in the Database Administration perspective), this does not really be create a new user or group, but creates an identifier into the IBM Data Studio GUI. This identifier should match an existing user or group created outside of DB2.

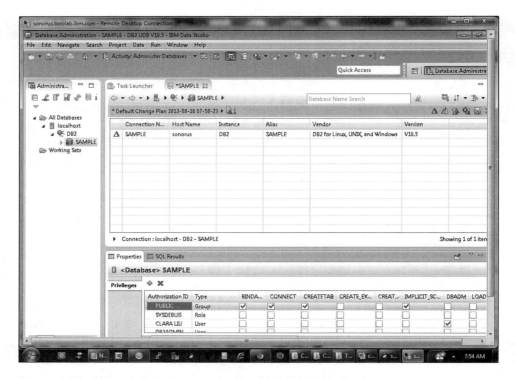

Figure 8.26   Managing database authorities from IBM Data Studio

To manage privileges for each individual database object, right-click the target object from IBM Data Studio and select **Manage Privileges**. The Properties tab at the bottom of the window displays the privileges for the object selected as shown in Figure 8.27.

To grant a privilege, click the corresponding box until a checkmark appears. If you want to grant the user the ability to grant the same privilege to others, click the box again until you see two checkmarks, one on top of the other. To revoke a privilege, click the box until you don't see checkmarks.

Case Study

In this case study, you practice with privileges, authorities, roles, and RCAC. Follow each section in order; they cannot be performed independently.

Working with Authorities and Privileges

You are asked to set up a database environment for a new team in your company. You will not be the permanent system administrator or DBA for any database in that system; however, you need to set it up and then pass control to members of a new team.

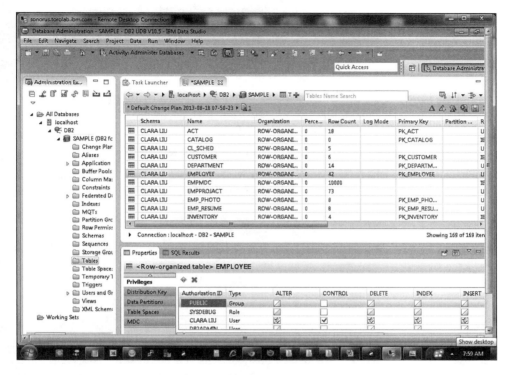

Figure 8.27 Managing database object privileges from IBM Data Studio

Say your user ID is *admin* and your password is *pswadmin*. You successfully install DB2 Enterprise with those credentials. Next, you review the following table, which contains the list of individuals in the team, the user ID and passwords assigned, and their responsibilities:

Name	User ID	Password	Responsibility	Operating System Group
<Your name>	Admin	adminpsw	Install DB2, set up other authorities	swatgrp
Cynthia Sommers	Cynthia	cynthiapsw	SYSADM	sysgrp
Mary Prescot	Mary	marypsw	SYSADM and DBADM	sysgrp
Peter Pang	Peter	peterpsw	SECADM	secgrp
Tom Arevalo	tom	tompsw	Tester	
Amna Jones	amna	amnapsw	Tester, then developer	

First, you create all of the users and groups in the table using operating system commands. Next, with your user *admin*, which is SYSADM, you create the database TSTDB using this command from the DB2 CLP:

```
create database tstdb
```

If you add `restrictive` at the end of the command, the PUBLIC group will have no access whatsoever on the database. Because we don't, any user can connect to the database. For example, if you issue this command from the DB2 CLP

```
connect to tstdb user cynthia using cynthiapsw
```

user Cynthia would be able to connect. Rather than using `restrictive`, if you don't want PUBLIC to do much on the database, you can revoke the CONNECT privilege (and other privileges) as follows:

```
connect to tstdb user admin using adminpsw
revoke connect, createtab, implicit_schema, bindadd on database from
public
```

The next time Cynthia tries to connect, she receives

```
connect to tstdb user cynthia using cynthiapsw
SQL1060N  User "CYNTHIA " does not have the CONNECT privilege.
SQLSTATE=08004
```

Because you created the TSTDB database, by default you are also the SECADM, and DBADM with DATAACCESS and ACCESSCTRL on the database. You can verify this from IBM Data Studio. After connecting to TSTDB, right-click it and choose **Manage Privileges**. You can then confirm from the privileges tab that you have these authorities.

You need to transfer SECADM to Peter and then have him revoke all of these authorities from you.

To give Peter SECADM authority, issue

```
connect to TSTDB user admin using adminpsw
grant SECADM on database to user peter
```

After you notify Peter, you ask him to remove you as SECADM, DBADM, DATAACCESS and ACCESSCTRL as follows:

```
connect to TSTDB user peter using peterpsw
revoke SECADM, DBADM, DATAACCESS, ACCESSCTRL on database from user
admin
```

You can verify you don't have these authorities anymore from IBM Data Studio (you might have to disconnect and reconnect to the database again), or you can try granting DBADM to Cynthia to just check if you are still SECADM:

```
connect to TSTDB user admin using adminpsw
grant DBADM on database to user cynthia
```

```
DB21034E  The command was processed as an SQL statement because it was
not a valid Command Line Processor command.  During SQL processing it
returned:
SQL0552N  "ADMIN" does not have the privilege to perform operation
"GRANT". SQLSTATE=42502
```

If you now try to create a table, will you be able to do it? Try and issue

```
create table t1 (col1 int)
```

```
DB21034E  The command was processed as an SQL statement because it was
not a valid Command Line Processor command.  During SQL processing it
returned: SQL0552N  "ADMIN" does not have the privilege to perform
operation "CREATE TABLE".  SQLSTATE=42502
```

This confirms you also don't have DBADM authority anymore.

Last, you would like to remove yourself from being a SYSADM in the instance where you created this database; at the same time you are making the members of group *sysgrp* the SYSADMs. This can be done with this command:

```
update dbm cfg using SYSADM_GROUP sysgrp
db2stop
db2start
```

At this point, you have absolutely no authorities nor privileges on the instance or the database. You can let Cynthia and Mary know that they are the new SYSADMs and that they should contact Peter (the SECADM) for any other security concern.

Mary contacts Peter and asks him to give her DBADM authority on TSTDB. Peter issues the following:

```
connect to TSTDB user peter using peterpsw
grant DBADM without DATAACCESS on database to user mary
```

ACCESSCTRL is granted by default when granting DBADM, so Mary is able to grant others access to objects. Now Mary tries the following:

```
connect to TSTDB user mary using marypsw
create table t1 (col1 int)
insert into t1 values (1)
select * from t1
```

Because Mary is DBADM, she can create a table in the database and insert into it. Because she created the table, she has full control on it, so she can also see the contents of the table when issuing a SELECT statement.

Because Mary has ACCESSCTRL, she can grant Tom CREATETAB as follows:

```
connect to TSTDB user mary using marypsw
grant CONNECT, CREATETAB, IMPLICIT_SCHEMA, BINDADD on database to user
tom
```

Now Tom issues the following:

```
connect to TSTDB user tom using tompsw
create table t2 (col1 int)
insert into t2 values (1)
select * from t2
```

Just like Mary, because Tom created table *T2*, he has full control on this table.

Now, let's see if Mary can read from *T2* (Tom's table):

```
connect to TSTDB user mary using marypsw
select * from tom.t2
```

```
SQL0551N  "MARY" does not have the required authorization or privilege
to perform operation "SELECT" on object "TOM.T2".  SQLSTATE=42501
```

This confirms that even though Mary is a DBADM, she is not allowed to see all the data in the database.

Finally, Mary can allow Tom to do anything he wants on her table *T1* using this statement:

```
connect to TSTDB user mary using marypsw
grant CONTROL on table t1 to tom
```

Tom can then try the following:

```
connect to TSTDB user tom using tompsw
insert into mary.t1 values (2),(3), (4), (5)
select * from mary.t1
```

All of this is successful, as expected.

Working with Data Encryption, Ownership Transfer, and Roles

A new company policy requires all data on transit to be encrypted to prevent eavesdropping. To do this, Mary updates the database manager authentication to DATA_ENCRYPT_CMP so that user IDs, passwords, and data are encrypted while on transit:

```
update dbm cfg using authentication DATA_ENCRYPT_CMP
```

She then stops and restarts the instance. Next, Mary configures each DB2 client using the following command. This assumes that the TCPIP node *dbsrv* had already been cataloged:

```
catalog db tstdb at node dbsrv authentication DATA_ENCRYPT
```

After a few months working in this environment, Tom quits the company, and Rob is hired as his replacement. Rob has a lot of problems accessing tables created by Tom, so Mary decides to transfer ownership of Tom's database objects to Rob. However, only a SECADM can do this, so she asks Peter to execute these commands:

```
connect to TSTDB user peter using peterpsw
transfer ownership of schema tom TO user rob preserve privileges
```

As months pass, more people join the team, and Mary and Peter find it challenging to manage security. One measure to simplify their administration is by using roles. Peter creates a role for testers and developers as follows:

```
connect to TSTDB user peter using peterpsw
create role tester
create role developer
grant select on table mary.t1 to role tester
grant update on table mary.t1 to role developer
```

When tester Amna and developer Bradley join the team, Peter issues these other two commands:

```
grant role tester to amna
grant role developer to bradley
```

When developer Bradley moves to a different position, Peter issues this command:

```
revoke role developer from bradley
```

At the same time, Amna is promoted from tester to developer, so Peter issues the following commands:

```
revoke role tester from amna
grant role developer to amna
```

Thus, the use of roles can help administrators manage security in their environments.

Working with RCAC

Peter feels very sick one day, but he has received approval from management to make Mary his backup. So Peter grants Mary SECADM:

```
connect to TSTDB user peter using peterpsw
grant SECADM on database to mary
```

Now Mary is both SECADM and DBADM. She has ACCESSCTRL, but not DATAACCESS.

To run tests that are more accurate to real-life scenarios, management would like to extract some data from the production database PRODDB and load it into the test database TSTDB. Specifically, you have to extract data from table EMPLOYEE, which has the following information.

FIRSTNAME	LASTNAME	SSN	SALARY
Meylin	Chong	111111111	50000
Isabelle	Chong	222222222	28000
Michael	Campodonico	333333333	35000
Marco	Zanforlin	444444444	70000

Mary is asked to perform this extraction, with the requirement that sensitive information such as Social Security Numbers (SSNs) are masked when accessed by anyone who is not part of the HR role. For this purpose, Mary creates the *EMPLOYEE* table in the TSTDB database and then loads the data. After loading the data she creates these two column masks:

```
connect to TSTDB user mary using marypsw;

create mask ssn_mask
  on employee
  for column SSN return
  case when verify_role_for_user(SESSION_USER, 'HR')= 1
       then SSN
       else
          'XXX-XX-' || substr(SSN,6,4)
   end
enable;


create mask salary_mask
  on employee
  for column salary return
  case when verify_role_for_user(SESSION_USER, 'HR')= 1
```

```
      then salary
      else
         NULL
   end
enable;
```

After Mary creates the masks, she tests but notices no changes. She then realizes she needs to activate RCAC for column access control. She issues

```
alter table employee activate column access control
```

When Mary tests this with the query:

```
select * from employee
```

she gets what is expected: Because she is not part of the HR role, she sees masked SSNs and the salary column containing only NULLs.

```
FIRSTNAME     LASTNAME         SSN              SALARY
-----------   ---------------  ------------     -------
Meylin        Chong            XXX-XX-1111           -
Isabelle      Chong            XXX-XX-2222           -
Michael       Campodonico      XXX-XX-3333           -
Marco         Zanforlin        XXX-XX-4444           -
```

Summary

This chapter introduced the DB2 security model. To connect to a DB2 database, user and password authentication is performed outside of DB2 using the security facility provided by the operating system of the DB2 server, by Kerberos, through customized security plug-ins or other external security facilities. Security plug-ins are loadable library modules that implement security mechanisms to be used for user authentication.

Setting the authentication type at the DB2 server and client determines where authentication takes place. At the DB2 server, authentication type is defined in the Database Manager Configuration file. DB2 clients specify an authentication type for each database it connects to when the database is being cataloged.

When a user is successfully authenticated, he or she must have appropriate database authorities and/or privileges before being able to perform database tasks and operations. Database authorities are required for a user to perform database administration tasks such as database creation or database backup.

Database privileges for various types of database objects are granted and revoked through the GRANT and REVOKE statements. The assignment and update of privileges are much simplified by granting privileges to roles instead of individual user IDs.

Label-Based Access Control (LBAC) lets you decide exactly who has read and write data access to individual rows and columns in tables. Row and Column Access Control (RCAC) provides similar security granularity as LBAC, but it also enables you to mask the data.

There are special considerations for a DB2 server on Windows configured in a Windows domain, for example, for local or global group lookup. DB2 enables you use the registry variable DB2_GRP_ LOOKUP to identify where the user is being enumerated for group resolution.

A trusted context is a database object that defines a trust relationship for a connection between the database and an external entity such as an application server. By using trusted contexts, the actual user's identity and database privileges are used for database requests performed by the middle tier on behalf of that user.

Review Questions

1. Where does DB2 store information about the users who can access DB2?

2. Besides performing user ID and password authentication at the DB2 server or DB2 client, what other authentication mechanisms does DB2 support?

3. When does a user need the BINDADD privilege on a database?

4. If *bob* is connected to a database and wants to create a table *foo* in the *ts1* table space, what privileges must he have to run the following statement?

   ```
   CREATE TABLE mary.foo (c1 INT, c2 INT) IN ts1
   ```

5. A user ID *bob* who is a member of operating system group *dba* is defined on the DB2 server. Why would the following fail to give SYSCTRL authority to user *bob*?

   ```
   update dbm cfg using sysctrl_group bob
   ```

6. In a Windows environment where a DB2 server is defined inside a domain called *dom-prod*, user ID *db2admin* is only defined in the domain controller as a member of the global group *glbgrp*. If you want to log on to the DB2 server as the domain user *dom-prod\db2admin* and perform tasks such as creating a new database, what are the three key steps you have to take?

7. You want to authenticate users at the clients. What are the three types of clients that the parameter TRUST_ALLCLNTS evaluates?

8. You have just created a database. Other than the members of the SYSADM group, you want to allow only *bob* to create new tables in the database. What DCL command do you have to issue?

9. *Mary* wrote an embedded SQL program with static SQL statements. A package is created and bound to the database. What privilege does *bob* need to use the package?

10. Given the following Database Manager Configuration parameters on your DB2 instance running on the Linux Server DBL1:

```
Database manager authentication        (AUTHENTICATION) = CLIENT
Trust all clients                      (TRUST_ALLCLNTS) = NO
Trusted client authentication          (TRUST_CLNTAUTH) = CLIENT
```

If you are connecting to the database from an untrusted client, where will authentication take place?

11. If you are connecting to a DB2 database on a UNIX server named DBX1 from a Linux client named DBL1, where will the user ID be authenticated by default?

   A. DBL1

   B. DBX1

   C. Both

   D. No authentication will be required

12. If you have configured DB2 with the authentication set to SERVER_ENCRYPT, which of the following describes what is encrypted?

   A. Data

   B. Data and user IDs

   C. User IDs and passwords

   D. Data, user IDs, and passwords

13. Given the following Database Manager Configuration parameters on your DB2 instance running on the Linux Server DBL1:

```
Database manager authentication        (AUTHENTICATION) = CLIENT
Trust all clients                      (TRUST_ALLCLNTS) = YES
Trusted client authentication          (TRUST_CLNTAUTH) = CLIENT
```

If you are connecting to the database from an untrusted client, where will authentication take place?

   A. The client

   B. The server

   C. Both

   D. None

14. Which two of the following DB2 authorities can select data from tables?

   A. SYSADM

   B. SYSCTRL

    C. SYSMAINT

    D. DBADM

    E. None of the above

15. Which of the following can be encrypted with DB2?

    A. User IDs

    B. Passwords

    C. All data

    D. User IDs, passwords, and data

16. Which of the following groups can create and drop event monitors?

    1. SYSADM

    2. SYSMON

    3. SYSCTRL

    4. SYSMAINT

17. Which of the following authorities cannot take a DB2 trace?

    A. SYSADM

    B. SYSMON

    C. SYSCTRL

    D. SYSMAINT

18. Given the following:

    • User1 grants CREATEIN privilege on the schema *foo* to Fred with grant option.

    • Joe grants CREATEIN privilege on the schema *foo* to Barney with grant option.

    • User1 revokes CREATEIN privilege on the schema *foo* from Fred.

    • Barney grants CREATEIN privilege on the schema *foo* to Wilma.

    • Wilma grants CREATEIN privilege on the schema *foo* to Betty.

Which of the following still have CREATEIN privilege on the schema *foo*?

    A. Barney

    B. Barney and Wilma

    C. Barney, Wilma, and Betty

    D. No one

19. Given the table space *tsp1* that is created with default options, which of the following sets of commands ensure only the group *grp1* can use the table space?

    A. GRANT USE OF TABLESPACE tsp1 TO grp1

    B. GRANT USER OF TABLESPACE tsp1 TO grp1 WITH GRANT OPTION

    C. REVOKE USE OF TABLESPACE FROM ALL, GRANT USE OF TABLESPACE tsp1 TO GRP1

    D. REVOKE USE OF TABLESPACE FROM PUBLIC, GRANT USE OF TABLESPACE tsp1 TO GRP1

20. If a DBA wants to find out whether user *bob* has CREATETAB privileges, which of the following system catalog tables should the DBA query?

    A. SYSCAT.TABAUTH

    B. SYSCAT.TABLES

    C. SYSCAT.DBAUTH

    D. SYSCAT.SCHEMAAUTH

21. Which of the following statements is true?

    A. RCAC is another name for LBAC

    B. RCAC controls access at the table space level

    C. LBAC uses row permissions and column masks to control access

    D. RCAC and LBAC are different security mechanisms to offer fine-grained access to your data

Understanding Concurrency and Locking

In a multiuser environment, a database system must ensure that data can be accessed concurrently by the users. Access should be granted while guaranteeing integrity of the data and good performance. For example, if three different users try to update the same row of data at the same time, how should the database system behave? DB2 utilizes locking mechanisms to handle such scenarios. A DB2 user can choose different locking behaviors depending on the needs of his application—an application that requires estimated values would have a different locking behavior than one that requires precise values. Locking behaviors are controlled in DB2 by using different isolation levels. DB2 uses four isolation levels. Choosing the appropriate isolation level dictates not only the behavior of how locks are taken and released, but also the level of concurrency supported. In this chapter we explore isolation levels, explain their differences, and provide some examples on how they can be used in an application. As a database administrator or an application developer, it is helpful to have troubleshooting skills to identify locking problems, and this chapter covers DB2 monitoring tools to do this.

In this chapter, you learn about

- The big picture of the DB2 locking mechanism
- Different concurrency scenarios
- The DB2 isolation levels
- How DB2 isolation levels affect locking
- Troubleshooting tools that identify locking problems
- Avoiding locking problems

DB2 Locking and Concurrency: The Big Picture

Figure 9.1 provides an overview of the DB2 locking mechanism using isolation levels. Isolation levels can be set by various methods. For example, you can specify the isolation level when you precompile a program or when you bind a package. These methods are illustrated at the top of the figure.

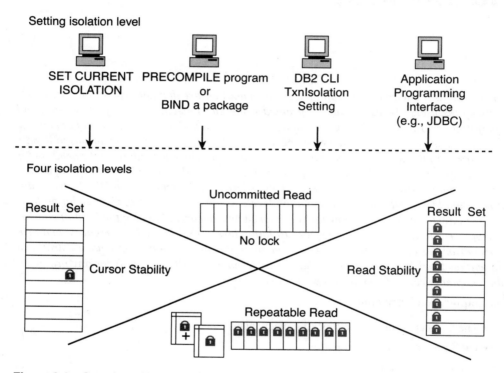

Figure 9.1   Overview of locking and concurrency

The bottom of the figure shows the four isolation levels. Depending on the isolation level specified, DB2 performs locking differently. The following sections discuss these in more detail.

Concurrency and Locking Scenarios

Like many other database systems, DB2 provides support for concurrent data access. While the database is being accessed and manipulated by multiple users, it is important to keep data integrity by using database locking. Before getting into detailed discussions about DB2 locking, you should first understand various concurrent data access scenarios you might encounter and how each DB2 isolation level can prevent these scenarios from occurring or allow these scenarios to occur, if desired.

Lost Updates

Assume there is an airline reservation system with multiple agents answering calls for seat reservations. A table called *RESERVATIONS* is defined to store flight numbers, seat assignments, and passenger names. Each seat on every flight is represented by a single row of data. Table 9.1 shows the *RESERVATIONS* table.

Table 9.1   Sample Content of the Reservations Table

Flight	Seat	Passenger_name
512	1C	John Smith
512	1D	Arnold Page
512	23A	Tim Chan
512	13B	Bernard Reid
512	4A	-

Suppose customer Harry Jones wants to reserve a seat on Flight 512 and calls the reservation center. An agent, Sam, receives the call and finds the only seat available, 4A, for Harry. While Harry is confirming the itinerary with his wife, Sam maintains the available seat on his screen. At this time, agent Mary is helping another customer, Billy Bee, to fulfill his request. Mary also finds 4A, the last seat on Flight 512.

Eventually, Harry decides to confirm the seat, and Sam assigns seat 4A to Harry. However, Mary does not see Harry's update, and she assigns the same seat to Billy. Both seat assignments are successful, but guess who gets the seat? If the list of seats is retrieved again, the second update overwrites the first one (see Table 9.2). Hence, Sam loses the seat assignment, and Harry doesn't get on the plane as he expects to.

Table 9.2   Sample Content of the Updated Reservations Table

Flight	Seat	Passenger_name
512	1C	John Smith
512	1D	Arnold Page
512	23A	Tim Chan
512	13B	Bernard Reid
512	4A	Billy Bee

This example demonstrates that if there is no mechanism in place to maintain the accuracy of data, it is possible to lose updates without knowing it or until the customers find out for themselves.

By default, DB2 acquires a lock on every record that the agent is updating. This default behavior cannot be changed. With this type of lock, no other agent can update the same row of data. If this reservation system is implemented in DB2, this scenario of lost update can never occur. When Sam is updating the record, all write operations to the same row of data wait until Sam's transaction is completed. Read operations might be allowed depending on the isolation level used. After Sam has committed the change, Mary sees the new seat assignment in her next data retrieval, so Billy cannot be assigned to the seat.

A few terms are introduced here that warrant some discussion. A **transaction** (also known as a **unit of work**) is a sequence of SQL statements that the database manager treats as a whole. Any reading from or writing to the database is performed in a transaction. At the end of a transaction, the application can COMMIT or ROLLBACK the changes. After you issue a COMMIT operation, changes are written to the database. A ROLLBACK operation causes the changes within the transaction to be rolled back.

> **NOTE**
>
> Transactions are discussed in more detail in Chapter 10, "Maintaining, Backing Up, and Recovering Data."

Uncommitted Reads

Using the same flight reservation example, assume Sam is updating a row to assign a seat. Because DB2 locks the row by default, no other agent can read or update the same record. Meanwhile, the manager wants to run a report to determine how many passengers are scheduled to fly on Flight 512. Assuming he just needs an estimate, he can use an application implemented to read uncommitted data. This way, the manager can run the report even if Sam has not completed his transaction. This type of read is called an **uncommitted read** or a **dirty read**. However, changes Sam makes are not guaranteed to be written to the database. Therefore, if he decides to roll back the changes, the manager gets a different result when running the report again.

Whether an uncommitted read is desireable or not, it is based on the application design. As you can imagine, applications with the ability to read uncommitted data can respond promptly because there is no need to acquire and wait for locks.

However, you must understand that the data retrieved is *not* committed data, which means that the data might not be the same the next time you query it.

Nonrepeatable Reads

Suppose Harry asks Sam to find an aisle seat on Flight 512. Sam issues a query and retrieves a list of available seats on the flight. Table 9.3 shows such a list where (the NULL value) in the *Passenger_name* column means the seat is not assigned.

Table 9.3   Available Seats on Flight 512

Flight	Seat	Passenger_name
512	5B	-
512	6E	-
512	8C	-
512	13E	-
512	15E	-

In this aircraft model, only C and D seats are aisle seats. There is only one aisle seat available on this flight, seat 8C. Before Sam reserves seat 8C for Harry, no lock is acquired on this row highlighted in Figure 9.4. At this time, Mary has assigned and committed the same aisle seat to another customer, Billy. When Sam is ready and tries to assign Seat 8C to Harry, the update fails because the seat is no longer available. If the same query is issued, Table 9.4 shows that seat 8C is no longer available.

Table 9.4   Updated Available Seats on Flight 512

Flight	Seat	Passenger_name
512	5B	-
512	6E	-
512	13E	-
512	15E	-

This is an example of a **nonrepeatable read** scenario for which a different result set is returned with the same query within the same transaction. To avoid this situation, all the rows returned from the result set, shown in Figure 9.4, should be locked. This way, no other user can update the rows currently being read until the transaction is completed. However, there will be a decrease in concurrency because of the extra locks being held.

Phantom Reads

A phantom read is similar to a nonrepeatable read: while rows currently read are not updatable or removable by another user, new rows *can* be inserted into the tables that fall under the query criteria.

The flight reservation application is designed in a way that all rows in a result set are locked. Due to the demand of this particular flight, the airline decides to upgrade the aircraft to a larger one so that more passengers can be served. Because more seats are added to the flight, the same query used before to obtain available seats now returns extra rows. If the aircraft upgrade is made in the middle of another query transaction, the next execution of the same query results in extra "phantom" rows. Depending on the situation, reading phantom rows might or might not be desirable with the application. To avoid this behavior, extra locking is required.

DB2 Isolation Levels

DB2 provides four isolation levels to control locking behavior. From the least restrictive isolation level to the highest these are

- Uncommitted read
- Cursor stability
- Read stability
- Repeatable read

These isolation levels use different locking strategies, so you can choose the level of data protection depending on the application design.

Uncommitted Reads

Uncommitted read (UR) is the lowest isolation level but provides the highest concurrency to the database applications. When you configure an application to perform uncommitted reads, the application does not acquire any row locks to read data. However, a nonrestrictive table lock is required (see the section, "DB2 Locking," for more information). Because no row locks are acquired, there is no conflict with any read or write operations undergoing on the same data. With this isolation level, uncommitted reads, nonrepeatable reads, and phantom reads can occur.

Figure 9.2 shows an example of two applications accessing the same row. Assume that App A locks row 2 for an update operation. No other application can make changes to row 2 until App A commits or rolls back. However, an uncommitted read is a valid concurrent operation that can be issued against row 2 as illustrated by App B.

No row lock is acquired for read operations for applications configured with the UR isolation level. For any update, insert, or delete operation, an application with UR still holds locks obtained to perform these operations until the transaction is committed or rolled back. App C in Figure 9.2 illustrates this.

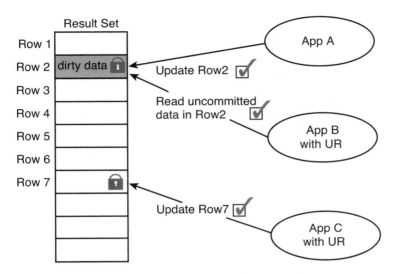

Figure 9.2 Concurrent data access with the uncommitted read isolation level

Cursor Stability

Cursor stability (CS) is the default DB2 isolation level. This isolation level works well with most applications because it uses a degree of locking sufficient to protect data, and at the same time it also provides a high level of concurrency. As the name of this isolation level implies, it uses a mechanism to provide a stable read on the latest row accessed. DB2 only locks the row currently being read.

A cursor can be viewed as a pointer to one row in a set of rows (also called a **result set**). You need to OPEN the cursor so that it is positioned just before the first row of the result set. To move the cursor to the next row, you execute a FETCH operation. As a best practice, you should CLOSE the cursor when it is no longer required.

Cursor stability has two behaviors depending on the setting of the db cfg parameter *currently committed* (CUR_COMMIT):

- Cursor stability without currently committed (CS without CC)
- Cursor stability with currently committed (CS with CC)

Figure 9.3 summarizes how contention is handled when two operations are accessing the same row using isolation CS without CC or CS with CC.

blocks	CS without CC		CS with CC (default)	
	Reader	Writer	Reader	Writer
Reader	No	Maybe	No	No
Writer	Yes	Yes	No	Yes

Figure 9.3   Comparing isolation-level CS without CC and with CC

In the figure, when using CS without CC:

- A reader (SELECT statement) does not block another reader but can block a writer (UPDATE statement).
- A writer blocks both a reader and another writer.

When using CS with CC:

- A reader does not block another reader nor a writer.
- A writer does not block a reader, but it blocks another writer.

A simple inspection of this table can tell you that CS with CC allows for more concurrency in your application. We explain each of the two behaviors in more detail in the next sections.

> **NOTE**
>
> Cursor stability with currently committed enabled (CS with CC) is the default DB2 isolation level.

Cursor Stability with Currently Committed Disabled

When CUR_COMMIT is OFF, currently committed behavior is disabled. This was the default behavior prior to DB2 9.7 or if the database is upgraded from DB2 9.7. In this situation, the CS isolation level is more restrictive. For example, a read operation could block an update operation from happening.

When a cursor is opened, no lock is acquired until the application fetches the first row of the result set. In the same unit of work, if the application fetches the second row, DB2 releases the previous row lock and acquires a lock on the second row. In Figure 9.3, App A with a CS isolation level fetches row 2. This application only locks the row it is reading—row 2. When App D tries to alter that particular row, it has to wait.

In Figure 9.4 App B holds a lock on row 7 for read (fetching). At the same time, App C obtains a share lock and can still read the same row. Therefore, with isolation-level CS, concurrent reads are still possible.

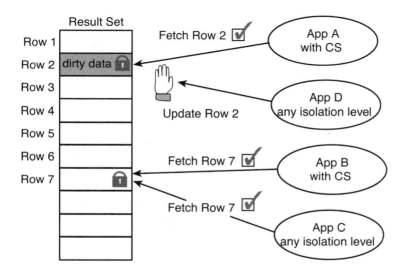

Figure 9.4 Concurrent read with two applications in cursor stability isolation level

Now you understand that a row lock is released when the application with CS reads the next row. But what happens if the application makes changes to a row while it is being read? Figure 9.5 illustrates this scenario.

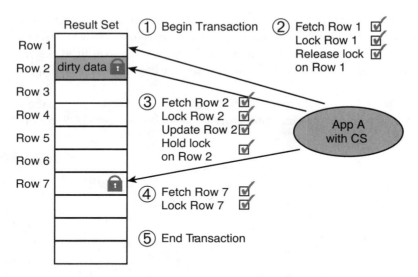

Figure 9.5   Reading and updating data with cursor stability isolation level

1. App A uses CS isolation level and starts a transaction.

2. App A locks row 1 for read. App A releases the lock on row 1 when it fetches row 2.

3. Row 2 is locked. During the read, App A decides to update the row. The lock is held until the current transaction is completed.

4. App A fetches row 7 and acquires a lock. At this point App A holds two locks: one for read of row 7 and one for update of row 2.

5. The current transaction is completed, and all locks are released.

Cursor Stability with Currently Committed Enabled

When CUR_COMMIT is ON, currently committed behavior is enabled. In this situation, the CS isolation level allows for more concurrency. For example, a read operation would not block an update operation from happening. If we look again at Figure 9.4, the figure would look exactly the same in this scenario, with the exception that App D would be allowed to update the row.

Likewise in Figure 9.5, in (3), when App A is performing the update on row 2, no other application could read the row. The reasoning behind this was that because the update is making changes to the row, a reader should wait until the update is finished to see the final committed value. With currently commit enabled, however, a reader can read the row. You might be wondering which value would be retrieved? The answer lies in the name of this parameter "currently committed." Any application performing a read would access the currently committed value. Following is an example to make this clearer.

Let's say you have a table called *EMPLOYEE* as shown in Table 9.5

Table 9.5   Table EMPLOYEE—Example of Cursor Stability with Currently Committed Semantics Behavior

FIRSTNAME	DEPARTMENT
Raul	Development
Clara	Planning

Say Raul changes departments and is now working in Sales. To reflect this change, App A is run with an UPDATE statement like this but does not commit:

```
UPDATE employee SET department = 'Sales' WHERE firstname = 'Raul'
```

Now say App B tries to read from this same row using this statement:

```
SELECT department FROM employee WHERE firstname = 'Raul' WITH CS
```

If currently committed were disabled, App B would wait on this statement until App A committed the update. However, with currently committed, this SELECT statement would actually return a value right away. Would it be Sales or Development? Because App A did not commit the change, Sales is not a committed value. The currently committed value is still Development ; therefore App B would return Development.

DB2 gives you the choice of what behavior your application should have. If you feel returning the currently committed value is not appropriate for your application, disable this feature.

Note that even though CS is the default isolation level, in the SELECT statement we used WITH CS for clarity. We discuss this clause in more detail later on in this chapter.

How is isolation CS with CC different than isolation UR for a SELECT? Isolation UR would return the uncommitted value. In the previous example, if App B tries this statement:

```
SELECT department FROM employee WHERE firstname = 'Raul' WITH UR
```

Because UR isolation is used, the value returned would be Sales, which is the uncommitted value.

Using isolation-level CS, nonrepeatable read and phantom read scenarios can still occur; however, the uncommitted read scenario is not possible.

For example, in the case where App A is performing DELETE operations that are not committed, and App B performs a SELECT that would access the rows that were deleted, by default the SELECT would not show the rows that were deleted. Therefore, the nonrepeatable read problem is still possible.

Similarly, in the case where App A is performing INSERT operations that are not committed, and App B performs a SELECT that would access the rows that were inserted, by default, the SELECT shows the new rows. Therefore, the phantom read problem is still possible.

Read Stability

Read stability (RS) is another isolation level DB2 uses to protect data. Unlike CS, RS not only locks the current row that is being fetched; it also applies the appropriate locks to all rows that are in the result set. This ensures that within the same transaction, rows that have been previously read cannot be altered by other applications.

Figure 9.6 shows that all the rows in the result set are locked even when the cursor is only processing a particular row. No wait is necessary if more than one application reads the same set of rows concurrently. However, any update operation must wait until the reads are completed. For example, in the figure you can see App A, App B, and App C can all perform read (fetch) operations on the result set. However, App D has to wait because it is trying to perform an update operation on row 2.

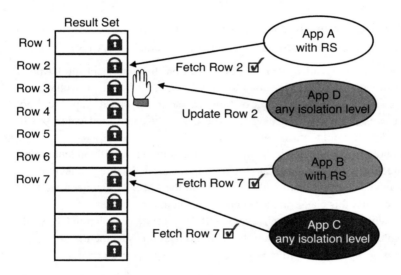

Figure 9.6   The read stability isolation level

RS causes DB2 to perform more locking than the UR or CS isolation levels. With RS, the uncommitted read and nonrepeatable read scenarios cannot occur; however, phantom reads can still happen.

Similar to the other isolation levels, if an application with RS updates a row, a lock is held until the transaction is completed.

Repeatable Reads

Repeatable read (RR) is the highest and most restrictive isolation level. It also gives you the lowest concurrency. Similar to RS, applications with RR force DB2 to lock all the rows in the result set as well as rows that are accessed to build the result set. For example, in a query that involves a two-table join, if DB2 decides to perform table scans on both tables to obtain the result, DB2 would lock all the rows in the two tables. If a row is read by the application using RR, no other application can alter it until the transaction is completed. This ensures that your result set is consistent throughout the duration of the unit of work. One consideration is that the additional locking can greatly reduce concurrency.

In Figure 9.7, you can see that behavior for applications A, B, C, and D is the same as RS. However, even if App E tries to update a row in table *T1* that is not in the result set, it still has to wait until the lock is released.

With repeatable read isolation level, none of the locking scenarios can occur. Applications with RR can only read committed data and perform repeatable read.

Table 9.6 summarizes the four isolation levels and locking scenarios that can occur.

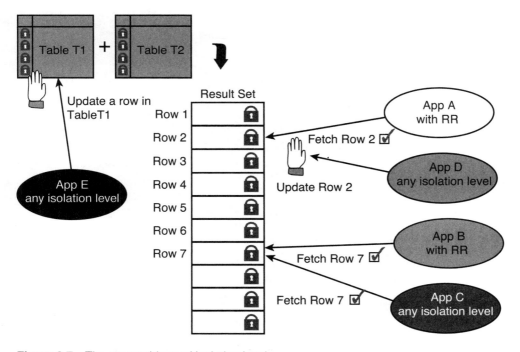

Figure 9.7 The repeatable read isolation level

Table 9.6   Four Isolation Levels and Locking Scenarios

Locking Scenarios	Uncommitted Read	Cursor Stability	Read Stability	Repeatable Read
Lost update	No	No	No	No
Uncommitted read	Yes	No	No	No
Nonrepeatable read	Yes	Yes	No	No
Phantom read	Yes	Yes	Yes	No

Changing Isolation Levels

The isolation level is not bound to a database. Each application and statements within an application can use a different isolation level so that a different locking mechanism can be applied. Isolation levels can be set at different levels:

- Session level
- Application level
- Statement level

The following sections describe each of these levels.

Using the DB2 Command Window

The current isolation level for any dynamic SQL statement issued within the current session is stored in a DB2 special register called CURRENT ISOLATION.

To obtain the current isolation level value, connect to the database and issue either of these statements:

```
VALUES CURRENT ISOLATION
SELECT CURRENT ISOLATION FROM sysibm.sysdummy1
```

The following are the possible values:

- UR (uncommitted read)
- CS (cursor stability)
- RS (read stability)
- RR (repeatable read)
- Blank (means that the default isolation level is used)

To change the isolation level, use the SET CURRENT ISOLATION statement. Listing 9.1 shows the syntax diagram for this statement.

Listing 9.1   Syntax Diagram for the SET CURRENT ISOLATION Command

```
       .-CURRENT-.                    .-=-.
>>-SET--+---------+---ISOLATION--+---+--+--+-UR----+---------------><
                                        +-CS----+
                                        +-RR----+
                                        +-RS----+
                                        '-RESET-'
```

Figure 9.8 demonstrates a few examples of how to set and obtain the current isolation level.

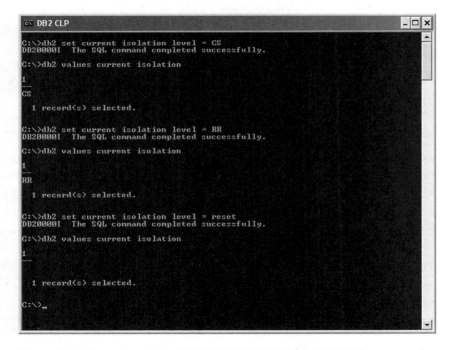

Figure 9.8   Examples of the SET CURRENT ISOLATION LEVEL command

It is important to understand that changes to this DB2 register affect only the current session. Subsequent dynamic SQL statements executed in this session use this isolation level. The change only applies for dynamic SQL statements. For static SQL statements or packages, you can control the isolation level through the DB2 `bind` command discussed in the next section.

Using the DB2 precompile and bind Commands

To execute an SQL statement, it must be compiled into an executable form that DB2 understands. This executable form of a statement is known as the **data access plan**. Data access plans are stored in database objects called **packages**.

Data access plans for dynamic SQL statements are created at execution time. DB2 uses the most current table and index statistics, configuration parameters, and DB2 register settings (such as `CURRENT ISOLATION`) to evaluate and generate the most optimal plan.

When an application with static SQL statements is precompiled, the prepared statements are stored in a bind file generated by the DB2 precompiler. To create the database access plan from the bind file, you need to invoke the bind utility. The utility takes the bind file as input, creates a package that contains the data access plan, and binds it to the database.

Both the DB2 `precompile` and `bind` commands enable you to specify some characteristics of how the package should be executed, like the query optimization level, use of row blocking, and the isolation level. For example, if you want to precompile or bind a package using a nondefault isolation level, use

```
precompile appfile.sqc isolation RR
```

or

```
bind bindfilename.bnd isolation RR
```

where *appfile.sqc* is an embedded C program containing static SQL, and *bindfilename.bnd* is a bind file containing SQL in internal format that is to be bound into a package.

When the package is bound, you can use the system catalog tables or IBM Data Studio to find out the isolation level specified.

Using the system catalog tables, you can issue the following query:

```
SELECT pkgschema, pkgname, isolation FROM syscat.packages
```

Using IBM Data Studio, from the Database Administration perspective, navigate to the folders Instance_name > Database_name > Application Objects > Packages. You should see the isolation level column on the right panel, as shown in Figure 9.9. For example, the package highlighted in the figure was bound with isolation-level CS.

Using the DB2 Call Level Interface

The DB2 call level interface (CLI) is the IBM callable SQL interface to DB2 database servers. It is a C/C++ application programming interface (API) for database access. If your application is using the DB2 CLI API, you can also set the isolation level with the CLI setting.

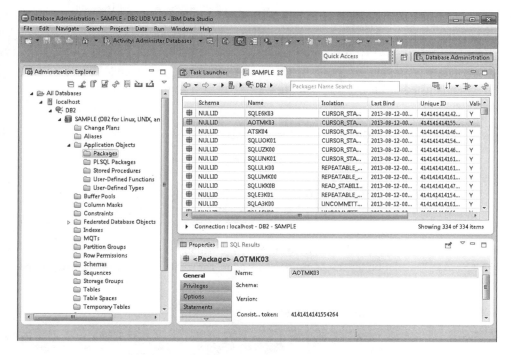

Figure 9.9   Using IBM Data Studio to retrieve the isolation level of packages

At the DB2 client, update the DB2 CLI initialization file (*db2cli.ini*). This text file is typically located at the DB2 install directory. Insert *TxnIsolation* under the database name you want and enter the isolation level you want to use. Each isolation level is identified by a number (see Table 9.7). The following example shows how to set the isolation for the SAMPLE database to repeatable read:

```
[SAMPLE]
DBALIAS=SAMPLE
TXNIsolation=8
```

Table 9.7   DB2 CLI Values for the Isolation Levels

	Uncommitted Read	Cursor Stability	Read Stability	Repeatable Read
TXNIsolation Value	1	2	4	8

Using the Application Programming Interface

In addition to CLI, DB2 provides various types of programming interfaces that your application can use. The Java Common Client for DB2 is one example. Most APIs such as Java Database Connectivity (JDBC) provide an option to specify the isolation level. A code snippet from a JDBC program is listed in Listing 9.2. For other APIs, check with the associated programming documentations.

Listing 9.2   Snippet of a JDBC Program to Specify an Isolation Level

```
Class.forName("com.ibm.db2.jcc.DB2Driver");
Connection con=null;
con = DriverManager.getConnection (jdbc:db2:sample,username,password);
con.setTransactionIsolation(TRANSACTION_READ_UNCOMMITTED);
```

The names of the isolation levels used in APIs are usually different from those used in DB2. JDBC and DB2 isolation level mappings are listed in Table 9.8. For other APIs, refer to the documentation.

Table 9.8   Comparable JDBC and DB2 Isolation Levels

JDBC	DB2
TRANSACTION_READ_UNCOMMITTED	Uncommitted read
TRANSACTION_READ_COMMITTED	Cursor stability
TRANSACTION_REPEATABLE_READ	Read stability
TRANSACTION_SERIALIZABLE	Repeatable read

Working with Statement Level Isolation Level

So far, you have seen that isolation level can be set for a connection. To provide more granular concurrency control, DB2 has the ability to specify isolation level at the statement level.

Suppose an application has started a transaction with CS isolation level. To increase concurrency of a particular statement, you want the statement to be executed with RR isolation level. To do so, use the isolation clause WITH RR:

```
UPDATE employee SET salary = 10000 WHERE empno='000010' WITH RR
```

Similarly, you can apply the WITH clause to the INSERT, DELETE, and SELECT statements. Note that the WITH clause cannot be used in subqueries. The same clause in the SELECT statement has an extra option for the RR and RS isolation level. Listing 9.3 shows the syntax diagram of the SELECT statement's isolation clause.

Listing 9.3   Syntax Diagram of the SELECT Statement's Isolation Clause

```
>>-+---------------------------------------+-----------------><
   '-WITH--+-RR--+----------------------+-+-'
          |       '-lock-request-clause-' |
          +-RS--+----------------------+-+
          |       '-lock-request-clause-' |
          +-CS------------------------+
          '-UR------------------------'
lock-request-clause:

>>-USE AND KEEP--+-SHARE-----+--LOCKS------------------------><
                +-UPDATE----+
                '-EXCLUSIVE-'
```

The `lock-request-clause` is optional and specifies the type of lock that DB2 will acquire and hold. The owner of a SHARE lock can read the row being locked. Concurrent processes can read the data in the locked object and can update it. The owner of an UPDATE lock can update the row being locked. Concurrent processes can only read the data in the locked object but cannot update it. EXCLUSIVE lock, on the other hand, is a more restrictive type of lock. It does not allow concurrent processes to acquire any lock on the data.

A SELECT statement with the isolation clause looks similar to the following:

```
SELECT empno, lastname, firstnme
  FROM employee
 WHERE deptno='A01'
  WITH RR USE AND KEEP EXCLUSIVE LOCKS
```

DB2 Locking

DB2 uses various levels of locking to provide concurrent data access and at the same time protect the data. Depending on the operations requested, the database manager can acquire locks on table rows, table blocks, tables, table spaces, buffer pools, and databases. Locks are acquired implicitly by DB2 according to the semantics defined by the isolation level.

> **NOTE**
>
> Table blocks are groups of records that block-based indexes point to. These block-based indexes are called multidimensional clustering (MDC) indexes.

Lock Attributes

This section explains the different objects that can be locked and the different lock modes.

DB2 can apply locks at different levels:

- Database (use the CONNECT statement)
- Table space (use the QUIESCE statement)
- Table (use the LOCK TABLE statement)
- Row (set by the isolation level)

You can explicitly lock a database, table space, and a table using the appropriate DB2 commands or statements. At the row level DB2 implicitly acquires and releases the locks for you based on the isolation level of your application.

To explicitly lock a database, use the CONNECT statement with the appropriate lock mode. For example:

```
CONNECT TO sample IN EXCLUSIVE MODE
```

This causes an exclusive lock to be applied to the database. It prevents concurrent applications from executing any operations at the database.

This lock mode is useful when exclusive administrative tasks must be performed. You can also connect to the database in SHARE MODE, which enables other concurrent connections to the database but prevents other users from connecting in exclusive mode.

> **NOTE**
>
> When you need to perform exclusive administrative tasks at the instance, rather than the database level, use the start database manager admin mode command as explained in Chapter 5, "Understanding the DB2 Environment, DB2 Instances, and Databases."

Table spaces for a particular table can be quiesced. **Quiescing** a table space is like locking a table space so that administrative tasks (for example, a load operation) can be performed. There are three quiesce modes, and their names explain how restrictive they are: Share, Intent to Update, and Exclusive. Depending on the quiesce mode selected, DB2 obtains different types of locks for the table and its associated table space(s). The syntax diagram of the QUIESCE TABLESPACES FOR TABLE command is presented in Listing 9.4.

Listing 9.4   Syntax Diagram of the Quiesce Table Spaces for Table Command

```
>>-QUIESCE TABLESPACES FOR TABLE--+-tablename-------+--------->
                                  '-schema.tablename-'


>--+-SHARE-----------+------------------------------------><
```

```
+-INTENT TO UPDATE-+
+-EXCLUSIVE--------+
'-RESET-----------'
```

If you have quiesced the table spaces with a restrictive mode, access to tables within those table spaces is not allowed. For example, this command

```
QUIESCE TABLESPACES FOR TABLE employee EXCLUSIVE
```

puts strict table space locking on the table space where table *EMPLOYEE* is stored and on the table *EMPLOYEE*. The state of the table space changes to QUIESCED EXCLUSIVE. No other access to the table spaces is allowed. This means that access to another table that is stored in the same table space is not allowed. You will receive the following error.

```
SQL0290N Table space access is not allowed SQLSTATE=55039
```

To unquiesce the table space, issue the same QUIESCE TABLESPACES FOR TABLE command but with the RESET option.

You can also lock a table explicitly with the LOCK TABLE statement. Similarly, different lock modes are available as shown in Listing 9.5. The LOCK TABLE statement locks the specified table until the transaction is completed.

Listing 9.5 Syntax Diagram of the LOCK TABLE Statement

```
>>-LOCK TABLE--+-table-name-+---IN--+-SHARE-----+--MODE--------><
               '-nickname---'        '-EXCLUSIVE-'
```

During normal data manipulation processing, DB2 uses row-level locking by default. You can override this rule to acquire table-level locking instead. The ALTER TABLE statement with the LOCKSIZE option forces DB2 to obtain a table level lock whenever the table is accessed. The statement looks like this:

```
ALTER TABLE employee LOCKSIZE TABLE
```

This setting is retained until you execute

```
ALTER TABLE employee LOCKSIZE ROW
```

Each lockable object can be locked in a different mode; this represents the type of access allowed for the lock owner. Different lock modes also control the type of access permitted for concurrent users of the locked object. This is explained in more detail in the next sections.

Table-Level Lock Modes

Table and row locks are the most common types of locks used. Figure 9.10 shows the table-level lock modes. The table lock modes IN, IS, IX, and SIX are used to support row-level locking. An application requires an IN lock on the table before it can perform an uncommitted read. The IS,

IX, and SIX locks permit row-level locking while preventing more exclusive locks on the table by other applications.

The other table lock modes—S, U, X, and Z—are strict table locking and do not use row-level locking. For example, if an application holds an X lock on a table, the lock owner can read or update any data in the table but cannot obtain a row lock. Refer to Table 9.10 for a summary of all table lock modes.

Table Lock Mode	Description	
IN	Intent **N**one	Row locking also used
IS	Intent **S**hare	Row locking also used
IX	Intent e**X**clusive	Row locking also used
SIX	**S**hare with **I**ntent e**X**clusive	Row locking also used
S	**S**hare	Strict table locking
U	**U**pdate	Strict table locking
X	e**X**clusive	Strict table locking
Z	Superexclusive	Strict table locking

Figure 9.10 Table lock mode compatibility chart

Row Lock Modes

Row lock modes require support of some kind of table lock. The minimum table locks DB2 must acquire before obtaining a row lock are listed in Table 9.9. For example, an application can lock a row in Share mode if it also holds an IS lock on the table.

Besides table and row locks, there are other types of objects DB2 locks. Table 9.10 presents a summary of lockable objects and lock modes. A *Y* means that the lock mode applies to that type of object; a dash means that it does not apply.

Table 9.9 Row Lock Mode Compatibility Chart

Row Lock Mode	Description	Minimum Table Lock Required
S	**S**hare	IS
U	**U**pdate	IX
X	e**X**clusive	IX
W	**W**eak Exclusive	IX

Row Lock Mode	Description	Minimum Table Lock Required
NS	Next Key Share	IS
NW	Next Key Weak exclusive	IX

Table 9.10 Lock Modes Summary

Lock Mode	Buffer Pool	Table Space	Table Block	Table	Row	Description
IN (Intent None)	–	Y	Y	Y	–	The lock owner can read any data in the object, including uncommitted data, but cannot update any of it. Other concurrent applications can read or update the table.
IS (Intent Share)	–	Y	Y	Y	–	The lock owner can read data in the locked object but cannot update its data. Other applications can read or update the object.
NS (Next Key Share)	–	–	–	–	Y	The lock owner and all concurrent applications can read but not update the locked row. This lock is acquired on rows of a table where the isolation level of the application is either RS or CS. NS lock mode is not used for next-key locking. It is used instead of S mode during CS and RS scans to minimize the impact of next-key locking on these scans.
S (Share)	–	–	Y	Y	Y	The lock owner and all concurrent applications can read but not update the locked data.
IX (Intent eXclusive)	–	Y	Y	Y	–	The lock owner and concurrent applications can read and update data. Other concurrent applications can both read and update the table.

Lock Mode	Buffer Pool	Table Space	Table Block	Table	Row	Description
SIX (**S**hare with **I**ntent e**X**clusive)	–	–	Y	Y	–	The lock owner can read and update data. Other concurrent applications can read the table.
U (**U**pdate)	–	–	Y	Y	Y	The lock owner can update data. Other units of work can read the data in the locked object but cannot update it.
NW (**N**ext Key **W**eak Exclusive)	–	–	–	–	Y	When a row is inserted into an index, an NW lock is acquired on the next row. The lock owner can read but not update the locked row. This lock mode is similar to an X lock, except that it is also compatible with W and NS locks.
X (e**X**clusive)	Y	–	Y	Y	Y	The lock owner can both read and update data in the locked object. Only uncommitted read applications can access the locked object.
W (**W**eak Exclusive)	–	–	–	–	Y	This lock is acquired on the row when a row is inserted into a table. The lock owner can change the locked row. This lock is used during insertion into a unique index to determine if a duplicate value is found. This lock is similar to an X lock except that it is compatible with the NW lock. Only uncommitted read applications can access the locked row.

Lock Mode	Buffer Pool	Table Space	Table Block	Table	Row	Description
Z (Super Exclusive)	–	Y	–	Y	–	This lock is acquired on a table in certain conditions, such as when the table is altered or dropped, an index on the table is created or dropped, and for some types of table reorganization. No other concurrent application can read or update the table.

Figures 9.11 and 9.12 (from the DB2 Information Center) present lock mode compatibility charts for table and row locks, respectively. NO means the requesting application must wait for the lock to be released, and YES means the lock can be granted.

Mode of Lock for App A \ Mode of Lock for App B	IN	IS	S	IX	SIX	U	X	Z
IN	YES	YES	YES	YES	YES	YES	YES	NO
IS	YES	YES	YES	YES	YES	YES	NO	NO
IX	(YES)	(YES)	NO	(YES)	NO	NO	NO	NO
S	YES	YES	YES	NO	NO	YES	NO	NO
SIX	YES	YES	NO	NO	NO	NO	NO	NO
U	YES	YES	YES	NO	NO	NO	NO	NO
X	YES	NO	NO	NO	NO	NO	NO	NO
Z	NO	NO	NO	NO	NO	NO	NO	NO

Figure 9.11 Table lock mode compatibility chart

Mode of Lock for App A \ Mode of Lock for App B	S	U	X	W	NS	NW
S	YES	YES	NO	NO	YES	NO
U	(YES)	NO	NO	NO	(YES)	NO
X	NO	NO	NO	NO	NO	NO
W	NO	NO	NO	NO	NO	YES
NS	YES	YES	NO	NO	YES	YES
NW	NO	NO	NO	YES	YES	NO

Figure 9.12   Row lock mode compatibility chart

Let's use an example to demonstrate how to use the charts. Assume that Application A is holding an IX lock on a table. Looking at the compatibility chart in Figure 9.11, you can see that another application can only lock the same table in IN, IS, or IX mode as highlighted with the circles in the figure.

If Application B requests an IS lock at the table level and tries to read some rows in the table, use the row lock chart in Figure 9.12 to determine the compatibility of concurrent data access. As long as Application A holds locks that are compatible with the lock mode Application B is requesting, both applications can work concurrently with each other. For example, if application A is holding a U lock on a row, application B can only obtain an S or NS lock (refer to compatibility values circled in Figure 9.12). Otherwise, Application B must wait for Application A to complete its transaction.

Lock Waits

A discussion of DB2 locking mechanisms is not really complete if lock wait and deadlock scenarios are not covered. As the number of concurrent applications increases, the possibility of running into situations with incompatible locks is relatively higher. In the examples used to describe the behavior of the different isolation levels, you saw how an application might have to wait for a lock. This is known as **lock wait**. Deadlocks are discussed in the next section.

It is generally not possible to totally avoid lock wait as concurrency increases. After all, DB2 relies on the locking mechanism to keep data integrity. However, you should minimize lock waits and each wait length as much as possible. They put a hold on processing the statements, hence, they affect performance.

Note that you should minimize lock waits and the duration of each wait. You can use the database configuration parameter called LOCKTIMEOUT to define how long an application is going to wait for a lock. By default, LOCKTIMEOUT is set to -1, which stands for infinite wait. We recommend setting it to a finite number that works well with your application and business requirement.

If an application reaches the LOCKTIMEOUT value, it receives the following message:

```
SQL0911N The current transaction has been rolled back because of a
deadlock or timeout.  Reason code "68".
```

Reason code "68" indicates the transaction is rolled back due to a lock timeout. LOCK-TIMEOUT applies to any application connecting to the database. In some cases, you might want to set the timeout duration for a given application rather than providing the same value for all applications. You can directly control how long an individual application waits for a lock using the set current lock timeout command. This command overrides the LOCKTIMEOUT parameter and stores the new value in the DB2 special register CURRENT LOCK TIMEOUT. This would be useful, for example, in a system where there is a mixed workload of long-running reports as well as update batch jobs. Listing 9.6 gives the syntax of the command.

Listing 9.6   Syntax Diagram of the Set Current Lock Timeout Command

```
        .-CURRENT-.                    .-=-.
>>-SET--+---------+--LOCK TIMEOUT--+---+----------------------->

>--+-WAIT------------------------+---------------------------><
   +-NOT WAIT------------------+
   +-NULL---------------------+
   | .-WAIT-.                 |
   +-+------+--integer-constant-+
   '-host-variable-------------'
```

You can set the lock timeout period to the following:

- WAIT specifies that the application waits infinitely for a lock.
- NOT WAIT specifies that the application does not wait for locks that cannot be obtained.
- NULL specifies that the application uses the value of the LOCKTIMEOUT database configuration parameter as the duration to wait for locks.
- WAIT integer_constant specifies an integer value of how long (in seconds) the application waits for a lock. The value -1 has the same behavior as WAIT (without an integer value). A value of 0 is equivalent to specifying NOT WAIT.

To review the value of the CURRENT LOCK TIMEOUT special register, you can use the VALUES statement:

VALUES CURRENT LOCK TIMEOUT

Deadlocks

Deadlock is a situation when two applications are waiting for locks that the other is holding. This is another undesirable lock scenario to avoid. Consider the situation illustrated in Figure 9.13.

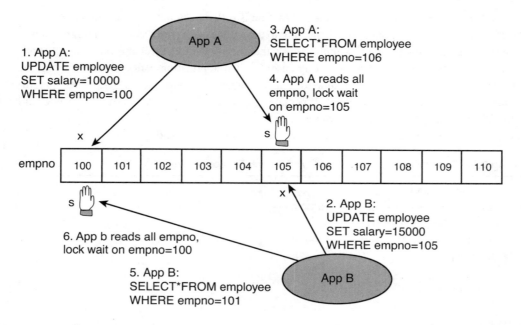

Figure 9.13   Example of a deadlock situation

1. App A starts a transaction and updates the record where *empno* = 100. The record is locked by App A with an X lock.

2. App B starts a transaction and updates the record where *empno* = 105. The record is locked by App B with an X lock.

3./4. In the same transaction as (1), App A queries the table and scans for *empno* = 106. Assume that DB2 chooses to use a table scan to read each *empno* and see if it is 106. To perform a read, App A needs an S lock on every row. An S lock cannot be obtained for *empno* = 105 because the row is locked by App B with an incompatible lock, X.

5./6. Similarly, App B is executing the same program to search for *empno* = 101. Assume that it also has to scan all the rows. App B stops and wait for *empno* = 100 that is being locked by App A.

Apps A and B in this example now encounter a deadlock situation. DB2 has a deadlock detector running around the clock to identify any deadlock. After one is detected, it randomly picks a victim and rolls back its transaction. By rolling back, all the locks that particular application is holding are released. This enables the other application that is involved in the deadlock to complete its processing.

The application that got rolled back receives the message

```
SQL0911N The current transaction has been rolled back because of a
deadlock or timeout.  Reason code "2".
```

Reason code "2" means that the transaction is rolled back due to a deadlock. The failed user application is then responsible to report the error and retry the transaction if necessary.

The deadlock detector is activated periodically as determined by the DLCHKTIME database configuration parameter. The default value for this parameter is 10,000 milliseconds (10 seconds).

To avoid deadlocks or any unnecessary lock waits, you need to understand your application. Design the application and tune the database in a way that the application only reads the data it requires. Going back to Figure 9.13 where two applications are manipulating data on different rows, why would they still encounter a deadlock? The key to this particular problem is that DB2 scans every *empno* value to see if the row qualifies the queries. If only a portion of the values are scanned, the applications might not run into a deadlock. This can be achieved by creating proper indexes and maintaining current database statistics so DB2 can choose a more efficient data access plan. Using the appropriate isolation level, for example, CS with CC might also help resolve deadlock situations.

A deadlock might still occur even with proper indexing and database maintenance. In such scenarios, consider enabling lock deferral as discussed in the next section.

Lock Deferral

You can enable lock deferral for CS or RS isolation level scans with the DB2_EVALUNCOMMIT-TED registry variable. With lock deferral, DB2 can evaluate the row before trying to lock it. To enable this feature issue the command

```
db2set DB2_EVALUNCOMMITTED=ON
```

To disable it issue

```
db2set DB2_EVALUNCOMMITTED=
```

Figure 9.14 shows that lock deferral no longer requires App A to put an S lock on *empno* = 105. App A can then read the *empno* = 106 row. Similar logic applies to App B.

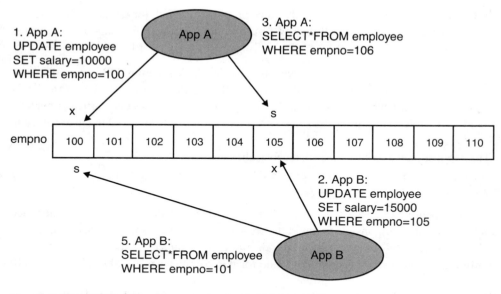

Figure 9.14   Deadlock problem resolved with EVALUNCOMMITTED enabled

To also skip all uncommitted deleted rows and uncommitted inserted rows, you should also set both the DB2_SKIPDELETED and DB2_SKIPINSERTED registry variables to ON.

```
db2set DB2_SKIPDELETED=ON
db2set DB2_SKIPINSERTED=ON
```

Lock Escalation

When DB2 acquires a lock on an object, it allocates memory for each lock from the database shared memory area called the **locklist**. A tunable database configuration parameter by the same name lets you indicate the maximum storage allowed for locks in each database. To resize the locklist, update the LOCKLIST parameter with a new value in units of 4K.

Regardless of the type of lock, each lock uses about 36 bytes of memory on 32-bit DB2 instances and 56 bytes of memory on 64-bit DB2 instances. As the number of locks being held by all applications connected to the database increases, it is possible that the locklist will get full. When this happens, DB2 attempts to free memory by allocating a table lock and releasing the row locks. This internal operation is called **lock escalation**.

Lock escalation degrades performance because it can significantly reduce database concurrency. When you monitor your database, you should ideally see very few to no escalations. It is important to tune the LOCKLIST parameter appropriately so that lock escalations are avoided.

Committing your transactions regularly is also a good practice to avoid unnecessary locking problems.

The MAXLOCKS database configuration parameter also has a direct effect on lock escalation. MAXLOCKS defines the percentage of the total locklist permitted to be allocated to a single application. Proper configuration of MAXLOCKS prevents any one application from using up all the memory available in the locklist. When the number of locks an application holds reaches the MAXLOCKS percentage, DB2 escalates the row locks of the particular application to a table lock. The table with the most row locks is escalated first. Lock escalation continues until the percentage of the locklist held is below the value of MAXLOCKS.

The database manager determines which locks to escalate by looking through the locklist for the application and finding the table with the most row locks. If after replacing these with a single table lock, the MAXLOCKS value is no longer exceeded, lock escalation stops. If not, escalation continues until the percentage of the locklist held is below the value of MAXLOCKS. The MAXLOCKS parameter multiplied by the MAXAPPLS parameter cannot be less than 100.

As the number of row locks being held increases, the chance of locking escalations occurring also increases. Take this into consideration when choosing isolation levels. For example, the RR isolation level locks all the rows in the result set as well as the rows referenced to build the result set. With this isolation level you should choose an appropriate value for your MAXLOCKS and LOCKLIST parameters.

You can simplify the task of memory configuration by using the AUTOCONFIGURE and self-tuning memory manager (STMM). When using these tools, MAXLOCK and LOCKLIST are set to AUTOMATIC by default, which means that the memory usage is dynamically sized as the workload requirements change.

Diagnosing Lock Problems

DB2 has a comprehensive set of tools that you can use to obtain information about locking. In the following sections we look at some of the tools that are available and how they can be used to troubleshoot locking problems.

Using the list applications Command

The list applications (or list application) command issued with the show detail clause shows the status of each application. Use this command as the first diagnostic step if you suspect a lock wait condition exists. You can also use IBM Data Studio to get similar information. From the IBM Data Studio Database perspective, right-click any database name in the Administration Explorer view, then choose **Monitor > Application connections**. This launches the IBM Data Studio Web Console. If you have not configured this console before, you might be asked to specify the databases to monitor and to provide appropriate credentials before you can see the list of applications.

Figure 9.15 shows the output of the `list applications show detail` command. The output is over 240 bytes wide; to understand locking behavior, focus on the output columns listed in Table 9.11.

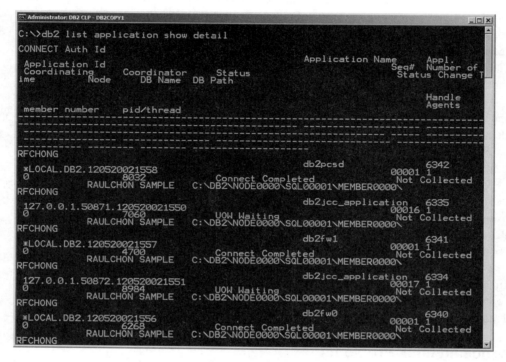

Figure 9.15   Output of the list applications show detail command

Table 9.11   Output Columns of the list applications show detail Command

Output Column	Description
Status	A value of *Lock-wait* means the application is blocked by a lock held by a different application. Don't be confused by a value of *UOW Waiting*, which means that the application (unit of work) is in progress and not blocked by a lock. It is simply not doing any work at the moment.
Status Change Time	This is of particular interest for an application with *Lock-wait* status. The value shows when the lock wait began. Note that the UOW monitor switch must be on for the status change time to be reported.

Output Column	Description
Appl. Handle	The handle is a unique ID for an active application. Being able to identify the application handle is important when it is holding locks that are causing contention problems. You can use the application handle in the FORCE APPLICA-TION command to terminate its current transaction.

Using the force application Command

You can use the force application command in conjunction with the list applications command to resolve concurrency problems. A typical scenario occurs when user *Bob* issues a query that does not COMMIT. He then goes for a one-hour coffee break, leaving other users unable to continue their work because his query is holding several locks on the same objects. In this scenario, a DBA can issue a list applications command to identify that the connection is from *Bob* by looking at the *Appl. Handle* column, as shown in Figure 9.16.

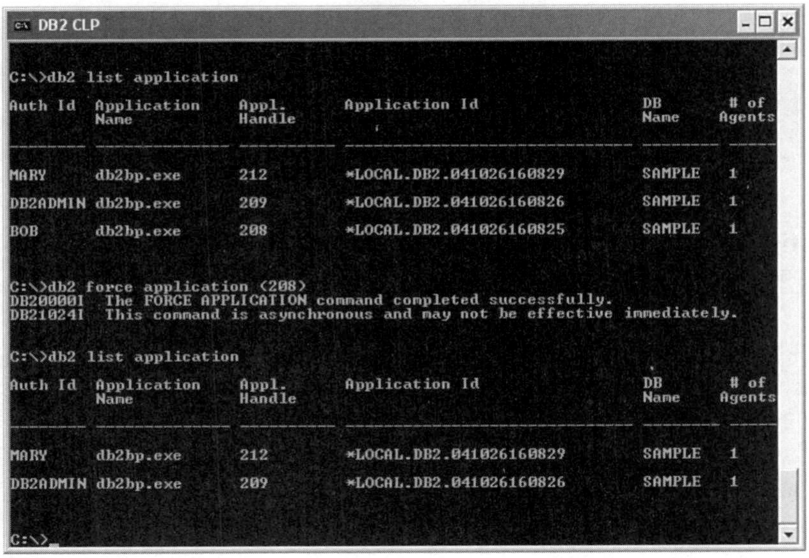

```
DB2 CLP                                                            _ □ ×

C:\>db2 list application

Auth Id  Application   Appl.      Application Id              DB       # of
         Name          Handle                                Name     Agents

MARY     db2bp.exe     212        *LOCAL.DB2.041026160829     SAMPLE   1

DB2ADMIN db2bp.exe     209        *LOCAL.DB2.041026160826     SAMPLE   1

BOB      db2bp.exe     208        *LOCAL.DB2.041026160825     SAMPLE   1


C:\>db2 force application <208>
DB20000I  The FORCE APPLICATION command completed successfully.
DB21024I  This command is asynchronous and may not be effective immediately.

C:\>db2 list application

Auth Id  Application   Appl.      Application Id              DB       # of
         Name          Handle                                Name     Agents

MARY     db2bp.exe     212        *LOCAL.DB2.041026160829     SAMPLE   1

DB2ADMIN db2bp.exe     209        *LOCAL.DB2.041026160826     SAMPLE   1

C:\>_
```

Figure 9.16   The force application command

Figure 9.16 shows there are three connections to the SAMPLE database. Next, the DBA identifies user *Bob* whose connection has the application handle of 208, and issues the command

```
db2 force application (208)
```

The command executes asynchronously, meaning it does not wait for the connection to be terminated to return. After a few seconds, when he issues the `list applications` command again, he sees that Bob's connection has been removed, allowing the other connections to continue their work.

To force several connections in one command use the syntax

```
db2 force application (Appl. Handle, Appl. Handle, ... )
```

There might be situations when you need to force all the connections against all the databases in the instance. In such situations, use the `all` option of the `force application` command:

```
db2 force application all
```

> **NOTE**
>
> The `force application` command does not prevent other users from connecting to a database. It always preserves database integrity, so only users who are idling or executing interruptible database operations can be terminated.

Using the Snapshot Monitor

You can use the Snapshot Monitor to capture information about a database and any connected applications at a specific time. Snapshot monitoring provides the majority of the useful information for dealing with lock issues. Before you can obtain snapshot information in full extent, you must turn on the database lock monitor switch. There are a few other monitor switches available for different use. In this section, we show you how to turn on all the monitor switches and only focus on the relevant commands required to continue with our lock diagnostic discussion.

Turn on all the monitor switches with this command:

```
db2 update monitor switches using bufferpool on lock on sort on
    statement on table on timestamp on uow on
```

To get a database snapshot, issue

```
db2 get snapshot for all on database_name
```

From the output of this command you obtain the following snapshot monitoring components in sequence. Snapshots that are most relevant to locking have an asterisk (*) after them.

- Database snapshot*
- Buffer pool snapshot
- Dynamic SQL snapshot
- Application snapshot*
- Table space snapshot
- Database lock snapshot*
- Table snapshot

The "database snapshot" section of the result contains a good summary of the locking information for the specified database. Listing 9.7 shows only the pertinent lines to locking from a sample database snapshot output.

Listing 9.7 Database Snapshot with Lock-Related Information

```
Database Snapshot
.  .  .  .

Locks held currently = 8
Lock waits = 0
Time database waited on locks (ms) = 315704
Lock list memory in use (Bytes) = 1692
Deadlocks detected = 0
Lock escalations = 0
Exclusive lock escalations = 0
Agents currently waiting on locks = 1
Lock Timeouts = 0
```

If you want to "zoom" into each application and understand the types of locks they are holding, examine the application snapshots. Listing 9.8 shows the most important subset of information for an application in a lock-wait situation.

Listing 9.8 Application Snapshot with Lock-Related Information

```
Application Snapshot

Application handle       = 14                                    (1)
Application status       = Lock-wait
Status change time       = 08-15-2012 14:30:36.907312
Snapshot timestamp       = 08-15-2012 14:30:43.414574
Time application waited on locks (ms)   = 6507                   (2)
```

```
Total time UOW waited on locks (ms)      = 6507
UOW start timestamp      = 08-15-2012 14:30:36.889356
Statement start timestamp        = 08-15-2012 14:30:36.890986
Dynamic SQL statement text:
select * from org                                      (3)

ID of agent holding lock         = 13
Application ID holding lock      = *LOCAL.DB2.011905182946
Lock name       = 0x02000200000000000000000054
Lock attributes         = 0x00000000
Release flags   = 0x00000001
Lock object type        = Table
Lock mode       = Exclusive Lock (X)                   (4)
Lock mode requested     = Intention Share Lock (IS)    (5)
Name of tablespace holding lock          = USERSPACE1
Schema of table holding lock             = CHONG
Name of table holding lock               = ORG
Lock wait start timestamp                = 08-15-2012 14:30:36.907318
```

In Listing 9.8,

1. You can see that application handle 14 is in a lock-wait state.

2. It has been waiting for 6,507 milliseconds for locks.

3. It is currently executing a SELECT statement and requesting an Intent Share (IS) lock on a table (5).

4. However, application handle 13 holds an exclusive (X) lock on the same table.

To further investigate the problem, you can use the list application command and see what application handle 13 is doing and check its application snapshot for more information.

Like the application snapshot, the database lock snapshot has a section for each connected application (see Listing 9.9).

Listing 9.9   Database Lock Snapshot

```
                Database Lock Snapshot

Database name                    = SAMPLE
Database path                    = C:\DB2\NODE0000\SQL00002\
Input database alias             = SAMPLE
Locks held                       = 3
Applications currently connected = 1
```

```
Agents currently waiting on locks      = 0
Snapshot timestamp                     = 03-04-2012 13:39:06.465057

Application handle                     = 18
Application ID                         = *LOCAL.DB2.01D3C4183155
Sequence number                        = 0007
Application name                       = db2bp.exe
CONNECT Authorization ID               = CLARALIU
Application status                     = UOW Waiting
Status change time                     = Not Collected
Application code page                  = 1252
Locks held                            = 3
Total wait time (ms)                   = 0

List Of Locks
  Lock Name                            = 0x02000500040000000000000052
  Lock Attributes                      = 0x00000020
  Release Flags                        = 0x40000000
  Lock Count                           = 1
  Hold Count                           = 0
  Lock Object Name                     = 4
  Object Type                          = Row
  Tablespace Name                      = USERSPACE1
  Table Schema                         = CLARALIU
  Table Name                           = EMPLOYEE
  Mode                                 = X

  Lock Name                            = 0x94928D848F9F949E7B89505241
  Lock Attributes                      = 0x00000000
  Release Flags                        = 0x40000000
  Lock Count                           = 1
  Hold Count                           = 0
  Lock Object Name                     = 0
  Object Type                          = Internal P Lock
  Mode                                 = S

  Lock Name                            = 0x02000500000000000000000054
  Lock Attributes                      = 0x00000000
  Release Flags                        = 0x40000000
  Lock Count                           = 1
```

Hold Count	= 0
Lock Object Name	= 5
Object Type	= Table
Tablespace Name	= USERSPACE1
Table Schema	= CLARALIU
Table Name	= EMPLOYEE
Mode	= IX

The snapshot in Listing 9.9 shows that application handle 18 is holding 3 locks. One of them is an exclusive (X) lock on a row in the employee table, another lock is an internal P lock, and the last one is an Intent Exclusive (IX) lock on the table *EMPLOYEE*. (Internal P locks are internal locks managed by DB2; there is nothing you can do about them.)

Using Snapshot Table Functions

You can also invoke SQL functions to produce locking information displayed in a table format. The function MON_GET_LOCKS produces one row for each lock held, and MON_GET_APPL_ LOCKWAIT produces one row for each lock-wait condition. Each row contains the same data that is provided in the snapshot monitoring output discussed in the previous section.

To invoke these snapshot table functions, use

```
SELECT * FROM TABLE ( MON_GET_LOCKS ('sample', 0) ) AS s
SELECT * FROM TABLE ( MON_GET_APPL_LOCKWAIT ('sample', 0) ) AS s
```

The first argument of the snapshot function specifies the database you want to monitor, and the second argument is the database partition number.

Using the Event Monitor

You can use a DB2 Event Monitor to obtain performance information on events as they occur on the server, such as statement or transaction completion and deadlock resolution. For DB2 locking issues, the Event Monitor is particularly useful for collecting deadlock information. Snapshots can provide counts on the number of deadlocks that are occurring. However, you need to obtain application details before the deadlock is detected and rolled back by the deadlock detector. The only way to guarantee that you get detailed information on each deadlock is to create and activate an Event Monitor for deadlocks with details.

Techniques to Avoid Locking

It is good to know how to diagnose locking problems, but it is even better to know how to prevent them. Avoiding locking problems requires a good application design. The following is a list of items you should consider when developing your applications. For a detailed explanation of these and other techniques, refer to the online DB2 manuals *(DB2 Information Center)*.

- Choose the appropriate isolation level: UR, CS, RS, or RR. As discussed earlier, UR allows for the most concurrency and the least number of locks required, and RR allows for the least concurrency and the most number of locks required. CS with CC, the default, is a good choice for most applications as it provides a good balance between concurrency and data stability. If your application is used for estimation purposes and the exact value of columns is not needed, isolation UR should be used. Choosing the correct isolation level guarantees that DB2 takes the right amount of locks that your application requires. In addition, catalog locks are acquired even in uncommitted read applications using dynamic SQL or XQuery statements.

- Issue `COMMIT` statements as frequently as the application logic allows. Issuing a `COMMIT` incurs I/O costs because data is flushed to disk, but it releases locks, allowing for more concurrency. Issue `COMMIT` statements even for read-only applications, given that S locks are taken (unless using UR Isolation).

- Specify the `FOR FETCH ONLY` clause in the `SELECT` statement. This clause prevents exclusive locks from being taken. The `FOR READ ONLY` clause is equivalent.

- Perform `INSERT`, `UPDATE`, and `DELETE` statements at the end of a unit of work if possible. These operations require exclusive locks, and they are kept until the end of the UOW (commit/roll back). Putting these statements at the end of a UOW allows for maximum concurrency.

- Avoid lock escalations impacting concurrency by using self-tuning memory manager or manually tune the `LOCKLIST` and `MAXLOCKS` database configuration parameters.

- When declaring cursors, be specific about their use. If the cursor is to be used only for reads, include the `FOR READ ONLY` clause in the declaration; if the cursor is to be used for updates, include the `FOR UPDATE` clause. In addition, you can specify the columns to be updated in the `FOR UPDATE` clause. For example

```
DECLARE mycur1 CURSOR FOR
    SELECT * FROM employee WHERE salary > 10000
    FOR UPDATE OF firstnme, lastname
```

By explicitly declaring the use of the cursor, DB2 chooses the correct locks.

- Enable optimistic locking in your application, a technique for SQL database applications that do not hold row locks between selecting and updating or deleting rows. The advantage of optimistic locking is improved concurrency because other applications can read and write those rows. Optimistic locking uses a new Row Identifier (`RID_BIT` or `RID`) built-in function and a new `ROW CHANGE TOKEN` expression with the SQL statements. The typical way that optimistic locking is used in your application is as follows
    1. In the initial query, `SELECT` the row identifier (using the `RID_BIT()` function) and `ROW CHANGE TOKEN` for each row you need to process.
    2. Release the row locks so other applications can `SELECT`, `INSERT`, `UPDATE`, and `DELETE` from the table.

3. Perform a searched UPDATE or DELETE on the target rows, using the row identifier and ROW CHANGE TOKEN in the search condition, optimistically assuming the unlocked row has not changed since the original SELECT statement.

4. If a row has changed, the UPDATE operation fails, and the application logic must handle the failure. For instance, retry the SELECT and UPDATE operations.

Case Study

You've been hired at Acme Inc. as a new DB2 DBA. On your first day, you are asked to review company procedures, get new IDs, and complete paper work. Unfortunately, that day two senior DBAs report they are ill, and the one other DBA is struggling to fix other problems related to other database vendor products. You rise to the challenge, and after you get your IDs sorted out, you are ready to handle any DB2 problem. Fortunately, the senior DBAs have taken advantage of DB2's autonomic features, so the databases are well-tuned, and STMM is handling changes in memory requirements well.

At 10:00 a.m., a developer, Mary, calls to indicate her application in test system Zebra is running very slow. You have a hunch that this could be related to a locking problem, so you issue

```
db2 list applications show detail
```

The output shows that only two applications are running, and one of them can be easily identified as Mary's. It is currently in LOCK-WAIT state. This confirms your suspicion that this was a locking issue. The other application is from user Rick who is testing his new application. When you give Rick a call, you find out that he has recently rebound his application to use isolation RR instead of isolation CS with CC, which was what he had before. This was apparently causing lock wait problems for Mary. Rick and Mary are actually on the same team, working on the same system. You let Rick and Mary know they need to understand and design their system to reduce contention. You also give them tips about how locking can be reduced. For now, Rick agrees you force his application off, so you issue

```
db2 force application (111)
```

where 111 is the application handle for Rick's application. After issuing this command, you feel the problem should be resolved; however it isn't! When you issue another list application command, you see another connection appear. You call Rick again, but he's off for lunch. When you talk to Mary, she confirms that Rick's application automatically tries to reconnect when a connection to the database is lost, so then you figure it is Rick's application causing the problem again. Mary knows Rick will be off for a long lunch, so she asks you for a quick solution. Given that this is a test system and that there are only two users working on it right now (Mary and Rick), you decide to issue a

```
db2stop force
```

This command forces all applications and also stops the instance. Start the *DB2* instance in `ADMIN MODE` so that only administrative tasks can be performed.

```
db2start admin mode
```

Next you rebind Rick's application back to isolation CS with CC, as this was the original problem. After the rebind operation completes successfully, unquiesce the instance to restore user access.

```
unquiesce <instance name>
```

Rick's application not interfering anymore, Mary is able to continue working with her application. Great job for your first problem in the company!.

But the day is not over yet. Later that day, another group in the company promotes an application from their Development environment to their Test environment. The application is a reservation system that is expected to handle requests from at most 200 users concurrently. On the very first run of the application, there are many locking issues, so you are asked to review the application design. Using monitoring information like snapshots, you first note that there is an incredible number of lock escalations. You review the `LOCKLIST` and `MAXLOCKS` parameters and decide to increase `LOCKLIST` by 50 percent. A second run of the application performs a lot better, and the snapshots for this run show there are no longer lock escalation problems, but still there are locking issues.

Next, you review the SQL issued by the application using the snapshots. All the cursors defined in the application are ambiguous; that is, they have not been defined with a `FOR READ ONLY` or `FOR UPDATE` clause, so DB2 might not be choosing the correct locking. You also note that the transactions are very long; in other words, `COMMIT` statements are not issued frequently enough. You voice these concerns to the application developers, who decide to stop the testing while they implement your suggestions. Congratulations on a successful first day in the company!

Exercises

The purpose of this exercise is to help you understand how the different isolation levels, locking scenarios, and parameters work using practical steps you can follow. In the instructions here we mention the DB2 Command Window available on Windows only, but if you are working on Linux or UNIX, you can follow along using a Linux/UNIX shell instead. The exercises in this section assume you follow all the steps and parts in sequential order.

Setup

Open a DB2 Command Window and follow these steps to set up the environment for this exercise:

1. Create a new database called TESTDB using default values. This will take a few minutes to complete.

```
db2 "create db testdb"
```

NOTE

At any time in this exercise if you make a mistake and don't know how to revert your changes, you can drop the database and start again from step 1. To drop the database issue:

```
db2 "terminate"
db2 "drop db testdb"
```

---

2. Connect to the database you just created:

```
db2 "connect to testdb"
```

3. Create a table called RESERVATION as follows:

```
db2 "create table reservation
 (flight varchar(5),
 seat char(3),
 passenger_name varchar(10)
 )"
```

4. Insert rows onto the table using this `insert` statement:

```
db2 "insert into reservation values
            ('512','1C', 'John'),
            ('512','1D','Arnold'),
            ('512','23A','Tim'),
            ('512','13B','Bernard'),
            ('512','4A',NULL)"
```

5. Verify the rows have been inserted correctly

```
db2 "select * from reservation"
```

The output should look like this:

```
FLIGHT SEAT PASSENGER_NAME
------ ---- --------------
512    1C   John
512    1D   Arnold
512    23A  Tim
512    13B  Bernard
512    4A   -
  5 record(s) selected.
```

6. Open another DB2 Command Window and position it below the first one you had opened as shown in Figure 9.17. You now have two windows open. We use these two DB2 command windows to simulate two different applications, trying to go after the same resources.

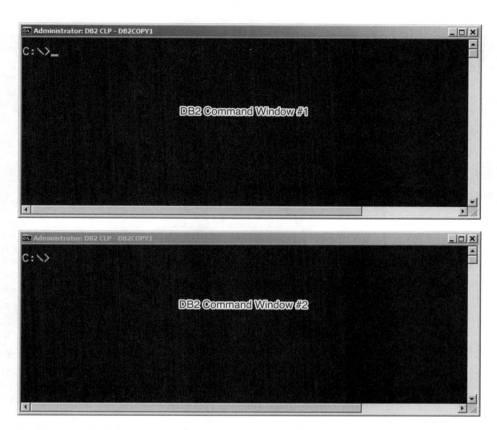

Figure 9.17 Two DB2 command windows simulating two different applications

7. Pick the top window and issue a list applications command. It is likely you only see one application with name db2bp.exe, which corresponds to Window #1. This is the only one appearing because from this window you issued a connect statement (see step 2).

8. From Window #2, connect to the database as follows:
   db2 "connect to testdb"

9. Issue again a list applications command from any of the windows. This time, you see two applications. Both applications are shown in Figure 9.18.

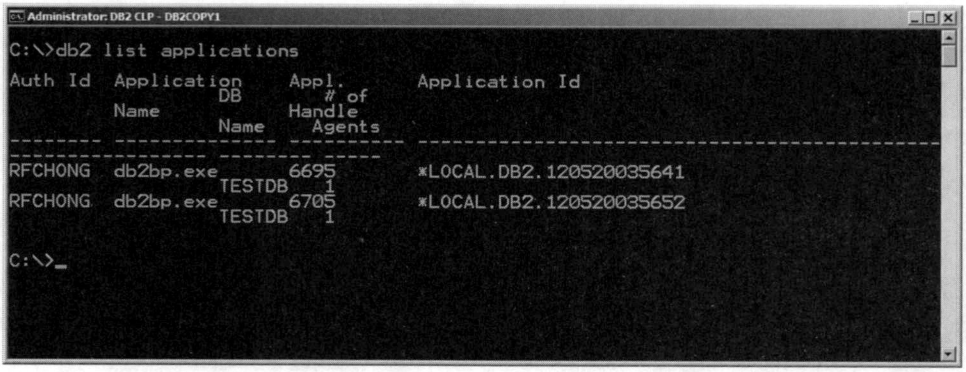

Figure 9.18   The list applications command showing two applications.

The DB2 Command Window tool has autocommit enabled by default. This means that after executing an SQL statement, the DB2 Command Window automatically issues a commit. For illustration purposes in this exercise, we use the +c flag to turn off autocommit and use the WITH <isolation level> clause after some SQL statements to override the default isolation. The DB2 Command Window uses isolation CS by default. To control if the behavior is with CC or without depends on the db cfg parameter CUR_COMMIT, which is enabled by default.

Part 1: Testing Isolation CS Without CC

1. Let's disable currently committed in our database TESTDB:

   ```
   db2 update db cfg using cur_commit off
   ```

   If you've been following all the steps up to now in order, you receive the following warning message:

   ```
   DB20000I  The UPDATE DATABASE CONFIGURATION command completed
   successfully.
   SQL1363W  Database must be deactivated and reactivated before
   the changes to one or more of the configuration parameters will
   be effective.
   ```

   Because we have two connections, for this change to take effect you need to disconnect all connections first, then new connections can use the new value. To disconnect all connections of all databases in your instance you can use

   ```
   db2 force applications all
   ```

   This is a powerful command you should only use when you are sure you will not be interfering with other users in the system.

2. Confirm there are no connections anymore by issuing a list applications command:

   ```
   db2 list applications
   ```

3. Connect again to the TESTDB database from both windows. Any SQL statement issued from any of these two windows should now be using isolation CS without CC.

4. From Window #1 (the writer), issue

```
db2 connect to testdb
db2 +c "update reservation set passenger_name = 'Raul' where
seat = '1D'"
```

5. From Window #2 (this is the reader), issue

```
db2 connect to testdb
db2 +c "select * from reservation"
```

This SELECT hangs waiting for the exclusive (X) lock to be released by the DB2 Command Window #1 application. The SELECT fetches each row, so it starts computing the result, but it gets "stuck" when it reach the row with seat 1D. As you can see, CS without CC allows for less concurrency than CS with CC. This is at the same time an example of a lock timeout.

6. Let's open for one minute a third DB2 Command Window, window #3, and from that window issue the command

```
db2 get db cfg for testdb
```

From the output, you find parameter LOCKTIMEOUT is set to -1:

```
Lock timeout (sec)                              (LOCKTIMEOUT) = -1
```

As discussed in the chapter, this means infinite wait. Changing the value of the parameter at this time would not resolve the hang because as mentioned earlier, the new parameter value would not take effect immediately (all connections have to be disconnected before the new value takes effect). Close window #3.

7. From window #1, issue db2 rollback. Watch quickly how window #2 starts displaying the results of the select. When the rollback was issued, locks were released; therefore the DB2 command window #2 was allowed to continue. Because a rollback was issued, note that the table was not changed by the update statement at all.

8. Clear the contents of both windows using cls (Windows) or clear (Linux/UNIX)

This ends this first part that demonstrated how CS without CC works and the concept of lock timeout.

Part 2: Different Access Paths, Different Locking

Application design (including how your write SQL statements) and choosing the appropriate isolation levels are important to minimize locking problems. In addition, you need to ensure you "help" DB2 choose appropriate access paths by creating database objects like indexes, or MQTs. In this part, we provide a simple scenario where the lack of an index causes contention.

1. From window #1, issue this UPDATE statement:

```
db2 +c "update reservation set passenger_name = 'Raul' where
seat = '1D'"
```

2. From window #2, issue this other UPDATE statement:

```
db2 +c "update reservation set passenger_name = 'Clara' where
seat = '13B'"
```

This second statement hangs. Why? Window #2 is going after a different row than window #1, and you are using isolation CS in both windows. Isolation CS should just be locking the row that it accesses. And indeed that is what it is doing. The problem is on the access path DB2 is choosing.

Because there are only 5 rows in the table and no indexes have been created, DB2 is performing a table scan. This means that DB2 is accessing one row at a time in the table until it finds the row it needs to update (think of an UPDATE statement as a SELECT statement plus performing the update). When it scans the table it hangs while fetching the second row (with seat 1D).

3. Issue a rollback statement from both windows:

```
db2 rollback
```

4. Now, from any window create an index in table RESERVATION as follows:

```
db2 "create index testix on reservation (seat)"
```

5. With the index created, repeat step #1 and #2. Now you see that this time, step #2 does not hang. In this case, DB2 is now choosing a different access path that involves using an index scan. This means that DB2 scans the index rather than the table itself, and when it finds the index for the row it is looking for, it locks and accesses the row.

6. Clear the contents of both windows using cls (Windows) or clear (Linux/UNIX).

This ends this part, in which demonstrated how different access paths can cause different locking situations.

Part 3: Simulating a Deadlock Situation

In this part, we simulate a deadlock. We continue from the state we left both applications from the previous part, where window #1 was locking the second row (with seat 1D), and window #2 was locking the fourth row (with seat 13B). You can go back to the setup section, step 4, to review the contents of the RESERVATION table so you visualize which rows are being locked. Basically, the two applications are locking two different rows of the table. Because we are using isolation CS and the access plan is using an index scan, only the rows being accessed are locked.

1. From window #1 issue this UPDATE statement:

```
db2 +c "update reservation set passenger_name = 'Raul' where
seat = '1D'"
```

2. From window #2 issue this other UPDATE statement:

```
db2 +c "update reservation set passenger_name = 'Clara' where
seat = '13B'"
```

3. From window #1, issue this SELECT statement:

   ```
   db2 +c "select passenger_name from reservation where seat =
   '13B'"
   ```

   This statement hangs LOCKTIMEOUT seconds because the SELECT statement is attempting to obtain a share lock (S lock) on this row, but this row has already been locked with an X lock when we issued an update from window #2. These two lock modes are not compatible.

4. From window #2, issue this SELECT statement:

   ```
   db2 +c "select passenger_name from reservation where seat =
   '1D'"
   ```

   This statement hangs LOCKTIMEOUT seconds because the SELECT statement is attempting to obtain a share lock (S lock) on this row, but this row has already been locked with an X lock when we issued an update from window #1. These two lock modes are not compatible. The two database connections are now involved in a deadlock situation!

   After 10 seconds (this interval is explained shortly) however, you receive this error from one of the windows:

   ```
   SQL0911N  The current transaction has been rolled back because
   of a deadlock or timeout.  Reason code "2".  SQLSTATE=40001
   ```

   At the same time, in the other window you see the result of the SELECT. As explained earlier, SQL0911N with reason code "2" means a deadlock has been detected. DB2 used an internal algorithm to pick which application needs to be rolled back and which application is allowed to continue.

5. Open a third window again for one minute and issue this statement:

   ```
   db2 get db cfg for testdb
   ```

   From the output, you find parameter DLCHKTIME is set to 10000 milliseconds (10 seconds):

   ```
   Interval for checking deadlock (ms)         (DLCHKTIME) = 10000
   ```

   As discussed in the chapter, this is the parameter that dictates how often DB2 needs to check for a deadlock situation and resolve it. This explains why after 10 seconds we got message SQL0911N.

6. Issue a rollback from the window where the SELECT was allowed to proceed so no changes are made to the table. If you are a bit confused which window was it, you can issue the rollback from both windows:

   ```
   db2 rollback
   ```

7. Clear the contents of both windows using cls (Windows) or clear (Linux/UNIX).

   This is the end of this part in which we demonstrated how a deadlock situation can arise and how DB2 resolves them.

Part 4: Testing Isolation CS with CC

In this part, we work with isolation CS with CC, and you can see the difference in behavior.

1. In Part 1, we turned CC off by changing the CUR_COMMIT db cfg parameter and disconnecting from all connections for the change to take effect. Let's now enable currently committed in our database TESTDB. From window #1 issue

   ```
   db2 update db cfg using cur_commit on
   db2 terminate
   ```

   The terminate command disconnects from the database

2. From window #2, issue

   ```
   db2 terminate
   ```

   At this point there are no connections to the database (you can confirm this with a list applications command). The next connection starts using the new value for CUR_COMMIT, which is ON, which means currently committed is enabled.

3. Let's repeat the same steps performed when testing isolation CS without CC, and compare the difference in behavior. From Window #1 (the writer) issue

   ```
   db2 connect to testdb
   db2 +c "update reservation set passenger_name = 'Raul' where
   seat = '1D'"
   ```

4. From window #2 (this is the reader), issue

   ```
   db2 connect to testdb
   db2 +c "select * from reservation"
   ```

   The SELECT completes successfully, returning the following:

   ```
   FLIGHT SEAT PASSENGER_NAME
   ------ ---- --------------
   512    1C   John
   512    1D   Arnold
   512    23A  Tim
   512    13B  Bernard
   512    4A   -
      5 record(s) selected.
   ```

Can you notice the difference in behavior? Previously, with isolation CS without CC, the SELECT statement would hang. However in this case, using isolation CS with CC, the SELECT was allowed to continue!

Note that the value of PASSENGER_NAME for row with seat 1D is Arnold. This is the currently committed value.

You might argue that if the application in window #1 issues a COMMIT, then the new value committed would be Raul, and therefore the value that the application in window #2 returned would be incorrect. This is true, but is an application design decision. If you prefer for window #2 to wait (hang) until window #1 commits, then you need to disable CUR_COMMIT and work as explained in Part 1 of this exercise.

Part 5: Testing Isolation UR

Continuing with the scenario in part 4, let's see what happens if the SELECT from window #2 was issued using isolation UR:

1. From window #2, issue

   ```
   db2 +c "select * from reservation with UR"
   ```

   Now you see the output displayed is

   ```
   FLIGHT SEAT PASSENGER_NAME
   ------ ---- --------------
   512    1C   John
   512    1D   Raul
   512    23A  Tim
   512    13B  Bernard
   512    4A   -

   5 record(s) selected.
   ```

   The second row shows passenger Raul instead of Arnold. Raul is the uncommitted value that can be displayed by isolation UR.

2. To clean up, from both windows issue

   ```
   db2 rollback
   ```

   This is the end of this exercise.

Summary

In this chapter, you learned about locking scenarios you can encounter when a database is accessed concurrently. Some scenarios might be desirable, and some others might not. To control the behavior of how DB2 handles concurrent database access, use the different isolation levels.

There are four types of isolation levels: uncommitted read (UR), cursor stability (CS), read stability (RS), and repeatable read (RR). Cursor stability has two semantics, one using currently committed and one not using it. Cursor stability with currently committed semantics is the default isolation level and provides a good balance between concurrency and data stability.

When an application is holding many locks that have exceeded its quota (through the setting of MAXLOCKS), lock escalation can occur. Lock escalation should be minimized as much as possible because it significantly reduces the concurrency of the database.

There are command line tools as well as graphical tools that can help you identify and solve locking problems, and you can implement techniques when developing your applications to avoid locking.

Review Questions

1. A batch operation is encountering lock escalations. If it is the only application running when the lock escalation occurs, which database configuration parameter can be used to reduce the lock escalations?

2. Sam issues a SELECT statement that returns the following result set of three rows:

   ```
   Name            Seat
   ----------------
   Liu             1A
   Chong           14F
   Dole            3B
   ```

   Without committing or rolling back the current transaction, he issues the same SELECT statement again. The following is returned:

   ```
   Name            Seat
   ----------------
   -               1A
   Chong           14F
   McQueen         3B
   ```

   Why is that?

3. What can be locked by a DB2 user explicitly using a DB2 command or statement?

4. If an application holds a U lock on a row, what lock must another application request to access this row concurrently?

5. What does error SQL0911N with reason code *68* mean?

6. What does error SQL0911N with reason code *2* mean?

7. A user complained about poor performance. With the DB2 Snapshot Monitor you obtained the following information:

   ```
   Locks held currently = 855
   Lock waits = 1123
   Time database waited on locks (ms) = 3157040000
   Lock list memory in use (Bytes) = 16920
   Deadlocks detected = 0
   Lock escalations = 103
   Exclusive lock escalations = 0
   Agents currently waiting on locks = 38
   Lock Timeouts = 2232
   ```

   How would you troubleshoot the high number of lock escalations?

8. What tools that come with DB2 can assist you in diagnosing lock problems?

9. The following is captured by the Snapshot Monitor. What does it tell you?

   Application Snapshot

   ```
   Application handle                        = 14
   Application status                        = Lock-wait
   Status change time                        = 08-15-2012
   14:30:36.907312
   Snapshot timestamp                        = 08-15-2012
   14:30:43.414574
   Time application waited on locks (ms)     = 6507
   Total time UOW waited on locks (ms)       = 6507
   UOW start timestamp                       = 08-15-2012
   14:30:36.889356
   Statement start timestamp                 = 08-15-2012
   14:30:36.890986
   Dynamic SQL statement text:
   select * from org

   ID of agent holding lock                  = 13
   Application ID holding lock               = *LOCAL.DB2.011905182946
   Lock name                                 =
   0x02000200000000000000000054
   Lock attributes                           = 0x00000000
   Release flags                             = 0x00000001
   Lock object type                          = Table
   Lock mode                                 = Exclusive Lock (X)
   Lock mode requested                       = Intention Share Lock
   (IS)
   Name of tablespace holding lock           = USERSPACE1
   Schema of table holding lock              = CHONG
   Name of table holding lock                = ORG
   Lock wait start timestamp                 = 08-15-2012
   14:30:36.907318
   ```

10. Bob connects to the *SAMPLE* database. He turns auto-commit OFF and issues the following statement:

    ```
    UPDATE employee SET salary = salary * 1.5 WHERE empno='000010'
    ```

    A database administrator, Mike, who had just joined the company is monitoring the system. He notices that Bob had acquired a table lock on the *EMPLOYEE* table. Because Bob had not committed or rolled back the transaction, no one can access the table (except for UR applications). Mike asks Bob to commit or roll back the transaction. That released the locks, and business goes on as usual. Then another user, Mary, issues the following statement:

    ```
    SELECT name, salary FROM employee WHERE empno = '000020'
    ```

Mary also has auto-commit turned `OFF` and doesn't commit or roll back the transaction. Once again, the *EMPLOYEE* table is locked.

Mike is concerned about these two locking incidents. Could you assist him with what might be the cause?

11. Which of the following is not a DB2 isolation level?

    A.   Uncommitted read

    B.   Cursor stability

    C.   Cursor with hold

    D.   Repeatable read

12. On which of the following objects does DB2 not obtain locks?

    A.   Row

    B.   Page

    C.   Table

    D.   Table space

13. Which of the following is the default isolation level in DB2?

    A.   Uncommitted read

    B.   Cursor stability

    C.   Read stability

    D.   Repeatable read

14. Which of the following isolation levels typically causes the most locks to be obtained?

    A.   Uncommitted read

    B.   Cursor stability

    C.   Read stability

    D.   Repeatable read

15. Which of the following isolation levels does not obtain row level locks?

    A.   Uncommitted read

    B.   Cursor stability

    C.   Read stability

    D.   Repeatable read

16. Which of the following isolation levels enables you see data that has been updated by other applications before it is committed?

    A.   Uncommitted read

    B.   Cursor stability

    C.   Read stability

    D.   Repeatable read

17. Given a transaction that issues the same SQL statement twice, which of the following isolation levels allow new rows to be returned in the result set but do not allow rows to be removed from the result set?

    A.   Uncommitted read

    B.   Cursor stability

    C.   Read stability

    D.   Repeatable read

18. If the current session has an isolation level of CS, which of the following changes the isolation level to UR for the current statement?

    A.   `select * from foo use UR`

    B.   `select * from foo with UR`

    C.   `select * from foo isolation UR`

    D.   `select * from foo UR`

19. Using the `alter table` statement, which two of the following can you change the locksize to?

    A.   Column

    B.   Page

    C.   Row

    D.   Index

    E.   Table

20. To specify that your application should return immediately rather than wait for a lock, which of the following commands must be used?

    A.   `Set lock timeout = nowait`

    B.   `Set lock timeout = not wait`

    C.   `Set lock timeout = NULL`

    D.   `Set lock nowait`

Maintaining, Backing Up, and Recovering Data

When working with a database, you insert, update, and delete data constantly. In the long run, you might find the performance of your queries start to degrade as more and more of these operations are performed. This chapter describes the DB2 utilities you can use to properly maintain your database to avoid these types of problems. In addition, while trying to improve the performance of your system, you might find that it would make more sense to move some data to a reporting system instead of keeping it in your day-to-day operations database, for example. DB2 has several utilities that can help you move data such as EXPORT, IMPORT, LOAD, and so on. Last, there is always some degree of risk when you manipulate important data. To prevent losing any critical information, it is always recommended to back up your databases. DB2 has robust backup and restore capabilities that we will discuss in this chapter.

In this chapter, you learn about

- The big picture of the DB2 data movement utilities
- The EXPORT, IMPORT, LOAD, and db2move utilities
- How to generate the Data Definition Language for a database
- The different data maintenance utilities such as RUNSTATS, REORG, REORGCHK, REBIND
- How to perform database backup, restore, and roll forward operations

DB2 Data Movement Utilities: The Big Picture

Moving data from one database server to another is a common task in a production environment and in almost every phase of the development cycle. For example, a developer might want to export data from a production database and load it into her tables for testing. In a production environment, a database administrator can export a few tables from production to a test database server to investigate a performance problem.

DB2 provides a number of utilities so that you can accomplish these tasks very easily. Figure 10.1 presents the big picture of the DB2 data movement utilities. The utilities provide a way to move data from one database to another. The source and target databases can be in the same instance, in different instances on the same server, on different servers on the same platform, or on different platforms entirely. For example, you can move data stored in DB2 on Windows to a database defined in DB2 on a Linux server. Data movement within DB2 is efficient and flexible.

Figure 10.1 shows that all data movement utilities use a file either for input or output. The file can be of types DEL, IXF, ASC, WSF, and CURSOR. In the case of the Ingest utility, the input cannot only be a file, but also a named pipe.

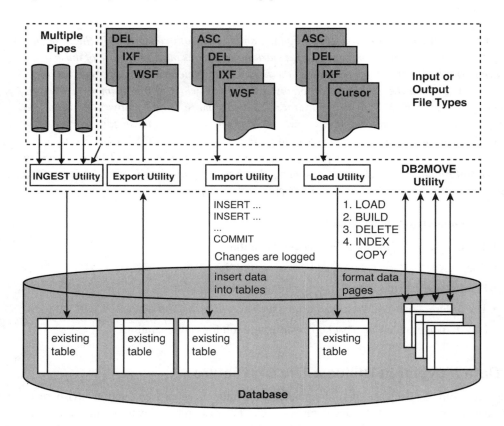

Figure 10.1   DB2 data movement utilities

To extract data from a table in a database, you use the EXPORT utility. The INGEST, IMPORT, and LOAD utilities insert data from the input files into a specified table. The table must exist prior to using these utilities. A batch version of the data movement utilities, db2move, can export, import, or load multiple tables with just one command. Each utility is discussed in more detail in the sections that follow.

In addition to the utilities illustrated in Figure 10.1, there are other tools worth mentioning:

- db2look: This tool is commonly used in conjunction with db2move. It can be used to generate a script file with the structure of database objects or the entire database. Later in the chapter we provide more details.

- db2relocatedb: Use this tool when you need to rename your database or in situations where you need to move the database from one instance to another in the same server or in different servers. The data is not moved by the tool, but the DB2 internal structures and configuration files are updated appropriately. For more information about this tool, refer to the DB2 Information Center

- The ADMIN_MOVE_TABLE stored procedure enables you to move a table while it is being used. For example, say you are running a business that requires your system to be up and running 24/7. At the same time, say you need to move your table so it uses faster and bigger disks. Because you cannot bring the table offline in this environment, the ADMIN_MOVE_TABLE stored procedure can be your best option.

Data Movement File Formats

Before learning about moving data between DB2 databases and/or other data sources, it is important to first understand the file formats that the data movement utilities use. You can choose from five different file formats:

- Delimited ASCII (DEL)
- Non-delimited ASCII (ASC)
- PC version of Integrated Exchange Format (PC/IXF)
- Worksheet format (WSF)
- CURSOR

Delimited ASCII (DEL) Format

As the name implies, this file format contains a stream of ASCII characters that are separated by row and column delimiters. The comma (,) is the default column delimiter, and the carriage return is the default row delimiter. For character strings, DB2 uses double quotes (" ") as the string delimiter. For example, a DEL file looks similar to Figure 10.2. Note that all the string data is surrounded by a pair of double quotes and each column value is separated by a comma.

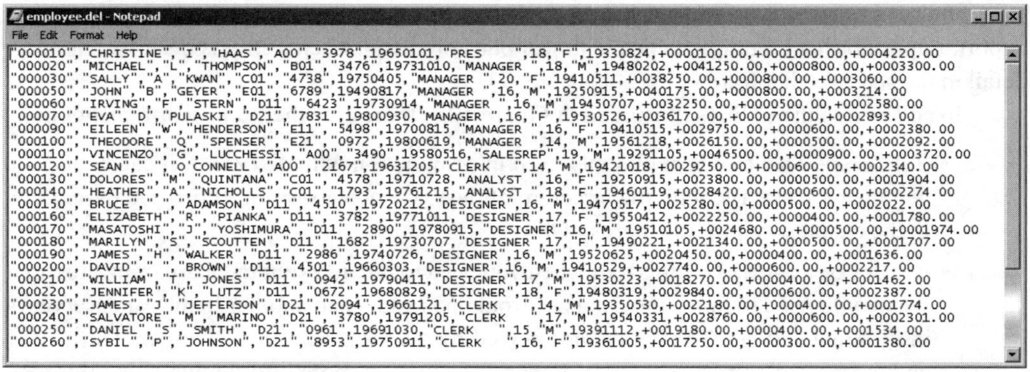

```
"000010","CHRISTINE","I","HAAS","A00","3978",19650101,"PRES    ",18,"F",19330824,+0000100.00,+0001000.00,+0004220.00
"000020","MICHAEL","L","THOMPSON","B01","3476",19731010,"MANAGER ",18,"M",19480202,+0041250.00,+0000800.00,+0003300.00
"000030","SALLY","A","KWAN","C01","4738",19750405,"MANAGER ",20,"F",19410511,+0038250.00,+0000800.00,+0003060.00
"000050","JOHN","B","GEYER","E01","6789",19490817,"MANAGER ",16,"M",19250915,+0040175.00,+0000800.00,+0003214.00
"000060","IRVING","F","STERN","D11","6423",19730914,"MANAGER ",16,"M",19450707,+0032250.00,+0000500.00,+0002580.00
"000070","EVA","D","PULASKI","D21","7831",19800930,"MANAGER ",16,"F",19530526,+0036170.00,+0000700.00,+0002893.00
"000090","EILEEN","W","HENDERSON","E11","5498",19700815,"MANAGER ",16,"F",19410515,+0029750.00,+0000600.00,+0002380.00
"000100","THEODORE","Q","SPENSER","E21","0972",19800619,"MANAGER ",14,"M",19561218,+0026150.00,+0000500.00,+0002092.00
"000110","VINCENZO","G","LUCCHESSI","A00","3490",19580516,"SALESREP",19,"M",19291105,+0046500.00,+0000900.00,+0003720.00
"000120","SEAN"," ","O'CONNELL","A00","2167",19631205,"CLERK   ",14,"M",19421018,+0029250.00,+0000600.00,+0002340.00
"000130","DOLORES","M","QUINTANA","C01","4578",19710728,"ANALYST ",16,"F",19250915,+0023800.00,+0000500.00,+0001904.00
"000140","HEATHER","A","NICHOLLS","C01","1793",19761215,"ANALYST ",18,"F",19460119,+0028420.00,+0000600.00,+0002274.00
"000150","BRUCE"," ","ADAMSON","D11","4510",19720212,"DESIGNER",16,"M",19470517,+0025280.00,+0000500.00,+0002022.00
"000160","ELIZABETH","R","PIANKA","D11","3782",19771011,"DESIGNER",17,"F",19550412,+0022250.00,+0000400.00,+0001780.00
"000170","MASATOSHI","J","YOSHIMURA","D11","2890",19780915,"DESIGNER",16,"M",19510105,+0024680.00,+0000500.00,+0001974.00
"000180","MARILYN","S","SCOUTTEN","D11","1682",19730707,"DESIGNER",17,"F",19490221,+0021340.00,+0000500.00,+0001707.00
"000190","JAMES","H","WALKER","D11","2986",19740726,"DESIGNER",16,"M",19520625,+0020450.00,+0000400.00,+0001636.00
"000200","DAVID"," ","BROWN","D11","4501",19660303,"DESIGNER",16,"M",19410529,+0027740.00,+0000600.00,+0002217.00
"000210","WILLIAM","T","JONES","D11","0942",19790411,"DESIGNER",17,"M",19530223,+0018270.00,+0000400.00,+0001462.00
"000220","JENNIFER","K","LUTZ","D11","0672",19680829,"DESIGNER",18,"F",19480319,+0029840.00,+0000600.00,+0002387.00
"000230","JAMES","J","JEFFERSON","D21","2094",19661121,"CLERK   ",14,"M",19350530,+0022180.00,+0000400.00,+0001774.00
"000240","SALVATORE","M","MARINO","D21","3780",19791205,"CLERK   ",17,"M",19540331,+0028760.00,+0000600.00,+0002301.00
"000250","DANIEL","S","SMITH","D21","0961",19691030,"CLERK   ",15,"M",19391112,+0019180.00,+0000400.00,+0001534.00
"000260","SYBIL","P","JOHNSON","D21","8953",19750911,"CLERK   ",16,"F",19361005,+0017250.00,+0000300.00,+0001380.00
```

Figure 10.2 Sample DEL file

Non-Delimited ASCII (ASC) Format

The ASC file format is also known as **fixed length ASCII file format** because each column length in the file has the same length as defined for the corresponding column definition in the table. For example, variable-length character column definitions in a table are padded with blanks in an ASC file and represented using their maximum length. Figure 10.3 shows the same data as in Figure 10.2 but in ASC format.

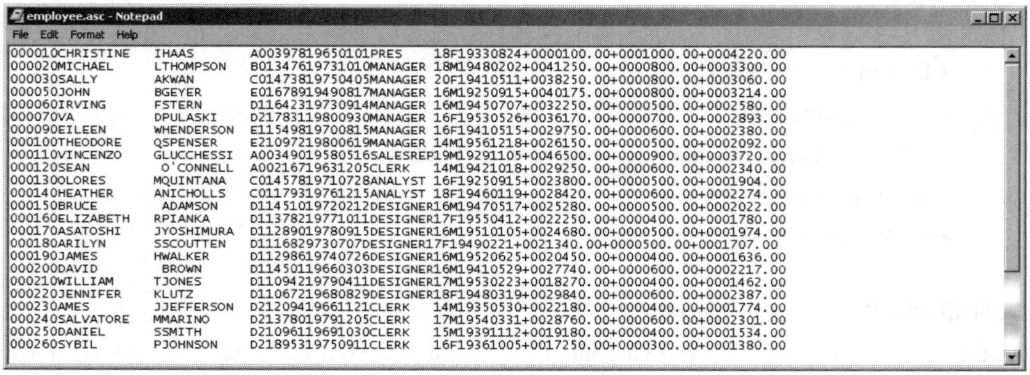

```
000010CHRISTINE   IHAAS           A00397819650101PRES    18F19330824+0000100.00+0001000.00+0004220.00
000020MICHAEL     LTHOMPSON       B01347619731010MANAGER 18M19480202+0041250.00+0000800.00+0003300.00
000030SALLY       AKWAN           C01473819750405MANAGER 20F19410511+0038250.00+0000800.00+0003060.00
000050JOHN        BGEYER          E01678919490817MANAGER 16M19250915+0040175.00+0000800.00+0003214.00
000060IRVING      FSTERN          D11642319730914MANAGER 16M19450707+0032250.00+0000500.00+0002580.00
000070VA          DPULASKI        D21783119800930MANAGER 16F19530526+0036170.00+0000700.00+0002893.00
000090EILEEN      WHENDERSON      E11549819700815MANAGER 16F19410515+0029750.00+0000600.00+0002380.00
000100THEODORE    QSPENSER        E21097219800619MANAGER 14M19561218+0026150.00+0000500.00+0002092.00
000110VINCENZO    GLUCCHESSI      A00349019580516SALESREP19M19291105+0046500.00+0000900.00+0003720.00
000120SEAN         O'CONNELL      A00216719631205CLERK   14M19421018+0029250.00+0000600.00+0002340.00
000130OLORES      MQUINTANA       C01457819710728ANALYST 16F19250915+0023800.00+0000500.00+0001904.00
000140HEATHER     ANICHOLLS       C01179319761215ANALYST 18F19460119+0028420.00+0000600.00+0002274.00
000150BRUCE        ADAMSON        D11451019720212DESIGNER16M19470517+0025280.00+0000500.00+0002022.00
000160ELIZABETH   RPIANKA         D11378219771011DESIGNER17F19550412+0022250.00+0000400.00+0001780.00
000170ASATOSHI    JYOSHIMURA      D11289019780915DESIGNER16M19510105+0024680.00+0000500.00+0001974.00
000180ARILYN      SSCOUTTEN       D1116829730707DESIGNER17F19490221+0021340.00+0000500.00+0001707.00
000190JAMES       HWALKER         D11298619740726DESIGNER16M19520625+0020450.00+0000400.00+0001636.00
000200DAVID        BROWN          D11450119660303DESIGNER16M19410529+0027740.00+0000600.00+0002217.00
000210WILLIAM     TJONES          D11094219790411DESIGNER17M19530223+0018270.00+0000400.00+0001462.00
000220JENNIFER    KLUTZ           D11067219680829DESIGNER18F19480319+0029840.00+0000600.00+0002387.00
000230AMES        JJEFFERSON      D21209419661121CLERK   14M19350530+0022180.00+0000400.00+0001774.00
000240SALVATORE   MMARINO         D21378019791205CLERK   17M19540331+0028760.00+0000600.00+0002301.00
000250DANIEL      SSMITH          D21096119691030CLERK   15M19391112+0019180.00+0000400.00+0001534.00
000260SYBIL       PJOHNSON        D21895319750911CLERK   16F19361005+0017250.00+0000300.00+0001380.00
```

Figure 10.3 Sample ASC file

PC Version of IXF (PC/IXF) Format

PC/IXF (or simply IXF) files cannot be edited with a normal text editor. They use the IXF data interchange architecture, which is a generic relational database exchange format that lets you move data among DB2 databases. PC/IXF can only be used for moving data between DB2 databases because it is an IBM proprietary format. In addition to data, the file also contains the data types and structure of the table.

> **NOTE**
>
> The PC/IXF format was commonly used with the `CREATE` and `REPLACE_CREATE` options of the `IMPORT` utility. With these options, the table did not need to exist before running the `IMPORT` utility because the utility would create the table using the information from the PC/IXF file prior to loading the data. The `CREATE` and `REPLACE_CREATE` options are now deprecated. Using these options to re-create a table did not create the tables with all its required structures.

WSF Format

WSF files use worksheet formats that the database manager supports. Any file names with these extensions are accepted: WKS, WK1, WRK, WR1, and WJ2. WSF files are mainly used for moving data between DB2 and these worksheets.

CURSOR

You can only use the CURSOR file format with the `LOAD` utility. The cursor must be declared with an SQL query first before it can be referenced in the `load` command. For example

```
DECLARE mycurs CURSOR FOR SELECT col1, col2, col3 FROM test.mytable1
LOAD FROM mycurs OF CURSOR INSERT INTO test.mytable2
```

The `LOAD` utility processes the entire result of the query associated with the specified cursor whether or not the cursor has been used to fetch rows.

The DB2 EXPORT Utility

The `EXPORT` utility extracts data from a table into a file. The `export` command supports many different options. Let's start with a simple export command and discuss how to use some options to customize the command. The following example of the `export` command exports all the rows in the *EMPLOYEE* table to the file *empdata.ixf* in IXF format.

```
export to empdata.ixf of ixf select * from employee
```

The following shows the sample output of running this command:

```
db2 => export to empdata.ixf of ixf select * from employee
SQL3104N  The Export utility is beginning to export data to file
"empdata.ixf".
```

```
SQL3105N  The Export utility has finished exporting "42" rows.
Number of rows exported: 42
```

All the keywords in this command are mandatory; that is, you have to provide the output file name, specify the file format, and the `SELECT` statement that will retrieve the rows to be exported. The exported file can be in a format of DEL, IXF, or WSF. The output file specified is created after executing the export in the directory where the command is executed. Using the optional `messages` clause, you can specify a file name where warning and error messages of the export operation are logged. If no message file accompanies the `messages` clause, the messages are written to standard output. Though optional, we highly recommend you use this clause so that all the messages generated by the utility are saved.

The `export` command also supports `SELECT` statements with joins, nested statements, and so on. Thus, if you want to export data from two tables, they can be joined as shown in the following example:

```
export to deptmgr.del of del messages deptmgr.out
   select deptno, deptname, firstnme, lastname, salary
     from employee, department
   where empno = mgrno
```

The preceding example joins the *EMPLOYEE* and *DEPARTMENT* tables to obtain information for each department manager. If the command is successfully executed, the number of rows exported is returned.

```
Number of rows exported: 8
```

When the command finishes successfully with no warning or error message, the message file *deptmgr.out* only includes entries that indicate the beginning and end of the utility execution.

```
SQL3104N  The Export utility is beginning to export data to file
"deptmgr.del".

SQL3105N  The Export utility has finished exporting "8" rows.
```

Specifying Column Names

The `method n` (column names) option is useful when a column is derived from one or more columns. For example, if you use the following `SELECT` statement in the `export` command:

```
select empno, firstnme, lastname, salary * 1.3
  from employee
 where workdept='A00'
```

The following shows what the output of the `SELECT` statement would be. Notice that the last column in the select list is a derived column that does not have a column name.

EMPNO	FIRSTNME	LASTNAME	4
000010	CHRISTINE	HAAS	130.000
000110	VINCENZO	LUCCHESSI	60450.000
000120	SEAN	O'CONNELL	38025.000

The IMPORT utility (which is discussed in a later section) can be executed with a create option that enables you to create the target table if it does not already exist before data is imported. The input file must also contain the definition of the table. If you were to import this result with the create option, the newly created table would have the fourth column named *4*. Rather than using a number, you can provide a more descriptive name using the AS clause in the select statement:

```
export to newsalary.ixf of ixf
  messages newsalary.out
  select empno, firstnme, lastname, salary * 1.3 as new_salary
    from employee
  where workdept='A00'
```

Alternatively, use the method n option to explicitly specify all the column names. This option is only supported when the export file format is IXF or WSF.

```
export to newsalary.ixf of ixf
  messages newsalary.out
  method n ('EMPLOYEENO', 'FIRSTNAME', 'LASTNAME', 'NEWSALARY')
  select empno, firstnme, lastname, salary * 1.3
    from employee
  where workdept='A00'
```

With the method n clause and the specified columns, the resulting file contains the new column names:

EMPLOYEENO	FIRSTNAME	LASTNAME	NEWSALARY
000010	CHRISTINE	HAAS	130.000
000110	VINCENZO	LUCCHESSI	60450.000
000120	SEAN	O'CONNELL	38025.000

The DB2 IMPORT Utility

The IMPORT utility inserts data from an input file into a table or a view. The utility performs inserts as if it were executing INSERT statements. Just like normal insert operations, DB2 validates the data and checks against the table definitions, constraints (such as referential integrity and check constraints), and index definitions. Triggers are also invoked.

The utility supports options and import modes that enable you to customize its behavior. The `import` command has many options. Let's review a simple `import` command example and discuss the mandatory options. To a certain degree, the `import` command is structured much like the `export` command: You have to specify the input file name, format of the file, and the target table name, for example

```
import from employee.ixf of ixf
  messages employee.out
  insert into employee
```

This command takes the file *employee.ixf,* which is in the IXF format, as the input and inserts the data rows from the file into the *EMPLOYEE* table. The `IMPORT` utility supports input files in ASC, DEL, IXF, and WSF formats. We also recommend that you specify the optional clause `messages` to save the error and warning messages and the import status. The message file can be used to identify where to restart an interrupted import operation.

Import Modes

The previous example uses `insert` to indicate that new data is to be appended to the existing *EMPLOYEE* table. Table 10.1 lists some of the modes supported by the `IMPORT` utility.

Table 10.1 Import Modes

Mode	Description
INSERT	Adds the imported data to the table without changing the existing table data. The target table must already exist.
INSERT_UPDATE	Adds the imported data to the target table or updates existing rows with matching primary keys. The target table must already exist defined with primary keys.
REPLACE	Deletes all existing data from the table and inserts the imported data. The table definition and index definitions are not changed.

Let's take a look at some examples of how to use the `import` command. In the example that follows, the input data file is `employee.del` of DEL format. The target table where all the rows will be imported into is the *EMPSALARY* table; this table must exist to use the `replace` mode. The `warningcount 10` option indicates that the utility will stop after 10 warnings are received. If this option is not specified or is set to zero, the import operation continues regardless of the number of warnings issued.

```
import from employee.del of del
  messages empsalary.out
  warningcount 10
  replace into empsalary (salary, bonus, comm)
```

In this next example, the `import` command deletes all the rows in the table, if table *NEW-EMPLOYEE* exists, and inserts the row contents. If the *NEWEMPLOYEE* table does not exist, the command creates the table with definitions stored in the IXF input file and inserts the row contents. The number of rows to be imported is limited to the first 1000 rows by using the `rowcount 1000` option.

```
import from employee.ixf of ixf
  messages employee.out
  rowcount 1000
  replace_create into newemployee
```

Select Columns to Import

There are three ways to select particular columns you want to import. `method 1` uses the starting and ending position (in bytes) for all columns to be imported. This method only supports ASC files; for example

```
import from employee.asc of asc
    messages employee.out
    method 1 (1 5, 6 14, 24 30)
    insert into employee
```

This command imports three selected columns of data into the *EMPLOYEE* table: bytes 1 to 5 for the first column, bytes 6 to 14 for the second column, and bytes 24 to 30 for the third column.

The other two methods specify the names of the columns (`method n`) or the field numbers of the input data (`method p`). `method n` is only valid for IXF files, and `method p` can be used with IXF or DEL files. The following examples demonstrate the `method n` and `method p` clauses in the `import` command, respectively.

```
import from employee.ixf of ixf
    messages employee.out
    method n (empno, firstnme, lastname)
    insert into employee (empno, firstnme, lastname)
```

```
import from employee.ixf of ixf
    messages employee.out
    method p (1, 2, 4)
    insert into employee (empno, firstnme, lastname)
```

Regular Commits During an Import

The `IMPORT` utility inserts data into a table through normal insert operations. Therefore, changes made during the import are logged and are committed to the database upon successful completion of the import operation. By default an import behaves like an atomic compound statement for which more than one insert is grouped into a transaction. If any insert fails, the rest of the inserts are not committed to the database.

If you were to import a few million rows into a table, you would need to make sure there was enough log space to hold the insertions because they are treated as one transaction. However, sometimes it is not feasible to allocate large log space just for the import. The `commitcount` n option can be used to force a commit after every *n* records are imported and thus release log space. With `commitcount  automatic`, the utility commits automatically at an appropriate time to avoid running out of active log space and avoid lock escalation.

Restarting a Failed Import

If you have import failures due to invalid input, you can, for example, use the message file generated from an `import` command that uses the `commitcount` and `messages` options to identify which record failed. Then you can issue the same `import` command with `restartcount n` or `skipcount n` to start the import from record *n*+1. Here is an example where `skipcount 550` is used so the import restarts from record 551.

```
import from employee.ixf of ixf
  commitcount 1000
  skipcount 550
  messages newemployee.out
  create into newemployee in datats index in indexts
```

The DB2 Load Utility

The `LOAD` utility is another tool you can use to insert data into a table. Note that you cannot run the `LOAD` utility against a view; the target must be a table that already exists. The major difference between a load and an import is that a load is much faster. Unlike the `IMPORT` utility, data is not written to the database using normal insert operations. Instead, the `LOAD` utility reads the input data, formats data pages, and writes directly to the database. Database changes are not logged, and constraint validations (except unique constraint) are not performed during a load operation. Triggers are also not fired.

The Load Process

A complete load process consists of four phases:

- Load phase
- Build phase
- Delete phase
- Index copy phase

In the *load phase*, the LOAD utility scans the input file for any invalid data rows that do not comply with the table definition—for example, if a table column is defined as INTEGER but the input data is stored as "abcd". Invalid data is not loaded into the table. The rejected rows and warnings are written to a dump file specified by the dumpfile modifier. Valid data is then written into the table. At the same time, table statistics (if the statistics use profile option were specified) and index keys are also collected. If the savecount option is specified in the load command, points of consistency are recorded in the message file. Consistency points are established by the LOAD utility; they are useful when it comes to restarting the load operation. You can restart the load from the last successful consistency point.

During the *build phase*, indexes are produced based on the index keys collected during the load phase. The index keys are sorted during the load phase, and index statistics are collected (if the statistics use profile option was specified).

In the load phase, the utility only rejects rows that do not comply with the column definitions. Rows that violated any unique constraint are deleted in the *delete phase*. Note that only unique constraint violated rows are deleted. Other constraints are not checked during this phase or during any load phase. You have to manually check them after the load operation is complete.

During the *index copy phase*, index data is copied from a system temporary table space to the original table space. This only occurs if a system temporary table space was specified for index creation during a load operation with the read access option specified.

The LOAD Command

The LOAD utility is powerful and has many options. In this book we take a look at the MESSAGES, WARNINGCOUNT, and SAVECOUNT options. Let's take a look at the example that follows that uses these options.

```
load from stock.del of del
   savecount 1000
   warningcount 10
   messages stock.out
   insert into stock(itemid, itemdesc, cost, inventory)
```

In the example, data in the stock.del delimited input file is loaded into a list of columns of table *STOCK*. The messages option specifies the filename stock.out to store warnings and errors encountered during the load operation. This particular load stops when the threshold of warnings specified by the warningcount option is encountered—in this example, after 10 warnings. You can check the output file for warnings and errors.

The savecount 1000 option establishes consistency points after every 1,000 rows are loaded. Because a message is issued at each consistency point, ensure that the savecount value is sufficiently high to minimize performance impact.

Consistency points are established during the load phase. You can use them to restart a failed or terminated load operation. By specifying the same `load` command but replacing `insert` with the `restart` option, the load operation automatically continues from the last consistency point.

To terminate a load, issue the same `load` command but use the `terminate` option in place of `insert`; for example

```
load from stock.del of del
  savecount 1000
  warningcount 10
  messages stock.out
  terminate
```

Loading from a CURSOR

The LOAD utility supports four file formats: IXF, DEL, ASC, and CURSOR. When using the CURSOR file type as demonstrated in the following example, the cursor must be already declared but does not need to be opened. The entire result of the query associated with the specified cursor will be processed by the LOAD utility. You must also ensure that the column types of the SQL query are compatible with the corresponding column types in the target table.

```
declare cur1 cursor as select * from oldstock;
load from cur1 of cursor
  messages curstock.out
  insert into stock
```

MODIFIED BY dumpfile and Exception Table

As mentioned earlier, the load process goes through four phases. During the load phase, data that does not comply with the column definition is not loaded. Rejected records can be saved in a dump file by using the `modified by dumpfile` modifier. If `dumpfile` is not specified, rejected records are not saved. Because the LOAD utility does not stop unless it reaches the warning threshold if one is specified, it is not easy to identify the rejected records. Hence, it is always a good practice to use the modifier and validate the message file after a load is completed. This example shows how to use `modified by dumpfile`:

```
load from stock.ixf of ixf
  modified by dumpfile=stockdump.dmp
  messages stock.out
  replace into stock
  for exception stockexp
```

Assume that the input file *stock.ixf* contains the data shown in Table 10.2.

Table 10.2   Data Stored in the Input File stock.ixf

Itemid	itemdesc	inventory
10	~~~	1
20	~~~	–
30	~~~	3
30	~~~	4
40	~~~	X
50	~~~	6
50	~~~	7
80	~~~	8

The target table *STOCK* is defined with three columns using this CREATE TABLE statement:

```
CREATE TABLE stock
        ( itemid     INTEGER NOT NULL
        , itemdesc   VARCHAR(100)
        , inventory  INTEGER NOT NULL
        , PRIMARY KEY (itemid) )
```

Notice that the second and fifth records in *stock.ixf* do not comply with the NOT NULL and numeric definitions, respectively. If the load command shown earlier is executed, a dump file (*stockdump.dmp*) is created to save rows that are not loaded due to incompatible data type and the nullability attribute. Table 10.3 shows that the dump file *stockdump.dmp* contains the rows not loaded.

Table 10.3   Rows not Loaded but Stored in the Dump File stockdump.dmp

Itemid	itemdesc	inventory
20	~~~	–
40	~~~	X

Recall that in the third load phase, the load process deletes rows that violate any unique constraint defined in the target table. You can save the deleted rows in a table called an **exception table** using the for exception option. If an exception table is not specified, the rows are discarded.

You need to create an exception table manually before you can use it. The table should have the same number of columns, column types, and nullability attributes as the target table to be loaded. You can create such a table with this command:

```
CREATE TABLE stockexp LIKE stock
```

Because the LOAD utility does not clean up the exception table, it contains invalid rows from previous load operations unless you remove existing rows before invoking the utility. To log when and why rows are rejected, you can add two other optional columns to the end of the exception table. The first column is defined as a TIMESTAMP data type to record when the record was deleted. The second column is defined as CLOB (32K) or larger and tracks the constraint names that the data violates. To add columns to the table, use the ALTER TABLE statement:

```
ALTER TABLE stockexp
  ADD COLUMN load_ts TIMESTAMP
  ADD COLUMN load_msg CLOB(32k)
```

Like the *dumpfile* modifier, it is a good practice to also use the exception table, especially if unique violations are possible. The exception table illustrated in Table 10.4 contains rows that violated the unique constraints.

Table 10.4   Exception Table stockexp

Itemid	Itemdesc	inventory
30	~~~	4
50	~~~	7

Figure 10.4 shows the big picture of the concepts of *dumpfile* and the exception table.

1. Create the target table *STOCK*.
2. Issue the `load` command with `modified by dumpfile`, `messages`, and `for exception` options.
3. Rows that do not comply with the table definition (NOT NULL and numeric column) are recorded in the *stockdump.dmp* file.
4. Rows that violated the unique constraint are deleted from the *STOCK* table and inserted into the exception table.
5. Four rows are successfully loaded into the *STOCK* table.

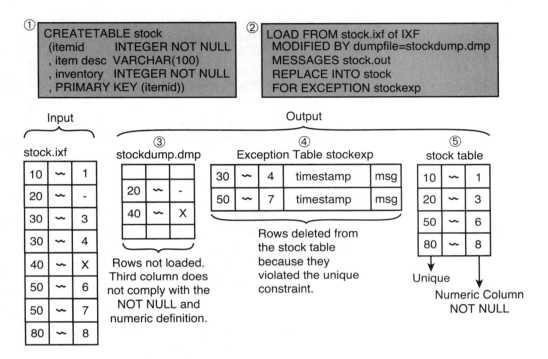

Figure 10.4 Loading data with dumpfile and an exception table

Loading from a Client

In all the examples you have seen so far, the load commands are executed from the database server, and the input files are located on the database server. You might sometimes want to invoke a load operation from a remote client as well as using a file that resides at the client. To do so, specify the `client` keyword in the command as follows:

```
load client from stock.ixf of ixf
  modified by dumpfile=stockdump.dmp
  rowcount 5000
  messages stock.out
  tempfiles path c:\loadtemp
  replace into stock
  for exception stockexcept
  lock with force
```

You cannot load a CURSOR file type from a client. The *dumpfile* and *lobsinfile* modifiers (discussed in the following sections) refer to files on the server even when the command includes the client keyword.

> **NOTE**
>
> Use the load client command when the input file resides on the client from which you are issuing the command. Use the *dumpfile, tempfile*, and *lobsinfile* modifiers for files located on the DB2 server.

The rowcount option works exactly the same as the one supported by the IMPORT utility. You can control the number of rows to be loaded with this option.

During the load process, the utility uses temporary files. By default, it allocates temporary files on the directory where the load command was issued. The tempfiles option shown in this example is used to explicitly specify a path for this purpose. Notice that the example also uses the replace mode, which replaces the old data in the target table with the new data.

Validating Data Against Constraints

The LOAD utility checks for invalid data and unique constraints during the load process. However, other constraints such as referential integrity and check constraints are not validated. DB2 therefore puts target tables defined with these constraints in check pending state, which forces you to manually validate the data before the tables are available for further processing.

The set integrity command gives you the ability to do just that. The command can be as simple as the following example, which immediately validates data against the constraints for table *STOCK*:

```
set integrity for stock immediate checked
```

There are many other options for this command; refer to the DB2 Information Center for more details.

Monitoring a Load Operation

During the phases of a load, the target table and its associated table spaces are in different states. By checking the state of the table and table space, you can tell which phase the load operation is currently in. Before introducing the tools to obtain this information, let's first discuss the different table and table space states.

Table 10.5 lists the states in which tables can be placed by the database manager. You can control some of these; others are set by the LOAD utility.

Table 10.5 Table States

Table State	Description
Normal	The table is in normal state.
Set Integrity pending	The table is placed in check pending because it has constraints that have not yet been verified. When the load operation begins, it places tables with constraints (foreign key constraint and check constraint) in this state.
Load in progress	Load is in progress on this table.
Load pending	A load operation has been activated on this table. However, it was aborted before data could be committed. Issue the load command with the terminate, restart, or replace option to bring the table out of this state.
Read access only	The table data is available for read access queries. Load operations using the allow read access option placed the table in this state.
Unavailable	The table is unavailable. You can drop or restore it from a backup. Rolling forward through a non-recoverable load operation places a table in this state.
Not load restartable	When information required for a load restart operation is unreliable, the table is placed in this state. This prevents a load restart operation from taking place. For example, a table is placed in this state when a roll forward operation is started after a failed load operation that has not been successfully restarted or terminated.
Unknown	The table state cannot be determined.

Table 10.6 lists the states in which table spaces can be placed by the database manager.

Table 10.6 Table Space States

Table State	Description
Normal	The table space is in normal state.
Quiesced: SHARE	The table space has been quiesced in SHARED mode.
Quiesced: UPDATE	The table space has been quiesced in UPDATE mode.
Quiesced: EXCLUSIVE	The table space has been quiesced in EXCLUSIVE mode.
Load pending	A table space is put in this state if a load operation has been active on one of its associated tables but has been aborted before data could be committed.
Delete pending	A table space is put in this state if one of its associated tables is undergoing the delete phase of a load operation but has been aborted or failed.

Table State	Description
Backup pending	A table space is put in this state after a Point In Time roll forward operation, or after a load operation with the `no copy` option. You must back up the table space before using it. If it is not backed up, then you cannot update the table space, and only read-only operations are allowed.
Roll forward in progress	A table space is put in this state when a roll forward operation on that table space is in progress. When the roll forward operation completes successfully, the table space is no longer in roll forward-in-progress state. The table space can also be taken out of this state if the roll forward operation is cancelled.
Roll forward pending	A table space is put in this state after it is restored or following an I/O error. After it is restored, the table space can be rolled forward to the end of the logs or to a Point In Time. Following an I/O error, the table space must be rolled forward to the end of the logs.
Restore pending	A table space is put in this state if a roll forward operation on that table space is cancelled or if a roll forward operation on that table space encounters an unrecoverable error, in which case the table space must be restored and rolled forward again.
Load in progress	A table space is put in this state if it is associated with a load operation. The load in progress state is removed when the load operation is completed or aborted.
Reorg in progress	A `REORG` operation is in progress on one of the tables associated to the table space.
Backup in progress	A backup is in progress on the table space.
Storage must be defined	For DB2 database manager internal use only.
Restore in progress	A restore is in progress on the table space.
Offline and not accessible	DB2 failed to access or use one or more containers associated to the table space, so the table space is placed offline. To take the table space out of this state, repair the containers.

Load Querying

DB2 has two utilities that you can use to obtain the table state, `load query` and `list utilities`. You can specify the following command to check the status of the load operation on table `stock` using `load query`:

```
load query table stock to c:/stockstatus.out
```

The output file *stockstatus.out* might look similar to Listing 10.1.

Listing 10.1   stockstatus.out Output File

```
SQL3501W  The table space(s) in which the table resides will not be
placed in backup pending state since forward recovery is disabled for
the database.
SQL3109N  The utility is beginning to load data from file "stock.del"
SQL3500W  The utility is beginning the "LOAD" phase at time "03-21-2013
11:31:16.597045".
SQL3519W  Begin Load Consistency Point. Input record count = "0".
SQL3520W  Load Consistency Point was successful.
SQL3519W  Begin Load Consistency Point. Input record count = "104416".
SQL3520W  Load Consistency Point was successful.
SQL3519W  Begin Load Consistency Point. Input record count = "205757".
SQL3520W  Load Consistency Point was successful.
SQL3532I  The Load utility is currently in the "LOAD" phase.

Number of rows read          = 205757
Number of rows skipped       = 0
Number of rows loaded        = 205757
Number of rows rejected      = 0
Number of rows deleted       = 0
Number of rows committed     = 123432
Number of warnings           = 0

Tablestate:
  Load in Progress
```

The `list utilities` command displays the list of active utilities on the instance. Use the `show detail` option to also display detailed progress information. Listing 10.2 illustrates sample output of this utility.

Listing 10.2   list utilities Command Output

```
list utilities show detail
ID                          = 1
Type                        = LOAD
Database Name               = SAMPLE
Partition Number            = 0
Description                 = OFFLINE LOAD Unknown file type
AUTOMATIC INDEXING INSERT COPY NO
Start Time                  = 03/15/2013 00:41:08.767650
Progress Monitoring:
```

```
Phase Number                     = 1
   Description                   = SETUP
   Total Work                    = 0 bytes
   Completed Work                = 0 bytes
   Start Time                    = 03/15/2013 00:41:08.786501
Phase Number [Current]           = 2
   Description                   = LOAD
   Total Work                    = 11447 rows
   Completed Work                = 5481 rows
   Start Time                    = 03/15/2013 00:41:09.436920
```

The report in Listing 10.2 indicates that a load was performed on the database *SAMPLE* and includes a brief description of the operation. *Progress Monitoring* tells you the current phase of the load and the number of rows already loaded and to be loaded.

The table space in which the load target table resides is placed in backup pending state if the COPY NO (the default) option is specified. The utility places the table space in this state at the beginning of the load operation. The table spaces stay in backup pending mode even when the load is complete until you perform a database or table space level backup.

Listing 10.3 shows how to retrieve the table space status using the list tablespaces command with the show detail option.

Listing 10.3   list tablespaces show detail Command Output

```
list tablespaces show detail

Tablespace ID                    = 2
 Name                            = USERSPACE1
 Type                            = System managed space
 Contents                        = Any data
  State                           = 0x0000
   Detailed explanation:
     Backup pending
 Total pages                     = 527
 Useable pages                   = 527
 Used pages                      = 527
 Free pages                      = Not applicable
 High water mark (pages)         = Not applicable
 Page size (bytes)               = 4096
 Extent size (pages)             = 32
 Prefetch size (pages)           = 16
 Number of containers            = 1
```

V10 The Ingest Utility

Modern data warehouses require continuous data input to ensure timely access to current business data. Batch loads usually require a window during which queries and database operations are locked out. For 24/7 global businesses, this is no longer acceptable. The ingest utility introduced in DB2 V10.1 offers improved data loading capabilities. The utility is also referred as Continuous Data Ingest (CDI). It specializes in high speed, continuous ingestion of data from files and named pipes into DB2 tables. It can move large amounts of real-time data without locking the target table. You don't need to choose between data concurrency versus availability. The ingest utility helps lower the amount of time you spend managing data movement between your transactional database and your data warehouse because it offers multiple advantages:

- It can run continually so it can process a continuous data stream through named pipes.
- It updates the target table with low latency in a single step. No additional storage is required for a staging table.
- It uses row-level locking, which has minimal interference with other user queries on the same table.
- It facilitates preprocessed data ingestion with high speeds, which is suitable for populating very large databases.
- It supports multiple data manipulation operations like INSERT, UPDATE, DELETE, REPLACE, and MERGE with SQL expressions.

Figure 10.5 shows how CDI is typically used. Data from the transactional database is exported into files or named pipes, which are then fed into the ingest utility as input sources. At super high speed, data is then ingested into the target warehouse database. The ingest utility supports three input data formats: delimited ASCII (DEL), non-delimited ASCII (ASC), and columns in various orders and formats.

You can use the ingest utility by issuing the INGEST command. Data that the INGEST command processes go through three phases:

1. **Transport:** The transporters read from the data source and put records on the formatter queues. If the operation is INSERT or REPLACE, there is one transporter thread for each input source, for example, one thread for each input file. If the operation is UPDATE, MERGE or DELETE, there is only one transporter thread.

2. **Format:** The formatters parse each record, convert the data into the format that DB2 requires, and put each formatted record on one of the flusher queues for that record's partition.

3. **Flush:** The flushers issue the SQL statements to perform the operations on the DB2 tables.

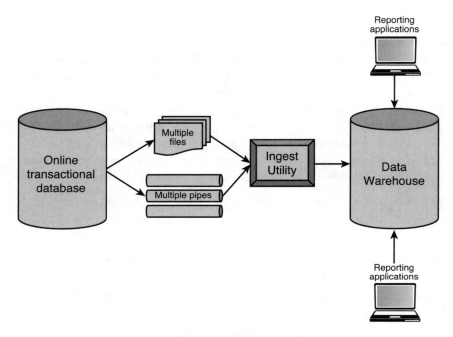

Figure 10.5   Continuous data ingest from a transactional database to a data warehouse

Listing 10.4 provides an example of the INGEST command.

Listing 10.4   INGEST Command

```
INGEST DATA FROM FILE retailTxn.del
    FORMAT DELIMITED
    (
        $field1 INTEGER EXTERNAL,
        $field2 INTEGER EXTERNAL,
        $field3 DECIMAL EXTERNAL,
        $field4 DATE,
        $field5 CHAR(1),
        $field6 INTEGER EXTERNAL
    )
    BADFILE exception_file.del
    MESSAGES message.txt
    INSERT INTO CDI.RETAIL_TRANSACTIONS
     (ID,
      CUSTOMER_ID,
```

```
ITEM_PRICE,
PURCHASE_DATE,
IS_RETURNABLE,
TOTAL_ITEM_PRICE)
VALUES ($field1,
       $field2,
       $field3,
       $field4,
       $field5,
       $field6);
```

This particular example takes a DEL file as the input source. The FORMAT clause specifies the list of field definitions. There are six fields to be expected for each row and each field is delimited by a comma. Field names start with a dollar sign ($). EXTERNAL for numeric field types indicate that the field value is specified as ASCII characters rather than in binary. If EXTERNAL is specified on any integer field, it must be specified on all other integer, decfloat, and float fields.

The BADFILE clause specifies that rows rejected by the formatters are to be written to the specified file. The formatters reject the rows due to errors. Errors such as syntax errors in the input or data cannot be converted to the specified field type. The MESSAGES clause specifies the file that will be recording informational or error messages during the ingest. The last clause specifies the target table and columns into which data is inserted.

Named pipe as illustrated in Figure 10.6 is the other input source that the ingest utility supports. A named pipe is a method of inter-process communication. It is also known as FIFO (first in, first out) for its behavior. To ingest data from a pipe, you first have to create the pipe. Next, write data from the source database into the pipe. Then use the ingest utility to write data from the pipe into the target database.

Listing 10.5 demonstrates another example of the INGEST command. In this example, the keyword PIPE is used to indicate that the input source is a named pipe. A MERGE SQL statement is used here. Refer to Appendix B, "An Introduction to SQL," for more information and examples about MERGE statements.

Listing 10.5   INGEST Command

```
INGEST FROM PIPE /home/db2inst/cdipipe
    FORMAT DELIMITED
     (
        $field1 CHAR(128),
        $field2 BIGINT   EXTERNAL,
        $field3 BIGINT   EXTERNAL,
        $field4 DECIMAL  EXTERNAL,
```

```
        $field5 SMALLINT EXTERNAL,
)
BADFILE exception_file.del
MESSAGES message.txt
MERGE INTO CDI.BPMETRICS
    ON BPNAME = $field1 AND MEMBER = $field5
  WHEN MATCHED THEN
    UPDATE SET (LOGICAL_READS, PHYSICAL READS, HIT_RATIO) =
        ($field2, $field3, $field4)
  WHEN NOT MATCHED THEN
    INSERT VALUES ($field1, $field2, $field3, $field4, $field5);
```

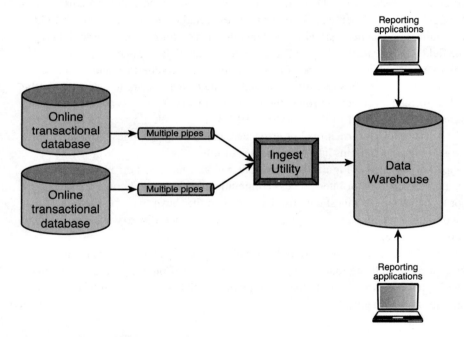

Figure 10.6   Ingest from named pipe

Table 10.7 summarizes and compares different attributes of the IMPORT, LOAD, and INGEST utilities that can be helpful to decide which tool to use.

Table 10.7   A Comparison of Different Utilities to Load Data

	IMPORT	LOAD	INGEST
Speed	Slow Uses sequential INSERTs	Very fast Writes directly to the data pages	Fast Uses parallel INSERTs
Logging	Yes	No (during load phase)	Yes
Concurrency	High, but some table level locking may occur	Low.	Very High Row Level locking used
Failure	Rollback Table accessible	Table is put in LOAD PENDING state. Manual intervention is required.	Rollback Table accessible
LOBs and XML handling	Yes	Yes	No

The db2move Utility

You can only operate the EXPORT, IMPORT, and LOAD utilities on one table at a time. To move a large number of tables between DB2 databases, use the db2move utility. Supported actions in the command are export, import, load, and copy. Based on the action you request, the utility calls the DB2 export, import, and load application programming interfaces (APIs) accordingly.

The db2move command can also be used without any options. This example exports all tables in the *SAMPLE* database:

```
db2move sample export
```

To import tables with schema *dbaadmin* and schemas that start with *dbauser*, you can specify the -tc option and provide a list of schema names; the command also accepts the wildcard (*).

```
db2move sample import -tc dbaadmin,dbauser*
```

You can also specify the *replace* mode and *lobpath*:

```
db2move sample load -lo replace -l c:\lobpath1,c:\lobpath2
```

There is no specific authorization prerequisite to invoke this utility. However, the user ID must have the correct authorization and/or privileges for the associated utility (EXPORT, IMPORT, and LOAD) to take action.

The behavior of the export, import, and load actions is exactly the same as described in the previous sections. The only action you probably are not familiar with is copy. It duplicates tables in a schema or schemas into a target database. Only tables with exactly the same schema names specified in the -sn option are copied (via export). If multiple schema names are specified, use commas to separate them without blank spaces. For example

```
db2move sample copy -sn db2inst1,prodschema
    -co target_db acctdb user peter using petepasswd ddl_and_load
```

The db2move command copies supported objects under the schema *db2inst1* and *prodschema*. The -co target_db option that follows makes the command more interesting. It specifies the target database in which the schemas are going to be copied. This option is mandatory when the copy action is specified. In addition, the target database must be different from the source database. You can provide the user and password with the user and using options when connecting to the target database.

By default, supported objects from the source schema are created, and tables are populated in the target database. This is the behavior of the ddl_and_load mode used in the preceding example. Two other modes are available: ddl_only and load_only. As the names imply, ddl_only only creates all the supported objects from the source schema, and load_only loads all specified tables from the source to the target database. Note that tables must already exist in the target database when this option is used.

Sometimes you might want to rename the schema when copying the objects to the target database. The schema_map option can be used for this purpose. You simply provide one or more pairs of schema mappings like the following:

```
schema_map ((source_schema1,target_schema1),(source_schema2,target_
schema2))
```

Extra attention is recommended when SCHEMA_MAP is used. Only the schema of the object itself is renamed; qualified objects inside the object body remain unchanged. For example, in the following view

```
CREATE VIEW FOO.v1 AS 'SELECT c1 FROM FOO.T1'
```

if the schema is renamed from *FOO* to *BAR*, only the schema of the view is changed. The underlying definition of the view is preserved. This example is mapped to the following. Note that BAR.v1 created in the target database might fail if FOO.T1 is not defined.

```
CREATE VIEW BAR.v1 AS 'SELECT c1 FROM FOO.T1'
```

A similar mapping idea also applies to table spaces. For example, you want the copied tables to be stored in a different table space name from the source database. The db2move command is extended to let you specify table space name mappings. Consider the following option:

```
tablespace_map ((TS1,TS2),(TS2,TS3), sys_any)
```

The preceding table space name mapping indicates that source TS1 is mapped to target TS2, and source TS2 is mapped to target TS3. The sys_any indicates that the remaining table spaces will use table spaces chosen by the database manager based on the table space selection algorithm. Let's put the pieces together in an example.

```
db2move sample copy -sn db2inst1,prodschema
    -co target_db acctdb user peter using petepasswd load_only
        schema_map ((db2inst1,db2inst2),(prodschema,devschema))
        tablespace_map sys_any
```

This command copies supported objects with the schema names *db2inst1* and *prodschema* from the *SAMPLE* database to the *acctdb* database. The authorization ID *peter* and the associated password are used to connect to *acctdb*. The target tables already exist in *acctdb*, and the tables are repopulated. All objects under the *db2inst1* and *prodschema* schemas are now under *db2inst2* and *devschema* respectively. Instead of using the table space name defined in the *SAMPLE* database, the default table space in *acctdb* is used instead.

Generating Data Definition Language

So far, this chapter has introduced tools and utilities that you can use to extract data and table definitions using export. In cases when you just want to extract the definition of a table, the db2look command comes in very handy.

db2look extracts the Data Definition Language (DDL) of database objects. Besides that, the tool can also generate the following:

- UPDATE statistics statements
- Authorization statements such as GRANT statements, also known as the Data Control Language (DCL)
- update commands for several Database Manager Configuration parameters and database configuration parameters
- The db2set command for several DB2 registry variables

The following examples demonstrate how the command can be used (the *SAMPLE* database is being used here):

- This command generates the DDL of objects created by *db2admin* under the schema *prod*. It also generates authorization statements. The output file *db2look.sql* captures this result.

```
db2look -d sample -u db2admin -z prod -e -x -o db2look.sql
```

- This command extracts the DDL from the *STAFF*, *DEPARTMENT*, and *EMPLOYEE* tables, and generates UPDATE statements used to replicate statistics of the tables and the associated runstats commands.

```
db2look -d sample -t staff department employee -m -r
```

- This command generates the DDL for all the database objects, including the authorization statements, and stores the result in *db2look.sql*.

```
db2look -d sample -xd -o db2look.sql
```

- This command extracts the DDL from the *CUSTOMER* and *PORDER* tables. It also exports all files necessary for XML schemas registration. The XSR objects are stored in *c:\xsddir*.

```
db2look -d sample -t customer porder -xs -xdir c:\xsddir
```

DB2 Maintenance Utilities: The Big Picture

Performing maintenance activities on your databases is essential to ensure that they are optimized for performance and recoverability. In this section, we introduce a few utilities that you should use regularly to ensure the database is healthy and optimized. Figure 10.7 provides an overview of the maintenance process that you should perform regularly against your database. The figure shows the typical order in which you should run database maintenance utilities: RUNSTATS, REORG, REORGCHK, REBIND, and FLUSH PACKAGE CACHE. Each of these utilities is explained in more detail later in the next sections.

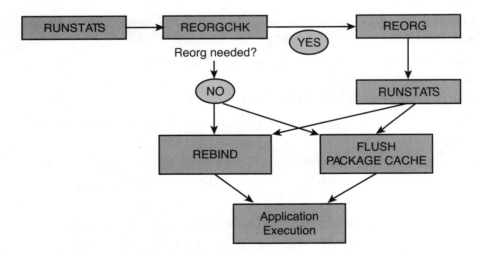

Figure 10.7 Database maintenance process

The RUNSTATS Utility

DB2 utilizes a sophisticated cost-based optimizer to determine how data is being accessed. Its decisions are heavily influenced by statistical information about the size of the database tables and indexes. Therefore, it is important to keep the database statistics up to date so that an efficient data access plan can be chosen. The RUNSTATS utility updates statistics about the physical characteristics of a table and the associated indexes. Characteristics include the number of records (cardinality), the number of pages, the average record length, and so on.

The following examples illustrate how to use this command:

- This command collects statistics on the table *db2user.employee* while letting readers and writers access the table while the statistics are being calculated.

```
runstats on table db2user.employee allow write access
```

- This command collects statistics on the table *db2user.employee*, as well as on the columns *empid* and *empname* with distribution statistics. While the command is running, the table is only available for read-only requests.

```
runstats on table db2user.employee with distribution
     on columns ( empid, empname ) allow read access
```

- The following command collects statistics on the table *db2user.employee* and detailed statistics on all its indexes.

```
runstats on table db2user.employee and detailed indexes all
```

- This command collects statistics on the table *db2user.employee* with distribution statistics on only 30 percent of the rows.

```
runstats on table db2user.employee with distribution
     tablesmple bernoulli(30)
```

You can be very specific when it comes to collecting statistics on the database objects. Different combinations of runstats options can be used to collect table statistics, index statistics, distribution statistics, sampling information, and so on.

To maintain efficient database operation, statistics should be collected regularly. You should find regular windows of reduced database activity so that database statistics can be collected without affecting the database performance. In some environments, this might not be possible.

Starting in DB2 9, automatic statistics collection allows DB2 to automatically run the runstats utility in the background to ensure the most current database statistics are available. The automatic statistics collection feature is enabled by default for any new database created. You can disable it by explicitly setting the AUTO_RUNSTATS database configuration parameter to OFF. To minimize the performance impact of automatic statistics collection, throttling of the runstats utility can be used to limit the amount of resources consumed by the utility. When the database activity is low, the utility runs more aggressively. On the other hand, when the database activity increases, the resources allocated to executing runstats are reduced. Here is an example of how to specify the level of throttling using the util_impact_priority option:

```
runstats on table db2user.employee
   with distribution default
   num_freqvalues 50 num_quantiles 50
   util_impact_priority 30
```

The acceptable priority value using `util_impact_priority` ranges from 1 (lowest priority) to 100 (highest priority, meaning unthrottled). The default priority level is 50.

The REORG and REORGCHK Utilities

As data is inserted, deleted, and updated in the database, it might not be physically placed in sequential order, which means that DB2 must perform additional read operations to access data. This usually requires more disk I/O operations, and we all know such operations are costly. To minimize I/O operations, you should consider physically reorganizing the table to the index so that related data are located close to each other.

An index is said to have a **high cluster ratio** when the data with equal or near key values is physically stored close together. The higher the cluster ratio, the better rows are ordered in index key sequence. Figure 10.8 shows the difference between indexes with high and low cluster ratio.

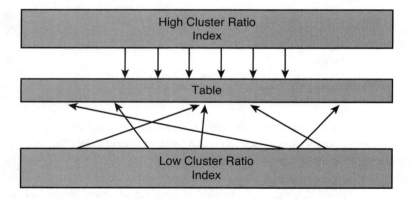

Figure 10.8   Indexes with high and low cluster ratio

An index's cluster ratio is part of the database statistics. Keeping database statistics is very important when it comes to performance. REORGCHK is a data maintenance utility that has an option to retrieve current database statistics or update the database statistics. It generates a report on the statistics with indicators identifying tables and indexes that should be reorganized (or defragmented). Using the statistics formula, REORGCHK marks the tables or indexes with asterisks (*) if there is a need to REORG.

For example, the following command generates a report of the current statistics on all tables that are owned by the runtime authorization ID:

```
reorgchk current statistics on table user
```

This command updates the statistics and generates a report on all the tables created under the schema *smith*:

```
reorgchk update statistics on schema smith
```

Figure 10.9 shows a sample output of a `reorgchk` command. You can see that the report contains table and index statistics. Every table and index defined in the database is listed. If statistics are not collected for the table or index, a dash (–) is displayed.

```
Table statistics:

F1: 100 * OVERFLOW / CARD < 5
F2: 100 * (Effective Space Utilization of Data Pages) > 70
F3: 100 * (Required Pages / Total Pages) > 80

SCHEMA.NAME                 CARD    OV      NP      FP ACTBLK      TSIZE  F1  F2  F3 REORG
------------------------------------------------------------------------------------------
Table: RFCHONG.ACT
                              18     0       1       1      -        648   0   - 100 ---
Table: RFCHONG.ADEFUSR
                               8     0       1       1      -        144   0   - 100 ---
Table: RFCHONG.CATALOG
                               0     0       0       1      -          0   0   -   0 ---
Table: RFCHONG.CL_SCHED
                               5     0       1       1      -        145   0   - 100 ---
Table: RFCHONG.CUSTOMER
                               6     0       1       1      -        648   0   - 100 ---
Table: RFCHONG.DEPARTMENT
                              14     0       1       1      -        840   0   - 100 ---
Table: RFCHONG.EMPLOYEE
                              42     0       1       1      -       3696   0   - 100 ---
------------------------------------------------------------------------------------------

Index statistics:

F4: CLUSTERRATIO or normalized CLUSTERFACTOR > 80
F5: 100 * (Space used on leaf pages / Space available on non-empty leaf pages) > MIN(50, (100 – PCTFREE))
F6: (100 – PCTFREE) * (Amount of space available in an index with one less level / Amount of space required for all key
F7: 100 * (Number of pseudo-deleted RIDs / Total number of RIDs) < 20
F8: 100 * (Number of pseudo-empty leaf pages / Total number of leaf pages) < 20

SCHEMA.NAME               INDCARD  LEAF ELEAF LVLS  NDEL    KEYS LEAF_RECSIZE NLEAF_RECSIZE LEAF_PAGE_OVERHEAD NLEAF_
------------------------------------------------------------------------------------------------------------------
Table: RFCHONG.ACT
Index: RFCHONG.PK_ACT
                              18     1     0    1      0      18            2             2               1568
Index: RFCHONG.XACT2
                              18     1     0    1      0      18            8             8               1048
Table: RFCHONG.CATALOG
Index: RFCHONG.PK_CATALOG
                               0     1     0    1      0       0            2             2               1568
Index: SYSIBM.SQL130812001007600
                               0     1     0    1      0       0            0             0               1894
Index: SYSIBM.SQL130812001007660
                               0     1     0    1      0       0            0             0               1894
Table: RFCHONG.CUSTOMER
Index: RFCHONG.CUST_CID_XMLIDX
                               -     -     -    -      -       -            -             -                  -
```

Figure 10.9 Sample output of the `reorgchk` command

To reorganize tables or indexes, use the REORG utility. It reorganizes data for a table and/or index. Although data is physically rearranged, DB2 provides the option of performing this online or offline.

By default, offline REORG enables other users to read the table. You can restrict table access by specifying the `allow no access` option. Online REORG (also called inplace REORG) supports read or write access to the table while the reorganization is happening. The reorganization is performed asynchronously; therefore, it might not be effective immediately. You can easily stop, pause, or resume the process with the appropriate options.

The following command reorganizes table *db2user.employee* and its index *db2user.idxemp*. The operation enables others perform writes to the same table:

```
reorg table db2user.employee index db2user.idxemp inplace allow write
access
```

To pause a REORG operation, issue the command with the same options but specify the pause option:

```
reorg table db2user.employee index db2user.idxemp inplace pause
```

You can also reorganize an index. If the cleanup clause is used as shown in one of the examples that follow, a cleanup is done instead of a reorganization:

```
reorg index db2user.idxemp for table db2user.employee allow write access
reorg index db2user.idxemp for table db2user.employee cleanup only
```

> **NOTE**
>
> The REORG utility rearranges the data physically but does not update the database statistics. Therefore, it is important to always execute a RUNSTATS upon completion of a REORG.

Other ways to obtain table reorganization information is to use the SNAPTAB_REORG administrative view and the SNAP_GET_TAB_REORG table function.

The REBIND Utility and the FLUSH PACKAGE CACHE Command

Before a database application program or a SQL statement can be executed, DB2 precompiles it and produces a package. A *package* is a database object that contains compiled SQL statements used in the application source file. DB2 uses the packages to access data referenced in the SQL statements. How does the DB2 optimizer choose the data access plan for these packages? It relies on database statistics at the time the packages are created.

For static SQL statements, packages are created and bound to the database at compile time. If statistics are updated to reflect the physical database characteristics, existing packages should also be updated. The REBIND utility enables you re-create a package so that the current database statistics can be used. The command is simple:

```
rebind package package_name
```

When you execute dynamic SQL statements, they are not known until the application is run and are precompiled at runtime and stored in the package cache. If statistics are updated, you can flush the cache so that dynamic SQL statements are compiled again to pick up the updated statistics. Use the following command:

```
flush package cache dynamic
```

Automatic Database Maintenance

Maintaining a database can be quite time-consuming to plan and execute. DB2 includes several automatic features, including the automatic maintenance capability, which can save time and keep your database in good shape automatically. They are enabled by default when you create a new database. The automatic database maintenance capability is adopted by most of the utilities, namely, database backups, update statistics, update statistics with statistics profiles, and data reorganization. In IBM Data Studio Version 3.1 or later, you can use the task assistant for configuring automatic maintenance. Task assistants can guide you through the process of setting options, reviewing the automatically generated commands to perform the task, and running these commands. For more details review the IBM Data Studio Information Center.

In addition to using IBM Data Studio, you can turn on or off automatic maintenance using the command-line interface by updating the following database configuration parameters and setting their values to `ON` or `OFF`. Note that if `auto_maint` parameter is set to `OFF`, then all the other parameters would also be turned off:

- Automatic maintenance (`auto_maint`)
- Automatic database backup (`auto_db_backup`)
- Automatic table maintenance (`auto_tbl_maint`)
- Automatic runstats (`auto_runstats`)
- Automatic statistics profiling (`auto_stats_prof`)
- Automatic profile updates (`auto_prof_upd`)
- Automatic reorganization (`auto_reorg`)

Database Backup, Recovery, and Roll Forward Concepts: The Big Picture

A power failure could hit your database system while it is busy processing. A user could accidentally drop an important table that you really need. What can you do to ensure that the data in the database remains consistent even when processing has been interrupted by a power failure? How can you recover a table that has been accidentally dropped? DB2's backup and recovery methods are designed to help you in these situations.

The most basic concept of recovery is ensuring that you can restore committed information, that is, information you explicitly saved using the `COMMIT` statement. This can be performed in different ways that might utilize backups (saved images of your entire database) and logs (saved operations performed against your database). Figure 10.10 shows the big picture of database recovery concept.

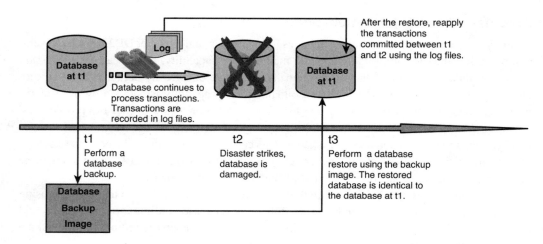

Figure 10.10   Basic concept of database recovery

At *t1*, a database backup operation is performed. This operation creates a database backup image. After the backup operation, the database continues to process transactions. These transactions change the data in the database. All changes are logged in files called log files.

At *t2*, a problem that damages the database occurs. To make the database accessible again, you can restore the database using the backup image taken at *t1*. The restored database is identical to the database at time *t1*. But what about the transactions that occurred between *t1* and *t2*? Because all transactions have been logged in the database log files, you might be able to replay the transactions by applying the log files on top of the restored database. If you replay the transactions to a point in time just before the disaster struck, then you will would be able to recover all committed data. This chapter builds on this basic scenario.

Recovery Scenarios and Strategies

To prevent the loss of your data, you need to have a recovery strategy, ensure that it works, and consistently practice and follow it. The following are some recovery scenarios you should consider:

- **System outage:** A power failure, hardware failure, or software failure can cause your database to be in an inconsistent state.

- **Transaction failure:** Users can inadvertently corrupt your database by modifying it with incorrect data or deleting useful data.

- **Media failure:** If your disk drive becomes unusable, you can lose all or part of your data.

- **Disaster:** The facility where your database server is located can get damaged by fire, flooding, power loss, or other catastrophe.

To plan your recovery strategy, ask yourself these questions:

- Can the data be loaded from another source?
- How much data can we afford to lose?
- How much time can we afford to be down?
- What storage resources are available for storing backups and log files?
- Can we have a server available to take over in the event of a failure?

The answers to these questions form the foundation of your recovery strategy.

Unit of Work (Transaction)

A unit of work (UOW), also known as a transaction, consists of one or more SQL statements that end with a COMMIT or ROLLBACK statement. All of the statements inside this UOW are treated as a complete unit, which ensures data and transactional consistency. A typical example used to explain this concept is that of a customer trying to transfer $100 from his savings account to his checking account. The UOW in this case would include all of the following to ensure consistency:

```
UPDATE Savings account set balance = balance - 100 dollars
UPDATE Checking account set balance = balance + 100 dollars
COMMIT
```

If these statements are not treated as a unit and a hardware failure occurs after the first update but before the second update, then this person loses $100! Because the statements are treated as a complete entity, this will never happen because DB2 knows that the unit of work did not complete if a COMMIT was not issued. When the system is restarted after the failure, DB2 automatically does a ROLLBACK all of the statements in the transaction, meaning it brings the database back to the state prior to the beginning of the transaction.

> **NOTE**
>
> An analogy for understanding the COMMIT statement is to compare it to the *Save* button in word processing software. When you click this button, you expect your text document to be saved. Changes made after you save the document are lost if your server crashes, but what was saved remains on disk. Similarly, when you issue a COMMIT statement, changes made to the database are guaranteed. If your server crashes, anything that was committed can be recovered, and anything that was not is lost.

Types of Recovery

There are three types of recovery in DB2:

- Crash recovery
- Version recovery
- Roll forward recovery

Each recovery type is discussed in detail in the next sections.

Crash Recovery

Crash recovery protects a database from being left in an inconsistent state following an abnormal termination. An example of an abnormal termination is a power failure. Using the banking example we just described, if a power failure occurred after the update statements but prior to the COMMIT statement, the next time DB2 is restarted and the database accessed, DB2 will VROLLBACK the UPDATE statements. Note that statements are rolled back in the reverse order that they were performed originally. This ensures that the data is consistent and that the person still has the $100 in his savings account.

By default, DB2 automatically initiates crash recovery when a database is accessed for the first time following an abnormal termination. You can disable the automatic crash recovery by setting the database configuration parameter AUTORESTART to OFF. If you do that, you need to perform crash recovery manually using the RESTART DATABASE command if the database terminates abnormally. If you do not restart the database manually in the event of a system crash, you receive the following error when you try to connect to the database:

```
SQL1015N The database must be restarted because the previous session
did not conclude normally.
```

Generally, leave AUTORESTART set to ON unless you have a specific reason to change it.

Version Recovery

Version recovery enables you to restore a snapshot of the database taken at a point in time using the BACKUP DATABASE command.

The restored database is in the same state it was in when the BACKUP command completed. If further activity was performed against the database after this backup was taken, those updates are lost. For example, assume you back up a database and then create two tables, *TABLE1* and *TABLE2*. If you restore the database using the backup image, your restored database will not contain these two tables.

Referring to Figure 10.10, at time *t3*, version recovery recovers all data in the database at *t1*. Any transactions that occurred after *t1* are lost.

Roll Forward Recovery

Roll forward recovery extends version recovery by using full database and table space backups in conjunction with the database log files. A backup must be restored first as a baseline, and then the logs are reapplied to this backup image. Therefore, all committed changes you made *after* you backed up the database can be applied to the restored database. Using the previous example with roll forward recovery, you have a number of choices to restore your database:

- You can restore the database using only the backup image. This is identical to version recovery. In this case, the restored database does not contain *TABLE1* and *TABLE2*.

- You can restore the database using the backup image and then roll forward the logs to the point after *TABLE1* was created. In this case, the restored database contains *TABLE1* but not *TABLE2*.

- You can restore the database using the backup image and then roll forward the logs to the point after *TABLE2* was created. In this case, the restored database contains *TABLE1* and *TABLE2* but no transactions after that point in time.

- You can restore the database using the backup image and then roll forward the logs all the way to the end of the logs. In this case, the restored database contains both *TABLE1* and *TABLE2* and all committed transactions that occurred on the database.

By default, crash recovery and version recovery are enabled. You learn how to enable roll forward recovery later in this chapter.

Referring back to Figure 10.10, roll forward recovery begins after time *t3* where version recovery has restored the database image from *t1*. Any transactions that were committed are applied to the database, and any transactions not committed are rolled back. The database is then at a consistent state, the same as it was just before the disaster occurred.

DB2 Transaction Logs

DB2 uses transaction logs to record all changes to your database so that they can be rolled back if you issue the ROLLBACK command or reapplied or rolled back in the event that you need to restore a database backup or during crash recovery.

NOTE

An analogy for understanding the use of transaction logs is to compare it to the *autosave* feature that many word processing software programs have. When this autosave feature kicks in, the word processing software is saving information for you. Similarly, with DB2, operations such as updates, deletes, and so on, are saved in log files whether they have been committed or not. If they were committed, they will certainly be saved.

Understanding the DB2 Transaction Logs

The ability to perform both crash recovery and roll forward recovery is provided by the database transaction logs. *Transaction logs* keep track of changes made to database objects and their data. During the recovery process, DB2 examines these logs and decides which changes to redo or undo.

Logs can be stored in files or on raw devices, although the latter is deprecated functionality. In this chapter, we use files in our examples for simplicity. To ensure data integrity and for performance reasons, DB2 uses a "write-ahead logging" mechanism to write to the logs before writing (externalizing) the database changes to disk and before returning control to the application. To illustrate this process, assume a user issues the following statements:

```
UPDATE t1 SET year = 2000 WHERE ID = '007'
UPDATE t1 SET year = 2001 WHERE ID = '011'
COMMIT
UPDATE t1 SET year = 2004 WHERE ID = '003'
```

Table *t1* and its index *ix1* are shown in the logical view of Figure 10.11.

As each statement is executed, the following takes place (Figure 10.11 uses the first UPDATE statement for illustration purposes):

- The DB2 optimizer parses the query and determines that using index *ix1* is the fastest way to retrieve the desired data. An index page access followed by a data page access is required.

- The statement and access plan information is stored in the package cache (1).

- The extent containing the desired index page (2) is brought from disk to the buffer pool (3) if the page is not already in the buffer pool. The index points to a record in the data page, and thus the extent containing the pertinent data page (4) is also brought from disk to the buffer pool (5) if it is not already in the buffer pool.

- The UPDATE operation takes place in the buffer pool.

- The UPDATE operation is recorded in the log buffer. The old and new values are kept in case the operation needs to be rolled back or undone (6).

- DB2 constantly checks to see if the log buffer is full or if one second has lapsed. If any of these events have occurred, the information in the log buffers is written to the log file on disk (7).

As you might have determined, log files contain committed and uncommitted changes. When crash recovery happens, DB2 undoes any statements that were not committed, and reissues any statements that were committed so that the database is left transactionally consistent.

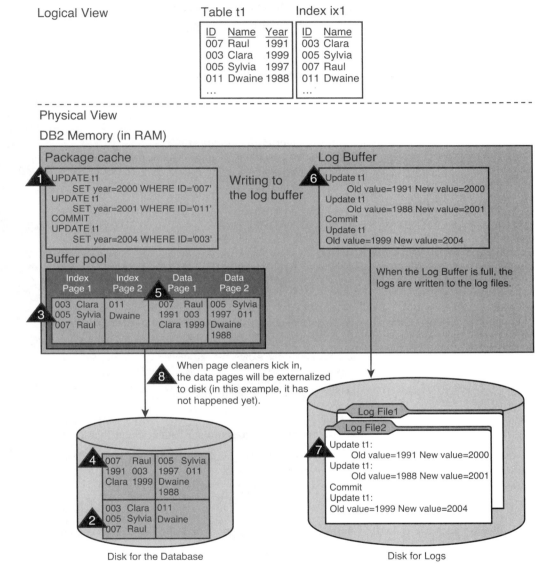

Figure 10.11   Concept of transaction logging

Note too that the rows that were changed in the buffer pool and that were recorded in the log files might not have been saved to the database disks. The changed rows can eventually be written to disk when "page cleaner" processes are run to "clean" the modified (or dirty) pages from the buffer pool (8). This is not done immediately after the statement is executed or when the transaction commits for performance reasons. DB2 is already storing the information in the log files on disk to ensure data integrity, and the change is reflected in the buffer pool, so there is no need to perform an I/O right away to store the changed pages to disk.

When data is committed and also saved to disk, the data is considered to be **externalized**.

Primary and Secondary Log Files

The *Disk for Logs* in Figure 10.11 is known as the *active log directory* or *log space*. Its location is specified in the database configuration parameter *Path to log files*.

The size of the log space is controlled by three database configuration parameters. Table 10.8 discusses what these parameters are.

Table 10.8   Log Parameters

Log Parameters	Description/Usage
LOGPRIMARY	Indicates the number of primary log files that are allocated in the active log directory.
	Primary log files are allocated during the first database connect or during database activation by the `ACTIVATE DATABASE` command.
LOGSECOND	Controls the maximum number of secondary log files that can be allocated in the active log directory.
	Secondary log files are allocated dynamically one at a time as needed, when there are no more primary logs available for transaction processing.
LOGFILSIZ	Specifies the size of the log files (in number of 4KB pages).

For example, let's say you have the following values in your database configuration:

```
Log file size (4KB)             (LOGFILSIZ)  = 1000
Number of primary log files     (LOGPRIMARY) = 3
Number of secondary log files (LOGSECOND)    = 2
Path to log files                            = C:\mylogs\
```

Because each file is 4MB (1000 × 4KB), and there are a total of 5 log files (3 primary logs and 2 secondary logs), the log space is 20MB.

NOTE

The maximum number of log files (logprimary + logsecond) cannot exceed 256 files. If infinite logging is set (as discussed later in the chapter), then `LOGPRIMARY` cannot exceed 256 files.

When the first connection is made to a database or the database is activated, the primary log files are created and allocated on disk. In the example configuration just given, as soon as the first connection to the database is established, three primary log files of 1000 4KB-pages each are allocated or initialized. If you examine the C:\mylogs directory, you see these three files:

```
2013-05-10 08:06p 4,104,192 S0000000.LOG
2013-05-10 08:06p 4,104,192 S0000001.LOG
2013-05-10 08:06p 4,104,192 S0000002.LOG
3 File(s) 12,312,576 bytes
```

Now, let's say you decide to perform the following transaction, which inserts a million records into a table:

```
INSERT INTO TABLE1 VALUES(1);
INSERT INTO TABLE1 VALUES(2);
...
INSERT INTO TABLE1 VALUES(1000000);
COMMIT;
```

DB2 fills up the first log file, continues with the second log file, and then the third log file. After it fills up the third log file, there are no more primary logs available (remember that LOGPRIMARY is set to 3, so a maximum of three primary logs can exist at any time). At this point DB2 dynamically allocates a secondary log file. After the first secondary log file is filled up successfully, DB2 attempts to allocate another secondary log file. When this second log file is filled, DB2 attempts to allocate a third secondary log file. However, because this example has LOGSEC-OND set to 2 and there are already two secondary log files allocated, DB2 cannot allocate another secondary log file. If LOGSECOND were set to a number more than 2, this process of allocating secondary log files continues until the maximum number of secondary log files is reached.

At the point when the maximum number of secondary log files is reached, if DB2 needs more log space to complete the transaction, a *log full* condition occurs. This means there is not enough room left in the logs to record and complete the transaction. The transaction encountering this log full condition is rolled back. In general, DB2 tries to reuse the old logs first, if possible, before creating a new one. DB2 uses an algorithm that reduces the chances of encountering a log full condition.

Log full is an undesirable condition. Not only is all of the work performed up to this point within the transaction lost, but the rollback also takes some time. For this reason, it is important to ensure that you allocate enough log space to accommodate your workload and particularly your longest or largest transactions; alternatively, if your application logic permits it, you should COMMIT often.

Generally, you do not want to allocate a huge number of PRIMARY logs because they are allocated or initialized when the database is activated. If you specify a large number, DB2 can spend some time creating/initializing these files, causing the first connection to the database to take a long time. If your transaction workload is generally small throughout the day, all that log space is wasted. You might want to specify enough LOGSECOND log files to handle a spike in your workload (for example, a heavier workload with long transactions at the end of a month) and have just enough primary logs to cover the normal workloads.

Another undesirable condition is a *log disk full* condition. Unlike a log full condition, where DB2 runs out of logging space because the maximum number of primary and secondary log files have been reached, a log disk full condition occurs when the drive or file system that hosts the active log directory is physically full, meaning no more log files can be created, even though the maximum numbers of primary and secondary log files might not have been reached. This condition could be caused by the file system being too small or the active log directory becoming filled by too many inactive (archive) log files. (You learn what inactive logs are in the next section.)

By default, a transaction that receives a log disk full error fails and is rolled back, just as in the case of a log full condition. However, you can change this behavior by setting the database configuration parameter BLK_LOG_DSK_FUL to YES. Setting this parameter to YES causes applications to block (or wait) instead of rolling back when DB2 encounters a disk full error when writing to the log files. While the applications are waiting (or blocked), DB2 attempts to create the log file every five minutes until it succeeds. After each attempt, DB2 writes a message to the administration notification log. The way to confirm that your application is blocked because of a log disk full condition is to monitor the administration notification log.

> **NOTE**
>
> The administration notification log is discussed in Appendix D, "Diagnosing Problems."

Until the log file is successfully created, any user application that attempts to update table data is not processed. Read-only queries might not be directly affected; however, if a query needs to access data that is locked by an update request or a data page that is fixed in the buffer pool by the updating application, read-only queries also appear to hang.

When you have determined that DB2 is waiting because the log disk is full, you can resolve the situation by deleting inactive log files, moving inactive log files to another file system, or by increasing the size of the file system so that a new log file can be created.

Active Logs

The state of a log is determined by whether the transactions that are recorded in it have been committed and whether or not they have been externalized to disk. There are three log file states: active, online archive, and offline archive.

A log is considered *active* if any of the following applies:

- It contains transactions that have not yet been committed or rolled back.
- It contains transactions that have been committed but whose changes have not yet been written to the database disk (externalized).

- It contains transactions that have been rolled back but whose changes have been written to the database disk (externalized).

In Figure 10.11, log file 2 is an active log because it contains a transaction that has not yet been committed (the last UPDATE statement). Log file 2 also contains a transaction that has been committed but has not been externalized to disk (the first two UPDATE statements).

Imagine that at this point a power failure occurs and everything in the buffer pool is lost. The only place where you can find a record of these transactions is in the database log files. When the database is restarted, it goes through crash recovery.

DB2 first looks at what is known in the log control file to determine the oldest of the following:

- The oldest committed transaction that has not been externalized
- The oldest uncommitted transaction that has been externalized

After determining the recovery starting point, it then determines what log contains this particular transaction.

DB2 will then redo or undo all transactions from that point forward until it reaches the end of the logs.

Figure 10.11 indicates that no page cleaning has occurred, so the committed and uncommitted transactions are still in the buffer pool and not externalized. DB2 then finds the oldest transaction needing recovery and identifies that it starts in log file 1. DB2 first opens log file 1 and reads its contents. DB2 will redo the transactions that have a COMMIT and undo the transactions that do not. Figure 10.11 shows DB2 will redo all of the updates in log file 1 and the first two UPDATE statements in log file 2. Because the last update was not committed, it is not replayed. All of the active log files, by definition, are required for crash recovery. If you lose the active logs, crash recovery cannot complete, and the database is inaccessible.

Active logs typically reside in the active log path. If you have enabled infinite logging, active log files might need to be retrieved from the archive site. (Infinite logging is discussed later in the chapter.)

Online Archive Logs

Online archive logs are files that contain only committed, externalized transactions. In other words, they are logs that are no longer active and therefore no longer needed for crash recovery.

Online archive logs still reside in the active log directory. This is why they are called "online." The term *online archive logs* might sound complicated, but all it means is that inactive logs reside in the active log directory.

Although these logs are no longer needed for crash recovery, they are retained for roll forward recovery. You see why in a later section in this chapter.

Offline Archive Logs

File systems and disk drives have limited space. If all of the online archive logs are kept in the active log directory, this directory is soon filled up, causing a log disk full condition. Therefore, the online archive logs should be moved out of the active log directory as soon as possible. You can do this manually, or DB2 can invoke a program or procedure to do this for you. After this has been done, these logs become offline archive logs.

Like the online archive logs, offline archive logs are also retained for roll forward recovery.

Logging Methods

DB2 supports three logging methods: circular logging, archival logging, and infinite active logging.

Circular Logging

Circular logging is the default logging mode for DB2. As the name suggests, in this method the logs are reused in a circular mode. For example, if you have three primary logs, DB2 uses them in this order: Log #1, Log #2, Log #3, Log #1, Log #2...

Note that in this sequence Log #1 and Log #2 are reused. When a log file is reused, its previous contents are completely overwritten. Therefore, a log can be reused if and only if the transactions it contains have already been committed or rolled back and externalized to the database disk. In other words, the log must not be an active log. This ensures DB2 has the necessary logs for crash recovery if needed. Figure 10.12 shows how circular logging works.

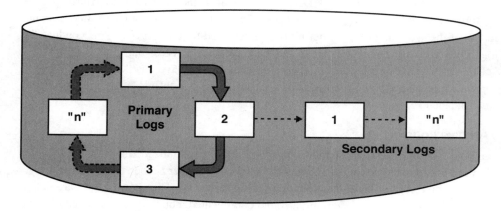

Figure 10.12   Circular logging

Although the ability to recover from a crash is assured, you cannot reapply the transactions that were in these logs because they have been overwritten. Therefore, circular logging only supports crash recovery and version recovery, not roll forward recovery.

Archival Logging

Archival logging keeps the log files even after they contain committed and externalized data. To enable archival logging, you can change the value of the LOGARCHMETH1 database configuration parameter. We discuss the possible values for the LOGARCHMETH1 parameter later in this section.

With archival logging, roll forward recovery is supported. The contents of inactive logs are saved rather than overwritten; therefore, they can be reapplied during roll forward recovery. Depending on the value set in LOGARCHMETH1, you can have the log files copied or saved to various locations. When the log is needed during roll forward recovery, DB2 retrieves it from that location and restores it into the active log directory.

With archival logging, if you have three primary logs in a database, DB2 allocates them in this order: Use Log #1, use Log #2, use Log #3, archive Log #1 (when no longer active), create and use Log #4, archive Log #2, create and use Log #5...notice that the log number increases as new logs are required. Figure 10.13 shows how archival logging works.

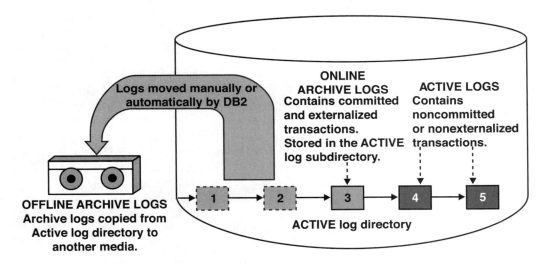

Figure 10.13   Archival logging

How DB2 archives and retrieves a log file depends on the value set in the LOGARCHMETH1 database parameter. The possible values are OFF, LOGRETAIN, USEREXIT, DISK, TSM, and VENDOR and are discussed in detail in Table 10.9.

Table 10.9   Additional Logging-Related Database Configuration Parameters

LOGARCHMETH1 Values	Description/Usage
OFF	Archival logging is disabled, and circular logging is used.
LOGRETAIN	The log files are retained in the active log directory.

Let's use the example in Figure 10.3 to demonstrate how LOGRETAIN works. DB2 starts with three primary logs: log #1, log #2, and log #3. When DB2 fills up all these three logs, it checks if log #1 has become inactive. If it has, DB2 renames log #1 to log #4. The set of primary logs then becomes log #2, log #3, and log #4. If log #1 is still active, DB2 creates log #4 as secondary log. When a new log is needed, DB2 checks if log #2 has become inactive. If it has, DB2 renames log #1 as log #5. If not, it creates log #5 as a secondary log. The process is repeated until LOGSECOND is reached, at which point the log full condition occurs.

Note with LOGRETAIN, inactive log files are never overwritten. In Figure 10.3, even though log #1 and log #2 have already become inactive, they still remain in the active log directory. (At this point, they are online archive logs.) You have to manually move them to a different location, or the active log directory will soon be filled up by these logs. However, you should never delete these logs without making a copy of them somewhere because they might be needed for roll forward recovery. After logs #1 and #2 have been moved to another location, they become offline archive logs. |
| USEREXIT | The archive and retrieval of the logs are performed automatically by a user-supplied user exit program called **db2uext2**.

The user exit program archives a log file to a different location as soon as it becomes full, even if it is still active. Archiving a log file simply means making a copy of it somewhere; the log itself still remains in the active log directory. If the log is still active, DB2 does not reuse it. If the log is inactive, when a new log is required, DB2 renames and reuses it.

Once again, let's use the example in Figure 10.3 to explain how the USEREXIT works. DB2 starts with three primary logs: log#1, log #2, and log #3. As soon as these logs are full, DB2 calls the user exit program to archive them. When DB2 needs a new log, it checks to see if log #1 is active. If log #1 is still active, DB2 creates secondary log #4. If log #1 is inactive, DB2 renames log #1 to log #4 and reuses it (instead of creating a new log #4). This helps to eliminate the overhead of creating a new file. There is no loss of data in reusing a log that has been archived because its copy can always be retrieved when needed.

When logs are needed during recovery, DB2 calls the user exit program to retrieve the necessary logs. Because everything is handled by the user exit program, you should not manipulate the log files manually. Doing so can potentially interfere with the user exit program.

There is no need to use user exit programs anymore, but user exit support is still available for backwards compatibility. |

LOGARCHMETH1 Values	Description/Usage
DISK:directory	With this setting, archival logging uses a similar algorithm as in USEREXIT. The only difference is instead of calling the user exit program, DB2 automatically archives the logs from the active log directory to the specified *directory*. During recovery, DB2 automatically retrieves these logs back to the active log directory.
TSM:[management class name]	With this setting archival logging uses a similar algorithm as in USEREXIT. The only difference is that the logs are archived on the local Tivoli Storage Manager (TSM) server. The management class name parameter is optional. If not specified, the default management class is used.
VENDOR:library	With this setting, archival logging uses a similar algorithm as in USEREXIT. The only difference is that logs are archived using the specified vendor library.

You can optionally configure the LOGARCHMETH2 parameter. This parameter specifies the secondary archive log method and can be set using the same values as for LOGARCHMETH1. If set, logs are archived to both this destination and the destination specified by the LOGARCHMETH1 parameter.

In addition to LOGARCHMETH1 and LOGARCHMETH2, Table 10.10 lists a number of other logging-related database parameters.

Table 10.10 Additional Logging-Related Database Configuration Parameters

DB CFG Parameters	Description
FAILARCHPATH	Failover archive path. Specifies a third target to archive log files if the primary and secondary archival paths fail. The medium must be disk. It is a temporary storage area for the log files until the primary path(s) becomes available again, at which time the log files are moved from this directory to the primary archive path(s). By moving the log files to this temporary location, log directory full situations might be avoided.
NUMARCHRETRY	Specifies the number of retries attempted on primary target(s) before archiving to FAILARCHPATH. The default is 5.
ARCHRETRYDELAY	Specifies the number of seconds between retry attempts. The default is 20 seconds.

DB CFG Parameters	Description
LOGARCHOPT1 and LOGARCHOPT2	Specifies a string that is passed on to the TSM server or vendor APIs. For TSM, this field is used to enable the database to retrieve logs that were generated on a different TSM node or by a different TSM user. The string must be provided in the following format: `"-fromnode=nodename -fromowner=ownername"` where nodename is the name of the TSM node that originally archived the log files, and ownername is the name of the TSM user who originally archived the log files. Each log archive options field corresponds to one of the log archive methods: LOGARCHOPT1 is used with LOGARCHMETH1, and LOGARCHOPT2 is used with LOGARCHMETH2.

Infinite Logging

Infinite active logging (Infinite logging) is built on top of archival logging. With circular logging and archival logging, log space can potentially be filled with active logs if you have very long running transactions. If you have long-running transactions, you can use infinite active logging so that you do not run out of log or log disk space.

To enable infinite active logging:

- Archive logging must be enabled with one of the automatic archival methods; that is, LOGARCHMETH1 must be set to one of USEREXIT, DISK, TSM, or VENDOR.
- Set the LOGSECOND database configuration parameter to -1.

When archival logging is enabled, a log is marked for archival as soon as it becomes full. However, DB2 leaves the log in the log directory until it becomes inactive for performance reasons and then renames the file for reuse. With infinite logging, DB2 still archives the log as soon as it is full, but it does not wait for it to become inactive before it renames the file for reuse. This guarantees that the active log directory never fills up because any logs can be reused after they are filled and archived. Note that the use of infinite active logging can prolong crash recovery times as active logs might need to be retrieved from the archive site.

Log Mirroring

Even with all the protection provided by DB2 logging, there is still a concern of someone accidentally deleting an active log file or a disk crash that causes data corruption in your database. Mirroring the log files helps protect your database from these potential disasters. Log mirroring enables you to specify a secondary path for the database to manage copies of the active logs. DB2 attempts to write the log buffer to the log files in both places. When one log path is damaged for whatever reason, DB2 can continue to read and write to the other log path, keeping the database up and running.

To enable log mirroring, set the MIRRORLOGPATH database configuration parameter to a valid drive, path, or device.

Make certain you place your secondary log path on a physically separate disk or disk array (preferably one that is also on a different disk controller and in a different cabinet). This way, the disk drive or disk controller cannot be a single point of failure. When log mirroring is first enabled, it does not become active and used until the next database restart. When there is a failure to either the active log path or the mirror log path, the database marks the failing path as "bad," write a message to the administration notification log and write subsequent log records to the remaining "good" log path only. The next time DB2 attempts to write to the "bad" path is when the current log file is full or truncated and it starts writing to the next log file. If the failure has been fixed at that time, then DB2 continues to write to both log paths. If the failure has not been fixed, then DB2 does not attempt to use the path again until the next log file is required. DB2 continues to perform this verification check on the "bad" path each time it starts a new log file until the failure is fixed and DB2 can write to both log paths again. DB2 does not synchronize the logs in the two log paths but keeps track of access errors that occurred so that the correct path is used when log files are archived. If one log path has already been marked bad and a failure occurs while the writing to the good path, the database stops.

Handling the DB2 Transaction Logs

DB2 logs are crucial for crash and roll forward recovery. A missing or corrupted log file causes crash recovery and rolls forward recovery to fail, which can potentially render the database inaccessible. We recommend that you do not manipulate any logs manually.

If it becomes necessary to work with the log files for some reason, exercise extreme care. Never remove log files based solely on their timestamps. Understanding how log files are time-stamped can save you from losing active logs and creating a potential disaster.

When the primary log files are created at database activation, they are *all* given a time-stamp based on the activation time. These timestamps do not change until DB2 writes transaction updates to the logs, one log file at a time. These logs are kept in the active log directory, even though they may be empty. For example, if LOGPRIMARY is set to 20, then 20 log files are created with timestamp A. Suppose transactions begin and write to logs 1 through 10 at timestamps greater than A. At this point in time, you still have 20 logs in the active log directory. Logs 1 through 10 have timestamps greater than A. Logs 11 through 20 have timestamps at exactly A. Assume that these logs (logs 1 to 10) span multiple days of work. In this scenario, you might think that logs 11 to 20 are older logs because of their older timestamps and can be removed. In fact, these logs are still active logs. If you remove them, and DB2 requires those logs (for example, the next log required would be log 11), the database crashes and marked as corrupted. The only way to recover is to restore from a recent backup. Therefore, we highly recommend you let DB2 handle the logs automatically.

To determine which log files are active and which ones are not, look at the value of the *First active log file* parameter in the database configuration. All the logs prior to the value are inactive; all the log files starting at the value are active—therefore, you should not touch them.

For example, if the first active log file is S0000005.LOG, then logs 0, 1, 2, 3, and 4 are inactive. All the logs starting at log 5 are active.

Recovery Terminology

Depending on the type of backups that you take, there are different methods you can use to recover your database in the event of an error. In addition, the configuration you choose for your database determines whether you can use the database logs to reapply transactions that might otherwise be lost if you need to restore your database from a backup.

Logging Methods Versus Recovery Methods

Circular logging supports only crash and version recovery. Archival logging supports all types of recovery: crash, version, and roll forward.

Recoverable Versus Nonrecoverable Databases

Recoverable databases can be recovered using crash or roll forward recovery, and as discussed before, archival logging is required to support roll forward recovery. Nonrecoverable databases do not support roll forward recovery and use only circular logging. Table 10.11 shows which logging and recovery methods work together.

Table 10.11   Summary of Logging and Recovery Methods

Logging Method	Supports Crash Recovery	Supports Version Recovery	Supports Roll Forward Recovery	Recoverable Database
Circular Logging (LOGARCHMETH1 = OFF)	Yes	Yes	No	No
Archival Logging (LOGARCHMETH1 = LOGRETAIN, USEREXIT, DISK, TSM, or VENDOR)	Yes	Yes	Yes	Yes

Performing Database and Table Space Backups

There are two different granularities that you can choose for your backups; you can choose to back up the entire database or one or more table spaces from within the database. You also have two different options for how the backup can be performed; you can choose whether the backup be taken online or offline. The next section discusses what an online or offline backup is. These options can be combined, and different choices are available depending on the type of logging method is selected, which provides you with a very flexible recovery mechanism for your databases.

Online Access Versus Offline Access

In the following sections we use the terms "online" and "offline" quite often. An *online backup* allows other applications or processes to connect to the database, as well as read and modify data while the operation is running. An *offline backup* does *not* allow other applications or processes to access the database and its objects while the operation is being performed.

Database Backup

A database backup is a complete copy of your database objects. In addition to the data, a backup copy contains information about the table spaces, containers, the system catalog, database configuration file, the log control file, and the recovery history file. Note that a backup does *not* contain the Database Manager Configuration file or the values of registry variables.

You must have `SYSADM`, `SYSCTRL`, or `SYSMAINT` authority to perform a backup using the `BACKUP DATABASE` command. Refer to the DB2 Information Center for details about this command.

To perform an offline backup of the *SAMPLE* database and store the backup copy in the directory d:\mybackups, use the following command on Windows. The d:\mybackups directory must be created before the backup can be performed.

```
BACKUP DATABASE sample TO d:\mybackups
```

To perform an offline backup of the *SAMPLE* database and store the backup copy in two separate directories, use the following command on Linux/UNIX:

```
BACKUP DATABASE sample                        (1)
  TO /db2backup/dir1, /db2backup/dir2         (2)
  WITH 4 BUFFERS                              (3)
  BUFFER 4096                                 (4)
  PARALLELISM 2                               (5)
```

where

1. Indicates the name (or alias) of the database to back up.
2. Specifies the location(s) where you want to store the backup file. DB2 writes to both locations in parallel.
3. Indicates how many buffers from memory can be used during the backup operation. Using more than one buffer can improve performance.
4. Indicates the size of each buffer in 4KB pages.
5. Specifies how many media reader and writer threads are used to take the backup.

If not specified, DB2 automatically chooses optimal values for the number of buffers, the buffer size, and the parallelism settings. The values are based on the amount of utility heap available, the number of processors available, and the database configuration. The objective is to minimize the time it takes to complete the backup operation.

Notice there is no keyword for OFFLINE in the syntax, as this is the default mode.

If you have a 24/7 database, shutting down the database is not an option. To perform backups to ensure the database's recoverability, you can perform online backups instead. You must specify the keyword ONLINE in the BACKUP DATABASE command as shown here:

```
BACKUP DATABASE sample ONLINE TO /dev/rdir1, /dev/rdir2
```

Because there are users accessing the database while it is being backed up, it is likely that some of the changes made by these users are stored in data and index pages in the backup image. A transaction might be in the middle of processing when the backup was taken. This means the backup image likely contains a database that is in an inconsistent state.

If this online backup is used to restore a database, as soon as the restore operation finishes, DB2 places the database in roll forward pending state. A roll forward operation must be performed to bring the database back to a consistent state before you can use it. To do this you must roll forward to at least the time when the backup completed.

If you have set LOGARCHMETH1 to USEREXIT, DISK, TSM, or VENDOR, DB2 automatically retrieves the logs into the active log directory. Otherwise, if LOGARCHMETH1 was set to LOGRE-TAIN, you must retrieve the log files manually before rolling forward the database. To perform the roll forward, all logs that were active at the time of the backup must be in, or copied into, the active log directory when needed.

> **NOTE**
>
> Archival logging must be enabled to perform online backups.

To backup the logs as part of the backup copy, use the INCLUDE LOGS option of the BACKUP DATABASE command. When you specify this option, the logs are backed up along with the database during an online backup operation. This ensures that if the archived logs are not available, the backup is still recovered to a minimum Point In Time (PIT) using the logs that are included in the backup image. If you want to restore to a later PIT, additional log files might be required.

For example, to take an online backup of the *SAMPLE* database along with the logs, using the destination directory /dev/rdir1, issue the command shown here:

```
BACKUP DATABASE sample ONLINE TO /dev/rdir1 INCLUDE LOGS
```

Table Space Backup

In a database where only some of your table spaces change considerably, you can opt not to back up the entire database but only specific table spaces. To perform a table space backup, you can use the following syntax:

```
BACKUP DATABASE sample
  TABLESPACE (syscatspace, userspace1, userspace2)
  ONLINE
  TO /db2tbsp/backup1, /db2tbsp/backup2
```

The keyword TABLESPACE indicates this is a table space backup, not a full database backup. You can also see from the example that you can include as many table spaces as desired in the backup. Temporary table spaces cannot be backed up using a table space level backup.

You should back up related table spaces together. For example, if using DMS table spaces where one table space is used for the table data, another one for the indexes, and another one for LOBs, you should back up all of these table spaces at the same time so that you have consistent information. This is also true for table spaces containing tables defined with referential constraints between them.

> **NOTE**
> Archival logging must be enabled to perform table space backups.

Incremental Backups

As database sizes continue to grow, the time and resources required to back up and recover these databases also grows substantially. Full database and table space backups are not always the best approach when dealing with large databases because the storage requirements for multiple copies of such databases are enormous.

To address this issue, DB2 provides incremental backups. An **incremental backup** is a backup image that contains only pages that have been updated since the previous backup was taken. In addition to updated data and index pages, each incremental backup image also contains all of the initial database metadata (such as database configuration, table space definitions, database history, and so on) that is normally stored in full backup images.

There are two kinds of incremental backups:

- In incremental **cumulative** backups, DB2 backs up all of the data that has changed since the last full database backup.
- In **delta** backups, DB2 backs up only the data that has changed since the last successful full, cumulative, or delta backup.

Figure 10.14 illustrates these concepts.

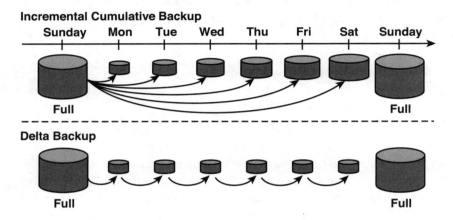

Figure 10.14   Incremental and delta backups

For incremental backups, if there was a problem with your database that would render it unusable, and this event happened some time after the incremental backup was taken on Friday, you would restore the first Sunday's full backup, followed by the incremental backup taken on Friday.

For delta backups, if there was a problem with your database that would render it unusable, and this event happened some time after the delta backup was taken on Friday, you would restore the first Sunday's full backup, followed by each of the delta backups taken on Monday through Friday inclusive.

To enable incremental and delta backups, the TRACKMOD database configuration parameter must be set to YES. This allows DB2 to track database modifications so that the backup utility can detect which database pages must be included in the backup image. After setting this parameter to YES, you must take a full database backup to have a baseline against which incremental backups can be taken.

To perform a cumulative incremental backup on the *SAMPLE* database to directory /dev/rdir1, issue

```
BACKUP DB sample
  INCREMENTAL TO /dev/rdir1
```

To perform a delta backup on the *SAMPLE* database to the directory /dev/rdir1, issue:

```
BACKUP DB sample
  INCREMENTAL DELTA TO /dev/rdir1
```

The Backup Files

The backup images are stored as files. The name of the backup file contains the following parts:

- Database alias
- Type of backup (0=Full database, 3=Table space, 4=Copy from LOAD)
- Instance name
- Database partition (always DBPART000 for a single-partition database)
- Timestamp of the backup
- The image sequence number

The naming convention applies to all platforms. In Figure 10.15, you can see the full file name of each backup image.

Linux/UNIX/Windows

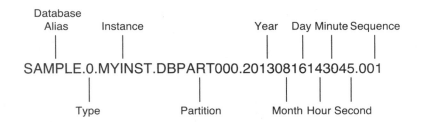

Figure 10.15 Backup file name hierarchy

For example, the following command (on a Windows server)

```
BACKUP DATABASE sample to C:\temp
```

produces the backup image shown in Figure 10.16.

```
08/16/2013  02:30 PM    <DIR>          .
08/16/2013  02:30 PM    <DIR>          ..
08/16/2013  02:30 PM      176,422,912 SAMPLE.0.DB2.DBPART000.20130816143045.001
              1 File(s)      176,422,912 bytes
              2 Dir(s)   6,767,071,232 bytes free
```

Figure 10.16 Backup file on Windows

The backup image can be found in the directory specified in the BACKUP DATABASE command or the directory where the command is issued from.

> **NOTE**
>
> Do not change the name of the backup file. You will not be able to restore your database if you do.

Performing Database and Table Space Recovery

You can restore a backup image using the RESTORE DATABASE command. You can choose to recover everything in the image, just an individual table space, or multiple table spaces.

Database Recovery

You can restore a database backup image using the RESTORE DATABASE command. You can restore the database into a newly created database, or you can restore on top of an existing database. To restore to a new database you need SYSADM or SYSCTRL authority. To restore into an existing database you need SYSADM, SYSCTRL, or SYSMAINT authority.

For example, to perform a restore of the *SAMPLE* database, you can use the syntax shown here:

```
RESTORE DATABASE sample             (1)
    FROM C:\DBBACKUP                 (2)
    TAKEN AT 20130428131259          (3)
    WITHOUT ROLLING FORWARD          (4)
    WITHOUT PROMPTING                (5)
```

where

1. Indicates the name of the database image to restore.
2. Specifies the location where the input backup image is located.
3. If there is more than one backup image in the directory, this option identifies the specific backup based on the timestamp, which is part of the backup file name.
4. If a database has archival logging enabled, a restore operation puts the database in roll forward pending state, regardless of whether the backup was online or offline. If restoring from an offline backup, you can choose not to roll forward. This option tells DB2 not to place the database in roll forward pending state. When restoring from an online backup, the "without rolling forward" option cannot be used, as you must roll forward to at least the time that the backup completed.
5. Specifies that the restore is to be performed unattended. Action that normally requires user intervention returns an error message. When using a removable media device, such as tape or diskette, you are prompted when the end of the device is reached, even if this option is specified.

Note that there is no keyword OFFLINE in the RESTORE DATABASE syntax, as this is the default mode. In fact, for the RESTORE utility, this is the only mode allowed if you are restoring a whole database.

When we talked about database backups, we mentioned that the INCLUDE LOGS option enables you to back up the logs needed for roll forward recovery. If you specified this option, when restoring the database, you need to provide a location to restore the log files with the LOG-TARGET option. You can also choose to only restore the log files without restoring the backup image.

For example, on Windows, to restore the *SAMPLE* database from a backup image residing in the C:\DBBACKUP directory and restore the log files to the directory C:\DB2\NODE0000\ SQL00001\SQLOGDIR, issue the following command

```
RESTORE DATABASE sample
   FROM C:\DBBACKUP
   LOGTARGET C:\DB2\NODE0000\SQL00001\SQLOGDIR
```

To restore just the logs to the same directory, issue

```
RESTORE DATABASE sample
   LOGS FROM C:\DBBACKUP
   LOGTARGET C:\DB2\NODE0000\SQL00001\SQLOGDIR
```

Table Space Recovery

You can restore table spaces either from a full database backup or from a table space backup. The following listing shows an example of a table space restore:

```
RESTORE DATABASE sample                     (1)
   TABLESPACE (mytblspace1)                 (2)
   ONLINE                                   (3)
   FROM /db2tbsp/backup1, /db2tbsp/backup2  (4)
```

where

1. Indicates the name of the database image to restore.
2. Indicates that this is a table space restore and specifies the name of the table space(s) to restore from the backup image.
3. Indicates this is an online restore. Note that for user table spaces, both online and offline restores are allowed.
4. Specifies the location where the backup file is located.

Table Space Recovery Considerations

After a table space is restored, it is *always* placed in roll forward pending state. To make the table space accessible, the table space must be rolled forward to its minimum PIT. This minimum PIT ensures that the table space is consistent with the system catalogs, for example

1. Say at time *t1* you took a full database backup that included table space *mytbls1*.

2. At time *t2* you created table *myTable* in the table space *mytbls1*. This set the minimum PIT for recovery of the table space *mytbs1* to time *t2*.

3. At time *t3* you decided to restore only table space *mytbls1* from the database backup taken at *t1*.

4. After the restore is complete, table space mytbls1 is placed in roll forward pending state. If you were allowed to roll forward to a point prior to the minimum PIT, table space mytbls1 would not contain the table *myTable*, but the system catalog would say that the table exists in that *mytbls1*. To avoid inconsistencies like this, DB2 forces you to roll forward at least to the minimum PIT when you restore a table space.

A minimum PIT for a table space is updated when DDL statements are run against the table space or against tables in the table space. To determine the minimum PIT of recovery for a table space you can do either of the following:

- Execute the `LIST TABLESPACES SHOW DETAIL` command
- Obtain a table space snapshot: `GET SNAPSHOT FOR TABLESPACE ON` dbname.

In offline mode, the system catalog table space (`SYSCATSPACE`) must be rolled forward to the end of logs to ensure that the database is consistent. We discuss more about the `ROLLFOR-WARD` command in the next section.

Redirected Restore

We mentioned earlier that a backup file includes information about the table spaces and containers. For example, let's say one of the table spaces, *ts2*, has a DMS file container */database/ts2/cont1*. This information is stored in the backup image. When you restore this backup image to a different server (or even to the same server using a different database name), DB2 tries to create the exact same container. If the directory does not exist, DB2 tries to create it. But most likely this fails because the instance owner does not have the proper authority.

In this case, a regular restore does not work. However, a **redirected restore** solves this problem. During a redirected restore, you can specify new paths for the table space containers, and data is restored to the new containers.

To change the container definitions during a redirected restore, you first need to obtain the current container definitions in the source database. Use the `LIST TABLESPACES` command to list all the table spaces including their table space IDs and then use the `LIST TABLESPACE`

CONTAINERS FOR tablespace ID command to obtain the container definition for each table space. After you have this information, you can proceed with the redirected restore operation.

A redirected restore is performed in three steps:

1. Start the restore operation, but pause it so that you can change the table space definitions. To do this, include the REDIRECT keyword as part of the RESTORE command. The following shows an example of the command and output:

```
RESTORE DATABASE DB2CERT FROM C:\DBBACKUP INTO NEWDB REDIRECT

SQL1277N Restore has detected that one or more table space
containers are inaccessible, or has set their state to 'storage
must be defined'.

DB20000I The RESTORE DATABASE command completed successfully.
```

2. Specify the container definition for any table space you want to change:

```
SET TABLESPACE CONTAINERS FOR 0 USING (FILE "d:\newdb\cat0.dat"
5000)
SET TABLESPACE CONTAINERS FOR 1 USING (FILE "d:\newdb\cat1.dat"
5000)
. . .
SET TABLESPACE CONTAINERS FOR n USING (PATH "d:\newdb2")
```

In this example, n represents an ID of one of the table spaces in the backup. When using redirected restore, you cannot change the type of the table space from DMS to SMS or vice versa. The types must stay the same.

3. Restore the data itself into the new containers by including the keyword CONTINUE in the RESTORE command:

```
RESTORE DATABASE DB2CERT CONTINUE
```

Rather than performing the preceding steps manually, the restore utility enables you to generate a redirected restore script by issuing the RESTORE command with the REDIRECT and the GENERATE SCRIPT options. When the GENERATE SCRIPT option is used, the restore utility extracts container information from the backup image and generates a CLP script that includes all of the detailed container information. You can then modify any of the paths or container sizes in the script and run the CLP script to re-create the database with the new set of containers.

For example, to perform a redirected restore of the DB2TEST database using a script, follow these steps:

1. Use the restore utility to generate a redirected restore script:

```
RESTORE DATABASE DB2TEST FROM C:\DBBACKUP INTO NEWDB REDIRECT
GENERATE SCRIPT NEWDB.CLP WITHOUT ROLLING FORWARD
```

This creates a redirected restore script called NEWDB.CLP. You can edit this script to fit your environment and then run it in the DB2 command window. An excerpt of the NEWDB.CLP script is shown in Listing 10.6.

Listing 10.6   Sample Redirected Restore Script Excerpt

```
-- ************************************************************
-- ** automatically created redirect restore script
-- ****************************************************************
UPDATE COMMAND OPTIONS USING S ON Z ON NEWDB_NODE0000.out V ON;
SET CLIENT ATTACH_DBPARTITIONNUM 0;
SET CLIENT CONNECT_DBPARTITIONNUM 0;
-- ****************************************************************
-- ** automatically created redirect restore script
-- ****************************************************************
RESTORE DATABASE DB2TEST
-- USER username
-- USING 'password'
FROM 'C:\dbbackup' TAKEN AT 20130516120102
-- ON 'D:'
-- DBPATH ON 'target-directory'
INTO NEWDB
-- NEWLOGPATH 'D:\DB2\NODE0000\SQL00001\SQLOGDIR\'
-- WITH num-buff BUFFERS
-- BUFFER buffer-size
-- REPLACE HISTORY FILE
-- REPLACE EXISTING REDIRECT
-- PARALLELISM n WITHOUT ROLLING FORWARD
-- WITHOUT PROMPTING
;
-- ****************************************************************
-- ** table space definition
-- ****************************************************************
-- ****************************************************************
-- ** Tablespace name = SYSCATSPACE
-- ** Tablespace ID = 0
-- ** Tablespace Type = Database managed space
-- ** Tablespace Content Type = All permanent data. Regular table space.
-- ** Tablespace Page size (bytes) = 4096
-- ** Tablespace Extent size (pages) = 4
-- ** Using automatic storage = Yes
```

```
-- ** Auto-resize enabled = Yes
-- ** Total number of pages = 16384
-- ** Number of usable pages = 16380
-- ** High water mark (pages) = 8872
-- ********************************************************************
-- ********************************************************************
-- ** Tablespace name = TEMPSPACE1
-- ** Tablespace ID = 1
-- ** Tablespace Type = System managed space
-- ** Tablespace Content Type = System Temporary data
-- ** Tablespace Page size (bytes) = 4096
-- ** Tablespace Extent size (pages) = 32
-- ** Using automatic storage = Yes
-- ** Total number of pages = 1
-- ********************************************************************
-- ********************************************************************
-- ** Tablespace name = USERSPACE1
-- ** Tablespace ID = 2
-- ** Tablespace Type = Database managed space
-- ** Tablespace Content Type = All permanent data. Large table space.
-- ** Tablespace Page size (bytes) = 4096
-- ** Tablespace Extent size (pages) = 32
-- ** Using automatic storage = Yes
-- ** Auto-resize enabled = Yes
-- ** Total number of pages = 8192
-- ** Number of usable pages = 8160
-- ** High water mark (pages) = 1888
-- ********************************************************************
-- ********************************************************************
-- ** Tablespace name = TBS1
-- ** Tablespace ID = 5
```

The "--" indicates a comment. The SET TABLESPACE CONTAINER command is only created for table spaces that are not set up to use automatic storage. For table spaces that use automatic storage, their containers are handled by DB2 automatically, so there is no need to reset them.

2. Open the redirected restore script in a text editor to make any modifications that are required. You can modify the restore options, as well as container layout and paths.

3. Run the modified redirected restore script as follows:

```
db2 -tvf NEWDB.CLP
```

The output of the script is written into a file called *dbname_nodenumber.out*. In our example, the filename is *db2test_000.out*.

Database and Table Space Roll Forward

If you have to restore your database or a table space in one of your databases, you will lose any changes made since the backup was taken unless you have archival logging enabled (which for table space backups is always required) and use the ROLLFORWARD command to replay the logs for your database.

Database Roll Forward

If a backup operation is performed online, there might be users connected to the database in the middle of a transaction. Thus, an online backup contains the backup image of a database that is potentially in an inconsistent state. After restoring an online backup image, the database is immediately placed in roll forward pending state. You must run the ROLLFORWARD DATABASE command to bring the database back to a normal state.

If you performed an offline backup but your database is configured to use archival logging, then the database is also placed in a roll forward pending state following a restore. In this case, you do not need to use the ROLLFORWARD command because an offline backup implies that the database is already in a consistent state. To avoid this, use the WITHOUT ROLLING FORWARD option in the RESTORE DATABASE command. You need SYSADM, SYSCTRL, or SYS-MAINT authority to execute the ROLLFORWARD command.

During the roll forward process, the transactions in the log files are applied. You can apply all the changes in the log files, that is, roll forward to the end of logs, or you can roll forward to a PIT. This means DB2 traverses the logs and will redo or undo all database operations recorded in the logs up to the specified PIT. However, you must roll forward the database to at least the minimum recovery time. This is the earliest point in time to which a database must be rolled forward to ensure database consistency. If you attempt to roll forward to an incorrect point in time, you receive the following error message:

```
SQL1275N The stoptime passed to roll-forward must be greater than or
equal to "timestamp", because database "dbname" on node(s) "0" contains
information later than the specified time.
```

The timestamp given in the error message is the minimum PIT to which you must roll forward the database. The minimum recovery time is automatically determined for you if you specify the END OF BACKUP option in the ROLLFORWARD DATABASE command.

During roll forward processing, DB2 does the following:

1. Looks for one log file at a time in the active log directory.
2. If found, reapplies transactions from the log file.
3. If the log file is not found in the active log directory, DB2 searches for the logs in the OVERFLOWLOGPATH, if specified in the ROLLFORWARD DATABASE command.
4. If the log file is not found in the overflow log path, use the method specified in the LOGARCHMETH1 database configuration parameter to retrieve the log file from the archive path.
5. If DB2 does not find the log file in the active log directory and you did not specify the OVERFLOWLOGPATH, then the logs have to be retrieved from their archive locations. The method used is determined by the LOGARCHMETH1 parameter. If it is set to LOGRETAIN, then you have to retrieve the logs manually. If it is set to USEREXIT, then the user exit program db2uext2 is called to retrieve the log file. If it is set to DISK, TSM, or VENDOR, then DB2 automatically retrieves the log file from the respective archive locations.

After the log is found in the active log directory or from the OVERFLOWLOGPATH option, DB2 reapplies the transactions it contains and then goes to retrieve the next file it needs.

Following are some examples of the ROLLFORWARD DATABASE command that perform a roll forward of the *SAMPLE* database.

```
ROLLFORWARD DATABASE sample TO END OF LOGS AND COMPLETE                        (1)
ROLLFORWARD DATABASE sample TO timestamp AND COMPLETE                          (2)
ROLLFORWARD DATABASE sample TO timestamp USING LOCAL TIME AND COMPLETE         (3)
ROLLFORWARD DATABASE sample TO END OF BACKUP AND STOP                          (4)
```

Example (1) rolls forward to the end of the logs, which means that all archived and active logs are traversed. At the end, DB2 completes the roll forward operation and brings the database from roll forward pending state to a usable state.

Example (2) rolls forward to the specified PIT. The timestamp used is in UTC (Universal Coordinated Time), which can be calculated as follows:

Local time—the value in the CURRENT_TIMEZONE special register

For example, to look at the value of the CURRENT_TIMEZONE special register, connect to the database and issue the following SQL statement:

```
db2 "VALUES (CURRENT_TIMEZONE)"
```

If the local time is 2013-09-29-14.42.38.000000, and CURRENT_TIMEZONE is -5, then the corresponding UTC time is 2013-09-29-19.42.38.000000.

Example (3) is similar to example (2), but the timestamp is expressed using local time.

Example (4) instructs DB2 to determine the minimum PIT that database *SAMPLE* is allowed to roll forward to and then will roll forward to that PIT and bring the database from roll forward pending state to a usable state.

Note that there is no keyword OFFLINE in the ROLLFORWARD command syntax, as this is the default mode. In fact, for the ROLLFORWARD command for databases, this is the only mode allowed.

Table Space Roll Forward

You can perform table space roll forward either online or offline, except for the system catalog table space (SYSCATSPACE), which can only be rolled forward offline. The following is an example of a table space ROLLFORWARD:

```
ROLLFORWARD DATABASE sample
   TO END OF LOGS AND COMPLETE
   TABLESPACE (userspace1) ONLINE
```

The options in this example have already been explained in the previous section. The only difference is the addition of the TABLESPACE option, which specifies the table space to be rolled forward.

Table Space Roll Forward Considerations

If the registry variable DB2_COLLECT_TS_REC_INFO is enabled, only the log files required to recover the table space are processed. The ROLLFORWARD command skips over log files that are not required, which can speed recovery time.

You can use the QUERY STATUS option of the ROLLFORWARD command to list the log files that DB2 has already processed, the next archive log file required and the timestamp of the last committed transaction since roll forward processing began, for example

```
ROLLFORWARD DATABASE sample QUERY STATUS USING LOCAL TIME
```

After a table space PIT roll forward operation completes, the table space is placed into backup pending state. A backup of the table space or database must be taken because all updates made to it between the PIT that the table space was recovered to and the current time have been lost.

Recovering a Dropped Table

You might accidentally drop a table that has data you still need. To recover such a table, you could perform a database (not a table space) restore operation, followed by a database roll forward operation to a PIT before the table was dropped. However, all of the changes you made after the table was dropped are lost. This process might be time-consuming if the database is large and the backup is old, and your database will be unavailable during recovery.

DB2 offers a dropped table recovery feature that makes recovering a dropped table much easier. This feature enables you to recover your dropped table data using table space-level restore and roll forward operations. This is faster than database-level recovery, and your database remains available to users.

For a dropped table to be recoverable, the table space in which the table resides must have the DROPPED TABLE RECOVERY option turned on. By default, dropped table recovery is enabled when a table space is created. To toggle this feature, use the ALTER TABLESPACE statement. To determine if a table space is enabled for dropped table recovery, you can query the DROP_ RECOVERY column in the SYSCAT.TABLESPACES catalog table:

```
SELECT TBSPACE, DROP_RECOVERY FROM SYSCAT.TABLESPACES
```

> **NOTE**
>
> The DROPPED TABLE RECOVERY option is limited to regular table spaces only and does not apply to temporary table spaces and table spaces containing LOBs, LONG VARCHARs, or XML data.

To recover a dropped table, perform the following steps:

1. Identify the dropped table by invoking the LIST HISTORY command with the DROPPED TABLE option. This command displays the dropped table ID in the Backup ID column and shows the DDL statement to re-create the table.
   ```
   LIST HISTORY DROPPED TABLE ALL FOR dbname
   ```

2. Restore a database-level or table space-level backup image taken before the table was dropped.
   ```
   RESTORE DB dbname TABLESPACE (tablespace_name) ONLINE
   ```

3. Create an export directory to which files containing the table data are to be written. In a partitioned database environment, this directory must either be accessible to all database partitions or exist on each partition.

4. Roll forward to a PIT after the table was dropped using the RECOVER DROPPED TABLE option on the ROLLFORWARD DATABASE command. Alternatively, roll forward to the end of the logs so that updates to other tables in the table space or database are not lost.

   ```
   ROLLFORWARD DB dbname
      TO END OF LOGS TABLESPACE ONLINE
      RECOVER DROPPED TABLE dropped_table_id
      TO export_directory
   ```

If successful, subdirectories under this export directory are created automatically for each database partition. These subdirectories are named NODEnnnn, where *nnnn* represents the database partition number. Data files containing the dropped table data as it existed on each database partition are exported to a lower subdirectory called *data*; for example:

`\export_directory\NODE0000\data`

The *data* file is a delimited file.

5. Re-create the table using the CREATE TABLE statement from the recovery history file, obtained in step 1.

6. Import the table data that was exported during the roll forward operation into the table.

    `IMPORT FROM data OF DEL INSERT INTO table`

The Recovery History File

DB2 keeps tracks of all the backup, restore, load, and roll forward operations performed on a database in a file called db2rhist.asc, also known as the *recovery history file*. There is a recovery history file for each database, and it is stored in the directory where the database resides. The file is automatically updated when any of the following events occurs:

- A database or table space is backed up
- A database or table space is restored
- A database or table space is rolled forward
- A database is automatically rebuilt and more than one image is restored
- A table space is created
- A table space is altered
- A table space is quiesced
- A table space is renamed
- A table space is dropped
- A table is loaded
- A table is dropped
- A table is reorganized
- A database is recovered

To see the entries in the recovery history file, use the LIST HISTORY command. For example, to list all the backup operations performed on the *SAMPLE* database, issue

`LIST HISTORY BACKUP ALL FOR sample`

Listing 10.7 shows the output of the LIST HISTORY BACKUP command:

Listing 10.7 Sample List History Backup Output

```
Op Obj Timestamp+Sequence Type Dev Earliest Log Current Log  Backup ID
-- --- ------------------ ---- --- ------------ ------------ ---------
 B  D  20130929122918001   D    D  S0000007.LOG S0000007.LOG
-------------------------------------------------------------------
 Contains 3 tablespace(s):

 00001 SYSCATSPACE
 00002 USERSPACE1
 00003 SYSTOOLSPACE
-------------------------------------------------------------------
   Comment: DB2 BACKUP SAMPLE OFFLINE
Start Time: 20130929122918
  End Time: 20130929122939
    Status: A
-------------------------------------------------------------------
 EID: 21 Location: d:\temp\SAMPLE.0\DB2\NODE0000\CATN0000\20130929
```

For each backup operation performed, an entry like the one shown in Figure 10.18 is entered in the history file. The following list summarizes the information that is recorded:

- The time of the operation: `20130929122918001`
- The command used: `DB2 BACKUP SAMPLE OFFLINE`
- The table spaces that were backed up: `SYSCATSPACE`, `USERSPACE1`, and `SYSTOOLSPACE`
- The location of the backup image: d:\temp\SAMPLE.0\DB2\NODE0000\CATN0000\ 20130929

If an error occurred during the operation, the error is recorded as well.

With the recovery history file, you can easily track all your backup operations, restore operations, and more.

Although you can manually prune and update the status of recovery history file entries, it is highly recommended that you configure DB2 to automatically do this for you to avoid manual errors.

To configure DB2 to automatically delete unneeded backup images:

1. Set the `AUTO_DEL_REC_OBJ` database configuration parameter to ON.
2. Set the `num_db_backups` database configuration parameter to the number of backups to keep (default is 12).

3. Set the `rec_his_retentn` database configuration parameter to the number of days of recovery history information to keep (default is 366).

The `num_db_backups` database configuration parameter defines the number of database backup images to retain for a database.

The `rec_his_retentn` database configuration parameter defines the number of days that historical information on backups are retained.

For example, if you take weekly backups on the *SAMPLE* database and would like DB2 to keep at least a month's worth of backups and prune everything older than 45 days, you can run the following commands:

```
db2 update db cfg for sample using auto_del_rec_obj on;
db2 update db cfg for sample using num_db_backups 4;
db2 update db cfg for sample using rec_his_retentn 45;
```

Database Recovery Using RECOVER DATABASE

The `RECOVER DATABASE` command combines the `RESTORE` and `ROLLFORWARD` operations into one step. The `RECOVER DATABASE` command automatically determines which backup image to use by referring to the information in the Recovery History file.

Figure 10.17 shows that the `RECOVER DATABASE` command combines the `RESTORE DATABASE` command and the `ROLLFORWARD DATABASE` command.

Let's look at some examples:

To recover the *SAMPLE* database from the most recently available backup image and roll forward to end of logs, use

```
RECOVER DB sample
```

To recover the *SAMPLE* database to the PIT 2013-09-21-14.50.00 (note that the PIT is specified in local time, not UTC time), issue

```
RECOVER DB sample TO 2013-09-21-14.50.00
```

To recover the *SAMPLE* database to a PIT that is no longer contained in the current history file, you need to provide a history file from this time period:

```
RECOVER DB sample
    TO 2013-12-31-04:00:00
    USING HISTORY FILE (/home/user/old2011files/db2rhist.asc)
```

If the `RECOVER` command is interrupted before it successfully completes, you can restart it by rerunning the same command. If it was interrupted during the roll forward phase, then the `RECOVER` command attempts to continue the previous recover operation without redoing the restore phase. If you want to force the recover utility to redo the restore phase, issue the `RECOVER DATABASE` command with the `RESTART` option to force the recover utility to ignore any prior recovery operation that failed to complete. If the recover utility was interrupted during the restore phase, then it starts from the beginning.

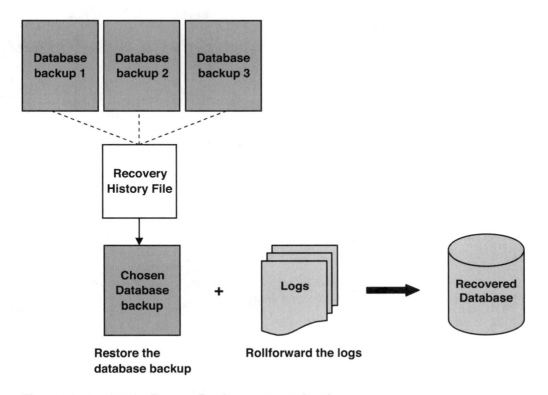

Figure 10.17   How the Recover Database command works

Case Study

Assume your company wants to deploy a new accounting application very soon, but the finance department director has demanded more thorough testing. The only test machine available for testing has DB2 for Windows installed. However, you need to obtain data from a DB2 for AIX database server. Because the source and target platforms are different, you cannot restore on Windows a DB2 backup image obtained from DB2 on AIX. In addition, because you don't need every table and view for your testing, you choose to use data movement utilities to move data to the Windows server.

First, you connect to the source server and then export the required tables with this command:

```
export to newsalary.ixf of ixf
  xml to xmlpath
  xmlfile acctdesc
  modified by xmlinsepfiles xmlchar
  messages newsalary.out
  select empno, firstnme, lastname, salary * 1.3 as new_salary
    from employee
   where workdept='A00'
```

You find out that the accounting application needs all of the 100 tables under the schema *acct*. To save the time and effort of typing the `export` command for each of the 100 tables, you choose to use the `db2move` command.

```
db2move proddb export -sn acct
```

Because the output files are in IXF format, you can create the tables and import data directly to the target database using the `IMPORT` utility:

```
import from newsalary.ixf of ixf
  xml from xmlpath
  xmlparse preserve whitespace
  messages newsalary.out
  create into newsalary in datats index in indexts
```

Note that a new table called *NEWSALARY* is created in the *datats* table space and that its indexes are stored in the *indexts* table space.

After the first few successful completions of the import operation, you realize you cannot finish all the imports within the estimated time. The `IMPORT` utility performs insert statements behind the scenes and thus activates constraint checking, logging, and triggers. The `LOAD` utility, on the other hand, goes behind the DB2 engine and loads the data directly to the pages. You can choose to perform logging as well as performing only primary and unique key checks. Thus, for the sake of performance, you decide to change the plan and use the `LOAD` utility instead.

To capture all rows that violated unique constraints of the target table, you create an exception table with this statement:

```
CREATE TABLE salaryexp
( empno CHAR(6), firstnme VARCHAR(12), lastname VARCHAR(15)
, new_salary DECIMAL(9,2), load_ts TIMESTAMP, load_msg CLOB(2K))
```

You issue the following `load` command:

```
load from newsalary.ixf of ixf
  modified by dumpfile=salarydump.dmp
  rowcount 5000
  messages salary.out
  tempfiles path c:\loadtemp
  create into salary
  for exception salaryexp
```

After the load is completed successfully, the table is not accessible (by default) due to table space backup pending. Therefore, you need to perform a table space or database backup. You choose to perform a simple offline database backup, assuming the database name is targetdb:`backup database targetdb`

If the table has any constraints defined, such as referential integrity and check constraint, you need to validate the data integrity with the following command:

```
set integrity for newsalary immediate checked
```

The target tables should be ready and accessible for testing.

As the testing is progressing, you realize that the performance of the report generator reduces after each monthly inventory update. You first reorganize the tables and update the statistics of the tables with the following commands:

```
reorg table inventory_parts indexes all keepdictionary

runstats on table inventory_parts
    with distribution default
    num_freqvalues 50 num_quantiles 50
    util_impact_priority 30
```

Because the table *inventory_parts* is enabled for row compression, the KEEPDICTION-ARY option is specified to preserve the dictionary. Rather than performing the maintenance tasks manually, you have decided to turn on automatic maintenance. You simply specify the maintenance window and the maintenance tasks you would like to enable, all through IBM Data Studio.

Summary

In this chapter, you were introduced to the different data movement utilities that come with DB2. The utilities support the following file formats: DEL, ASC, IXF, WSF, and CURSOR.

The EXPORT utility extracts data from a table or view into a file. The export command can be very simple. At a minimum, you should specify the output file name (where exported data is stored), its file format, the message file name, and a SELECT statement.

The IMPORT utility, on the other hand, inserts data into a specified table or view from a file. You can choose to import to an existing or new table (or view). By default, DB2 only issues one COMMIT at the very end of the import operation. In case of failure during the import, all the changes will be rolled back, and you must restart the import from the beginning. Alternatively, you can use options such as commitcount, restartcount, and skipcount to enable the ability of restarting an import.

The LOAD utility is another method to insert data into a specified table or view and is much faster. The utility formats the data pages while bypassing DB2 buffering and logging. The utility is composed of four phases: load, build, delete, and index copy. You can check the load message file or the status of the table or use the load query command to monitor the load operation.

The db2move utility can be used to move more than one table using just one command. The utility enables you specify the action: export, import, or load. This utility comes in handy when many tables need to be moved.

The RUNSTATS, REORG, and REORGCHK utilities are very important data maintenance utilities that should be performed regularly to ensure that the most optimal data access plans are used. You should also review the automatic database maintenance capabilities DB2 provides. It saves you a lot of time in planning and scheduling maintenance activities.

In this chapter you also learned about units of work, (UOW), logging methods, and different backup and recovery strategies.

A unit of work (UOW) is composed of one or more statements and completed by a COMMIT or ROLLBACK statement. If a UOW is interrupted in the middle of processing, all statements executed up to that point are rolled back. This ensures data integrity.

When a database is activated, DB2 allocates a number of primary logs based on the setting of the LOGPRIMARY database configuration parameter. When the primary log space fills up, DB2 allocates secondary logs one at a time. When the maximum number of secondary logs is reached, specified by the LOGSECOND database parameter, DB2 encounters a log full condition. At this point, uncommitted transactions are rolled back.

There are three types of database recovery: crash, version, and roll forward recovery. Crash recovery and version recovery are the defaults. To enable roll forward recovery, you need enable archival logging.

There are three logging methods available in DB2: circular, archival, and infinite active logging. Circular logging is the default logging method. However, it does not support roll forward recovery. Archival logging is enabled by setting the LOGARCHMETH1 database configuration parameter. Both archival logging and infinite active logging support roll forward recovery. Log mirroring is valuable in maintaining a redundant active log path.

The RECOVER DATABASE command combines both the RESTORE and ROLLFORWARD commands into one easy step. The RECOVER DATABASE command can continue where it left off if it is interrupted. Alternatively, it is possible to start the recover process from the beginning by specifying the RESTART option.

Review Questions

1. Which data movement utility supports the CURSOR input file type?

2. What other privileges are needed to load a table if the person already has LOAD authority?

3. Bob creates the *STOCK* table:

```
CREATE TABLE stock ( id        INTEGER NOT NULL
                   , name      VARCHAR(10)
                   , bandlevel INTEGER NOT NULL
                   , PRIMARY KEY (id) )
```

He then loads the table with this load command:

```
load from stock.del of del
    modified by dumpfile=stockdump.dmp
    messages stock.out
    replace into stock
    for exception stockexp
```

The input file *stock.del* looks like this:

```
10, "AAA", 30
20, "BBB", -
30, "CCC", 3
30, "DDD", 4
40, "EEE", x
```

After the load command is executed, which rows are stored in the *stockdmp.dmp* file?

4. With the same target table definition, load command and input file as in question 3, which rows are stored in the *stockexp* exception table?

5. A table is created with the following statement:

```
CREATE TABLE employee
    ( id    SMALLINT NOT NULL
    , name VARCHAR(10)
    , job  CHAR(5) CHECK (job IN ('Sales', 'Mgr', 'Clerk') )
    , PRIMARY KEY (id))
```

If this load command is issued, what state would the *EMPLOYEE* table be in?

```
load from emp2.del of del insert into emp2
```

6. A table is created with the following statement:

```
CREATE TABLE employee
    ( id    SMALLINT NOT NULL
    , name VARCHAR(10)
    , job  CHAR(5) CHECK (job IN ('Sales', 'Mgr', 'Clerk') )
    , PRIMARY KEY (id))
```

   If this `import` command is issued, what state would the *EMPLOYEE* table be in?

```
import from emp2.del of del insert into emp2
```

7. What will this command do?

```
db2look -d department -a -e -m -x -f -o db2look.sql
```

8. Bob just completed a load operation to insert 300,000 rows of data into various tables. He performs a `RUNSTATS` to update the database statistics so that the DB2 optimizer knows about the new data. However, when the user logs in and runs the application, the performance is not acceptable. The application is mainly coded in static SQL and SQL stored procedures. What can Bob do to improve performance?

9. Bob tries to execute the following command:

```
import from largeinputfile.ixf of ixf
    messages import.out
    create into newtable in datts index in indexts
```

However, he receives log full errors. What can he do to solve this problem?

10. What is the prerequisite for a table to be imported with the `insert_update` option?

11. Besides crash recovery, what are the other two types of database recovery?

12. Which option enables you to back up the logs along with the database?

13. When are secondary logs created and destroyed?

14. What condition triggers the logs to be flushed from the log buffer to log files?

15. Which of the following tools read data from an ASCII file and add them to a table?

   A. insert

   B. merge

   C. load

   D. export

   E. import

16. Which of the following tools read data from an ASCII file and add them to a view?

    A. insert

    B. merge

    C. load

    D. export

    E. import

17. You want to import the following rows of data in the file *foo.txt* into the table *foo*:

    ```
    "Hello"|"World"
    "Goodbye"|"Cruel World"
    ```

    Which of the following commands must you run?

    A. `Import from foo.txt of txt insert into foo`

    B. `Import from foo.txt of del insert into foo`

    C. `Import from foo.txt of pipedel insert into foo`

    D. `Import from foo.txt of del modified by coldel insert into foo`

18. Which of the following are true?

    A. The LOAD utility locks the whole table space for the table being loaded.

    B. The LOAD utility locks the whole table being loaded.

    C. The LOAD utility by default locks only the existing data in the table until the load completes.

    D. The LOAD utility allows read access to all data that existed in the table before the load was run.

19. Which of the following database configuration parameters specifies the redundant active log path?

    A. FAILARCHPATH

    B. LOGARCHOPT1

    C. MIRRORLOGPATH

    D. LOGARCHMETH1

20. Which of the following activates infinite active log space?

    A. LOGSECOND = 0

    B. LOGPRIMARY = 0

    C. LOGSECOND = -1

    D. LOGPRIMARY = -1

Solutions to the Review Questions

This appendix contains the answers to the review questions from each chapter.

Chapter 1 Answers

1. DATABASE 2 (DB2) was used to indicate a shift from hierarchical databases (such as the Information Management System) to the relational databases.

2. IBM PureData System for Transactions is powered by the DB2 pureScale technology.

3. Yes. All DB2 editions have a set of core modules that are the same; therefore, an application that works with DB2 Express will work against DB2 Enterprise.

4. No. DB2 Connect is required only in one direction: when connecting from a DB2 LUW to DB2 for z/OS or other host server like DB2 for i, DB2 for VM, and VSE.

5. DB2 with BLU Acceleration is a memory-based column store that leverages parallel vector processing power, dynamic memory capabilities, and advanced storage disk technology.

6. No. Separate installation and entitlement of InfoSphere Federation Server is not needed to federate DB2 LUW data and an Informix data source.

7. IBM makes various offerings in the PureData System because different type of workload requires systems to be optimized differently.

8. No. Even though more than 90 percent of the code is common among these platforms, each platform has its own file used for installation for the appropriate platform.

9. The database partitioning functionality enables you to partition your data within a single server or across multiple servers running the same operating system. This provides scalability.

10. Contact your IBM marketing representative or call 1-800-IBM-SERV and indicate that you would like to buy a permanent license for your DB2 product.

11. **D**. The minimum software required on the Windows client is the IBM Data Server run-time client. This is required to *run* any application, other than an application using the JDBC type 4 driver, to connect to a remote DB2 database server.

12. **C**. The Data Server Driver for JDBC and SQLJ.

13. **D**. DB2 Advanced Workgroup (and DB2 Advanced Enterprise) offers database parti-tioning and warehouse functionalities.

14. **B**. DB2 Express-C does not include SQL replication. An optional renewable 12-month subscription license can be purchased for DB2 Express-C to obtain IBM DB2 Technical support (24/7) and also support for the SQL replication and the High Availability and Disaster Recovery (HADR) functionality.

15. **D**. DB2 Enterprise (and DB2 Advanced Enterprise) do not have system resource usage limitations. They are targeted for enterprise-class solutions.

16. **C**. DB2 Developer Edition fits their needs. With the DB2 Developer Edition, the licensed developer can install and run tests against any DB2 edition comes with DB2 Developer on multiple servers. If the company decides to use DB2 in production envi-ronments, they would have to acquire the appropriate edition and license.

17. **D**. DB2 Developer Edition includes DB2 Connect Enterprise Edition capability and entitlement, which allows the connection to host servers. It also includes all the DB2 LUW clients. Typically DB2 Developer Edition is more cost-effective and suitable for software development companies.

18. **A** and **C**. A System z server with a LPAR running the Linux operating system can run DB2 for Linux, UNIX, and Windows, and DB2 Connect.

19. **A**. The Data Server Driver Package supports applications using ODBC, CLI, .NET, OLE DB, PHP, Ruby, JDBC, and SQLJ. This driver on Windows also has the merge modules for embedded installation support.

20. **All of them**. All the drivers on the list provide JDBC and SQLJ support, both JDBC 3.0 and JDBC 4.0.

Chapter 2 Answers

1. They are classified in four categories: DB2 system commands, DB2 CLP commands, DB2 CLP Plus commands, and DB2 Text Search commands.

2. There are three different classes of SQL statements: Data Definition Language (DDL), Data Manipulation Language (DCL), and Data Control Language (DCL).

3. A partitioned database environment manages data in parallel using a shared-nothing architecture. Data is distributed across partitions. On the other hand, in a DB2 pureScale environment, DB2 members access data that is shared by other members and stored on a clustered of shared disks.

4. The `db2icrt` command creates a DB2 instance on the server where the command is run.

5. CLPPlus provides a quick and easy way for database administrators (DBAs) and application developers familiar with Oracle's SQLPlus to work with scripts and run command-line reports.

6. The `db2ilist` command lists all instances that exist on a server, whether they have been started or not.

7. When you install DB2 on a Windows server, the installation program automatically creates an instance named *DB2* on the server.

8. RDMA (Remote Direct Memory Access) technology is used to achieve interrupt-free communication between members. It allows one host to access memory of another host directly.

9. The DB2 environment can be configured by changing values of parameters in different areas:
   * Environment variables
   * DB2 registry variables
   * Database Manager Configuration (dbm cfg) file and
   * Database configuration (db cfg) file

10. DB2 Advanced Workgroup Server Edition and DB2 Advanced Enterprise Server Edition come with a comprehensive set of advanced tools to make database design, configuration, tuning, and monitoring more easily.

11. **C.** The `db2start` command starts the current DB2 instance.

12. **B.** The `db2set -all` command lists all of the currently configured registry variables.

13. **D.** The command `list db directory on C:` examines the local database directory, which is not removed when the instance is dropped, and lists all of the databases on that drive/filesystem.

14. **D.** You must catalog the database before you can connect to it. To catalog the database in this situation, you must specify the drive or directory where the local database directory exists. In this case it is C:, so use the command `catalog db sample on C:`.

15. **C.** You must set the DB2INSTANCE environment variable to the instance you want to work with, in this case *inst2*, so the command is `export db2instance=inst2`.

16. **B.** Cluster services run on every member and CFs in the pureScale cluster. It detects member failure, drives automated recovery, and manages access to shared data.

17. **B.** The `db2_all` command runs the specified command on all database partitions in the database.

18. **B.** Federated support is turned on using the dbm cfg parameter FEDERATED.

19. **C.** DB2NODE.

20. **A.** The CURRENT DBPARTITIONNUM special register provides this information.

Chapter 3 Answers

1. Two methods for Windows are available: the DB2 Setup Wizard and Silent install. Four methods for Linux and UNIX are available: the DB2 Setup Wizard, Silent install, the db2_install script, and manual installation of DB2 payload files.

2. No. DB2 image is always placed in the $HOME/sqllib directory, where $HOME represents the non-root user's home directory.

3. The default instance name is db2inst1. The user owner ID db2inst1 is created as well. If db2inst1 already exists, DB2 tries db2inst2, db2inst3, and so on.

4. You can run the db2prereqcheck command on the system you are going to install DB2 on. The command checks if the system requirements are met.

5. By default, three logs are generated under the /tmp directory: db2setup.his, db2setup.log, and db2setup.err. To redirect the logs to a different location, run the db2setup program with the –l option.

6. By default, two logs are generated under the My Documents\DB2LOG directory: db2.log and db2wi.log. To redirect them to a different location, run the setup program (from the DB2 installation media) with the –l option.

7. DB2ADMNS and DB2USERS.

8. You need to run the db2iupdt command for all of your DB2 instances after you install a DB2 fix pack to update the instance with the new libraries and to update the logical links to the installed libraries.

9. The following user rights are granted to the instance owner:
   - Act as part of the operating system
   - Create token objects
   - Increase quotas
   - Lock pages in memory
   - Log on as a service
   - Replace a process-level token

10. The user who is installing DB2 must have Local Administrator authority. If you want to have the DB2 Setup Wizard create a domain user account for the Instance owner or the DAS user, the installation ID must have the authority to create domain user accounts.

11. **B**. The DB2 Setup Wizard and the Silent install are the only two methods available on Windows.

12. **C**. A response file is a text file containing all the options to be used during the install process. Use this file as input during a silent install.

13. **C**. 50000 is the default.

14. **D**. You need root authority.

15. **A**. The DAS User ID.
16. **B**. The db2_install script is not a valid method of installation on Windows.
17. **C**. The db2_install script.
18. **A**. `db2setup -r response_file`
19. **A**. The `db2licm -a` command
20. **C**. The db2ls command can list the DB2 products and features installed on your Linux and UNIX systems, including the DB2 HTML documentation.

Chapter 4 Answers

1. The IBM Data Studio Web Console lets you schedule scripts containing SQL statements and/or DB2 commands to be run at specific times.
2. There is no equivalent DB2 tool in the Linux/UNIX platforms. The Linux/UNIX shell would be equivalent to the DB2 Command Window.
3. The registry variable is DB2OPTIONS.
4. When you plan to copy a command or statement that has carriage returns and then paste it into the CLP, it is best to use this method.
5. The terminate command.
6. The CLPPlus is a command-line user interface that enables you to do everything CLP supports. The one key benefit CLPPlus provides is that it supports SQL*Plus scripts that many DBAs and application developers are familiar with.
7. The database routine editor that is available from the IBM Data Studio can be used to develop SQL user-defined functions.
8. Yes. The IBM Data Studio provides collaborative database development tools for DB2 for z/OS, DB2 for i, Informix database, and of course, DB2 for LUW. The support for all of these is at the same level of service and features.
9. The IBM Data Studio Web Console enables you to drill down into alerts, filter the display of alerts by time period, database, or alert type.
10. Access the Information Center from the Internet:

    For DB2 10.5: http://pic.dhe.ibm.com/infocenter/db2luw/v10r5/index.jsp
11. All the answers are correct.
12. **B**. The default termination character is a semi-colon (;).
13. **E**. By default the CLP has auto-commit enabled, and this causes the CLP to issue a `commit` statement automatically after every statement. Therefore, in this case, the CLP issues a `commit` four times, once after each entry in the input file.
14. **D**. The Query Tuner Workflow Assistant enables you to capture statements of interest, invoke the advisor, and review the access plan graphs.

15. **A** and **B**. The web console tasks are view health summary, view alerts, view application connections, and manage database jobs.

16. **A**. By default the CLP has auto-commit enabled, which causes the CLP to issue a commit automatically after every statement. However, the +c flag tells the CLP to disable auto-commit; therefore, in this case, the CLP does not issue a `commit`. Because there is no explicit `commit` statement, there are no `commits` during the processing of this file.

17. **B**. To set a termination character you need to use the -td option, and to set the input file you need to use the -f option. However, if you specify a value for an option, you cannot string the options together. Therefore the correct answer is **B**.

18. **C** and **D**. `db2 ? SQL-911` is not commonly used, but it works. `db2 ? SQL911N` is most often used. Note that the *N* after the 911 is optional.

19. **D**. Repeat is not a DB2 CLP command and can't be run in interactive mode.

20. **C** and **D** are allowed from the CLP in interactive mode. **A** is not allowed because you cannot prefix the command with `db2` when in interactive mode. **B** is a DB2 system command, and it can only be executed from the Command Window or the Linux/UNIX shell.

Chapter 5 Answers

1. The DB2INSTANCE environment variable determines the current active instance, that is, the instance for your current session to which your commands would apply.

2. You can set up your DB2 environment in Linux/UNIX by adding the db2profile (for the Bourne and Korn shells) or *db2cshrc* (for the C shell) in the .login or .profile initialization files. You should also modify the db2profile file to set the DB2INSTANCE variable to the name of the instance you want active by default.

3. `db2set DB2COMM= -g`

4. `db2ilist`

5. To create a new instance with the `db2icrt` command on Linux or UNIX, you must have root authority.

6. To create a new instance with the `db2icrt` command on Windows, you must have Administrator authority.

7. The `db2idrop` command removes the DB2 instance from the list and remove all DB2-related executables and libraries from the instance owner's home directory.

8. You should connect to the database first. CONNECT TO <dbname>

9. Issue the `db2start` command with the ADMIN MODE USER userID option.

10. An attachment is required to perform operations at the instance level, and a connection is required to perform operations at the database level.

11. **C**. The db2set -lr command lists all of the registry variables that DB2 recognizes.

12. **A** and **D**. Sort heap threshold (SHEAPTHRES) and maximum query degree of parallelism (MAX_QUERYDEGREE) are both database manager (instance)-level configuration parameters.

13. **D**. Each instance is a separate DB2 operating environment, so errors in one instance cannot affect the other instances. Therefore, to ensure that problems that you normally encounter in development do not affect your production system, put these databases in separate instances.

14. **B**. To get the current, effective setting for each configuration parameter along with the value of the parameter the next time the instance is stopped and restarted, use the show detail option of the get dbm cfg command.

15. **D**. To update the DAS configuration, use the command db2 update admin cfg.

16. **D**. To change the DAS configuration back to its default values, use the command db2 reset admin cfg.

17. **C**. db2stop force forces all applications off the databases and prevents new connections from happening. Then it stops the active instance.

18. **A**. The list applications command requires an instance attachment.

19. **D**. The db2 get db cfg command is used to review the contents of the database configuration (db cfg) file. If you are not connected to the database, you need to specify the name of the database in the command.

20. **B** and **D**. The values of YES and ON are equivalent, but a *1* is not allowed. Also, INTRA_PARALLEL is a Database Manager Configuration parameter; therefore, **D** is incorrect.

Chapter 6 Answers

1. The system database directory contains all the databases you can connect to from a Data Server client machine.

2. To view the content of the database directory on the H: drive, you use the command list db directory on H:.

3. An entry type of *indirect* means that this entry corresponds to a local database.

4. To determine which port is being used, look for the string db2_cDB2 in the *services* file.

5. TCPIP can be used as the communication protocol to connect from a DB2 Connect gateway to a DB2 for z/OS server.

6. DB2 Connect Enterprise Edition can be installed once on a gateway machine to enable all 1,000 clients to connect to the DB2 for i server, while DB2 Connect Personal Edition is licensed only to be installed at the Data Server client machine.

7. To remove an entry from the DCS directory, you can use the command `uncatalog dcs db dbname`.

8. To remove an entry from the node directory, you can use the command `uncatalog node <nodename>`.

9. DB2 Connect Enterprise Edition can be installed once on a gateway machine. You should check the `db2comm` registry variable by issuing `db2set -all` to verify that the communication protocol is set correctly.

10. After creating or changing database and node directory entries, issue the `terminate` command to refresh the cache. This ensures the new configuration and setting is used.

11. **D**. This command puts an entry into the node directory that points to the remote server and port that the instance uses for inbound connections.

12. **D**. When an instance is dropped, the database is not dropped; however, you need to ensure the system database directory points to the right place. When the instance was recreated, the system database directory is empty. To populate it with an entry that point to the MYDB database, use the `catalog db MYDB on <path where database resides>` command.

13. **B**. You should use the value specified in the SVCENAME parameter in the command as shown in B.

14. **C**. When a database is created, an entry of type *indirect* is inserted into the system database directory.

15. **A** and **B** are required. **A** specifies the port number used by the instance. **B** turns on the TCP/IP listener.

16. **A** and **D**. The IBM Data Server clients support DB2 for LUW, DB2 for z/OS, and Informix data servers.

17. **A** and **B**. Named Pipes or TCPIP can be used as the communication protocol to connect from a DB2 on Windows client to a DB2 on Windows server.

18. **B**. This is the only catalog statement that is correct.

19. **B**. IBM Data Server Driver for JDBC and SQLJ. This provides the smallest footprint. You do not need to install any software—simply copy the driver to the appropriate path.

20. All of them.

Chapter 7 Answers

1. **C**. Because no schema is explicitly specified, the schema is the authorization ID for the connection. The authorization ID, also known as the connection ID, is the user ID used to connect to the database. Therefore, the table name is foo.t1.

2. **B**. There is no object named IBMDEFAULTSPACE. When a database is created, DB2 creates the table spaces SYSCATSPACE, USERSPACE1, and TEMPSPACE1; the partition groups IBMCATGROUP, IBMTEMPGROUP, and IBMDEFAULTGROUP; and the buffer pool IBMDEFAULTBP.

3. **C**. An identity column GENERATED ALWAYS and defined as primary key ensures uniqueness, but only within a table. A sequence generates a unique value that is across the whole database and can therefore be used with multiple tables.

4. **D**. The statement `alter table t1 activate not logged initially with empty table` deletes all rows from the table and does not log the deletions. This enables it to deliver the fastest response time. Table *t1* must have been created with the `activate not logged initially` clause for the `alter table` to work.

5. **B**. Although you can enforce this by specifying the T or F constraint by creating a view (if all inserts are done using a view), this will not prevent you from inserting a different value if you insert into the table directly. To ensure that no other values are entered into this column, you need to define a check constraint.

6. **B**. The `CASCADE` option will delete all referenced rows in the child tables.

7. **B** and **D**. Both a unique constraint and a primary key constraint can be referenced by a foreign key constraint.

8. **C**. The statement inserting a value of 300 into the productno column will fail as this is an identity column GENERATED ALWAYS, so there will be two rows successfully inserted into the table.

9. **C**. The default precision and scale are 5, 0 if not explicitly specified in the `CREATE TABLE` statement.

10. **A**. INBETWEEN is not a type of trigger.

11. **C**. Each database has its own set of logs and system catalogs, and a schema is created within a database. However, the registry variables are set for all instances or at the instance level and control all databases in the instance.

12. **B**. The `CREATE TABLE` statement creates the table/data object for the database. Since there is a primary key clause in this statement, an index will also be created to support the primary key. This statement creates two objects.

13. **B**. There are two server names in the *db2nodes.cfg* file; therefore, the database is partitioned across two servers.

14. **D**. You need to connect to the database and create the buffer pool with a 16K page size before you can create a table space with a 16K page size.

15. **A** and **B**. A package is stored in a database and contains the executable SQL statements and the access path the DB2 optimizer will choose to retrieve the data.

16. **D**. Object names must be unique within a schema, but since the schema is the high-level qualifier for the object name, objects can have the same name as long as they are in different schemas.

17. **B** and **C**. seq1.next and seq1.nextValue are not valid options.

18. **D**. A user temporary table space created with the CREATE USER TEMPORARY TABLESPACE statement is needed before global temporary tables can be declared. Global temporary tables are created with the DECLARE GLOBAL TEMPORARY TABLE statement.

19. **D** and **E**. CREATE TABLE and ALTER TABLE will enable compression, actual compression of the rows will not occur until data is loaded and dictionaries are automatically built.

20. **A**. DETACH. After issuing a DETACH followed by a COMMIT, changes will take place immediately where the partition (a.k.a range) will become a stand-alone table.

21. **D**. Distribute by. This is used for the database partitioning functionality.

22. **A**. DB2 supports 4K, 8K, 16K and 32K page sizes

Chapter 8 Answers

1. DB2 relies on operating system security or an external security mechanism and does not store user IDs and passwords in the database.

2. DB2 supports Kerberos security service. You can also use your own security service plug-in. The plug-in is loaded at instance startup. Other external facilities can also be used.

3. When a new package is bound to the database, for example, when creating a SQL stored procedure, BINDADD is required.

4. He must have CONNECT privileges to connect to the database and CREATETAB privileges to create a new table in the database. Because he is trying to create a table that has a different schema than the authorization ID (i.e., *bob*), he must have IMPLICIT_SCHEMA privileges if schema *mary* does not already exist. If it does exist, then CREATEIN privileges on the schema *mary* are needed. In addition to all of this, *bob* also needs to have USE privileges on the table space *ts1*.

5. DB2 SYS* authorities must be set to a user group. The command is executed successfully, but *bob* does not receive the authority. It must be set to the group *dba* like this:
   ```
   update dbm cfg using sysctrl_group dba
   ```

6. First, a local group with a name like *db2dba*, defined on the DB2 server is required. Second, add the global group *glbgrp* as a member of the local group *db2dba*. Third, update the Database Manager Configuration parameter to set SYSADM to *db2dba*.

7. The first type is called untrusted clients, which do not have a reliable security facility. The second type is called trusted clients, which have a reliable security facility. The third type is called DRDA clients, which are clients on host systems (z/OS and iSeries) with reliable security facility.

8. CREATETAB is granted to PUBLIC implicitly when a database is created. To allow only *bob* to create tables in the database, you must first revoke CREATETAB from PUBLIC and GRANT CREATETAB to *bob*.

```
REVOKE CREATETAB FROM PUBLIC;
GRANT CREATETAB TO USER bob;
```

9. Regardless of the SQL statements performed in the program, *bob* only needs EXECUTE privileges on the package. *Mary* needs the associated privileges to perform all the SQL statements in the program. In addition, BINDADD is required to bind the new package to the database. If the package contains embedded dynamic SQL, some special considerations might apply, which can be configured using the DYNAMICRULES BIND option.

10. Because TRUST_ALLCLNTS is set to NO, only trusted clients can be authenticated on the client. Untrusted clients must be authenticated on the server.

11. **B.** The default authentication takes place on the server, so in this case the user ID is authenticated on the DBX1 server.

12. **C.** The SERVER_ENCRYPT authentication type encrypts only the user ID and password that is sent during an authentication request; it does not encrypt the data.

13. **A.** Because TRUST_ALLCLNTS is set to YES, users are authenticated on the client to see if they do exist.

14. **E.** None of the above. Having SYSADM or DBADM authorities is not enough now to see data. You also need DATAACCESS authority.

15. **D.** You can encrypt user IDs, passwords, and data. Data can be encrypted on transit or at rest.

16. **A.** The user who wants to create or drop an event monitor must hold either SYSADM or DBADM authority.

17. **B.** Only SYSMON does not have the ability to take a DB2 trace.

18. **C.** When a privilege is revoked from a user, it does not cascade to users who received privileges from this user. Therefore, be careful who you give WITH GRANT OPTION permission to. In this example, Barney, Wilma, and Betty have the privileges.

19. **D.** By default, PUBLIC is granted use of a table space when it is created. Therefore, to ensure only the group *grp1* can use the table space, you must revoke use of the table space from PUBLIC.

20. **C**. CREATETAB is a database level privilege; therefore, information about its grantee is stored in the SYSCAT.DBAUTH table.

21. **D**. RCAC and LBAC are different. LBAC is primarily intended for defense applications. LBAC requires that data and users be classified and implements a fixed set of rules. RCAC is a general-purpose security model that is primarily intended for commercial customers. RCAC enables you to create your own security rules.

Chapter 9 Answers

1. Increasing MAXLOCKS (the percentage of the lock list that an application can use before escalation occurs) and increasing LOCKLIST can reduce the chances of getting lock escalations.

2. Sam is likely using isolation-level UR in his application, which means he can read uncommitted data.

3. A DB2 user can lock a database, a table space, and a table using commands as follows:

   Databases: CONNECT TO dbname IN EXCLUSIVE MODE

   Table spaces: QUIESCE TABLESPACE FOR TABLE tabname INTENT FOR UPDATE

   Tables: LOCK TABLE tabname IN EXCLUSIVE MODE

4. U lock is compatible with S and NS lock only. (Refer to the Row lock mode compatibility chart in the chapter.)

5. It means that the current transaction has been rolled back because of a lock timeout.

6. It means that the current transaction has been rolled back because of a deadlock.

7. There are two database configuration parameters that can cause locks to be escalated. Make sure LOCKLIST is sufficiently large. If LOCKLIST is full, lock escalation occurs. Next check if MAXLOCKS is set appropriately. This value defines the percentage of the total LOCKLIST permitted to be allocated to a single application. If any application holds locks more than this percentage, lock escalation also occurs. If both values are set appropriately, you might want to check the isolation level used in the application or maybe the application design.

8. DB2 comes with various troubleshooting and diagnosing tools. Those that are particularly useful for locking-related information are the list applications command, the Snapshot Monitor, snapshot table functions, and Event Monitor. Note that Event monitors for detecting deadlock events have been deprecated since DB2 9.7.

9. Application handle 14 is currently in a lock-wait status. It has been waiting for locks for 6507 ms. The dynamic SQL statement that this application is executing is SELECT * FROM org. It is requesting an IS lock on the table *org*.

10. By default, DB2 uses row-level locking. Unless a lock escalation is required, table lock is not requested. In this case, it is most likely that the table *employee* was altered to perform table-level locking rather than row-level locking. If row-level locking is the desired behavior, Mike can issue the following statement:

    `ALTER TABLE employee LOCKSIZE ROW`

11. **C.** Cursor with Hold is not a DB2 isolation level.

12. **B.** DB2 for LUW does not obtain page-level locks. If lock escalation occurs, a number of row-level locks is turned into a table-level lock.

13. **B.** If you do not specify the isolation level for your application, DB2 defaults to cursor stability. In addition, because databases have `CUR_COMMIT` enabled by default, then the default behavior is cursor stability with currently committed.

14. **D.** Because repeatable read must guarantee the same result set within the same unit of work, it retains locks on all rows required to build the result sets. Therefore, this typically causes many more locks to be held than the other isolation levels.

15. **A.** Uncommitted read obtains an intent none (IN) table-level lock but does not obtain row-level locks while scanning your data. This enables DB2 to return uncommitted changes because it does not have to wait for locks on rows.

16. **A.** Uncommitted read allows access to changed data that has not been committed.

17. **C.** The read stability isolation level allows new rows to become part of the result set but does not allow rows to be deleted that are part of the result set until the transaction completes.

18. **B.** The `WITH` isolation clause changes the isolation level for the statement to the specified value.

19. **C** and **E.** You can set the lock size for a table to be either an individual row or the whole table. For batch operations that update a large number of rows in a table, it is sometimes beneficial to set the lock size to the table level first.

20. **B.** The option `NOT WAIT` specifies that the application does not wait for locks that cannot be obtained immediately.

Chapter 10 Answers

1. The load utility supports CURSOR as the input. The cursor must be already declared before the load utility is invoked. The entire result of the query associated with the specified cursor will be processed by the load utility.

2. When the load utility is invoked in `INSERT` mode, you need `INSERT` privileges on the target table. If `REPLACE` mode is used, `INSERT` and `DELETE` privileges on the target table are also required.

3. Rows that do not comply with the table definition are not loaded and placed in the dump file. Therefore *stockdump.dmp* contains

```
20, "BBB", -
40, "EEE", x
```

4. Rows that violated the unique constraint are deleted and inserted into the exception table. Because the ID column was defined as a primary key, which implies uniqueness by definition, then the *stockexp* has the following row:

```
30, "DDD", 4
```

5. The table will be in CHECK PENDING state because only unique constraints are validated during the load operation. If a constraint is defined in the table like the CHECK constraint in the example, the utility places the table in CHECK PENDING statement. You need to issue the SET INTEGRITY command to validate the data before the table is available for further processing.

6. The table is accessible after the import command is successfully executed. No other command is required because data is already validated during the import operation.

7. The command generates the DDL for all objects in the database *department*, the UPDATE statements to replicate the statistics on all tables and indexes in the database, the GRANT authorization statements, the UPDATE statements for the Database Manager Configuration and database configuration parameters, and the db2set statements for the registry variables. The output is stored in the file *db2look.sql*.

8. The step that Bob missed is to REBIND the packages. Packages for static and SQL stored procedures are created at compile time. When the packages are bound to the database, data access plans are determined. Because the large amount of data is inserted into the database and database statistics have been updated, data access plans for these packages are still based on the outdated statistics. A REBIND of all packages that already exist ensures that the latest statistics are used, hence more optimal data access paths. Nonetheless, Bob might need to further tune the system by creating new indexes to further improve performance on this larger table.

9. He can either increase the size of the log files (or the number of logs) sufficiently large enough to hold all the changes made during the import. Alternatively, he could include the commitcount option:

```
import from largeinputfile.ixf of ixf
    commitcount 1000
    messages import.out
    create into newtable in datats index in indexts
```

10. The option insert_update means that the utility adds imported data to the target table or update existing rows with matching primary keys. Therefore, the table must already exist with primary keys. Otherwise, the import fails.

11. Besides crash recovery, DB2 also supports version recovery and roll forward recovery.

12. You can back up the transaction logs along with the database by using the INCLUDE LOGS option in the BACKUP DATABASE command.

13. Secondary logs are created when needed (for example, for long running, non-committing transactions) and are deleted when the database is restarted.

14. Log buffer is flushed to log files when the log buffer is full.

15. **C** and **E**. The load and import tools can read ASCII data from an input file and then insert them in a table in your database.

16. **E**. Only the import tool can insert records from an input file into a view. The load tool can only add data to a table, not a view.

17. **D**. The default column delimiter is a comma, so you need to modify the column delimiter as in answer D to import this data successfully.

18. **B** and **D**. By default, the load utility locks the target table for exclusive access until the load completes. If the allow read access option is specified, it allows read access to data already existing in the table before the load was run. However, you cannot see the newly loaded data until the load completes.

19. **C**. Log mirroring enables you to specify a secondary path for the database to manage copies of the active logs.

20. **C**. Infinite active logging is activated by setting LOGSECOND to -1.

Introduction to SQL

Structured Query Language (SQL) was invented by IBM in the 1970s in support of relational databases. SQL allows users to retrieve data by expressing what they are looking for without having to indicate how to get to it. The SQL database engine is treated as a black box that figures out how to retrieve data the fastest. SQL has become the de-facto database language, with thousands of IT professionals using it worldwide.

In this Big Data era, surprisingly SQL has not lost its popularity. Recognizing that sharp learning curves to learn new Big Data languages and programming paradigms is an inhibitor to technology adoption, several companies have worked to develop SQL dialects so that programmers can use their beloved SQL to query Big Data. For example, Hive, donated by Facebook to the open source community, has a SQL dialect called HiveQL. HiveQL is a great way to get started with Big Data using SQL; however, it lacks in richness and suffers in performance. In 2013 IBM launched "Big SQL" as part of its Big Data platform offering. Big SQL is SQL for Big Data. As it continues to evolve, Big SQL should reach a level of SQL support similar to what is offered to standard relational databases. Big SQL is being designed to deliver better performance. It gives users the ability to choose whether to run SQL in local mode or in Map-Reduce mode. For example, if you are running a simple query that does not need to be run on a cluster, choose local mode; otherwise choose Map-Reduce mode.

In this appendix, you learn about

- The SELECT SQL statement used to query data
- The INSERT, UPDATE, and DELETE SQL statements used to modify table data
- Recursive SQL statements
- How to query data that just got inserted, updated, or deleted in the same SQL statement
- The MERGE SQL statement used to combine insert, update, and/or delete operations in one statement

This appendix shows you how to leverage the power of SQL to work with relational data that is stored in DB2 databases; however most of what is covered here also applies to Big Data through Big SQL. The examples provided in this appendix use the SAMPLE database.

> **NOTE**
>
> If you are following the examples in this appendix using the Command Line Processor (CLP) or the Command Window, these tools have autocommit enabled by default, so the changes you make are stored permanently to the table. Refer to Chapter 4, "Using Database Tools and Utilities," for more information.

> **NOTE**
>
> The purpose of this appendix is to provide you a good introduction to SQL. For more advanced SQL topics, refer to the DB2 Information Center.

Querying DB2 Data

You use the SELECT statement to query tables or views from a database. At a minimum, the statement contains a SELECT clause and a FROM clause. The following are two examples of SELECT statements. This first example uses the wildcard symbol (*) to indicate that all columns from the *EMPLOYEE* table are selected:

```
SELECT * FROM employee;
```

In this example, the column names *empno, firstname*, and *lastname* are specified in the SELECT statement:

```
SELECT empno, firstnme, lastname FROM employee;
```

Derived Columns

When data is retrieved from a table using the SELECT clause, you can derive or calculate new columns based on other columns. The DESCRIBE command is handy to display table definitions, which for this section, can help you determine how to derive other columns based on existing ones. Let's find out what columns are defined in the *EMPLOYEE* table.

```
DESCRIBE TABLE employee
```

The output of this command would be:

```
db2 => describe table employee
```

Column name	Data type schema	Data type name	Column Length	Scale	Nulls
EMPNO	SYSIBM	CHARACTER	6	0	No
FIRSTNME	SYSIBM	VARCHAR	12	0	No
MIDINIT	SYSIBM	CHARACTER	1	0	Yes
LASTNAME	SYSIBM	VARCHAR	15	0	No
WORKDEPT	SYSIBM	CHARACTER	3	0	Yes
PHONENO	SYSIBM	CHARACTER	4	0	Yes
HIREDATE	SYSIBM	DATE	4	0	Yes
JOB	SYSIBM	CHARACTER	8	0	Yes
EDLEVEL	SYSIBM	SMALLINT	2	0	No
SEX	SYSIBM	CHARACTER	1	0	Yes
BIRTHDATE	SYSIBM	DATE	4	0	Yes
SALARY	SYSIBM	DECIMAL	9	2	Yes
BONUS	SYSIBM	DECIMAL	9	2	Yes
COMM	SYSIBM	DECIMAL	9	2	Yes

```
  14 record(s) selected.
```

Listing B.1 illustrates how to derive the column *totalpay* by adding the *salary* and *comm* columns.

Listing B.1   Example of a Derived Column

```
SELECT empno, firstnme, lastname, (salary + comm) AS totalpay
  FROM employee

EMPNO   FIRSTNME      LASTNAME          TOTALPAY
------  ------------  ---------------   ------------
000010 CHRISTINE     HAAS               156970.00
000020 MICHAEL       THOMPSON            97550.00
000030 SALLY         KWAN               101310.00
000050 JOHN          GEYER               83389.00
000060 IRVING        STERN               74830.00

. . .
```

Note that *totalpay* is the name for the derived column specified in the SELECT statement. If it is not specified, DB2 uses the column number as the column name. In the following example, *(*salary + comm*)* is the fourth column in the SELECT list, hence a number 4 is used as the column name.

```
SELECT empno, firstnme, lastname, (salary + comm) FROM employee
```

The SELECT Statement with COUNT Aggregate Function

The COUNT option enables you to get a row count of the result set. For example, the SQL statement in Listing B.2 returns the number of rows in the *SALES* table whose *region* column has the value *Quebec*. In this case, there are 12 records that match this criteria.

Listing B.2   Example of a SELECT Statement with COUNT Aggregate Function

```
SELECT COUNT(*)
  FROM sales
 WHERE region = 'Quebec'


1
- - - - - - - - - - -
         12
  1 record(s) selected.
```

The SELECT Statement with DISTINCT Clause

To eliminate duplicate rows in a result set among the columns specified in the SELECT statement, use the DISTINCT clause. The SQL statement in Listing B.3 selects the distinct, or unique values, of the *region* column of the *SALES* table.

Listing B.3   Example of a SELECT Statement with DISTINCT Clause

```
SELECT DISTINCT region FROM sales

REGION
- - - - - - - - - - - - - -
Manitoba
Ontario-North
Ontario-South
Quebec
  4 record(s) selected.
```

You can also use the DISTINCT clause in the SELECT statement with COUNT function. For example, the SQL statement in Listing B.4 returns the number of distinct or unique values in the *region* column of the *SALES* table.

Listing B.4   Example of a SELECT Statement with COUNT Function and DISTINCT Clause

```
SELECT COUNT (DISTINCT region) FROM sales

1
-----------
          4

 1 record(s) selected.
```

The output shows that there are four distinct values for the *region* column in the *SALES* table. This value is the same as we saw with the SELECT DISTINCT region FROM sales result obtained in Listing B.3.

DB2 Special Registers

DB2 special registers are memory values/registers that allow DB2 to provide information to an application about its environment. These registers can be referenced in SQL statements. Table B.1 lists the most commonly used special registers. For a complete list of DB2 special registers, refer to the *DB2 SQL Reference Guide*.

Table B.1   DB2 Special Registers

DB2 Special Registers	Descriptions
CURRENT DATE or CURRENT_DATE	A date based on the time-of-day clock at the database server. If this register is referenced more than once in a single statement, the value returned will be the same for all references.
CURRENT ISOLATION	Identifies the isolation level for any dynamic SQL statements issued within the current session. This special register can be modified using the SET CURRENT ISOLATION statement.
CURRENT LOCK TIMEOUT	Specifies the number of seconds that an application waits to obtain a lock. This special register can be modified using the SET CURRENT LOCK TIMEOUT statement.

DB2 Special Registers	Descriptions
CURRENT PACKAGE PATH	Identifies the path to be used when resolving references to packages. This special register can be modified using the SET CURRENT PACK-AGE PATH statement.
CURRENT PATH or CURRENT_PATH	Identifies the SQL path used to resolve proce-dure, functions, and data type references for dynamically prepared SQL statements. The value of this special register is a list of one or more schema names. This special register can be modified using the SET PATH statement.
CURRENT SCHEMA or CURRENT_SCHEMA	Identifies the schema name used to qualify unqualified database objects in dynamic SQL statements. The default value is the authoriza-tion ID of the current user. This special register can be modified using the SET CURRENT SCHEMA statement.
CURRENT TIME or CURRENT_TIME	A time based on the time-of-day clock at the database server. If this register is referenced more than once in a single statement, the value returned will be the same for all references.
CURRENT TIMESTAMP or CURRENT_TIMESTAMP	A timestamp based on the time-of-day clock at the database server. If this register is referenced more than once in a single statement, the value returned will be the same for all references.
CURRENT USER or CURRENT_USER	Specifies the authorization ID to be used for statement authorization.
SESSION_USER	Specifies the authorization ID to be used for the current session. This is the same as the USER special register.
SYSTEM_USER	Specifies the authorization ID of the user who connected to the database.
USER	Specifies the runtime authorization ID used to connect to the database.

To display the value of a special register, use the following statement:

```
VALUES special_register
```

For example, to display the value of the CURRENT TIMESTAMP special register, issue

```
VALUES CURRENT TIMESTAMP
```

SQL also supports expressions using DB2 special registers. Listing B.5 uses the CURRENT DATE register to derive the *retiredate* column.

Listing B.5   Example of Using DB2 Special Registers in a SELECT Statement

```
SELECT empno, firstnme, lastname
     , (salary + comm) AS totalpay
     , CURRENT DATE AS retiredate
  FROM employee


EMPNO   FIRSTNME      LASTNAME            TOTALPAY      RETIREDATE
------  ------------  ----------------  ------------  ----------
000010  CHRISTINE     HAAS                156970.00  10/12/2006
000020  MICHAEL       THOMPSON             97550.00  10/12/2006
000030  SALLY         KWAN                101310.00  10/12/2006
000050  JOHN          GEYER                83389.00  10/12/2006
000060  IRVING        STERN                74830.00  10/12/2006
.  .  .
```

As indicated in Table B.1, some of the special registers are updatable. For example, to change the value of the CURRENT ISOLATION special register to RR (Repeatable Read), issue:

```
SET CURRENT ISOLATION RR
```

Scalar and Column Functions

Invoking a function against the column values can be useful to derive new column values. Consider the following example where you want to obtain the name of the day for each employee's hire date. You can use the DAYNAME built-in function supplied by DB2, as shown in Listing B.6.

Listing B.6   Example of a Scalar Function

```
SELECT empno, firstnme, lastname
     , (salary + comm) AS totalpay
     , DAYNAME(hiredate) AS dayname
  FROM employee


EMPNO   FIRSTNME      LASTNAME            TOTALPAY      DAYNAME
------  ------------  ----------------  ------------  ----------
000010  CHRISTINE     HAAS                156970.00  Sunday
000020  MICHAEL       THOMPSON             97550.00  Friday
000030  SALLY         KWAN                101310.00  Tuesday
```

```
000050 JOHN        GEYER                 83389.00 Friday
000060 IRVING      STERN                 74830.00 Sunday
. . .
```

In Listing B.6, the `hiredate` column is defined with a `DATE` data type. Invoking the `DAY-NAME` function on the `hiredate` column retrieves the name of the day for that date. The function `DAYNAME` is called a scalar function. A *scalar function* takes input values and returns a single value. Another type of function, called a *column function*, operates on the values of an entire column. The example in Listing B.7 shows how to calculate the average value of the *salary* column in the *EMPLOYEE* table.

Listing B.7　Example of a Column Function

```
SELECT DECIMAL( AVG(salary), 9, 2 ) AS avgsalary
  FROM employee

AVGSALARY
-----------
   58155.35
  1 record(s) selected.
```

The `AVG` column function, which is a built-in function, calculates the average of a specified column. In this example, it calculates the average of all the salary values in the *EMPLOYEE* table. Notice that the `DECIMAL` function is also used; this casts the average result to a decimal representation with a precision of 9 and scale of 2. Casting is discussed in the next section.

The CAST Expression

There are many occasions when a value with a given data type needs to be converted to a different data type. For example, when manipulating data using the `DATE` and `TIMESTAMP` data types, `TIMESTAMP` might need to be cast to `DATE`. Listing B.8 illustrates such an example.

Listing B.8　Example of a CAST Expression

```
SELECT CURRENT TIMESTAMP, CAST(CURRENT TIMESTAMP AS DATE)
  FROM SYSIBM.SYSDUMMY1

1                          2
-------------------------- ----------
2006-10-12-12.42.16.828000 10/12/2006

  1 record(s) selected.
```

DB2 provides many built-in functions you can use. In addition, you can create your own user-defined functions (UDFs). For more information, refer to the DB2 Information Center.

The FROM Clause

The FROM clause is used to specify the table or tables from where column information will be retrieved. When specifying multiple tables after FROM, you are dealing with JOIN operations explained later in this appendix. In addition, after a FROM clause you can enter another SELECT statement or even a function call as long as the output is another table. Later in the appendix you see examples of this.

The WHERE Clause

For better performance, you should always write your SQL statements so that only the required data is returned. One way to achieve this is to limit the number of columns to be retrieved by explicitly specifying the column names in the SELECT statement (as illustrated in previous examples). The other way is to limit the number of rows to be retrieved using the WHERE clause. Listing B.9 illustrates an example of a SELECT statement that returns employees who are managers with a salary greater than $1,000.00.

Listing B.9   Example of a WHERE Clause

```
SELECT empno, firstnme, lastname
  FROM employee
 WHERE salary > 1000
   AND job = 'MANAGER'


EMPNO   FIRSTNME      LASTNAME
------  ------------  ---------------
000020  MICHAEL       THOMPSON
000030  SALLY         KWAN
000050  JOHN          GEYER
000060  IRVING        STERN
000070  EVA           PULASKI
000090  EILEEN        HENDERSON
000100  THEODORE      SPENSER
  7 record(s) selected.
```

Using FETCH FIRST *n* ROWS ONLY

Sometimes the result set returned contains hundreds or thousands of rows, and you might only need the first few rows from the result set. Use the FETCH FIRST *n* ROWS ONLY clause of the SELECT statement to accomplish this. For example, to only return the first three rows from the example illustrated in Listing B.9, use the statement shown in Listing B.10. Note that the actual result of the query does not change, but you instructed DB2 to return only the first *n* rows of the result set. This is also helpful for performance.

Listing B.10   Example of FETCH FIRST n ROWS ONLY

```
SELECT empno, firstnme, lastname
  FROM employee
 WHERE workdept > 1000
   AND job = 'MANAGER'
 FETCH FIRST 3 ROWS ONLY

EMPNO  FIRSTNME     LASTNAME
------ ------------ ---------------
000020 MICHAEL      THOMPSON
000030 SALLY        KWAN
000050 JOHN         GEYER
   3 record(s) selected.
```

The LIKE Predicate

The LIKE predicate enables you to search for patterns in character string columns. In SQL, the percent sign (%) is a wildcard character that represents zero or more characters. It can be used any place in the search string and as many times as you need it.

    The other wildcard character used with the LIKE predicate is the underline character (_). This character represents one and only one character. For example, the SQL statement in Listing B.11 returns all the rows in the employee table where the *lastname* column starts with the letter M or the *workdept* column contains three characters starting with 'D2'.

Listing B.11   Example of a LIKE Predicate

```
SELECT empno, firstnme, lastname, workdept FROM employee
WHERE lastname LIKE 'M%' OR workdept LIKE 'D2_'

EMPNO  FIRSTNME     LASTNAME         WORKDEPT
------ ------------ ---------------- --------
000070 EVA          PULASKI          D21
000230 JAMES        JEFFERSON        D21
000240 SALVATORE    MARINO           D21
000250 DANIEL       SMITH            D21
000260 SYBIL        JOHNSON          D21
000270 MARIA        PEREZ            D21
```

```
000320 RAMLAL        MEHTA               E21
200240 ROBERT        MONTEVERDE          D21
   8 record(s) selected.
```

The BETWEEN Predicate

The BETWEEN predicate enables you to search for all the rows whose value falls between the values indicated. For example, the SQL statement in Listing B.12 returns all the rows from the employee table whose salary is between $40,000 and $50,000.

Listing B.12   Example of a BETWEEN Predicate

```
SELECT firstnme, lastname, salary FROM employee
WHERE salary BETWEEN 40000 AND 50000

FIRSTNME     LASTNAME          SALARY
------------ ---------------- ----------

SEAN         O'CONNELL          49250.00
MASATOSHI    YOSHIMURA          44680.00
JENNIFER     LUTZ               49840.00
JAMES        JEFFERSON          42180.00
SALVATORE    MARINO             48760.00
DANIEL       SMITH              49180.00
SYBIL        JOHNSON            47250.00
WING         LEE                45370.00
JASON        GOUNOT             43840.00
DIAN         HEMMINGER          46500.00
EILEEN       SCHWARTZ           46250.00
  11 record(s) selected.
```

The IN Predicate

The IN predicate enables you to search rows based on a set of values. The SQL statement in Listing B.13 returns all the rows from the *SALES* table where the value in the *sales_date* column is either *03/29/1996* or *04/01/2006*.

Listing B.13   Example of an IN Predicate

```
SELECT * FROM sales
WHERE sales_date IN ('03/29/1996', '04/01/2006')
```

```
SALES_DATE SALES_PERSON     REGION          SALES
---------- ---------------  --------------- -----------
03/29/1996 LEE              Ontario-North             2
04/01/2006 LUCCHESSI        Ontario-South             3
04/01/2006 LUCCHESSI        Manitoba                  1
04/01/2006 LEE              Ontario-South             8
04/01/2006 LEE              Ontario-North             -
04/01/2006 LEE              Quebec                    8
04/01/2006 LEE              Manitoba                  9
04/01/2006 GOUNOT           Ontario-South             3
04/01/2006 GOUNOT           Ontario-North             1
04/01/2006 GOUNOT           Quebec                    3
04/01/2006 GOUNOT           Manitoba                  7

  11 record(s) selected.
```

The ORDER BY Clause

SQL does not return the results retrieved in a particular order; the order of a result can be different each time a SELECT statement is executed. To sort the result set, use the ORDER BY clause as shown in Listing B.14.

Listing B.14   Example of an ORDER BY Clause

```
SELECT empno, firstnme, lastname
  FROM employee
 WHERE job='MANAGER'
 ORDER BY lastname ASC

EMPNO  FIRSTNME      LASTNAME
------ ------------- ---------------
000050 JOHN          GEYER
000090 EILEEN        HENDERSON
000030 SALLY         KWAN
000070 EVA           PULASKI
000100 THEODORE      SPENSER
000060 IRVING        STERN
000020 MICHAEL       THOMPSON

  7 record(s) selected.
```

You can specify column names or column numbers in the ORDER BY clause, so in the previous query, ORDER BY lastname ASC could be replaced with ORDER BY 3 ASC.

Notice that *LASTNAME* is sorted in ascending order. You can explicitly specify the keyword ASC or omit it because it is the default behavior. To sort the result set in descending order, simply use the DESC keyword instead.

The GROUP BY...HAVING Clause

When you need to group multiple rows into a single row based on one or more columns, the GROUP BY clause comes in handy. Let's use an example to explain the usage of this clause. Listing B.15 sums up the salary of all the employees. The GROUP BY clause groups the results by *workdept*, which returns the total salary of the employees for each department.

The HAVING clause then specifies which of the combined rows are to be retrieved. You can think of it as a WHERE clause that is applied only to the GROUP BY clause group. In the statement in Listing B.15, only department names starting with *E* are retrieved.

Listing B.15   Example of GROUP BY and HAVING Clauses

```
SELECT workdept, SUM(salary) AS total_salary
  FROM employee
 GROUP BY workdept
HAVING workdept LIKE 'E%'


WORKDEPT TOTAL_SALARY
-------- --------------------------------
E01                               80175.00
E11                              317140.00
E21                              282520.00

  3 record(s) selected.
```

Joins

Sometimes information you want to retrieve does not reside in a single table. You can join the rows in two or more tables in a SELECT statement by listing the tables in the FROM clause. Consider the example in Listing B.16.

Listing B.16   Example of an INNER Join

```
SELECT empno, firstnme, lastname, deptname, mgrno
  FROM employee, department
 WHERE workdept = deptno
   AND admrdept = 'A00'
```

EMPNO	FIRSTNME	LASTNAME	DEPTNAME	MGRNO
000010	CHRISTINE	HAAS	SPIFFY COMPUTER SERVICE DIV.	000010
000020	MICHAEL	THOMPSON	PLANNING	000020
000030	SALLY	KWAN	INFORMATION CENTER	000030
000050	JOHN	GEYER	SUPPORT SERVICES	000050
000110	VINCENZO	LUCCHESSI	SPIFFY COMPUTER SERVICE DIV.	000010
000120	SEAN	O'CONNELL	SPIFFY COMPUTER SERVICE DIV.	000010
000130	DELORES	QUINTANA	INFORMATION CENTER	000030
000140	HEATHER	NICHOLLS	INFORMATION CENTER	000030
200010	DIAN	HEMMINGER	SPIFFY COMPUTER SERVICE DIV.	000010
200120	GREG	ORLANDO	SPIFFY COMPUTER SERVICE DIV.	000010
200140	KIM	NATZ	INFORMATION CENTER	000030

```
    11 record(s) selected.
```

Listing B.16 retrieves a list of employees, their department names, and manager's employee numbers whose administrative department (*admrdept*) is *A00*. Because the *EMPLOYEE* table only stores the department number of the employees and not the department names, you need to join the *EMPLOYEE* table with the *DEPARTMENT* table. Note that the two tables are joined in the FROM clause. Only records with matching department numbers (*workdept = deptno*) are retrieved.

This type of join is called an *inner join*; it results in matched rows that are present in both joined tables. The INNER JOIN keywords can be omitted as demonstrated in Listing B.16. If you choose to explicitly use the INNER JOIN syntax, an example can be seen at the bottom of Figure B.1, which also illustrates the information that is retrieved when using this type of join.

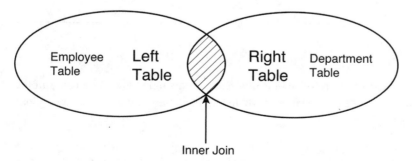

```
SELECT empno, firstnme, lastname, deptname
   FROM employee INNER JOIN department
      ON workdept = deptno
```

Figure B.1   Example of an INNER join

Note that the `INNER JOIN` clause is used in the `FROM` clause. The ON keyword specifies the join predicates and categorizes rows as either joined or not-joined. This is different from the `WHERE` clause, which is used to filter rows.

> **NOTE**
>
> When joining tables, it is good practice to provide alias names to the tables being joined. This is particularly useful when you need to distinguish between columns that have the same column names on different tables. For example, in the `SELECT` statement below, we use alias 'E' for table employee, and alias 'D' for table department. Then the columns can be prefixed with the appropriate table alias.
>
> ```
> SELECT empno, firstnme, lastname, deptname
>    FROM employee E INNER JOIN department D
>        ON E.workdept = D.deptno
> ```

There are three other types of joins: `LEFT OUTER JOIN`, `RIGHT OUTER JOIN`, and `FULL OUTER JOIN`. Outer joins are useful when you want to include rows that are present in the left table, right table, or both tables, in addition to the rows returned from the implied inner join. A table specified on the left side of the `OUTER JOIN` operator is considered the left table, and the table specified on the right side of the `OUTER JOIN` operator is considered the right table.

A left outer join includes rows from the left table that were missing from the inner join. A right outer join includes rows from the right table that were missing from the inner join. A full outer join includes rows from both the left and right tables that were missing from the inner join. Figure B.2, B.3, and B.4 demonstrate information to be retrieved and an example of each join.

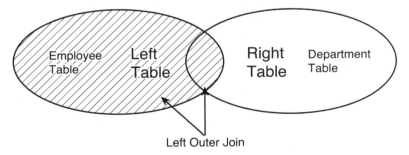

Left Outer Join

```
SELECT empno, firstnme, lastname, deptname
   FROM employee LEFT OUTER JOIN department
      ON workdept = deptno
```

Figure B.2   Example of a LEFT OUTER join

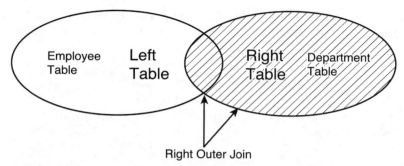

Right Outer Join

```
SELECT empno, firstnme, lastname, deptname
  FROM employee RIGHT OUTER JOIN department
    ON workdept = deptno
```

Figure B.3　Example of a RIGHT OUTER join

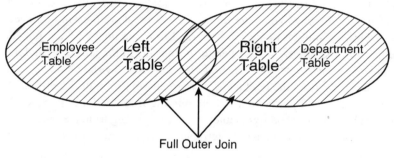

Full Outer Join

```
SELECT empno, firstnme, lastname, deptname
  FROM employee FULL OUTER JOIN department
    ON workdept = deptno
```

Figure B.4　Example of a FULL OUTER join

Working with NULLs

A NULL in DB2 represents an unknown value. The following is an example of how to return all rows where the value of *midinit* is NULL.

```
SELECT empno FROM employee WHERE midinit IS NULL
```

When working with NULL values, the COALESCE function comes in handy: It checks whether the input is NULL and replaces it with the specified value if it is NULL. See Listing B.17 for an example that returns 0 if the value in the *comm* column is NULL.

Listing B.17　Example of the COALESCE Function

```
SELECT id, name, COALESCE(comm, 0) AS comm
  FROM staff
```

```
FETCH FIRST 6 ROWS ONLY

ID      NAME        COMM
------  ---------   --------------
    10 Sanders              0.00
    20 Pernal             612.45
    30 Marenghi             0.00
    40 O'Brien            846.55
    50 Hanes                0.00
    60 Quigley            650.25

  6 record(s) selected.
```

The CASE Expression

When you want to perform different operations based on the evaluation of a column or value, you can use the CASE expression in an SQL statement to simplify your code. Listing B.18 introduces this expression.

Listing B.18 Example of a CASE Expression

```
SELECT firstnme, lastname,
  CASE
    WHEN salary IS NULL  THEN 'Salary amount is missing'
    WHEN salary <= 40000 THEN 'Need a raise'
    WHEN salary > 40000 AND salary <= 50000 THEN 'Fair pay'
    ELSE 'Overpaid'
  END AS comment
FROM employee

FIRSTNME        LASTNAME          COMMENT
------------    ---------------   ------------
MAUDE           SETRIGHT          Need a raise
RAMLAL          MEHTA             Need a raise
WING            LEE               Fair pay
JASON           GOUNOT            Fair pay
DIAN            HEMMINGER         Fair pay
GREG            ORLANDO           Need a raise
KIM             NATZ              Overpaid
KIYOSHI         YAMAMOTO          Overpaid
  . . .
```

In Listing B.18, the values of the *salary* column are evaluated. If the value is less than or equals $40,000, the string *Need a raise* is returned. If the value is between $40,000 and $50,000, *Fair pay* is returned. For all other values, *Overpaid* is returned.

Adding a Row Number to the Result Set

Recall that the `FETCH FIRST` n `ROWS ONLY` clause enables you to return only the first n rows. What if you want to return rows higher than 35? The `ROWNUMBER` and `OVER` functions solve this problem. Listing B.19 shows a column derived with sequential row numbers generated by `ROWNUMBER() OVER()`. Some rows are not displayed in the figure to save space.

Listing B.19   Example 1: Using ROWNUMBER() OVER()

```
SELECT ROWNUMBER() OVER() AS rowid, firstnme, lastname FROM employee

ROWID                  FIRSTNME     LASTNAME
-------------------- ----------- ----------------
                   1 CHRISTINE    HAAS
                   2 MICHAEL      THOMPSON
                   3 SALLY        KWAN
                   4 JOHN         GEYER
                   5 IRVING       STERN
                   6 EVA          PULASKI
                     . . .
                  38 ROBERT       MONTEVERDE
                  39 EILEEN       SCHWARTZ
                  40 MICHELLE     SPRINGER
                  41 HELENA       WONG
                  42 ROY          ALONZO
     42 record(s) selected.
```

To return rows higher than 35, use the `ROWNUMBER()OVER()` expression to the `FROM` clause. Listing B.20 shows this trick.

Listing B.20   Example 2: Using ROWNUMBER() OVER()

```
SELECT rowid, firstnme, lastname
  FROM ( SELECT ROWNUMBER() OVER() AS rowid, firstnme, lastname
         FROM employee ) AS temp
 WHERE rowid > 35
```

```
ROWID                   FIRSTNME     LASTNAME
--------------------    ------------ ---------------
              36 KIYOSHI          YAMAMOTO
              37 REBA             JOHN
              38 ROBERT           MONTEVERDE
              39 EILEEN           SCHWARTZ
              40 MICHELLE         SPRINGER
              41 HELENA           WONG
              42 ROY              ALONZO
   7 record(s) selected.
```

Modifying Table Data

You modify table data using the INSERT, UPDATE, DELETE, and MERGE statements. Most of the clauses and functions described in the previous section also work with these statements. We use some examples to explain their basic usages.

You can specify all the column values in the INSERT statement like this:

```
INSERT INTO employee
VALUES ( '000998', 'SMITH', 'A', 'JOHN',  NULL, NULL, NULL, NULL, 18,
         'M', NULL, NULL, NULL, NULL )
```

Alternatively, you can explicitly specify the column list for which values are provided in the INSERT statement:

```
INSERT INTO employee (empno, firstnme, midinit, lastname, edlevel)
VALUES ( '000999', 'SMITH', 'A', 'JOHN', 18 );
```

For columns that are not named in the INSERT statement, NULL or default value if defined are inserted for a nullable column. On the other hand if a NOT NULL column has a default value defined, that value will be inserted. Otherwise, the INSERT fails with *SQL0407 Assignment of a NULL value to a NOT NULL column is not allowed.*

You can also insert multiple rows in one INSERT statement as shown here:

```
INSERT INTO employee (empno, firstnme, midinit, lastname, edlevel)
   VALUES ( '000999', 'SMITH', 'A', 'JOHN', 18 )
        , ( '000998', 'LOPEZ', 'M', 'JEN' , 18 )
        , ( '000997', 'FRASER', 'B', 'MARC', 28 );
```

A multi-row insert can also be achieved with values obtained from a SELECT statement:

```
INSERT INTO employee_temp ( SELECT * FROM employee );
```

It is fairly straightforward to update one or more rows in a table by simply assigning the new values in the SET clause of an UPDATE statement:

```
UPDATE employee SET salary = salary * 1.5, comm = 0
 WHERE empno='000999';
```

The next UPDATE statement updates the *EMPLOYEE* table and sets the *hiredate* with value of the DB2 special register CURRENT DATE. It also sets the *workdept* to the department number selected from the *DEPARTMENT* table.

```
UPDATE employee
   SET (hiredate, workdept) = (SELECT CURRENT DATE, deptno
                                 FROM department
                                 WHERE deptname='PLANNING')
 WHERE empno='000999';
```

The DELETE statement is used to delete rows from a table. To remove all rows from the *EMPLOYEE* table, use the following statement:

```
DELETE FROM employee;
```

To remove only certain rows, use the WHERE clause to filter the rows:

```
DELETE FROM employee WHERE workdept IS NULL;
```

To remove rows with a relative position greater than 100 when ordered by *empno*, use the ROWNUMBER()OVER() functions like this:

```
DELETE FROM
 (SELECT ROWNUMBER() OVER(ORDER BY empno) AS rowid
   FROM employee)
WHERE rowid > 100
```

Selecting from UPDATE, DELETE, or INSERT

Although the INSERT, UPDATE, and DELETE statements change data in the specified tables, they only return a message indicating whether or not the statement completed successfully and an indicator of the number of rows being affected. If the statement completed successfully, you need to issue a separate SQL statement to find out what changed. In the next example, to determine which rows are to be deleted, you first issue a SELECT statement to capture the rows you will be deleting with a subsequent DELETE statement. Both statements have the same WHERE condition to filter the same rows.

```
SELECT empno, firstnme, lastname FROM employee WHERE workdept = 'A00';
DELETE FROM employee WHERE workdept = 'A00';
```

Rather than issuing two separate statements, they can be optimized to use just one SQL statement like this:

```
SELECT empno, firstnme, lastname
  FROM OLD TABLE (DELETE FROM employee WHERE workdept = 'A00');
```

The preceding statement deletes the rows and reports to you what was deleted. Because of referential integrity in the *SAMPLE* database, this DELETE will not work in this case, but you can practice with this command with other tables of your own.

Whenever a table is inserted, updated, or deleted, DB2 maintains one or more internal temporal tables known as transition tables. You specify the transition tables with the NEW TABLE and OLD TABLE clauses. Depending on the SQL operation, different transition tables are available. Refer to Table B.2 for a summary of their availability.

Table B.2   Availability of Transition Tables Depending on the SQL Statement Issued

SQL Statement	NEW TABLE	OLD TABLE
INSERT	Yes	No
UPDATE	Yes	Yes
DELETE	No	Yes

To demonstrate a SELECT from UPDATE query, consider the following example in which you want to increase the salary of all the employees in department A00. If you use the OLD TABLE clause, you can perform the update and return the old salaries as they were before the update. This is good for building an audit table to track the changes to important tables.

```
SELECT salary
   FROM OLD TABLE (UPDATE employee
                     SET salary = salary * 1.1
                   WHERE workdept = 'A00')
```

Similarly, if you want to retrieve the new salary, you can use the NEW TABLE clause instead:

```
SELECT salary
  FROM NEW TABLE (UPDATE employee
                    SET salary = salary * 1.1
                  WHERE workdept IS NULL )
```

> **NOTE**
>
> This can now be also achieved with the Time Travel Query feature explained in Chapter 7, "Working with Database Objects."

SELECT from INSERT works just like the preceding example:

```
SELECT salary
   FROM NEW TABLE (INSERT INTO employee
         (empno, firstnme, midinit, lastname, edlevel, salary)
      VALUES ( '000999', 'SMITH', 'A', 'JOHN', 18, 45000 ))
```

You cannot retrieve the new and old salary values using both the NEW TABLE and OLD TABLE clauses. To do this, use the INCLUDE clause.

```
SELECT salary as new_salary, old_salary
  FROM NEW TABLE ( UPDATE employee INCLUDE (old_salary DECIMAL(9,2))
                   SET salary     = salary * 1.10,
                       old_salary = salary
                 WHERE workdept = 'A00')
```

The INCLUDE clause in the nested UPDATE statement creates a new column that can be selected using the outer SELECT statement. You can see that the *old_salary* gets the old salary value, and the table column *salary* is increased by 10 percent.

Finally, let's look at the FINAL TABLE clause. When executing an INSERT, UPDATE, or DELETE statement, there can still be AFTER triggers or referential constraints that result in further modification of data in the table. Using FINAL TABLE can prevent these types of changes.

For instance, assume that an AFTER trigger is defined to delete all rows from the *EMPLOYEE* table when an employee's salary is updated. If FINAL TABLE is used, the UPDATE statement will fails. This protects you from any unforeseen side-effects not visible to the application.

For example, an error is received if the following SQL statement is issued:

```
SELECT salary
  FROM FINAL TABLE ( UPDATE employee
                     SET salary = salary * 1.1
                   WHERE workdept = 'A00')
SQL0989N  AFTER trigger "AUDIT_TRIG" attempted to modify a row in table
"EMPLOYEE" that was modified by an SQL data change statement within a
FROM clause. SQLSTATE=560C3
```

> **NOTE**
>
> Trigger is a type of application database object that defines a set of actions to be performed in response to an insert, update, or delete operation on a specified table. Triggers are discussed in Chapter 7, "Working with Database Objects."

The MERGE Statement

The MERGE statement combines an INSERT statement with an UPDATE or DELETE statement. For example, if a row in table *T1* also exists in table *T2*, the existing row in *T2* should be updated. If a row in *T1* does not exist in *T2*, it should be inserted into *T2*. A new and efficient way to code this logic can be implemented with one statement: the MERGE statement. Listing B.21 shows this MERGE statement.

Listing B.21   Example of a MERGE Statement

```
MERGE INTO T2 as target
    USING (SELECT ... FROM T1) AS source
        ON target.id=source.id
    WHEN NOT MATCHED THEN
        INSERT INTO T2 ...
    WHEN MATCHED THEN
        UPDATE T2 SET ...
```

Listing B.22 illustrates the syntax of the MERGE statement. The MERGE statement has many clauses; see the *DB2 SQL Reference* manual for more examples and additional information.

Listing B.22   Syntax of the MERGE Statement

```
>>-MERGE INTO--+-table-name-------+--------------------------->
               +-view-name--------+
               '-(--fullselect--)-'


>--+-----------------------+--USING--table-reference---------->
   '-| correlation-clause |-'

>--ON--search-condition--------------------------------------->

   .------------------------------------------------------------.
   V                                                            |
>----WHEN--| matching-condition |--THEN--+-| modification-operation |+>
                                         '-signal-statement---------'

   .-ELSE IGNORE-.
>--+-------------+--------------------------------------------><
```

NOTE

Refer to Chapter 1, "Introduction to DB2," for a description of the DB2 syntax diagram conventions.

The UNION, INTERSECT, and EXCEPT Operators

UNION, INTERSECT, and EXCEPT are operators that can be used to obtain the union, intersection, and difference among *fullselect*, *subselect*, or *values-clause*. Listing B.23 shows the syntax diagram of the UNION, INTERSECT, and EXCEPT operators.

Listing B.23   Syntax Diagram of the UNION, INTERSECT, and EXCEPT Operators

```
>>-+-subselect---------+----------------------------------------->
   +-(fullselect)------+
   '-| values-clause |-'


   .----------------------------------------------.
   V                                              |
>----+-----------------------------------------+-+-+----------->
     '-+-UNION---------+--+-subselect---------+-'
       +-UNION ALL-----+  +-(fullselect)------+
       +-EXCEPT--------+  '-| values-clause |-'
       +-EXCEPT ALL----+
       +-INTERSECT-----+
       '-INTERSECT ALL-'


>--+-----------------+--+-------------------+---------------><
   '-order-by-clause-'  '-fetch-first-clause-'
```

The UNION and UNION ALL Operators

A UNION operation combines two sets of columns and removes duplicate rows. Specifying UNION ALL gives the same result as the UNION operation, but it also includes the duplicate rows. Consider the two tables, R1 and R2, in Listing B.24.

Listing B.24   R1 and R2 Tables

```
R1                     R2
-----------            -----------
Apple                  Apple
Apple                  Apple
Apple                  Banana
Banana                 Banana
Banana                 Banana
Cranberry              Cranberry
Cranberry              Mango
Cranberry
Orange
```

Listing B.25 shows the results of the UNION and UNION ALL operations on the two tables illustrated in Listing B.24. As you can see, the UNION operator removes duplicates.

Listing B.25   Examples of UNION and UNION ALL

```
SELECT R1 FROM R1 AS R1_UNION_R2
 UNION SELECT R2 AS R1_UNION_R2 FROM R2
 ORDER BY R1_UNION_R2


R1_UNION_R2
------------------
Apple
Banana
Cranberry
Mango
Orange


SELECT R1 AS R1_UNION_ALL_R2 FROM R1
 UNION ALL
SELECT R2 AS R1_UNION_ALL_R2 FROM R2
 ORDER BY R1_UNION_ALL_R2


R1_UNION_ALL_R2
------------------------
Apple
Apple
Apple
Apple
Apple
Banana
Banana
Banana
Banana
Banana
Cranberry
Cranberry
Cranberry
Cranberry
Mango
Orange
```

The INTERSECT and INTERSECT ALL Operators

An INTERSECT operation retrieves the matching set of distinct values from two columns; INTERSECT ALL returns the set of matching rows. The examples in Listing B.26 use tables R1 and R2 from Listing B.24.

Listing B.26 Examples of INTERSECT and INTERSECT ALL

```
SELECT R1 AS R1_INTERSECT_R2 FROM R1
INTERSECT SELECT R2 AS R1_INTERSECT_R2 FROM R2
 ORDER BY R1_INTERSECT_R2


R1_INTERSECT_R2
------------------
Apple
Banana
Cranberry


SELECT R1 AS R1_INTERSECT_ALL_R2 FROM R1
INTERSECT ALL
SELECT R2 AS R1_INTERSECT_ALL_R2 FROM R2
 ORDER BY R1_INTERSECT_ALL_R2


R1_INTERSECT_ALL_R2
-----------------------
Apple
Apple
Banana
Banana
Cranberry
```

The EXCEPT and EXCEPT ALL Operators

An EXCEPT operation retrieves the set of distinct values that exist in the first table but not in the second table. EXCEPT ALL returns the set of rows that exist only in the first table. The examples in Listing B.27 use tables R1 and R2 from Listing B.24.

Listing B.27 Examples of EXCEPT and EXCEPT ALL

```
SELECT R1 AS R1_EXCEPT_R2 FROM R1
EXCEPT
SELECT R2 AS R1_EXCEPT_R2 FROM R2
ORDER BY R1_EXCEPT_R2
```

```
R1_EXCEPT_R2
------------------
Mango


SELECT R1 AS R1_EXCEPT_ALL_R2 FROM R1
EXCEPT ALL
SELECT R2 AS R1_EXCEPT_ALL_R2 FROM R2
ORDER BY R1_EXCEPT_ALL_R2


R1_EXCEPT_ALL_R2
----------------------
Apple
Cranberry
Cranberry
Mango
```

Recursive SQL Statements

Recursive SQL is a powerful way to query hierarchies of data. Organizational structures, bills-of-material, product classifications, and document hierarchies are all examples of hierarchical data. It can also be used to generate random data. Recursive SQL is implemented using *common table expressions (CTE)*, which temporarily store data as the query execution progresses. Multiple common table expressions can be specified following the single WITH keyword. It can also be referenced in other places within the query. Each use of a specific CTE within a complex query shares the same temporary view. Listing B.28 illustrates the syntax of a common table expression.

Listing B.28 Syntax of a Common Table Expression

```
>>-table-name--+-----------------+----------------------------->
               |        .-,-----------.      |
               |        V            |      |
               '-(----column-name-+--)-----'
>--AS-(--fullselect--)-------------------------------------->< 
```

Let's use an example to demonstrate how a recursive SQL statement is written. Assume that there is a table called *CHILDREN* with definitions and data, as shown in Listing B.29.

Listing B.29   Sample Data in the children Table

```
CREATE TABLE children ( person_id  INTEGER
                      , name       VARCHAR(50)
                      , age        INTEGER
                      , gender     CHAR(1)
                      , parent_id  INTEGER ) ;


SELECT * FROM children;


PERSON_ID    NAME      AGE          GENDER PARENT_ID
-----------  --------  -----------  -----  -----------
          1  Apple              10  F               10
          2  Zoe                11  F                3
          3  John               30  M               13
          4  Mary               25  F               24
          5  Peter              14  M                4
          6  Jenny              13  F                4
         24  Robert             60  M               30


  7 record(s) selected.
```

To retrieve the ancestors of *Jenny*, you would use the recursive query shown in Listing B.30.

Listing B.30   A Recursive SQL Example

```
WITH temptab (person_id, name, parent_id) AS          (1)
     (SELECT person_id, name, parent_id               (2)
        FROM children
       WHERE name = 'Jenny'


     UNION ALL                                         (3)


     SELECT c.person_id, c.name, c.parent_id           (4)
       FROM children c, temptab super
      WHERE c.person_id = super.parent_id


) SELECT * FROM temptab                                (5)
```

In Listing B.30, the CTE is called *temptab*, and it is created with the `WITH` clause on line (1). The definition of the CTE is specified at lines (2), (3), and (4) inside the parentheses.

Line (2) obtains the initial result set that contains the record with the name `'Jenny'`. Then, the recursion takes place by joining each row in *temptab* with its parents (4). The result of one execution of this recursion is added to *temptab* via `UNION ALL` at line (3).

The final query (5) extracts the *person_id*, *name*, and *parent_id* out of the *temptab* CTE.

The recursive SQL returns Jenny's parents and their parents, as shown in Listing B.31.

Listing B.31   Result of a Recursive SQL

```
PERSON_ID    NAME                          PARENT_ID
-----------  ----------------------------  -----------
SQL0347W  The recursive common table expression "DB2ADMIN.TEMPTAB" may
contain an infinite loop.  SQLSTATE=01605

        6 Jenny                           4
        4 Mary                           24
       24 Robert                         30


  3 record(s) selected with 1 warning messages printed.
```

Notice that a warning message is also returned indicating that the CTE might contain an infinite loop. To avoid an infinite loop, you can specify the maximum number of recursive levels in the query. For example, in Listing B.32 the maximum number of recursive levels must be fewer than 5.

Listing B.32   A Recursive SQL Example with a Maximum Number of Recursive Levels

```
WITH temptab (person_id, name, parent_id, level) AS
    (SELECT person_id, name, parent_id, 1
      FROM children
     WHERE name = 'Jenny'

   UNION ALL

   SELECT c.person_id, c.name, c.parent_id, super.level + 1
     FROM children c, temptab super
    WHERE c.person_id = super.parent_id
      AND level < 5

) SELECT * FROM temptab
```

A Comparison of DB2 and Oracle Terminology

The purpose of this appendix is to aid Oracle-skilled individuals learn DB2 faster using their existing skills. The appendix has tables comparing Oracle and DB2 terms and concepts. In addition, it has sections with more details about compatibility features built into DB2 to easily migrate Oracle databases and applications to DB2.

> **NOTE**
>
> The IBM Redbook® *Oracle to DB2 Conversion Guide: Compatibility Made Easy* (http://www.redbooks.ibm.com/abstracts/sg247736.html) is an excellent source of information explaining how to migrate from Oracle to DB2 and more.

Product and Functionality Mapping

Table C.1 has three columns showing a mapping of Oracle to DB2 products and options. The third column provides more detail when needed.

Table C.1   Product and Functionality Mapping

Oracle	DB2	Comment
Oracle 11g Release 2 Enterprise Edition	DB2 10.5 Enterprise Server Edition	No limits for memory/storage/CPU for both products.
Oracle 11g Release 2 Express	DB2 10.5 Express-C	Both are free. Resource limitation per their license: Oracle Express—per the Oracle Express website (http://www.oracle.com/technetwork/products/express-edition/overview/index.html) at the time of writing: 1 CPU, 1GB RAM, 11GB db size limit DB2 Express-C—per the DB2 Express-C website (http://www-01.ibm.com/software/data/db2/express-c/?cm_sp=MTE2083) at the time of writing: 2 cores, 16GB RAM, no db size limit
Oracle Gateway	IBM InfoSphere Federation Server	Access to data in diverse sources.
Active Data Guard	DB2 HADR	Provides High Availability and disaster recovery by the use of standby servers.
Oracle TimesTen	IBM SolidDB	These are in-memory databases: TimesTen—Oracle-specific SolidDB—Universal cache
Oracle SQL Developer	IBM Data Studio	Both are free. Graphical IDE that simplifies database administration and development tasks.
Oracle Audit Vault	DB2 Audit tool	These tools help monitor data access to protect against and discover unknown or unacceptable behavior when working with the database.
Oracle Parallel	Database Partitioning (formerly known as DPF)	Support to node partitioning.

Oracle	DB2	Comment
Oracle XML DB	DB2 pureXML	Oracle 11g—CLOB/Shredded/Binary XML

DB2 10.5—Native XML storage |
Oracle Partitioning	Range (or table) Partitioning	Enables tables and indexes to be split into smaller parts.
Automatic Storage Management (ASM)	DB2 Automatic Storage	Simplifies storage management.
Automatic Memory Management	DB2 Self-Tuning Memory Manager	Automatically manages shared memory allocation by different consumers.
Oracle Advanced Compression	DB2 Row Compression (Classic and Adaptive)	Oracle—block level compression

DB2—Row compression with table and page level dictionaries |
| Oracle Label Security | DB2 Label-Based Access Control (LBAC) | Mandatory Access Control (MAC) implementation.

DB2 also has RCAC (Row Column Access Control). |
| Oracle Spatial | DB2 Spatial Extender | Ability to store, access, manage and analyze location-based information. |

Terminology Mapping

Table C.2 has three columns showing a mapping of Oracle to DB2 terms and concepts. The third column provides more detail when needed.

Table C.2   Terminology Mapping

Oracle	DB2	Comment
Instance	Instance or Database Manager (DBM)	Processes and shared memory. A DB2 instance can have *multiple* databases. Oracle instances can only have *one* database.
startup nomount	`db2start`	The command that starts the instance.
Database	Database	In Oracle, multiple instances can use the same database, and an instance can connect to one and only one database.

In DB2, multiple databases can be created and used concurrently in the same instance. |

Oracle	DB2	Comment
Control files and .ora files (init.ora) and Server Parameter File (SPFILE)	Database Manager (DBM) and Database configuration	In Oracle, files that name the locations of files making up the database and provide configuration values. In DB2, each instance (DBM) and database has its own set of configuration parameters accessible via DB2 commands (`get dbm cfg` and `get db cfg`, respectively).
ORACLE_SID environment variable	*DB2INSTANCE* environment variable	This is the same concept.
Data Dictionary	Catalog	Metadata of the database.
Data Buffer Cache	Buffer Pools	Caches table space data in memory to reduce I/O. In DB2 you can have as many buffer pools of any page size you like.
Table spaces	Table spaces	Defines where the table data is stored.
SYSTEM table space	*SYSCATSPACE* table space	*SYSCATSPACE* contains the system catalog.
Data files	Containers (DMS table spaces)	DB2 data is physically stored in containers, which contain objects.
Segment	Storage Object	Oracle—set of extents that store a logical structure. This is the same concept.
Extents	Extents	Set of contiguous blocks/pages.
Data block	Data Page	Smallest storage entity in the storage model.
Redo log	Transaction log	The transaction log records database transactions and can be used for recovery.
active log	active log	This is the same concept.
archive log	offline-archive log	This is the same concept.
inactive log	online-archive log	This is the same concept.
archive log mode	log archiving	This is the same concept.
noarchive log mode	circular logging	This is the same concept.
actual parameter	argument	This is the same concept.
formal parameter	parameter	This is the same concept.

Oracle	DB2	Comment
created global temporary table	created global temporary table	This is the same concept.
cursor sharing	statement concentrator	This is the same concept.
Oracle Call Interface (OCI)	Call Level Interface (CLI)	CLI is a C and C++ application programming interface that uses function calls to pass dynamic SQL statements as function arguments. In most cases, you can replace an OCI function with a CLI function and relevant changes to the supporting program code.
Procedural Language/Structured Query Language (PL/SQL)	SQL Procedural Language (SQL PL)	SQL PL is a subset of the SQL Persistent Stored Modules (SQL/PSM) language standard. Oracle PL/SQL statements can be compiled and executed using DB2 interfaces.
database link	nickname	A nickname is an identifier that refers to an object at a remote data source (a federated database object).
materialized view	materialized query table (MQT)	An MQT is a table whose definition is based on the results of a query and is meant to be used to improve performance.
partitioned tables	partitioned tables	This is the same concept.
local index	partitioned index	This is the same concept.
global index	nonpartitioned index	This is the same concept
dual table	dual table	This is the same concept.
synonym	alias / synonym	
role	role	This is the same concept
session	session; database connection	This is the same concept
alert log	administration notification log	Logs informational, warning, and error messages. A DBA can use this info to diagnose problems or to tune or monitor a database.
bdump directory	diagnostic log (db2diag.log)	db2diag.log is intended for use by DB2 Support for troubleshooting purposes.
dynamic performance views	snapshot monitor SQL administrative views	Snapshot monitor SQL administrative views, which use schema SYSIBMADM, return monitor data about a specific area of the database system. For example, the SYSIBMADM. SNAPBP SQL administrative view provides a snapshot of buffer pool information.

Oracle	DB2	Comment
SQL*PLUS	DB2 CLPPlus	Command-line interface
system global area (SGA)	instance shared memory and data-base shared memory	Instance shared memory and database shared memory can be loosely mapped to the SGA. The instance shared memory stores all of the information for a particular instance, such as lists of all active connections and security information. The database shared memory stores information for a particular database, such as package caches, log buffers, and buffer pools.
program global area (PGA)	application shared memory and agent private memory	Application shared memory stores information that is shared between a database and a particular application: primarily, rows of data being passed to or from the database. Agent private memory stores information used to service a particular application, such as sort heaps, cursor information, and session contexts.
user global area (UGA)	application global memory	Application global memory comprises application shared memory and application-specific memory.
data dictionary cache	catalog cache	This is the same concept.
large pool	utility heap	The utility heap is used by the backup, restore, and load utilities.
library cache	package cache	The package cache, which is allocated from database shared memory, is used to cache sections for static and dynamic SQL and XQuery statements on a database.

DB2 Compatibility Features

Starting in DB2 9.7, there were many features and capabilities developed in DB2 to make it easier for Oracle databases and applications to be migrated to DB2. You must first enable these features by setting the DB2_COMPATIBILITY_VECTOR registry variable to the value of ORA as follows:

```
db2set DB2_COMPATIBILITY_VECTOR=ORA
db2stop
db2start
```

Data Types, SQL, and Packages Support in DB2

Oracle types, such as NUMBER, VARCHAR2, VARRAY, and more, are supported in DB2. Similarly, several Oracle proprietary SQL statements such as CONNECT BY, ROWNUM, and more are also supported in DB2.

Many of Oracle's conversion and formatting functions, datetime arithmetic functions, string manipulation functions, and other functions are supported in DB2. The same applies to packages, built-in packages, and SQL*PLus scripts. For more details, refer to the DB2 Information Center.

PL/SQL Support in DB2

Oracle's PL/SQL can run in DB2 with minimal or no changes required. DB2 has a built-in PL/SQL compiler, as shown in Figure C.1.

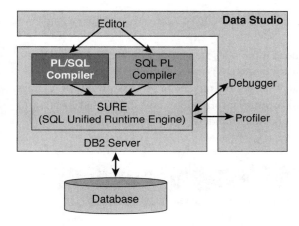

Figure C.1   DB2's support for Oracle's PL/SQL

The figure illustrates you can develop either a PL/SQL or SQL PL program, and depending on which language is used, DB2 chooses the appropriate compiler. Data Studio can be used as the IDE to develop the program and includes debugger and profiler capabilities. Alternatively, you can run PL/SQL from CLPPlus. You cannot combine PL/SQL with SQL PL in the same program.

Concurrency Control

DB2's default for isolation level is Cursor Stability with Currently Committed (CS with CC). This isolation level behaves very similar to Oracle's default locking algorithms; therefore, applications migrated to DB2 should not experience many issues after migration. CS with CC is described in detail in Chapter 9, "Understanding Concurrency and Locking."

IBM Database Conversion Workbench

The IBM Database Conversion Workbench (DCW) is a no-charge plug-in that adds database migration capabilities to IBM Data Studio. DCW helps you move your Oracle databases to DB2 for LUW in a much shorter time. The tool was designed in a framework that is based on best practices from field experts.

Additionally, DCW can also help to move existing DB2 databases to other DB2 environments such as DB2 pureScale and IBM PureData System for Transactions.

DCW integrates number of database migration tools into a single development environment. The end-to-end conversion process offered by the DCW is categorized into three main tasks:

1. Data Definition Language (DDL) Extraction

2. Assessment and Conversion

3. Data Movement

DCW provides an integrated help guide that provides step by step instructions through the entire conversion process. Figure C.2 demonstrates the DCW task launcher.

Under each task, DCW takes you through the entire conversion process from DDL extraction to final verification of the conversion. For more information about DCW and location to download the tool, visit ibm.com/developerworks/data/ibmdcw. (See Appendix E.)

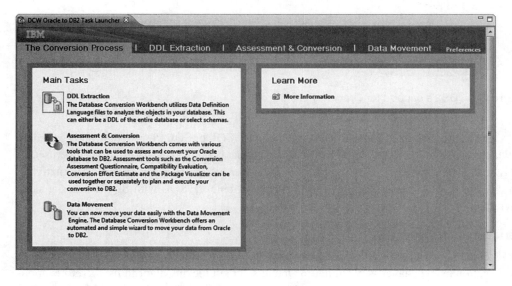

Figure C.2   Data Conversion Workbench Task Launcher

Diagnosing Problems

Inevitably when working with any kind of software, you will encounter at one point or another some problem or performance degradation that you must resolve. This appendix describes how to investigate issues you may encounter while working with DB2 and how to troubleshoot them using DB2 diagnostic information.

In this appendix, you learn about

- The big picture of DB2 problem diagnosis
- Obtaining more information about an error message, including how to use the help (?) command
- Collecting diagnostic information: First Occurrence Data Capture (FODC) and other troubleshooting tools
- The db2support tool
- The trace facility
- Searching for known problems

Problem Diagnosis: The Big Picture

Figure D.1 provides an overview of the actions that you should perform to investigate any issues you encounter when working with DB2. The following sections describe the items in the figure in more detail.

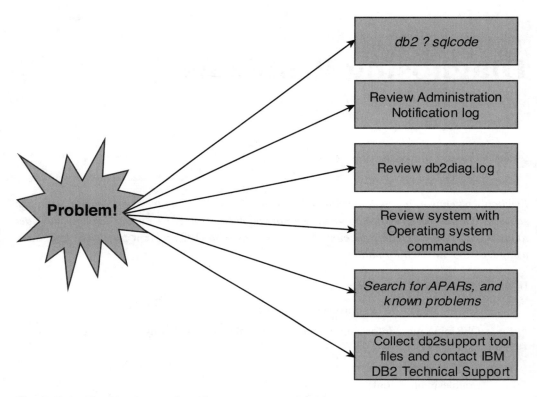

Figure D.1   The big picture of problem source identification and resolution

Typically when working with DB2, a problem is manifested by an error message. The error message might be reported immediately to the user, or it might be written to some diagnostic file like the administration notification log. Some problems might not report any error message at all. For example, if the DB2 instance abnormally hangs or the response time is very slow, you might need to run diagnostic tools or DB2 traces to further troubleshoot the problem.

The Help (?) Command

The help command, which is invoked with a question mark (?), is useful to obtain more information about a message returned by DB2 from the CLP. For example, let's say you issue the SQL statement `select from employee` in the DB2 CLP. As shown in Figure D.2, you receive an error message SQL0104N that indicates that there is a syntax error in the statement (column names have not been specified).

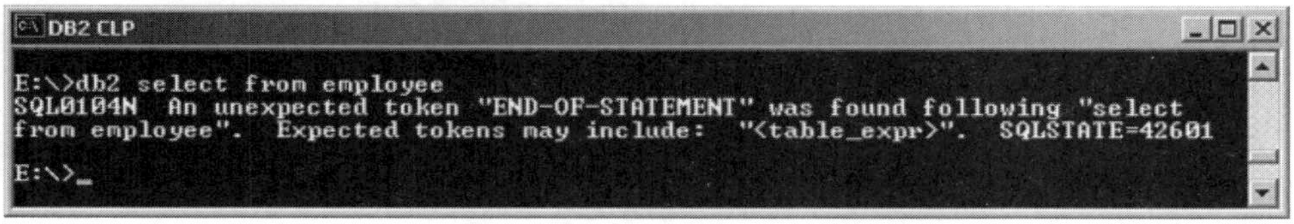

Figure D.2 An error message reported by DB2 from the CLP

You can get more information about SQL0104N by invoking the help command in any of the following ways:

```
db2 ? SQL0104N
db2 ? SQL104N
db2 ? SQL-0104
db2 ? SQL-104
db2 ? SQL-104N
db2 ? sql0104
```

The component keyword, in this case SQL, needs to prefix the message code. Negative numbers can be suffixed with the letter *N*. Figure D.3 shows the output that is displayed when you use any of these help commands.

Figure D.3 Using the help (?) command

DB2 First Occurrence Data Capture (FODC)

First Occurrence Data Capture (FODC) is a general term applied to the diagnostic information that DB2 captures automatically when messages occur. This information reduces the need to reproduce errors to get diagnostic information. The information captured by FODC is stored in the following files:

- Administration Notification log
- db2diag.log
- DB2 dump files
- Trap files
- Core files (Linux/UNIX only)

Administration Notification Log

When significant events occur, DB2 writes information to the administration notification log. The information is intended for use by database and system administrators. Many notification messages provide additional information to supplement the SQLCODE that is provided. The type of event and the level of detail of the information gathered are determined by the NOTIFY-LEVEL Database Manager configuration parameter. (The NOTIFYLEVEL parameter is discussed in the next section.)

- On Windows systems, the DB2 administration notification log is not created as a separate file; instead, its entries are incorporated into the Windows event log and can be viewed using the Windows Event Viewer.
- On Linux and UNIX, the administration notification log for the instance is called *instance_name*.nfy.

db2diag.log

Diagnostic information about messages is recorded in the db2diag.log text file. This information is more detailed than the administration notification log and is intended for DB2 technical support, but it can be useful for experienced database administrators. The level of detail of the information is determined by the DIAGLEVEL Database Manager configuration parameter. (The DIAGLEVEL parameter is discussed in the section "DB2 Instance Level Configuration Parameters Related to FODC".)

Trap Files

The database manager generates a trap file if it cannot continue processing because of a trap, segmentation violation, or exception.

On Linux and UNIX, trap file names begin with the letter *t* followed by the thread ID (TID) that caused the trap. They have the file extension *nnn*, where *nnn* is the partition number.

On Windows systems, trap files begin with the letter *P* followed by the TID and the file extension *TRP*.

For example

- Linux/UNIX: t<tid>.nnn (t023945.000)
- Windows: p<tid>.nnn (P023945.TRP)

The trap file contains the function sequence that was running when the error or exception occurred. This is sometimes called the function call stack or stack trace back. These files are intended for use by DB2 technical support only.

Dump Files

For some error conditions, extra information is logged in external binary files named after the failing process ID or thread ID. These files have the file extension *nnn*, where *nnn* is the partition number. For single-partitioned environments, this extension is always 000. Dump files are intended for use by DB2 technical support only.

Core Files (Linux/UNIX Only)

When DB2 terminates abnormally, the operating system generates a core file. The core file is a binary file that contains information similar to the DB2 trap files. Core files might also contain the entire memory image of the terminated process. These files are intended for use by DB2 technical support only.

DB2 Instance Level Configuration Parameters Related to FODC

The following Database Manager Configuration parameters are related to FODC:

- NOTIFYLEVEL
- DIAGPATH
- DIAGLEVEL
- DIAGSIZE

The NOTIFYLEVEL Parameter

The NOTIFYLEVEL parameter specifies the type of notification messages that are written to the administration notification log. On Linux/UNIX platforms, the administration notification log is a text file called *instance.nfy*. On Windows, all administration notification messages are written to the Event Log. These messages can be written by DB2. User applications can cause DB2 to write messages on its behalf. Table D.1 lists the valid values for this parameter. You might want to increase the value of this parameter to gather additional problem determination data to help resolve a problem.

Table D.1   Values for the NOTIFYLEVEL Parameter

Value	What It Captures
0	No administration notification messages (this setting is not recommended).
1	Only fatal and unrecoverable errors.
2	Everything captured at NOTIFYLEVEL 1, plus conditions that require immediate attention from the system administrator or the database administrator. If the condition is not resolved, it could lead to a fatal error. Notification of very significant, non-error activities (for example, recovery) might also be logged at this level.
3	Everything captured at NOTIFYLEVEL 2, plus conditions that are nonthreatening and do not require immediate action but might indicate the system is not optimal. This is the default.
4	Everything captured at NOTIFYLEVEL 3, plus informational messages.

The DIAGPATH Parameter

The DIAGPATH parameter specifies the fully qualified path in which DB2 puts the FODC information. The default value for DIAGPATH is a null string. We recommend you keep this default value. If you choose to change the value, keep this information separate from where you store your data, indexes, or even backup images and use a centralized location, especially if there are multiple database instances.

When the value of DIAGPATH is a null string, the diagnostic log information is placed in the following locations:

- For Windows operating systems

    If the DB2INSTPROF environment variable is *not* set, the information is placed in the folder DB2PATH*instance_name*, where DB2PATH is the environment variable that indicates where DB2 is installed on a Windows system.

    If the DB2INSTPROF environment variable *is* set, the information is placed in DB2INSTPROF*instance_name*, where DB2INSTPROF is the environment variable that indicates the location of the instance owner's home directory. The DB2INSTPROF variable is normally not set; therefore, instances on Windows are created under the directory specified in DB2PATH.

- For Linux/UNIX operating systems

- The information is placed in *$HOME*/sqllib/db2dump, where *$HOME* is the home directory of the instance owner.

- We recommend you compress or clean out the DIAGPATH directory files periodically to keep them from becoming too large.

The DIAGLEVEL Parameter

The DIAGLEVEL parameter specifies the type of diagnostic messages that are recorded in the db2diag.log file. Table D.2 lists the valid values for this parameter. The default level is 3. DB2 support might request you set your DIAGLEVEL to level 4 when they are helping you troubleshoot a problem. Level 4 produces additional informational messages that can provide a clue to identify the problem or can help verify if a given feature is enabled. It is not recommended to run your daily environment at level 4 because the additional informational messages can grow the size of the db2diag.log file quickly.

Table D.2   Values for the DIAGLEVEL Parameter

Value	What It Captures
0	No diagnostic data.
1	Only severe errors.
2	All errors.
3	All errors and warnings (this is the default).
4	All errors, warnings, and informational messages.

The DIAGSIZE Parameter

By default, there is only one db2diag.log file and one *<instance_name>*.nfy (Linux/UNIX only) file, which can grow as much as there is space in the file system. The DIAGSIZE parameter provides a way to split db2diag.log and *<instance_name>*.nfy entries into a number of rotating files with at most 10 files in the rotation. The file names have the format *db2diag.n.log* and *<instance_name>*.n.nfy, where *n* represents an integer. For example, at any point in time you could find file names like this:

db2diag.4.log, db2diag.5.log, ...,db2diag.13.log

and

<instance_name>.0.nfy, *<instance_name>*.1.nfy,...*<instance_name>*.9nfy

When db2diag.14.log is generated, db2diag.4.log is deleted. Likewise, when *<instance_name>*.10.nfy is generated, *<instance_name>*.0.nfy is deleted. This keeps the number of files to a maximum of 10 for each. The DIAGSIZE parameter specifies the maximum size in megabytes that each of these files can hold.

Administration Notification Log Examples

Listing D.1 illustrates a sample administration notification log entry in the notification log on a UNIX system.

Listing D.1   Example of Administration Notification Log

```
2013-03-22-02.05.48.322796       Instance:db2inst1     Node:000
PID:25692(db2star2)     TID:1      Appid:none
base sys utilities    DB2StartMain       Probe:911


ADM7513W      Database manager has started.
```

You interpret these entries as follows:

- The message was generated at *2013-03-22-02.05.48.322796*.
- The instance name is *db2inst1*.
- The partition number is *0* as indicated by the field *NODE : 000*.
- The process ID (PID) is *25692*.
- The process name is *db2star2*.
- The thread ID (TID) is *1*.
- The component identifier is *base sys utilities*.
- The DB2 function identifier is *DB2StartMain*.
- The unique error identifier (probe ID) within the function is *911*. This indicates where in the DB2 source code the error or warning is logged. This information is used only by DB2 Technical Support.

This message is logged when the Database Manager Configuration parameter NOTIFY-LEVEL is set to 3 and indicates that the instance has started.

On Windows, you need to open the Windows Event Viewer to view the DB2 administration notification log entries. The method to launch the Event Viewer differs depending on the type of Windows operating system you are running.

db2diag.log Example

Listing D.2 illustrates an example of a db2diag.log entry at a diagnostic level of 3.

Listing D.2   Example of a db2diag.log Entry

```
2013-04-01-18.22.40.663000-240    I6636H441          LEVEL: Error
PID    : 2268                      TID  : 5124        PROC : db2syscs.exe
INSTANCE: DB2                      NODE : 000
APPHDL  : 0-665                    APPID: *LOCAL.DB2.061007222240
AUTHID  : RFCHG
```

```
FUNCTION: DB2 UDB, buffer pool services, sqlbDMSDoContainerOp, probe:810
MESSAGE: ZRC=0X8402001E=-2080243682=SQLB_CONTAINER_NOT_ACCESSIBLE
          "Container not accessible"
```

Here is a breakdown of the entries in this db2diag.log:

- The message was generated at *2013-04-01-18.22.40.663000.*
- The process ID (PID) is *2268.*
- The thread ID (TID) is *5124.*
- The process name is *db2syscs.exe.*
- The instance name is *db2.*
- The partition number is *0* as indicated by the field *NODE : 000.*
- The component identifier is *buffer pool services.*
- The DB2 function identifier is *sqlbDMSDoContainerOp.*
- The unique error identifier (probe ID) within the function is *810.* This indicates where in the DB2 source code the error or warning is logged. This information is used only by DB2 Technical Support.

The last part of the message entry is a message that often includes error codes, page dumps, or other detailed information. Sometimes this information is complex, but usually it gives you an idea of the type of operation that is causing the failure, along with some supporting information to help the investigation. In this example, you can see that a table space container is not accessible. If you look at the next entry in the db2diag.log (see Listing D.3), you find out why the table space container is not accessible. An error occurred when DB2 was trying to check container 0 for table space 2. In fact, we changed the permissions of the container file to create this error message. Notice that the path to the container file was provided. In this case, you should have enough information from the error entry to investigate and resolve this error message.

Listing D.3   Useful db2diag.log Entry

```
2013-04-01-18.22.40.663000-240   I7079H466          LEVEL: Error
PID     : 2268                    TID  : 5124        PROC : db2syscs.exe
INSTANCE: DB2                     NODE : 000
APPHDL  : 0-665                   APPID: *LOCAL.DB2.061007222240
AUTHID  : RFCHG
FUNCTION: DB2 UDB, buffer pool services, sqlbDMSDoContainerOp, probe:810
DATA #1 : String, 100 bytes
Error checking container 0
(C:\DB2\NODE0000\SAMPLE\T0000002\C0000000.LRG) for tbsp 2. Rc = 860F000A
```

Tools for Troubleshooting

There are a host of DB2 problem determination and analysis tools available to troubleshoot any abnormality within your database and/or database manager. These tools can be used separately for specific conditions or used in conjunction to troubleshoot complicated issues.

DB2VAL

The db2val command can be used to validate the core functionality of your instance or database by checking the state of installation files, instance setup, and local database connections. For example, to validate the instance MYINST and database MYDB in that instance issue:

```
db2val -I MYINST -b MYDB
```

DB2DIAG

The db2diag.log entries can be quite long and difficult to analyze. The db2diag tool provides a way to filter the information in this log. You can filter the logs based on the name of a database, the process ID, the message level, and so on. For example, to find the logs with sever error messages for process ID 1234, issue

```
db2diag -g level=Severe,pid=1234
```

The db2support Tool

The db2support tool is a *Problem Analysis and Environment Collection* tool. It collects all diagnostic information, including the db2diag.log, dumps, and traps in one single compressed archive file called *db2support.zip*. DB2 Technical Support usually requests this zip file for problem determination and troubleshooting purposes. With this handy tool, you do not have to look for the diagnostic files manually. It also has an optional interactive "Question and Answer" session, which poses questions about the circumstances of your problem.

The syntax of the db2support command is

```
db2support output_path -d db_alias options
```

This creates the file *db2support.zip* under *output_path* for the database *db_alias* after the command completes. The following options are usually required when running the db2support command:

- -g collects all files under the DIAGPATH directory. This includes the *db2diag.log*, dump files, trap files, and the DB2 administration notification log.
- -s collects detailed hardware and operating system information.
- -c attempts to connect to the specified database (default is no).

Type db2support -h to get all the supported options. The db2support tool collects the following information under all conditions:

- db2diag.log
- All trap files
- Locklist files
- Dump files
- Various system related files
- Output from various system commands
- db2cli.ini

Depending on the circumstances, the db2support utility might also collect other files. One particular file of interest in the compressed .ZIP file is the *db2support.html* file. You can view it in any browser, and it provides an excellent summary of your environment.

> **NOTE**
>
> The db2support utility should be run by a user with SYSADM authority, such as an instance owner, so that the utility can collect all of the necessary information without an error. If a user without SYSADM authority runs db2support, SQL errors (for example, SQL1092N) might result when the utility runs commands such as QUERY CLIENT or LIST ACTIVE DATABASES.

The DB2 Trace Facility

Sometimes the information in the FODC files is not enough to determine the cause of a problem. Under normal circumstances, you should only take a trace if asked by DB2 Technical Support. The DB2 trace uility is useful when debugging reproducible problems. The process of taking a trace entails setting up the trace facility, reproducing the error, collecting the data, and turning off the trace facility.

The command to turn on the DB2 trace is

```
db2trc on options
```

Use db2trc -h to display all the available options. DB2 Technical Support usually requires you to perform the following steps to collect a trace:

1. Turn on the DB2 trace to collect the last 8MB of information in the trace:
   ```
   db2trc on -l 8M
   ```

2. Recreate the error.

3. Dump the trace information into a binary file:
   ```
   db2trc dmp db2trc.dmp
   ```

4.   Turn off the DB2 trace:

     ```
     db2trc off
     ```

5.   Format the trace dump file into a text file that sorts the records by process/thread:

     ```
     db2trc fmt db2trc.dmp filename.fmt
     ```

6.   Format the trace dump file into a text file that sorts the records chronologically:

     ```
     db2trc flw db2trc.dmp filename.flw
     ```

You are then asked to send the files named filename.fmt and filename.flw to DB2 Technical Support for analysis.

> **NOTE**
>
> Be aware that tracing slows down the DB2 instance. The amount of performance degradation depends on the type of problem, your current workload, and how busy your system is during the trace operation.

The db2dart Tool

You can use db2dart to inspect the whole database, a table space in the database, or a single table. When the inspection ends, it presents the results in a nicely organized report, deposited in the directory where the db2dart command was issued (on Linux/UNIX), or the *db2_install_dir\instance_name*\DART0000 directory (on Windows). The report has the name *dbalias.RPT*.

You can only use the db2dart tool when the database is offline, so no connections are allowed while the database is being inspected.

The syntax for the command is

```
db2dart DBALIAS [OPTIONS]
```

Type db2dart from the command line to see the list of all available options.

The following are some ways you can use db2dart.

* To perform an inspection on all objects in the *SAMPLE* database, issue

  ```
  db2dart sample
  ```

* To inspect table space USERSPACE1 in the *SAMPLE* database, issue

  ```
  db2dart sample /TSI 2
  ```

  where 2 is the table space ID for table space USERSPACE1. Table space IDs can be found in the LIST TABLESPACES command output.

* To inspect the *SALES* table in the *SAMPLE* database, issue:

  ```
  db2dart sample /TSI 2 /TN "sales"
  ```

If `db2dart` reports some data pages being corrupted, restore the database using a good backup image.

The INSPECT Tool

The `INSPECT` tool is the online equivalent of the `db2dart` tool, which can run while the database is online. The `INSPECT` tool inspects databases for architectural integrity and checks the pages of the database for page consistency. The inspection checks that the structures of table objects and table spaces are valid. However, it cannot be used to mark an index invalid or fix possible data corruptions like the `db2dart` tool can.

The results file of the inspection is generated in the DB2 diagnostic data directory (that is, where the *db2diag.log* file is). It is a binary file that needs to be formatted with the `DB2INSPF` command. If no errors are found, by default, the results file is erased after the `inspect` operation is complete, unless the `KEEP` option is used.

- To inspect the *SAMPLE* database and write the results to a file called *inspect.out*, issue

```
CONNECT TO sample
INSPECT CHECK DATABASE RESULTS inspect.out
```

- To inspect the table space with table space ID *2* and keep the results and write it to the file *inspect.out*, issue:

```
CONNECT TO sample
INSPECT CHECK TABLSPACE TBSPACEID 2 RESULTS KEEP inspect.out
```

- To format the results file, issue:

```
DB2INSPF results_file output_file
```

where results_file is from the `inspect` command and output_file is the name of the output file generated.

DB2COS

The `db2cos` script, which stands for "DB2 call out script," is invoked automatically when the database manager cannot continue processing due to a panic, trap, segmentation violation, or exception that causes the database manager to stop executing. By default, the `db2cos` script runs the `db2pd` tool to collect information in an unlatched manner, which means it does not affect the performance of your database system while the script is running. You can edit the `db2cos` script to collect more or less information. If you want to capture a complete picture of what was happening when the DB2 software failed, you can simply put in the `db2cos` script `db2pd` `-everything`, and DB2 dumps every option available to the `db2pd` tool. The `db2cos` script is located in the DB2PATH\bin directory on Windows and $INSTHOME/sqllib/bin directory on UNIX/Linux platforms.

When the default db2cos script is called, it produces an output file called *db2cosXXXYYY. ZZZ,* where *XXX* is the process ID (PID) relating to the process that is failing, *YYY* is the thread ID (TID) identifier, and the *ZZZ* is the database partition number (000 for single partition databases.) You can turn on db2cos to run automatically (on by default) or invoke it manually during a DB2 hang condition, for example. The default path is specified by the DIAGPATH database manager configuration parameter.

For example, Listing D.4 shows a *db2diag.log* entry where db2cos is invoked.

Listing D.4   Sample Entry with db2cos in db2diag.log

```
2013-12-14-08.38.11.19952-300   I19441A349          LEVEL: Event
PID     : 843287                 TID  : 1            PROC : db2sysc
INSTANCE: db2inst1               NODE : 000
FUNCTION: DB2 UDB, trace services, pdInvokeCalloutScript, probe:10
START   : Invoking /home/db2inst1/sqllib/bin/db2cos from oper system
Services sqloEDUCodeTrapHandler
```

The output file is called *db2cos843287000001.000.* Listing D.5 shows a sample db2cos output using the default db2cos script. Additional db2pd information follows but is not shown. The output information depends on the commands specified in the db2cos script.

Listing D.5   DB2 Administration Notification Log Entry on Windows

```
2013-12-14-08.38.11.19952
PID     : 782348                 TID  : 1            PROC : db2cos
INSTANCE: db2inst1               NODE : 0            DB   : SAMPLE
APPHDL  :                        APPID: *LOCAL.db2inst1.025714167819
FUNCTION: oper system services, sqloEDUCodeTrapHandler, probe:999
EVENT   : Invoking /home/db2inst1/sqllib/bin/db2cos from
oper system services sqloEDUCodeTrapHandler
Trap Caught
Instance db2inst1 uses 64 bits and DB2 code release SQL09010
...
Operating System Information:
OSName:   AIX
NodeName: n1
Version:  5
Release:  2
Machine:  000966594C00
```

DB2PDCFG

The `db2pdcfg` (short for DB2 problem determination configure) command enables you to influence the detail of information collected during a DB2 software failure. You can use `db2dbcfg` with the `-cos` option to set the `db2cos` options, such as turning on or off the automatic call by the database manager during a database manager trap. The `db2pdcfg` command can also be used to "catch" particular SQLCODEs and perform specific actions based on those codes.

There are many options available to customize your problem determination requirements. The following are a couple of examples of how to use the `db2pdcfg` command.

- If you wanted to call `db2cos` whenever a deadlock condition arises, you can use the command

  ```
  db2pdcfg –CATCH -911, 2 DB2COS
  ```

- If you wanted to catch a lock timeout condition caused by a particular lock name

  ```
  db2pdcfg -911,68 LOCKNAME=000200030000001F0000000052
  ```

- To dump out all available information when a table space full condition is encountered, specify

  ```
  db2pdcfg -CATCH -289
  ```

DB2FODC

First Occurrence Data Capture, represented as `db2fodc`, is a tool to collect and capture data when an outage or error condition is detected.

The `db2fodc` utility can be initiated either automatically or manually. Outages involving traps, panics, or data corruptions invoke an automatic FODC call. You can initiate a manual FODC call during a hang condition where the database and DB2 commands are unresponsive. When invoked, the `db2fodc` utility captures symptom-based data about the outage or error condition and writes the information to a FODC package. The FODC package is a set of diagnostic information collected into a specific location during a manual or automatic FODC invocation. The diagnostic information, such as log, trace, trap, or dump files are be stored into a new subdirectory under the DB2 instances' diagnostic path (for example, $INSTHOME/sqllib/db2dump on UNIX/Linux). The new subdirectory path has a name like *FODC_<outage type>_<timestamp>*. For example, *FODC_Trap_2013-05-12-17.34.50.171938*, where the outage type is a trap and the timestamp is indicated as 2013-05-12-17.34.50.171938. The four outage types available include TRAP, PANIC, DATA CORRUPTION, and HANG.

Additional data collected by the `db2fodc` utility is controlled by the `db2pdcfg` utility's FODC options. For example, you might want to dump the shared memory data, which includes Database Manager (instance) shared memory, Fast Communication Manager's buffers, Fenced Mode Process memory set, Database memory, and Application memory, if you suspect a memory corruption in your recent database crash. You can set this option with the following command:

```
db2pdcfg -FODC DUMPSHMEM=ON
```

If you want to collect data during a potential hang condition for all databases without stopping the database manager, specify

```
db2fodc -HANG -ALLDBS
```

If you want full details for a potential hang condition on the SAMPLE database, specify

```
db2fodc -DB sample -HANG FULL
```

When the execution of the `db2fodc` command completes, the `db2support` tool must be run to prepare and collect the resulting diagnostic files and prepare the package for submission to IBM support for further analysis. By default, `db2support` collects all *FODC_<outage type>_<timestamp>* directories found under the diagnostics data directory path. This is done to avoid additional requests from IBM Support for diagnostic information.

Table D.3 summarizes the major tools used for problem determination discussed in this appendix.

Table D.3   Summary of Problem Determination Tools

Problem Determination Tool	When to Use It
db2val	Validate the core functionality of instances and databases.
db2support	Invoke the db2support utility to automatically collect all DB2 and system diagnostic information available.
DB2 Trace Facility	Invoke the db2 trace facility to acquire detailed information about a reproducible problem operation you are investigating.
db2dart	Use the db2dart tool to determine and fix possible data corruptions.
inspect	Use the INSPECT tool to determine possible data corruption.
db2cos	The db2cos script is invoked by default when the database manager cannot continue processing due to a panic, trap, segmentation violation, or exception.
db2pdcfg	Use the db2pdcfg command to configure how much information to collect or how DB2 will handle certain problems or failures.
db2fodc	Invoke the db2fodc tool manually during a hang condition where the database and DB2 commands are unresponsive. The database manager invokes the db2fodc tool when you set it to be used automatically.

Other tools that can help with specific problems are

- `db2mtrk`: Provides a complete report of memory usage.
- `db2ckbkp`: Checks if a backup image is in good shape.
- `db2top`: Good to check for performance issues by monitoring databases, table spaces, buffer pools, locks, and so on.

Searching for Known Problems

After you have collected some information about your problem, you can research if similar cases have been previously reported by other customers and learn about workarounds and fixes. These are the steps you can follow to resolve your problem:

1. Confirm if the product is working as designed by reviewing the DB2 documentation using the DB2 Information Center (http://pic.dhe.ibm.com/infocenter/db2luw/v10r5/index.jsp).

2. Search the Internet for problems reported by other DB2 users.

3. If your environment allows it, apply the latest fix pack, which you can download for free from the DB2 for Linux, UNIX, and Windows Technical Support site (www-306.ibm.com/software/data/support/). Fix Packs are cumulative, and they also come with an *aparlist.txt* file describing the authorized program analysis reports (APARs) that were fixed with the fix pack. (An APAR is simply the official method that IBM uses to acknowledge a defect in the product.)

4. If you cannot apply the fix pack in your environment at the moment, besides reviewing the aparlist.txt file, you can also research for related problems in the DB2 Technical Support site. This site includes FAQs, technical notes, and flashes, and you can also search for specific APARs.

5. Ask in DB2 forums or newsgroups such as `comp.databases.ibm-db2` for problems similar to the one you are encountering. The DB2 for Linux, UNIX and Windows DeveloperWorks® forum be found at http://www.ibm.com/developerworks/forums/forum.jspa?forumID=842.

6. Try DB2 Blog sites such as www.planetdb2.com/ for hints and tips.

7. If your research doesn't lead to any hits and you suspect it is a product defect issue, contact DB2 Technical support at 1-800-IBM-SERV or use the IBM support website at http://www-947.ibm.com/support/entry/portal/Overview/Software/Information_Management/DB2_for_Linux,_UNIX_and_Windows).

Resources

*This appendix lists the website resources referenced in this book as well as additional resources, including traditional course offerings, computer-based training courses, free tutorials, and other information. The document WebsiteResources provided on this book's website (*www.ibmpress-books.com/title/9780133461909*) contains all the websites listed in this section so you can copy and paste the URLs directly into your browser.*

Table E.1 lists the website resources referenced in this book. It provides a brief description of each website and notes the chapter in which it was referenced.

Table E.1 Websites Referenced in This Book

Resource Name	Description	URL	Chapter
DB2 Express-C	Main page for DB2 Express-C	ibm.com/software/data/db2/express-c/.	1
Data Server Client	Data Server Client download page	www-01.ibm.com/support/docview.wss?uid=swg27016878	1
IBM passport advantage	Main page for IBM passport advantage	ibm.com/software/howtobuy/passportadvantage/	3
How to buy	How to buy IBM software	ibm.com/software/rational/howtobuy/index.html	3
DB2 trial download	DB2 for LUW overview, features and benefits, and download page	ibm.com/software/data/db2/linux-unix-windows/download.html	3

Resource Name	Description	URL	Chapter
DB2 for Linux, UNIX, and Windows main web page	Information about DB2 products	ibm.com/db2	1
IBM DB2 Support website—FixPaks	Place to obtain DB2 clients and Fix Packs and to search for APARS, fixes, and whitepapers	ibm.com/support/entry/portal/Overview/ Software/Information_Management/ DB2_for_Linux,_UNIX_and_Windows	3, Appendix D
IBM Data Studio features description by data server and component	Data Studio features description	w-01.ibm.com/support/docview. wss?uid=swg27038175	4
The DB2 Information Center	Search engine for searching in the DB2 manuals	**DB2 database product documentation:** www.ibm.com/support/docview. wss?rs=71&uid=swg27009474 **Version 10.5:** pic.dhe.ibm.com/ infocenter/db2luw/v10r5/index.jsp **Version 10.1:** pic.dhe.ibm.com/ infocenter/db2luw/v10r1/index.jsp	4
DB2 Documentation (on the DB2 Technical Support website)	PDF versions of the DB2 manuals	www.ibm.com/support/docview. wss?rs=71&uid=swg27009474	Appendix D
DB2 Technical Support website	Search for DB2 known problems	ibm.com/software/data/db2/udb/ support.html	Appendix D

To prepare for the DB2 database administration certification exams, there are free tutorials you can take. Table E.2 lists the IBM Professional Certification program website and the tutorial websites for all available certification exams.

Table E.2   IBM Certification Program and Tutorials Website

Website Name	URL
IBM's Professional Certification Program	www.ibm.com/certify
DB2 10.1 Fundamentals Certification (Exam 610) Tutorial	www.ibm.com/developerworks/views/data/libraryview.jsp?sort_order=1&sort_by=Title&series_title_by=db2+10.1+fundamentals+certification+exam+610+prep
DB2 10.1 Database Administration Certification (Exam 611) Tutorial	www.ibm.com/developerworks/views/data/libraryview.jsp?sort_order=1&sort_by=Title&series_title_by=db2+10.1+DBA+certification+exam
DB2 9 Fundamentals Certification (Exam 730) Tutorial	www.ibm.com/developerworks/offers/lp/db2cert/db2-cert730.html
DB2 9 DBA Certification (Exam 731) Tutorial	www.ibm.com/developerworks/offers/lp/db2cert/db2-cert731.html
DB2 9 Application Development Certification (Exam 733) Tutorial	www.ibm.com/developerworks/offers/lp/db2cert/db2-cert733.html
DB2 9.5 SQL Procedure Developer (Exam 735)	www-01.ibm.com/software/data/education/735tutorials.html?ca=selfstudy

Table E.3 lists some of the traditional classroom courses for DB2 database administration and performance tuning offered by IBM Learning Services. For more information, see the DB2 Education website at www.ibm.com/software/data/education.html.

Table E.3   Course Offerings

Course Number	Course Name
CL484	DB2 10.1 for Linux, UNIX, and Windows Quickstart for Experienced Relational DBAs
CL313	DB2 10.1 for LUW New Features and Database Migration Considerations
CL2X3	DB2 10 for LUW: Basic Administration for Linux and Windows
CL413	DB2 for LUW Performance Tuning and Monitoring Workshop—DB2 10.1
CF202	DB2 9 Database Administration Workshop for Linux
CF212	DB2 9 Database Administration Workshop for UNIX
CF232	DB2 9 Database Administration Workshop for Windows
CF241	DB2 UDB Multi Partition Database Administration Workshop for UNIX
CF413	DB2 9 for Linux, UNIX, and Windows Performance Tuning and Monitoring Workshop

Course Number	Course Name
CF443	DB2 UDB for UNIX Multi Partition Performance Workshop
CF460	DB2 UDB Advanced Database Administration for Experts Workshop
CF491	DB2 UDB Advanced Recovery for Single Partition Databases

Table E.4 lists resources that provide articles, books, whitepapers, brochures, and so on about DB2. It also includes information about news groups.

Table E.4   DB2 Technical Resources, Magazines, and News Groups

Resource Name	Description	URL
IBM Software Support	One-stop shop for any software support resources	www.ibm.com/software/support
DeveloperWorks	DB2 articles of interest	www.ibm.com/developerworks/db2
IBM Redbooks	Free books about IBM technology	www.redbooks.ibm.com
DB2 Technical Materials Library	Books, whitepapers, brochures, consultant reports, technology overviews, and so on	www.ibm.com/software/data/pubs/
IBM Information Management Best Practices	The Information Management best practices portal for best practice publications for Information Management products	www.ibm.com/developerworks/mydeveloperworks/ groups/service/html/communityview?communityUuid =4ec897c9-a742-4186-b371-4528f4fc4c31
IBM DB2 for LUW Forum	A place to exchange ideas and share solutions with DB2 peers and IBMers	www.ibm.com/developerworks/ community/forums/html/forum?id= 11111111-0000-0000-0000-000000000842
DB2 News Group	News, forums about DB2	www.channeldb2.com/forum/ topics/807741:Topic:3761
	comp.databases.ibm-db2 Google Newsgroup	groups.google.ca/group/comp.databases.ibm-db2/ about

Resource Name	Description	URL
IBM Data Magazine	A magazine about DB2. Each issue contains a variety of features on technical and business topics for the DB2 community, plus columns with tips and techniques on data mining, programming, system administration, content management, and more. The magazine is available in print as well as on the Web.	www.idmdatamag.com
DB2 database on the Cloud	Main page of DB2 database on the Cloud	www.ibm.com/software/data/db2/linux-unix-windows/cloud/
Big Data University	A free community educational portal with free online courses about DB2, Cloud and Big Data. Register (free) and enroll in any of the free courses.	bigdatauniversity.com

You can participate in user groups and DB2 conferences to keep up to date with the latest features of DB2. Table E.5 lists the two most popular resources.

Table E.5 DB2 User Groups and Conferences

Resource Name	Description	URL
International DB2 Users Group (IDUG)	DB2 user group organization	idug.org
DB2 and other IBM Technical Conferences	Technical conference with sessions of interest about DB2 and other products	ibm.com/services/learning/conf/us/index.html

For IBM Business Partners, Table E.6 lists relevant websites.

Table E.6   IBM Business Partners Information

Resource Name	Description	URL
IBM PartnerWorld Home Page	Home page for IBM Business Partners support	ibm.com/partnerworld

For blogs about DB2, Table E.7 lists relevant websites.

Table E.7   Blogs About DB2

Resource Name	URL
Blogs about DB2	blogs.ittoolbox.com/database/db2luw
Blog aggregator about DB2 worldwide	planetdb2.com
Blog about SQL Tips for DB2 LUW	ibm.com/developerworks/community/blogs/ SQLTips4DB2LUW/?lang=en
An Expert's Guide to DB2 Technology	idug.org/p/cm/ld/fid=113

Index